THE NEW JEWISH TEACHERS HANDBOOK

Audrey Friedman Marcus
and Rabbi Raymond A. Zwerin,
Editors

A.R.E. Publishing, Inc.
Denver, Colorado

Published by:
A.R.E. Publishing, Inc.
Denver, Colorado

Library of Congress Catalog Number 94-70560
ISBN 0-86705-033-0

© A.R.E. Publishing, Inc. 1994

Printed in Canada
10 9 8 7 6 5 4 3 2 1

All rights reserved. No part of this book may be reproduced in any form or by any means without permission in writing from the publisher.

Beth Sholom Religious School
805 Lyons Blvd.
Fredericksburg, VA 22406

DEDICATION

To our parents (*Zichronam Livrachah*) who were our teachers:
to our children who are our students;
to our grandchildren who will be our teachers.

ACKNOWLEDGEMENTS

We wish, first of all, to thank the outstanding educators who contributed their expertise to this volume, as well as all of those individuals who helped them with their chapters.

We are grateful for the help of Anita Wenner, Librarian at Congregation Emanuel in Denver, Colorado, who checked every reference for accuracy and created many of the bibliographies herein. Without her, this book could not have come to fruition. We also thank Carolyn Starman Hessel, Director of the Jewish Book Council, Toby Rossner, Media Coordinator, Bureau of Jewish Education of Rhode Island, and Barbara Leff, Library Director at Stephen S. Wise Temple, Los Angeles, for their help with resources.

Thanks, too, to Renae Levin, for reading the manuscript and providing some very useful feedback.

CONTENTS

In The Beginning

Introduction – Raymond A. Zwerin ... ix

Classroom Environment

1. Creating Community in the Classroom – Ron Wolfson ... 1
2. Designs for Jewish Learning Spaces – Joel Lurie Grishaver and Joyce Seglin ... 12
3. Parent Involvement – Audrey Friedman Marcus ... 20
4. Classroom Management – Audrey Friedman Marcus ... 26
5. Effective Bulletin Boards – Elyce Karen Azriel ... 38

Background for Teachers

6. About Child Development – Miriam Roher Resnick ... 43
7. Dealing with Children at Risk – Steven Bayar and Fran Hirschman ... 52
8. Faith Development: A Jewish View – Roberta Louis Goodman ... 64
9. Encouraging Moral Development – Earl Schwartz ... 75

Special Populations

10. Teaching Children of Interfaith Families – Saundra Heller ... 89
11. Providing for the Jewish Gifted – Zena W. Sulkes ... 98
12. Reaching and Teaching Adults and the Elderly – Audrey Friedman Marcus and Kerry M. Olitzky ... 108

Teaching Methods and Strategies

13. Listening Skills, Lecture, and Discussion – Audrey Friedman Marcus ... 119
14. Cooperative or Collaborative Learning – Carol K. Ingall ... 127
15. Jewish Creative Thinking Skills – Robin Eisenberg and Zena W. Sulkes ... 136
16. Classroom Learning Centers – Audrey Friedman Marcus and Deborah Levy ... 146

17. Using Games in the Classroom – Joel Lurie Grishaver	160
18. Values Clarification – Audrey Friedman Marcus	169

Creating and Using Materials

19. Planning Lively Lessons – Audrey Friedman Marcus	188
20. Evaluating and Choosing Learning Materials – Ronald Wolfson	201
21. Creative Use of Textbooks – Stan J. Beiner	209

Hebrew

22. Issues in Hebrew Language Instruction – Dina Maiben	215
23. Games and Other Learning Activities for the Hebrew Class – Hillary Zana	240

The Arts

24. Drama in the Classroom – Joyce Klein	255
25. Theater as an Educational Tool – Elaine Rembrandt	261
26. Teaching with Puppets – Rita Kopin	269
27. Storytelling: Role and Technique – Peninnah Schram	281
28. Creative Writing – Audrey Friedman Marcus	299
29. Music and Jewish Education – Jeffrey Klepper	305
30. Creative Movement Activities – JoAnne Tucker and Susan Freeman	310

Supports for the Teacher

31. Using the Library Creatively as a Door to the Future – Barbara Y. Leff	323
32. Working with Teen Aides – Helene Schlafman	351

Subject Matter

33. The Challenge of Teaching about God – Sherry H. Blumberg	362
34. Of Prayer and Process: One Model for Teaching Jewish Prayer – Stuart Kelman and Joel Lurie Grishaver	372

35. Beyond Bible Tales: Toward Teaching Text – Joel Lurie Grishaver   392

36. Expanding the Jewish Social Studies – Fradle Freidenreich   410

37. M'Korot: Teaching Jewish History with Primary Sources – Seymour Epstein   427

38. Teaching about Death and Dying – Audrey Friedman Marcus   437

39. Teaching Jewish Current Events – Linda K. Shaffzin and Stephen Schaffzin   446

In Conclusion

40. Student Assessment: A Rewarding Experience – Norman J. Fischer   451

Resources for Jewish Educators   459

INTRODUCTION
Raymond A. Zwerin

In Judaism, the medium is not the message. The message is Torah, and Torah must be taught over and over again, using the best, the most sophisticated, the most gripping and engaging media and other educational techniques available at the time. Torah unstudied is just an object — soulless, a dust collector. But Torah taught well, ignites the spirit. Torah learned, brings the Eternal into the here and now.

Torah and *Morah* come from the same Hebrew root letters as if to teach us that teaching Torah is a very significant calling. It is not accidental that Moses is called *Rabbenu* — our teacher. He is not refered to as our law giver or our savior/redeemer or our prophet even though he served in every one of those roles. Instead, we are enjoined to focus on what he taught us, but how he taught is also instructive. Before passing Torah to Israel, he made certain that his students, the Children of Israel, were settled and sheltered, fed and watered, and that their basic needs had been met.

Then he became master pedagogue employing excellent teaching techniques. He gathered the people together and commanded their attention through the auditory sense — "Shema!" He was a master at the use of audio-visual aids — ten plagues, spliting the sea, lightning and thunder all about the mountain as Torah was received. He understood values clarification — "Behold, I have set before you this day life and death . . . blessing and curse . . . therefore, choose . . ." The entire 40 years in the desert can be seen as an engaging simulation experience — a brilliantly conceived experiential exercise in redemption and revelation. And he understood confluent education principles. Who was likely to forget the experience of being among the people standing on Mt. Gerizim and Mt. Ebal shouting "Amen" in response to the blessings and curses pronounced by the priests in the valley of Shechem?

As Moses, our first teacher of Torah, is a master teacher, so all teachers of our Jewish heritage should have access not only to words of Torah, but to as much information and as many techniques, ideas, educational tools, insights, methods, strategies, and resources as possible. That is what this book is about.

HISTORY

In 1980, Audrey Friedman Marcus wrote and edited the first of her trilogy of teaching manuals entitled *The Jewish Teachers Handbook*. In 1981 and 1982, Volumes II and III followed. In them, articles written by the best minds in Jewish education were gathered. Each volume was a treasury of ideas on involving students and parents, on creating the classroom environment and managing it, on specific subject matter and how best to present it, and on resources and references for the Jewish educational setting.

For well over a decade, these three handbooks were the primary if not the sole teaching tool for Jewish educators in supplementary schools and day schools everywhere in the English speaking world. Jewish education was then only ten years into the revolution to bring our schools out of a "dark ages" in terms of materials and techniques. So, when these handbooks first saw the light of day, they were exactly on target for that generation of teachers. Now, a new generation of teachers enters our classrooms. They bring with them a sense of what was and is valid and usable in the classrooms of the 1990s and what is now passé.

As we at A.R.E. Publishing began to contemplate the needs of Jewish teachers and schools not only in this decade, but for the first decades of the next century, it became clear that they, too, will need and should be provided with the latest and the best teaching tools available. Therefore, it was decided to renew, refresh, and revise the volumes written in the 1980s. Whatever was out of date in the old volumes was to be deleted, whatever was of continuing practical use was to be updated with completely new Bibliographies and source materials, and whatever was new in the field and therefore essential to today's teachers was to be added. What's more, we wanted to put all of this information into one easy to find and easy to use volume so that there would be no guessing as to which volume contained what chapters. We are proud to say that our efforts have resulted in this major tome. Extensively altered and improved, it certainly merits its title, *The New Jewish Teachers Handbook*.

While this *Handbook* is intended primarily for use by the classsroom teacher, it will also be of considerable benefit to those involved in informal Jewish education — youth groups, camping, retreats, "Shul-ins" and *Shabbatonim*, family education and family life education, Jewish Community Center programs, and the like. Teachers of adults will also find this book useful. Every teacher, regardless of his or her teaching venue, will want to make frequent use of the Bibliographies found at the end of each chapter and of the Resources for Jewish Educators found at the end of this book.

ABOUT THIS BOOK
Format

The chapters in this handbook are divided into ten sections: Classroom Environment, Background for Teachers, Special Populations, Teaching Methods and Stragegies, Creating and Using Materials, Hebrew, The Arts, Supports for the Teacher, Subject Matter, and In Conclusion.

In the section Classroom Environment, you will find chapters that will help you to build a sense of community in your classroom, arrange your learning space in such a way that it fosters learning, involve the parents of your students so as to make them partners with you in educating their children Jewishly, manage the classroom effectively in terms of preventing discipline problems and coping with such problems when they do arise, and to create bulletin boards to enliven the classroom environment.

Background for Teachers provides vital information on child development, how to recognize and deal with children at risk, a Jewish view of faith development, and ways to encourage moral development.

How to teach the many children of intermarried families in today's classrooms is the first chapter in the section Special Populations. This is followed by chapters on providing for the Jewish gifted and teaching adults and the elderly.

Many ways to enliven your classroom are covered in the section Teaching Methods and Strategies. There is a chapter that includes ways to encourage listening skills, to lecture in an effective manner, and to conduct lively discussions. There are also chapters on cooperative learning, fostering Jewish creative thinking skills, initiating classroom learning centers, using games in the classroom, and employing values clarification techniques.

Under Creating and Using Materials, you will find suggestions for designing lively lessons, evaluating and choosing learning materials, and using textbooks in innovative and meaningful ways.

The section on Hebrew contains an in-depth and scholarly overview of Hebrew decoding, followed by a practical chapter on using games and other learning activities in Hebrew classes.

Under the rubric of The Arts, you will find two chapters on drama in the classroom, as well as chapters on teaching with puppets, telling stories effectively, using creative writing as a teaching technique, including music, and introducing creative movement activities.

A very comprehensive chapter on how to make good use of the library and one on working effectively with teen aides comprise the section on Supports for the Teacher.

Specific curricular areas included in the section called Subject Matter are God, Prayer, Bible, Social Studies, Jewish History, Death and Dying, and Current Events. Each of these chapters contains background information, as well as many practical ways of teaching these topics.

The final section, In Conclusion, contains an important chapter on the critical area of assessing students to see what they have learned. This is followed by a list of resources for Jewish educators, which is made up of a selective listing of Jewish publishers, periodicals, and audiovisual distributors.

CONCLUSION

While this book is intended to be comprehensive, it is not meant to be encyclopedic. It cannot possibly contain all known teaching techniques and methods, much less every possible curricular topic. What is assured is that the methods, ideas, hints, strategies, modalities, and resources found in these pages have been successfully used in Jewish learning situations. Chances are, they will enrich your teaching, too, if you pick and choose carefully and interface the subject matter with the appropriate methodology, if you become knowedgable about and comfortable with a method before you use it, if you do not overuse any one technique to the exclusion of all others, and if you strive for variety in your classroom presentations.

This is meant to be a practical book. Theory is blended in where needed, but usually as a rationale to support applications — the doing. Aware of the immense challenge that faces Jewish education in the decades ahead — less class time, more secular and personal distractions, changes in the social structure, changes in the family and in family life, conflicting values, the dying out of the older generation which frequently served as positive Jewish role models, intermarriage, the list is endless — we as educators of Jews have to maximize every minute given to Jewish education and make exceptional use of every teaching opportunity. To help in that effort is the undergirding reason for this *Handbook*.

Therefore, we invite you to read *The New Jewish Teachers Handbook* with an eye toward adapting and incorporating its insights into your teaching; we encourage you to treat it as you would any significant teaching manual — make notes in its margins and underline what you consider to be salient points. This book reflects our enthusiasm for the future of Jewish education which is all about putting our ageless heritage into the hands and hearts of twenty-first century Jews. We hope that this book will help you to accomplish your teaching mission, that it will enable you to put more class in your teaching and . . . more teaching in your class.

Raymond A. Zwerin is President of A.R.E. Publishing, Inc., and founding Rabbi of Temple Sinai in Denver.

CLASSROOM ENVIRONMENT

CHAPTER ONE

CREATING COMMUNITY IN THE CLASSROOM

Ron Wolfson

Sometimes it seems everybody cares about Jewish education except the kids. Teachers, Rabbis, synagogues, Bureaus of Jewish Education, even some parents care enough about Jewish education to spend millions yearly and countless hours of planning and meeting, teaching and preaching, all in an attempt to transmit Judaism to the young people of the next generation.

And the kids don't care. They don't care because so much of what they learn in Religious School has little or no impact on their personal life experiences. They don't need or value what we offer in Jewish education.

Look at it from the youngsters' point of view. Who needs to learn to speak Hebrew in America? Why learn to read Hebrew if most religious services are conducted in English? What's the use of five years of Religious School to prepare for Bar/Bat Mitzvah when everyone knows all someone has to do is memorize some tape recording of a Haftarah to chant what can seem like so many nonsense syllables?

But do we not also teach about holiday observances, *mitzvot,* Jewish peoplehood, and values? The problem is: where does the American Jewish child actually see these things being acted upon? In the Jewish community? What Jewish community? Children don't see a vibrant Jewish community. We have to take them on field trips to the lower East Side in New York or the Fairfax District in Los Angeles to show them a Jewish neighborhood with kosher meat markets and bakeries, *shuls,* and shops. The suburbs have spread Jews all over the place.

Perhaps students could find outlets for Jewish expression in the family. Certainly, in some families, Jewish life is still alive. Yet many of our students come to us from intermarriages, from homes shattered by divorce, from upwardly mobile families who live apart from large extended families which once provided support for traditional values and observances.

The question then remains: why should kids take Religious School seriously if they cannot relate what they learn to a Jewish family or Jewish community experience? Moreover, what difference does a Jewish education mean to these students personally? They know that public school is important for future college and professional goals, but Religious School? Everyone knows Religious School is second class education. Socially, the kids do not usually see Religious School as a place to develop meaningful relationships with fellow students or with the adults who are found there. Intellectually, these Jewish youngsters become easily bored with a curriculum which centers almost exclusively on the past and is transmitted passively through books.

Religious School education used to make sense. At one time our Jewish students came to our schools with a positive Jewish identity, from actively Jewish homes, living within the context of a vibrant Jewish community. The task of the Religious School was to fill in the details of their Jewish knowledge. The central problem with Jewish education today is that the school still tries to teach the details of Judaism. But the audience, by and large, comes to the Religious School without a positive Jewish identity, from homes that are religiously dormant and without the context of a vibrant Jewish community. In the absence of these three key factors, the facts we teach in Religious Schools are taught in a vacuum and frequently fall on deaf ears.

What we need to do is rethink our conceptualization of Jewish education and the task of the Jewish school. Certainly, we must teach the content of Jewish life to our students. But first we must provide some meaningful context in which the students can absorb this information if Jewish education is to be maximally effective.

I believe we can begin by creating "substitute" Jewish communities in our Jewish schools and classrooms. The Jewish school can become a place where the student feels it's great to be Jewish, where it's important to be Jewish, and where he/she feels a sense of belonging to a group of fellow Jews. Believe it or not, a Jewish classroom can be a place where kids want to be, where they can belong to a Jewish peer group, where they can enjoy a warm relationship with a model adult Jew, where they can learn how to live Jewishly within the context of a personal Jewish community.

A CLASS IS ALSO A GROUP — A SOCIAL ENTITY.

While the place to begin is in the classroom, we will need to have a radically different notion of what a classroom is. We need to see the classroom as more than a four-walled room, populated by kids, a teacher, some textbooks, desks, and chalkboards. A class is also a group — a social entity with certain roles, patterns of interaction, norms, attitudes, and affiliations.

In this group, there are issues of membership and identity, content and process, goals and expectations. And there is the potential for community — Jewish community — depending on how well these factors are identified and developed.

What do you see in a classroom? Try this simple exercise now. Take a piece of blank paper and draw a teacher teaching students in a classroom. When you have finished, check back and ask yourself these questions:

1. Who is the teacher? Is it you?
2. Is the teacher drawn in greater detail than the rest of the picture?
3. Are there students in your picture? Do they look alike or are they "individuals"?
4. Does the teacher dominate the picture? If so, why?
5. Are the students active or bored?
6. Is the teacher close to the students or at a distance?
7. What kinds of relationships can you see between teacher and students? Between students and students?
8. Is there any content in the classroom?
9. How are the seats arranged?
10. Is there any indication of "community?"

Now let's discuss what it is we seek in creating a sense of community in the classroom. A classroom community is a group of people in which (1) there is face-to-face interaction, (2) each person is aware of his/her own membership in the group, (3) each person is aware of the membership of others in the group, and (4) everyone is receiving some satisfaction from participating in the activities taking place. Ultimately, the classroom community in the Jewish school is a group of people who know each other well, who care about each other, who want to be together in a Jewish framework.

In order to achieve this goal, the classroom teacher must assume the role of group leader in addition to his/her responsibilities as instructor. A good group leader is not only the catalyst for much of what happens, but he/she is also an integral member of the group itself. A camp counselor is not a camper, but is identified by all as a member of a particular cabin as well. The youth group leader is not just one of the kids, and yet, he/she is an accepted part of the group. The role of the teacher in creating a classroom community centers on the ability of the teacher to establish a social group in which he/she is both a member and the acknowledged leader.

The first objective of the classroom leader is to establish a positive climate for community development in the group. There are aspects which are necessary to such a classroom group: (1) Open Communication, (2) Expectations, Attraction, and Mutual Influence, (3) Agreed upon Norms and Group Process, and (4) Goal Orientation.

To get to a point where the group exhibits all of these characteristics is a long and gradual process. It does not happen overnight. One factor does not necessarily lead to another. There is, no simple recipe for which steps to take first in trying to establish this climate for group-building. Nevertheless, let's attempt to outline some of the basic things teachers can do to begin to create community in the classroom based on these essential four aspects of a positive classroom climate.

OPEN COMMUNICATION
Verbal Communication

Good lines of communication are absolutely crucial if individuals are to become a group.

Most students are conditioned to speak only when called on, only to the teacher, and only about the subject matter at hand. In the ideal classroom community, students and students as well as students and teacher will engage in many levels of discourse about many things, all characterized by the give and take of dialogue.

To get to that point takes some planning and practice. The place to start is on the very first day of class when the teacher not only introduces himself/herself, but when the students get to know each other personally, too. There are many excellent sources for "ice-breakers" and many effective games and strategies. Here are three easy ways for your classroom members to get to know each other.

Make a Name Tag

You'll need construction paper, scissors, marking pens, and string. Ask each person to cut out a shape of paper which tells something about himself/herself (e.g., a round shape may indicate an interest in baseball). Each should decorate the shape and write the name he or she wishes to be called in class. Each student then punches two holes in either side of the name tag, adds a length of string, and wears the tag like a necklace. Have each person pair with someone they don't know and explain the name tag. Pairs spend a few minutes getting to know each other. Then each person introduces his/her new friend to the group by explaining the friend's name tag and what it stands for.

Name Whip

Arrange the group in a circle. You sit in the circle, too. Start with the first student to your right and ask his/her name and a simple question answerable with one word. For example: "What's your name and what's your favorite TV show?" (or "What's your favorite book?" or "Who is a person you admire?" or "What's your favorite toy?") The first student will say: "My name is Michael and I like 'The Simpsons.'" The second student must remember what the first student's name and favorite show were and then respond for him/herself. "His name is Michael and he likes 'The Simpsons.' And my name is Judy and I like 'Beverly Hills 90210.'" The third student starts with the first person and says "His name is Michael and he likes 'The Simpsons.' Her name is Judy and she likes 'Beverly Hills 90210.'

And my name is Sandy and I like MTV," etc. Depending on the size of the group, the people at the end of the circle may worry about remembering each person's name and favorite show. When this occurs, ask the group to help out. Keep it light and fun. Above all, don't forget to participate in the exercise as well. The leader has the last turn and no doubt will forget some of the answers. That's O.K. If the group can't remember what a particular person said, let that person remind them. By the time this exercise is over, everyone should know the names of everyone else in the group. To test it out, ask the first three students to go around the circle and give names and favorite shows.

Who's in the Group Form

This exercise is excellent for reinforcing name recognition and learning something about each person in the group. Create a list of things people in your class have probably done or characteristics they have. For example:

A person in this group who has gone to summer camp is _____.

A person in this group who likes bananas is _____.

A person in this group who has been to a Jewish wedding is _____.

A person in this group who owns an electronic game is _____.

A person in this group who has been to Israel twice is _____.

Have as many items as there are people in the group. Copy enough forms for everyone.

The object of the exercise is for each participant to interview every other one in order to discover something that person has or has not done. A student might ask one question or five questions of another student until an affirmative answer is forthcoming. The person's name is then written into the proper space and the questioner moves on to the next available person. Each person must talk to every other person until all blanks are filled with different people's names. If there are 15 students, each of 15 questions will have one of the student's names attached to it. (Note: The exercise calls for students to be out of their seats and talking to one another. There will be quite a bit of constructive noise.)

When it appears that most of the students have completed their lists, ask the group to reconvene. Start with Question 1 and ask, "Who knows a person in this group who has gone to summer camp?" and let the students call out the names of people in the group who have been to camp. Do this for each question on the form. Conclude by remarking at the wide variety of shared experiences in the group and how interesting it is to get to know each other better.

The purpose of these exercises is two-fold. First, it is critical that the members of the group learn each other's names as soon as possible. For the students, a series of these "get-to-know-you" exercises will usually do the trick. They are helpful for the teacher, too, since it is vital to learn the students' names immediately. Study the class roster before you meet the students for the first time so that you have their names fresh in your memory. Then participate in the exercises to gain some practice attaching names to faces.

The second objective of these exercises is to set the tone for the group dynamics in the class. This is a class in which students are expected to participate, to get to know each other, to communicate with not only the teacher, but with fellow classmates as well.

CLASSROOM SET-UP AND INTERACTION

The way a classroom is set up can do much to determine the type of communication found there, and perhaps even influence the way students perceive their group.

(For more on classroom set-ups, see Chapter 2, "Designs for Jewish Learning Spaces.")

Look at these diagrams of two classrooms:

```
            T

    S   S   S   S
    S   S   S   S
    S   S   S   S
    S   S   S   S

       CLASSROOM A
```

What types of communication are facilitated or hindered in each? Classroom A represents the so-called "traditional" seating arrangement of straight rows of students, all pointed toward the teacher in the front. This configuration directs the attention of the students to the teacher and facilitates teacher-directed dialogue

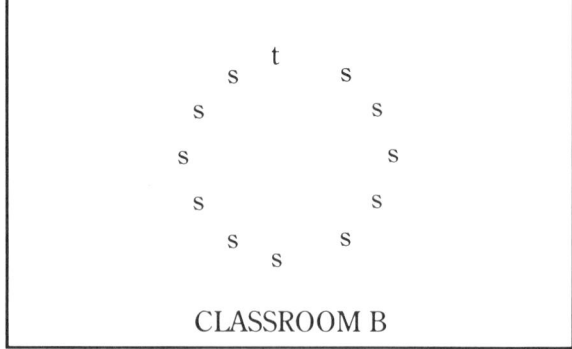

CLASSROOM B

with one student at a time. This setting hinders student-student communication.

Classroom B, set in a circle that includes the teacher, certainly facilitates face-to-face interaction among all people in the group. Here there are no impediments to student-student communication and the teacher assumes a coequal place in the physical setting. In addition, the circle arrangement sends a message to the students that this is, in fact, one group.

For the purposes of group-building, Classroom B is clearly superior. Variations of this setting include a horse-shoe design, a semi-circle and even small circles of three or four students each. It is advisable to vary the setting occasionally, depending on the content of the lesson. But it is good practice to bring the entire group together in a circle at least once during each class period to reinforce the message that this class is building a community.

The key to the success of any group, is the establishment of effective patterns of interaction between its members. In classroom groups this is especially important if a sense of community is to be developed. But, it is interesting to note that the types of communication patterns found in effective groups are rarely found in Religious School classrooms.

Most of the time someone is talking in classrooms. And fully two thirds of that time, the someone talking is the teacher. Most of this teacher-talk is either lecture or management instructions directed at the students. When students talk, it is mostly in response to the teacher. Student-initiated talk is rare. Rarer still is a situation where students talk with other students in the formal give-and-take of classroom discussion. And yet, this is precisely what is desired.

Most classroom talk follows a one-way communcation pattern — the teacher talks to the student. What we are after is a two-way communication pattern wherein the teacher and students dialogue among each other. Better stil is a three-way configuration with teacher and students responding to each other and students responding to other students.

To achieve this takes a great deal of retraining for both teacher and students. Teachers must learn how to present curricular material which demands student initiation and discussion. Teachers must learn to listen, really listen, to what students are saying. Too often it is tempting to listen only for the "right" answer or to half ignore student comments while mentally projecting ahead to the next teaching move. Teachers will need to encourage small group discussions which allow maximum student-student interaction. And finally, teachers can create the expectation and norm that students can, in fact, talk to each other in class.

Verbal interaction is only one of the factors that influence open communication in the class room. Also important are inclusion, getting to know your students, and encouraging personal disclosure. Included in the discussion which follows each of these factors are several easy exercises which will foster their development. These are drawn from the many excellent resources which provide training in communication skills and suggest exercises for classroom use. (See the Bibliography at the end of this chapter for a representative sample of this literature.)

Inclusion

The content of classroom interaction is usually subject matter. But in trying to establish a sense of community, teachers must also encourage communication which promotes inclusion and group development. This type of communication requires that specific skills be taught to students, that all members who wish to participate in a group discussion are included, and that all communications within a group be clear and mutually understood.

Here's a simple exercise which demands this type of communication. The objective of this exercise is to see how well and how quickly a group can work together. Announce to the group that a simple task will be given. After the task is completed, an analysis will follow. The task is: "You are to calculate the average height of this group. You must work together as one group and everyone in the group must agree on one answer. When you have the answer, appoint one person to submit it to the teacher."

What usually follows is a mild panic. There is no appointed leader to help the group organize for the task, yet a leader or two will probably emerge. Then one of two things will happen: the "leader" will arbitrarily announce how the average height is to be figured out or a discussion will ensue about how to arrive at an answer. Eventually, a decision on how to proceed is reached and the group engages the task. Depending on how smoothly this goes, consensus is either easily reached or never agreed upon. Ultimately, you may have to call time after about 15 minutes of struggle. In excellent working groups, a solution will have been reached in several minutes.

Lead the group in an analysis of how it approached the task. Did a leader emerge? Was he/she needed? What problems did the group have in getting organized? What part did each group member have to play in order to solve the problem? How could the group solve the problem faster next time?

Three points should be emphasized: (1) a person exhibiting leadership functions is useful to a group, (2) it is important to listen to each other, and (3) every group member has important contributions to make to the group process and should be included.

Other exercises that promote inclusion can be found in *Learning Discussion Skills through Games* by Gene and Barbara Stanford, a useful collection of step-by-step exercises for acquiring communications skills and developing groups. I particularly recommend the "Murder Mystery Exercise."

Getting To Know Your Students

All of the communication exercises described here will help the members of your classroom group get to know each other better. They will be especially useful for you, the leader of the group. The importance of learning about your students cannot be overestimated. The more you know about them, the greater the opportunity

> ENCOURAGE VERBAL INTERACTION, PROMOTE INCLUSION.

you have to establish a point of communication with each person.

There are several things a leader can do to learn about class members. The most obvious strategy is to ask about them directly via an autobiographical questionnaire. Compile 10-15 questions on a handout for students to complete. Ask questions that reveal information which can be useful to you in establishing communication points, such as:

What are your hobbies?

What do you do in your spare time?

What kinds of activities do you do with your family?

In what sports do you enjoy participating?

What is your favorite TV show?

Have you recently seen a movie you liked?

What is your favorite rock group?

Besides a written questionnaire, you can interview students personally. This can be done individually before or after school, perhaps over a lemonade at a nearby restaurant. Or, try inviting a small group of students to your home for Shabbat dinner. The informal atmosphere will help the students open up and share with you and with each other.

Of course, you can learn about class members from sources other than the students themselves, including school records, the Director of Education and/or previous teachers, and parents.

Data you may need to have from these sources includes special academic concerns or needs, physical or emotional problems requiring medication, or special handling and each student's family status. (A word of caution: Beware of "teacher's lounge" gossip about students; it can create unfair expectations of students.)

Encouraging Personal Disclosure

The third area of communications skills critical to group development centers on social relations. One goal in building classroom groups is to establish effective personal relationships within the community. To do this, teacher and students must learn about themselves and each other within the context of the group. This is called "personal disclosure."

Personal disclosure is the process of getting in touch with one's own feelings and emotions. During many of the activities in the classroom community, private thoughts will be triggered. It is perfectly acceptable for students to keep such information private.

The second level of disclosure occurs when group members feel comfortable enough to share these types of thoughts and feelings. Try the following simple communication exercise to illustrate this.

Divide the group into pairs. Ask one person to be "A" and the other "B." The "A's" will speak first and the "B's" will listen. Each "B" must listen very carefully since he/she will be asked to paraphrase what "A" says. Define "paraphrasing" as a process of repeating back what you hear without additions, interpretations, or judgments. "A" will get one minute to speak on the subject "Something I like about myself." After one minute, tell the "B's" to paraphrase back to their partners what they heard. Now switch roles. Let the "B's" speak on the same or a similar topic as the "A's" listen and then paraphrase. Afterward, discuss the difficulties in each role, how paraphrasing helps in understanding what another person is trying to say, and what each learned about the other.

The third level of personal disclosure is "mutual self-disclosure." Here, the teacher/leader gets into the act by exchanging personal information with the students. Try this adaptation of the "Public Interview," an effective Values Clarification technique, for demonstrating this process.

Ask for a volunteer to be in the public spotlight. Explain the ground rules for conducting this mutual interview. The teacher asks the student one personal question. The student can either answer or request a different question. Then the student may ask the teacher a personal question. The teacher has the same right to answer or to request a different question. The process can continue with several questions for the same student or can be conducted with the entire group participating. The type of question you ask sets the tone. Begin with low-threat questions like "How much TV do you watch?" or "If you had an extra $500 what would you do with it?" Progress to more serious questions as the exercise warms up: "How many children would you like to have?" "Do you ever get teased?" "Do you believe in life after death?" The students usually welcome the opportunity to answer these kinds of questions and enjoy asking them of the teacher.

Several important points must be made with regard to personal disclosure. People will not disclose personal information about themselves publicly unless they feel an atmosphere of acceptance and trust. The levels of disclosure will progress slowly as this climate begins to be established in the group.

Begin personal disclosure exercises by asking questions which are easy to answer. As time goes on, people will feel more comfortable with questions requiring more personal risk taking.

People must always be free to pass by not answering any question or participating in any exercise of this type. You must not force personal disclosure.

Encourage personal disclosure by example. The more students see you are comfortable discussing serious personal concerns, the freer they will feel about it. Certainly, teachers must maintain some privacy, too, and you should exercise the right to pass whenever appropriate. But, the more mutual self-disclosure there is, the more human you and your classroom become.

EXPECTATIONS, ATTRACTION, AND MUTUAL INFLUENCE

Most students have expectations of their Religious School class. For some, it is the expectation of the excitement of learning a new language. For many it is the expectation of another boring year of repetitive curriculum and unimaginative teaching.

Teachers have expectations, too. For some, it is the expectation of a challenging group of inquisitive students. For many, it is the expectation of another year facing a group of tired, uninterested kids.

Ask yourself: what are your own expectations of teaching in Jewish schools? And what do you think your students expect of you and your classroom?

There are several important points to make about expectations and how they can affect the group-building process. First, expectations are natural — the important thing is to be aware of them and the ways they influence us. How do you think the expectations you just thought about could influence your approach to teaching?

Second, beware of the self-fulfilling prophecy. Treating students according to our expectations can influence them to behave in exactly the way we expect them to behave.

Third, it is possible to modify expectations based on new information. You may have heard from last year's teacher that Sammy was a "trouble-maker." But the Director of Education reports that Sammy had a great summer at camp and has turned over a new leaf. Your expectations of Sammy will probably change.

Finally teachers can create positive expectations for individuals and the group. You might tell your students that in your class they will get to know each other better than in any previous year. Or you might make it a practice to tell them at the very beginning of each class what new things they will learn or what experiences they will have that day. Or you might create an air of expectation at the end of class by posing a question that will be answered the following week. The important point is that you as the classroom leader can create positive expectations by your directions and actions. However, never fail to follow through on your promises or your credibility will suffer greatly.

To understand the concept of attraction, put yourself in your students' shoes — just for a moment — and ask yourself this simple question: "Why should I want to come to this class?" Now think of some probable answers: "My parents force me," "I have to go in order to become Bar or Bat Mitzvah," "I get to see my friends."

The question is really rather basic: what attracts students to your class? Again, once aware of the reasons that students might possibly be attracted to your class, you may be able to increase both the attractiveness of the group and your own attractiveness as well.

Let's begin with the group. For many students, Religious School is the only time they get to see Jewish friends from other public schools or neighborhoods. Sometimes, in spite of attempts by teachers and administrators to disrupt cliques of friends, the kids nevertheless find ways to socialize, to create and maintain friendships. In the attempt to build community in the classroom, the development of friendship groups is not only desirable, it is critical.

Friendships are the bases upon which groups are built. Most people look for somebody to be friends within a group. Belonging to a small friendship subgroup helps individuals connect with the larger group, thereby increasing feelings of attraction to the class.

Students in a Religious School classroom will usually know their classmates. This may or may not indicate they have friends in the group — people they genuinely want to be with. Even if they do, it is up to the teacher/leader to help develop friendships among all the students and thereby increase the attractiveness of the group.

The first step in the process of creating friendships is to discover those friendship patterns which already exist. This can be done through a simple sociometric technique.

If you have open seating in your classroom, make a chart of where students sit each time you meet with them. By analyzing several of these charts, you should be able to distinguish friendship dyads, triads, and small groups. Other facts which might help identify friends are class lists from past years. Find out who was in same Religious School class last year and in years past. Sometimes youngsters have become friends simply by virtue of being together throughout Religious School. Ask the student three important questions: (1) What public school do you attend? (2) Where do you live? and (3) With whom do you carpool to Religious School? Students who share the same neighborhoods, schools, and carpools are likely to be friends, although this is not always so. Sometimes familiarity breeds contempt. Finally, simply ask the kids to identify their three closest friends in the group.

Knowing this information will help you greatly in trying to build a network of friendships in the group. Ideally, everyone in a classroom community is friends with everyone else. Realistically, this is very hard to accomplish. Yet, there are several specific strategies teachers can use to help create friendships.

Allow time and effort for friendships to develop. A teacher must be willing to spend time in class on group process exercises and on social situations that arise in the group.

EMPHASIZE EXPERIENTIAL LEARNING OPPORTUNITIES.

Ensure that the students participate in enjoyable activities together, whether in class or in extra-curricular activities. Arrange to take the group for ice cream after class on a Sunday. Take them ice skating on a Saturday night, or invite them to your home for a Friday night Shabbat dinner. Organize a weekend retreat, where perhaps the best environment exists for group building. Someday your students may not remember much about your class, but they will recall with fond memories the teacher who provided these opportunities for friendship development.

Each member of the group has some strengths and talents. Discover what they are and accentuate them in the group. Try to build lessons and experiences which include the opportunity for your students to utilize their talents and skills in the class work. Students with similar hobbies or talents may be attracted to each other, but only if they know they share these interests. Encourage all students to appreciate the unique abilities of each of their classmates.

Be sure that each person feels positive self-esteem and respect when they participate in the group. Of course, this is easier said than done, but by accentuating individual strengths and giving people a sense of competence, a higher degree of group attraction will result.

Above all, the people must share common experiences together to develop group friendships. By participating in mutual experiences, the members of the group will be building shared group memories — the glue which binds most friends together.

There are aspects of the class environment beyond seating designs which can also be fashioned to be more attractive to students. The classroom meeting space should be physically attractive. The common decor of most Religious School classrooms consists of a worn Aleph-Bet chart, an old JNF poster and a Jewish calendar from the local mortuary. Who can be attracted to that environment? Make it a class project to decorate the bulletin boards with murals, projects, and art work. In elementary grades, be sure to put up student's work. Visit one of your student's public school classes. If your Religious School classroom is not as attractive, there is work to be done. (For a more detailed discussion of bulletin boards, see Chapter 5, "Effective Bulletin Boards.")

An attractive space is only the beginning of creating an attractive classroom. The curriculum itself must be stimulating, interesting, and relevant to student's needs. An emphasis should be placed on experiential, activity-oriented learning opportunities. Perhaps there will also be a sense of surprise in the curriculum. Don't tell the students about everything you'll do in advance —

create a sense of anticipation. Students should feel that something interesting and worthwhile is likely to happen at each class meeting.

It is important for students to feel a sense of ownership toward the group. It is somewhat difficult to identify exactly what contributes to this feeling, but one factor seems critical. Students need to feel they have a voice in what happens in the group. In a group of teenagers, this might be manifested by giving students a role as junior decision makers in the group process. In elementary grades, students who have choices about what and when they will learn (e.g., in learning centers) or even choices from among teacher-determined alternatives, are likely to have a sense of ownership. And, of course, teachers can encourage students to view the class as their group by referring to it as such. Teachers need not refer to the group solely as "my class." It is "our class"; we belong to it and it belongs to us. If students feel this sense of mutual influence, their investment in the success of the group will increase.

Students will be attracted to a classroom group where they encounter success — not only academic success, but social success as well. Teachers must ensure that each student has a feeling of success and that the class is viewed as a successful group. Look for opportunities for group praise. For example, at the end of a particularly good session, you might remark, "We worked really well today. I look forward to an even better session next week." People enjoy belonging to a "good" group.

Finally, let us examine how the teacher can increase his/her own attractiveness:

Students are attracted to teachers who are likable, respectable, consistent, and trustworthy.

Teachers should show genuine interest in individual class members and in the success of the group.

Attractive teachers are empathetic. They can see things from the student's point of view and accept students where they are at.

Teachers who are aware of the kids' culture can be attractive to students. Keep up to date on sports, current events, movies, records, television, and fads. Show that you are generally a "with it" person, aware of the world beyond the classroom.

It is important for the teacher to establish a relationship with each and every individual in the classroom. You can never hope to lead the group if you don't enjoy a working relationship with each of its members.

Participate in every activity in which the group engages. This is absolutely critical. Always include yourself in group activities as a participant as well as a leader. If you ask students to do a particular communications exercise, you do it, too. If you ask them to create an art project, you do it, too. If you ask them to share information about themselves, you share information about yourself as well. Never ask class members to do something you would not do. Be a model of the behavior and attitudes you expect, and watch your attractiveness as a teacher grow.

AGREED-UPON NORMS AND GROUP PROCESSES

A good working group operates according to a set of agreed-upon norms. These standards of conduct include (1) rules for group behavior, (2) expectations of academic achievement, and (3) setting a tone for group participation and interaction.

It is generally up to the teacher or leader to establish the ground rules for group activities. Depending on the level of your students, these standards may take the form of a set of rules for behavior established by teacher direction (no talking out of turn, one person leaves the room at a time, etc.) or they may emerge as the need arises.

Another way of arriving at a set of norms is by discussing the requirements of living together as a group. This necessitates attention to the group process. At an early meeting of the group, this issue can be raised and dealt with through a process of mutual decision making. There may be certain rules of the school which must be followed. There may also be a set of conditions you, the teacher, wish to see observed in the group. And the students themselves, based on their experiences with classroom rules, will contribute their ideas for good group behavior. Once all the rules have been stated, have the group attempt to consolidate them into a few basic standards for classroom conduct. Ask the group to agree upon the norms, verbally or in a written contract. Impress upon them that the job of ensuring adherence to these standards is not the teacher's alone, but is a group responsibility.

It is also important to set norms for academic achievement in the group. This relates to the previous discussion on expectations, but deserves special notice. The classroom community is not just a discussion group. Most kids in Jewish schools are bright and underchallenged. The activities, projects, and learning experiences must be at levels of interest which encourage student involvement and commitment.

Finally, the teacher/leader has a critical role to play in setting a tone of acceptance and good feelings in the group. It is not unusual for subgroups and cliques to form in the early stages of classroom community's development. It is also not unusual for certain students to be isolated, even scapegoated by others in the group. The teacher should model a standard of acceptance of all students and work to break down walls of separation which may develop. While some students will be friendlier with certain others, the overall tone of the class should be one of togetherness as one group. The exercises suggested here, the effects of participation in group activities, and the attention to group process throughout the life of the group will all assist in creating this atmosphere in the class.

GOAL ORIENTATION

Most effective groups are organized with specific goals or tasks in mind. Classroom groups are no different. In fact, the curriculum of good classroom groups can be outlined through a process of realistic goal setting.

There are various levels of goals in any group. Each individual has personal goals for participating in the group — e.g., a student may come to your class to meet Jewish friends. The group itself has goals for itself and its members — e.g., the school has created the class to teach its members Hebrew. Sometimes the individual's goals and the group's goals are similar; sometimes they differ. Then, of course, each individual may have different personal goals, creating at variety of needs and expectations.

That is why it is advisable to attempt to introduce a "superordinate goal" for the class, a goal which overrides all other individual and group goals and creates one unifying group task or project. Such a project will allow each student to participate in the group's activities and contribute to the achievement of the goal. Moreover, the best superordinate goals are those which emerge from the students themselves for they are then more likely to feel the project is "theirs."

Examples of superordinate goals include: planning and producing a class play, filming an original movie, preparing a graduation program, organizing a field trip.

Even if superordinate goals are difficult to establish, an effective group is usually capable of identifying goals and organizing itself to achieve them. This "task-orientation" helps to focus group activity and gives members a unifying purpose. The teacher must assist the group in providing or identifying individual and group goals which are desirable, achievable, and agreed-upon by most of the group members.

CONCLUSION

There are many more things to be said about the complicated process of creating community in the classroom. The sources listed in the Bibliography offer excellent guidance and creative examples.

The rewards of the successful establishment of a community feeling in the class are considerable. The most amazing result is that kids begin to care about coming to meetings of the community, their class. A new, more positive attitude about their involvement at Religious School begins to manifest itself. Students begin to enjoy learning about Judaism, because within the context of their own personal Jewish community, the knowledge and experiences encountered there make sense.

Perhaps more importantly, lifelong friendships are created which can exert enormous influence over important aspects of students' lives. Students begin to consider how their actions and attitudes fit with their primary Jewish group. The teacher, having established a warm, caring relationship with each student, maintains a powerful influence over each person's thoughts and actions. And, in many cases, the group makes a commitment to continue their associations with each other, the school, and Jewish life.

One final point. The Jewish teacher today, perhaps unfairly, is asked to do many things. He/she must not only teach about Judaism; in many cases, he/she is asked to provide kids with a sense of Jewish identity as well. All this is to be done with limited support, resources, and time. For many, the addition of another task for the already overburdened Jewish teacher may seem a luxury. But, if the arguments presented above ring true, then the task of creating community in each and every Jewish classroom is no luxury; it is an absolute necessity. For, if we fail to provide our kids with a sense of belonging to a personal Jewish community, then the noble efforts of Jewish educators may be for naught, and another generation of Jews will continue to shrug off Judaism with an apathetic "who cares?" In whatever way and at whatever level that is comfortable with our own teaching styles, each of us can begin this process in our own classrooms. To the extent that we succeed, our students will appreciate the experience of being together in a Jewish community — now and for many years to come.

Ron Wolfson is the Director of the Shirley and Arthur Whizin Institute for Jewish Family Life and Vice President of the University of Judaism. He is the author of The Art of Jewish Living series published by the Federation of Jewish Men's Clubs and the UJ.

BIBLIOGRAPHY

Brophy, J. *Classroom Organization and Management*. Washington, D.C.: National Institute of Educational, 1982.

Johnson, David W., and Roger Johnson. *Learning Together and Alone*. 3d ed. Englewood Cliffs, NJ: Prentice Hall, Inc., 1990.

Johnson, David W., et al. *Circles of Learning: Cooperation in the Classroom*. Alexandria, VA: ASCD, 1984.

Schmuck, Richard A., and Patricia A. Schmuck. *Group Processes in the Classroom*. Dubuque, IA: William C. Brown Co., 1992.

Stanford, Gene, and Barbara Dodds Stanford. *Learning Discussion Skills through Games*. New York: Citation Press, 1969.

Stanford, Gene. *Developing Effective Classroom Groups*. New York: Hart Publishing Co., 1977.

Wolfson, Ronald G. "A Description and Analysis of an Innovative Learning Experience in Israel — The Dream and the Reality." Unpublished Ph.D dissertation, Washington University, St. Louis, Missouri, 1974.

CHAPTER TWO

DESIGNS FOR JEWISH LEARNING SPACES

Joel Lurie Grishaver and Joyce Seglin

Every classroom has a wardrobe. It is dressed in its wardrobe (or designed and redesigned) by the teacher every time it is used. The wardrobe can be "store-bought," coordinated and fashionable, or homemade, free flowing and eclectic. It can be custom tailored to maximize potential (and to disguise weaknesses) and it can be up-to-date, influenced by the times and by current styles. It is the responsibility of the teacher to shape the classroom into an inviting space, a place which encourages and enhances Jewish learning in meaningful ways.

While there will always be compromise caused by school regulations and budgetary limitations, every teacher can evolve a teaching space which enhances instruction. This chapter will present some of the possibilities for doing so.

Regardless of how a room starts out, no matter what chairs happen to be in it, no matter how much gum has piled up and no matter what is on the walls, no matter where in the building it is located and no matter how dark, dismal, dungeon-like, and dirty it seems, space can be shaped and improved by the teacher. To begin such a transformation, it is necessary to have a vision of what our classroom might become. We need to begin with a sense of the ideal place for our class to meet. Then we need to move this ideal into an achievable reality. Few schools, if any, enable us physically to build or rebuild our teaching areas. Indeed, many of us share our spaces, or work in spaces which are not meant to be classrooms at all. Yet all of us can rearrange chairs, pin, tape, tack, staple, hook, or otherwise attach objects to the wall. And all of us can buy or make things to beautify our rooms. Thus we begin to outfit our classroom.

The first step in designing an ideal learning space is to collect data on the key elements: the teacher, the subject, the students, and the physical space. Below is an outline for a needs assessment. It will provide you with some key areas to consider as you plan your ideal environment.

JEWISH LEARNING ENVIRONMENTS NEEDS ASSESSMENT
First Impressions

Consider first the age and grade of your students, what students are like at this age, and the subject of the course. Be aware of the number of students in the class and the number for whom the room is designed. From this basic information you can draw some quick conclusions.

Which of the following statements about instructional needs will be true for you? My classroom will:

1. be overcrowded.
2. have adequate room in which to work.
3. be mine alone to do with as I wish.
4. be shared with one or two other teachers.
5. consist of makeshift space, existing only when the class meets.
6. house students for one period at a time.
7. house the same students all day for all subjects.
8. be the location for the same (or similiar) lessons happening more than once on a given day.
9. house the same students for two or three periods each time schools meets.
10. be the location for many different types of lessons directed by me.
11. change locations from period to period, meaning that my environment has to be carried (or rolled) around.
12. be "destroyed" by another class which uses the room.

13. contain extremely active students.
14. by the middle of the day, be filled with youngsters who will need a change of activity.
15. contain munchkins whose bathroom needs have to be considered.
16. contain tired, burned out kids who have already been to school, dancing, swimming, and/or soccer practice.
17. contain not-yet-awake, dragged-out-of-bed kids who refuse to take off their jackets and who try to sleep.
18. contain unwashed youngsters who bring the locker room environment with them.
19. contain carefully dressed kids who are afraid to get dirty.
20. be bothered by all kinds of external distractions.
21. have to contend with the effects of climatic conditions (e.g., snow boots, umbrellas, mud, roof leaks, and other teaching hazards).
22. need to contain specific resources necessary for my subject.
23. need to provide the possibility for use of specific equipment, such as audiovisual hardware.
24. be mysterious to me until I know more.
25. be an environment that I can design and manage.

Based on what you have learned from these considerations, decide what kind of a room would best suit your needs. Request the ideal space.

Content Needs

The subjects you teach make demands on the classroom environment. Think about the answers to these questions for each subject that you teach:
1. What materials will the students be using in class? (books, workbooks, worksheets, audiovisual aids, etc.)
2. What kind of working area do these materials demand?
3. What kind of storage will be needed for materials?
4. What kind of possibilities for visual display are needed? (chalkboards, flip charts, TV/VCR, projectors, etc.)
5. What support facilities do these require? (electrical outlets, window shades for darkness, wall space, etc.)
6. What kind of display space will be needed on an ongoing basis for charts, maps, models, pictures, student projects, etc.?
7. What kinds of access, storage, and security will be required?
8. How can you avoid carrying in the needed items each time the class meets?
9. What tools will you and your students need on a regular basis? (art supplies, writing utensils, various kinds of paper, hole punches, folders, etc.)

The classroom is not only a place to learn, it is also a setting in which to be Jewish. Before continuing, think about the things your classroom needs for you to foster the development of Jewish feelings and actions, e.g., *mezuzah, tzedakah* box, an Ark, posters, Israeli flag, etc.

Teacher Needs

On a certain level, a classroom needs to belong to the teacher. It is as personal as an office or a workshop. You have the right to invest some effort in making it a place which reflects your personality and goals and which makes you comfortable. In this regard, you will want to consider the following:
1. What will you want to have in your room to make it yours? (pictures, coffee mugs, an objet d'art for the desk, posters, etc.)
2. What kinds of privacy needs do you have? Will there be areas that are off limits to students?
3. What teaching styles will you utilize?
   a. Lecture (don't feel guilty — it's a good technique)
   b. Lecture-demonstration
   c. Lecture-discussion (Socratic or free flowing)
   d. Lecture-activity
   e. Media presentations to the whole class (with or without teacher participation)
   f. Worksheets to be gone over by the whole class
   g. Student presentations to the whole class
   h. Games for the whole class directed by the teacher or a proxy
   i. Small group work (each group does the same task)
   j. Small group work (each small group does a piece of the whole)
   k. Small group work (each group rotates through a progression of tasks)
   l. Small group tasks which are competitive or interactive (debates, games, simulations)

m. Small group tasks with motivation or skill level adapted to the specific needs of each group
n. Individualized instruction (each student completes the same material at his/her own pace)
o. Individualized instruction (each student completes similar material with various units added or deleted based on individual needs)
p. Individualized instruction (each student works toward the same objective and chooses the learning tasks that facilitate mastery)
q. Individualized instruction (each student receives a set of materials which have been customized to meet his/her needs and interests)

YOUR TEACHING STYLE DETERMINES HOW YOU ORGANIZE YOUR ROOM.

The teaching styles you use will determine how you organize your room. For each of the styles outlined above, two choices are possible. The student can go to a specific area in the room and complete his or her work there. Or the student can pick up material at a central storage/display area to use at his/her seat. Combinations of these two procedures are possible. Materials can also be passed out by the teacher to each student.

Items (a) through (h) describe frontal teaching, meaning that the attention of the class is focused in one place. Items (1) through (m) describe cluster learning, meaning students are learning in small, interactive groups. Items (n) through (q) describe individualized learning formats in which students are individually paced and directed. Most teachers use a combination of these techniques. Think about the teaching styles you use and estimate the percentage of time you will spend utilizing each. When you design your room, decide which format is the dominant one and to which other styles the room needs to be able to adapt.

Student Needs

While the classroom may "belong" to the teacher, it must also be a setting which supports the students' needs. Things to consider in this area are:

1. How big are your students and what kinds of furniture can they comfortably sit in or on?
2. What kind of energy level can you anticipate? Will you need to contain or excite?
3. What kinds of classrooms are students used to? How have their weekday schools and their previous religious school rooms been arranged and structured? (You will need to evaluate whether a change will enhance or confuse.)
4. What socialization needs do your students have? Do they socialize in groups of two, three, five, or by the roomful? (Here you will have to balance nurturing and restraining student needs.)
5. What time of day do you teach the children — morning, afternoon or evening? Is it before other things they want to do or after important things they have already done?
6. For how many hours will you have a group? Anticipate how many activities it will take to fill that time slot.
7. What are the privacy needs of your students? Are there things you want them to be able to put away during class that neither you nor their peers know anything about? What kind of privacy should they have from other students and from the teacher?
8. Is there a problem child of whom you are aware? How will he or she affect your room?
9. In what way will you allow both the individual students and the group as a whole define the room (and/or portions of the room) as theirs?

Based on the insights that these questions trigger, decide what design factors you want to add to your master plan.

BETWEEN THE REAL AND THE IDEAL
Your Classroom

So far, as a first step, we have been collecting data related to instructional needs. Your answers reflect the kind of place you want your classroom to be. Now envision the room you have been assigned. Visualize the furniture, storage, display areas, chalkboards, bulletin boards, movie screen, electrical outlets, lighting, overall appearance (dark, bright, small, cavernous, cold, etc.), available space, and built-in distractions. Analyze the problems you think you might face. Determine the gaps between the real classroom which you inherited and the ideal one you imagined earlier.

Several solutions are possible to the problems you anticipate. Perhaps you can have different furniture brought into you room. You might request additional electrical outlets or other minor alterations. Some of the difficulties may be alleviated by buying or building some items or by changing the wall surfaces with paint, posters, or Contact paper. If the situation is really untenable, request a different room. It never hurts to try!

Resources

The second step, once you have completed your needs assessment, is to obtain a catalogue of classroom supplies. There are available catalogues filled with thousands of useful items — classroom decorations, storage pieces, instructional aids, student awards, and items which defy categorization. Remember that any item which was designed for secular education can be adapted to Jewish education. Furthermore, almost all of the expensive items which are pictured (other than the electronic items) were probably first made by a classroom teacher out of shelf paper, cardboard, or other scrounge materials. Your challenge will be to figure out how to make or acquire your own version of those items that you feel will enrich your classroom. In the Bibliography at the conclusion of this chapter, you will find several helpful resources. If you are fortunate enough to live in a community which has a Jewish Teacher Center, visit and begin to network with other caring teachers who share ideas and resources.

In the next section, we will examine several elements essential to a well dressed classroom.

ELEMENTS OF A WELL DRESSED CLASSSROOM
Learing Centers

A learning center can be a physical location where a student can go (alone or in groups) to work on particular kinds of activities. It can also be a place where students obtain certain types of materials which they utilize or complete in their own work space.

A learning center can be a place for drama. It may be only a pile of cast-off clothes for costumes, or it may contain scripts or role play cards.

A learning center can be a shoe box filled with objects for students to sort, categorize, and identify. The shoe box can also contain items which make up a "historical puzzle." Students are asked to figure out where and when in history the person who used the items lived.

A learning center can be a place to read. It can be any quiet corner of the room — with or without a rug, sofa, or pillows — where students can read a specific story, or choose from among a variety of materials. (You might want to supply ear muffs to help make it a quiet place.) Worksheets or activity sheets can provide accountability for the reading that students complete.

A learning center can be a place to listen to tapes or watch a video. It can be stocked with elaborate equipment, enabling many students to work at one time, or it can simply be a small area for one student at a time. Such a listening center can generate questions, projects, and feelings. Directions can be given on a tape recorder. When a second tape recorder is added, students can fill in their own answers. (If you don't have a tape recorder, draft a teenager, a student who needs extra attention, or a parent to read to students.)

A learning center can be a chalkboard. It can be a group writing a story together or in turn. It can be (especially with colored chalk) a place for Hebrew language exercises. And it can be a place where values are expressed.

A learning center can be a window shade which has pockets glued to it. Students sort cards into the correct pockets or take the cards out of the pockets, completing suggested tasks back at their seats.

A learning center can be a collection of art supplies and "scrounge" materials. The materials can be used in an open ended way, or task cards and worksheets can outline instructions for specific projects.

A learning center can be a suitcase or table full of educational games.

A learning center can be a map. Students can use pins to trace routes on wall maps or grease pencils to write on laminated floor maps. Maps can be copied from 3-D models, or 3-D models can be made from maps. Maps can have layers of transparencies. Students can also trace maps on transparencies for their own use.

A learning center can even be just four sheets of poster board, each with directions for tasks students can complete.

BREAK UP YOUR SPACE WITH BOOKSHELVES, CABINETS, CUBBIES.

A learning center can be a place for content or interests, required or optional work, scrap paper art, pantomine, music, creative writing, investigation, drills and skills, poetry, programmed materials, construction (as in building), choosing a topic, doing research, and writing private journals. Centers can even be places to take tests and quizzes!

A room alive with learning centers becomes an inviting environment in which to learn. In such a room students will be learning in corners, on or under tables, in bookcases, at desks or on the rug. They will be hanging or standing or lying, working in an enriched classroom with a variety of resources including books, worksheets, projectors, computers, art supplies, games, chart stands, flash cards, manipulatives, and hands-on materials.

(For more on learning centers, see Chapter 16, "Classroom Learning Centers.")

Bulletin Boards

A bulletin board is a good way to utilize wall space for display and decoration. Besides the usual cork board, window shades, pegboard, windows, table edges, the back of chalkboards on wheels, cardboard boxes and ceilings can also be used for the same purposes. Bulletin boards can also be interactive, providing opportunities for sorting, ordering and reordering, hanging up answers (and questions) and so on. (For more on the subject of bulletin boards, see Chapter 5, "Effective Bulletin Boards.")

Storage Areas

The way we store our materials can affect (a) the way we decorate our classroom, (b) the kind of instruction we provide, (c) the kinds of things we can keep in our classroom, and (d) the kind of freedom our students will have there.

Storage areas can be the most attractive or the most unattractive places in our classrooms. They can be brightly decorated, displaying creative materials and learning possibilities, or they can be cluttered centers of chaos and confusion.

Our storage areas can define the ways we teach. Where we put books, files, paper, pencils, maps, crayons, and the like, determines who can get them. If they are accessible to students, then the classwork flows in one manner. If they are managed by the teacher, the classwork will proceed in a different manner.

The kinds of supplies a teacher keeps in the room are determined by budget, space, and security. Keeping a tape recorder, a set of reference books, a paper cutter, and other similar materials in the classroom necessitates the creation of ways to store them.

Unless they are built into the walls, storage places take up floor space. By placing bookcases, cabinets, cubbies, and the like creatively around the room, you can break up the space into subareas and you can enhance or limit movement.

Pencils can be put in tin cans, shoe boxes, pockets on boards, paper cups, or even in actual pencil holders.

Papers can be stored in cupboards, drawers, stacking trays, old filefolder boxes, hang-up folders, or paper caddies, anything an office uses, a cardboard version of anything an office uses, liquor boxes with sections, and dishpans.

Games, materials, and other junk can be put away in suitcases, milk crates, any kind of box, ice cream containers, shelves, file drawers, and corners of the room.

Bookcases can be made of boxes, crates, bricks and boards, cardboard cubes, confiscated skateboards. Real bookcases can also be used.

Inventories are stored in the teacher's mind.

Seating

Chairs, tables, benches, rugs, pillows, mats, and counters are meant for sitting. There are many different seating possibilities. Each of these will influence the tone, learning style, and management of a room. A few guiding principles, however, will help you more than a graph:
1. Circles are only good if you really want your students looking at and talking to each other.
2. The closer to the floor students are, the quieter and more controlled they will be.
3. A classroom can be arranged to support pairs of teaching styles such as these:
   a. Group work and frontal teaching: Furniture is arranged in clusters. All of the clusters face a single focus in the room.

b. Individual and group learning: Chairs or desks are clustered in groups of no more than four students per cluster.
   c. Lecture and individual work: Chairs and desks are in rows. (Such arrangements will rarely support a third style of teaching without moving furniture around.)
4. If a seating arrangement doesn't work, try another. If one way no longer seems to work, change it. If one way has been working well for a long time, change it just for variety.

TEACHING IN A NON-CLASSROOM

Teaching is most difficult in spaces which are not really meant to be classrooms. Many teachers face their students in hallways, alcoves, sections of social halls, and other "creative" spaces. Those of you who work in places like these have a special burden. It is a vital, though difficult, task to make both you and your students comfortable and at home in whatsoever forsaken corner you have been allotted. The three problems you will face in such a situation are distractions, ownership, and storage.

Distractions

When you work in "public" space, it is necessary to find ways to cut off the rest of the world. Doing so enables students to focus in on the lesson and the interaction that is taking place. In settings such as these, it is likely that you will have problems with noise from adjoining areas. You may also have problems with visual distractions — people who wander by in the course of the session, classes on their way to music or Hebrew, visiting parents, etc. If the ceiling is high (as it often is in a social hall), you may find students gazing into the vastness while listening to each noise echoing. Additionally, almost every shared environment contains temptations that your students are forbidden to touch, but which they find far more fascinating than anything you have to offer. The following will be helpful when dealing with distractions:
1. Avoid frontal teaching. Have students focus on papers or projects and work in small groups.
2. Work as close to the floor as possible. As mentioned before, the lower a group of students sits, the easier it is to control. They will also feel more together.
3. Limit the space you use even if there is room to spread out. The closer and more limited the working environment, the less distracting outside factors will be. Hold class in a corner made with a folding or rolling partition or construct a natural barrier of tables.
4. A carpet and dividers will draw students together and define the area. The chalkboard should be placed so that it directs your students away from, and not toward, distractions. Thoughtful placement of chairs will also help here.

Ownership

Your students will obviously be aware that yours is not a real classroom. Their first reaction will be to decide that if it is not a real room, then it will probably not be real school. Until they own the space, they won't own the learning process. If, however, students help to create or shape their learning space, they will feel better about being in it and working in it. Some ways of involving your students in the process of ownership are:
1. Roll out sheets of butcher paper and each week let students write, draw, cut, paste, color, paint, etc.
2. Together make a patchwork rug which can become the focal point of your portable room.
3. With your students, decorate the items which regularly roll in or are carried into your temporary classroom (e.g., blackboard, desk, cart, etc.).
4. Ask students to be responsible for carrying in materials and for transforming the space each week.

Storage Again

It is very demoralizing to have to pick up your classroom and put it back into your car trunk after every session. You feel as if you could do a lot more with the class, but that it is just not worth it to drag everything up all those stairs only to bring it back down. Not having one's own closet in the classroom can get the best teacher down. Some of the following suggestions may help:
1. If you don't have a "real" classroom, you nonetheless need, and have the right to have, a permanent storage area for all your materials.

2. Ask your school for a cart, a little red wagon, or for a rolling, folding bookcase. This will enable you to have both a drawer and a closet.
3. If your storage unit is inadequate, consider suitcases, milk crates, and, even as a last resort, boxes from reams of paper. Contact paper helps to make such cardboard containers look nice and the room less tacky.

SNAPSHOTS – A PORTFOLIO

Thus far in this chapter, we have discussed wardrobes and accessories for the classroom. But classroom designs go beyond color coordination. We'll end with a few total concepts. These are a few of our favorite learning places. They are places where the form (the design of the room) really does determine the content (the way the learning takes place). Enjoy these snapshots.

Ralph's Room

Ralph is fifty years old and earns his living as a salesperson. He is the type of guy who can tell you endless stories, most of which you enjoy the first time or two. Ralph loves to teach Religious School, and specializes in teaching values to upper junior high school students. He is good at talking with kids about sex, drugs, politics, and relationships, and tying these to Jewish values. When Ralph taught ninth grade (on a Tuesday evening), he requested the following: "Put the chairs in a circle. It doesn't matter if they are armchairs or folding chairs. Do not supply desks and make sure there is a chalkboard on which I can write. Put a coffee pot, cups, cream and sugar in the room." When the principal questioned serving coffee to ninth graders, Ralph explained, "They won't drink it. We'll sacrifice a pot of coffee every session, but they'll feel like adults and our conversations will go better."

Gila's Room

Gila teaches in a double room. Half of it is a "formal classroom" with desks in rows that face her desk and the chalkboard. The back half of the room has pillows and milk crates and a carpet. In the front half of the room, Gila gives lectures and tests and has the students work in workbooks. In the back half, the students stretch out and do their reading assignments. Here they also gather to do group projects. They frequently present plays and act things out. Gila also keeps a costume box in her room.

Once she was working on the rug doing research with some students. They were looking at some maps. She found herself chalking some additional maps onto the floor as she explained things. The following week her students were busy using the floor tiles as a grid on which multi-colored fabric tape was forming a huge world map. Once the class had finished the map, it served as the basis for a number of lectures and a variety of games. The room became an ongoing play-research area, symbolizing the interaction of teacher and student in the learning process.

David's Room

The first week of school, David sends a note home to parents telling them that the shirts and ties and dresses the children are used to wearing to Religious School will not be appropriate for his class. The following Sunday, the kids arrive in torn jeans and overalls. David arrives with hammers, saws, wood, and lots of tri-wall cardboard (the material out of which refrigerator boxes are made). The students build a box-like fort out of the tri-wall. Over the course of the year, that box is transformed into a sukkah, a model of the Tabernacle, part of Solomon's Temple, a modern synagogue, and a time machine. In David's class, the learning environment is the content.

Nate's Room

Nate teaches in a basement room. It is the one he wanted. He had often gotten in trouble for the amount of noise generated by his class. Nate's room has track lighting, a bunch of milk crates, some clipboards, a large area rug, and some risers. Nate doesn't teach in any one particular way. He uses every technique from group games to lectures, raps to role play. What he does is to shape, with his students, an intense emotional environment every week. Nate's empty state classroom is the perfect place for him to create the multiple realities through which his students learn.

CONCLUSION

By now you have seen the connections between the environment and the learning process. You have probably thought of dozens of ways to improve and enrich the environment in which you teach. Be sure to begin with a careful assessment of the physical surroundings, the content of the course, your needs and those of your students. Send for catalogs which will provide the necessary materials and resources. Then organize your room into learning centers, solve your storage problems, and decide on methods for display and decoration. The care you take to dress your classroom well will pay off in increased learning and student involvement.

Joel Lurie Grishaver is the Creative Director of Torah Aura Productions and the author of a myriad of materials for Jewish schools, including *The Life Cycle Workbook* and *Tzedakah, Gemilut Chasadim and Ahavah* (A.R.E.) He also teaches Bible and Rabbinics at the Los Angeles Hebrew High School.

Joyce Seglin is the Director of Education at Temple Sinai, Tenafly, New Jersey.

BIBLIOGRAPHY

Gareau, M., and C. Kennedy. "Structure Time and Space To Promote Pursuit of Learning in the Primary Grades." *Young Child*, May 1991, pp. 46-51.

Preparation of Inexpensive Teaching Material, 3d ed. Carthage, IL: Fearon Teacher Aids, 1988.

Resource

Teacher Created Materials, Inc, 6421 Industry Way, Westminster, CA 92683-3608.

Video

Tips for Improving School Climate. Arlington, VA: American Association of School Administrators, n.d.

CHAPTER THREE

PARENT INVOLVEMENT

Audrey Friedman Marcus

Long ago Rabbi Mordecai Kaplan, who arguably had the most significant intellectual influence on twentieth century Judaism, reminded us that to educate a child without educating and involving the parents and the entire family system can be compared to heating a house while leaving the windows open. I became convinced of this insight when, during one particular year of teaching Religious School, I realized that I had never met, or even seen, the parents of more than half of my students! This conviction has been bolstered by many studies and articles which point out a compelling correlation between academic progress, attitude, and parent involvement. Some educators, in fact, are suggesting that children taught by their parents, either before or after starting school, dramatically outperform their peers.[1]

This chapter does not include a discussion of family education programming. Family education is generally content oriented, often involves the whole family, links families with other families, and is geared to helping families become comfortable with and competent in integrating Jewish experiences and practice into their own lives.[2] That exciting trend in Jewish education is certainly related to parent involvement, but it is generally organized by the Director of Education or a Family Education Coordinator, rather than by the teacher. The discussion herein will be limited to suggestions for how teachers can establish and maintain contact with parents, interesting them in their child's Jewish education, helping them to understand and thereby to be able to reinforce the child's learning, and to bring them into the classroom for significant experiences.

WHAT IS PARENT INVOLVEMENT?

Parent involvement occurs when parents are involved in planning, implementing, and participating in Religious School activities which may or may not involve learning. Parent involvement also means communication between school and parents, the translation of school programs to the home. In other words, parent involvement refers to the attempt to join school and parents in a partnership venture which we call Jewish education.

It is true that many parent involvement activities are also organized by the school administration; yet, there is much that the individual classroom teacher can do. The purpose of this chapter is to suggest a variety of ways that you can develop and enhance parent awareness, interest, participation, and support. There are four areas in particular which present possibilities for parent involvement. These are communication, cooperation, participation/education, and evaluation. While there is a slight amount of overlap between these headings, they work quite well on the whole. Of vital importance is the fact that in each category, parent support and involvement has to be earned. Parents need to feel that you appreciate and care for their child and that you are deeply concerned about his or her development as a knowledgeable and committed Jew.

Communication

The first and most important area of parent involvement is the area of communication. If parents are to become interested in what is going on in your class, they need to be invited early and often to share in the important work of their child's Jewish education. A good way to begin is to write a brief letter to parents at the beginning of the school year. Be warm and friendly and open; this communication sets the tone for all the interaction to follow. Introduce yourself and describe the course of study for the year. Outline a few suggestions of ways they can share in your task and describe some opportunities for involvement. Invite them to stop by and introduce themselves and assure them that they are always welcome to visit while class is in session. Parents with several students in the same Religious School are sometimes uncertain as to which child's teacher you are, so sign your name and include the grade you teach and the room number of your classroom. If your group is not too large, you may prefer to telephone parents instead of writing them.

Instead of, or in addition to, writing letters, many teachers organize an orientation meeting for parents before or shortly after the beginning of the school year. These get-togethers can be held at school or in a home, with or without the children present. More ambitious teachers like the idea of holding an orientation breakfast before one of their class sessions. However you structure your orientation meeting, explain your goals and provide examples of the kinds of activities in which the children will be engaged. Discuss the importance of a positive attitude toward religious education on the part of parents, and help parents see their role as the teachers who have the ultimate responsibility for their child's Jewish education. Allow time for questions and discussion and an opportunity to socialize. If students are present, plan a separate activity for them at some point. While they are supervised by an aide, you can speak alone with parents.

One creative California preschool teacher, Diane Rauchwerger, arranged her orientation in such a way that each child and his/her parent(s) spent 20 minutes alone with the teacher. She greeted them and took them on a "tour" of the classroom. The child picked something to play with while parent and teacher talked. Before each family left, another family came. The two children were introduced and had a chance to play together before the next tour began. In this manner, each youngster knows at least one other child on the first day of school.

As the year progresses, you will want to stay in touch with parents on a regular basis. One way of doing this is to send home an occasional newsletter or bulletin which describes what is happening in class. This can be created wholly by the students, by you alone, or by you and the students together. Include some creative writing by students, as well as ideas for home activities, ways to observe a holiday together (e.g., how to build a *sukkah* or bake *challah*), blessings, art projects, recipes, discussion ideas, family trips, suggestions for enriching the Jewish home. Advertise a family poster contest or *sukkah* building contest in your newsletter.

Inform parents of available adult classes and upcoming community events. Recommend books and magazines on child rearing, Judaism, and other appropriate subjects, and suggest records and tapes for home use and subscription publications, such as *Home Start*, and *Jewish Family*. For sure, see that parents are aware of *The Jewish Parents' Almanac* by Danan. (See the Bibliography under "Resources for Parents" for a listing of these and other appropriate materials.) Encourage your school to set up a video home lending library so that parents can check out videos of Jewish interest.

Still another way to foster communication is to create a bulletin board specifically for parents. On it you can display various aspects of the curriculum, as well as current student work. Or, plan an attractive and informative poster on the classroom door each week, making sure that parents know that this is there for them when they drop off and pick up their children. Now and then you might prepare information sheets, placing these in a folder tacked to the poster. These can outline the lesson in still more depth and provide some follow-up activities and discussions for home. In the case of both bulletin boards and posters, students can be responsible for part, or even all, of both planning and preparation.

Some new commercially published materials contain components for each lesson geared to involving parents. You can easily design such components yourself when they are not provided. For examples, see the section "Involving the Family" in *Teaching Torah: A Treasury of Insights and Activities* and *Teaching Tefilah: Insights and Activities on Prayer*, both by Kadden and Kadden and published by A.R.E.; the parent guides that

INFORM PARENTS ABOUT CLASSES AND EVENTS, BOOKS AND VIDEOS OF JEWISH INTEREST.

accompany the *Building Jewish Life* series published by Torah Aura Productions; and *Why Be Different? Family Guide* by Rosenbeck from Behrman House.

These are just a few ideas for helping you communicate with parents. Your Director of Education and Rabbi can help you originate other methods of doing so. See the Bibliography for some resources on the topic for teachers.

Cooperation

Cooperation means the involvement of parents as helpers. Many schools still find that the appointment of one or two Room Parents for each class an effective way to involve people and to establish a network of communication among parents. If your school does not do so, send home a sign up sheet which lists all the ways that parents can assist (e.g., becoming a Room Parent, joining the Religious School Committee, driving for field trips, baking with the children, decorating the *sukkah*, helping with Shabbat dinners/holiday programs/specific events, making phone calls, planning and participating in family education programs, sharing talents, speaking to the class). Ask that the list be returned to you promptly and then be sure to call on everyone who volunteers at some point early in the school year. Include a request for any items you need, such as clothes and props for the costume box, fabric scraps, and other items for art projects, large cartons, smocks, refreshments, etc.

By all means invite parents to help in the planning and execution of all social and educational events such as Shabbat dinners, holiday celebrations, carnival booths, retreats, and *Shabbatonim*. Their input and help is invaluable and can also serve to draw them into the life of the school. Parents can help, too, with the preparation of games and hands-on and manipulative materials for the classroom. They can act as chaperones for field trips, as shoppers, and as library assistants. Ask them to read stories to non-readers and to take dictation from them during creative writing activities.

Invite parents (and grandparents, too) to teach a mini-course or a segment of a day's lesson or to give a talk about a subject in which they have expertise. Students will enjoy hearing about Jewish life as it used to be, interesting Jewish experiences, hobbies, or about trips to Israel or other sites of Jewish interest which are illustrated by slides.

Participation/Education

Similar to cooperation, participation refers to joint activities for parents and children times when parents are invited to share a celebration or learning experience.

Every holiday offers opportunities for parents and children to celebrate together in school. At least once a year, organize a class Shabbat dinner prior to services. Parents can plan the menu and buy the food. After blessings, a delicious dinner, and *zemirot*, all can attend services together. Many schools initiate such dinners for younger grades only. Junior high students enjoy such occasions, too, as long as the proceedings are kept on a high level and kids have an opportunity to socialize.

Congregation Am Shalom in Glencoe, Illinois, under the leadership of their educator Sharon Morton, has an extensive program of parent involvement and family education. One of these activities offers a delightful variation on the usual Shabbat family dinner. As a part of their study of Shabbat and the Jewish home, each first grader creates and decorates a Shabbat Box containing a *challah* cover, a *Kiddush* cup, candleholders, and a vase for flowers. Each child then invites his/her family (including grandparents) to a Shabbat dinner on a Friday evening before services. The group celebrates a Kabbalat Shabbat, using the Shabbat Boxes made by each child. The children light candles and are blessed by their parents. The children, in turn, then bless their parents. (In other congregations, a Shabbat Basket containing items similar to those in the Shabbat Box is sent home each week with a different child as an encouragement to parents to do a table service at home.)

During the year, you (or more than likely your school administration) will want to schedule a back-to-school event or open house or two for parents. Give parents as much notice as possible so that they can add these events to their busy calendars at the start of the year. If they come without their children to an evening function, this is an excellent time to have a discussion on such topics as child development, problems encountered when raising children, teaching Jewish values, synagogue skills, ways to give positive reinforcement at home to the efforts of the school, and so on. If desired, invite the Director of Education and/or an outside expert to participate. You can also display children's work and/or show a videotape of a class activity.

If children are also present at the open house, use this opportunity to engage parents and children in a learning experience at the same time as you demonstrate what the class has been studying. Students can conduct discussions, demonstrate newly learned skills, show original slides shows, put on plays and participate in arts and crafts activities, games, and learning centers with their families. Include parents whenever you can in review sessions or in a *siyyum* (a celebration marking the culmination of a unit of study).

An intergenerational retreat for the students and their families is a wonderful way to form close bonds and create a sense of community and purpose. Such an undertaking requires considerable planning — another opportunity for parent involvement.

Don't overlook the possibility of including parents in field trips as participants, learners, and contributors, instead of just as chaperones. They will enjoy and gain from accompanying the class to a Jewish museum, a bagel factory, a Jewish agency, a cemetery, or to services at another synagogue.

Whether the event is an in-class learning experience, a party, a retreat, or a field trip, be sure to make arrangements for all children whose parents do not participate to be "adopted" by a surrogate family.[3]

Whenever your students participate in an assembly, sing in the choir, conduct a service, or act in a play, be sure to notify parents and invite them to come. Include parents also in all recreational and cultural activities initiated by your class or by the school or community, such as Jewish art festivals, book affairs, film festivals, carnivals, fairs, and bazaars.

Arrange occasions after school during which your class can visit the library with their parents. This encourages both children and parents to read and enjoy Jewish books. If this is not a practical time because of carpools, arrange a library corner in your room which includes some adult books. Invite parents to come ten minutes early to browse and check out books. (For other creative ways of using the library, see Chapter 31, "Using the Library Creatively as a Door to the Future.")

Your school administration undoubtedly spearheads some family education programs. Nonetheless, you might want on occasion to prepare home kits that parallel your curriculum or that deal with a particular holiday. These might contain history and observances, an interesting reading, tape recordings of songs and blessings, worksheets for families to complete together, and suggested discussion topics. Parents could be involved in the preparation and distribution of these.

Consider introducing Torah Aura's "JET" cards, sets of activity cards to send home for parents and children to do together. The teacher keeps a class record of each card completed, and at the end of the year those who have completed the entire set receive a certificate. Or, discuss with your Director of Education starting a home reading program for families. One such program, *The Parent Connection*, has been published by the Boston Bureau of Jewish Education.

Some teachers use what is referred to as the "refrigerator curriculum." A list of things to be learned, such as the Ten Commandments, a particular blessing, or other item is sent home with the children to be hung on the refrigerator. Each family member is obligated to repeat the items on the list before opening the refrigerator door. You might suggest to the Director of Education the promotion of a school-wide "car pool curriculum" consisting of various questions of Jewish interest and import to be discussed on the way to and from Religious School.

In every way that you can, encourage families to do Jewish things together, to investigate their own history, to talk about Jewish ideas, values, and issues at home.

ENCOURAGE FAMILIES TO DO JEWISH THINGS TOGETHER.

Evaluation

The final category of parent involvement is evaluation. Frequent evaluation of students will help parents to be aware of and involved in their child's progress. There are many ways to share evaluations with parents. Report cards remain the most frequently used method, and are usually sent at the end of the school year. In addition, make every effort to send an additional report home at mid-year so that parents will know how their children are doing early on. Where letter grades are awarded, it is especially important to add anecdotal comments which inform about the child's attitude and participation. Furthermore, don't wait until report card time to send home a note praising a student's progress or describing a particular accomplishment, or a certificate honoring the child for a specific achievement.

Face-to-face parent teacher conferences represent another excellent way of working together with parents to achieve student success. (On occasion, such conferences can also include the child.) As preparation for parent conferences, you might consider sending home a questionnaire to be completed by parents and returned to the shcool a few days before the meeting. On this questionnaire, parents can check off or briefly describe their concerns to alert you to specific areas they would like to discuss.[4]

You will increase the involvement of parents in still another vital way, and win their admiration as well, if you ask them to help you evaluate the accomplishments and failings of the year. This can be done via a questionnaire sent through the mail, at individual meetings, by phone, or at a gathering of all the parents.

CONCLUSION

In all of the areas delineated above, it is important for the teacher, Director of Education, and Rabbi to work hand-in-hand to encourage parent involvement. Urge parents to attend Religious school PTA/PTO meetings or open meetings of the Religious School Committee. And become an advocate for the sponsorship by your school of joint and parallel classes for parents and children, for involving families in Bar/Bat Mitzvah programs, for frequent family services, and for *Shabbatonim* and retreats.

Audrey Friedman Marcus received her Masters Degree in Jewish Education from the Rhea Hirsch School of Education of Hebrew Union College-Jewish Institute of Religion in Los Angeles. She has been a teacher, junior high school coordinator, curriculum coordinator, family educator, and Director of Education. The co-founder of A.R.E. Publishing, Inc., Audrey is the author of many children's books, mini-courses, and articles on Jewish education.

NOTES

1. R. Barker Bausell, "Teaching Your Child," *Rocky Mountain News*, February 18, 1981, p. 45.
2. Janice Alper, "Characteristics of Jewish Family Education," *Jewish Education News* 14 (1), Winter 1993, p. 31.
3. Martha Aft, "Parental Partnership," *Compass*, Spring 1979, p. 10.
4. Sharon Schanzer and Beverly Bernstein, "Tips for Productive Parent-Teacher Communication," *Compass* 15 (1), Fall 1992, p. 21.

BIBLIOGRAPHY

Books and Articles on Parent Involvement

Alper, Janice P. "Celebrating the Jewish Holidays with Your Family." *Compass* 16 (1), Fall 1993, pp. 11-13.

Cervone, B.T., and K. O'Leary. "A Conceptual Framework for Parent Involvement." *Educational Leadership*, November 1982.

Cohen, Burton I. *Case Studies in Jewish School Management: Applying Educational Theory to School Practice*. West Orange, NJ: Behrman House, Inc., 1992.

Kane, Gerald M. "Moving from Dropping Off to Jumping In." *Compass* 16 (1), Fall 1993, pp. 9-11.

Kaye, Joan, proj. dir. *The Parent Connection*. Newton, MA: Boston Bureau of Jewish Education, 1988. (Preschool and primary editions)

Kelman, Stuart L. "Parent Motivation." In *What We Know about Jewish Education*. Los Angeles: Torah Aura Productions, 1992, pp. 187-196.

Miller, Betty L., and Ann L. Wilmshurst. *Parents as Volunteers in the Classroom: A Handbook for Teachers*. 2d rev. ed. Palo Alto, CA: R & E Research Associates, Inc., 1984.

Miller, Miriam. *Mothers and Education, Inside Out? Exploring Family-Education Policy and Experience*. New York: St. Martin's Press, Inc., 1993.

Reitz, R. *Parent Involvement in the Schools*. Bloomington, IN: Center on Evaluation, Development and Research, 1990.

Reimer, Joseph. "Between Parent and Principal: Social Drama in a Synagogue." *Contemporary Jewry* 13, 1992, pp 60-73.

Schanzer, Sharon, and Beverly Bernstein. "Tips for Productive Parent-Teacher Communication." *Compass* 15 (1), Fall 1992, p. 21.

Subscription Publications

Chanover, Hyman, ed. *Home Start*. West Orange, NJ: Behrman House, 1985/1987. (Level One, nursery and kindergarten; Level Two, Grades 1 and 2)

Jewish Family. Los Angeles: Torah Aura Productions. (6 issues a year)

Resources for Parents

Books

Bell, Roselyn, ed. *The Hadassah Magazine Jewish Parenting Book*. New York: Free Press/Avon, 1989/1991.

Danan, Julie Hilton. *The Jewish Parents' Almanac*. Northvale, NJ: Jason Aronson Inc., 1993.

Donin, Hayyim Halevy. *To Raise a Jewish Child*. New York: Basic Books, 1977.

Greenberg, Blu. *How To Run a Traditional Jewish Household*. 2d ed. Northvale, NJ: Jason Aronson Inc., 1989.

Isaacs, Ron. *The Jewish Family Game Book for the Sabbath and Festivals*. Hoboken, NJ: Ktav Publishing House, 1989.

Kushan, Neil. *Raising Your Child To Be a Mensch*. New York: Macmillan, 1987.

Mandelkorn, Nicolas D., and Vicki Weber. *The Jewish Holiday Home Companion: A Parent's Guide to Family Celebration*. West Orange, NJ: Behrman House, 1994.

Olitzky, Kerry M., and Ron Isaacs. *The How-to Handbook for Jewish Living*. Hoboken, NJ: Ktav Publishing House, 1993.

Syme, Daniel B. *The Jewish Home: A Guide for Jewish Living*. New York: UAHC Press, 1988.

Together 1: A Child-Parent Kit. New York: Melton Research Center, 1990. (Kit for 8 and 9-year-olds and their families on life cycle, celebration, and Jewish values)

Windows: 2. New York: Melton Research Center, 1990. (Four booklets for 11 and 12-year-olds and their parents)

Wolfson, Ron. *The Art of Jewish Living*. New York: Federation of Jewish Men's Clubs, 1985-present. (Books on Passover, Chanukah, and Shabbat are available.)

CHAPTER FOUR

CLASSROOM MANAGEMENT
Audrey Friedman Marcus

No handbook for teachers would be complete without a discussion of classroom management. Yet, this is such an extensive topic that a full discussion would require many volumes instead of one single chapter. I have chosen to solve the dilemma by including a brief chapter divided into three sections. The first section is a list of suggestions for advance planning, classroom organization, and creative teaching, all of which can prevent some discipline problems from occurring. The second section provides suggestions for dealing with those discipline problems that do occur. In the third section, you will find an overview of three particular methods for coping in the area of discipline: Dr. Thomas Gordon's Teacher Effectiveness Training (T.E.T.); Assertive Discipline, developed by Lee Canter; and Discipline with Dignity, created by Richard L. Curwin and Allen N. Mendler. It is hoped that readers will follow up on this limited introduction to classroom management by consulting some of the books on the topic that are listed in the Bibliography.

As I have met with and conducted workshops for Jewish teachers in the United States, Canada, and England, discipline is most frequently mentioned as the greatest single problem teachers face. They point out the difficulties of coping with students who don't want to be in their classrooms, but are forced to attend. They are angry that so much time is wasted on discipline and readily admit that they feel powerless and overwhelmed when students are rude and insolent. They wonder at the disbelief parents often express when misbehavior is reported to the home. They resent it greatly when instead of backing up the school, parents make excuses for their children and accuse teachers of conducting boring lessons. Teachers complain that mothers and fathers seem to expect religious education to engage their youngsters' attention in the same way as "Sesame Street," the Simpsons, Barney, or Little League. Faculty members assert that parents ignore attendance standards and do little to reinforce, or even show interest in, their children's religious studies or Hebrew lessons. Teachers are hurt and disappointed when open houses and back-to-school nights are poorly attended, particularly by parents of upper grade students. Perhaps the most frustrating realization of all is that we can offer no motivation comparable to acceptance in college which spurs our students to excel in secular or private school.

The entire matter is further complicated by the nature of today's Jewish students. These children represent an aggravating combination of the wonderful and the terrifying. On the one hand, they are bright, interesting, attractive, and eager. And on the other, they are spoiled, rude, precocious, easily bored, and annoying. What is more, mobility, the high rate of divorce, and abuse of varying sorts among Jewish families have thrust into our schools a large number of youngsters with emotional and behavioral problems. (For a fuller discussion of these issues, see Chapter 7, "Dealing with Children at Risk.") I think the Rabbis must have had contemporary teachers in mind when they said that teachers of young children are destined to sit at the right hand of God!

PREVENTING DISCIPLINE PROBLEMS

In the book *Looking in Classrooms*, the authors state, ". . . the key to classroom-management success lies in the things the teacher does ahead of time to create a good learning environment and a low potential for trouble."[1] From the literature and from my own experience, I have gathered a list of some important ways that teachers can avoid discipline problems. Since many of these methods are covered in detail in other chapters in this volume, mention here will be brief and will include a cross-reference to the related chapter or chapters.

1. Build a sense of community in your classroom. Encourage good listening skills, open communication, respect, trust, and agreed upon norms and goals. Show your students that you value them and care for them as individuals. Be there to greet them warmly when they arrive. Get to know them through discussions and individual conferences. Be interested in their lives and really listen to them when they speak. Accept them and be nonjudgmental about their opinions and beliefs. Share your own background, interests, hobbies, and views so that they can in turn know you as a person.

    Be affectionate, particularly with younger children. Since some older students resent being touched, and since there is risk these days in having your touches misunderstood, try bending down close to them when you are communicating. Initiate opportunities to be with your class outside of school — at a party or a picnic, or invite them in groups to your home for Shabbat or for another holiday or special occasion.

    In his book *How To Be a Jewish Teacher*, Sam Joseph asserts that the way students treat a teacher is usually a reflection of the way that teacher treats those students. He goes on to say that in a Jewish school we are trying to nurture future *menschen*, individuals who value human dignity and justice, who treat people with respect, and who believe in community. Joseph asserts, "It is important that the Jewish classroom live by the values it is obligated to teach. It is also important to note that the classroom that manifests these values is an environment in which learning will take place."[2]

    (For related ideas, see Chapter 1, "Creating Community in the Classroom" and Chapter 13, "Listening Skills, Lecture, and Discussion.")

2. Consider the physical environment in your classroom. Be sure it is a safe place to be. Arrange the room in a neat, cheerful, and attractive way so that students will be comfortable and receptive to learning. Be sure the room is light enough and that it is kept at the proper temperature. Mount attractive bulletin boards, wall decorations, posters, murals, and display work, and be sure that these are hung at the eye level of your students. Store equipment in convenient locations and make certain that traffic moves without confusion, delays, or obstructions. Designate a quiet corner for reading and thinking that is separate from the area where noisier activities take place. (For more suggestions on the learning environment, see Chapter 2, "Designs for Jewish Learning Spaces" and Chapter 5, "Effective Bulletin Boards.")

3. Plan your lessons thoroughly and conduct your class in a well organized manner. Always prepare a lesson plan, even if doing so is not required by your school. Be sure to have more material on hand than you will need in case an activity is unsuccessful or takes less time than you had thought. Begin with a good opener and involve students in closure. Give clear directions. Ask students to repeat the directions so that you can be sure they are understood. (See Chapter 19, "Planning Lively Lessons.")

4. Use a variety of teaching methods that interest, involve, and challenge students. Vary the pace of activities and the mode of interaction, and integrate the cognitive, affective, and psychomotor domains. Stimulating lessons will result in reduced boredom and fewer discipline problems. And, if you find that a particular activity you have planned is not succeeding, don't hesitate to switch quickly into something else. (See Chapter 21, "Creative Use of Textbooks," and all of the chapters in the sections "Teaching Methods and Strategies" and "The Arts.")

5. Keep your students alert by calling on each of them during a class session. After a response from one student, ask another student, "Do you agree with _____?" or "Is _____ right?" Now and then ask for mass unison responses, such as "How many of you saw *The Diary of Anne Frank* on television last night?"[3]

USE DIFFERENT TEACHING METHODS AND VARY THE PACE.

6. Initiate cooperative learning in your classroom (see Chapter 14, "Cooperative or Collaborative Learning").
7. Build in opportunities for students to release energy through active involvement in games, Israeli or interpretive dance, values clarification exercises that require moving around. Give them time for a stretch, organize a relay race or a run around the block, provide a snack, a break, or a recess. When energy is high, read a story, sing a song, play music, do role playing, put on a play, use puppets, or move students into learning centers. (See Chapter 16, "Classroom Learning Centers," Chapter 17, "Using Games in the Classroom," Chapter 18, "Values Clarification," and all the chapters contained in the section called "The Arts.")
8. Help children to know what to expect by giving a warning a few minutes before you plan a change in activity. Don't let the transition between one activity and another drag on or interrupt the flow of your lesson. (Effective teachers take no longer than 30 seconds for a routine transition, resulting in little misbehavior during the transition period. Less effective teachers spend as much as four to nine minutes between activities, during which time there is often misbehavior.)[4] Delays can be avoided by writing diagrams on the blackboard before class and setting out in advance all necessary equipment and materials.

DEALING WITH DISCIPLINE PROBLEMS

Regretfully, following all of the suggestions above will not completely eliminate all discipline problems. Here are some ideas for coping when problems do arise.

1. Gain early control. Some classroom veterans have adapted the well known public school adage and advise new teachers, "Don't smile until Chanukah." While this may be overly harsh, there is no doubt that students take great joy in testing a new teacher. After the brief "honeymoon" at the start of the year, behavioral problems tend to increase. When teachers practice effective management skills during this critical period, misbehavior falls and levels off.[5]

2. In conjunction with #1 immediately above, set behavior standards early in the year. Give reasons why certain behaviors are not acceptable. It is most effective to have students draw up their own code of behavior with the teacher acting as facilitator. Be sure that rules and expectations are clearly understood by all. Have students make a chart of the rules and post it in a prominent place in the classroom.

3. Enforce the rules fairly and consistently from the outset. Try to anticipate misbehavior. When unacceptable behavior occurs and disrupts the class, punish immediately. Many studies have shown that when punishment is administered early, students are hesitant to go on. On the other hand, don't overreact or blow a small matter out of proportion, or become angry over things you can't change. There are times when it is better to ignore minor misbehavior; calling attention to every single infraction tends to poison the atmosphere in the classroom. Kids are kids and it is natural for them to joke, sing, whistle, chew gum, show off, giggle, pinch, pull hair, etc.! It often helps to give a student who is causing a disturbance permission to do what he or she is doing at a future time — after the work is completed, during recess, after school, on the retreat, etc. Contracts which negotiate individual behavioral goals can also be effective.

4. Don't threaten students with punishments unless you intend to carry out your threat. Especially avoid promising a punishment that you do not have the authority to carry out, such as suspending a child from school. Never humiliate or embarrass students.

5. Be mature and controlled. Don't give mixed messages. Instead, model the kind of behavior that you expect from your students. If you don't want students to speak in loud voices or lose self-control, then speak softly and stay controlled. Don't use put-downs or sarcasm. Be warm and friendly and helpful and your students will imitate your behavior. Show your enthusiasm for learning and it is likely that your students will also be enthusiastic.

6. Don't stand in one place all the time. Move around the room. Stand next to a child who is acting up. Change the seating arrangement when students misbehave. Seat a troublesome youngster next to a responsible student, an easily distracted child next to a quiet, diligent one.
7. Don't always react in the same way. Make a surprise move — respond positively instead of negatively when a child disturbs the class; make a joke, ignore the incident and keep on with the lesson, and so on.
8. Use "desists" — actions taken by the teacher as an immediate response to misbehavior. These can take the form of a nonverbal cue, a verbal directive, or some other form of punishment. Carl and Ladonna Wallen have organized desist techniques on "stair steps" from minimum (eye contact) to maximum forcefulness (sending the child to another teacher's room):[6]
   Establish eye contact
   Frown at student
   Shake your head
   Move closer to student
   Gently place hand on student's shoulder
   Write student's name on the board
   Call student to your desk
   Scold
   Refer student to posted rules
   Remind student of earlier agreement
   Say "Sh"
   Call student's name
   Threaten loss of recess
   Inform of later conference
   Threaten trip to office
   Threaten call to parent
   Change instructional activity
   Take student outside to confer
   Take away privileges or jobs
   Provide adjustment time: exercise, drink, etc.
   Have student place head on desk
   Stand silently and wait for behavior change
   Send to counselor
   Move other catalytic students
   Move student to front or rear
   Move student to semi-isolation
   Place student at desk outside door (check with your Director of Education to be sure this is acceptable)
   Send to office
   Send to another teacher's room (need prior approval)

   Desist techniques should be used sparingly, as frequently used desists have a diminishing effect. Sometimes just making eye contact will be sufficient to cause a student to stop misbehaving.
9. Don't argue. Explain and discuss in a calm and firm way, but never argue with a child.
10. Use positive reinforcement. Stress and reward appropriate behavior, allowing every student many opportunities for success in both academic and behavioral areas. Use verbal reinforcers such as "Thank you," "That's wonderful," "Wow," "I like the way you work," "You did so well you're ready to...," "I really appreciate your participation in...," "When you are involved and not acting up, it really makes a difference to the class." Give positive reinforcement to the whole class with such statements as, "You are such good listeners," and "I'm so glad to see so many helpers." Use nonverbal reinforcers such as standing close by, smiling, nodding, thumbs up, or okay signals.[7] Give stars, smiling faces, happy notes to take home. Award free time, extra privileges, a chance to play a favorite game or participate in a prized classroom activity, or assign a special job to students who demonstrate appropriate behavior. When chastising, do so quietly at the child's desk, in order not to embarrass him or her. When praising, do it publicly, allowing the child to bask in the praise in front of classmates.
11. Initiate a system for quieting down the class when they become rowdy. One method, familiar from its use by Girl Scouts, is now a technique of cooperative learning. The teacher raises a hand, then each student stops talking and raises a hand until everyone's hand is in the air. (You can time the students as they do this — the entire class should be able to respond in 5-10 seconds, and they'll enjoy the race.) Another way is to do a countdown with the students from five to one. By the count of one, all mouths should be closed.
12. Don't wait to involve parents. Enlist their support when a problem first arises. When speaking to a parent, don't make accusations. Say instead, "I need your help. By working

together, I think we can help Becky behave the way we all want her to." (For more on relationships with parents, see Chapter 3, "Parent Involvement.")
13. Admit errors. Your students will appreciate your honesty and humanity and will respect you more.
14. Most important — maintain a sense of humor!

THREE APPROACHES TO DISCIPLINE

In an effort to cope with the growing discipline problems in schools, educators, philosophers, and psychologists in the last several decades have produced a seemingly endless variety of approaches. Some of these are listed in the Bibliography. I have chosen to discuss three quite different methods here. Each has its dedicated adherents who have found the system they advocate to be very effective. I believe we can learn many valuable insights from a look at each of these methods.

Teacher Effectiveness Training (T.E.T.)[8]

Teacher Effectiveness Training is based on the teachings of John Dewey and Carl Rogers. T.E.T. stresses the personhood of the students and the undesirability of power-based authority.

T.E.T. STESSES THE PERSONHOOD OF THE STUDENTS.

Developed by Dr. Thomas Gordon, the originator of Parent Effectiveness Training (P.E.T.), this method of solving classroom problems provides teachers with a new way of communicating with students. Dr. Gordon believes that the use of power and authority destroys relationships. For this reason he proposes a problem solving method which enables both parties to a conflict to join together in search of a solution that is acceptable to both, one that requires no one to lose. The method is not only applicable in the classroom, but can be used by parents, husbands and wives, employers and employees, and by anyone else dealing with a conflict situation.

Before using Gordon's No-Lose Method of Conflict Resolution, teachers need to learn and practice the skills of active listening. They must avoid what Dr. Gordon calls the twelve roadblocks to communication (responding by ordering, warning, moralizing, analyzing, cross-examining, etc.). Active listening means decoding the real message of what is going on inside the student and feeding it back. (See Chapter 13, "Listening Skills, Lecture, and Discussion.")

Secondly, teachers need to know how to state their own needs clearly and honestly by sending good "I-messages." There are three components of an I-message.
1. The sender of the message informs the receiver in a nonjudgmental way what is creating the problem (e.g., "When I hear talking in the back of the room . . . " or "When I get interrupted while I give instructions . . . "
2. The sender pins down the tangible or concrete effect on him or her of the specific behavior described in the first part of the message (e.g., "When the paints are not returned to the cupboard (nonjudgmental description), I have to waste a lot of my time collecting them and putting them away" (tangible effect).
3. The sender states the feelings generated within him or her because he or she is tangibly affected (e.g., "When you have your feet in the aisle (nonjudgmental description), I'm apt to trip over them (tangible effect) and I'm afraid I'll fall and get hurt" (feeling).

The No-Lose Method is derived from John Dewey's problem solving method. It is comprised of six separate steps.
1. Define the problem or conflict. This is vital to the whole process. Tell students what you need without giving your solution.
2. Generate possible solutions. To do this, involve all of those who are part of the conflict in brainstorming ways to solve the problem. Write down all suggestions without evaluating them.
3. Evaluate the solutions. Say, "Now is the time to say which of these solutions you like or don't like. Do you have any preferences?" Cross off any solutions with a negative rating from anyone, whatever the reason. Use active listening, state your own feelings, and send I-messages. Allow participants to argue the case for their solutions. Don't rush this step; let everyone have a say.
4. Make the decision as to which is the best solution. Often, everyone will agree upon one obvious best solution. If not, don't arrive at

the decision by a vote. Work toward consensus or at least an agreement to try one particular solution. Write down the agreed upon decision.
5. Determine how to implement the decision. Ask, "What do we need in order to get started?" or "Who is going to be responsible for what? And by when?" Write down who does what and the time schedule.
6. Assess the success of the solution. After trying the solution, see if the problem has disappeared, if progress is bring made, if the solution is a good one, and if the parties are happy with it.

The last important aspect of Dr. Gordon's method is the Rule-Setting Class Meeting which he recommends for the first day of school. During this meeting, students are involved in setting the rules and regulations for the class. Some guidelines for conducting the meeting, along with a full explanation of the method outlined above, are included in Dr. Gordon's book.

Assertive Discipline[9]

Assertive Discipline is the second approach to discipline to be discussed here. It has its roots in Assertion Training, which is a system designed to help individuals learn to express their wants and feelings more effectively. Thus assertive teachers are trained to communicate their wants to students clearly and firmly and to reinforce their words with appropriate actions. When teachers are assertive, they create a positive classroom atmosphere, striking a balance between their rights and those of the children and between firm limits and warmth and support.[10]

The first step for an assertive teacher is the setting of limits. This means determining the behaviors that you need from your students in order to function to your maximum potential in your classroom. Teachers are asked to make a list of no more than five of these behaviors.

The second step is to learn how to make more assertive verbal responses to student behavior. An effective message includes not only the verbal instruction, but the use of the student's name, eye contact, touch (a hand placed on the arm or shoulder), and a gesture with the free hand. Despite all efforts to sidetrack the teacher, the request is repeated to the student in a calm voice, like a broken record, and prefaced by such phrases as, "I understand, but . . . " or "That's not the point, I . . . " if the student still does not do what he or she is being asked to do, it is time to back up the request with a promise of action. Notice that it is a promise, not a threat.

The promise of action, or limit-setting follow-through, is done by giving students a choice, for example, "Karen, I want you to stop talking while I am speaking. If you continue to talk, you will choose to sit by yourself at the far table." Responsibility is placed where it belongs — on the students. They make the choice. Either they do as the teacher asks or they take the consequences. Teachers need to be comfortable with the consequences they employ. Consequences should be offered to the child as a choice and must not be harmful. They should be provided matter of factly, and without hostility as soon as possible after a child chooses to disregard the teacher's request and every single time this happens. Some suggested consequences are: time out (isolation to a corner of the room for 15-20 minutes), removal of a privilege or favorite activity, loss of recess privileges, a trip to the Director of Education's office, or a note or call to parents and negative consequences at home. (A "severe clause" enables the teacher to suspend immediately a student who willfully hurts another student, destroys school property, stands up and interferes with the learning process, or decides to refuse to do what the teacher asks.)

Assertive teachers are trained to give praise whenever students behave appropriately (see #10 under "Dealing with Discipline Problems" above). These positive assertions are delivered with eye contact, touch, and using the student's name. As students receive the attention they want for good behavior, inappropriate behavior begins to fade away and a positive classroom environment results. Parents are also sent notes or called when students demonstrate good behavior. Awards, special privileges, candy, toys, and special treats at home are also used when behavior is good. The entire class is rewarded for appropriate behavior with a party, a video, a special activity, or trip.

COMMUNICATE YOUR WANTS TO STUDENTS CLEARLY AND FIRMLY.

The proponents of Assertive Discipline recommend that teachers make a discipline plan just as they make a lesson plan. This plan should include the list of behaviors they want students to eliminate, the negative and positive consequences they plan to employ, and an outline of the steps that are necessary to implement the plan.[11] On the first day of school, the plan is presented to the class. The list of behaviors is posted in front of the room. Students are asked to copy the rules and to take them home for parents to read, sign, and return.

The class is told that when one of them does not follow directions, that child's name will go on the board. In secular school, this usually means that the student is required to stay after school for five minutes. Unfortunately, carpools make it virtually impossible to keep students after Religious School or Hebrew School. (More's the pity, I feel, since this disruption of parents' schedules might do wonders to straighten out children's behavior!) Another negative consequence may have to be substituted for detention. If the student chooses to disrupt again, a check mark is placed beside the name. This means an additional loss of privilege (or ten minutes after school). If a name has more than two check marks during a session, the parent is called. No discussion or complaint is permitted by the child. Names and check marks are put on the board with a minimum of disruption and without a break in the continuity of the lesson. Positive consequences (the reward system) should also be explained on the first day of class.

ALWAYS MAINTAIN THE DIGNITY OF EACH STUDENT.

Three-Dimensional Discipline — Discipline with Dignity[12]

Richard L. Curwin and Allen N. Mendler are the creators of Three-Dimensional Discipline, or as it is sometimes called, Discipline with Dignity. This philosophy of discipline encompasses a variety of theories and approaches, including Rudolf Dreikur's logical consequences, and is based on the authors' beliefs "that the best decisions for managing student behavior are based on a value system that maintains the dignity of each student in all situations" and that "behaving responsibly is more valued than behaving obediently."[13] The following description of this system of discipline is drawn from the book *Discipline with Dignity* by Curwin and Mendler.

The three dimensions are: (1) the prevention dimension, (2) the action dimension, and (3) the resolution dimension. The prevention dimension means having a plan for discipline that is structured and directed, yet flexible. The authors outline the stages of prevention: Increasing self-awareness on the part of the teacher (getting in touch with who you are and your mannerisms and teaching style); increasing awareness of students (getting to know them through school records, their interests and hobbies); learning to express feelings; discovering and recognizing alternatives (e.g, research, models, and philosophies of discipline); motivating students to learn; establishing social contracts (a list of rules and consequences governing behavior made for students by the teacher and made for the teacher by the students); implementing the social contracts; and dealing with stress associated with disruptive students.

The action dimension takes cognizance of the fact that despite all the efforts of both teacher and students, conflicts will inevitably occur. When this happens, teachers implement the consequence associated with a rule violation as outlined in the social contract. They also use the occasion as an opportunity to revisit the social contract and see if it requires revision. Consequences should be logical, instructive, and related to the rule that was broken. It is vital that consequences differ from punishments (e.g, a consequence for breaking a rule by talking when someone else is talking might be to have to wait five minutes before speaking; a punishment for violating this rule might be to sit in the hall for the entire period).

Positive consequences are an important aspect of the social contract formula, which can state not only what happens when a rule is broken, but what good things happen when the rule is followed. When a rule is broken, the authors urge consistency. State the rule and the consequence. Deliver the consequence in a soft voice while standing close to the child and making eye contact. (Every now and then deliver praise in this same manner.) Don't embarrass the student, be firm and anger free, and do not accept excuses, bargaining, or whining.

The resolution dimension is comprised of activities designed to reach the out-of-control student. The authors offer many creative solutions for dealing with such individuals, including role reversal, using humor, using nonverbal messages, audio or videotaping your class, audio playback, and using older students as resources.

The three overviews above were necessarily very brief, leaving out or skimming over many important details. Nonetheless, the descriptions provided should enable you to assess whether or not you think you could be comfortable using any of these techniques or a combination of some or all of them.

CONCLUSION

To be successful, any discipline method requires the involvement of every administrator and staff member, the Director of Education, the Religious School Committee, and the parents. All these stakeholders must work together to come up with a method suitable to your particular situation. (See the Appendix for the behavior guidelines developed under the aegis of the Religious School Committee for the Temple Sinai Religious School in Denver.)

Classroom management involves teaching creatively and motivating your students, as well as dealing effectively with the discipline problems that arise in your classroom. To enhance your skills in the area of creative teaching, read the other chapters in this book. Attend in-service training sessions available through your synagogue, day school, central agency, and secular education community. Attend the annual CAJE conference. To become more proficient in dealing with discipline problems, read some of the books and articles listed in the Bibliography. Improve your skills by attending training sessions on a specific system of discipline. Be patient; results will not be immediate. But you will be helped over the rough spots that every teacher faces by your enthusiasm, your love of children, and your increased knowledge and capability.

Audrey Friedman Marcus earned a Masters Degree in Jewish Education from the Rhea Hirsch School of Hebrew Union College-Jewish Institute of Religion in Los Angeles. She has given workshops on classroom management for many groups of teachers.

APPENDIX
Behavior Guidelines

Children in our congregation are entitled to a sound Jewish education. to help facilitate such, there are several basic behavioral guidelines for our Religious School students.

Students must attend school regularly, arrive on time, and be on time for every class and activity that is part of the school program. Parents should assure their children's regular punctual attendance and avoid early dismissal requests. Administration will contact the home when the situation warrants, and teachers will assign make-up work as necessary.

Students are expected to remain in the building during Religious School hours except when taking part in a school activity under staff or parental supervision.

Students must dress appropriately, behave with appropriate decorum, and follow the instructions of teachers and staff members. Every child must be respectful of adults, peers, and property. Disruptions, property destruction, and disregard for safety will not be permitted.

Food or drink may not be brought into the building or the classrooms unless requested by a teacher for a class activity.

Inappropriate behavior which cannot be resolved between the teacher and student will be dealt with as follows:

First Time	Child is removed from the classroom situation and will speak with the Director of Education. Teacher, student, and Director of Education will meet after class.
Second Time	Parents are notified by telephone. (The child may do the calling.)
Third Time	Parent will be called by the Director of Education. The child will be readmitted to class only when brought to the Religious School office or classroom by a parent.
Fourth Time	Parent must accompany the child to school, and remain with the child throughout the entire session.

NOTES

1. Thomas L. Good, and Jere E. Brophy, *Looking in Classrooms*, 5th ed. (New York: HarperCollins Publishers, Inc., 1990), p. 165.
2. Samuel Joseph, *How To Be a Jewish Teacher: An Invitation To Make a Difference* (Los Angeles: Torah Aura Productions, 1987), p. 73.
3. William J. Gnagey, *Motivating Classroom Discipline* (New York: Macmillan Publishing Co., Inc., 1981), pp. 69-70.
4. Bob F. Steere, *Becoming an Effective Classroom Manager: A Resource for Teachers* (Albany, NY: State University of New York Press, 1988).
5. Gnagey, op. cit., p. 64.
6. Carl J. Wallen and LaDonna L. Wallen. *Effective Classroom Management*. (Boston: Allyn and Bacon, 1978).
7. Keith D. Osborn and Jamie Dyson Osborn, *Discipline and Classroom Management* (Athens: Education Associates, 1977), pp. 96-98.
8. Thomas Gordon, *T.E.T.: Teacher Effectiveness Training* (New York: David McKay, 1975).
9. Lee Canter, with Marlene Canter, *Assertive Discipline* (Los Angeles: Lee Canter and Associates, Inc., n.d.).
10 Ibid., p. 37.
11. Ibid., pp. 94-95.
12. Richard L. Curwin and Allen N. Mendler, *Discipline with Dignity* (Alexandria, VA: ASCD, 1988).
13. Ibid., p. 20.

BIBLIOGRAPHY

Brophy, Jere E. *On Motivating Students*. East Lansing, MI: Institute for Research on Teaching, College of Education, Michigan State University, 1986.

Bull, Shirley, and Jonathan Solitys. *Classroom Management*. New York: Chapman and Hall, 1987.

Canter, Lee, with Marlene Canter. *Assertive Discipline*. Los Angeles: Lee Canter and Associates, Inc., n.d.

Curwin, Richard L., and Allen N. Mendler. *Discipline with Dignity*. Alexandria, VA: ASCD, 1988.

Dobson, James. *Dare To Discipline*. rev. ed. Wheaton, IL: Tyndale House Publishers, 1991.

Dreikurs, Rudolf, and Pearl Cassel. *Discipline without Tears: What To Do with Children Who Misbehave*. New York: NAL/Dutton, 1990.

Dreikurs, Rudolf, and Loren Gray. *Logical Consequences: A New Approach to Discipline*. New York: NAL/Dutton, 1990.

Dreikurs, Rudolf, et al. *Maintaining Sanity in the Classroom: Classroom Management Techniques*. New York, HarperCollins College, 1990.

Ernst, Ken. *Games Students Play (and What To Do About Them)*. Berkeley, CA: Celestial Arts Publishing Co., 1990.

Fromberg, Doris, and Maryanne Driscoll. *The Successful Classroom: Management Strategies for Regular and Special Education Teachers*. New York: Teachers College Press, Columbia University, 1985.

Georgiady, N. "What is the Most Effective Discipline?" *Principal*, Summer 1991, pp. 49-50.

Ginott, Haim. *Teacher and Child*. New York: Avon, 1976.

Glasser, William. *Reality Therapy: A New Approach to Psychiatry*. New York: HarperCollins, 1975.

———. *Schools without Failure*. New York: HarperCollins, 1975.

Gnagey, William J. *Motivating Classroom Discipline*. Lanham, MD: University Press of America, 1990.

Good, Thomas L., and Jere E. Brophy. *Looking in Classrooms*. 5th ed. New York: HarperCollins Publishers, Inc., 1990.

Gordon, Thomas. *Discipline that Works: Promoting Self-Discipline in Children at Home and at School*. New York: NAL/Dutton, 1991.

———. *T.E.T.: Teacher Effectiveness Training*. New York: David McKay, 1975.

Grossnickle, Donald R. *Preventive Discipline for Effective Teaching and Learning: A Sourcebook for Teachers and Administrators*. Reston, VA: National Association of Secondary School Principals, 1990.

Grubaugh, S., and R. Houston R. "Establishing a Classroom Environment that Promotes Interaction and Improved Student Behavior." *Clearing House*, April 1990, pp. 375-378.

Hawley, Susan, and Robert C. Hawley. *Ten Steps for Disciplining Difficult Students*. Amherst, MA: Education Research Associates, 1985.

Innovative Discipline. Washington, DC: National Education Association, 1994.

Joseph, Samuel. *How To Be a Jewish Teacher: An Invitation To Make a Difference*. Los Angeles, CA: Torah Aura Publications, 1987.

Hoppenstedt, Elbert M. *Teacher's Guide to Classroom Management*. Springfield, IL: Charles C. Thomas Publishing, 1991.

———. *Teachers Guide to Cooperative Discipline*. Springfield, IL: Charles C. Thomas Publishing, 1989.

Kreider, William. *Creative Conflict Resolution: More than 200 Activities for Keeping Peace in the Classroom*. Glenview, IL: Scott Foresman, 1984.

Maurer, Richard E. *Elementary Discipline Handbook: Solutions for the K-8 Teacher*. West Nyack, NY: Center for Applied Research in Education, 1985.

Mendler, Allen N. *What Do I Do When . . . ? How To Achieve Discipline with Dignity in the Classroom*. Bloomington, IN: National Education Service, 1992.

Osborn, Keith, and Janie D. Osborn. *Discipline and Classroom Management*. 3d ed. Athens, GA: Daye Press, Inc., 1989.

Rogers, Dorothy M. *Classroom Discipline: An Idea Handbook for Elementary Teachers*. West Nyack, NY: Center for Applied Research in Education, 1987.

Rossel, Seymour. *Managing the Jewish Classroom: How To Transform Yourself into a Master Teacher.* Los Angeles, CA: Torah Aura Publications, 1988.

Steere, Bob F. *Becoming an Effective Classroom Manager.* White Plains, NY: Longman Publishing Group, 1993.

CLASSROOM ENVIRONMENT

CHAPTER FIVE

EFFECTIVE BULLETIN BOARDS

Elyce Karen Azriel

Illustrated by Joanne Hemmer

There is nothing deadlier than a "dead" bulletin board in a classroom! In an otherwise drab schoolroom, attractive bulletin boards and display areas create a warm atmosphere and complement the learning which goes on there.

Effective bulletin boards are of an even greater value in the Jewish school. Much of the material taught in the Jewish classroom is remote from the students' daily lives; these visual aides help concretize such material.[1] With the use of simple designs and inexpensive materials, even the inexperienced teacher can construct an effective bulletin board.

A successful bulletin board can be created with the slightest amount of time, energy and money. Constructed correctly, it will simply and effectively express the subject or theme to be projected. Almost every subject that can be taught in the religious school can be depicted by means of a bulletin board. The beginning teacher will need the following components of creativity: inspiration, imagination, and inventiveness. Possible ideas for bulletin boards are everywhere — in daily conversation, events, holidays, etc. With time and practice, any teacher can become a skillful bulletin board manager.

The bulletin board in the classroom serves to motivate the student, interpret material, reward and recognize student work, and supplement lessons and units of study. It is a means of communicating students' and/or teachers' ideas through visual construction. It serves as a beginning to energize the interest of the students. A display of attractive pictures and articles will promote student interest in the subject being taught.

THREE KINDS OF BULLETIN BOARDS

There are three general types of bulletin boards: (1) teacher-made, (2) student-made, and (3) a combination of both.

For teacher-made bulletin boards, the teacher provides the ideas and leadership and carries out the task fully (see figure 1 below). Less tangible topics such as ethics, law, and atonement are usually better managed by the teacher alone. (For over 60 original bulletin board ideas for the Jewish school cross-referenced by topic and skills needing reinforcement, see *Original Bulletin Boards on Jewish Themes* by Moskowitz.)

Figure 1
A teacher-made bulletin board for an ethics unit

Student-made bulletin boards require student input from the very beginning, i.e, when the initial design is being visualized.

Students are responsible for content and presentation. The teacher allows them a free hand in the construction of the actual bulletin board, even though some of the materials may turn out to be slightly lopsided. In other words, teacher participation is not acceptable, even if it may improve the appearance of the final product. Some feel that the strategy of involving students in this process will result in increased interest in the final product. (See figure 2 below.)

Figure 2
A student-made bulletin board
for a unit on Israel

The third kind of bulletin board is created when the teacher provides the ideas and leadership and, whenever it is appropriate, asks for student involvement. A class discussion is a good stimulus, encouraging the sharing of the entire project and an equal partnership between teacher and student in creating the display. (See figure 3 below.)

Figure 3
A combination (teacher/student)
bulletin board (for Tu B'shevat)

WHERE DO I BEGIN?

The following represent the five steps necessary in the creation of bulletin boards. Each will be discussed in more detail.
1. Decide upon the purpose and subject.
2. Work out a caption.
3. Make a sketch of the entire bulletin board including locations, lettering, and colors.
4. Gather materials.
5. Execute and evaluate.

Purpose and Subject

Decide on the subject to be headlined and have a clear-cut idea of the purpose. The subject which is presented should include only one thought or idea. Possible topics which can be broadened into bulletin board topics and from which activities can emanate are: holidays and special events, centers of interest, the Jewish and general community, current events, a unit of study. Everything on the bulletin board should accentuate the principal idea that you choose.

The Caption

Select or create a caption that is short, captivating, and thought provoking. The caption is your selling point; it should tell at a glimpse what the display is about and should begin to generate curiosity and interest. Unusual and exciting captions can do a great deal to create initial interest in the bulletin board. Try using a question: How did Samson do it? Or a play on words: Israel Is Real. Or play on a current TV show, using "Family Feud" to portray the Joseph story or "The Match Game" to illustrate Noah's ark.

Rough Sketch

Begin to make a sketch, keeping in mind the size of the bulletin board. The sketch shows you how the materials can best be placed, and what the overall combination will look like. It will also give you an indication of whether the bulletin board appears overcrowded and if the parts tie together to produce a blended effect. Be careful that the board is not too "busy." A good bulletin board will have an orderly plan of arrangement. The sketch should include wording and location of caption, lettering and colors. Just as a bulletin board must have only one main topic, every display should have a visual area of emphasis, a main point of interest. This can be a large word, a bright color, or an unusual shape. Lines or arrows can play up the point of emphasis.

Bulletin boards should communicate their purpose, but it is also good to include a short summary of the purpose. Make it large enough for all to read and put it in a place where it can be read at eye level.

Gather the Materials

When gathering materials for a display, two main concerns should be variety of materials and color/texture. A variety of materials will maintain interest. It will help to collect and keep a file of all kinds of pictures and prints, as well as three dimensional objects such as pamphlets, models and craft items. When choosing colors, stick with those that are complementary. Choose a color scheme that is stimulating and tasteful, but do not use colors in such a way that parts of the board are competing with one another.

> BULLETIN BOARDS SHOULD COMMUNICATE THEIR PURPOSE.

Choose colors that are harmonious. If the colors do not blend well, both the viewer and the message may be lost. In warm weather, "cool" colors should be used: blues, greens, violets, grays, and white. In cold weather, the "warm" colors should predominate: reds, oranges, and yellows.

The background must be subordinate to the main display, but at the same time promote interest and vitality for the exhibit. Simple, inexpensive materials work very effectively and can be found easily. Textured materials, as color, should be chosen carefully so as to enhance the display and not overpower it.

The viewers should be able to see all letters from a distance. Therefore, a sharp contrast between letters and background is desirable. Lettering should be planned along with your art work; it should not be an afterthought.

Always have an eye open for something which can be used in your display. Don't be afraid to ask for what you want. Parents and congregants are more than happy to donate materials which they would otherwise throw out. The variety of materials to be used is practically inexhaustible. Here are a few suggestions for background materials:

Cloth Products
Colored burlap or burlap sacks – interesting texture, can be found at supermarkets.
Felt
Tablecloth
Colored cheesecloth
Fabric – can be found in clothing and garment factories. (Try to build up a network of suppliers. Eventually, these people will give you ideas for the displays!)[2] Use a dull knife to push raw edges under the frame of the bulletin board.
Old sheets – ask hospitals and linen companies for donations.[3]

Paper Products
Poster Board – Stationery stores, school supply stores, artists' supply dealers.
Construction paper
Tissue paper, crepe paper
Holiday or plain gift wrap
Shelf paper
Wax paper, aluminum foil
Wallpaper samples – from wallpaper or paint store
Newspaper – from doctor's office or bookstore
Road maps – from your neighborhood gas station, or from AAA

Paint – Cover an old bulletin board with latex paint or spray paint. It's washable and long wearing! Sometimes paint stores sell their returned or mismatched paints inexpensively.

Think of all the different materials that you and your family throw out each day. What about the colorful pages from your favorite magazine? Or the white plastic egg from pantyhose? Why not use all these easily accessible items?

Here are a few suggestions for lettering materials:
Sandpaper
Cut-outs
Pipe cleaners
Chalk letters
Yarn
Graph paper
Rope
Construction paper

Execution and Evaluation

As you create your final display, the following guidelines can be helpful.
1. Make the bulletin board express a single idea. If using more than one thought, section the bulletin board.
2. Make neatness in arrangement a governing principle. Don't worry if you're not a great artist!

3. Avoid crowding the board with too much material. Confusion does not communicate. Keep away from a scrambled effect.
4. See that the material posted is firmly secured in place.
5. See that the board is changed frequently. In a one to two day a week school, the board should stay up no more than a month.

Figure 4 below is a sketch for a bulletin board that indicates the locations of caption and illustrations, colors, lettering, and materials. The background is made of yellow and orange fabric, and the caption of red burlap letters. Other materials include a soup can, foil, a bowl, and yellow construction paper.

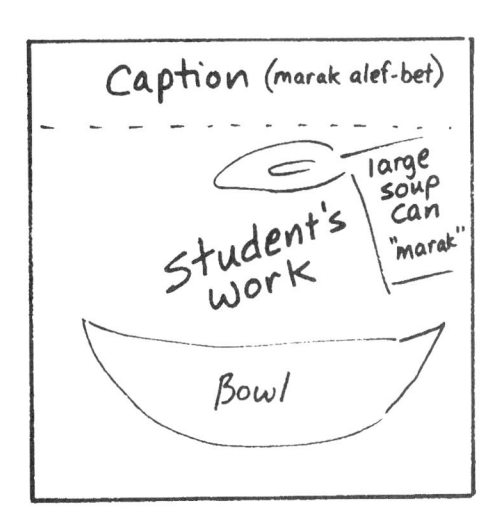

Figure 4

In evaluating your display, some of the best suggestions come from your own pupils and other teachers. Take note of the comments made when you first display the board. Then, when you no longer want the materials on display, take a close look and evaluate. Ask yourself these questions: Does the bulletin board have eye appeal? Does it attract attention? Are all elements well thought out? Is the board neat, orderly, and uncluttered? Are the captions short, concise, easy to read, and properly spaced? Does the board draw reactions from pupils? Is the material relevant, accurate, and up-to-date? Is the theme apparent at a glance? Is the display in good taste both in design and material?[4]

Storage

There is no reason why you cannot reuse many materials. This is especially practical for paper backgrounds, cutouts, letters, and numbers. The bulletin board itself can be put up each year for different classes.

Here are a few easy and practical ideas for saving displays:

1. Staple two pieces of posterboard together to form folders. File the folders in an upright position. Label. Attach an envelope filled with the letters and small pieces.
2. Use large plastic bags with heavy posterboard in front and in back of all materials. Staple to close. Label.
3. Draw a rough sketch on 3" x 5" cards and file by subject. This type of sketch is valuable for the re-creation of the bulletin board at a later date.[5]
4. Place pictures in a large manila folder or large envelope. Label the folders on the tabs and the envelopes in the upper right hand corner.
5. To remember the arrangement and color combinations from year to year, take colored photographs of each completed bulletin board. Attach to stored pieces.

SUMMARY

Either alone or with your students, every teacher can create effective displays for classroom enrichment. Using topics ranging from Torah to Tu B'Shvat, you need only invent a catchy caption and gather eye-catching, diverse materials to bring together one of the most effective learning starters.

The attractive, enriching bulletin board you add to your classroom is well worth the small investment of time and materials.

Elyce Karen Azriel has a degree in Jewish Studies from Spertus College and the University of Illinois, and a Master Teacher's Certificate from the Board of Jewish Education of Baltimore in conjunction with Baltimore Hebrew College. As a "Community Teacher," she teaches Hebrew as a foreign language under the auspices of the Jewish Federation of Omaha and the Omaha Public Schools. In addition she is a teacher and supervisor of Hebrew at Temple Israel in Omaha and Supervisor of their Bar/Bat Mitzvah program.

NOTES

1. Moses Zalesky. *Teacher's Kit No. 10 — The Bulletin Board,* (Cincinnati, OH: Bureau of Jewish Education, 1950), p. 1.
2. Linda Campbell. *Library Displays* (Jefferson, NC.: McFarland and Co., Inc., 1980), p.5.
3. Delores Kohl Education Foundation. *Teacher Centering: Ideas Shared by the Kohl Jewish Teacher Center* (Wilmette, IL: Delores Kohl Education Foundation, 1978), p. 10.
4. Ward Phillips and John H. O'Lague. *Successful Bulletin Boards* (Dansville, NY: F.A. Owen Publishing Co., 1966), p. 14.
5. Alice Rusk. *Easy Ways To Displays* (Baltimore, MD: Catholic University of America, Master of Science in Library Science Dissertation, 1958), p. 49.

BIBLIOGRAPHY

Black, Barbara. *Bulletin Boards To Brag About.* Glenview, IL: Goodyear Books, 1985.

Britton, Coleen. *Create and Use Bulletin Boards that Teach.* Prescott, AZ: Educational Ministries, 1990.

Commins, Elaine. *Bloomin' Bulletin Boards.* Atlanta, GA: Humanics Ltd., 1992.

Dungey, Joan M. *Interactive Bulletin Boards as Teaching Tools.* Washington, DC: National Education Association, 1989.

Glickstein, Barbra. *Bulletin Board Extravaganza.* Carthage, IL: Good Apple Publishing, 1981.

Moskowitz, Nachama Skolnik. *Original Bulletin Boards on Jewish Themes.* Denver: A.R.E. Publishing, Inc., 1986.

Nowlin, Susan, and Mary E. Sterling. *Think & Do Bulletin Boards.* Westminster, CA: Teacher Created Materials, Inc., 1988.

Skaggs, Gayle. *Bulletin Boards and Displays.* Jefferson, NC: McFarland and Co., Inc., 1993.

BACKGROUND FOR TEACHERS

CHAPTER SIX

ABOUT CHILD DEVELOPMENT

Miriam Roher Resnick

Once upon a time, there was an eighth grade Religious School class whose leaders were Dan, Jeff, Mike, and David. They became known as the Teacher Eaters. They "consumed" four successive teachers in four successive months through the use of creative misbehavior. As misbehavior is contagious, the whole class of 30 boys and girls eventually caught it.

After a frantic search, a young man not yet out of college was coaxed and cajoled into taking the job of teaching this class. Amazingly, he disarmed the boys the first time he appeared in the classroom by imposing a no-holds-barred discipline. A budding playwright, he transformed Jewish history into dramatic games. And, most importantly, he remembered how he had been as a bright, restless thirteen-year-old.

Although this is a true story, it happened many years ago. (No current Religious School class suffers such problems, does it?) Dan, Jeff, Mike, and David are now, respectively, a doctor, a lawyer, a successful businessman, and an electronics engineer. Three of them are fathers, struggling to deal with their own children. No doubt they have all forgotten what went on in that Religious School classroom. In that respect, they are like the rest of us. We don't remember very much about our childhood. Certainly, some incidents remain vivid. But we're adults now. Kid stuff – it's to be laughed off.

But it isn't so funny. As teachers, we are obliged to remember what young people are like because it is young people whose minds and hearts we are trying to reach. In order to do so, we need to know "where they're at" — their mental and emotional stages. It may seem too obvious to mention, but the emotional and intellectual capacity of a fourth grader is different from the capacity of an eighth grader. Even a five-year-old is quite different from a four-year-old. Chronological (actually maturational) age affects every aspect of the child who sits or squirms in the classroom seat, namely:

1. Intellectual capacity – what kinds of concepts can the pupil be expected to grasp?
2. Language ability – what words does the pupil understand and what is the real meaning of the words the child uses?
3. Emotional capacity and moral development – how does a typical youngster behave at various ages and what approaches are most effective at various stages?

A teacher also needs to know something about the genetic and environmental influences that could affect each child's mental and emotional development. Classroom strategies that work with most children of a given age might be a total failure with some others.

This one chapter cannot answer all the fascinating and important questions about child behavior, gleaned from a century of scientific research and theorizing. But a brief survey of the characteristics of the various ages/stages can at least provide initial illumination on major factors in child development.

PRESCHOOL: AGES 3 TO 5
Physical and Motor Development

Studies show that the level of physical and motor development of a preschooler has a great deal to do with the child's capacity to learn. It is important to know the norms of motor capacity, not only to spot those children who will be less easy to reach, but also to plan activities that will be within the ability of the majority. Many classroom games have been devised to teach Judaism to young children. But let the game match the child's capacity.

At three, a youngster can construct a tower nine blocks tall and might even be able to make a bridge. The child is able to catch a ball with straight arms, use a spoon without spilling, pour from a pitcher. A three-year-old can usually unbutton a sweater, put on shoes, copy a circle, draw a straight line, walk on tiptoes, jump down a 12-inch step, stand on one foot, hop with both feet, and ride a trike.

At four, most youngsters can cut on a line with scissors, make designs and crude letters, and dress without help. The four-year-old is able to gallop, walk down steps alternating feet as an adult does, and might do stunts on a tricycle.

The five-year-old is able to copy designs, letters, numbers; button clothing; fold paper into a double triangle; walk a straight line, skip, and hop on one foot.

Perceptual and Sensory Development

A teacher or parent cannot teach an average preschooler to read Hebrew or English or any other language because maturation governs the time when children will be able to discriminate one letter from the other. Stimulation by teacher or parents does play a certain role in developing a child's skills. But there is a limit as to how far the developmental timetable can be pushed.

COGNITION IS DEPENDENT ON MATURATION.

Discrimination of complex forms is just beginning around the age of three-and-a-half. Form discrimination, of course, is important for dealing with any symbols — words, numbers, signs. Preschoolers do seem to be aware of differences in the shape of forms, but they have trouble with orientation. For example, the letters b, p, and d are hard for a child to tell apart. Likewise, W and M are confusing. In all these cases, the shapes are the same but orientation in space is different. A great increase in ability to make such distinctions comes gradually between the ages of three and six. In general, children are not ready to read until the age of five.

Listening accuracy is also developmental. Often, young children simply do not hear little words or contractions. A teacher is not necessarily having a discipline problem when Judy or David closes the door after being told, "Don't close the door!" The child doesn't hear the don't.

A young child also has trouble ignoring noisy distraction. The problem is developmental, not willful. The youngster is physically unable to shut his or her ears to what is not relevant.

Appreciation for auditory rhythm is innate, according to researchers. A teacher of preschoolers can make good use of music and dancing to convey information.

While all the senses are present at birth, the most highly developed sense, even in the newborn, is probably the sense of touch. Thus, the famous Montessori Schools for preschoolers use many tangible objects as learning tools — cones, pyramids, three-dimensional wooden letters, textures.

Cognitive Development

Cognition is the ability to think and reason logically and to understand abstract principles. Cognition, too, is dependent on maturation. According to Jean Piaget, the major theorist on cognitive development, from the ages of two to seven, children are in a period he calls preoperational thought. This means that children of preschool age are characteristically egocentric. The child is not necessarily selfish, only unable to see beyond his or her own point of view.

A classic experiment illustrates this limitation. Take two identical glasses of water, put them side by side, and ask a four-year-old to describe them. The child rightly says they are alike. Then, with the child watching, pour the water from one of the glasses into a taller, narrower container. Seeing the higher water level, the child will say the new container has "more" water than the untouched original!

This inability to reverse events in one's mind is characteristic of the limited thinking ability of a preschooler. It explains young children's squabbles about who has more juice or more cake. Don't expect logical thought from three or four-year-olds. They can only think in terms of what they themselves have experienced.

Time is a concept that is usually beyond a preschooler. "Tomorrow" is any time in the future. Time is not tangible and little children are oriented to things they can see or touch. And they rely on the most vivid impressions.

A young child's world is concrete and absolute; the youngster is guided mostly by visual clues. Objects are more important than words. Abstract concepts and relative terms are beyond them.

The following anecdotes illustrate childish thinking.

A researcher asked a preschool child: "Who do you think made the world?"
A. God.
Q. Who's God?
A. He flies in the sky all the time.
Q. Is God an airplane?
A. No . . . He flies like a bird. God is just a bird.

Or:

A four-year-old, riding in a car with grandpa, said: "Oh, there's an American flag!"

Grandpa, affectionately, "It certainly is. And you're a nice American girl."

The little girl: "No, I'm not an American girl, Grandpa. I'm a Jewish girl!"

The absolutes that dominate a three-year-old child's thought processes begin to break up between the ages of four and seven. During this transitional period, children begin to doubt their previously positive judgments. They start to consider other perspectives. With the help of adults, they can decenter their thinking, grasp more than one aspect of a situation. Gradually, logic is developing.

Language Development

Semantic development — learning what words mean — has a close relationship to cognitive development. Both involve the ability to handle concepts. And the development of both proceeds from the concrete to the abstract. Here are some examples:

Preschoolers understand first and last before they understand before and after. If you tell a young child to move a blue object first, move the red one last, the instruction is more likely to be understood than if you said: "Before you move the red one, move the blue one."

Youngsters, even six-year-olds, respond to the word order of a command. For instance, confusion will result from two sentences like, "The girl is helped by the boy" and "The girl helps the boy." The word order makes a stronger impression than the active and passive verbs.

No one can count on preschoolers to grasp the difference between *different* and *same*. They also have a hard time with negatives. *No* is easy, but *not* might be lost in a sentence that contains concrete words like *red* or *toys* or *eat*. Cause and effect are hard to grasp. "Don't touch the dough because it will make the little *challah* tough." The child might even repeat the warning and then touch the dough anyway. The preschooler can verbalize the caution, but cannot yet conceptualize it.

While reading is beyond the average preschooler, this does not mean that three to five-year-olds cannot learn some spoken Hebrew.

After all, children begin to learn their own native tongue in infancy. Preschoolers characteristically acquire languages with impressive ease, possibly because of the early plasticity of the brain. Teaching a second language very early also takes advantage of the fact that children do not seem to transfer their native accent to a foreign language. One recommendation as to teaching technique is to duplicate the process whereby children develop physical behavior: "Clap your hands!" or "Look at what the Rabbi is wearing!"

Teachers of preschoolers must be constantly aware of the fact that the pupils are not ready for abstract concepts. Show them, wherever possible: a Torah, *matzah*, a *chanukiah*.

Social and Moral Development

In terms of behavior, in school the teacher is a major model, just as in the home, Mommy and Daddy are the models. In spite of preschoolers' developmental limitations, in many ways teaching them about their Jewish heritage can be more rewarding than dealing with almost any other age group. According to respected theorist Erik Erikson, they are at the psychosocial stage, a period during which they have a powerful desire to master new tasks. Their will to achieve is fresh and new. At this age, they are not captives, but delighted participants. This is also the age when self-identity is being established, a prime time to realize that "I am a Jew!" That self-concept lasts a lifetime.

Morally, however, a preschooler's behavior is anchored by maturational limitations. Theorist Piaget points out that a child of four is apt to judge the rightness of an act in terms of physical consequences, a reflection of the child's cognitive development. Rules of behavior are fixed, like the rising and setting of the sun. A young child sees an action as either totally right or totally wrong. And some acts are wrong because they will lead to punishment. Very young children do not understand "do unto others," and they will not understand that concept for many years.

CHILDHOOD: AGES 6 TO 11

Children in the primary grades continue to be products of their own maturation. Some ideas they can cope with; some concepts are beyond them. Emotionally, they are more advanced than they were in kindergarten, but they still have the limitations natural to the immature human organism.

Cognitive Development

Between the ages of 7 and 11 is the beginning of thinking as we adults understand the process. Children in this age range are capable of reversible, relativistic thinking, although they are still somewhat limited in their ability to reason abstractly. But they are beginning to understand the use of symbols — numbers, words — to represent something else. They have progressed from egocentrism to relativism. They no longer think only in terms of absolutes. In the water level experiment, they would be able to realize that there is no more liquid in the taller, narrower container than there was in the original glass. They can generalize — understand that some people are Jews, some belong to other groups, but all can be Americans.

By seven, children can perceive a situation from more than one point of view and even think hypothetically: "What if . . ." Nevertheless, these abilities come gradually. The capacity to deal with the abstract and the symbolic does not develop all at once. A teacher must be sensitive to the cognitive limitations of some members of the class. Even in the third grade, some children may see God as a white-bearded fellow who lives in a cloud or behind the Torah.

Perceptual Development

Primary school children are also far from fully mature in terms of visual perception. Inexperience is one cause, developmental ability is another.

A study of second graders and sixth graders presented them with pairs of colored animal forms in a viewer and asked them to say which were alike and which were different. They were also asked to pair the animals for color likeness and form likeness. The older children were much better at the job than the younger ones.

The lesson for the Religious School teacher is that illustrative materials have to be kept simple. Details might well be beyond the ability of the younger children to grasp. Only gradually does an individual acquire the ability to discriminate and attend to relative cues.

Listening accuracy, too, continues to develop until about the age of nine. The increase in a child's ability to sort out one verbal message from several may not necessarily come from better hearing, but from more experience with language. And classroom disturbance continues to be a problem for most children; they simply cannot tune out distractions.

Learning Ability

A teacher can put to good use the impressive ability of most elementary school children to use and understand language. For example, experimenters have shown that when children between the ages of five and seven were taught to mention a relevant cue — put it into words — they had an easier time carrying out instructions. Similarly, a child who puts an inaccurate mental label on, say, an illustration in a book will remember the picture inaccurately.

Look and *say* is a valuable teaching technique. Words can also be a help in enforcing discipline. One study showed that impulsive children who were trained to talk to themselves actually were able to become more self-controlled.

The best combination for promoting memorization is both words and pictures. Even a sixth-grader finds it easier to remember objects than words. In any case, children's ability to remember seems to improve with age, perhaps as part of the process of cognitive development. The most successful teacher explains while showing.

Every primary grades teacher must be constantly aware of children's cognitive limitations. For example, kindergartners through fifth-graders were asked to tell how they would go about finding a lost jacket at school. About a third of the fifth-graders answered that they would try to remember where they had last had it and would try to work forward through their activities after that time. Very few of the younger children were able to map out such a strategy. The ability to formulate a hypothesis and try it out is related to the age of a child. Kindergartners usually cannot do it. But most fourth-graders can.

Investigators confirm that, as we have all suspected, films and television are aids to youthful learning. But they have also found that it is important to supplement film with other techniques, such as putting the "moral" into words or having children role play what they have seen. Verbal labeling promotes the learning of abstract issues and values, to supplement what has been viewed on a screen.

The best films portray characters with whom the pupils can identify. The older the child, the better able to understand film characters' feelings and motivation. Many of the things children see in the media or witness in real life are over their heads. Children often miss asides, whether they are visual or verbal or humorous. What an adult finds attractive may seem irrelevant or incomprehensible to a child or it may just slide by unnoticed.

There are developmental reasons why the primary grades are probably the easiest for Religious School teachers. Erik Erikson believes that the pre-adolescent is in a stage he calls basic sense of industry versus basic sense of inferiority. In other words, during these years, motivation and productivity, a child's normal desire to learn and to accomplish, are challenged by a normal fear of failure. Thus, the average child is really anxious to learn in Religious School and is just waiting for the teacher to help fulfill this need. But in childhood there are also many challenges to self-concept and self-esteem. So the teacher is in an ideal position to help pupils develop a sense of themselves as Jews who are proud of their heritage and their identity.

Moral Development

A teacher who moves from the kindergarten to a grade school class will soon become aware of the development of moral judgment with maturation. But children's moral standards are still very different from those of adults, even though progress is evident. While four-year-olds usually judge an act in terms of physical consequences, nine-year-olds are likely to judge intent to do harm. A very young child sees an action as either totally right or totally wrong and thinks everyone has the same view, but the older child accepts the possibility that opinions differ.

The probability of punishment is no longer the criterion of bad behavior for a grade schooler who deems an act to be bad because it violates a rule or harms other people. Not until ten do children have the idea that they should treat others as they have been treated. When this idea does take shape, however, it is likely to be acted out concretely, as in hitting back.

Also, an older child no longer thinks of severe punishment as a means of making up for wrongdoing. The child is now more likely to favor redress in the form of restitution or even attempts to reform the wrongdoer.

Can children be taught to be honest? A pioneering study in New York more than 50 years ago still seems relevant today. Investigators worked out 14 situations that might reveal who would cheat in school, in athletics, in games, at parties, and on school homework. They found that there are no totally honest children and no totally dishonest children. No connection was found between cheating and a child's moral code. They all had the same conventional ideas about what was right and what was wrong.

Children who regularly attended Religious School were no more honest than children who rarely went. But there did seem to be some connection between the very fact of Religious School enrollment and a better level of conduct. The investigators suggested that this might mean that families with higher standards at least try to send their children to Religious School classes. Thus, family training may be the responsible factor.

The only strong correlation the researchers found was in comparing the homes of the 50 most honest and the 50 most dishonest children. The cheaters' homes were full of discord, there was no discipline, and the family economic and social situation tended to be chaotic or changing. However, the attitudes of teachers did seem to have an influence. The pupils of cooperative, sympathetic teachers were likely to be more honest than students in classes where teachers were arbitrary and/or dictatorial.

ADOLESCENCE

The troublesome boys who led off this chapter were all early adolescents. This is the age group that is notorious in Religious School circles not only for misbehavior in class, but also for outright refusal to attend Religious School. Nobody has a surefire recipe for dealing with these youngsters. But understanding their developmental status could help a teacher cope and even to teach.

Physical Development

The physical status of adolescents is an important influence on their behavior. The period from 12 to 15 or 16 is a time of uneven but highly significant change: inordinately slow, inordinately rapid, differently timed as between the two sexes, different from one individual to another, and uneven for each individual. Bodily changes (often ill-understood by the individual who is undergoing those changes), the difference in change between one boy and another and one girl and another (also ill-understood), the difference between girls and boys of the same chronological age, all has a profound psychological effect on young people. And it influences their behavior both in class and outside of class.

The most notable distinctions between boys and girls begin at about the age of 10. By 12 or 13 most girls' earlier development is apparent, as sexual characteristics appear. But among 12-year-old boys, there are great differences. Some are maturing fast, some hardly at all. Different parts of a boy's body may show different stages of maturity. Many girls have become womanly by age 14, but most boys of that age are usually still in transition. Generally, therefore, adolescence is characterized by a growth spurt that is unique for each individual. Development comes in fits and starts, although the whole period is a spurt compared to the growth that has preceded it in childhood.

ADOLESCENCE IS A PERIOD OF EGOCENTRISM AND IMAGINED IMMORTALITY.

In general, girls are developmentally older than their male classmates for several difficult years. During the senior high school years, students of the same age have a range of at least six years in maturational age.

All this translates into the behavior problems which can plague the teachers of these adolescents. Many youngsters have adjustment problems because social and cultural standards presume equal development and conformity. Peers, parents, teachers, and society as a whole unrealistically expect everybody the same age to have similar interests, to look basically the same, and to do the same things in the same fashion. Both personality and self-esteem are affected by whether a girl or boy matures early or late. Either way, each sees himself or herself as "different" from others.

Cognitive Status

Cognitively, however, most adolescents are gratifyingly ready to undertake logical and abstract reasoning. Their thinking has become methodical; they are leaving trial and error behind. They can, if they wish, make a plan instead of rushing headlong into a project.

The absolute world of the child — "Jews are the best people" – has broken up during adolescence. The change comes from the newly developing ability to think in terms of probability, possibility, and proportion. This is the period when an individual can get a much more comprehensive hold on "what if?" situations. "What if a leader like Moses had not appeared?" "What if I fall in love with a Christian?"

Nevertheless, this does not mean that during adolescence all people come to full cognitive maturity. It is peculiar to adolescents' thinking that they show a unique kind of egocentrism that accounts for self-conscious behavior and belief in their own invulnerability.

A typical adolescent thinks everyone else is looking at him/her and concentrating on his/her behavior. Adolescents are self-conscious in the extreme. They are forever playing to imaginary audiences. They think they are special and may even keep a diary for posterity. In fact, they feel immortal: death, injury, serious illness can never strike them. They do dangerous things, protected by their feeling of invulnerability.

Some of what emerges from this behavior is funny, some can be tragic, since a whole catalog of misfortunes can follow in the train of the teen-ager's egocentric belief that "it can't happen to me." And some can be extremely annoying to a serious teacher.

Another consequence of adolescent egocentrism is a faulty sense of the past and future. Now is the only time many a teen-ager recognizes. It is difficult to think about the realities of college, of Confirmation, of a parent's concern if a group stays too late over pizzas after a youth group dance.

Identity Crisis

The most notorious aspect of adolescence, a product of the adolescent's developmental stage, is the familiar identity crisis of the teenage years. "Who am I?" is a question that relies on the newly developed ability to think about probability and possibility. As part of the quest, teen-agers try to separate themselves, from the rules and roles of society, their parents, the Religious School. They question everything and everybody. The adolescent is caught between conformity, egocentrism, and formal reasoning. All hypotheses are now subject to testing.

According to Erik Erikson's theories, adolescence encompasses a recognizable psychological stage in life. The teen-age years are characterized by the need to achieve a stable sense of self. Therefore, the constant testing of self and of everyone around, including the Religious School and its teachers, is entirely normal and necessary.

Sex roles are another complication in adolescent behavior. Teen-agers typically begin to worry about various aspects of their masculinity or feminity and those concerns, too, affect their behavior in Religious School.

In general, all the morals, values, beliefs, and relationships so painstakingly instilled into children during earlier years are called into question when they are teen-agers. Young people are all looking for an answer to the question "Who am I?" and they are trying on all sorts of possible new roles. A teacher cannot count on meeting the same pupil in the classroom two weeks in a row. The same body may show up, but new behavior is being tried on.

During all this turmoil of the adolescent's attempt to develop a realistic self-concept, warm, sympathetic teachers can help. Real communication between the adolescent and significant adults appears to be a must if a viable self-concept is to be developed.

However, not every adolescent has to have a violent identity crisis. Some theorists believe that the identity crisis is not even common and that adolescent problems are exaggerated. Not every member of the tenth grade Religious School class is going through turmoil. Still, some of them certainly are. These troubled souls are the most disruptive and also the most creative and the most useful as a yeast for the bubbling classroom mix. But it takes a patient, compassionate, and creative teacher to take advantage of the peculiar strengths of class members and to work sympathetically with their weaknesses.

Moral Development

Troublesome though some adolescents may be, they could be a delight to a teacher who would like students to become seriously involved in the moral questions which are, after all, at the basis of religious education. Teenagers are developmentally ripe for serious debate on ethical issues.

Like Piaget, Lawrence Kohlberg, a leading thinker about moral development, sees a clear relationship to cognitive development. But he divides moral development into three levels.

On the *preconventional* level, which includes the childhood years through early puberty, young peoples' moral judgments depend on considerations like punishment and unquestioning deference to authority. The basis is not so much moral as practical — to avoid punishment or to satisfy one's own needs.

The next level is dubbed *conventional* by Kohlberg, who theorizes that it begins in late adolescence and continues into adulthood. Not everyone remains at this stage, but many do. Respect for authority is paramount. A person behaves well simply to please others. Some individuals at this level even move on to a slightly more elevated stance. They begin to think about the needs of society as a whole and strive to live up to social rules for their own sake. The orientation is toward law and order. Youngsters at this stage would condemn mercy killing because the law and religious teachings frown on euthanasia.

A very small proportion of late adolescents and adults reach the post-conventional level described by Kohlberg: belief in higher principles of justice, independent of personal consequences. Some take the position that society depends on a complex network of agreed-upon rules of conduct and that even if one does not agree personally, one still has an obligation to conform and to work to secure change through means provided by the system. They would, for instance, register for the draft, even if they disapprove, but work through the system to get the draft eliminated.

Very few, according to Kohlberg, reach the stage of adhering to universal ethical principles, whereby they believe that one's own conscience is the sole criterion of right conduct. Such individuals have strict standards: logical, comprehensive, universal, consistent. In effect, the law is considered subordinate to those higher principles. Such people — there aren't many — can be troublesome but a delight to the teacher who strives for a good class discussion. (For a more detailed discussion of moral development, see Chapter 9, "Encouraging Moral Development.")

AN IDEAL TEACHER

The influence of a Religious School teacher's personality on classroom learning cannot be underestimated. The teacher is a "model" who can be imitated by all students, particularly the younger ones. What would an ideal teacher be like, to motivate not only the younger children but also those difficult teen-agers?

One educational psychologist called for a warm, orderly, systematic individual, able to influence pupils indirectly through question asking, a good organizer of the material to be learned. But it may well be impossible to draw a picture of an academic Moses. The chances are that good teachers are all somewhat different and that different teachers may be effective with different children. Given these provisos, professional educators nevertheless have provided many tips about how various kinds of teacher behavior affect children.

A teacher's approval or disapproval can have a significant effect on motivation, though more for first-graders than for fifth-graders. A child may be afraid to speak out in the classroom, not because of lack of knowledge but because of fear of criticism. Praise has the opposite effect, particularly if it is "labeled" so that children know just what they are being praised for.

Skilled teachers can make use of normal curiosity as a motive to help children learn. Colorful materials, a "different" approach are advised. But too much curiosity can be detrimental. Too many posters, too much noise, too much coming and going may distract the class.

Some teachers create anxiety, particularly in children who are themselves anxious. When the teacher pushes for achievement, an already anxious pupil becomes frightened and less productive. But a responsive teacher is effective with children who are interested in rewards. Thus, teachers must learn to cope with different kinds of children and to tailor their approach to individuals.

One educational study appeared to show that teachers' preconceived expectations had an effect on how well pupils learned. The research project gave teachers false information about their pupils' IQs. The result was that the supposedly brighter children, expected to do more, actually did do better, and vice versa. While the study has been criticized for its statistical methods, the principle probably holds: a teacher with legitimate expectations based on students' ability can influence the children's performance.

INDIVIDUAL DIFFERENCES

No responsible student of child development would peddle gross generalizations to either parents or teachers. It is a given that every pupil is an individual, as different from everyone else as his or her fingerprints. Possible exceptions are identical twins, who do tend to be very much the same. But fraternal twins differ as much as any other two siblings.

Every child who comes to Religious School is a product of a distinctive heredity, a distinctive home life, distinctive life experiences. A teacher with a large class might be driven, through practical necessity, to treat everyone the same. But ideally, a teacher should develop a one-on-one relationship with each child.

Does this mean that the theorists who have worked out developmental norms have created an impractical fiction? Of course not. All the generalizations about what happens when to a child — physically, cognitively, in terms of socialization — are valuable guides to the behavior and potentialities of the pupils in the Religious School class. There *are* types of behavior to be expected in a given age range. There *are* limitations on the learning and motivation of youngsters in particular age groups. Even the kinds of differences among pupils, especially adolescents, are predictable. Thus, the norms and descriptions of pupils from preschool age through Confirmation age and beyond could b immensely useful to a conscientious and creative teacher.

But for the full story about child development, the teacher should turn to the textbooks and special studies that now abound in this field. This chapter is only a brief teaser.

Mirian Roher Resnick (z"l) was the author of two high school textbooks, and a college text called *The Child: Development through Adolescense.* She also edited numerous publications, including *The Jewish Community News* and the bulletin of Temple Emanuel in San Jose, California.

BIBLIOGRAPHY

Bjorklund, David, and Barbara Bjorklund. *Looking at Children: An Introduction to Child Development*. Pacific Grove, CA: Brooks-Cole, 1992.

Caine, Renate Nummela, and Geoffrey Caine. *Making Connections: Teaching about the Human Brain*. Alexandria, VA: ASCD, 1991.

Cavalletti, Sofia. *The Religious Potential of the Child*. New York: Paulist Press, 1983.

Charles, C.M. *Teacher's Petit Piaget*. Carthage, IL: Fearon Teaching Aids, 1974.

Dunn, Rita, et al. *The Giftedness in Every Child: Unlocking Your Child's Unique Talents, Strengths and Potential*. New York, NY: John Wiley and Sons, Inc., 1992.

Dworetzky, John P. *Introduction to Child Development*. Saint Paul, MN: West Publishing Co., 1993.

Elkind, David. *A Sympathetic Understanding of the Child: Birth to Sixteen*. Needham Heights, MA: Allyn and Bacon, 1978.

Kagan, J. "Yesterday's Premises, Tomorrow's Promises." *Developmental Psychology* 28:990-7, November 1992.

Miller, Joan. *Your Baby's Development*. Philadelphia, PA: Transatlantic, 1993.

Miller, Patricia M. *Theories of Developmental Psychology*. New York: W.H. Freeman and Co., 1993.

Moran, Gabriel. *Religious Education Development*. Minneapolis: Winston Press, 1983.

Piaget, Jean. *Judgment and Reasoning in the Child*. Lanham, MD: Littlefield, 1976.

Pulaski, Mary Ann Spencer. *Understanding Piaget: An Introduction to Children's Cognitive Development*. rev. and expanded text. New York: Harper & Row, 1980.

Rathers, Spencer A., and Peter Favaro. *Understanding Child Development*. New York: HarperCollins Publishers, 1988.

Salkind, Neil J. *Child Development*. 6th ed. New York: HarperCollins Publishers, 1990.

Schickedanz, Judith, et al. *Understanding Children: School Age and Adolescence*. 2d ed. Mountain View, CA: Mayfield Publishing Co., 1992.

Shkedi, A. "Teachers Workshop Encounters with Jewish Moral Texts." *Journal of Moral Education* 1:19-30, 1993.

Siegler, Robert, and Eric Jenkins, eds. *How Children Discover New Strategies*. Hillsdale, NJ: Lawrence Erlbaum Associates, Inc., 1989.

Skolnik, Arlene S. *Psychology of Human Development*. New York: HarperCollins Publishers, 1986.

Slonim, Marueen B. *Children, Culture and Ethnicity: Evaluating and Understanding the Impact*. New York: Garland Publishing, Inc., 1991.

Smith, Peter, and Helen Cowle. *Understanding Chld Development*. Cambridge, MA: Blackwell Publishing, 1988.

Thomas, R. Murray. *Comparing Theories of Child Development*. 3d ed. Belmont, CA: Wadsworth Publishing Co, 1992.

Vasta, Ross, ed. *Six Theories of Child Development: Revised Formulations and Current Issues*. Bristol, PA: Taylor and Francis, Inc., 1992.

Winger, Lucien T., and Jaan Valsiner. *Children's Development within Social Contexts*. Hillsdale, NJ: Lawrence Erlbaum Associates, Inc., 1991.

Woodhead, Martin, and Paul Light, eds. *Growing Up in a Changing Society*. New York; Routledge, Chapman and Hall, Inc., 1991.

Zigler, Edward F., and Matia Finn-Stevenson. *Children in a Changing World: Development and Social Issues*. 2d ed. Pacific Grove, CA: Brooks-Cole, 1993.

CHAPTER SEVEN

DEALING WITH CHILDREN AT RISK

Steven Bayar and Francine Hirschman

"May you live in interesting times," is an old Chinese saying. It can be taken as a blessing or a curse. Unfortunately, many of our students live with "interesting" challenges and difficulties far beyond what we might consider to be normal adolescent dilemmas. They come to our schools with emotional and physical baggage which, just a few years ago, we would never have imagined possible, including profound depression and chemical, food, sexual/physical abuse.

It would be foolish for the day school educator, let alone the supplementary school teacher, to believe that he or she can remedy all or even some of the ills which might possibly afflict our students. Yet, it would be cowardly if not morally wrong for us not to be aware of and alert to such conditions and to try to be of help.

When it comes to dealing with a child at risk, it's natural to want to rationalize away suspicions and avoid the signs and signals. The thoughts that come most easily to mind are: "It's probably not that serious," "It's a passing phase," "Just a natural part of adolescence," "This is none of my business," "How can I be certain that what is being implied here is really happening?" "The child is just angry at parents and this is a way of getting back at them," and so forth. Yet, when the signs persist, rationalizing needs to desist.

STUDENTS WITH PROBLEMS
General Warning Signs

Depending on which statistics you accept, given a class of 20 students, a fourth to a half may have physical, emotional, or learning problems. Just the thought of so many in any class being potentially afflicted is alarming. Is it any wonder then that the number of students who exhibit attitudes and behaviors which are deemed disruptive or unmanageable seems on the increase?

Since our task is to educate an entire class, we tend to focus immediately on the negative behavior itself. Classroom management techniques, much as in any damage control situation, would call for isolating the behavior — removing the child — so that we can go back to teaching. Yet, if we could but take the extra minute to be less reactive and more proactive, if we had the patience or the insight to ascertain the causal factors behind a child's negative attitudes and behaviors, we might actually be able to do more to influence that child's life than we could with all the lesson plans we ever implement. To remove the child from class is to make him/her more unreachable. Ironically, it is those who disturb us the most who could most benefit from our compassion and understanding.

Our first task, then, if we are to impact students who have problems, is to identify those students. Their behavior is the key. While they may try to hide anger, frustration, and fear, it will find release in some form. Thus, in working with students, look for any of the following signs:

1. changes in behavior
2. difficulty in paying attention
3. difficulty in making eye contact
4. peer social problems
5. not working up to expected ability
6. reluctance to share information about home life
7. consistent behavior problems
8. excessive absences
9. totally immersed in one activity to the exclusion of other activities, or lack of involvement in anything
10. writing assignments or drawings that consistently reflect negative or dark thoughts and deeds

Students exhibiting such signs are not necessarily ill or being victimized in any way, they simply bear watching closely. Remember, too, that students undergo many changes in the course of a school year. It is possible that a student might exhibit such behaviors for a short period of time because of a temporary life situation. As a general rule, however, should anyone persist in any of the above for an extended period of time, consider that he/she may be in need of attention and help.

Resources

Teachers have limitations. We are not expected to be well versed in law, psychology, or enforcement policies. Therefore, problems which require such expertise should not be handled alone. Every teacher should maintain an up-to-date resource list — a card file — in which at least the following phone numbers are listed:

1. your Director of Education and Rabbi
2. a lawyer (preferably one knowledgeable in criminal law)
3. a social worker and/or psychologist (preferably one who works with the age group that you teach)
4. Police Department
5. alcohol and drug abuse hot lines
6. Rape Hot Line
7. Social Services

Don't be surprised by entry #1. Before you take any action, always contact your supervisors first so as to help them be aware of and become a part of the situation at hand. They may have more expertise and experience in handling such problems. They may have information about a family which you lack. They may be aware of steps already being taken which address the situation.

Unfortunately, a teacher is sometimes the last professional to know what is going on. Therefore, it is especially important that a teacher not make decisions or take actions without input and support.

What follows is a partial list of problems facing students today, what signals to look for, and how to respond. This is not an all inclusive listing so much as a general guide.

LEARNING DISABILITIES

It is estimated that 10% of all students have some sort of learning disability. Even if that number is an overestimation, it is likely that every teacher will confront at least one student with learning disabilities every year.

Students with learning disabilities tend to be bright and capable in some areas, while showing weaknesses in cognitive, verbal, and/or motor skills. A student may be unable to write down correct or legible answers, even though we know that he/she knows them. A student, though obviously bright, may be unable to concentrate on an activity for an extended amount of time. The following case study demonstrates this problem.

> **TEN PERCENT OF ALL STUDENTS HAVE SOME SORT OF LEARNING DISABILITIES.**

Joshua

Joshua, a junior high school student, seemed withdrawn and quiet. He had an eye tic which a parent said was "nervousness." He was constantly getting into trouble with older students for "making remarks," and all of his teachers said that he seemed unable to concentrate in class and was doing poorly.

The Director of Education and social worker looked into the situation and found that there were two components to Joshua's condition: a medical and a learning problem. The tic (and Joshua's verbal outbursts to older students) were symptomatic of Tourette's Syndrome, and the concentration problem was Attention Deficit Disorder (ADD) — a learning problem often associated with his medical illness.

What To Look For

Following are the signals to look for when suspecting learning disabilities:

1. A student who seems to be performing well below his or her ability.
2. Significant differences in ability in different subjects, e.g., the student cannot learn to read Hebrew, yet can learn and understand complex aspects of Jewish history and Bible.
3. Tremendous effort leading to tremendous frustration — a student who tries hard, yet finds little or no success.
4. A student who avoids performing by acting out in class, or by causing a distraction

CHAPTER SEVEN   53

which will circumvent his/her being forced to perform.

Resources

Every school should have a list of referral possibilities for students with suspected learning disabilities. Aside from private psychologists, your local Jewish Family Service, university, or other communal institutions may have educational testing services available. Good resources for the individual teacher or Director of Education include special education teachers from local public and day schools, psychologists, pediatric physical therapists, and occupational therapists. When making a referral recommendation, remind the parents to keep the school in the loop by sharing reports and evaluations. The school will assure the parents that all such reports will be treated as confidential.

DRUG AND ALCOHOL ABUSE

"Jews don't drink!" How many of us grew up believing that statement to be fact? Today we know that many Jews drink, do drugs, and fall prey to the same temptations and problems as the rest of the world. Worse, these behaviors may start as early as elementary school and are much more common among our high school students than teachers would like to believe.

What To Look For

Students who drink or do drugs come from every part of the socio-economic spectrum. They may act tremendously exhausted and sleepy all the time, or they may always seem to be "up." They may have dramatic mood swings and be unable to concentrate or finish a task. They may be secretive and spend long amounts of time in the bathroom or alone in a classroom. If you do suspect drugs or alcohol, contact your Director of Education, Rabbi, or guidance counselor/school expert on the subject (if you have such a person on staff). The accusation of drug or alcohol use should not come from the teacher alone. Often the first hint of such a problem may come from the student's peers. Such confidences must be carefully protected. Be aware that parental denial is the almost invariable reaction to such an accusation.

It's the Law

It is important to be aware of the following:

In many localities, if you know, or have sufficient knowledge to suspect, that a student is abusing alcohol and/or drugs and you do not report it, you may be held partially responsible for any actions they take or crimes they commit.

Resources

JACS (Jewish Alcoholics and Chemically Dependent Persons and Significant Others) is one of the few organizations under Jewish auspices which deals with alcohol and substance abuse. Alcoholics Anonymous has teen programs, and your local Y, Jewish Center, or Federation may have educational programs for prevention and/or ongoing help for students addicted or at risk. Getting to know the Community Patrol Officer or Youth Officer in your local police precinct is, surprisingly, often a good way to get effective referral possibilities. Make sure that you know your legal responsibility to report drug problems, and know the local rulings on what action you may take with regards to searches, confiscation, etc.

PHYSICAL AND SEXUAL ABUSE

More than in any other area, when it comes to abuse the law requires that a teacher be aware. Every teacher should know the state laws regarding reporting abuse. The issue should be discussed by the Director of Education or Rabbi with the staff before each school year.

Physical abuse at home is more than just an occasional spanking of a young child. Physical abuse may or may not leave marks on the student. A child who is being abused may explain away multiple bruises or injuries as being the result of various accidents. Confronting the student even with assurances that "nothing will happen to if you tell," is not enough. Abused children, for whatever reason, will often protect the abusive parent. Health professionals should be involved in any evaluation; a teacher or educator has the same reporting responsibility as the pediatrician or family doctor.

Sexual abuse is even more devastating and harder to detect. The acting out component of this sort of abuse may be promiscuous behavior or severe timidity or even suicidal intimations. This case study exemplifies such a situation.

Melody

A new student in the school, Melody was extremely pretty, bright, and admired by her peers. Yet, from the outset, she was always late to school, argued with teachers about class requirements, and violated most school rules. Her attire for school was inappropriate — low cut blouses, jeans with rips in the seat, and excessive make-up. Her language, especially when boys were around, which was most often, was seen as being provocative. When confronted by the Director of Education about these issues, she said, "That's the way I am. If you don't like it, you'll have to change. I won't." When her parents were called in, they threw up their hands in frustration. They could not control Melody at home either, and she was rude to them in front of the Director of Education. It was obvious that she had no respect for any kind of authority. After this behavior continued for several months, she was asked to leave school.

This might have been the end of the story had it not been for a concerned administrator who, even after she left the school, made a psychological referral for Melody. It was discovered in those sessions that when Melody was raped by a cousin when she was four. Her parents moved from the city and neither dealt with the incident themselves, nor got her counseling or help. Melody has no memory of that rape.

When Melody was about seven, she was bullied for over a year by another relative, and the parents did not intervene. In therapy, Melody said, "You couldn't protect me. You didn't help me," talking about the later incident, but obviously prompted by some hidden memory of the earlier rape.

Obviously, Melody had no reason to respect authority; it had never been able to protect her. Hence, her tremendous disdain for rules and authority

What To Look For

If you suspect abuse of any sort, look for the following signs:
1. inappropriate sexual behavior
2. exaggerated fearfulness and shyness
3. a preoccupation with sexual and physical matters
4. serious social adjustment problems and problems with authority

It's the Law

It is incumbent upon every teacher to know the legal aspects and the obligations concerning physical and sexual abuse, because, as a general rule, the law (in the United States) mandates reporting evidence or even suspicions of same. Of course, laws do vary from state to state, so it is vital that you check your local statutes. However, every teacher must be aware of the following general guideline: If you have reason to suspect that a child is being abused, unless you have overwhelming evidence to the contrary (and who has?), you must report the alleged offense to your local state agency.

While we might gasp at the thought of getting so directly and personally involved in these legal matters, perhaps a more compelling reason for taking appropriate actions is that, as teachers, we are models for the tradition we represent. Therefore, we should be bound by the ethic we purport to inculcate in our students. So, to suspect that a child is being abused (or has an eating disorder or is suicidal) and ignore it, in effect places that life at risk, which is morally indefensible.

Resources

If there is behavior which may indicate abuse, you must know your legal obligations. Do not let yourself be talked out of taking action. Anyone dealing with adolescents should have the name of a good pediatrician with connections to a university affiliated hospital with adolescent facilities, psychologists and/or psychiatrists who can be called on for advice, and legal advisors who specialize in family matters.

Do not think that abuse that has ended is damage that is over. As Melody's case clearly shows, the effects of abuse clearly outlive the abuse itself.

DEPRESSION AND SUICIDE

Depression is the feeling of overwhelming sadness, worthlessness, and hopelessness that can affect anyone sometimes, but becomes a serious illness when it takes over a person's life. With adolescents, it is one of the surest and clearest warning symptoms of impending suicide.

Suicide has reached epidemic proportions among American teenagers. Jewish teens are at the same risk as others, so no teacher who suspects/hears about a suicide threat can take it lightly. Teenagers are most susceptible to attempting suicide when their lives seem hopeless or out of control (often the same motivation as in anorexia or bulimia, the eating disorders which threaten the lives of teenage girls), or following the loss of someone important to them, or as a result of abuse they have suffered.

Suicide is often glorified in teen literature, movies, or music, and, consequently, seems romantic and dangerous. Twice as many girls as boys attempt suicide; more boys are successful. Three quarters of those who commit suicide have threatened or attempted to commit suicide beforehand. The following is a case in point.

Gary

Gary was a young man from a seriously troubled family. He had lost a younger brother and there was another sick child in the family. Lost in their grief and bitterness, the parents were unaware of how little attention their oldest child was receiving. When Gary entered high school, there were two significant things noticed: his poor academic performance and his "invisibility." He seemed to shrink against the walls, he slouched, he wore his oversized coat indoors — you literally could not see the person inside.

As the year wore on, Gary's constant sadness and sense of unworthiness seemed to be a cloud floating around him. He could neither perform, nor be upset about not performing. He seemed to disappear a little more each day. No teacher seemed able to reach him.

Gary's behavior and performance indicated a deep depression, and he eventually did tell the school social worker that he really had no reason to live. But even without elucidating this thought, Gary's behavior was a cry for help. He felt guilty over his brother's death, guilty over the next child's illness, guilty over his parents' arguments, and even guilty about his own continuing existence. These feelings paralyzed him and pushed him to shrink and disappear, first in the sense of his physical presence, and then possibly out of life itself. This was a young man who needed serious counseling, both individually and as part of a family, and that was the recommendation that was made by the school.

LONELY, TROUBLED, AND ANGRY KIDS ARE MOST AT RISK FOR CULTS.

What To Look For

Not every suicidal adolescent will "wear" his depression as clearly as Gary did, but adolescents are especially at risk for both depression and suicide. There are certain behaviors and warning signs which must be taken seriously as possible indications of suicidal intent or need for immediate professional consultation. One or more of the following signs are danger signals:
1. depression, withdrawal, mood swings
2. changes in normal behavior and friendships
3. giving away prized possessions
4. writing/reading death and suicide related poetry
5. extreme preoccupation with death

Resources

Keep handy your local suicide prevention hot line number. Make sure all of your students have it, too. The student contemplating suicide may not call, but his or her best friend may. Let your students know who they can see or call *immediately* if they or a friend is feeling very depressed.

CULTS

It is estimated that there are over 5,000 cults in the United States today. While many are small organizations with few members and little influence, a goodly number of well-organized, well-funded "communities" do exist which recruit in many local areas.

Complicating the matter in recent years have been the successful attempts of several of the largest and best known cults to achieve a sort of mainstream status. The Moonies own one of the two daily newspapers in Washington D.C., offering clergy and lay leaders expense paid trips to "leadership sessions." L. Ron Hubbard's Scientology literature has found its way into school curricula. Well-known actors and actresses publicize EST. The list is very long.

Cults tend to use common symbols and idealistic language and causes to lure the unsuspecting "prospect." Once enticed, the newcomer is worked on by an amazingly modern array of mind control techniques.

Students most at risk are those who are lonely, troubled, and angry. They may be the very students who seek justice and are imbued with the spirit of "*tikkun olam*" (fixing the world). It is common for such a student to be approached to work on some social action project by an

56 DEALING WITH CHILDREN AT RISK

organization he/she never heard of. Once involved in a first project or a first meeting, the indoctrination begins. Jason/Sanji demonstrates such a sad situation.

Jason/Sanji

Jason's mother and stepfather moved into town and went to visit the local synagogue. Jason, thirteen years old, had never been given a Jewish education. His mother explained that she had only just come back to Judaism. Her first husband was Jewish, but anti-religious. Could Jason become a Bar Mitzvah?

Jason attended an exclusive private school with a schedule that did not allow him to enter seventh grade with his peer group at the synagogue. After much discussion, a private tutor was engaged, a system of study and service attendance was devised, and the Bar Mitzvah ceremony was tentatively set for a little after his fourteenth birthday.

The tutor, in monthly reports, remarked how interested Jason seemed in social action projects. When attending services, people noticed that Jason aggressively criticized his peers for "not caring enough" about the world. Jason's mother complained that Jason was not getting a "spiritual feeling" from his Jewish education.

The Rabbi, after several months, suggested that Jason attend a Jewish summer camp to develop friendships and have a more intense religious experience. Jason replied that he already attended a religious summer camp with his father each year.

The truth, as it came out, was that Jason's father and mother were cult members and had raised their son within it. When his mother left the cult and divorced his father, she took Jason with her. The terms of the divorce agreement mandated that Jason spend each summer with his father at the cult's summer encampment. At that time, he dressed as a cult member and went by another name — "Sanji."

Jason believed himself still to be a member of the cult and was unsure of his Jewish identity. He did not accept his becoming a Bar Mitzvah as anything other than an accommodation to his mother.

What To Look For

Be alert to the following signs, which may signal involvement in a cult:

1. literature of or meeting notices for a group which is unfamiliar; get a copy and take notice of what it says.
2. talk about a charismatic person or leader of a group; find out about him/her.
3. a student suddenly has a friend (often older by a year or two) of the opposite sex who is taking him/her to the meetings.

Resources

There are too many cults to list here. Their symbols and methods of operation are also too varied to list. The Citizens Freedom Foundation in Chicago (312 267-7777) has newspaper files on every cult in the United States. For a small fee they will send you a copy of their files. Also, the local Anti-Defamation League, Community Relations Committee, or American Jewish Committee will have information about cults operating in your area.

JEWS FOR JESUS AND CHRISTIAN MISSIONARIES

The gravest concern to those who are aware of the goals and methods of Jews for Jesus and Christian missionaries is that very few outsiders seem to take the threat seriously. It is often held that the Jews for Jesus represent a fringe group of social misfits who have no clear purpose. Nothing could be farther from the truth.

There is a great deal of money and clear motivation behind the attempt of Jews for Jesus to lure Jews away from their religion. There are also many more such groups than we realize. One of their main goals is to achieve recognition by the Jewish community as informed and respected teachers. Thus, their first target is Jews who are not familiar with scripture. This includes most who attended supplementary school and not a few ex-day school students as well.

There are several fundamentalist groups which train their members to "witness" to those who are not "saved." Some of these, e.g., Seventh Day Adventists, have written pamphlets which detail "how to witness to your Jewish friends." These booklets show the missionary how to reword Christian theological terms into less "loaded" expressions, what specific arguments to employ when debating religion, and what phrases to use to begin a conversation on the topic of Jesus. To the unsuspecting, these groups can and do pose a clear and present danger. Mindy could have been a victim of a cult had her Rabbi not intervened.

Mindy

The Rabbi met Mindy, one of her Confirmation students, at the supermarket. Mindy was very distraught. In school that week, one of her friends had given her a pamphlet about a Rabbi who had converted to Christianity. The cover of the pamphlet, with the friendly face of an Orthodox man, was filled with quotes concerning his rebirth. How could such a pious and observant man be wrong?

The Rabbi wrote away to the Jews for Jesus, who had published the pamphlet, for more information about this Rabbi. It turned out that this Rabbi had graduated from the Hebrew Union College in 1895. While the questions concerning his conversion still existed, the blatant lies concerning his observance, the attempt to portray him as Orthodox, and neglecting to mention that only one Rabbi in the last hundred years converted to Christianity, did much to allay Mindy's fears and frustrations.

What To Look For

When suspecting involvement in a Jews for Jesus or other Christian missionary group, watch out for:
1. pamphlets and other written materials brought to class.
2. questions about religion that would not otherwise come up in class.

Resources

There is a helpful organization called Jews for Judaism, which works to counter the Jews for Jesus movement. (The address of their main office is P.O. Box 15059, Baltimore, MD 21208.) Write them for information and for addresses of branches in other cities.

AIDS AND COMMUNICABLE DISEASES

In all the other categories discussed in this chapter, we have presented a case to illustrate our text. The cases available to us for AIDS and communicable diseases are too tragic and painful to portray, all the more so because in each and every instance they were preventable. Today's teens have already become infected and will carry these plagues forward, infecting the unwary.

Here again, the first rule, is — yes, Jewish teenagers are at risk. Concerning AIDS, ignorance can be terminal. Proper education, which a child may or may not receive at home, is imperative. Abstinence is the first and best line of defense. But, realistically, teenagers now need to know about safe sex, about not using/sharing needles, and about the risks of homosexual and heterosexual sex. Informal synagogue programming should encourage discussions on all the problems that teenagers face. The Religious School classroom is also a valid venue for such discussions.

Concerns about sexual behaviors and choices can and should be aired in discussions between students and respected Jewish educational professionals who can bring both their moral outlook and practical advice to bear. Just as we need to inform students about condoms and other precautions, we must also lead them to consider the moral implications of their choices.

Resources

The first resources in this instance are your Director of Education and/or Rabbi. Will he/she support your educational efforts? If not, know where to send the students to find out what you may not be able to tell them. Know a good AIDS speaker. Know about the local clinics, doctors, and testing centers. Know enough so as not to be shocked when kids speak to you, but know also the limits of your ability to help or to answer questions.

DEATH OF A LOVED ONE

You may assume that the death of a family member or close friend, or even a death in the family of a close friend, will create tension and behavior changes in students. This is a normal part of the grieving process, a process that can take months, even years, to restore balance in a young mind.

In many of the other situations described above, some type of aggressive action is usually recommended. In the case of grief work, giving the student time to feel the pain and hurt is perhaps the best strategy to use. Many tend to hurry along the process, becoming impatient with a child's inability to cope with a life process they themselves cannot fully comprehend. They demand responses and communication which only complicate an already trying time.

This is not to say that a student should be allowed to wallow in self-pity. Nor should a student be left to feel alone in sorrow. An understanding attitude and the message that you care and are there as a support, will bear fruit down the road. The case study of Phyllis is about a teenager whose father died.

Phyllis

Phyllis was thirteen years old when her father died suddenly. An outstanding student and a very responsible young woman, she helped her mother with her four brothers, and continued to excel in her studies. The only visible effect of her loss was a significant weight gain.

It took a crisis three years later for the Rabbi to see what was behind the "coping" front Phyllis had adopted. She had fought with her father the night before he died, and for three years she had lived with (and stuffed herself over) the guilt she felt for "causing" his death. Once she spoke about this problem — and realized how silly it sounded to her — she was ready to do the real grieving she did not do at the time of her father's death. She was ready to stop punishing herself by overeating, overworking, and overcompensating in every other aspect of her life, and to begin trying to rethink this critical point in her life. A recommendation for further counseling was made and brought her back to "life."

What To Look For

Any of the following signs should be taken as danger signals:
1. lingering depression
2. constant weeping or weeping for no apparent reason
3. inability to concentrate
4. preoccupation with death in conversations, writings, or drawings
5. a total lack of affect — no emotion about anything

In most instances, time and emotional support from others should be enough the help the student through the grieving process. Should the grieving dynamic continue for an overextended period of time, action should be taken. Also, if the student exhibits no behavioral changes and carries on as though nothing has happened, be concerned.

Resources

The Director of Education and/or Rabbi should have been apprised of the loss. Keep them informed as to what happens in class. A skilled therapist is another member of the support team to be utilized as needed. In many communities there are Jewish support groups which normally meet for six to ten sessions. Most suggest that a mourner begin with such a group no sooner than six months after a loss. The Rabbi or the Jewish Family Service would know about such a group.

EATING DISORDER

Anorexia nervosa and bulimia are psychological disorders that manifest themselves as compulsive starvation, overeating, and self-induced vomiting. They are most often associated with young women and are frequently seen in Jewish adolescent females. They are life threatening.

Anorexia is increasingly perceived as a disturbed adolescent's attempt to exert control over herself when she is unable to control a chaotic or hostile environment. By starving herself the adolescent can retard the physical changes of maturity and can prevent or delay sexual development. The issue is never whether or not the girl is overweight; her self-image is so distorted that an emaciated, hospitalized teenager weighing 70 pounds can still see herself as being too fat.

Bulimia, the purging cycle, can be found independently or in conjunction with anorexia. It is not up to a teacher or Director of Education to make a certain diagnosis, and treatment is certainly not within the educator's purview. Indeed, a cure may not be possible by medical professionals either. However, with these diseases, standing aside altogether is tantamount to participating in a suicide.

Chavi's story is a sad one.

Chavi

In junior high school, Chavi was a plump, happy student. She started changing in many ways during her sophomore year of high school. She lost a great deal of weight — which first

INFORM YOUR DIRECTOR OF EDUCATION AND RABBI ABOUT PROBLEMS.

appeared to be a major improvement in her appearance — became withdrawn, was often late to school and to class, and was frequently absent because of illness. By the end of that year, she was pale, sickly looking, and very thin.

Chavi's teachers and principal were concerned about these changes, as were her friends. Several of them spoke to members of the faculty about the fact that Chavi spent long periods of time in the bathroom and seemed to be eating little.

The principal decided to discuss with Chavi the changes she had seen, but Chavi denied any problems. With the aid of the school psychologist, a conference was set up with the parents. They also denied any problems. Chavi had always been and was still a perfect daughter, a perfect student.

Chavi was also the perfect example of an anorexia/bulemic student, starving and gorging, vomiting repeatedly to make herself really "perfect." The parents made some cursory attempts at medical evaluation, but have, to this point, refused to deal with the main problem. And Chavi's behavior continues.

What To Look For

If you see any of the following signs, an eating disorder is a possibility:
1. students who never eat, especially when others do
2. binge eating following by bathroom visits
3. student gossip about destructive eating habits

Note: Conversation among students is invaluable for dectecting problems. These symptoms are most often manifest outside the classroom. Students talk a great deal about each other and almost always know when someone exhibits the symptoms of eating disorders.

Resources

There are many types of health professionals. In this case you need someone who specializes in eating disorders. Many hospitals have (inpatient) eating disorder clinics.

INAPPROPRIATE RELATIONSHIPS AND SEXUAL HARASSMENT

In preparation for writing this chapter, we consulted with our resources and spoke to many lay people, including our students. We asked them to list what they thought were the most pressing problems facing them as individuals and groups. While in most instances we anticipated their answers, one unforeseen response involved sexual harassment and inappropriate relationships. Many of them related anecdotal material concerning teachers of one gender becoming too familiar verbally or physically with students of the opposite sex. Several spoke about relationships between teachers and students which were questionable at best and criminal at worst.

Rachel

Rachel, the youngest child of a widower, is the only Jewish teenager in a small town. The lone congregation is served by Brad, a student Rabbi. Brad drives in twice a month to lead services and to teach the few children.

Rachel is very interested in Judaism because of her dead mother's strong identity. She also had time on her hands because she was not part of the "in" crowd at high school, and because her father had little time for her. She and Brad, who was lonely in an isolated and uninteresting pulpit, became friends.

After Brad's ordination, Gary took his place in the congregation. Rachel and Brad, still very close, enter into a dating relationship. Rachel visits Brad at his new home and neglects all other interests and people in favor of him.

Rachel's father talks to her about her relationship with Brad, and Gary also confronts Brad on the inappropriateness of this relationship. Brad and Rachel stop seeing one another, but no one emerges from the situation unscathed.

At what point does a friendly, supportive relationship cross the line? Indeed, it is often difficult for the person engaging in a behavior to be fully aware of how inappropriate it may be. For example, a young male teacher who "innocently" flirts with his female high school students, may be leading a particularly vulnerable student to interpret the flirting as an invitation to a "special" relationship. Observers on the scene can often be more objective in assessing the behavior of the teacher and warning of its potential for harm.

What constitutes sexual harassment? As this question remains subjective in the courts, we certainly do not have specific answers either.

But most of us know the difference between appropriate and intentionally inappropriate behavior, between constructive and destructive language, and between that which is respectful and that which is embarrassing or provocative. Most of us know what it means to be a *mensch*.

What To Look For

When suspecting an inappropriate relationship or sexual harassment the general rules to follow are:
1. If it looks questionable, question it.
2. If it appears unhealthy, it probably is.
3. Don't hesitate to confront a colleague.
4. Don't begin rumors or allow rumors to fester.

Resources

First and foremost, contact the Director of Education and/or Rabbi. They need to know what is (or what you suspect is) happening. Whatever action is taken must come from them.

DIVORCE AND SEPARATION

We deal last with the category which is first among our concerns. Of all the possible problematic situations with which an educator can be faced, the issues surrounding the children of divorce and separation are at the same time most prevalent and most often ignored. Perhaps this is because so many of our students come from single parent homes or live with combined families (thus giving them three parents and six grandparents). Perhaps this is because many Jewish educators are also single parents who deal with the realities of the situation every day, and thus acknowledging in other children the problems that they and their children cope with at home.

For whatever reason, we must be especially vigilant in attending to the unique concerns of these students who are stretched and pulled by every adult around them.

Allen

Allen was a personable junior high school student who, while frequently involved in small acts of mischief, seemed unaffected by the anger or discipline of his teachers. His grandmother, the adult responsible for him, called frequently to check on his progress, but her concerns were often ignored. Allen's parents did not attend parent-teacher conferences and were detached from their son.

Allen's continued acts of mischief finally aroused several faculty members. At the January staff meeting, all concerned admitted they did not understand the child or the family dynamics. It was determined that the school social worker would look into the matter.

Some detective work revealed the nature of Allen's world. His parents divorced shortly after he was born. His father moved across the country. His mother worked long hours and had moved near her mother for support, but no longer had any relationship with her except through Allen. Allen spent after school time with his grandmother. She supervised homework, watched out for him, gave him supper, and sent him home to his mother at night and on weekends. He spoke to his father once a week and spent summers with him. His parents were not on speaking terms.

Unravelling Allen's complex world, we understand that he had learned to negotiate his life through separate universes: his mother's, his grandmother's, and his father's. He had become adept at playing one off against the other; and, sadly, he had no consistent parenting, expectations, or demands from any of these adults. His school experience was like an extension of his home life — compartmentalized, with no one person laying down consistent rules.

The principal decided to begin an aggressive approach for this young man. Allen's school would really act *in loco parentis*, providing a unified network of rules and expectations. During the next months, Allen's behavior and performance improved.

Although Allen's case is a markedly unusual and exaggerated, every divorce or separation brings fragmentation into the lives of the youngsters affected. Although the home situation prior to the divorce was probably less than ideal, at least there was one home with (hopefully) one set of rules. Two (or, in this case, three) homes with different expectations and "cultures" seriously compound the confusion, guilt, and anxiety of the child of divorce. He or she can become severely confused, anxious, or, like Allen, adept at maneuvering among warring parties (or engaging in anti-social behaviors such as lying, cheating, stealing, drugs, etc.). The school must be aware and able to deal with some of the child's conflict.

The behaviors that signal problems for a child living in this dynamic are similar to symptoms described in categories shown above. The proper responses are also similar. Identifying the problem and working (sometimes with the parents, sometimes despite the parents) with the child, present the greatest challenges.

CONCLUSION

All of the above may make you say, "Stop, I just wanted to teach Hebrew/Chumash/History"! But consider: a good teacher doesn't teach topics, he/she teaches students. Students today seldom enter the classroom with undivided focus on the subject at hand. Their lives are "interesting" and so, beyond the curriculum, they often need our concern, support, and . . . intervention. That doesn't mean you don't teach Hebrew/Chumash/History. It just means that you may be called upon to teach other life lessons as well. And it is those lessons that can make a decided difference to our students.

Steven Bayar is the Rabbi of Congregation B'nai Israel of Millburn, New Jersey. He is the co-author of *Teens and Trust,* published by Torah Aura Productions, and various articles on Jewish education and the Rabbinate. He is also the B Side Director of Camp Ramah in New England.

Fran Hirschman is the Principal of the Ezra Academy in Flushing, New York. She is a doctoral student at Azrieli Graduate Institute of Yeshiva University, and is co-author of *Teens and Trust.*

BIBLIOGRAPHY

Allen, Nancy H., and Michael L. Peck. *Suicide in Young People*. West Point, PA: American Association of Suicidology, Merck Sharp & Dohme. (Pamphlet)

Bayar, Steven, and Francine Hirschman. *Teens & Trust: Building Bridges in Jewish Education*. Los Angeles: Torah Aura Productions, 1993.

Cohen, Susan, and Daniel Cohen. *Teenage Stress*. New York: M. Evans & Company, 1984.

Conway, Flo, and Jim Siegelman. *Snapping, America's Epidemic of Sudden Personality Change*. New York: Dell Publishing, 1976.

Galbraith, Ronald E., and Thomas Jones. *Moral Reasoning: A Teaching Handbook*. Minneapolis: Greenhaven Press, 1976.

Giffin, Mary, and Carol Felsenthal. *A Cry for Help*. Garden City, NJ: Doubleday & Co., 1983.

Gordon, Sol. *When Living Hurts*. New York: UAHC Press, 1985.

Grollman, Earl A. *Suicide: Prevention, Intervention, Postvention*. rev. ed. Boston: Beacon Press, 1988.

Kaplan, Aryeh. *The Real Messiah: A Jewish Response to Missionaries*. New York: National Council of Synagogue Youth, 1985.

Klagsbrun, Francine. *Too Young To Die*. New York: Pocket Books, 1985.

Kubler-Ross, Elisabeth. *On Children & Death*. New York: Macmillan Publishing Company, 1983.

Levy, Stephen Jay, ed. *Addictions in the Jewish Community*. New York: Federation of Jewish Philanthropies, 1986.

Schwartz, Earl, *Moral Development: A Practical Guide for Jewish Teachers*. Denver: A.R.E. Publishing, Inc., 1983.

(Note: For in-depth case studies on these and similar topics, please see *Teens & Trust: Building Bridges in Jewish Education* by Bayar and Hirschman. The authors would like to thank Dr. Marilyn Sperling and Sara Shuter for their help with this chapter.)

BACKGROUND FOR TEACHERS

CHAPTER EIGHT

FAITH DEVELOPMENT: A JEWISH VIEW

Roberta Louis Goodman

Our students of all ages are continuously deriving meaning out of their lives. They are answering questions about life and death; developing their value systems; determining how they want to live their lives, connecting to Judaism, cultivating relationships with people, creating their own views of (or dialogue with) God, forming their views about what is sacred and central to their lives. They are doing this naturally, whether or not we as Jewish educators choose to intervene in the process.

I am guided by faith development theory which suggests that making meaning out of our lives is what it means to be human. We are meaning making beings.

Meaning making can be nurtured. Faith development theory offers ways of approaching the task of nurturing meaning making. Other theories provide guidelines for developing curriculum which are age appropriate in terms of cognitive, social, or even moral development. But these theories usually leave out concerns central to Judaism: the connections between ethical values and God, Torah, and Israel; our spiritual longings — a sense of the holy; and the role of symbols, rituals, and traditions. Faith development theory provides us with a way of addressing these concerns and understanding the human being's quest for meaning and how we as educators can nurture people's journeys.

In this chapter, I will (1) present faith development theory as it helps us understand the process of people's meaning making, (2) describe a rubric of activities for nurturing faith, and (3) offer suggestions of actual activities for nurturing faith.

FAITH DEVELOPMENT THEORY

Faith development theory was devised by Dr. James Fowler, a minister, teacher, and thinker. He formed his theory from interviews with people of both genders and different ages, from different religious groups as well as unaffiliated individuals, and from different socioeconomic backgrounds. All of his subjects lived in North America.

Faith development is about meaning making. "Faith or 'faithing' is the process by which a person finds and makes meaning of life's significant questions and issues, adheres to this meaning and acts it out in his or her life" (*A Test of Faith* by Goodman, p. 1). Faith is common to all people. Yet, we each choose a particular path in pursing this universal phenomenon.

Faith has a narrative quality. We are continuously creating and recreating a story or stories about who we are. These stories embody our meaning making systems. They reveal to others and to ourselves, our values, struggles, conflicts, and hopes. These stories guide our daily decisions, life choices, and actions.

Faith formation occurs in relation to others. These others can be individuals, such as family members, friends, classmates, workplace associates, youth group workers, Rabbis, and/or educators. Or, these others can be groups such as a synagogue, team, youth group, school, and/or havurah.

What Fowler calls "shared centers of value and power" mediate the relationship between the individual and others. These centers of value and power include: trust, fairness, financial gain, possessions, recognition, strength, beauty, integrity, humanism, holiness, and/or God. Fowler identifies God as one possible center of value and power. By doing so, his theory overcomes the split between rationality and passion, religion and secularism, that has characterized the modern era since the Enlightenment. According to Fowler, all people, whether they are atheists or religious zealots, have faith. How we organize these centers of value and power, whether we assign more importance to financial gain than to fairness, or to beauty than to integrity, or to humanism than to holiness, reflects who we are and how we conduct our lives.

Faith encompasses the whole human being, binding together the rational, affective, kinesthetic, cognitive, conscious, and unconscious. Just as faith binds together these components, so, too, these components can be conduits through which faith is nurtured.

Faith changes over time, both in its content and structure. Faith development theory examines the structural changes in one's faith. Fowler outlines six "stages of faith" which describe people's faith (see below). Although our formal schooling may end, faith, or meaning making, is a lifelong process. The choice, perhaps the obligation, is for us as educators to intervene in people's meaning making processes. We have an important role to play in nurturing faith. By understanding how people construct their faith, we can better address their needs in this area.

THE STAGES OF FAITH

Faith development is similar to other theories, such as those of Piaget and Kohlberg, in that there are stages to the process. Fowler outlines one pre-stage and six "stages of faith." These stages are sequential and hierarchical, meaning that one goes through them in order. People do not skip around from one stage to another. A higher stage is considered more adequate than a lower.

The faith stages are structural. The stages tell how people structure their meaning making system. The stages reveal little if anything about the content of each stage. Their structural orientation gives them their universal quality as they encompass people of all religious groupings. We do not go through faith stages in the abstract. We each pursue a path filled with particular ideas, beliefs, experiences, practices, symbols, rituals, and customs. Stage 3 Catholics and Stage 3 Jews share a way of organizing, presenting, discussing, and thinking about their lives, irrespective of the content. In the same way, a concrete operational thinker who is Mexican-American and a concrete operational thinker who is Anglo-American think about the math concepts of sets or addition similarly.

Age is not equated with stage. A person *develops* stage structures, rather than *grows* into a particular stage automatically upon reaching a certain age or phase in his/her life. Therefore, not everyone goes through all six of Fowler's stages. Most people get through at least Stages 1 and 2. Few reach Stages 5 and 6.

The stages of faith are outlined in this chapter accompanied by Jewish educational implications for each stage. Fowler claims that the role of education or of any intervention, is not to move a person from one stage to the next. Rather, the task is to fill out each stage. For example, imagine the person who in Stage 1 is not introduced to any Jewish rituals or symbols until she or he is in a higher stage, and obviously older. This person who lacks an early introduction to Jewish symbols and rituals is likely to feel a void in his or her Jewish upbringing. The introduction of ritual and symbols into a Stage 3 person's life must be done differently than with a Stage 1 person. A Jewish education needs to address a person at every stage of his or her faith development to bring out the richness of our heritage. Different faith issues, transitions, crises, and dangers can arise at each stage. The stages of faith help us appreciate the importance of lifelong Jewish education.

ALL PEOPLE HAVE FAITH, SAYS FOWLER.

Pre-Stage: Undifferentiated Faith or Primal Faith

Fowler calls this a pre-stage because it is essentially kinesthetic, and non-verbal or "pre-talking." This pre-stage focuses on trust and mistrust. The infant develops a sense of routine, ritual, and mutuality through feeding, dressing, bathing, and sleeping. The interaction between caretaker and child establishes a foundation for images of God.

Stage 1: Intuitive Projective Faith

The use of language and symbols to communicate about objects and experiences signals the onset of Stage 1. A Stage 1 person is self-centered: the world revolves around him or her. Individuals view their perspective and that of others as the same.

At this stage, emotions are central and intense. Individuals have a great sense of mystery, awe, and fear. These underlie their views of God. The ability to think logically is not present. They often do not distinguish between reality and fantasy. This gives free reign to the imagination. Life has an episodic and mysterious quality to it. Rituals create an alliance between the moral and the sacred. One obeys out of a desire to avoid punishment.

Jewish Educational Implications for Stage 1

As Stage 1 individuals are just learning the names of things, their new verbal capabilities provide an opportunity for introducing Judaism's culture code. They will as easily learn a Hebrew word or expression as an English one. Stage 1 individuals are open to the mysteries of rituals, symbols, stories, and prayers. When talking about symbols, remember to have concrete examples present. Stage 1 individuals flourish on repetition and routine. Their views of God can be quite anthropomorphic. God is a wonderful topic for discussion with those who are at this stage. Their desire for playing and pretending makes them receptive to a variety of experiences through role playing and imitating others. They enjoy fairy tales. As their comprehension of stories is episodic, do not overemphasize the importance of sequencing of events. Although you as teacher may distinguish between Bible stories and *midrash*, between what is in the biblical text and what is not, making such a distinction is superfluous to this stage.

Stage 2: Mythic Literal Faith

The emergence of concrete operational thinking which includes the ability to distinguish between reality and fantasy generally stimulates the transition to Stage 2. Stage 2 individuals are able to differentiate their perspective from that of others. Life is linear and predictable. Narrative or stories which have a beginning, middle, and end, as opposed to the episodic quality of the previous stage, become a favored way of grasping meaning. Stories of my people give an individual a sense of identity. Stories are understood literally. Meaning is both carried and trapped in the narrative. This stage can be self-righteous. Prejudice emerges at this stage.

Symbols are one-dimensional. Stage 2 individuals take pride in participating and helping in the celebration of holidays and life cycle events, or in performing acts, as with the *mitzvot* (commandments).

Events have a cause and effect relationship. Good is rewarded and bad is punished. A reciprocal fairness emerges. God appears to be like a consistent, fair, and caring ruler or parent.

Jewish Educational Implications for Stage 2

The sequencing of stories is important to this age group. They can tell the difference between fairy tales and true to life stories and between the biblical text and *midrash*. The stories of their people, especially their heroes and heroines, provide a source of pride and connection for this stage. Their interpretations of texts are still very literal. They can grasp a tremendous number of details and concepts. They can understand a concept like *Hachnasat Orchim* (welcoming strangers) in a literal way through concrete examples.

Although some of the mystery and awe of symbols is lost in this stage, individuals at this stage do enjoy participating and assisting in rituals or celebrations. This comes in part from their desire to please authority figures, such as parents or teachers. They respond to the images of the good emulated by adults. *Mitzvot* provide a tangible and concrete way of enacting behaviors that both authority figures and the community value.

Stage 3: Synthetic-Conventional Faith

The emergence of interpersonal perspective taking, the ability to see another person's perception of oneself — the preoccupation with looking at oneself in the mirror, often signifies the beginnings of this stage. How the person appears to others is all absorbing. At this stage, an individual can construct the interiority of oneself and of others. Identity and meaning are functions of roles and relations, yet not held in critically reflective ways. Approval and acceptance from others is sought and valued. Authority is external, coming from the group or selected authority figures, rather than from within oneself. This stage often sees the formation of a personal relationship to an authority figure other than one's parents — youth group leader, Director of Education, Rabbi, coach, teacher, gang leader, or cult leader. Those at this stage are susceptible to the loss of self to the group, as with gangs, and to total commitment to an authority figures, as with cult leaders.

Formal operational thinking, the ability to think abstractly, emerges at this stage. With that capability comes a sense of the future and an awakening to death. Values and beliefs are tacit and unexamined. These values and beliefs are often fleeting and piecemeal, unsystematic. Sometimes individuals at this stage get stuck in seeing the world and themselves in one way; they fail to imagine alternatives. Symbols are evocative and reflect one's identity. Wearing a *chai* or *Magen David* is one example. God is perceived in mainly interpersonal terms: God as friend, the One who knows and understands me.

Jewish Educational Implications for Stage 3

Stage 3 individuals have the ability to think abstractly which leads to contemplating their futures, and brings out fears and concerns about: death, messiah, the afterlife, their contribution to society, taking responsibility for their lives and destinies, suicide, making life meaningful, the sacred and the profane, and God. Although capable of thinking abstractly, Stage 3 individuals are neither systematic or systematized thinkers, nor are they particularly critically reflective. When presenting or discussing these topics, getting the Stage 3 individual to raise questions, see options, and think through statements is essential. In terms of options, the Stage 3 individual who rejects God as an old man with a white beard needs to be shown that our views change and that other views of God exist.

Getting Stage 3 individuals to think critically is tricky, because they are sensitive to how others perceive them. They have a tendency (1) to not express any opinion, or (2) to get stuck making some outrageous pronouncement that they feel compelled to defend. As a preferable alternative to "attacking" one of their viewpoints, take a text or statement of an unknown party, and critique it. Until they become comfortable or trusting of the instructor and their classmates/studymates, they may be slow to open up to criticism of their views. It is crucial to provide opportunities for creative writing, expository, journal writing, or art, with the assurance of acceptance rather than critique.

At this stage, individuals search for a personal God. God has an imminent quality of knowing one and caring for one. Hasidic tales are a favorite of this stage, as they present a close and caring personal relationship to God. This stage is often marked by an acknowledgement of the unfairness of a God who allows children to die of cancer or hunger. Stage 3 individuals struggle with ideals and realities, and can be opened to the complexities of life and God.

Stage 4: Individuative–Reflective Faith

Clashes with and exposure to other value systems leads to the formation of Stage 4. The individual becomes critically reflective of his/her own ideas and views, and those of others. The meanings behind (the why of) symbols and rituals become important while, at the same time, these symbols and rituals lose their evocative power and their mystery. Stage 4 individuals construct systems or theories of belief and meaning which must be internally consistent and defensible. Views become explicit. This stage tends toward rationality and individuality. They can display over confidence in critical thought and in the rational, conscious mind.

Membership in a group or organization results from an individual's choosing. The individual takes responsibility for and control over his/her commitments, life-style, beliefs, and attitudes.

Jewish Educational Implications for Stage 4

Stage 4 individuals look for systems of thought. So they are receptive to reading or learning about the works of a Buber, Heschel, Maimonides, and so forth, on far ranging topics, such as forgiveness, *tzedakah*, and God. They construct their own theology or philosophy of Judaism and life. Introduction of texts on issues relevant and useful to their lives, such as biomedical ethics, business ethics, caring for the elderly, and the like, can influence their actions as they carry out their daily responsibilities. Stage 4 individuals hold up the standards of scholarship or scientific works, whether of electrical engineers or philosophers, commonly found in the university. They judge these religious or theological systems on the basis of internal consistency, truth, insightfulness, and presentation. They freely critique and reflect on the meanings expressed by others and themselves.

They develop explanations for their actions, for their adherence to ritual and traditions. Their search for answers and understanding motivates them to learn. "Why" needs to be explicitly answered for them — why do we light two candles on Shabbat? Why do we recite blessings over four cups of wine? etc.

Stage 5: Conjunctive Faith

Dissatisfaction with the flatness and sterility of the orderly meanings and systems that one serves and a recognition of the complexity of life can lead to transition into Stage 5. This stage brings a second naivete, a receptivity to symbolic power reunited with conceptual meanings. This provides an opportunity for introducing and experimenting with new rituals. Multiple names and metaphors for the holy emerge. Experiencing God goes beyond the rational.

An awakening to life's paradoxes and an openness to discovering new meanings from strangers or those unlike oneself occurs. Life is dialectical. The language is of "both" rather than "either/or." Stage 5 individuals show an uncertainty, a doubting. This stage is multi-systemed. Stage 5 individuals tolerate differences and inconsistences which have implications for realizing *K'lal Yisrael*. The tolerance of Stage 5 can lead to passivity, inaction, cynicism, and complacency.

> THERE'S NO WAY OF PREPARING A PERSON TO BE A STAGE 6 INDIVIDUAL.

Jewish Educational Implications for Stage 5

Stage 5 presents the possibility for awakening to and active experimentation with new rituals and traditions in the home and synagogue. Exploring and uncovering deep and rich meanings of symbols and observances can enrich the lives of Stage 5 individuals. God, holiness, the mystery of life, spirituality, and mysticism are topics of interest to this stage. The receptivity of Stage 5 individuals allows the educator to introduce far-reaching views and writings. This stage presents the opportunity for sharing the worship experiences, customs, and valued writings of Judaism's various branches.

Stage 6: Universalizing Faith

A search for a transforming world vision and the willingness to live that vision leads to this stage. Jewish concept terms for people who are at Stage 6 are *lamed vavnik* (one of the hidden 36 righteous who sustain the world) or *tzaddik*. Few people reach this stage. Stage 6 is characterized by an at-oneness with God, a uniting of self and God. Transcendence and imminence of God are experienced as intertwined. These individuals share their unconditional love and commitment to absolute justice. Particularism, in the sense of feeling distinct or different from another human being, is lost. The experience is of one human family. A social consciousness leads to the loss or detachment of self, as seen with Gandhi, King, and Heschel. God's presence is felt in the presence of these individuals.

Jewish Educational Implications for Stage 6

How do you educate for or continue to stimulate the development of a Stage 6 individual? The entire world, both in terms of interactions with people of all religions and beliefs and all texts Jewish and non-Jewish, is the material upon which a Stage 6 individual draws. In reality, there is no way of preparing one to be a Stage 6 individual. If you think you are a *lamed vavnik*, you probably are not one. Similarly, if you are self-conscious that you are a Stage 6 individual, then you probably are not.

A CRITIQUE OF THE STAGES OF FAITH

Perhaps the most common critique of the stages is the feminist critique of Stages 3 and 4. Fowler presents Stage 3 as a more communal and relationship oriented stage, whereas Stage 4 is much more individually and independently oriented. Gilligan's feminist critique of Kohlberg (Gilligan, 1982) applies here, too. Gilligan claims that women tend to be relationship and group oriented, whereas men are more independent and individually oriented. To claim that one orientation is a lesser stage than another is to make women look morally inferior in the case of Kohlberg's moral development, and, extrapolating, is to relegate women's faith to a lesser form of development. (For more on Gilligan, see Chapter 9, "Encouraging Moral Development.")

THE TEACHER/FACILITATOR AND PARENT

Teacher/facilitator and parent are roles which involve transmitting the content of Judaism and nurturing faith, meaning making. Stages of faith can be helpful in understanding how our students/learners and children structure meaning. Often, we structure meaning in ways different from our students. Stages of faith help make us aware of these developmental differences and can guide our expectations, preparation, and presentation as we teach and preach.

Good teachers overlap strategies for auditory, visual, and kinesthetic learners. In the same way, we need to overlap strategies for people at different faith stages.

In the main, the task is to enrich a person's meaning making processes at a particular stage, rather than moving people from one stage to the next. No educational or spiritual advantage is derived from having people in one stage versus another. The richer and deeper the Jewish experience at each stage, the more our lives are filled with meaning. This approach deepens, strengthens, and renews our commitment to living a Jewish life as evidenced by our actions, values, and beliefs.

A RUBRIC OF ACTIVITIES FOR NURTURING FAITH

The key to nurturing faith is helping the individual make connection between himself/herself and the array of experiences, symbols, rituals, and texts that Jewish life has to offer. This represents an entire approach to Jewish education. Nurturing faith has a cognitive, concrete, and conscious side, even though it involves the whole person (including the affective and the unconscious). This tangible side of faith makes nurturing faith look similar to teaching other Judaic subjects. Certain activities better fit a faith nurturing approach to Jewish education. Outlined below is a rubric of activities for nurturing faith.

The Arts

Music, creative writing, dance, sculpture, painting, and all other art forms are implicitly expressive and interpretive.

Nature

Appreciating nature gives us a sense of rhythm, movement, mystery, power, growth, renewal, and origins. By sensing the mystery and wonder in the world, we discover that the world is more than people. Nature presents a physical reality that parallels a psychic understanding.

Narratives or Stories Including Metaphor

Stories model the relationship between God and the Jewish people and the relationships among individuals. Stories show us how we got and get from the past to the present. Stories provide a way of knowing about a whole.[1] Embedded within stories are a microcosm of the Jewish world view and values. Stories teach without being didactic. They are entertaining.

Metaphor allows us to make explicit our perceptions and explore new meanings. With stories and metaphor, we are both limited and freed by language. Metaphor and stories are expressive.

Symbols, Rituals, and Prayer

Symbols both hold past meaning and offer the possibility for new meanings. Through ritual and blessing, we act out the symbolic meaning. For example, blowing the shofar on Rosh HaShanah: "The symbol makes a connection between what God commands us or expects, what we as Jews do, and how in the doing, we make our lives special."[2]

Prayer is a spiritual, meaning making activity; it too can be taught and processed.

Experience and the Experiential

Experience draws upon the life one has lived. Experience is important because we are all meaning makers. Sharing something explicitly adds a different quality, and often adds understanding to the experience.

The experiential occurs when we try to create or simulate an experience, i.e., crossing the Sea of Reeds. The experiential puts one in another person's perspective, another time or space. The experiential extends one's imagination. It has an affective component.

Both experience and the experiential are emotive and whole person oriented; they get on the inside, the interiority of one's inner life.

PRAYER IS A SPIRITUAL ACTIVITY THAT CAN BE TAUGHT.

Definitions, Descriptions, and Categories

Creation, loving, caring, thanksgiving, and *Gemilut Chasadim* are examples of categories. Deriving definitions, descriptions, and categories is the work of theologians. This approach closely examines a phenomenon, trying to figure out what something is, striving for common understanding.

Dialogue, Discussion, and Questioning

Dialogue, discussion, and questioning are the most common techniques used (and often

CHAPTER EIGHT **69**

overused) in a meaning making approach. They make the issue public and conscious. They help form understanding and insight. They are essentially inquiry oriented, inquisitive.

MEANING MAKING ACTIVITIES BY STAGE

Following are activities by stage that promote meaning making.

Stage 1: Intuitive Projective Faith

Note: All activities for Stage 1 are reprinted with permission from "God and Prayer and Faith Development" by Goodman, found in *The Jewish Preschool Teachers Handbook*, Revised Edition, by Sandy Furfine Wolf and Nancy Cohen Nowak, © 1991 A.R.E. Publishing, Inc., pages 139-148. Many activities other than those reproduced here can be found in that chapter.

B'tzelim Elohim (In the Image of God) – A Visual Art Activity

Objective

The students will associate the creation of human beings *B'tzelem Elohim* with the responsibility for showing caring behavior.

Activity

An important concept in Jewish theology is that human beings are made in the image of God. This concept is introduced in the creation story. God cares for human beings and, like God, we care for each other. Collect and show photographs of people.

Have the preschoolers identify pictures that show caring behavior.

Hospitality — A Story Activity

Objective

The students will practice being hospitable to strangers and friends, imitating Sarah and Abraham.

Activity

Have a "Be Kind to Strangers Day" at school. Invite "strangers" — the elderly, another class, grandparents — to visit on that day. Send invitations. Prepare a program. Act out the story of Abraham and Sarah and the three visitors. Share a snack. Come dressed in biblical costumes.

Performing Ritual Acts

Objective

The students will practice doing ritual acts.

Activity

Play *Follow the Leader* using motions that pertain to rituals: washing hands, affixing a *mezuzah* to a doorpost, lighting Shabbat candles, drinking *Kiddush* wine, walking to synagogue for services, climbing steps to the *bimah*. Go over what the motions represent.

Music Videos

Objective

The students will interpret key concepts in prayers or songs in expressive and creative ways.

Activity

Learn a song, such as "*Oseh Shalom*," "Prayer Is Reaching," or "*Hineh Mah Tov*." Sing the song. Go over the words. Discuss how students can act these out. Focus on the main concepts. With "*Oseh Shalom*," for example, concentrate on how we show things are peaceful: hug, kiss, shake hands, hold hands in a circle. Sing the song and do the motions. As an option, videotape the production for a real music video.

Stage 2: Mythic Literal Faith
Miracle of the Week Bulletin Board: Stories and Visual Arts

Objective

Students will find evidence of the mystery of creation and life by sharing pictures and stories of miracles in their lives and surroundings.

Activity

Assign a student a week to come up with a picture or story that illustrates a miracle in their lives or surroundings. These pictures or stories can be photographs, drawings, newspaper stories, a story that happened to them, and the like.

Brachah Busters Scavenger Hunt: Nature

Objective

The students will link the *Birkot HaNehenim* with items found in nature.

Activity

The students are given a list of the *Birkot HaNehenim*, such as the blessing on smelling fragrant woods or barks, on smelling fragrant plants, on seeing the rainbow, at the sight of sea, on hearing thunder, on seeing a sage distinguished for knowledge of Torah, on affixing a *mezuzah*. Send the students out into the woods or streets to find evidence of these *brachot*. Be creative — not just literal!

Hiddur Mitzvah Corps: Symbols and Rituals
Objective
  The students help maintain and prepare ritual objects for use in prayer services.

Activity
  Hiddur Mitzvah refers to paying attention to the aesthetic beauty involved in performing *mitzvot*. This activity actually has the students beautify and prepare ritual objects and settings for use. Have the students polish silver Torah ornaments. Dust prayer books, *Chumashim*, and non-silver ritual objects. Set the Torah to its place for the next reading. Straighten up the sanctuary. If ritual objects are on display elsewhere in the synagogue, those too can be cleaned.

God's Top Ten: Stories
Objective
  The students will associate a story with each of the Ten Commandments.

Activity
  God's Top Ten by Goodman (Torah Aura) exemplifies each commandment by using a biblical or *midrashic* story, or folktale. Throughout each story are questions that make the students analyze the story as they grapple with meaning making issues and try to understand each commandment better.

Stage 3: Synthetic Conventional Faith
God is Like . . . : A Metaphor Activity
Objective
  The students will increase their understanding of God's character and being through a metaphor activity.

Activity
  Have the students make a list of famous people. Then have them write or answer aloud: God is like (insert name of a famous person) because . . . . Keep doing this with several different examples. Then try: God is not like (insert name of a famous person) because . . . . Compare the two lists.

A Spiritual Interview
Objective
  The students will critique an individual's understanding of his/her spirituality and views on spiritual issues, such as: prayer and praying, life after death, God, Israel, finding meaning in life, relationships, marriage.

Activity
  One week the students make up questions on these different topics, then interview a person. Before the next week, the teacher interviews the person and provides a transcript. Have two or three students take the excerpts from the transcript on each topic (i.e., prayer, God, life after death). The students must be prepared to explain and defend the person's views. Once they are ready, go around the room having one group at a time read their section of the transcript. The other students ask them questions and challenge their views.
  An alternative way of doing this exercise is to take excerpts from famous Jewish philosophers/theologians and do the same thing.
  On a third week (if the students are ready), have students interview one another in pairs, using the questions they devised.

Create a Prayer
Objective
  The students will write prayers about personal events or experiences that happen in their lives.

Activity
  Look at a variety of different prayers: blessings, prayers of thanksgiving, petitions. Make a list of events and occurrences that happen in people's lives for which no particular prayer exists: getting your driver's license, a friend moves away, finishing school, passing an examination, a birthday, travel to a special place, and so forth. Write a prayer or two for these occasions.

Panel on God – Discussion
Objective
  The students will hear and respond to a panel's presentation on some meaning making issues.

Activity
  Invite some important or prominent members to speak on this panel. (No Rabbis, Jewish edu-

cators, Cantors, Judaic studies professors, or other Jewish professionals should be on the panel.) Ask panelists to prepare a few minute presentation on their relationship to God, spiritual experiences, earliest memories of God, etc.

After the presentations, open up the panel for questions. Encourage dialogue as much as possible.

Stage 4: Individuative-Reflective Faith
Tray of Symbols
Objective

The participants will describe their connections to various symbols.

Activity

On a tray or table, place a number of symbols associated with prayers and blessings: *kipah*, *tallit*, Shabbat candlesticks, *challah* cover, *Kiddush* cup, *tefillin*, shofar, *Seder* plate, prayer book, Torah, or *Chumash*. In pairs, ask people to give their responses in 90 seconds or less, explaining to their partners why they selected a particular symbol for the following sentences:

Choose a symbol that you are comfortable using.

Choose a symbol that you are uncomfortable or less comfortable using.

Choose a symbol that connects you to other Jews.

Choose a symbol that brings you close to God.

As a total group, process the responses.

My Own Jewish Book of Why
Objective

The participants will make explicit why they observe certain rituals and customs.

Activity

Around a room, place sheets of posterboard or butcher paper with a ritual or custom written on them. (These can be rituals and customs such as: lighting Shabbat candles, not eating *chametz* on Passover, affixing a *mezuzah*, etc.) Have people circulate, writing on each sheet, why they do or do not observe each ritual. Give people the opportunity to move around and read the responses. Have a discussion of the whys and why nots of ritual observances. Allow for stories to emerge. Focus on the meaning that people derive from these observances and what barriers may be standing in the way for others.

Using *The Jewish Book of Why* by Kolatch, introduce a more "traditional" Jewish view as opposed to a personal view of the whys of these same rituals and customs. Discuss the meaning making reasons that these practices emerge from the view of Jewish tradition.

Discuss where people's explanations and the traditional explanations of why intersect and diverge.

Pirke Avot — *A New Anthology for Future Generations: Creative Writing*
Objective

The participants will articulate their views on a number of meaning making topics.

Activity

Read a few excerpts from *Pirke Avot* on topics that relate to how people live their lives. Create a list of topics that theologians commonly deal with and add some of the group's concerns: justice, truth, meaning of life, righteousness, *tzedakah*, work, family, education, blessing, and joy. Then have participants write their own "*Pirke Avot: Sayings of Our Ancestors.*" Share the writings.

Modern Midrashim
Objective

The participants will create their own *midrashim*, tying today's problems to biblical themes.

Activity

In one bag, written on separate sheets of paper, write movie titles with which people are likely to be familiar. In another bag, written on separate sheets of paper, write quotable verses or commandments from the Torah.

In small groups, have each group pull out a movie title and a biblical verse. Give them time to create a modern *midrash*. Have each group act out their *midrash* which connects the movie's plot or characters to the biblical verse. The movie title and the verse must be recited at some point during the play.

Stage 5: Conjunctive Faith
An Illuminated Prayer Book – Visual Arts
Objective

The participants will each interpret a prayer or prayers from the *Siddur* through the visual arts.

Activity

Look at some illuminated or illustrated *Haggadot*. Give each person a prayer in Hebrew or Aramaic and English on a sheet of paper that can be cut out. Using various art materials, have the participants create an illuminated prayer page. You may want to arrange the prayers so that you cover an entire service or service section, e.g., the *Amidah*.

A Spiritual Will: Creative Writing
Objective

The participants will each write their own spiritual will.

Activity

We have living wills and ethical wills, as well as inheritance wills. Ask participants to write their spiritual wills.

Experiment with a Ritual or Custom
Objective

The participants will try out a ritual or custom that is new for them and will report on the experience.

Activity

This activity takes two sessions. During the first session, introduce participants to the idea of trying out a ritual or custom that is new to them. The ritual or custom may be something they want to continue doing, such as Havdalah, or it may be something that they anticipate trying only once, i.e., wearing a *kipah* for an entire day, laying *tefillin*, going to a weekday service, washing their hands before they eat.

Have each participate report on his/her experience.

Interpreting Prayers through Modern Dance
Objective

The participants will explore the meanings and interpretations of prayers through modern dance. (See Chapter 30, "Creative Movement Activities" for ideas on this topic.)

Activity

Have live or taped music available of five or six different melodies to the same prayer or song (i.e., *Shema* or *Adon Olam*). Sing the prayer or song a few times using a familiar tune. Go over the words. Then sing the song using different tunes. In small groups, play one tune and interpret the music through modern dance. You can use a combination of stretching, motion, drama and dance. Have the dancers and then the audience comment on what they experienced, saw, felt, and learned.

Stage 6: Universalizing Faith

Suggesting specific activities for Stage 6 is complex. As stated earlier, few people are or ever will be at Stage 6, and one cannot be intentionally prepared to be a Stage 6 individual. The deliberate effort of becoming Stage 6 contradicts the loss of self, the at-oneness with the world and God, that characterize the Stage 6 individual. Yet, Stage 6 people continue to grow and learn from others. In this sense, they have become "students." All meetings or encounters with people, and all texts regardless of their origin, provide sources of stimulation for Stage 6 individuals. To label these experiences and textual readings as facilitated educational "activities" is too limiting.

CONCLUSION

Faith development theory is a tool. It offers us a way of understanding human meaning making. People are constantly in motion, constantly making meaning out of their lives. We as Jewish educators can enter this ongoing internal dialogue, nurturing people's meaning making processes. A meaning making approach to Jewish education will help create responsive and committed Jews.

Roberta Louis Goodman is a Field Researcher for the Council for Initiatives in Jewish Education (CIJE). She is a graduate of the Rhea Hirsch School of Education of Hebrew Union College–Jewish Institute of Religion in Los Angeles. She studied faith development with Dr. James Fowler at Emory University, and is presently a doctoral candidate at Teachers College Columbia University, in Adult Education.

NOTES

1. Robert N. Bellah, et al, *Habits of the Heart* (Berkeley: University of California Press, 1985), p. 302.

2. Roberta Louis Goodman, "God and Prayer and Faith Development," in *The Jewish Preschool Teachers Handbook* by Sandy Furfine Wolf and Nancy Cohen Nowak. rev. ed. (Denver: A.R.E. Publishing, Inc., 1991), p, 141.

BIBLIOGRAPHY

Bellah, Robert N., et al. *Habits of the Heart.* Berkeley: University of California Press, 1985.

Dykstra, Craig, and Sharon Parks, eds. *Faith Development and Fowler.* Birmingham, AL: Religious Education Press, 1984.

Fowler, James W. *Stages of Faith: The Psychology of Human Development and the Quest for Meaning.* San Francisco: Harper & Row Publishers, 1981.

Fowler, James W., et al. *Stages of Faith and Religious Development.* New York: Crossroad, 1991.

Gilligan, Carol. *In a Different Voice.* Cambridge, MA: Harvard Press, 1982.

Goodman, Roberta Louis. "Faith Development." In *What We Know about Jewish Education*, Stuart Kelman, ed. Los Angeles: Torah Aura Productions, 1992, pp. 129-135.

———. "God and Prayer and Faith Development." In *The Jewish Preschool Teachers Handbook.* by Sandy Furfine Wolf and Nancy Cohen Nowak. rev. ed. Denver: A.R.E. Publishing, Inc., 1991.

———. "Test of Faith: An Instant Lesson Faith Development." Los Angeles: Torah Aura Productions, 1985.

Grossman, Barbara. "Faith and Personal Development: A Renewed Link for Judaism." *Journal of Psychology and Judaism*, Vol. 16, No. 1, Spring 1992.

Osmer, Richard Robert. *Teaching for Faith: A Guide for Teachers of Adult Classes.* Louisville, KY: Westminster/John Knox Press, 1992.

Rossoff, Donald. Handouts on "Stages of Faith," prepared for a workshop at the 1986 NATE Conference in Chicago.

Shire, Michael. "Faith Development and Jewish Education." *Compass*, Vol. 10, No. 1, Fall 1987, pp. 17-18, 24-25.

BACKGROUND FOR TEACHERS

CHAPTER NINE

ENCOURAGING MORAL DEVELOPMENT

Earl Schwartz

Introductory Note: Lawrence Kohlberg was professor of education and social psychology at Harvard. His work stood at the forefront of the field of moral education throughout the 1960s and 1970s. Around the time this chapter first appeared, a flurry of critiques and extensions of Kohlberg's research were published, including those of Carol Gilligan and James Fowler. The ensuing debate between Kohlberg and his critics has tended to obscure the significance of Kohlberg's initial studies and the influence his work continues to exert, directly as well as through the work of his colleague-critics. Lawrence Kohlberg died in January 1987, but his voice lives on in the ground breaking research he conducted and in his eloquent advocacy of education for justice.

One Sunday morning, a few years back, I told a group of nine and ten year olds the famous story of how Hillel, unable to pay for his daily Torah lesson, listened to the lecture through a skylight (*Yoma* 35b). I chose the story because I felt that Hillel's actions were a wonderful expression of devotion to *Talmud Torah*. I assumed that Hillel's behavior could not help but evoke each listener's empathy. You can therefore imagine my surprise when on this particular morning the empathy I evoked was rather tepid. In fact, I soon found myself scrambling to defend Hillel against a volley of accusations. Instead of seeing Hillel as a model of piety, several students derided him as a cheat and a coward who had ripped off a lesson via the skylight. In their eyes Hillel was no better than someone who sneaks into a movie theater through the exit. I left class quite befuddled. How could I have so grossly miscalculated my students' reaction to the story?

About a year before giving this lesson on Hillel, I had begun work on a dilemma-discussion moral development curriculum for use in Jewish schools. The curriculum is in large part based upon the research of Lawrence Kohlberg, whose theory of moral development proposes that:

1. "... there is a natural sense of justice intuitively known by the child."[1]
2. "... moral judgment develops through ... (a) culturally universal invariant sequence of stages."[2]
3. "... the existence of moral stages ... provide(s) a universal or non-relative and nonarbitrary approach to moral education. They define the aim of moral education as that of stimulating movement to the next stage of moral development ... the process for doing this ... rests on having students discuss moral dilemmas in such a way that they confront the limits of their reasoning and that of their fellow students."[3]
4. "One important stimulus to moral development is ... the sense of uncertainty which arises when one's easy judgments lead to contradiction or uncertainty when facing difficult decisions. A second stimulus is exposure to the next stage of reasoning above one's own."[4]

On the basis of these four principles, Kohlberg maintains that moral development should be understood as a process whereby a person's moral judgment develops through a set series of stages. Each of these stages is typical of a particular period in one's overall maturation, but they are not strictly correlated with specific ranges of age. This is because moral development is also a learning process: one must acquire, stage by stage, ever more adequate structures of moral logic. Kohlberg's research suggests that this type of learning is achieved by the thoughtful consideration of moral dilemmas.

Through the first year of my curriculum's development I had yet to witness a dramatic confirmation of Kohlberg's findings. But in mulling over what might have been behind the lack of empathy for Hillel on the part of my class, it occurred to me that perhaps the confirmation I was looking for was now staring me in the face. The lesson on Hillel had, in fact, turned into a discussion of a moral dilemma, the question being: is simple egalitarianism always an adequate measure of justice? Perhaps I had expected of my students a moral judgment for which they were cognitively unprepared.

To test this hypothesis, the story about Hillel was transformed into a dilemma about a child who is confined to a wheelchair and is thus barred from attending school by architectural rather than financial barriers. I wanted to see if my class would empathize with such a child any more than they had with Hillel. Specifically, I asked the class whether money which had been set aside for use by the student body as a whole should be used to make the necessary architectural changes for this one new child. At first the discussion of this "new" story followed the same line of reasoning with which poor Hillel had been "done in," but at a crucial point in the discussion two concepts were introduced that turned the whole thing around.

First, one student was unable to maintain his argument against making the architectural changes when I asked him whether the child in the wheelchair had a right to attend the school. Immediately following this, another student wondered aloud whether the *brit* (covenant) at Sinai, which mandated that *Talmud Torah* be made available to all Jewish children, was more important than simple "fairness." The second child was actually struggling to apply the concept of rights to this dilemma. With this concept at their disposal, several of the students began to see the dilemma in a very different light. Before the idea of rights was introduced, most of the students did not have the conceptual tools necessary to understand the virtue of Hillel's behavior. When these tools were provided, those who were prepared to do so quickly scampered up a step in moral judgment. At the end of the discussion I was convinced that I had witnessed what Kohlberg's cognitive-developmental theory predicts: the development of moral judgment through guided exploration of a moral dilemma.

THE DILEMMA-DISCUSSION MODEL IN TRADITIONAL JEWISH SOURCES

Examples of teaching ethical principles through discussion of moral dilemmas are found throughout Jewish literature. Rabbinic sources make frequent use of the dilemma-discussion model (*Baba Metzia* la, 60b; *Ketuvot* 17a). In the Torah such discussions often flow from a dilemma over which God and a prophet meet in dialogue. Abraham's attempt to save Sodom (Genesis 13), the case of the daughters of Zelophehad (Numbers 27, 36), and chapter four of the book of Jonah (note how it ends with a question) are all examples of this process.

In many of these dialogues the participants' lines of reasoning are quite explicit. In the discussion between God and Abraham about the fate of Sodom, for instance, Abraham uses a *kal vahomer* argument ("Will the Judge of all the earth not do justice?!") to secure God's commitment to spare the innocent. Another such discussion in which a *kal vahomer* argument plays a significant role comes in the wake of Miriam's bout with leprosy (Numbers 12). Here Miriam is punished with leprosy for showing disrespect toward her brother Moses. Moses, being the most humble of all people (Numbers 12:3), is *mohel al k'vodo* and thus prays for Miriam's immediate recovery. God, however, suggests to Moses that if he were to be successful in his intercession it would seem as though Moses could be taunted with impunity. This, in turn, would undermine the just authority of both God and Moses. God reinforces the point with a *kal vahomer* argument: If Miriam had been reprimanded by her father, wouldn't she have born the consequences for at least a week? How much more so, then, when the prestige of "My servant Moses" (Numbers 12:7, 8) is at stake!

But the most dramatic and complete example of the dilemma-discussion method found in Jewish sources is the confrontation between Nathan and David in II Samuel, chapter 12. Here we have it all — an actual dilemma (David, in effect, murders Uriah and takes

> RABBINIC SOURCES USE THE DILEMMA-DISCUSSION MODEL.

Bathsheba as his wife) transformed into a hypothetical problem (the poor man and his lamb), an initial reaction to the dilemma (David's exclamation: "Someone who would do that deserves death!"), guidance from a morally superior source (Nathan's reply: "You are that man!"), and moral advancement (David's admission: "I have sinned against the Lord.").

Three Possible Problems

We have seen how the dilemma-discussion model is frequently found in the classic Jewish sources, but three important questions remain to be considered before the method can be prescribed for use in our schools:
1. Does the dilemma-discussion method threaten the norm-setting authority of the traditional sources?
2. To what extent do the stages of moral development which Kohlberg has derived from his cross-cultural research correspond with a classic Jewish hierarchy of values?
3. Does this method fail to connect knowing what is right with doing what is right?

Let us consider item #1 first. Does the dilemma-discussion method threaten the normsetting authority of the traditional sources?

To this point, Saadia Gaon commented . . . "we inquire and speculate in matters of our religion for two reasons: (1) in order that we may actualize what we know in the way of imparted knowledge from the prophets of God; (2) in order that we may be able to refute those who attack us on matters connected with our religion. For our God (be God blessed and exalted) instructed us in everything that we require in the way of religion, through the intermediacy of prophets . . . . God also informed us that by speculation and inquiry we shall attain to certainty on every point in accordance with the truth revealed through the words of His messenger."[5]

Saadia presages modern cognitivists like Kohlberg when he maintains that a concept is not fully "actualized" unless it is rationally integrated into one's existing thought structure. He can therefore confidently assert that teachers of Torah have nothing to fear from rational inquiry. On the contrary, the speculations that pass between teacher and student are the heartbeat of the living Torah, as in the Rabbinic dictum "Even what an advanced student points out to his teacher sometime in the future has already been told to Moses at Sinai."[6]

The central element of each unit of my moral development curriculum is a dilemma story, but each unit also includes a collection of references from traditional sources which touch upon the particular value concept at stake in the dilemma. These traditional sources are not meant to be used simultaneously with the dilemma-discussion portion of the unit, as this might cut short the process of inquiry which we seek to encourage. Rather, the sources are meant to be used by teachers at some time after the initial discussion to guide and reinforce the students' own judgment. The curriculum does presuppose a set hierarchy of Jewish values (as is expressed in the traditional sources), but is built on the assumption that it is preferable for students to develop an understanding of the function and need for these values (in Saadia's terms, to "actualize" them) rather than simply to present Jewish values as a "bag of virtues."[7]

Professor A. Arzi of the Hebrew University has suggested that Talmud should, in fact, always be taught in this manner. Arzi maintains that Talmudic problems should, whenever possible, first be posed orally, "garbed as an example drawn from everyday life . . . students ought to be called upon to examine the problem purely on the basis of their own, unprejudiced judgment, without searching for the support of Talmudic precedents . . . only after the class has examined the issue in this manner for itself should the students be given the task of studying the Talmudic exchange from the written text . . . The opinions of the sages will no longer be viewed as heteronomous, imposed upon the student from the outside, but rather as autogenous, arrived at by the student through his or her own reasoning and sense of justice."[8]

Point #2 deals with the extent to which the stages of moral development which Kohlberg has derived from his cross-cultural research correspond with a classic Jewish hierarchy of values.

On the next page in figure 1 are Kohlberg's six stages of moral reasoning. Note that each stage has a distinct cognitive basis for moral judgments. After Kohlberg's stages is a selection from Maimonides' commentary on the Mishnah. Here, too, we have a series of cognitive-developmental stages, with each stage characterized by a particular type of rationale for doing *mitzvot*. In comparing these two sets of stages, we see that Maimonides and Kohlberg agree that:

KOHLBERG'S SIX STAGES OF MORAL REASONING[9]
Classification of Moral Judgment into Levels and Stages of Development

Levels	Basis of Moral Judgement	Stages of Development
I	Moral value resides in external, quasi-physical happenings, in bad acts, or in quasi-physical needs rather than in persons and standards.	**Stage 1:** Obedience and punishment orientation. Egocentric deference to superior power or prestige, or a trouble-avoiding set. Objective responsibility.
		Stage 2: Naively egoistic orientation. Right action is that which instrumentally satisfies the self's needs and occasionally the needs of others. Awareness of relativism of value to each actor's needs and perspective. Naive egalitarianism and orientation to exchange and reciprocity.[10]
II	Moral value resides in performing good or right roles, in maintaining the conventional order and the expectancies of others.	**Stage 3:** Good-boy orientation. Orientation to approval and to pleasing and helping others. Conformity to stereotypical images of majority or natural role behavior, and judgment by intentions.
		Stage 4: Authority and social-order maintaining orientation. Orientation to 'doing duty' and to showing respect for authority and maintaining the given social order for its own sake. Regard for earned expectations of others.
III	Moral value resides in conformity by the self to shared or shareable standards, rights or duties.	**Stage 5:** Contractual legalistic orientation. Recognition of an arbitrary element or starting point in rules or expectations for the sake of agreement. Duty defined in terms of contract, general avoidance of violation of the will or rights of others, and majority will and welfare.
		Stage 6: Conscience or principle orientation. Orientation not only to actually ordained social rules but to principles of choice involving appeal to logical universality and consistency. Orientation to conscience as a directing agent and to mutual respect and trust.

Figure 1

1. Reasoning is an essential part of moral behavior.
2. Human beings pass through stages of moral development.
3. There is some correspondence between age and stage.
4. The thrust of moral development is from physical rewards, through "good roles" to principled behavior.

COGNITIVE–DEVELOPMENTAL STAGES IN MAIMONIDES[11]

Imagine a child who is brought to a teacher to teach him Torah. This is actually the most important element in his development, but because he is young and intellectually weak he doesn't understand its value and how it will contribute to his development. Therefore, the teacher (who is more developed than he) is forced to motivate him to study through things which he *does* find desirable, as befits his young age. So [the teacher] says, "Read, and I'll give you some nuts and dates, and I'll give you a little honey," and for this he reads and makes an effort — not for the sake of the reading itself, because he doesn't appreciate its value, but rather, so that he can get the food. Eating these sweets is more valuable to him than reading, and certainly much superior to it, so he considers studying a burdensome chore which he's willing to put up with in order to get the desired result: a nut or a little honey.

When he grows and his intellect becomes stronger and he thus loses interest in the thing which had previously been important to him and is no longer obsessed with it, you have to motivate him through something that he does find desirable. So his teacher says to him, "Read, and I'll get you some nice shoes or some attractive clothes," and for this he'll try to read — not for the sake of the study itself, but for the clothing, which is more important to him than the Torah, and which is therefore his reason for reading.

When he's more intellectually developed he'll come to think lightly of this as well and will then set his heart on something superior to it, and thus his teacher will say, "Learn this passage or chapter and I will give you a dinar or two," and for that he'll read and make the effort — to get the money. That money is more important to him than the study, because the purpose of studying is to get the money that was promised to him for it.

When he becomes quite knowledgeable and he doesn't think much of this (the money) because he knows that it's really of little value, he will desire something more worthwhile, and so his teacher will say to him, "Learn this so that you can become a head of the community and a judge. People will respect you and stand up when you go by, like so and so." So he'll read and make the effort, so that he might reach this rank. His purpose will be to gain respect and praise from others.

But all of this is unbecoming . . . our sages have warned us that one should not have some ulterior motive in serving God and doing a *mitzvah* . . . . Antigonos of Socho said, "Don't be like servants who serve the master so that they might receive a reward, but rather, like servants who serve the master even though they don't receive a reward." What I mean to say is that one should believe the truth for the sake of its truth, and this is what is called "service out of love."

HaRav A.I. Kook also understood Jewish education in developmental terms. Commenting on the Mishnah, "At five years of age a child is ready for Tanach, at ten for Mishnah," etc. (*Avot* 5:21). Kook contended that "a person should be trained in forms of worship and religious study by precisely those means that bring their basic purpose within the range of that person's comprehension, proceeding to the study of more sophisticated matters when more sophisticated purposes can be comprehended. For if a person is trained to bear with forms of worship and study whose purposes fail to leave even a trace of an impression, we plant the faulty and destructive notion — God forbid — that such things need no purpose, and have none. When that person grows older and becomes convinced that . . . one should not expend effort in pursuit of the pointless, the pillars of his zeal will buckle, along with his development . . . thus a child from five to ten years of age, whose tender intellect is in the early stages of its development, is ready to sense the beauty and splendor of the plain meaning of biblical texts . . . but is still far from being able to see the point to the righteousness of the specific actions enumerated in the Mishnah. However, by the age of ten, one acquires the ability to distinguish between good deeds and their opposites, and one recognizes the need for study to guide one in learning about the specifics of good behavior and the need to be cautioned concerning the specifics of bad behavior, and thus is ready to be taught Mishnah. But one's intellect is not yet sufficiently mature to recognize, beyond an elementary grasp of good and bad actions, the need to further explore their many implications, working from what is explicit to the implicit. However, at around the age of fifteen one's intellect has been sufficiently awaked to the breadth of subtleties attendant upon actions, virtues, and attitudes, and can therefore be taught by way of the Talmud. In this way one grows in the study of God's Torah with joy and satisfaction . . . ."[12]

> MAIMONIDES AND HARAV COOK HAVE VIEWS SIMILAR TO KOHLBERG.

Taken together, Maimonides and HaRav Kook still offer only two perspectives on the subject, but they are exceedingly important ones. The striking similarities between their views of moral maturation and Kohlberg's taxonomy of cognitive moral development suggest an essential compatibility between contemporary cognitive developmental findings and classical Jewish thinking about moral education.

Item #3 above has to do with whether or not the dilemma-discussion method fails to connect knowing what is right with doing what is right. In an address to the National Catholic Education Association in 1975, Kohlberg made the rather daring assertion that the gap between having moral principles and acting upon them is bridged by "faith." The fact that people who had reached the highest stage of moral development also tended to be people who were "deeply religious" led him to concur with James Fowler's hypothesis that there exists a series of "faith stages" running roughly parallel to his own set of moral stages. Kohlberg concluded that these two sets of stages complement one another: "Moral principles . . . do not require faith for their formulation or for their justification. In some sense, however, to ultimately live up to moral principles requires faith. For this reason, we believe, the ultimate exemplars of Stage 6 morality also appear to be men of faith."[13]

This formulation of faith, as that which empowers us to act on our principles, is very close to the biblical notion of *emunah*. Here, "faith" is not the substance of our values, but rather, the state of mind and spirit that allows for their fulfillment, developing parallel to the values we may hold at any given stage. A teacher of moral principles must therefore not only be concerned with a student's cognitive moral development, but must also nourish that student's existential sense of *emunah*. The teacher of Torah should strive to be a model of faithfulness to persons and principles: *ne'eman* (faithful), as was Moses our teacher. In this way we may help to enlarge our students' range of *emunah*.

The paradigm, then, is: Talmud Torah + *emunah* → *Ma'asim* (learning + faith lead to deeds). Which brings to mind the famous *baraita* (Rabbinic story): "When Rabbi Tarfon and the sages were dining in the upper chamber of the house of Nitzah in Lydda, this question was asked of them: 'What is greater, study or practice?' Rabbi Tarfon answered, 'Practice is greater.' Rabbi Akiba answered, 'Study is greater.' Then all the sages said, 'Study is greater because study leads to practice.'"[14]

HOW TO CHOOSE OR COMPOSE A DILEMMA STORY

Kohlberg's taxonomy identifies six basic stages of moral development. Each stage is characterized by a particular sort of moral reasoning, and movement through these stages is understood as both a maturational and a learning process. In Stage 1, for instance, moral judgments tend to be made on the basis of obedience vs. punishment, whereas in Stage 2 they are oriented toward "satisfying the self's needs."

This taxonomy is often misunderstood as describing types of people. Not so. Kohlberg's stages describe moral premises and lines of reasoning, not types of people. A second common misunderstanding is the assumption that a person's moral reasoning must fit into precisely one stage at any given time. In fact, Kohlberg's findings tend to suggest that one's moral judgment is a composite of previous, predominant, and anticipated stages.

Knowing this, then, Kohlberg's categorization of types of moral reasoning is educationally valuable to the extent that it suggests what type of reasoning a given student will find most developmentally challenging. The taxonomy helps teachers ask the questions which are within "walking distance" of the students' present cognitive structure. You can parachute a Stage 5 line of reasoning into a Stage 2 argument, but it will leave no permanent structural tracks for the student to trace back to Stage 5. Moral challenges are most effective when they are "local," i.e., from the next highest stage, and the taxonomy can serve as a road map in this regard.

From ages seven through fourteen, most children reason in ways which are characteristic of the middle stages: 2, 3, and 4 (5 and 6 are mostly post-adolescent stages; Stage 1 is typical of early childhood). There are formal tests available for ascertaining levels of moral reasoning, but informed observations of a few preliminary dilemma-discussions should give a teacher a very good sense of the class members' predominant stages of reasoning. With this information teachers can then decide which sorts of dilemmas are most appropriate for their classes. For instance, a dilemma which simply poses the question of whether pure accidents and intentional acts are morally equal will not be developmentally challenging for a child who usually reasons at Stage 4, since a moral appreciation of intentionality is achieved at Stage 3. Likewise, the use of a dilemma which can only be understood as centering on a conflict between contract and conscience would be developmentally premature, and therefore ineffective, for students who are most at home in a Stage 3 values structure.

Dilemma stories can be obtained from a variety of sources. On occasion, Kohlberg has used selections from the Bible. Other researchers have taken stories from basal readers and literature texts. Sets of dilemmas have been published which are specifically designed for use as part of a moral development curriculum.

You may also choose to compose your own dilemmas. Writing your own dilemmas allows you to tailor the stories to the specific needs and experiences of your class. I have already mentioned how the story of Hillel was transformed into a dilemma about a child in a wheelchair. That dilemma is now part of a unit in my moral development curriculum.

Whether you choose to use dilemmas which have been written by others or decide to compose your own, you may find the following suggestions helpful:

1. Try to avoid characterizations which the students might understand stereotypically. Characters engaged in questionable activities should not be gratuitously stigmatized. Once, in the course of evaluating a dilemma that I had written, the reviewer noticed that I had managed to choose Teutonic names for every dubious character in the story, names which might sound particularly harsh to Jewish ears. One researcher who used filmstrips to present her dilemmas found that a particular group of students were seriously distracted from the actual dilemma by the color of one of the characters (although this, of course, is a moral dilemma in its own right).
2. Try to avoid characterizations which strongly suggest individuals with whom the students are personally acquainted. Recognizing a character makes it much more difficult to be objective about that character's role in the dilemma.
3. A well crafted narrative makes for an easier presentation of the dilemma. Too many extraneous details can be distracting. Unless such details are an integral part of the story, or the material is also being considered from a literary point of view, it is probably best to skip them.
4. The dilemma should end with a clear and relatively specific question concerning one of the character's actions, e.g., "Should David take the money?" "Did Sandra do the right thing?" etc.

LEADING A DISCUSSION OF A DILEMMA

Earlier it was stated that it is preferable for a class which is discussing a moral dilemma to be made up of members who are not all at the exact same level of moral reasoning. This is because exposure to reasoning one step higher than one's own is a crucial element in the development of moral judgment. If a few articulate class members come up with a solution to a dilemma which is one step above the position of the majority, the discussion will contain the type of cognitive tension which Kohlberg has identified as a highly significant factor in moral development. Thus, if you find that your students all tend to employ the same line of reasoning in solving a particular dilemma, it becomes your responsibility to introduce this tension into the discussion. It is clearly preferable that this process be the product of differences between peers, but when students are all in agreement, the task of suggesting a higher stage solution to the dilemma falls to the teacher. However, we should be careful in this regard not simply to bulldoze the discussion toward a higher stage solution.

The dilemma-discussion method emphasizes growth in reasoning and this takes time and tact. It is important that a dilemma be looked at from many different angles so that no one leaps to artificial, unreasoned solutions. During this process of fully sizing up the dilemma there should be adequate opportunity for the teacher to hint at, probe for, or, as a last resort, suggest a higher stage solution. The first and most important principle in the procedure is simply to challenge every conclusion with "Why?" — *mai tama?*

One other important point about dilemma-discussions: it's very easy to get sidetracked. One suggestion I have in this regard is that you may sometimes wish to provide your students with a limited number of solutions to the dilemma. This might seem to be an unwarranted restriction on the free exercise of their reasoning skills, but it can help to prevent them from inventing ways of slipping out of the dilemma without really confronting the problem. Try to provide at least one choice which is typical of the stage of reasoning of the majority of your students and one choice which is typical of the stage that comes after that one.

EVALUATION OF A DILEMMA-DISCUSSION UNIT

In evaluating a dilemma-discussion moral development unit, keep in mind that the focal point of the approach is the development of moral reasoning. This means that it is not the students' immediate expression of appreciation for a particular value which validates the approach. but, rather, long-term development in the way students think about moral questions. This sort of development can only be spotted in the context of subsequent discussions: traditional sources, whether biblical, *aggadic,* or *halachic,* can be very useful in this regard. A discussion of a point of *halachah* which is related to a previous dilemma may provide the teacher with a sense of how well students have integrated the new moral schema into their own thought structures. For instance, an important Stage 3 concept is "intentionality." Following up a dilemma on intentionality with a discussion of the Rabbinic dictum: "*Mitzvot* must be intended" (*Berachot* 13a), may give a teacher a good idea of how deeply the dilemma has "sunk in." Remember, however, that this type of evaluation will be most revealing if the passage of several intervening lessons obscures the connection between the initial dilemma and the follow-up discussion.

KOHLBERG AND HIS CRITICS

Modern educational theory and practice have been formed, in large measure, around the widely accepted premise that learning is a developmental process. Kohlberg's contention that programs in moral education should also be shaped by developmental considerations has met with wide acceptance as well. However, the specifics of Kohlberg's taxonomy of development have met with vigorous criticism.

Carol Gilligan has become the most prominent of these critics. Gilligan's criticism of Kohlberg is centered on Kohlberg's contention that "the central moral value of the school, like that of the society, [is] justice," and that "Justice, in turn, is a matter of equal and universal human rights."[15]

Early in her career, Gilligan worked with Kohlberg on moral development research projects. It was this experience that led her to believe that Kohlberg's definition of cognitive moral development was too narrow. Gilligan came to be convinced that certain approaches to moral problem solving identified by Kohlberg as "conventional" were, in fact, as cognitively "adequate" as a post-conventional system of "equal and universal rights." In particular, Gilligan maintained that a person whose moral thought was consistently channeled through an ethic of "relationship" and "responsibility" was not necessarily less morally mature than a person who employed a moral frame of reference centered on the rights of individuals. Rather, such a perspective constituted a "different voice," more characteristic of women than men.

Gilligan also found that persons who emphasized "relationship" and "responsibility" over independence and rights tended to resist reducing the concrete specifics of moral problems to abstractions. So, for instance, a mother and child in a moral problem remained "mother" and "child" throughout the problem solving process, rather than being transformed into abstract persons "A" and "B." Kohlberg considered this type of transformation a sign of cognitive maturity, since abstract identities help to distance the persons in the problem from the biases of the problem solver. Gilligan, however, rather than seeing this tendency as evidence of an inability to form and employ abstractions, contended that it was in the nature of relationship-centered moral problem solving to emphasize the specific and concrete over the abstract.

Since the publication of her initial findings in 1977, Gilligan and her colleagues have worked to refine this "tow-track" theory of moral development. Kohlberg, for his part, responded to Gilligan's initial findings, along with those of James Fowler in the area of faith development, by suggesting that the development of moral *judgment* ultimately emerges from a "broader valuing process" that includes "religious thinking about human nature and the human condition as well as moral judgment and reasoning."[16] Kohlberg theorized that to the extent that Gilligan's research suggested an alternate taxonomy of moral development, it was actually reflecting aspects of this broader process, and not the particulars of moral reasoning per se. In terms of moral reasoning alone, Kohlberg continued to maintain that even in its most mature forms, an ethic of relationship and responsibility "still requires principles of fairness to resolve justice dilemmas."[17]

In more recent years, the popularization of the work of Gilligan and Fowler signaled a reduction in Kohlberg's direct influence on the field of moral development. However, many of the issues that emerged with the publication of the initial research of Gilligan and Fowler remain outstanding. In a lengthy reply to Gilligan, published in 1984, Kohlberg concluded, "The work of Gilligan and her colleagues has added depth to the description of moral judgment focused on responsibility and caring, but we do not believe that it defines an alternative morality. More than justice is required for resolving many complex moral dilemmas, but justice is a necessary element of any morally adequate resolution of these conflicts."[18] Nona Plessner Lyons, one of Gilligan's research colleagues, characterizes the outstanding issues in this way: "Although Kohlberg has identified a developmental patterns of a morality of justice, he has not elaborated the understanding of relationships."[19] After acknowledging an indebtedness to Kohlberg, Lyons concludes, "What remains, then, is the task of examining the developmental patterns of a morality of justice and of care within a framework of relationship."[20]

SUMMARY

Moral education is not simply another item on the already cluttered agenda of Jewish education — it is of its essence. Our values define us as a people: "Anyone who has compassion upon creatures is certainly a descendant of Abraham our father, and anyone who does not have compassion upon creatures is certainly not a descendant of Abraham our father."[21] Lawrence Kohlberg's work has engendered a great deal of hope, as well as controversy and criticism. Recent extensions of Kohlberg's research have broadened the field of cognitive developmental moral education in important ways. But throughout this process, the basic guidelines for moral education pioneered by Kohlberg and his colleagues have remained sound. This is especially true in the area of Jewish education, inasmuch as a cognitive developmental approach to moral education is, as we have seen, well rooted in classical Jewish sources.

It is clear that discussions of dilemmas, in and of themselves, cannot transform people into paragons of virtue. Even after acquiring a rational appreciation of a certain value, a person must be sustained by "good faith" if she or he is to act in accordance with that understanding. This is especially the case when strong contrary influences are also present. But the need for *emunah* does not cancel out the need for understanding. In a *talmid(ah) chacham(ah)* (a wise person), *emunah* and *havanah* (faith and understanding work hand in hand).

Earl Schwartz is on the faculties of the Talmud Torah of St. Paul and Hamline University. He is the author of *Moral Development: A Practical Guide for Jewish Teachers* (A.R.E.) and, with Rabbi Barry Cytron, of *When Life Is in the Balance: Life and Death Decisions in Light of the Jewish Tradition* and *Who Renews Creation* (United Synagogue).

APPENDIX

The following is the dilemma which was composed as a result of the criticism by my students of Hillel's "eavesdropping" on a Torah lesson through a skylight. Also included is a section on how to use the dilemma.

Dilemma:

The Talmud Torah (Religious School) is run on a budget. This means that each year a certain amount of money is available for operating the school. The Talmud Torah can spend only as much money as is in the budget.

In the spring, the Board of Directors meets to decide on a budget for the coming year. One spring, the Board finds that it will be able to meet all expected costs for the following year and still have a considerable amount of money left over. The Board decides to poll the student body on what they would most like to see done with the extra money.

At this point, solicit a few suggestions from the class as to what they would want done for the school with surplus funds. Have the class choose the suggestion they like best. The class's choice can then stand for the result of the "poll."

The Board of Directors decides that (whatever the class has chosen) is a worthwhile use of the extra money, and directs the appropriate committee to go ahead with its use for that purpose.

Over the summer, Susan signs up to attend the Talmud Torah. Susan's legs are paralyzed and she uses a wheelchair to get around. She's a proud child who likes to do things for herself, but this sometimes requires special equipment — ramps or elevators instead of steps, support railings in the bathroom, a desk that can fit her wheelchair, etc. Until this year, Susan had been studying with a private tutor hired by her parents, but she now wants to attend Talmud Torah classes like everyone else.

At its summer meeting, the Board of Directors is informed of Susan's application. The question is raised as to how the Talmud Torah could pay for special equipment for Susan, since the coming year's budget had already been allocated. At this point, the Board member who was overseeing the "extra money" states that it had not yet been spent and was still in the bank. Perhaps this money could be used to make the accommodations for Susan. Another Board member responds: But is it right to deprive all of the other students of something which is valuable to the school for the benefit of one child? The Board decides to poll the students again.

Here is the question they asked:

A child has applied to the Talmud Torah who is confined to a wheelchair. If she is to attend classes here several items must be purchased to meet her special needs. It has been suggested that the money which you had decided should go for _____ could be used to make these purchases. Do you think this money should be used for this new purpose?

Poll the class on this new question.

Discuss their respective positions on the issue.

Re-poll the class at the end of the period to see if anyone's position has changed, and if so, why.

Suggested Procedure:

1. Read the dilemma-story to the class. Follow the instructions in italics as each comes up in the story.
2. During the discussion at the end of the story listen for an implicit or explicit suggestion that Susan has "rights." If the students don't bring it up themselves, you might want to say something like: "Does Susan have a right to come to Talmud Torah? If so, what are the consequences of that right?"
3. Interject the following "what-ifs" into the discussion:
   a. What if Susan's parents could themselves pay for the necessary adaptations, but are not willing to do so?
   b. What if no other children (unless they were also confined to a wheelchair) would be allowed to use Susan's special equipment (the elevator, for example)?

NOTES

1. Lawrence Kohlberg, "Education, Moral Development, and Faith," *Journal of Moral Education,* 4:5, January, 1975.
2. Moshe M. Blatt and Lawrence Kohlberg, "The Effects of Classroom Moral Discussion Upon Children's Level of Moral Judgment," *Journal of Moral Education,* 4:129, February, 1975.
3. Lawrence Kohlberg, "Education, Moral Development, and Faith," p. 9.
4. Ibid.
5. Saadia Gaon, introduction to *Emunot V'Deot.*
6. *Jerusalem Talmud,* Peah 2:6.
7. "Bag of virtues" is Kohlberg's term for the inculcation of a given set of arbitrarily chosen, non-developmentally structured values.
8. A. Arzi, "A Talmud Lesson," in *Hora'at Ha-Torah She-B'al Peh*, Y. Heineman, ed. (Jerusalem: School of Education, Hebrew University, 1960), p. 61.
9. Lawrence Kohlberg, "Education, Moral Development and Faith," *Journal of Moral Education*, January, 1975, pg. 7.
10. i.e., the social focus of this stage remains egoistic. What is right or "fair" is: (1) serving one's own needs; (2) serving other people's needs when they do not conflict with one's own interests; or (3) serving others' interests as an instrument for the serving of one's own interests, by means of "fair deals."
11. *Mishnah Commentary, Perek Helek.*
12. Abraham Isaac Kook, *Selected Comments on Siddur,* Zvi Y'hudah HaCohen Kook (Jerusalem: Mossad HaRav Kook, 1983).
13. Lawrence Kohlberg, "Education, Moral Development and Faith," *Journal of Moral Education* 4 (January 1975) :14.
14. *Kiddushin* 40b.
15. Lawrence Kohlberg, *The Philosophy of Moral Development* (New York: Harper & Row, 1981), p. 39, o.p.
16. Ibid., p. 354.
17. Ibid., p. 352.
18. Lawrence Kohlberg, *The Psychology of Moral Development* (New York: Harper & Row, 1984), p. 370, o.p.
19. Carol Gilligan, et al, *Mapping the Moral Domain* (Cambridge, MA: Harvard Press, 1990), p. 24.
20. Ibid.
21. *Betzah* 32b.

BIBLIOGRAPHY

Books

Berkowitz, Marvin W., and Fritz Oser. *Moral Education: Theory and Application.* Hillsdale, NJ: Lawrence Erlbaum Associates, Inc., 1985.

A collection of essays and research papers on a wide range of theories propounded by Kohlberg and others on the subject of teaching morals.

Chazan, Barry. *Contemporary Approaches to Moral Education: An Analysis of Alternative Theories.* New York: Teachers College Press, Columbia University, 1985.

A discussion of the intersection of Jewish approaches to moral issues with contemporary theories of moral development.

Cytron, Barry D., and Earl B. Schwartz. *When Life Is in the Balance: Life and Death Decisions in Light of the Jewish Tradition.* New York: United Synagogue, 1986.

A wide-ranging set of texts drawn from classical Jewish sources are presented and applied toward the resolution of a series of moral dilemmas concerning triage, abortion, suicide, euthanasia, capital punishment, and life threatening violence. (For the secondary grades and adults)

Edward, Carolyn P. *Promoting Social and Moral Development in Young Children.* New York: Teachers College Press, Columbia University, 1986.

An overview of concrete ways to promote moral development among young children.

Fowler, James W. *Stages of Faith and Religious Development.* New York: Crossroad Press, 1991.

Fowler is the leading theorist of faith development. His work was embraced by Kohlberg.

Garrod, Andrew, ed. *Approaches to Moral Development.* New York: Teachers College Press, Columbia University, 1993.

In this collection, different authors expound on a variety of ways to encourage social and moral growth.

Gilligan, Carol. *In a Different Voice.* Cambridge, MA: Harvard University Press, 1982.

An overview of Gilligan's theory concerning "an ethic of care" and the early research that led to it.

Gilligan, Carol, et al. *Mapping the Moral Domain.* Cambridge, MA: Harvard University Press, 1990.

This collection of essays and research updates and elaborates upon Gilligan's initial findings and conclusions.

Hass, Glen, ed. *Curriculum Planning: A New Approach.* Needham Heights, MA: Allyn and Bacon, Inc., 1993.

A fine collection of articles on curriculum planning, including several articles on the cognitive development approach.

Kohlberg, Lawrence. *Moral Development, Child Psychology and Early Childhood.* White Plains, NY: Longman Publishing Group, 1987.

The leading proponent of moral development examines how to apply his research and techniques to very young children.

Kohlberg, Lawrence, with Thomas Lickona. *Stages of Ethical Development: From Childhood through Old Age.* San Francisco, CA: Harper, 1986.

This volume reviews all the research and methods that have been identified with Kohlberg.

Kohlberg, Lawrence, et al. *Moral Education: Justice and Community*. New York: Columbia University Press, 1989.

Kohlberg and others discuss the potential impact on community as Kohlberg's research is applied.

Riemer, Joseph, et al. *Promoting Moral Growth: From Piaget to Kohlberg*. 2d ed. Prospect Heights, IL: Waveland Press, 1990.

An examination of the roots, implications, and potential of Kohlberg's work.

Schwartz, Earl B. *Moral development: A Practical Guide for Jewish Teachers*. Denver: A.R.E. Publishing, Inc., 1983.

This collection of moral dilemma teaching materials for elementary and secondary grade students is based on the psychological and educational premises and goals outlined in this chapter.

Articles

Bieler, Jack. "Sensitizing Day School Teachers to Issues in Values Education." *Ten Da'at* VI (1): 5-11, Spring 1992.

A consideration of ways to adapt moral development theories to day school audiences.

Holtz, Barry W. "Of Reading, Values and the Jewish School." *Jewish Education News* 14 (3): 10-13, Summer 1993.

The author looks at the relationship between primary sources and our daily lives.

Kohlberg, Lawrence. "Education, Moral Development, and Faith." *Journal of Moral Education* 4: 5-16, January 1975.

An edited version of an address to the National Catholic Education Association in which Kohlberg discusses the relationship between faith and moral development.

Levitan, Sonia. "The First International Symposium on Jewish Children's Literature: Jewish Values and Cultural Transformation: Four Key Questions." *Judaica Librarianship* 7 (1-2): 28-30, Spring 1992-Winter 1993.

The author looks at communicating Jewish values through the use of library materials and discusses how these materials transmit a specific set of cultural values.

Lieberman, Dov. "Kohlberg's Theory of Moral Development: A Blueprint for Value Judgments within a Humanistic Context." *Humanistic Judaism* XX (IV): 14-19, Autumn 1992.

In his exploration of the relationship between humanism and Kohlberg's stages of moral development, the author looks at the process and goals of each.

Rosenzweig, Linda W. "Toward Universal Justice: Some Implications of Lawrence Kohlberg's Research for Jewish Education." *Jewish Education* 45 (3): 13-19, Summer-Fall 1977.

An overview of Kohlberg's levels and stages of moral development with recommendations for awareness of his theories in relationship to Jewish learning, specifically in the areas of ethics and history.

Schapiro, Susan. "Values, Morals and Ethics." *Reform Judaism*, Fall 1991, p. 26.

Values, morals, and ethics are often grouped together. In this article the author explains the differences between them, and how each can convey a different message. She also discusses ways to approach each area in an educational setting.

Schein, Jeffrey. "Moral Education." In *What We Know about Jewish Education*. Stuart L. Kelman, ed. Los Angeles, CA: Torah Aura Productions, 1992.

A concise analysis of present possibilities for moral education in Jewish settings.

Schnaidman, Mordecai. "Values in Orthodox Yeshivot and Day Schools." *Pedagogic Reporter* 32: 16-19, Fall 1980.

Briefly analyzes the need for Jewish moral education, and describes some of the available resources.

Social Education 40 (4): 213-215, April 1976.

This issue contains a special section on the cognitive developmental approach to moral education. An introduction by Kohlberg and an extensive bibliography are also included.

Sosevsky, Moshe Chaim. "Kohlberg Moral Dilemmas and Jewish Moral Education." *Jewish Education* 48 (4): 10-13, Winter 1980.

The author suggests adapting Kohlberg's theories to Jewish education by presenting *midrashic* and *Halachic* data along with the dilemmas.

Strum, Johan C. "Education Between Indoctrination and Emancipation." *Religious Education* 88 (1): 40-51.

A look at the impact on the moral development of students of the various approaches used in religious education to convey morals.

"The Wisdom of Women." *Reconstructionist Magazine*, January-February, 1990.

An exploration of images and themes relating to "wise women" in the Book of Samuel in light of contemporary research on moral development.

Journal
Journal of Moral Education
P.O Box 2025, Dunnellon, FL 32630

SPECIAL POPULATIONS

CHAPTER TEN

TEACHING CHILDREN OF INTERFAITH FAMILIES

Saundra Heller

Although the blessings brought about by cultural pluralism are significant, so are the challenges to Jewish life which it engenders. Among these challenges is the ever increasing number of intermarriage households. An intermarriage household is one in which one parent is a Jew and the other is of another religion, usually Christian. The reality of intermarriage certainly demands our full attention.

The 1990 National Jewish Population Study conducted by the Council of Jewish Federations[1] revealed that the choice of marriage partners has changed dramatically over the last few decades. In recent years, over half of born Jews who married, at any age, chose a spouse who was born a Gentile and has remained so, while less that 5% of these marriages include a non-Jewish partner who became a Jew-by-choice. Here are other grim statistics:

Since 1985, twice as many mixed couples have been created as Jewish couples.

More people are converting out of Judaism than are converting in.

Intermarriage complicates Jewish identification.

A majority of all new Jewish households formed in America between 1983-1990 include a non-converted, non-Jewish spouse.

Since it is clear that a great percentage of families in our synagogues are included in this relatively recent phenomenon, it is safe to say that intermarriage most definitely impacts our centers, our synagogues, and our schools.

There are many ways to interpret the effect that intermarriage will have on the Jewish community. Some see intermarriage as a threat to Jewish survival that must actively be fought. These individuals feel that we must discourage all intermarriages at all costs. Funds must be used only for strengthening Judaism from within — extensive education for our children from an early age, preschools, day schools, Jewish camping, Israel experiences, youth groups, college programming, etc.

Others see intermarriage as a fact of life. In an open society, it comes with the territory, and nothing we do can stem the tide. Instead, we must adopt an attitude of welcoming acceptance and we must develop programming that draws singles and intermarried couples to Judaism and to Jewish observances. Jewish money, time, and commitment should be invested in both outreach and inreach.

Still others are tentative and conflicted. The ever increasing numbers of intermarried are frightening and overwhelming, yet real. How do we walk that fine line between rejecting in concept and yet welcoming in practice those who have intermarried? On the one hand, the Jewish community must not be perceived as giving permission, of greasing the skids, and of providing resources which might encourage interfaith marriages. Yet, on the other hand, once faced with the actuality of so many such marriages, how can we ignore them or their needs?

THE JEWISH SCHOOL

Jonathan Woocher, Executive Vice President of JESNA, wrote in an article titled "Intermarriage and Jewish Education": "Jewish education must deal with intermarriage, not merely as a future life decision it seeks to prevent, but as a present reality in the lives of hundreds of thousands of Jewish children and adults. How shall Jewish education respond to the demographic and pedagogic challenges this poses?"[2]

Jewish day schools and supplementary schools are already teaching and working with

Jewish children who have non-Jewish relatives. The relatives may be parent, step-parents, grandparents, aunts, uncles, or cousins. The percentage of such children enrolled in our schools varies greatly, of course, from one institution to another. Likewise, from school to school, policies with regard to this population also vary greatly.

Some schools ignore the interfaith population, pretending that there are no special considerations needed for those children. Some schools take the interfaith population seriously and consider the needs of the child and family alongside the concerns of endogenous families. Can a Jewish school advance the message of Judaism to children of endogenous marriages without stigmatizing and alienating children from a dual religion family? Sometimes the answers lie in rethinking the process: intermarried families rely more heavily on the school for the most basic of information about holidays, blessings, foods, the how-to of Jewish life. Schools may have to offer *Sedarim* and Shabbat dinners as instructional/modeling tools to lead less knowledgeable families into Jewish practices at home.

BECOMING SENSITIVE TO THE ISSUE

ASSESS YOUR OWN FEELINGS ON INTERFAITH ISSUES.

While many schools now provide an exposure to interfaith issues during teacher in-service programs, still, to a great extent the teacher must secure his/her own information about this. A first step in addressing yourself to this subject would be to assess your own attitudes and feelings.

The following questions might be helpful in your self-assessment. Take a few minutes to jot down your answers and the reasons behind your responses.

1. Is a convert to Judaism Jewish?
2. Are children with a Jewish father and non-Jewish mother Jewish if they are raised and educated in Judaism? If they are not raised and educated in Judaism?
3. Are only those born of a Jewish mother Jewish?
4. What are your feelings about intermarriage?
5. Under what conditions should children of intermarriage be registered in your school?

Ask yourself: Can I teach the interfaith child with the dignity and respect each person deserves and not view him/her as a category? Can I assume that the child placed in a Jewish school warrants my best efforts to provide tools and to convey the meaning and beauty of living a Jewish life? If I find my position incompatible with working with such children, can I be honest with myself and the school I represent?

In order to expand your thinking concerning interfaith issues, you may want to hold discussions with other professionals and to do some reading in the field (see Bibliography below for suggestions). Increased knowledge on the subject will enable you to have a greater influence on the children you teach and their interfaith parents.

POLICY STATEMENTS OF THE SCHOOL

Every teacher should have a clear understanding of the policies, attitudes, and expectations of the school with respect to children of interfaith families and children with non-Jewish relatives. Be familiar with the theological stance of your school. An Orthodox school may not knowingly accept children of Jewish patrilineal descent, while the child of a Jewish mother and non-Jewish father may be accepted. The liberal school may accept children of either matrilineal or patrilineal descent if the child is being raised in Judaism. If there is a written position paper on the subject put out by the school, read it. Decide if you are comfortable with the school's position.

Ask your Director of Education for an in-service training during which the staff can process thoughts and attitudes. Such a discussion can be a positive way with which to begin a new school year. It can start the process of team building and of helping staff to become invested in the school. At the very least, it can provide teachers an opportunity to get acquainted, and the lively discussion will ensure that everyone on the faculty receives the same message.

Families are complex, and there are many variables in family situations. Some families may not be entirely truthful to themselves and may not provide accurate registration information. Unresolved matters or anger may serve as a destructive force in a marriage. If this condition exists, the child becomes the pawn. However, in all cases the teacher can best serve the child if he/she knows the family background. Ask your administrator to inform you about each student's particular circumstances.

CLASSROOM SCENARIOS

The following scenarios may be useful in helping you think about possible classroom situations and how you might respond:

In a fifth grade Sunday school class during December, a teacher asked the children to draw pictures of symbols they have in their home. As the teacher walked around the room, she stopped in front of one child, grabbed his picture of a Christmas tree, held it up, and said, "This is not appropriate."

How do you react to this scenario? What other ways could the teacher have approached this situation? How could the child have been validated? What message do you think the other children received from this situation? How could Jewish values been exemplified in this situation?

Sue was a fourteen-year-old girl who had been attending Religious School since she was nine years old. One day, her friends were whispering and giggling at their table. When she came over, they grew quiet. When she asked, "What's going on?" she was told that she wasn't really Jewish because her mother wasn't Jewish. The child went home devastated. When her parents heard the story, they came to the school angry.

How might this situation have been avoided or addressed once it occurred? List four values you consider Jewish and important. Be prepared to tell why. Think of ways that these values could become lessons in the classroom. Make a "wish" list for children of interfaith parents in your Jewish classroom. Does it differ from your "wish" list for all the children in your class? In what ways?

FAMILIES (PARENTS)

Although the dynamics and circumstances for each interfaith family is different, there are some general observations that warrant our attention. These are among the myriad permutations of possibilities among interfaith families. It may help you in your dealing with the interfaith child in your classroom to bear these in mind when teaching your class.

1. Children of interfaith families usually have two heritages. They have the right to know and respect both. They have a right to be accepted for who they are as individuals. Their self-esteem as individuals must be fostered. However, if enrolled in a Jewish school, it is assumed that the religion of the child, the heritage which informs his/her value system and identity is solely Judaism.

2. It is not unusual for the non-Jewish mother to be the one who brings the family into Judaism for one or more of the following reasons: her interest in Judaism, because she wants one unifying religion for her children, or because of an insistence by the father or by his side of the family. As teacher of the child, you will deal with her and not him. She may not fully understand the vocabulary, concepts, values, practices of Judaism. Be patient, consistent, and understanding.

3. A father who has insisted (directly or by inference) on his children being raised Jewish, may be ambivalent about his personal practice of Judaism and, therefore, not supportive of his family's Jewish observances. Yet, he may fully expect his wife, who is a Jew by Choice or non-Jewish, to raise their children as Jews. Because of this dichotomy, the wife may feel lost, confused, conflicted, peeved, betrayed, and abandoned. She may not be pleasant in her dealings with the school. It is often not personal. It may be her anger at her home situation more than her disappointments with teacher or school.

4. The non-Jewish parent may have acquiesced to raising a Jewish child without understanding what that meant, and now harbors resentment. Again, be patient, helpful, and welcoming when explaining the nuances of our heritage to her.

5. The non-Jewish parent, mother or father, may have opted for conversion before marriage because of pressure from the Jewish side of the family, rather than from an understanding of Judaism and personal conviction. Resistance and anger may have developed. This person especially needs acceptance and a feeling of being welcome at every turn.

6. A Jewish parent, mother or father, may have the support and blessing of the non-Jewish parent to raise the children as Jews. That parent may, however, still follow his/her own religion. Do not put the child in a position of having to defend either parent's actions or to choose one over the other.

7. Parents themselves are seeking spirituality. While discussing their child, be aware that you are addressing a parent who is searching for answers to the whys and wherefores of life.

8. Divorced interfaith families have the usual (often horrendous) divorce issues, plus the religious concerns that can now be very messy.
9. The family may be see themselves as Jewish with one parent living a Jewish life without formal conversion. The formal conversion will not take place until after the death of a non-Jewish grandparent. Sometimes conversion takes place for the parent at the time of their child's Bar or Bat Mitzvah. That parent wants to feel a part of the Jewish community. Even though he/she may not be permitted to participate in all ways in Jewish public worship or in community leadership roles, it is important that he/she does not fell discounted, ignored, or put down.
10. Often a parent is open to Judaism but cannot get past the hurt or injury carried from past family encounters with the Jewish family. When this is so, a caring Jewish mentor can reverse the past and open doors to help the person move ahead. In such cases, a teacher or Director of Education is more often sought out for acceptance and understanding than a Rabbi.
11. Raising a Jewish child can build Jewish experience, memories, and identification for the non-Jewish or converted spouse. Heritage, culture, and peoplehood can unify and heal.
12. Some parents are insecure and embarrassed about their own lack of knowledge and Jewish skills. Teach the basics often. Refer to such information sessions as a review.
13. Family commitment to Judaism, i.e., home and synagogue observances and participation, can provide the child with security and a strong sense of identification. Encourage this.
14. Some children will not have the opportunity to live Judaism in their homes. Teach it in the classroom with the same love you would bring to these observances in your own home.
15. Grandparents can influence children greatly. They often provide continuity and a sense of connectedness to Judaism. Welcome them to the classroom, to assemblies, and to worship services, too.
16. Ongoing communication with parents, openness, honesty, and respect enhance a child's sense of belonging and his/her ego strength.

TEACHERS

As mentioned above, a teacher (as well as the Director of Education) enhances a family's experience in Jewish life by presenting a welcome, warm, accepting environment for the parents. And, just as he/she is responsible for the Jewish education of the children, Jewish education for the parents (especially in intermarried families) is equally crucial . . . if not more so.

Therefore, at the very least, do the following:
1. Invite the parents to a first session where they can hear and discuss your goals for their children as well as the philosophy and curriculum of the school. Hand out the copies of the school's policy. This can take some of the mystery out of Jewish education for the newcomer. It can also help all parents become aware of what is expected of them and of their children, thus making your job easier during the year.
2. Provide an activity through which parents can mingle with each other and talk.
3. Ask parents what they especially want their child to gain during the school year. Ask what they as parents would like to gain personally from parents' meetings and parent/teacher conferences. Write their responses on a chart. Use parent input as the basis for creating a parent network. Get your parent volunteers for each class at this time.
4. Offer monthly or periodic forums where parents meet and discuss curriculum content/Jewish issues and become comfortable with one another. You will need a strong parent ally and leader to oversee this. Arrange a substitute for the teacher so that he/she can attend such meetings for a part of the time.
5. Offer two or more parent/child days when parents join their children in class to participate and learn as a family. Better still, have regularly scheduled family education programs for parents and children to share.
6. Let it be known that the child deserves the support and presence of both parents at these family programs.
7. Extend an invitation for all parents to visit the classroom with the provision that the

teacher receive 48 hours prior notification and that the parents come ready to participate in the classroom experience.

(For more ideas on involving parents, see Chapter 3, "Parent Involvement.")

THE CHILD

In their book *The Intermarriage Handbook,* Petsonk and Remsen write, "For many children and for many adults, religion is an important part of self-definition. Religion gives people a common history, values, traditions, rituals, stories, and jokes. This shared system gives them an anchor in the world — an identity."[3]

If parents have unresolved tensions around interfaith issues, the child can be caught between them; the child can receive mixed messages.

When parents can't resolve their conflicts and ambivalence, it is not uncommon for them to sluff all responsibility for religious choice off onto the child . . . Jewish or Christian? These parents say, "Oh, we'll do nothing and let the child decide when he/she is old enough." That puts a horrendous weight on the child! He/she is asked to decide what to be without the emotional or intellectual wherewithal to do so. Such situations can leave the child feeling responsible for the parents or feeling disloyal. Following are some personal thoughts about additional complexities that can exist especially for children of interfaith families:

1. Children need parental guidance, family unity, and approval to develop a clear sense of religious identity and a feeling of security.
2. Children can feel abandoned or controlled by grandparents, causing confusion and conflict.
3. Grandparents can be the main source of emotional strength and/or religious support and continuity.
4. Children may not have Jewish home rituals, holiday celebrations, cultural experiences, or discussions to support Religious School learning.
5. Children may be diminished by attitudes of their peers (you're not really Jewish) in the Religious School.
6. Children need to know that they are "okay" and entitled to respect as individuals.
7. Children need opportunities to be honest about their feelings of identity and religion.
8. Children need to know other children of interfaith families.
9. Children may be ambivalent about Religious School.
10. Children may seek attention and approval or act out negative behavior.
11. Children's sense of acceptance, comfort, belonging in the Jewish school is crucial in building self-esteem and ego strength. It can stabilize the child's identity factor.

THE CLASSROOM: A JUST, CARING COMMUNITY

Justice is an operative principal of Judaism; the classroom should exemplify this principal. A classroom that fosters caring, trust, risk-taking, respect, and independent thinking reflects justice. (See Chapter 1, "Creating Community in the Classroom" for ways to create a just, caring classroom.)

A teacher once told me that she often feels as if she is walking on eggshells in her classroom because she doesn't want to offend the interfaith child. The following strategies can help children look at issues and differences, and, while doing so, help build a trust level so that children can openly express who they are and how they feel.

A CHILD IN AN INTERFAITH FAMILY MAY BE CAUGHT IN THE MIDDLE.

Suggested Lesson: First Day of Class

Teacher might begin class by saying something to this effect:

Since we have all been part of a class before, we each have ideas and feelings about what we like or dislike, what makes a class comfortable, workable, and enjoyable. I have a very special kind of class in mind for all of us. I would like each of you to help me develop the idea, and then to see if over the months we can make it work for us. I call this a "just, caring class community." I see this classroom as a place in which learning can take place and be enjoyed.

Some rules and regulations are given to us by the school such as behavior in the halls, tardiness, dress code, and fire drills. But the structure we set for our class will be ours.

Let's first define the words I've used.

On the board, list "Just," "Caring," "Community." Under each word, list the children's concepts of the words. "Let's see how close we come to other definitions." Read the dictionary definitions.

"Just" means honorable and fair in one's dealing and actions; what is morally right; valid within the law. "Just" come from the word "justice" — which has always been an important Jewish value. (The book *The Alef-Bet of Jewish Values* by Kipper and Bogot, pages 24-25, is an excellent resource for teaching about justice. Other values in the book can be highlighted for other sessions dealing with a just, caring community.)

Write the Hebrew word "*Mishpat*" under "Just" on the chart. Tell the class:

Hebrew is the language of the Jewish people. We will hear, see, and use many Hebrew words during the year. The Torah is written in Hebrew. The Torah records laws for the people then and now. One goal of the laws is justice. Justice exists when actions are based on fairness. The Torah tell us that every person is entitled to justice. Jewish people believe in justice and work for justice.

(Have a miniature Torah and pictures of the Torah displayed. Give background information on the Torah.) Continue speaking:

There are many references to the word "justice" in the Torah. One from the book of Deuteronomy: "Justice, justice Shall Thou Pursue." (Explain this quotation.) At another time we will learn more about the Torah, and I'll have you find references about justice in Leviticus, Exodus, and in the Prophets, and we'll talk about what is written there.

Write the following question on the board: How do we judge what is fair? List student responses. You may have to help students clarify their meanings and consider consequences.

Ask: Do you think justice for every person is something God wants for everyone? Why?

Conduct a class discussion eliciting different views. Take opportunities to point out differences in thinking and feeling. Emphasize that respect of another's opinion and listening are important in the class values.

Define "caring" and "community," using examples. Discuss with the class and ask students for examples of each.

Write the phrase: Where Learning Can Take Place and Be Enjoyed. Ask: Why are you here? Can you enjoy learning? Can you enjoy each other? Tell us about a time when you left a classroom feeling good. Continue speaking to the class:

Now we're ready to set some rules to help our class become a just, caring class community where learning can take place and be enjoyed.

Have children offer rules. Encourage clarification by asking whys and hows. List on a chart. Some rules might be:

We will not talk when someone is speaking.
We will listen.
We will respect each person.
We will ask questions and try to understand.
Each person is responsible for her or himself.
Each person can help others.

If there are too many rules, have the class prioritize them. Hang the chart in the room. Use it frequently throughout the year for reference. The language words and concepts have to be grade appropriate. The above example could be used for Grades 1-3.

This lesson may take the entire class time, but will give a positive start for setting the tone of creating a classroom in which everyone will be respected and his/her opinions will be listened to.

For Grades 4-6, more sophisticated material can be used. The classroom scenarios presented earlier might be adapted for the class to deal with as a dilemma or as a role play.

For older students, bring to class a book or magazine article which contains a caution or disapproval of intermarriage. Present varying views to enhance understanding, create cognitive conflict, to "wear another's shoes," and to involve the children personally. Be open, honest, and sensitive to issues and feelings, thereby the just, caring community can develop. Teachers no longer have to walk on eggshells, because the process gives students ownership of their class attitudes and the way in which they attack and discuss issues. The teacher's role in this is to do the following:

Help students review and process material.
Help students understand how the class content can be useful in their everyday lives.
On a weekly basis, bring in socially sensitive materials to discuss as a class.
Continue to promote acceptance of differences.
Continue to promote the value of each person.

Help children to know they can take intellectual risks.

Help children to recognize that there is not always only one answer.

Seek clarification of student's answers, thoughts, and feelings.

Help children process class activities.

Praise respect.

Teach active listening (see Chapter 13, "Listening Skills, Lecture, and Discussion").

Promote sensitivity to language and what it can convey.

Help students plant roots, i.e., develop feelings of belonging to the class and to Judaism — its history, people, language, values, religion.

RESOURCES

There are several organizations and individuals whose work is most helpful in this relatively new field.

The Center for Jewish Outreach to the Intermarried (CJOI) in Iowa, and The Center for Jewish Studies at The Graduate School of City University of New York, headed by sociologist, Dr. Egon Mayer, prime mover in the field, provide important information for lay people, leaders, and professionals, working with the interfaith population. Dr. Mayer, author of *Love and Tradition: Marriage Between Jews and Christians*, is considered the leading researcher of Jewish/Christian marriage.

The CJOI bridges all denominations of Judaism and serves as a "think tank" for open debate and discussion about issues pertaining to intermarriage by leading scholars and communal professionals. The information compiled from conferences sponsored by these two groups, and ten other Jewish organizations, is available through CJOI (see Bibliography for address).

One of the earliest programs to deal with the interfaith issue is "Stepping Stones — To a Jewish Me." Begun in the mid-1980s as an outreach offering of the Denver Jewish community, this is a two year program for unaffiliated interfaith children and their parents. It offers classes, kindergarten through high school, from September through May. Highly experiential, its purpose is to expose children and their parents to all aspects of Judaism — prayer, history, values, culture, Hebrew, etc.

Stepping Stones has become the model for programs in nine other cities throughout the United States. The Union of American Hebrew Congregations (UAHC) has adopted the program, and through its Outreach and Education Departments, has developed educational materials for and compiled anecdotal information from interfaith and converted families enrolled in Jewish schools. Contact the UAHC for more information on these families and on the Stepping Stones program.

Excellent literature on interfaith and conversion is available for adults and there are a few books for children. Although I have provided a Bibliography at the conclusion of this chapter, I would like to highlight several of these.

The Interfaith Handbook by Petsonk and Remsen is easy to read and contains thoughtful information and exercises. Professional writers, the authors are both intermarried, but not to each other. They went across country to interview professionals working in the field of intermarriage. The book is the result of their findings.

Mixed Blessings: Overcoming the Stumbling Blocks in an Interfaith Marriage by Cowan and Cowan, is a heartrending compilation of the accounts of children, parents, grandparents of interfaith families. The authors own journey is included. The book is an important contribution to the field.

Between Two Worlds: Choices for Grown Children of Jewish-Christian Parents by Goodman-Malamuth and Margolis is a provocative book that provides the reader with insights about the feelings and needs of adults who were children of intermarriage. Especially important are the stories of those who still feel the bind of choosing one parent over the other by choosing one religion. This dilemma is often reflected in the confusion of young children. Who better to inform us than adults who have been in this situation themselves?

CONCLUSION

Interfaith families and their children are very much a part of our school. We need to see these families as people, not problems. The way in which they are received and made to feel welcome and encouraged to participate will greatly influence their involvement, enjoyment, and their commitment to Jewish life.

The teacher is often the person with whom these families have their first and/or most personal contact. How you respond to them, welcome them, show them, educate them, hear them, can make all the difference.

Saundra Heller is Outreach Director of Congregation Emanuel, Denver, where she facilitates groups for interfaith couples and Jewish parents of children in interfaith relations. She developed and implemented the original "Stepping Stones - To a Jewish Me" program. She holds a Master of Arts in Religion from the Iliff School of Theology.

NOTES

1. *Highlights of the CJF National Jewish Population Survey,* 1990.

2. Woocher, Jonathan. "Intermarriage and Jewish Education." *Jewish Spectator,* Winter 1991-92, p. 12.

3. Petsonk, Judy, and Jim Remsen. *The Intermarriage Handbook: A Guide for Jewish and Christians* (New York: Quill William Morrow, 1988), p. 19.

BIBLIOGRAPHY

Books and Articles

Cowan, Paul, with Rachel Cowan. *Mixed Blessings: Overcoming the Stumbling Blocks in an Interfaith Marriage.* New York: Penguin Group, 1987.

Coles, Robert. *The Spiritual Life of Children.* New York: Houghton Mifflin, 1990.

Fowler, James W. *Stages of Faith.* New York: Harper & Row, 1981.

Goodman-Malamuth, Leslie, and Robin Margolis. *Between Two Worlds: Choices for Grown Children of Jewish-Christian Parents.* New York: Pocket Books, 1992.

King, Andrea. *If I'm Jewish and You're Christian, What Are the Kids?: A Parenting Guide for Interfaith Families.* New York: UAHC Press, 1993.

Kipper, Leonore C., and Howard I. Bogot. *The Alef-Bet of Jewish Values.* New York: UAHC Press, 1985.

Kosmin, B., et al. *Highlights of the Council of Jewish Federations Population Study.* New York: Council of Jewish Federations in association with The Mandell Berman Institute-North America Jewish Data Bank, The Graduate School and University Center, CUNY, 1991.

Kushner, Harold S. *When Children Ask about God.* New York: Schocken Books, 1976.

Mayer, Egon, ed. *Jewish Intermarriage, Conversion and Outreach.* New York: The Center for Jewish Studies, The Graduate School and University Center of the City University of New York, 1991.

Mayer, Egon. *Love and Tradition: Marriage Between Jews and Christians.* New York: Plenum Press, 1985.

Mayer, Egon, ed. *The Imperatives of Jewish Outreach: Responding to Intermarriage in the 1990's and Beyond.* New York: The Jewish Outreach Institute and The Center for Jewish Studies, the Graduate School of the City University of New York, 1991.

Melzer, Shelley Kniaz. *Principles and Compassion: Guidelines and Casebook for Teaching with Children of Intermarried Parents in Our Synagogue School.* New York: Commission on Jewish Education of the United Synagogue, 1993.

Petsonk, Judy, and Jim Remsen. *The Intermarriage Handbook: A Guide for Jews and Christians.* New York: Quill William Morrow, 1988.

Romanoff, Lena. *Your People, My People: Finding Acceptance and Fulfillment as a Jew by Choice.* Philadelphia: The Jewish Publication Society, 1990.

Simon, Sidney B.; Leland W. Howe; and Howard Kirschenbaum. *Values Clarification: A Handbook of Practical Strategies.* New York: Hart Publishing Co., Inc., 1978.

Wilcox, Mary M. *Developmental Journey: A Guide to the Development of Logical and Moral Reasoning and Social Perspective.* Nashville: Abingdon, 1979.

Woocher, Jonathan. "Intermarriage and Jewish Education." *Jewish Spectator,* Winter 1991-92.

Organizations

The Center for Jewish Outreach to the Intermarried (CJOI), 2000 Financial Center, Des Moines, IA 50309.

Union of American Hebrew Congregations, 838 Fifth Avenue, New York, NY 10021.

SPECIAL POPULATIONS

CHAPTER ELEVEN

PROVIDING FOR THE JEWISH GIFTED

Zena W. Sulkes

In our continuing effort to be part of the successful middle class of American society, Jews have typically stressed school, learning, and achievement. Along the way, we have perpetuated the image of all of our children as high achieving, talented students. How many times have we heard the statement "All Jewish children are gifted"?

The fact that there has been a growing trend in our country to recognize special and individual needs of students has brought about increased study, funding, programs, and literature about the gifted. "We Americans are justly proud of our egalitarianism . . . but we are equally proud of our goal of individualization to fit the program to the child's needs."[1] Jewish educators need to be aware of the direction that secular education is taking in this area, its implications and applications to the Jewish educational setting.

DEFINING THE GIFTED

Before we deal with the needs of the gifted students in our Religious Schools, we need to have some understanding of the population about whom we are concerned. Educational researchers, teachers, and governmental agencies have recommended many methods of identification. Although Religious School administrators do not have the responsibility for identifying exceptional children, they have traditionally asked parents to share information about their child's school performances. Religious School parents have frequently been reluctant to share with us information about school related problems and labels attached to their children such as "learning disabled," "emotionally disturbed," etc. However, they have usually been most eager to share the label "gifted" and/or "talented," and to tell us proudly about accelerated or enriched secular school programming.

In 1972, the United States Office of Education report to Congress created a National Office of Gifted and Talented and delineated six general areas of gifted and talented abilities. This report suggested that any person who possessed superior ability in any of these general categories, or any combination of them, should be considered gifted.[2] These categories are:

1. General Intellectual Ability: This kind of giftedness corresponds roughly to I.Q. Any child in your classroom who performs very well in almost every academic area falls into this category.
2. Specific Academic Ability: A child fits this category who does outstanding work in math, language arts, or other specific areas, and yet is an average pupil in other subjects.
3. Creative Thinking: This category refers to the divergent thinker — the child who comes up with extraordinary responses even to very ordinary questions.
4. Leadership Ability: You know the kind of student who is gifted in this area — the child who naturally and consistently assumes a positive leadership role.
5. Visual and Performing Arts Ability: This gifted child is consistently outstanding in aesthetic production in one or more areas, such as the graphic arts, sculpture, music, and dance.
6. Psychomotor Ability: A child fits this category who displays mechanical skills or athletic ability superior to other children in the school.

In 1978, Congress redefined gifted and talented students in Public Law 95-561. This law stated: " For the purpose of this part, the term gifted and talented children means children and, whenever applicable, youth, who are identified at the preschool, elementary, or secondary level as possessing demonstrated or potential abilities that give evidence of high performance and capability in areas such as intellectual, creative, specific academic, or leadership ability, or in the performing and visual arts, and who by reason thereof require service or activities not ordinarily provided by the school."

The application of these definitions to students to determine which students require special services, is not, of course, the responsibility of the Religious School. However, the many models available which enable us to recognize these children are varied and often confusing. The major procedures recommended in the 1972 U.S. Office of Education report are:
1. Teacher observation and appointment
2. Group school achievement test scores
3. Group school intelligence test scores
4. Previously demonstrated accomplishments (including school grades and cumulative records)
5. Individual intelligence test scores
6. Scores on tests of creativity

In addition, behavior rating scales, parent recommendations, and peer recommendations are sometimes utilized.

Standardized group tests of intelligence and achievement are easy to use, but have several drawbacks. Tests such as these are basically designed for the average student, and their objectivity is based on limiting responses to a selection of "correct" answers. Gifted students tend to see beyond these answers. Pegnato and Birch found that group I.Q. tests failed to identify nearly fifty percent of the students who scored about 125 on individual I.Q. tests.[3] Although they focus on general intellectual ability, individual I.Q. tests such as the Stanford-Binet or the WISC-R, are usually the final screening in most schools.

In the area of creativity, the most widely used instruments are the Torrance Tests of Creative Thinking. These tests look for fluency, flexibility, originality, and elaborated skills. Test items are usually open-ended questions and task completion exercises. These tests are usually administered by a school psychologist or specially trained teachers of the gifted and the results of these evaluations help the secular school design appropriate educational programs.

A release form signed by parents can provide information to the Religious School which can aid in designing appropriate programs of Jewish education. Teachers should ask the Director of Education to secure such information, and a consultant should help with the interpretation if necessary. Characteristics of the gifted and talented students are almost as numerous as the number of students themselves. Most descriptions of the gifted refer to the characteristics found most often among them. Gifted individuals, however, do not necessarily possess all characteristics. The gifted child is likely to possess the following abilities:[4]

1. Reads earlier and with greater comprehension of nuances in the language.
2. Learns basic skills better, faster, and needs less practice. Overlearning can lead to boredom.
3. Makes abstractions when other children at the same age level cannot.
4. Delves into some interests beyond the usual limitations of childhood.
5. Comprehends, with almost nonverbal cues, implications which other children need to have "spelled out" for them.
6. Takes direction independently at an earlier stage in life and assumes responsibility more naturally.
7. Maintains much longer concentration periods.
8. Expresses thought readily and communicates with clarity in one or more areas of talent, whether verbal, numerical, aptitudinal, or affective.
9. Reads widely, quickly, and intensely in one subject or in many areas.
10. Expends seemingly limitless energy.
11. Manifests creative and original verbal or motor responses.
12. Demonstrates a more complex processing of information than the average child of the same age.
13. Responds and relates well to peers, parents, teachers, and adults who likewise function easily in the higher level thinking processes.
14. Has many projects going, particularly at home, so that he or she is either busily occupied or looking for something to do.

OVER 10% OF GIFTED AND TALENTED CHILDREN ARE JEWISH.

15. Assumes leadership roles because the innate sense of justice gives them strengths to which other young people respond.

Undoubtedly you have taught students who have demonstrated these characteristics. On first reading, these traits may appear to be totally positive. Yet there are problems inherent in each. For instance, a student who learned to read very early and is far advanced in that skill (characteristic #1) may find the usual Religious School textbook for his/her grade level too simple and be bored by its approach. In this case, teachers should find a book with similar content at a higher reading level.

Similar problems exist in other categories. A student who displays characteristic #7, and is thus able to maintain concentration on a specific content area for a long period of time, might be reluctant to move on to another activity with the majority of the class. The child who exhibits characteristic #10 and expends seemingly limitless energy requires firm and consistent handling and many positive learning outlets for his/her energy.

In February of 1982, the Education Consolidation Act resulted in the closing of the Office of Gifted and Talented, and gifted education was merged with 29 other programs. The result was that educational effort on behalf of gifted shifted from the federal to the state level.

The majority of the states do not use the broad six-area definition of the federal definition, but choose to define giftedness to include three areas: general intellectual ability, creativity, and leadership (Sisk).

JEWISH IDENTITY AND GIFTEDNESS

In an age in which cultural pluralism and ethnic identity seem to be at odds with one another, studies often examine the differences in racial and ethnic groups. While we find that gifted and talented students come from all different types of homes and all racial and ethnic groups, they are more likely to be found in some groups than others. Groups with the highest percentages of gifted students are those that place a great emphasis on intellectual areas and values. These families tend to have more extensive opportunities to develop those talents and skills that are already present in the child.[5] Adler (1967) in a review of studies designed to relate intelligence to ethnic groups, found that high ability students can be found in every racial and ethnic group. However, there are clear differences in the proportion of students that are identified as gifted in different racial and ethnic groups. According to Adler, the highest ranking in terms of gifted students identified were: Jewish, German, English, and Scottish origins. Terman and Oden noted a very high incidence of Jewish children in their now classic longitudinal study conducted from 1920-1960. Their research indicated that over ten percent of the sample was Jewish which is far larger than population incidence would indicate. Terman and Oden state:

"The conclusion suggested by these detailed comparisons is that the Jewish subjects in the study differ little from the non-Jewish except in their greater drive for vocational success, their tendency toward liberalism in political attitudes, and somewhat lower divorce rate."[6]

While it is precisely in the area of motivation that we may find the key difference between groups, updated studies are clearly needed. Current trends which point to a rapidly increasing Jewish divorce rate and a turning away by Jews from the liberalism of the past make Terman and Oden's conclusions somewhat suspicious for contemporary times.

While genetic factors may be considered as a source for the different ethnic proportions found in identifying the gifted, the genetic pluralism of European society and the nature of intelligence indicate that it is more likely that cultural influences are the determining factor. Strodbeck (1953) compared family and cultural values and found that Jewish families doubled their numbers in the professional classes in one generation. He concluded that Jewish family values produce more achievers because they stress:
1. A belief that the world is orderly and amenable to rational mastery.
2. A willingness to leave home to make one's way in life.
3. A preference for individual rather than collective credit for work done.
4. The belief that individuals can improve themselves through education and that one should not readily submit to fate
5. Greater equality in the power structure between the mother and the father in the family.[7]

PROGRAMMING FOR THE GIFTED

Assuming that we are able to identify the gifted and talented students in our Religious Schools, the next step is determining how we can best provide for their special needs within that setting. Gallagher states that there are three types of changes a school can make: (1) the content, (2) the method of presentation, and (3) the learning environment.[8] These changes are particularly appropriate in a Religious School setting. Yet, we need to remember that all students can benefit from an approach which considers their best learning style, includes involvement, and provides flexibility for individual interests and needs.

Programs for the gifted in Religious School are: alternate classes, honors sections, enrichment classes, in-class independent study, self-contained classes, special enrichment in classes, tracking, tutors and aides, and resource people. In the remainder of this chapter, these alternatives will be discussed with particular emphasis on school and on specific appropriate methodologies.

Alternative classes provide a different setting and curriculum which complement the regular Religious School classroom. Such classes may be optional or required and should have a specially trained, knowledgeable instructor. Take for example, a sixth or seventh grade class whose major curriculum area is Jewish History and which utilizes *My People: Abba Eban's History of the Jews*, adapted by David Bamberger (Behrman House). An alternate class on Jewish history could be offered to bright and identified gifted students. This class could provide an expanded view of the subject and perhaps even use a variety of textual approaches using the original Abba Eban text from which the younger version is drawn.

This model is limited to a larger Religious School where space, funding, and the number of students is large enough to accommodate such a plan. The group might consist of an honors class of students who have demonstrated excellence in academic studies and express an interest in a more challenging class of the same curriculum. In an enrichment class, cross-grade groups for three grade levels meet on a regularly scheduled basis as part of the school. For example, a group of fourth, fifth, and sixth grade students, clearly identified as gifted, can switch for a 30 to 45 minute segment of the regular class to enrichment activities. This program can include curricular areas from all three of the grades that are part of the class. It can involve a specialist in gifted who works with the entire school on a rotating basis, dealing with bright students, grouped by approximate ages, and involved in the special enrichment class for a regularly scheduled time.

The drawback to cross-grade groups is the time absent from the regular classroom. It is also necessary to decide whether students are responsible for the regular class program as well as the enrichment class. Is there opportunity for the teachers of both groups to meet, share, and discuss what will benefit the students most? Any type of additional programming for gifted students should include specialized staff, additional planning time, and involvement of all teachers and staff working with a given child.

Kough has listed requirements that he feels should be met if an enrichment model for the regular classroom is to be implemented.[9] Questions to be answered are:

1. Has the classroom teacher identified students who are gifted?
2. Can the classroom teacher describe specific curriculum modifications?
3. Does some specific person have responsibility for the entire program?
4. Are students, Rabbi, parents, teacher, Director of Education, and the Religious School Committee in support of the plan? Do they know what is involved?
5. Are the parents of the students in the program involved in its process of creation and are they aware of the specifics of the program?

Any program worth doing is worth doing well; this involves planning, specifics, and evaluation.

Tracking can allow students who are gifted in a specific area to be grouped together for part of their Religious School educational program, but remain with their own age group for other areas. This is the most commonly utilized method for Hebrew instruction which, as a skill, can be assessed. Students can then be grouped by achievement levels. These same students may quite possibly be grouped by grade level for Judaic studies.

A national study was conducted by Cox (1985)

for the Richardson Foundation in Fort Worth. This study, which surveyed the types of programs that existed for high-ability students, points to some interesting program ideas for Religious Schools.

In the Richardson study, the following program types were used:
1. Enrichment in the regular classroom
2. Part-time special class
3. Full-time special class
4. Independent study
5. Itinerant teacher
6. Mentorships
7. Resource rooms
8. Special schools
9. Early entrance
10. Continuous progress
11. Nongraded school
12. Moderate acceleration
13. Radical acceleration
14. College Board and Advanced Placement
15. Fast-paced classrooms
16. Concurrent or dual enrollment

The Richardson study found that the most commonly offered program option was the part-time special class, or "pull-out" model. The Richardson study recommended comprehensive programming for gifted students with flexible pacing and multiple options. A step-by-step curriculum development plan is suggested to assist school districts in program planning efforts: (1) involvement of key individuals, (2) development of definition, (3) conducting needs assessment, (4) development of a philosophy, (5) development of program goals, (6) selection of program types, (7) development of objectives and strategies, and (8) development of evaluation procedures. When gifted education is added to the local school offerings, the study concludes, other students benefit as well.

STRATEGIES FOR TEACHING THE GIFTED

Many Religious School settings do not afford us the opportunity for special programs for the gifted. When this is the case it then becomes the responsibility of the classroom teacher to help his or her own gifted students. Religious School teachers can effectively use traditional techniques with gifted children in a heterogeneous classroom and still meet their needs through a differentiated curriculum.

Religious School teachers who want to help their gifted students can: (1) make it a point to use open-ended, divergent questions and activities; (2) get out of the gifted pupil's way, so he or she can learn things that are truly new and not a rehash of previously learned material; (3) pay attention to gifted students (they need you — your touch, your approval, your interest); and (4) examine your attitudes toward the gifted student. Learn to relax and enjoy the challenge they provide.

It is possible for a gifted student to participate with the classroom teacher in designing, executing, and evaluating curricular modifications appropriate to his or her needs and still be an active classroom participant. Programs devised can involve a wide range of sensory experiences such as trips, films, books, records, pictures, charts, maps, art, etc. Students who find a particularly exciting learning experience can make this an area for independent study.

Independent study is one of the best models for the gifted because it builds on the gifted student's desire for self-initiated learning. The teacher's role is limited to that of encouraging gifted students to initiate projects of their own, to supervise and monitor the process, and to share in the product. Figure 1 is a sample contract form for monitoring independent study.

Perhaps the greatest advantage to independent study is that the gifted student can acquire motivation and skills which will help him or her become a continuous Jewish learner throughout life.

Games have long been recognized as a valuable tool for educators. Particularly useful for gifted students are activities that simulate real life. Simulations have high motivational value because students see an immediately useful reason to learn — to succeed and win. Such games afford the gifted: (1) opportunities for high level thinking (critical, creative, and logical thinking); (2) opportunities for teaching social values because although competition is present, cooperation is the common goal; (3) opportunities for gifted children to act and interact. While students become involved in the facts, the process, and the key concepts to be learned in the game, they are engaged in exciting and satisfying play.

The key features of a simulation are:

CONTRACT

Name of student or students involved in this activity:
_____

What I want to find out: (content to be studied)
_____

What I need to do: (resources to be used)
_____
_____

What I will do with what I have learned: (method of sharing)
_____
_____
_____
_____

Date begun: _____
Anticipated date of completion: _____

_____
Teacher's Signature

_____
_____
Student Signatures

Figure 1

1. It must clearly be focused on selected concepts and processes.
2. It should involve the students in a simulation of a reality based situation.
3. It must involve the dramatic qualities of a game.
4. Rules should be divided into several of the following kinds:
   a. procedural rules that tell how a game is to be played
   b. behavioral rules which tell what one player can do and the role specifications for each player
   c. goal rules that clearly delineate the goals and means of achieving the goals
   d. rules that specify consequences to a player when any of the game's rules are broken

A format for designing your own simulation games for gifted and other students follows:[10]

Name of the Game
_____

Statement of the Problem
_____

Objectives of the Game
_____

Scenario: Include past events, background information, the present time and setting, the conditions that may affect the game.

Characters and their Goals: Give a brief description of the physical characteristics, the personality, and the player's goals for the game:
_____
_____

A Point in Time: The exact place and time when the game begins.
_____

Resources: Props for the game — physical, social, economic, political, or personal.

Rules and their Administration: To govern players, the game pattern and scoring and how they are implemented.

Evaluation and Feedback: Were objectives reached; can the game be improved?

Inquiry is another strategy appropriate for teachers in regular classrooms for gifted and other students. The best lesson will not reach the student and create a commitment to learning until he/she has become personally involved in the learning process. Learning is an active process requiring a personal commitment through the inquiry oriented strategy of teaching as endorsed by Arthur Combs.[11] This engages the pupil in decision making regarding his or her own instruction. It sees the student as seeking, probing, and processing data from his or her own environment.

The process of inquiry involves first identifying and narrowing a problem of some kind to be studied. Then hypotheses are proposed by the gifted students to help guide their investigation. This is followed by proposals for the gathering of data. These processes are evaluated and then data are gathered and summarized about the hypotheses. The role of the teacher is that of guide, counselor, or consultant. The teacher helps by providing situations and materials that create questions in the minds of students. An example of inquiry for middle school students might be to investigate whether there were really "righteous Christians" during the Holocaust. What methods would students employ, what processes would they use for gathering data, what do they think the data would show?

Another strategy appropriate for gifted students helps them to develop strategies to facilitate more effective problem solving. Synectics is a technique devised by W.J.J. Gordon.[12] The term denotes a process to stimulate creativity through analysis. Synectics can be thought of as specific stages or as skills. The first stage requires active listening skills and is characterized by feedback. A typical Synectic session might be: (1) problem formulation — one person defines a problem and indicates what has been tried and the type of ideas wanted; (2) group ideation — group members share the essence of ideas, and these are collected; and (3) potential goals identified — potential valuable goals are identified by the problem giver. The teacher may introduce speculation or creative ideas which might help spur on the process. This is known as excursion, and the students may be asked to think of analogies in a different environment. For example, Religious School students attempting to gain a better understanding of ancestors and anti-Semitism might be asked to pretend that they are a pair of J.C. Penney "plain pocket jeans" hanging on a rack with Guess, Jordache, and other designer blue jeans. Their reactions as to how this might feel takes them away from the reality of the problem of being different and they may return to it shortly, refreshed and with new insights.

Enrichment activities can include individualized encounter lessons, bonus tables, "Super Heroes," and working as tutors and aides.

Encounter lessons are activities that stimulate creativity and utilize gifted students' inner strengths and their perceptions of these inner strengths to aid in the further development of their feelings and values. An encounter lesson is based on four principles which can be expressed in terms of teacher behavior.[13] The teacher will help:

1. the student think about who he or she is and what he or she can and ought to do.
2. the student feel valuable and worthwhile.
3. the student to see learning as relevant to his or her individual needs.
4. the student to develop and maintain a learning atmosphere that reflects psychological safety and freedom.

Encounter lessons are short in duration, lasting from twenty to thirty minutes. They are made up of an "involving" activity in which the students, usually in small groups, actively see, hear, taste, touch, smell, and react to ideas and others. The activities should be as open-ended as possible, thus providing each student an opportunity to bring his or her uniqueness to task.

Encounter experiences are particularly suited to the Religious School setting as part of a lesson used to introduce or to motivate, or as a culmination. They can be adapted to all levels, preschool through seniors. A specific example:

Lesson: The Torah

Objectives
To foster understanding
To implement self-awareness
To identify with the Torah and experience it in a unique way.

Procedure
Introduce the idea of the Ark as a resting place for the Torah. The scene is set and five students are selected at random and asked to stand next to each other facing the remainder of the group. They are then asked to imagine themselves as Torahs in an Ark. Each student should respond to the following sample questions:
1. The Ark door is closed; it is dark and the sanctuary is quiet. How do you feel? What are your thoughts?
2. It is Shabbat morning. The Rabbi and Synagogue President approach the Ark to open it and remove one Torah for the reading of this week's portion. Why should they pick you?
3. Tonight is Simchat Torah. The congregation is in attendance and eager to celebrate. You are about to be taken from the Ark and placed in the arms of one of the members. What do you want to tell this person who will carry you?

Evaluation
This is an important part of any encounter lesson. Discuss such questions as: To what extent did you become involved in this exercise? Did your awareness level change?

Bonus tables can be used to keep bright students who finish assignments very quickly involved in meaningful activities. A section for sixth/seventh grade might include one on American Jewish History. Students could be asked to choose between the following activities (resource *America: The Jewish Experience* by Sandra Leiman, UAHC Press, 1994):
1. Investigate the history of your synagogue and present it in a dramatic form, in a short story, or in a mural.
2. After investigating the major events in American Jewish History, create a time line of at least ten major events.
3. Research the lives of the following important Jews in America past and present: Jacob Rothschild, Abraham Joshua Heschel, Benjamin Cardozo, Rabbi Alexander Schindler, Moses Montefiore, Mordecai Kaplan. Create a booklet in which you briefly describe each life.

Another suggestion for a bonus table activity is a "Thing To Do Box." This is usually developed around a central stimulus material such as a book, a tape or C.D., a play, or filmstrip. (While filmstrips are not generally used in classrooms today, many excellent ones can be found in some closet in your building.) The box lends itself to both elementary, middle, and high school levels. It can be used as an extender and as enrichment for the regular classroom curriculum or to allow students to pursue an interest in a given subject.

Prepared sheets, flash or task cards, records, or tapes with headsets, books, etc., are appropriate for these individualized, enriching activities.

CONCLUSION

A number of different methods and ideas have been presented in this chapter. It is up to the individual teacher to incorporate into the curriculum those with which he or she is comfortable. In the past, education of gifted children in our Religious Schools may have been hampered by criticisms of elitism. Our gifted students need a better Jewish education so that they will provide future leadership for our communities and because education that has been adapted to their needs will mean that they can lead happier and more satisfying Jewish lives. If we can accept the premise that the purpose of Jewish education is to promote excellence and ensure the preservation of Judaism, then an educational system that is appropriate takes into account individual needs and differences.

OUR GIFTED STUDENTS NEED A BETTER JEWISH EDUCATION.

Zena Sulkes, Ph.D. serves as Director of Education of Congregation Rodeph Shalom in Philadelphia. She is a Past President of the National Association of Temple Educators, a member-at-large of the CAJE Board, serves on the Editorial Boards of *Agenda: Jewish Education, Shofar,* and *Compass,* and is the author of *Mitzvah Copy Pak*™ and *Proud and Jewish* (A.R.E.)

NOTES

1. James J. Gallagher, *Teaching the Gifted Child* (Boston: Allyn & Bacon, 1975), p. 9.
2. S. P. Marland, *Education of the Gifted and Talented* (Washington, DC: U.S. Office of Education, 1972), p. 261.
3. Carol W. Pegnato and Jack W. Birch, "Locating Gifted Children in the Junior High Schools: A Comparison of Methods," *Exceptional Children* 25: 300-304, March 1959.
4. Paul Plowman, and others, California State Department of Education, 1971.
5. M.A. Adler, "A Study of the Effect of Ethnic Origin on Giftedness," *Gifted Child Quarterly* 7: 98-101, 1963.
6. L. Terman and M. Oden, "Genetic Studies of Genius," Vol. 5 in *The Gifted Group at Mid Life* (Stanford, CA: Stanford University Press, 1960), p. 310.
7. F. Strodbeck, "Family Interaction, Values and Achievement," in *Talent and Society*, edited by B. McClelland (Princeton: Van Nostrand, 1958), pp. 186-190.
8. Gallagher, op. cit., p. 72.
9. J. Kough, "Administrative Provision for the Gifted," in *Working with Superior Students: Theory and Practices*, edited by B. Shertzer (Chicago: Science Research Associates, 1960), p. 147.
11. Arthur Combs, *Perceiving, Behaving and Becoming* (Washington, DC: ASCD, 1962).
12. W.J.J. Gordon, *Synectics* (New York: Harper & Row, 1961).
13. Dorothy Sisk, *Teaching Gifted Children* (Federal Grant Title V., The State of South Carolina, 1978), p. 6.

BIBLIOGRAPHY

Books and Articles

Adler, M.A. "A Study of the Effect of Ethnic Origin on Giftedness." *Gifted Child Quarterly* 7:98-101, 1963.

Barbe, W.B., ed. *Psychology and Education of the Gifted: Selected Readings*. 3d ed. New York: Irvington Press, 1981.

Combs, Arthur. *Perceiving, Behaving, and Becoming*. Washington, DC: ASCD, 1962.

Cox, Ann. "The Gifted Student: A Neglected Presence." *Teacher*, November/December, 1979, pp. 75-76.

Cox, June, et al. *Educating Able Learners: Programs and Promising Practices*. Austin, TX: University of Texas Press, 1985.

Davis, Gary A., and Sylvia Rimm. *Education of the Gifted and Talented*. 2d ed. Englewood Cliffs, NJ: Prentice-Hall, 1989.

Feldhusen, J., and S. Hoover. "The Gifted at Risk in a Place Called School." *Gifted Child Quarterly* 28: 9-11, Spring 1984.

Garfinkel, Alan, et al. "Foreign Language for the Gifted." *Roeper Review* 15:235-8, May/June 1993.

Greenlaw, M. Jean, and Margaret E. McIntosh. *Educating the Gifted: A Sourcebook*. Chicago: American Library Association, 1988.

Guilford, J.P. *Intelligence, Creativity, and Their Educational Implications*. San Diego: Knapp, 1968.

Kitano, Marjorie, and Darrell Kirby. *Gifted Education: A Comprehensive View*. Glenview, IL: Scott Foresman, 1987.

Kramer, Alan H., ed. *Gifted Children: Challenging Their Potential*. Unionville, NY: Trillium Press, Inc., 1981.

Maker, C. June. *Teaching Models in the Education of the Gifted*. Austin, TX: PRO-ED, 1982.

Pegnato, C.W., and J.W. Birch. "Locating Gifted Children in Junior High Schools: A Comparison of Methods." *Exceptional Children* 25: 300-301, 1959.

Plowman, Paul, and J.P. Rice, Jr. *Final Report: California Project Talent*. Sacramento: California Department of Public Instruction, 1969.

Renzulli, J. *The Enrichment Triad Model: A Guide for Developing Defensible Programs for the Gifted and Talented*. Storrs, CT: Creative Learning Press, 1977.

———. *A Guidebook for Evaluating Programs for the Gifted and Talented*. Los Angeles: National State Leadership Training Institute on Gifted and Talented, n.d.

Renzulli, J., et al. *Recommended Practices in Gifted Eduation: A Critical Analysis.* New York: Teachers College Press, Columbia University, 1991.

Renzulli, J., and L. Smith. "Revolving Door: A Truer Turn for the Gifted." *Learning* 9 (3):91-94.

Sisk, Dorothy. *Creative Teaching of the Gifted.* New York: McGraw-Hill Book Co., 1987.

Smith, Constance K. "Parents and Teachers in Partnership." *Gifted Child Today* 16:16-19, 1993.

Tuttle, Frederick B., Jr., and Laurence A. Becker. *Characteristics and Identification of Gifted and Talented Students.* 3d ed. Washington, DC: National Education Association, 1988.

Wenger, Win. *How To Increase Gifted Students' Creative Thinking and Imagination.* Manassas, VA: Gifted Education Press, 1984.

Winebrenner, Susan. *Teaching Gifted Kids in the Regular Classroom: Stragegies and Techniques Every Teacher Can Use To Meet the Academic Needs of the Gifted and Talented.* Minneapolis, MN: Free Spirit Publishing, Inc., 1992.

Organizations
THE ASSOCIATION FOR THE GIFTED
The Council for Exceptional Children,
1411 S. Jefferson Davis Highway, Suite 900,
Arlington, VA 22202

THE GIFTED CHILD RESEARCH INSTITUTE
300 West 55th St., New York, NY 10019

NATIONAL ASSOCIATION FOR GIFTED CHILDREN
4175 Lovell Rd., Suite 140, Circle Pines, MN 55014

NATIONAL STATE LEADERSHIP TRAINING INSTITUTE ON GIFTED AND TALENTED
Hilton Center, 900 Wilshire Blvd., Suite 1142, Los Angeles, CA 90017

Journals
EXCEPTIONAL CHILDREN
The Council for Exceptional Children
1920 Association Drive, Reston, VA 22091

GIFTED CHILD QUARTERLY
National Association for Gifted Children
1155 15th St. N.W., Suite 1002, Washington, DC 20005

GIFTED CHILD TODAY
G/C/T, Inc.
Box 6648, Mobile, AL 36660

JOURNAL FOR THE EDUCATION OF THE GIFTED
University of North Carolina Press
P.O. Box 2288, Chapel Hill, NC 27515

SPECIAL POPULATIONS

CHAPTER TWELVE

REACHING AND TEACHING ADULTS AND THE ELDERLY

Audrey Friedman Marcus and Kerry M. Olitziky

Jewish survival may depend on adult Jews who are secure in their identity, knowledgeable about Judaism, and well informed on issues that affect the Jewish community. In the face of a diminishing Jewish population, a high rate of assimilation and intermarriage and rising currents of anti-Semitism, the necessity for such an educated constituency has become ever more pressing. Thus, it seemed to us that the inclusion of a chapter aimed specifically at those who teach Jewish adults as well as those who serve the educational needs of the growing aging population in our midst was especially important.

We plan no further polemic on the need for Jewish education for adults. Nor will we discuss in detail the nature of the adult learner or the theoretical underpinnings of adult education. Instead, this very practical discussion will include a brief consideration of aspects of a positive learning environment, a listing of nearly fifty methods and strategies which can be employed when teaching adults, and finally, some specifics on the particular educational needs of the elderly. The Bibliography at the end of the chapter includes books on teaching, addresses of the major national Jewish organizations that are involved in adult Jewish education, and a few helpful resources for the classroom. The material in this chapter is aimed at those who teach adults in every setting where Jewish learning takes place — in synagogues, in Jewish Community Centers, in adult institutes sponsored by communities, in homes for the aged, and at retreats.

THE LEARNING ENVIRONMENT

Adult Jewish learners attend Jewish classes because they want to be there and out of a desire to learn more about our heritage. Some may come for the sociability as well. How we manage our classroom and the kind of atmosphere we encourage will in large measure determine the frequency of attendance and influence future registrations in adult classes on Judaism. Therefore it is incumbent upon us to bear in mind at all times the comfort and enjoyment of our participants, as well as their intellectual growth. Here are several ways to promote a desirable learning environment.[1]

First and foremost, we need to create an atmosphere that is warm and friendly, inviting and informal, yet serious about learning. Allow time for introductions and one or two get acquainted exercises before you begin the first session. Maintain an accepting and non-judgmental attitude, encouraging students to share their views and to participate in class discussions. Consider serving refreshments at each session; this also contributes to a friendly and fun atmosphere.

Don't overlook the physical comfort of your students. Be sure that chairs are comfortable and that seating is arranged in a way that maximizes interaction between group members. Later we'll talk about some aspects of environment that require special attention when teaching the elderly.

In most adult Jewish classes, students come with varying backgrounds, interests, and abilities. You will want to provide extra reading or research projects for advanced students and to offer special help to those who need it. Most important, strive for a stimulating intellectual level and don't talk down to your students. Participants will gain the most from their studies when they are able to relate the subject matter to their own life experiences.

Your good grasp of the subject matter and enthusiastic approach to it will strongly influence your students. Encourage a high level of participation and vary the techniques that you use. Attention to all of these aspects of the learning environment will increase student satisfaction and enjoyment and contribute to a high level of learning.

METHODS OF TEACHING ADULTS

Many teachers of adults rely exclusively on lecture and discussion in their classes, maintaining that a variety of approaches is unnecessary for this age group. While lecture and discussion are useful and appropriate methods, the use of other techniques in addition can result in greater learning and increased student participation.

Adults today are used to the visual excitement provided by television just as our young people are. When they become bored with a particular program or subject, they have only to switch to another channel. Their educational level is for the most part high and they desire challenging classes which involve them deeply. Individuals who attend classes in adult Jewish studies seek interaction with others and an opportunity to get to know peers better. These factors point up the need for using a variety of techniques in adult education.

The list which follows contains a brief description of a large number of techniques that can be used when teaching adults. These are grouped under the headings Presentation Methods, Audience Participation Methods, Discussion Methods, Simulation/Participation Methods, and Practice and Research Methods. The categories and strategies were drawn mainly from *The Modern Practice of Adult Education* by Knowles. Other strategies were suggested in *40 Ways To Teach in Groups* by Martha M. Leypoldt, and by other chapters in this volume. Remember that two or more of the techniques can often be used in combination. Whatever the method, it is vital that it fulfills the objectives and matches the needs and abilities of your students.

Presentation Methods

Lecture: An oral discourse by the teacher or a guest lecturer on a particular topic. Interaction is sometimes permitted during the lecture and most often, a forum (free, open discussion) follows.

Panel: Several persons with special knowledge informally discuss an assigned topic in front of the group. A panel is a good technique when there is a need to present a number of different views. A forum can follow. (Remember, students make good panelists, too!)

Dialolgue: A "conversation" between two people on a specific topic, on which they may or may not agree. The audience can be encouraged to participate throughout or a forum can follow.

Symposium: A series of speeches given by as many speakers as desired, or as there are aspects of a problem or issue to cover. A symposium can be followed by one or several reactors, by a forum, or by a dialogue.

Colloquy: Three to four people selected from the group present various aspects of a problem to three or four resource people who respond. Or questions can be designed by small groups and asked by their chosen representatives.

Debate: Speakers with opposing views, either students or outside experts, present their views for an equal length of time and then have a chance for rebuttal. A debate is followed by a forum.

*Interview: A*n expert gives facts and opinions freely in response to questions from the teacher or from the group. The interview is followed by a forum. Variations: Telephone interviews, interactive television, group interviews.

Demonstration: One or more people show the group how to do something. A demonstration is often combined with a lecture and/or followed by a forum.

Film Forum: A movie or filmstrip, or a chosen segment, is shown and then discussed by the group. (See the Bibliography at the end of the book for addresses of distributors.)

Slide Forum: A slide show or slide tape presentation originated by the teacher, an invited expert, or the students. Sets of slides may be borrowed from personal collections, from YIVO Slide Bank, or other sources.

USING A VARIETY OF METHODS LEADS TO GREATER LEARNING AND PARTICIPATION.

Tapes and CD's: A tape recording of the teacher, an outside expert, an interview, a selection of music, or a spoken word recording of a famous speech, historical event, or play. These can be listened to by the whole group, a small group, or by one student individually. Recordings can be stopped for questions, discussions, and clarification. A forum can follow.

Videotape/Videodisc: A videotape or videodisc can be shown on a subject pertinent to the curriculum. These can be recorded from television shows/or made by a master teacher or expert on the subject. A forum follows.

Exhibit: An exhibit is prepared for class members by a group of students or the teacher. Documents, photographs, written materials, and artifacts can be used to teach the content area. A forum follows.

Reading: Pertinent material from a textbook, magazine, or journal, or literature from any other primary or secondary source is read aloud by the teacher or student. A forum follows.

Note: All presentations are greatly enriched by the use of the blackboard or a flip chart, as well as by pictures, posters, photographs, charts, and/or maps, an overhead or opaque projector.

Audience Participation Methods
Forum: A free and open discussion by the group.

Question and Answer: Questions are asked by the teacher to determine students' knowledge, to help them understand concepts and draw conclusions, and to discover their opinions and values.

Buzz Groups: Pairs, triads, or groups of four to six or even twelve to fifteen participants, identify problems or raise questions for a speaker to address. They can react to a presentation, exchange ideas and experiences, test solutions, and/or arrive at a conclusion or solve a problem. A reporter is called on from each group. Other groups can question the reporting group after their report or after all the reports. When there are many buzz groups, reporters can volunteer to report or can mention only new points when reporting.

Listening Teams: The group is divided into several groups, each of which listens to the presentation with a different aspect of the subject matter in mind. Or one group listens for points that need clarification, another for points with which they disagree, a third for points they wish more information about, and the fourth for practical applications they wish to discuss. After the presentation, teams buzz for a few minutes, then choose a reporter to report to the group as a whole.

Reaction Panel: Several chosen members of the group react briefly to the lecture or other presentation. Or the reactors may be permitted to interrupt the presentation for clarification. A forum can follow.

Audience Role Play: Pairs or small groups role play all at the same time a specific situation related to the presentation.

Expanding Panel: Various members of the group, or the whole group, join the panel and add their views on the subject.

Discussion Methods
Dyadic Discussion: Two people share ideas, or solve a problem, reporting to the group as a whole if desired.

Group Centered Discussion: Discussion takes place with little guidance. The leader acts as a facilitator and resource person and may even participate as a group member.

Guided Discussion: The instructor leads students toward certain conclusions through discussion.

Book-Centered Discussion: All participants read the same assigned portion of the textbook or other fiction or non-fiction material and then discuss the reading together.

Socratic Discussion: The teacher and the students attempt to reach certain truths through a dialectic process of conversation and debate. In the central role, the teacher asks questions which force the students to generalize and which require the group to test the generalizations or the logic that was used.

Problem Solving Discussion: The teacher outlines a problem or poses a question. Students solve the problem or answer the question in small groups or in one large group.

Case Discussion: Information regarding a real life situation is presented to the group. Participants analyze all aspects of the situation, providing a solution, deciding if another course of action might have been better, etc. Cases can be designed by the teacher or the students. Variation: Value Sheets – a sheet consisting of a value issue, problem, or dilemma and a series of questions about it.

Circle Response (Whip): The teacher poses a question to the group or asks for a reaction. After a few moments, each person in turn responds briefly. No one can speak for a second time until all have had a turn.

Brainstorming: Students call out ideas in response to a given question or solutions in response to a problem. No evaluation of ideas is permitted and wild ideas are encouraged. Students may "hitchhike" on the ideas of others by adding to them and enlarging on them. Ideas are categorized, analyzed, and, if appropriate, acted on.

Fishbowl: Learners form an inner and an outer circle. For ten minutes, the inner circle tries to solve a problem or wrestles with an open-ended question. Outer circle participants act as observers and report on the quality of the discussion and the roles of each participant in the inner circle. Together, both groups evaluate the discussion.

Work Group: Two or three or four to six students discuss an assigned topic, define a problem or question, develop a list of possible goals, refine ideas, or develop solutions to problems. (Same as Buzz Group)

Simulation/Participation Methods
Role Play: Students spontaneously act out a situation related to the subject matter. Students learn to understand situations and feelings as well as test out ideas, solutions, and plans of action.
Critical Incident Process: An incident from an unfamiliar case (see Case Discussion above) is presented by the teacher. Students ask questions to find out the rest of the information about the case. The teacher gives out the facts of the case only in response to the questions.

Simulations: Students participate in a social model of an actual or hypothetical social process involving taking a role (e.g., immigration to America, Aliyah Bet, synagogue board meeting, etc.)

Games: Students participate in board games, team games, or games such as puzzles and riddles which test knowledge or require solutions to problems.

Values Clarification: Participatory strategies which help learners clarify their values on aspects of the subject matter (e.g., Forced Choice, Continuum, Rank Order, Sentence Completions, etc.).

Milling: Students mill around the room seeking someone who agrees/disagrees with them on an issue or who has the answer to a question they have. Milling can also be used to share written responses to a question or problem.

Group Drawing: In small groups, students, arrive at some shared ideas about the subject matter. They express these through a group drawing executed by one or all of the members. Drawings are then shared with the rest of the class.

Group Writing: Similar to a group drawing, except that ideas are expressed as a poem, a prayer, or other form of creative writing.

Field Trip: Students take trips to other sites for learning, such as a museum, an old section of town, another synagogue, or a community event. Excursions should be preceded by good briefings so that students know what they are expected to learn. Students should summarize their new learnings after the trip.

Practice and Research Methods
Drill: Learning something by repeated practice or repetition.

Recitation: The teacher asks questions to determine what students know about the subject based on a presentation, the textbook, homework, discussion, etc.

Peer Teaching (Chevruta): Students work in pairs, helping each other master subject matter.

Team Learning: Small groups of five to eight students cooperatively try to teach themselves facts and concepts, working from several paragraphs of prepared material and questions. A student from one group reads a question an a student from another responds using the answer decided on by his/her group. Other groups add only responses that have not already been read.

Group Investigation or Report: Students work together in small groups for one or more sessions, seeking answers or solutions to problems or concerns. Groups can do research, analyze a survey, etc. Each group chooses a leader, draws up plans, assigns duties, identifies necessary resources, gathers and analyzes information, and shares its findings with the rest of the class.

Individual Investigation: Research assignments are made to individual students. Investigations are done under the guidance of the teacher and can be in the form of a report, book review, survey, annotated bibliography, audiovisual presentation, etc. The product is presented to the rest of the group upon completion.

Independent Study: A student works on a topic of his/her choice that relates to the subject matter or extends it into an area of particular interest. The student determines the objectives and chooses the resources and activities. The teacher provides guidance as the student works in a self-paced way. Independent study can also be done by a small group.

TEACHING THE ELDERLY

Contrary to popular belief, you *can* teach an old dog new tricks. Understanding this cliche in our own terms, older people are not too rigid to learn, as long as you know how to teach them. Older learners, as a group, are no different from younger adult learners. There are older people who learn quickly, and there are those who learn more slowly. However, there are certain factors which must be taken into consideration when teaching the elderly.

Older people require increased repetitive stimulation in the learning environment in order to achieve a high retention level. Thus, it is better to employ the kind of techniques and learning experiences which provide any learner with such stimulation, making any modifications that are necessary for the older learner. Although older people may be more disciplined than young children in the sense that they can sit for a lengthy lecture, lecturing is probably the least effective means of teaching the older adult.

According to Edgar Dale, Professor of Education at Ohio State University, those educational experiences which involve the learner as doer are most effective. Contrived experiences such as simulation games and role plays are more effective than field trips and film. These, in turn, are still more effective than recordings, and, of course, than lectures.

While the older learner may require this increased stimulation, some research suggests that intelligence increases into the sixth and seventh decade of life. In addition, it has been determined that older learners have greater verbal ability than young learners. For example, once learned, the older learner can assimilate new words (in his/her vernacular) more readily and more easily. Of course, this can facilitate the learning process.

Old people are an ideal target group for educational activities. Most of them are either retired or have very flexible schedules. Many are eager to fill their unscheduled hours. They come on a voluntary basis and thus are highly motivated. Some have already established a life-long commitment to Jewish education. But they must be taught on their level. Never underestimate the older learner based only on what you see. The sage Judah HaNasi said that while he learned from his teachers and from his colleagues, he learned the most from his students. As we teach the elderly, we can appreciate the truth of his statement. Older people have considerable knowledge and a wealth of interesting experiences to contribute. The enrichment we gain from contact with them and with all they have to share represents one of the many joys of teaching the aged. An effective teacher of the elderly learns with his or her students, at the same time assisting them to become independent learners. Our most important goal when teaching older adults should be the establishment of a supportive environment. This may be difficult at first for the younger teacher. Elderly learners may sometimes seem critical. Yet they are equally ready to compliment and "stroke" their teacher. Once respect as a competent instructor has been earned, it will seldom be challenged. And the result will be extensive group participation and good attendance, both of which teachers of the young crave.

Teaching the elderly has its problems, too. Because people age at different rates, chronological age may not be a good indicator in evaluating your learning audience. Hearing and visual acuity are important items to keep in mind. Unusual names or unfamiliar terms may have to be pronounced slowly or written on the board. Written materials must be well typed, evenly spaced, and typed on large non-glare paper. Material must be "sensed" to be learned. Make sure that those with significant impairment are seated, without embarrassment, in a position which will enhance their ability to learn.

Educational methods may have changed since the elders you teach last participated in a formal educational experience. Thus you may need to describe in detail each approach you plan to employ prior to its use. Additionally, older learners may need a period of adjustment to the learning environment. College students are used to taking notes and having frequent tests. Older people may not be accustomed to these aspects of systematic education.

Furthermore, health factors which affect the elderly learner have to be constantly monitored. Lighting, for instance, must be intense, but without glare. Because older bodies do not adjust as rapidly to changes in room temperature, the degree of heat or cold needs to be kept as constant as possible. Every aspect of the environment must be taken into consideration in the creation of a supportive environment for the aged learner.

With all of this in mind, which methods and activities are most appropriate for use with older learners? Whatever the method, one particular technique is indispensable. The "pairing technique," as we call it, utilizes any two different methods in order to teach/emphasize the same subject. This takes into consideration the necessity for intense, repetitive stimulation. For example, if role playing with discussion has been used in order to teach the Jewish way of mourning and bereavement, a follow-up film or field trip is in order. One technique has thus been used to supplement the other. This pairing facilitates learning for the older adult.

Most of the techniques which are successful in the teaching of adults (such as those outlined earlier in this chapter) can be used in the teaching of the elderly. Some modification may be necessary and, of course, special consideration of the problems of aging must be made. For example, if a retreat is scheduled, it must take place in a facility which will enhance independence rather than foster dependence on the part of the elderly individual. If the dialogue method is used, proper, good quality sound amplification must be used in order to ensure that all learners can hear the presentation. Speakers should be given tips on speaking to hard-of-hearing individuals prior to any presentation. Buzz Groups represent a particularly good technique because of this hearing problem. If learners are made aware of what subjects will be discussed prior to a presentation, they may be more apt to catch words and phrases that might otherwise be unintelligible for them. Independent study and outside readings are good for the aged group because of the vast differences in learning abilities. Through this method students can pursue areas of interest at their own rate of speed. Adequate follow-up and monitoring by the teacher is essential. (Note: Avoid blues and blue-greens together in color presentations which use transparencies and duplicated materials. Some research suggests that the older eye tends to be unable to distinguish between these two colors.)

> **NEVER UNDERESTIMATE THE OLDER LEARNER.**

SAMPLE TOPICS OF INTEREST

The following list provides ideas and titles for classes and workshops which will interest older adults:

Jewish Foods and Older Adult Nutrition
Filling Retirement Hours Creatively
Grandparenting
Dealing with New Dependence
Social Visibility and the Older Adult
Suicide: Crying for Help
The Jewish Community Network of Service for the Older Adult
Parashat Hashavua
The Great Books of History

The Great Book: The Bible
Creating Poetry in Motion
Jewish Art and Art Forms
A Tour of Your Jewish Community
Reevaluating Values in Old Age
Senior Sexuality
Who Is a Jew?
Jewish Identity: Expressions in Old Age
Why I am a Jew . . . Why I Choose To
    Remain a Jew
Jewish Genealogy: Tracing Backward and
    Forward
Drugs and Drug Abuse
Ethical Wills: What I Really Want To Leave
    My Children
Relearning Yiddish
Hebrew for New Beginners
The Modern Jewish Short Story
Textual Study
I Give My Life to You: Sharing Oral Histories
Crucial Jewish Issues of Today
An Overview of Jewish History
A History of Anti-Semitism: You Were There
The Inner City Jew
The Jewish Life Cycle
The Jewish Calendar
Understanding Today's Teens
Women in Judaism
Holiday Workshop Series

Some ideas for ongoing programs are:
   The Elder Adult Bar/Bat Mitzvah Program
       for 83 Year Olds (3 score plus 10 + 13)
   The Rabbi and Me (weekly current event
       discussions with the Rabbi)

SEVEN STEPS TO HEALTHY OLD AGE (A Seven Week Program)
1. Nutrition
2. Exercise
3. Drugs and Substance Abuse
4. Accident Prevention
5. Filling Out Forms
6. Fighting Loneliness
7. Torah Study and *Siyyum*

JEWISH MUSIC
1. Appreciating Jewish Music: A How-to Session
2. Cantorial and Liturgical Music
3. Art Music
4. Folk Music
5. Cantillations, *Niggun,* and *Nusach*
6. Singing Along

RETREATS

An increasing number of synagogue and community institutions are experimenting with kallot for elderly people. Such weekend or overnight retreats provide excellent opportunities for learning, as well as for socializing. Suggested schedules for two retreats follow. For additional information on this approach, consult *My People Jacob: Thy Tents Have Grown Old: A Manual For Planning Weekend Kallot For Older People* by Zola and Olitzky.

Sample Weekend Retreat Schedule
Theme: "Kicking the 'A.K.' Habit: The Key to Successful Aging"

Friday
4:30   Arrival at *Kallah* location
        Orientation and tour of facility
5:15   Preparation for Shabbat
6:30   Preparation for Shabbat Dinner
7:00   Shabbat Dinner
8:00   Zemirot
8:30   Shabbat Evening Service
9:00   Keynote presentation (speaker or
        discussion)
10:00   Oneg Shabbat and mixer
11:00   *Lailah Tov*

Saturday
8:30   *Boker Tov*
9:15   Breakfast
10:00   Shabbat Morning service with
        d'var Torah
11:00   Workshop #1: The Health Optimist
        (includes tips on exercise, nutrition,
        drugs)
12:00   Prepare for Lunch
12:30   Lunch
1:15   Song session
1:30   Free Time
2:30   Workshop #2: Role Changing and
        Social Supports (includes grandparenting, retirement, widowhood programs,
        and resource banks)
3:30   Free Time
4:30   Shabbat Electives on Jewish Topics
        (includes Current Events, *Parashat HaShavua,* Jewish History, etc.)

5:30	Prepare for Dinner
6:00	Dinner
7:00	Song Session
7:30	Havdalah
8:00	Israeli Dancing and Coffeehouse
9:30	Campfire
10:30	Snacks and Free Time

Sunday
8:30	*Boker Tov*
	Packing and clean-up
9:15	Breakfast
9:45	Songs
10:00	Weekday service
10:30	Wrap-up and Evaluation
11:30	Prepare for lunch
12:00	Lunch
12:45	Friendship Circle
1:15	Departure

Sample Overnight Retreat Schedule
Theme: "The Older Jew: Contributions to a Challenging Civilization"

Sunday
9:00	Arrival at *Kallah* site
	Orientation and Tour of facility
10:00	Keynote Speaker
10:30	Discussion and Role Plays
11:00	Exercise Education
12:00	Relax and recuperate
12:30	Lunch
1:30	Song session
2:00	Free Time

4:00	Workshop #1: How To Do What You Really Want To Do If You Haven't Already Done It
5:30	Prepare for Dinner
6:00	Dinner
7:00	Workshop #2: Communication
8:00	Israeli Dancing and Coffeehouse
10:00	Free Time

Monday
8:30	*Boker Tov*
	Clean-up and pack
9:30	Breakfast/brunch
10:00	Wrap-up and Evaluation
11:00	Friendship Circle
12:00	Departure

Rabbi Kerry M. Olitzky, D.H.L. is Director of the School of Education at Hebrew Union College-Jewish Institute of Religion, New York, where he also directs the Graduate Studies Program. He writes and lectures widely on topics related to innovative religious education, aging, and spiritual renewal. Rabbi Olitzky is the founding editor of the *Journal of Aging and Judaism*, and the editor of *The Safe Deposit and Other Stories about Grandparents, Old Lovers and Crazy Old Men* (Markus Weiner).

Audrey Friedman Marcus received her Masters Degree in Jewish Education from the Rhea Hirsch School of Hebrew Union College–Jewish Institute of Religion. She is the co-author and editor of many teacher manuals, mini-courses, and workbooks.

NOTES

1. Some of the ideas in this section were suggested by Malcolm S. Knowles in *Informal Adult Education* (New York: Association Press, 1950), pp. 32-36.

BIBLIOGRAPHY

Books

Adult Jewish Learning Reader. New York: JESNA, 1993.

Coberly, Lenore M., et al. *Writers Have No Age: Creative Writing with Older Adults*. New York: Haworth Press, 1984.

Cross, K. Patricia. *Adults as Learners; Increasing Participation and Facilitating Learning*. San Francisco: Jossey-Bass, 1992.

———. *Beyond the Open Door*. Ann Arbor, MI: Books on Demand, n.d.

Curry, Robert C. *Training for Trainers: Serving the Elderly, the Technique*. Durham, NH: New England Gerontology Center, 1980.

Fishman, Sylvia Barack, and Alice Goldstein. *When They Are Grown They Will Not Depart: Jewish Education and the Jewish Behavior of American Adults*. Research Report 8, Brandeis University and JESNA, 1993.

Frances, Doris. *Will You Still Need Me, Will You Still Feed Me, When I'm 84?* Bloomington, IN: Indiana University Press, 1984.

Herman, Dorothy G. *From Generation to Generation: An Experiential Approach to the Teaching of the Elderly*. Miami: Central Agency for Jewish Education, 1985.

Houle, Cyril. *The Literature of Adult Education: A Bibliographic Essay*. San Francisco, CA: Jossey-Bass, 1992.

———. *Patterns of Learning: New Perspectives on Life Span Education*. San Francisco: Jossey-Bass, 1984.

Jones, Elizabeth. *Teaching Adults: An Active Learning Approach*. Washington, DC: National Association for the Education of Young Children, 1986.

Joyce, Bruce R., and Marcia Weil. *Models of Teaching*. 4th ed. Needham Heights, MA: Allyn and Bacon, 1992.

Knowles, Malcolm. *The Adult Learner: A Neglected Species*. Fourth Edition. Houston: Gulf Publications, 1990.

———. *The Modern Practice of Adult Education: From Pedagogy to Andragogy*. rev. ed. Englewood Cliffs, NJ: Cambridge Books, 1988.

Leypoldt, Martha M. *40 Ways To Teach in Groups*. Valley Forge, PA: The Judson Press, 1967.

Long, Huey B. *Adult Education in Church and Synagogue*. New York: Syracuse University of Continuing Education, 1973.

———. *Adult Learning: Research and Practice*. New York: University Press, 1988.

McKenzie, Leon. *Adult Education and Worldview Construction*. Melbourne, FL: Krieger, 1991.

Myerhoff, Barbara. *Number Our Days*. New York: Simon and Schuster, 1980.

———. *Storytelling and Growing Older*. Ann Arbor, MI: University of Michigan Press, 1992.

Olitzky, Kerry M. *Interfaith Ministry to the Aged: A Survey of Models*. New York: Human Science Press, 1988.

Olitzky, Kerry M., ed. *"The Safe Deposit" and Other Stories about Grandparents, Old Lovers and Crazy Old Men*. New York: Markus Wiener, 1989.

Peterson, David A. *Facilitating Education for Older Learners*. San Francisco, CA: Jossey-Bass, 1983.

Peterson, R.E., and Associates. *Lifelong Learning in America*. Ann Arbor, MI: Books on Demand, n.d.

Smith, Robert M. *Handbook of Adult Education: Toward a Learning Society*. New York: McGraw Hill, 1973.

———. *Helping Adults Learn How To Learn*. San Francisco, CA: Jossey-Bass, 1983.

———. *Learning To Learn across the Life Span*. San Francisco, CA: Jossey-Bass, 1990.

Stephens, Michael. *Adult Education*. New York: Cassell, 1990.

Verduin, John R. *Curriculum Building for Adult Learning*. Carbondale, IL: Southern Illinois University Press, 1980.

Verduin, John R., Jr., and Thomas A. Clark. *A Distance Education: The Foundation of Effective Practice*. San Francisco, CA: Jossey-Bass, 1991.

Vogel, Linda J. *The Religious Education of Older Adults*. Nashville, TN: Discipleship Resources, 1984.

———. *Teaching Older Adults: A Guide for Teachers and Leaders*. Nashville, TN: Discipleship Resources, 1989.

White, Martha. "Adult Education." In *The Jewish Principals Handbook*. Audrey Friedman Marcus and Raymond A. Zwerin, eds. Denver: A.R.E. Publishing, Inc., 1983.

Wickett, R.E. *Models of Adult Religious Education Practice*. Birmingham, AL: Religious Education Press, 1992.

Wlodkowski, Raymond. *Enhancing Adult Motivation To Learn*. San Francisco, CA: Jossey-Bass, 1993.

Zola, Gary P., and Kerry M. Olitzky. *My People Jacob: Thy Tents Have Grown Old: A Manual For Planning Weekend Kallot For Older People*. New York: Union of American Hebrew Congregations, 1981.

Periodicals

Burstyn, Joan N., and Louis J. Zachary. "Adult Jewish Learning: Then and Now." *Jewish Education*, Vol. 60 (2):10-13, Summer 1993.

Cohn, Edward P. "Vatikim: Sages, Elders, Mature Adults — Human Resources for Eduational Enrichment." *Journal of Psychology and Judaism*, Vol. 17 (4): 273-278, Winter 1993.

Foley, G. "Going Deeper: Teaching and Group Work in Adult Education." *Study in the Education of Adults*, Vol. 24: 143-61, October 1992.

Goodman, Roberta L. "The Neglected Learner: The Adult in Our Community." *Compass*, Vol. 16 (1):20-22, Fall 1993.

Greenberg, E.M. "Meeting the Needs of Diverse Adult Learners — A Symposium." *Liberal Education*, Vol. 78:2-52, September/October 1992.

Hassan, Abraham, and Moshe Kupetz. "The Use of Midrash in Adult Education." *Jewish Observer*, Vol. XXVI (4):37-41, May 1993.

Olitzky, Kerry M. "Renewing Jewish Education for Older Adults." *Compass*, Vol. 16 (1):23-25, Fall 1993.

Sandmann, L.R. "Building Communities to an Improved Future: 5 Key Challenges for the Adult Educator." *Adult Learning*, Vol. 4 (1): 9-22, March/April 1993.

Newsletters

Aging Concerns. Produced by the UAHC Gerontology Committee, 838 Fifth Avenue, New York, NY 10021.

Passages. Produced by the CCAR Committee on Aging.

National Organizations Involved in Adult Jewish Education

AGUDATH ISRAEL OF AMERICA
84 William St., New York, NY 10038

Publishes educational guides and texts, such as the Talmud, and provides materials and assistance for Soviet Jewish arrivals.

AMERICAN JEWISH COMMITTEE
INSTITUTE OF HUMAN RELATIONS
165 E. 56th St., New York, NY 10022

Works in the field of human relations, interprets Israel to all Americans, assists Jews to be fully integrated into American society, and provides educational services to the adult population. Publisher of *Commentary* magazine.

AMERICAN JEWISH CONGRESS
15 E. 84th St., New York, NY 10022

Offers adults opportunities to increase their knowledge of Israel, eliminate religious bigotry, and increase Jewish cultural survival. Publisher of *Congress Monthly* and *Judaism* magazines.

AMERICAN ZIONIST FOUNDATION
110 E. 59th St., New York, NY 10022

The mission of this agency is to educate about Israel and to promote *aliyah*. Through scholar-in-residence programs and resource materials, they reach out to the adult community.

ANTI-DEFAMATION LEAGUE
823 United Nations Plaza, New York, NY 10017

As part of its work in the fields of prejudice reduction and justice for all citizens of their countries, ADL publishes an extensive collection of books, pamphlets, and audiovisual materials for use by adults who want to expand their knowledge of these issues. Publisher of *Dimensions*.

B'NAI B'RITH
1640 Rhode Island Ave. N.W.
Washington, DC 20036

Offers programs designed to expand and ensure the preservation of the Jewish community in the U.S. and in over 45 other countries. They provide a series of texts for use in adult study groups. Publisher of *International Jewish Monthly*.

CLAL — NATIONAL JEWISH CENTER FOR LEARNING AND LEADERSHIP
47 W. 34th St., 2nd Floor, New York, NY 10021

Prepares materials to enable leaders of the Jewish community to respond to the issues facing American Jewry and Israel. In addition to print materials, lectures are available on audiotape. Publisher of *News* and *Perspectives*.

HADASSAH, THE WOMEN'S ZIONIST ORGANIZATION OF AMERICA, INC.
50 W. 58th St., New York, NY 10019

Provides basic Jewish education, supports and interprets Israel, as well as supporting hospitals in Israel and the U.S., Young Judaea and Zionist youth camps. Publisher of *Hadassah Magazine*, *Textures*, and *Bat Kol*, which is focused on adult education guides.

NATIONAL COUNCIL OF JEWISH WOMEN
53 W. 23rd St., New York, NY 10010

Publishes and distributes educational materials in the U.S. on a wide range of topics facing Jewish women today. Acts as an advocate for issues pertaining to women and children.

UNITED SYNAGOGUE OF CONSERVATIVE JUDAISM
Book Service
155 Fifth Ave., New York, NY 10010

Publishes and distributes books and other materials for the Conservative Movement. Adult learning materials are available through its Departments of Education, Synagogue Programming, and Administration. Study guides for adult Jewish groups are available. Publisher of *United Synagogue Review*.

UNION OF AMERICAN HEBREW CONGREGATIONS
UAHC Press
838 Fifth Ave., New York, NY 10021

This publishing arm of the Reform Movement provides books, auidovisual aids, pamphlets, and music, and publishes *Reform Judaism*. The Commission on Jewish Education has a commitment to lifelong learning. Both Women of Reform Judaism and the National Federation of Temple Brotherhoods are sources for study guides on holidays and Jewish observances. (For a listing of publications of the UAHC Committee on Older Adults, write Rabbi Richard F. Address at UAHC, 117 South 17th St., Suite 2111, Philadelphia, PA 19103.)

UNION OF ORTHODOX JEWISH CONGREGATIONS OF AMERICA
333 Seventh Ave., New York, NY 10001

This national center for Orthodox synagogues provides educational materials about Orthodox Judaism and observances through its various departments, such as the Women's Branch or the Institute for Public Affairs. Publisher of *Jewish Action Magazine*.

WOMEN OF REFORM JUDAISM
(formerly National Federation of Temple Sisterhoods)
838 Fifth Ave., New York, NY 10021

Offers study guides for the holidays and other topics, as well as a course called "Bat Kol: Voice of Learning" for individual or group study on many aspects of Judaism.

TEACHING METHODS AND STRATEGIES

CHAPTER THIRTEEN

LISTENING SKILLS, LECTURE, AND DISCUSSION

Audrey Friedman Marcus

One speaker began a lecture by saying to the audience, "I'm here to speak and you're here to listen. I just hope you don't finish before I do!"

As teachers, we have all experienced being tuned out. Our students do this as easily as they flip the TV dial from one channel to another. For this reason, I have chosen to begin this chapter on lecture and discussion techniques with a brief section on the development of good listening skills.

LISTENING SKILLS

Listening, like any other skill, can be taught. Showing students how to be good listeners early in the school year can make the difference between a successful and not so successful teaching experience. Listening practice will result in a higher level of attentiveness and fewer disruptions. Additionally, the quality of your class discussions will dramatically improve as students exercise the important skills of active and sensitive listening.

When asked to describe some rules for good listening, even the youngest children will be able to point out most of the following guidelines, sometimes called Focus Rules:

1. Look at the person speaking; maintain eye contact
2. Be accepting; show with your facial expression and body language that you hear and understand — nod, smile, lean forward, etc.
3. Encourage the speaker; help the person to feel safe and comfortable. Give understanding responses such as "Uh huh" and "Mmmmm."
4. Draw the speaker out. Try to understand his/her point of view. Ask clarifying questions such as, "I understand your position to be . . . " or "I hear you saying . . . " Ask the speaker for additional facts, feelings.
5. Make no judgments or "killer statements" such as, "That's a stupid idea," or worse, "You're stupid."
6. Don't ask manipulating questions such as, "Don't you think that . . . " or "Wouldn't it be better if . . . "
7. Don't steal the focus away from the speaker by saying something like, "Say, a similar thing happened to me, too. One day I was . . . "

Once your students have outlined good listening techniques, provide them with some opportunities to practice the Focus Rules. Divide the group into "Sharing Trios." In each group of three, give each person in turn a chance to speak on an assigned topic or question for three minutes. The other two group members must listen attentively, using the Focus Rules. Time the speakers and inform participants when to switch roles.

After the exercise, ask how many felt that they were really listened to. Find out how many thought that they in turn really gave total attention to others. Discuss how it feels to listen and to be listened to, which they prefer, and why.

Following this debriefing, allow students a chance to give each other positive feedback. They can praise each other for good listening and/or complete such sentences as, "I like it when you said . . ." or "I found you likeable when you said . . ." Young people rarely give each other positive strokes. Often this is because they don't know how. Encourage them to validate each other and each other's views whenever possible.

Students can join Sharing Trios again and again to discuss issues and share viewpoints.

This technique fosters the building of trust and respect and helps you to create a nourishing and pleasant environment in your classroom. Moreover, many children in our Religious Schools seldom have attention focused on them at home or at school even for three minutes. The opportunity to speak and have others listen can go a long way toward strengthening ego and building confidence.

Listening skills can also be taught to young children in Kindergarten and Grades 1 and 2 through the use of a variation on Sharing Trios.[1] Begin in a manner similar to "Show and Tell." Ask one youngster at a time to bring an object from home and talk about it in front of the class. A Jewish ritual object would be ideal. Some children may prefer to speak about something that happened, such as a holiday celebration at home or a visit to grandparents. Draw the "focus child" out, asking clarifying questions to elicit information. Reflect back to the child the feelings you hear him/her express. Ask if the rest of the children in the group have any questions for the focus child. The youngsters, modeling your behavior, will soon find questions to ask. Then say positive things about the focus child, inviting the others to do likewise. All of the children will thus become skilled at giving compliments.

After four or five sessions, children can meet in table groups of 8-9, allowing more of them a chance to be the focus person. Ask for volunteers and move around from group to group to keep things going. Finally, divide the class into groups of 4-5 for listening sessions. (This size group is less threatening to younger children.) Meet as a total group now and then in order to continue to model ways of drawing out a speaker and giving positive feedback. These meetings will also foster group coherence.

There are, of course, many other ways to encourage good listening. There is that wonderful children's game called *Telephone*. A whispered message is passed from one child to the other. The last child to receive it states it aloud. The final statement is then compared to the original message. In a variation of *Telephone*,[2] children sit in a circle. The starter has two small objects — a piece of chalk and an eraser will do. He or she passes the first object *to the right*, saying, "I found a *dreidle*" (or other object or symbol). The second player says, "A what?" The first repeats, "A *dreidle*." The second player starts the second object around *to the left*, saying, "I found a *Kiddush* cup." You can imagine the pandemonium that occurs as the two objects near each other! When one object is returned to the starting player, that child begins again naming a new object.

In a Story Relay,[3] students A, B, and C leave the room. A short story is read to the class. (Of course, tell a Jewish story, or read a paragraph from your textbook.) Then A is called in and asked to listen as someone who heard the story relates it. Following this, B enters and A tells the story to B. Then C enters and B tells it to C. Finally, those who first heard the story determine if the original story was changed as it was passed from one student to another.

Some time ago, Sylvia Porter discussed listening in her nationally syndicated column. She quotes the following suggestions for good listening which were developed by Sperry Corporation. Although these guidelines are geared to improving job performance and money management skills, they are applicable for students as well, providing useful suggestions for listening to lectures and participating in discussions. Your older students can discuss and analyze the Sperry list and make up their own Do's and Don'ts.

DON'T tune out "dry" subjects. Be an opportunist and ask, "What's in it for me?" What you don't ask can hurt you in the long run.

DON'T judge the speaker's delivery. Instead, pay attention to the content. You may not like how your boss talks, but you can learn a lot from what he/she says.

DON'T be argumentative. Stay quiet until you have completely understood what the speaker is really saying. This will give you time to think of constructive comments and to make a positive impression when you do enter the discussion.

DO listen for ideas, not only to facts. If you restrict your attention to facts alone, you may completely miss the point. Not only that, common sense will tell you that at times, facts can be exceedingly deceiving.

DO keep your mind open. Try not to overreact to emotional words or the emotional impact of certain words. Instead concentrate on why your speaker is using them.

DO capitalize on the fact that thought is four times faster than speech. You can use this time to challenge, anticipate, mentally summarize, and listen between the lines to the speaker's tone of voice as well as to what the speaker is saying.

DO, finally, work at listening. The more you exercise your "listening muscles," the better your skills become.

Once students understand the nature of good listening and have ample time to practice their listening skills, you can proceed with confidence to lecture and conduct classroom discussions.

LECTURE

During a lecture, the teacher gives an oral presentation of facts or principles. A lecture is often a useful way to introduce a subject, to cover a lot of material, to reinforce or to expand previous learning. When lecturing, the teacher is the expert, imparting information and wisdom to the students.

Some teachers lecture during every class session and do so successfully. We have all heard charismatic college lecturers, the kind who speak for an hour without a note and who are able to keep listeners wide awake, spellbound, and coming back for more. Most lecturers, however, are not so talented. Lecturing to today's students is particularly difficult because their attention spans are seldom more than twelve minutes long — the time between commercials! Thus, it is imperative that we use lecture infrequently and for brief periods of time and that when we do, we involve our students in an active and enjoyable learning experience. Lectures need not be boring and dry. They can be stimulating, creative, and effective.

The first rule of good lecturing is not surprising — it's that old Boy Scout motto, "Be prepared." The better organized you are, the better your lecture will be. This doesn't mean you need write down every word. If you are confident of the subject and good at extemporaneous speaking, a simple outline will suffice. Some of us do, however, need to write everything out in advance, even though we might glance at it only once or twice during our talk. The main thing is to proceed in the manner that seems most comfortable for you.

The best suggestions I have ever heard for public speaking are these:
Tell them what you are *going* to tell them.
Tell them.
Then tell them what you *told* them.
When you introduce your topic, explain to the students what they will be learning and why it is important. Tell them how long you plan to speak and stick to your estimate. It is worthwhile to find out where students are in relationship to the subject about which you plan to lecture. This can be accomplished by asking a few questions of the group before you begin, or by requesting "I Wonder Statements" (see Chapter 18, "Values Clarification").

At the start, give your students a task to do while they listen. You may want to provide them with an outline or fact sheet to follow as you speak. Ask them to take brief notes or to list the two or three most important points you make. Or assign every class member to a "Listening Team." Each of these small groups pays special attention to a particular aspect of your talk, reporting on that area to the rest of the class when the lecture is over.

If you are speaking on a controversial topic, you might label one side of the room "Agree" and the other side "Disagree." Ask students to sit on the side which best reflects their reaction to the views you express as you lecture. Each time an individual changes his or her mind during the talk, he or she moves a chair to the opposite side. As you might guess, this can turn into a very dynamic and rambunctious experience. However, if you know your group and don't overuse the technique, the results can be exciting and different.

> **LECTURE INFREQUENTLY AND FOR BRIEF PERIODS OF TIME.**

Tell your students what you want them to do after the lecture is over, e.g., write a paragraph on . . . , create a situation which . . . , write a short story or poem about . . . , get together with 4-5 others to discuss the subject further, or (for younger students), draw a picture about the lecture. Listeners can also be asked to summarize what they heard by telling the person next to them one thing they learned from the talk.

A good beginning will reward you with the attention of the group. Perhaps you will write a controversial statement on the board to arouse interest and curiosity. A case study, dramatic reading, poem, or recent news item are also good openers.

As you are "telling the group what you are going to tell them," don't try to cover too much material. Two or three important points are sufficient and each of these should be repeated several times. In the column referred to above,

Sylvia Porter cited tests which indicated that after listening to an oral presentation, the average consumer or employee had heard, understood, properly evaluated, and retained only half of what was said. Within 48 hours, this figure slips another 50%. It is likely that retention is even less for students, since the lecture topic may not necessarily be of high interest to them. Merrill Harmin, one of my most creative teachers, reminds us to be brief and succinct when he refers to "lecturettes" instead of lectures.

As you outline each of your major points, thoroughly explain and enlarge upon them. Give concrete examples that are meaningful to the age group you are addressing. Whenever possible use visual aids. This is especially important since some students do not internalize information that is heard unless they see it as well. The use of flat pictures, charts, maps, slides, transparencies on an overhead projector, portions of a video, the blackboard, and newsprint will help every type of learner to learn and will keep student attention focused on the subject.

Move around during your lectures. Be warm and friendly and enthusiastic about your topic. Show your emotions and demonstrate a high level of involvement. Emphasize important points with your voice, your facial expressions and with gestures. Look up often, making eye contact and connecting with your students. The occasional use of humor can relieve tension, refocus attention, and create a mutual bond.[4] Lecture in as informal a manner as possible, encouraging students to ask questions during the presentations. Pause frequently to ask questions of the students and to check out the reactions of the group. During such lectures, students are not passive listeners; they are involved and active participants.

Conclude your lecture by summarizing. In other words, tell the group what you told them. You might want to leave them with a quotation, or a problem to think about, or a question.

These simple guidelines can help you to lecture in an effective and creative way, avoiding the pitfalls that may lead to student boredom and restlessness.

DISCUSSION

Besides lecture, discussion is the method on which teachers rely most frequently. And with good reason. For a lively discussion involves students to the fullest, giving each class member a chance to participate and enabling all present to gain new insights. A very special kind of exhilaration accompanies this kind of interaction. Furthermore, students are learning and practicing a wide variety of intellectual processes as they organize facts, ask penetrating questions, and think reflectively on the relationships between their own ideas, the ideas of others and the realities of the situation.[5] Before considering some suggestions for enlivening classroom discussions, let us look at the different kinds of discussions that exist. In their book *Learning Discussion Skills through Games*, Gene Stanford and Barbara Dodds Stanford have provided us with a useful description of four basic categories of classroom discussion: recitation, inductive questioning, open-ended questions, and problem solving.[6]

Recitation

Recitation serves as a test or review, enabling the teacher to discover what the students know about a subject. The questions asked are usually fact questions and the answers are either correct or incorrect. As a general rule, the teacher stands in front of the whole class and one student answers each question he or she poses. Thus the dialogue is between teacher and student.

Inductive Questioning

The purpose of this second type of discussion is to help students develop a concept. Here, too, there is a right answer and the teacher tries to lead the students to it. This kind of discussion does not test what the students already know. Instead, it leads them to draw conclusions from the information they possess. The teacher, standing in front of the whole class, determines the goal of the discussion and completely structures it.

Open-ended Questions

In this type of discussion, the teacher asks a general question that has no right or wrong answers and students state their opinions. The teacher might ask, "Was Moses justified in killing the Egyptian?" "Would you have joined with the Maccabees in their fight against Antiochus?" "Had you been a Jew in Spain during the fifteenth century, what would have been your response to Christian efforts to convert you?" As students respond to these open-ended questions, they examine their values and opinions as well as those of their classmates. The teacher is the facilitator who keeps this non-directed discussion going, encouraging students to direct their responses to each other. Frequently, students can discuss without raising their hands or being called on. Open-ended questions can be discussed in one large group or in smaller discussion units.

Problem Solving

In a discussion geared to problem solving, the teacher sets the objective for the group. Students attempt to reach the objective by solving the problem or answering the question. This can be done in one large group, but is best accomplished in several smaller ones. The teacher may or may not serve as the discussion leader. However, the group remains free to come up with its own answer or solution and to devise the steps leading to it. Participants share ideas and then reach consensus. This method enables students to synthesize concepts which they have learned. Some examples of problems students might be asked to solve are:

1. Devise a plan to encourage families to observe the Shabbat more fully.
2. Create a ritual for divorce which offers emotional and psychological support in the same way that Jewish mourning rituals do.
3. Decide which of twelve proposed individuals should receive a kidney transplant.
4. Design ten additional commandments suitable for Judaism in the Computer Age.

As you can see, in the first two types of discussions, Recitation and Inductive Questioning, the organization of the discussion and the follow-through are entirely up to the teacher or leader. Thus it is always essential for that person to be very well prepared. Inductive Questioning requires particularly exacting preparation, since the teacher must guide the students toward a particular answer or view. When making your lesson plan, always list in order all of the questions you think you might ask. Practice answering them to see if they can be answered intelligently and what sort of responses you may get. Phrase your questions clearly and keep them short, direct, and concrete. Remember, though, that these are your focus questions.

While they will provide a framework for the discussion, they are not necessarily all-inclusive. Nor are they written in stone. Other excellent questions may suggest themselves during the course of the discussion and digressions based on student responses can be both interesting and meaningful.

Asking good questions is an art. Many teachers rely only on factual questions, overlooking thought provoking higher level questions that involve reasoning. These questions begin with such phrases as "To what extent . . .," " To what degree . . .," "Under what conditions or circumstances . . ." Ask your students to compare, describe, agree or disagree, and summarize. Have them apply the information they have learned to another situation. Personalize the issues, asking hypothetical questions to draw each person into the situation. These might include, "Suppose you had . . . what would you . . . ?" "Assume that you . . . how would you . . . ?" "Pretend you are . . . how will you . . . ?"

Questions such as these involve the more advanced levels of Benjamin S. Bloom's Taxonomy of Educational Objectives, such as interpretation, application, analysis, synthesis, and evaluation. They promote student growth and greatly enrich classroom discussions.[7]

Avoid questions that require only a yes or no answer. These questions often begin with the words "Is . . . " or "Are . . . " Some educators also prefer not to begin questions with "Why," feeling that this word puts students immediately on the defensive.

Ask your questions of the whole class and then choose the person to respond. Otherwise, the entire group besides the individual called upon will tune the question out. Be non-judgmental and try to accept at least a part of every student response.

There is a considerable amount of contemporary educational literature about something called "wait time." This is the amount of silent time a teacher allows to pass while waiting for a student response to a question. Most teachers, it seems, wait as little as one second before repeating or rephrasing the question, asking another student to reply, asking a different question, or answering the question himself/herself. After a student response, most teachers wait only .09 seconds before moving on to another question. Research indicates positive and dramatic results from waiting 3-5 seconds. Students give longer and more thoughtful answers. They exhibit more confidence and fewer of them fail to respond. Answers are more appropriate and children make more inferences from evidence. Additionally, all students, including slower learners, ask more questions and offer more responses.

To determine the length of your own wait time, tape record a class discussion and time the waiting periods which follow your questions. If your wait time is not at least three seconds long, you need to work on extending it. You can train yourself to increase the wait time by counting slowly after you ask each question, "One thousand one, one thousand two, one thousand three."[8] Then learn to wait at least three additional seconds after a student response before commenting on it or asking another question. You might want to suggest a practice session to include role playing for the next in-service training event at your school.

Mary Budd Rowe, who has been researching wait time for a number of years, also recommends the avoidance of positive and negative verbal signals such as, "Isn't it true that . . . ? " and "Don't you think that . . . ?" Another common negative cue she suggests eliminating is the prod, "Think!" Rowe also discourages mimicry, repeating a student's response, and suggests doing away altogether with verbal rewards such as "OK," "Fine," "Good," "Right" and that old standby, "Yes, but," which signifies rejection of a student's ideas. It is also her view that sustained eye contact is not a good idea because it generally favors a small select group of students who are called into action through its use by the teacher.[9]

Not everyone agrees with Rowe, despite her research. Many educators strongly advocate repeating and rephrasing a student's response. They feel that this repetition clarifies and summarizes and that it also demonstrates that the teacher really hears and accepts what is said.[10] Some theorists assert that praise and encouragement offered immediately encourages student participation and reinforces the desire to be actively involved in class discussions. Many recommend the use of nonverbal signals such as eye contact, a wave of the hand, or a nod. Based on an awareness of the alternatives and after some experimentation, you will be able to decide on your own approach, arriving at a procedure that is comfortable for you and for your students.

Open-ended Questioning and Problem Solving discussions are more student centered than Recitation and Inductive Questioning. The flow of communication is circular — among the students, rather than between teacher and student. The teacher acts as a facilitator and resource person, introducing the topic, clarifying issues, involving reluctant youngsters, keeping the discussion focused on the subject, and summarizing the proceedings.

Just as they need to be helped to practice and appreciate good listening, students need to understand and work at good discussion techniques. The book *Learning Discussion Skills through Games* by Stanford and Stanford provides many exercises which give students practice in a sequence of discussion skills that includes getting acquainted, organizing for action, recognizing the value of all contributions, taking responsibility to contribute, responding to other contributions, careful listening to perceive differences and agreements, encouraging contribution rather than argument, learning new roles, and arriving at consensus. This book is highly recommended; the use of the techniques it recommends can lead to greatly improved classroom discussions.

Even if you do not obtain and use the book by the Stanfords, you might wish to ask your students to list some reasons why a discussion fails. Following this, they can outline how to avoid these difficulties. Together, come up with a set of guidelines for good discussions. These can be posted in front of the room and students can also copy them into their notebooks.

Another way to help students understand the discussion process is called the fishbowl method. Divide students into two groups, an inner and an outer circle. Give the inner circle ten minutes to solve a problem or wrestle with an open-ended question. Using the students' own guidelines for good discussions, the participants in the outer circle act as observers and evaluate the discussion. If desired, each observer can be given a particular task. One can determine the role in the discussion of each inner circle participant (e.g., questioner, idea contributor, central-issue guide, arbitrator, good summarizer, independent thinker, etc.). Others can list the outstanding contributions of each group member or observe and report on body language. Still another observer can list the things that group members did that led (or didn't lead) toward the achievement of the purpose of the discussion. When the ten minutes are over, both groups can evaluate the discussion using the data obtained by the observers. Finally, the two groups of students switch roles and the process is repeated.

As stated above, Open-ended Questioning and Problem Solving discussions are most effective in small groups of two, three, four, or six. In these smaller units, students have a greater chance for involvement. There are many ways to arrange small groups. You can ask students to count off or to draw colored or numbered chips from a box. Groups can be chosen by birthdates or by the color of students' eyes or socks. Youngsters can be asked to find two other class members whom they don't know well. During informal educational programs, pass out gumballs in different colors and have participants find their partners by the color of their tongues! Students themselves can think of other original ways to make group assignments.

Once the small groups are formed, you might wish to start things off by giving students a few moments to think about the question or problem. Or you can ask each small group to whip around the circle, giving each group member a chance to make one initial comment about the subject. Groups then proceed to discuss the issue informally until the time limit is over.[11] You can move from group to group, helping as needed. The class might have to establish some procedures for coping with noise, such as holding up hands to signify that the noise level is too high, or arranging for low music to play in the background.

Don't allow the discussions to continue for too long a time. It is better to stop with some questions still unanswered and students still eager for more. Vary the procedure for reporting the results of the small groups. Call on one person from each group or invite general comments from anyone who wishes to respond. Groups can make a collage describing their discussion or they can post their findings on a chart. Two small groups can be asked to join each other to share ideas.

CONCLUSION

With practice, your students will become good listeners. And, if you follow some of the suggestions outlined in this chapter, you will improve your skills as a lecturer. Likewise, as they become more competent, your students will increasingly enjoy and benefit from classroom discussions. Each of these techniques will augment your repertoire of teaching strategies, as well as and enrich your students' Religious School experience.

Audrey Friedman Marcus received her Masters Degree in Jewish Education from the Rhea Hirsch School of Education of Hebrew Union College-Jewish Institute of Religion in Los Angeles. She studied values clarification under the tutelage of its creators, Sidney Simon and Howard Kirschenbaum, and Confluent Education with George Brown.

NOTES

1. Saville Sax and Sandra Hollander, *Reality Games* (New York: Popular Library, 1972), pp. 176-177.
2. *Learning*, December 1979, p. 14.
3. Ibid., p. 20.
4. Robert L. Gilstrap and William R. Martin, *Current Strategies for Teachers: A Resource for Personalizing Instruction* (Santa Monica: Goodyear Publishing Co., Inc., 1975), p. 9.
5. Ibid., p. 18.
6. Gene Stanford and Barbara Dodds Stanford, *Learning Discussion Skills through Games* (New York: Citation Press, 1969), pp.10-13.
7. Naomi F. Faust, "Handling Youth through Questioning," *Discipline and the Classroom Teacher* (Port Washington: Kennikas Press, 1977), pp. 110-115.
8. Craig Pearson, "Can You Keep Quiet for Three Seconds?" *Learning,* February 1980, p. 41.
9. Ibid., pp. 42-43.
10. Harry V. Scott, "Conducting Classroom Discussions: Some Useful Competencies," *Kappa Delta Pi Record* (April 1974), p. 103.
11. Louis E. Raths, Merrill Harmin, and Sidney B. Simon, *Values and Teaching: Working With Values in the Classroom* (Columbus, OH: Charles E. Merrill Publishing Company, 1978), p. 134.

BIBLIOGRAPHY

Books and Articles

Brooks, Jacqueline Grennon, and Martin G. Brooks. *In Search of Meaning: The Case for Constructivist Classrooms*. Alexandria, VA: ASCD, 1993.

Dillon, J. T. *The Practice of Questioning*. New York: Routledge, 1990.

———. *Questioning and Teaching*. New York: Teachers College Press, Columbia University, 1988.

Gourley, T.J., and C.S. Micklus. *Problems, Problems, Problems: Discussion and Activities To Enhance Creativity*. Glassboro, NJ: Creative Publications, 1982.

Griggs, Donald L. *Teaching Teachers To Teach*. Nashville, TN: Abingdon, 1982.

Harmin, Merrill. *Inspiring Active Learning: A Handbook for Teachers*. Alexandria, VA: ASCD, 1994.

Heimlich, Joan E., and S.D. Pittelman. *Semantic Mapping: Classroom Applications*. Newark, DE: International Reading Association, 1988.

Raths, Louis, et al. *Teaching for Thinking: Theory, Strategies and Activities for the Classroom*. 2d ed. New York: Teachers College Press, Columbia University, 1986.

Sanders, Norris M. *Classroom Questions: What Kinds?* New York: Harper & Row, 1966.

Schrank, Jeffrey. *Teaching Human Beings: 101 Subversive Activities for the Classroom*. Boston, MA: Beacon Press, 1972.

Stanford, Gene, and Barbara Dodds Stanford. *Learning Discussion Skills through Games*. New York: Citation Press, 1969.

Weissglass, Julian. "Constructivist Listening for Empowerment and Change." *Education Forum* 54: 351-70, Summer 1990.

Video

Teaching Skills for the Jewish Classroom: The Art and Science of Questioning. 52 min. Los Angeles: Rhea Hirsch School of Hebrew Union College-Jewish Institute of Religion, n.d.

CHAPTER FOURTEEN

COOPERATIVE OR COLLABORATIVE LEARNING

Carol K. Ingall

Cooperative learning is more than the latest fad to sweep secular education, or a panacea to cure the moral rot that has corroded the American body politic. It is a truly Jewish way of teaching our children. Cooperative learning builds group skills while stressing individual accountability. In addition to acquiring these important social skills, children in cooperative classrooms learn as much, or more, than in traditional classrooms.

Although cooperative learning has been around since the days of Colonel Francis Parker in the 1890s, it has captured the public imagination since the early 1980s. Its advocates see cooperative learning as an antidote to the rampant "me-firstism" of the yuppie decade, a form of moral education that creates a first-hand experience with democracy. The Attleboro, Massachusetts public schools are so convinced of the efficacy of cooperative learning, they have mandated its application for twenty percent of each teacher's instructional time.

Detractors see cooperative learning as yet another fad. They raise concerns for the gifted child, the loner who is uncomfortable in group situations, the suitability of all subjects to cooperative learning techniques, the necessity of retraining of teachers in the technique, and the potential of sacrificing skills to content. Should the group rewards in cooperative learning be extrinsic ones, like bonus points or prizes, or intrinsic? Is cooperative learning a set of techniques or a philosophy of living?

This chapter will address these questions by reviewing the current literature in the field. It will also provide readers with *tachlis* — examples of how cooperative learning can be applied to the curriculum of the Jewish school.

WHAT IS COOPERATIVE LEARNING?

Let's begin with a definition of cooperative learning. You have been teaching using groups for years. Students in Jewish history work on group reports; you divide your Hebrew language students into slow and bright groups. This is cooperative learning, right? Wrong.

One of the hallmarks of cooperative learning is positive interdependence. Positive interdependence means the creation of a "we" instead of a "me" atmosphere. The atmosphere can be created by establishing mutual goals. An example of a mutual goal is that all students must learn a given amount of material (e.g., ten vocabulary words from *Parshah Toldot*) and see to it that *all* members of the group have mastered the material.

A second example of the creation of positive interdependence is the introduction of joint rewards. For example, if each person scores above 70% on a quiz based on the vocabulary in *Toldot*, each member of the group will receive five bonus points.

A third method of effecting positive interdependence is for the teacher to limit materials and information. By sharing resources, students have to depend on each other. The students working on a biography of Herzl would turn in *one* report. Each member of the group might have been assigned a specific role: one to research Herzl's life and work before his "conversion" to Zionism, a second to study the impact of the Dreyfus Affair on the young journalist, a third to deal with Herzl's efforts in setting up the Zionist Congress. Students might be assigned one copy of a text to interpret, forcing them to sit "eye-to-eye and knee-to-knee."

A fourth method of fostering positive interdependence is to assign roles to students in the group. Thus in the *Toldot* vocabulary example, one student might be responsible for teaching the English translation of the words, a second for teaching the Hebrew spelling, and a third for conducting the practice drills and checking the completed work.

Another characteristic of cooperative learning is individual accountability. There are no "hitchhikers" in cooperative learning groups. Not only does each student have an integral role, but each student must also show mastery over the entire body of material. Our Herzl project would not be completed by the students working on their discrete assignments, binding them together, and turning in their project. In addition, each student would be responsible for sharing her area of expertise with the other members of the group. To assure individual accountability, the teacher might give each group member individual exams, or the teacher might randomly select one member of the group to summarize for the entire group. (Of course, the group would be given time to prepare for this method of evaluation.)

A third characteristic of cooperative learning is building social skills. Cooperative learning groups may be somewhat noisy. They should be. There is a lot of face-to-face interaction going on. Students are summarizing for each other, quizzing one another, explaining material to each other. Sounds familiar? This aspect of cooperative learning is old-fashioned *hevrusah* learning. In *yeshivot*, *hevrusah*, or learning with a partner, is the norm. For hundreds of years, Jews have been explicating their texts with study partners. The exchange of divergent views, the "ownership" of a text gained through teaching it to another, and the bonus of camaraderie are easily transplanted from the *bayt midrash* to the secular or religious school.

Cooperative learning differs from *hevrusah* in that the teacher has a responsibility for teaching the social skills needed for collaboration. Cooperative learning practitioners must address the questions of teaching how to develop leadership, how to make effective decisions, and how to resolve conflicts.

A fourth characteristic of cooperative learning is group processing. Students must have the opportunity and know-how to assess how well they and their groups are functioning. This aspect, although critical to the cooperative learning experience, is most often lacking. The groups can process their effectiveness individually through self-assessment forms turned into the teacher immediately after the experience or through student journals. The group can evaluate itself. One member can serve as evaluator, giving his/her report as to how many times each member participated, whether or not members added their remarks onto those of previous speakers, or noting "put-up's" instead of "put-down's." A further method of group processing is to have the teacher circulate with a checklist while the groups are working. She can then report on her findings to the class. Still another method is to review the group processing with the entire class. The teacher would pose the Ed Koch question, "How are we doing?" and facilitate a class-wide assessment.

A warning: this group processing is one of the most valuable aspects of cooperative learning, one which is usually sacrificed in the interests of time. Bypass it at your own peril. You lose the community building which is so valuable, particularly in Jewish schools, and you run the risk of having your cooperative learning experience become routine group work.

By now you should have the idea. Cooperative learning moves the locus of authority from the teacher to the students. Practitioners call this "student as worker; teacher as coach." The teacher is no longer the showman or actress, but the facilitator. The heavy duty work is done before class: creating the groups, assigning the roles, structuring the materials to provide positive interdependence, deciding how to insure individual accountability, determining which social skills would be taught as well as how to encourage and assess them, and finally, building group processing into your lessons. Needless to say, you have to determine what aspects of your curriculum are amenable to cooperative learning. Don't overdo it; it is but one arrow in your quiver of strategies. Lecture has its place, as does individualized activities, and healthy competition.

A REVIEW OF THE CURRENT LITERATURE

Among the original gurus of cooperative learning were David Johnson and Roger Johnson. They popularized the concept through workshops given for the Association of Supervision and Curriculum Development, by their contributions to the literature, and through their Minnesota center. They helped create the vocabulary that characterizes cooperative learning, such as positive interdependence, individual accountability, shared leadership, emphasis on task, and maintenance[1] — all of which describe learning "eye-to-eye and knee-to-knee." Their bias was a social one: cooperative learning was good for what ailed democracy. Social skills could not be assumed by the teacher; they had to be taught.

Robert Slavin of Johns Hopkins University came to cooperative learning from a different perspective. Originally interested in mainstreaming learning disabled students, his concern was achievement rather than community building. He writes: "Once thought of primarily as social methods directed at social goals, certain forms of cooperative learning are considerably more effective than traditional methods in increasing basic achievement outcomes, including performance on standardized tests of math, reading and language."[2] Unlike the Johnsons, who advocate cooperative learning for both the three R's and interpretive realms, Slavin concentrates on the three R's. Like most of the advocates of cooperative learning, Slavin insists on heterogeneity in grouping. He is opposed to ability or homogeneous grouping for pragmatic reasons: it doesn't work, even though teachers seem to feel that it does. "It is surprising to see how unequivocally the research evidence refutes the assertion that ability-grouped class assignment can increase student achievement in elementary schools."[3]

Alfie Kohn has challenged Slavin's assumptions and techniques. Like the Johnsons, Kohn is more concerned with a philosophy of living rather than a set of techniques. Kohn criticizes Slavin for his team-centered learning modalities, all of which use group rewards, or as Kohn would say, grade grubbing. He feels that using group rewards has a hidden cost: a diminution of creativity. Trophy-chasing is unnecessary; the process is itself the prize.[4]

A recent newcomer to the debate is John Myers. Writing in *Cooperative Learning*, Myers raises a semantic question. He asks us to differentiate between cooperative learning a la Slavin and collaborative learning a la Kohn/Johnsons. The former is concerned with techniques, product, and transmission; the latter with a *Weltanschauung*: process and transformation. Preferring the British nomenclature of collaborative learning to differentiate the transformational from the transmissional, Myers is an advocate of collaborative learning. He says: "I contend that the dispute is not about research, but more about the morality of what *should* happen in schools."[5]

APPLICATIONS FOR JEWISH SCHOOLS

If you wish to apply cooperative or collaborative learning techniques to your classroom, reflect on the following questions:[6]
1. What do I want my students to know and be able to do? How will I know? What will I measure? Is there a balance between social skills and content skills?
2. Is this task appropriate for cooperative or collaborative learning? Have I built in positive interdependence and individual accountability?
3. Have I clearly defined the criteria for success for the students and for myself?
4. Have I built in time for group processing?

Start modestly. Your groups should consist of no more than three or four students. Watch for a heterogeneous mix; consider ability, cliques, neighborhoods and gender — then mix them accordingly. Spend about twenty minutes on the first project.

If you want to practice before committing yourself to a long-term experience, you might want to try Think-Pair-Share. Ask a question that requires a thoughtful opinion, not one for which there is a right or wrong answer. For example, "Why has Chanukah, a minor Jewish holiday, become so important in the United States?" Give students a minute or so to ponder, then ask them to jot down their thoughts. (They may decide it's the American love of the underdog, the similarity of the American Revolution to the Hasmonean Rebellion, or just the proximity of Christmas.) Then give students a few minutes to share their ideas with a partner, pool them, and come up with an answer each pair agrees to. The teacher can then call on the pairs to share their conclusions with the entire class. Think-Pair-Share guarantees reflection and participation. You can graft processing onto this technique by asking students what new insight they gained by working with a partner or how they resolved conflict in their dyads. Think-Pair-Share can be used in any part of the curriculum that requires interpretation: *Chumash*, Hebrew literature, *mitzvot* or values, Jewish history, or current events.

Another task which builds consensus is to have students analyze a Jewish text using the following questions:
1. What does the text say?
2. What does the text mean?
3. What does the text mean to me?
4. What word or phrase is central to the understanding of the text? Why?

"Jigsaw" is a technique developed by Elliot Aronson. The Herzl project described earlier in this article is an example of adapting "Jigsaw" to the study of Jewish history. In "Jigsaw," students are assigned to four to six member teams to work on academic material that has been broken down into sections. For example, Sukkot might be broken down into the laws of building a *sukkah*, *ushpizin*, biblical references to Sukkot, *berachot*, traditional Ashkenazi and Sephardi foods eaten on the holiday. Each team member is assigned one of the five areas in which to gain expertise. If there are 25 students in the class, there would be five teams each having a *sukkah*, *ushpizin*, Bible, *berachot*, and foods expert. Team members would study their materials individually, then meet in "expert groups" to discuss and master their sections. (All five Sukkah experts, the five *ushpizin* experts, etc.) Then all the experts would return to their team to teach their teammates their expertise so that all the material is covered. The teacher could then evaluate each team on their mastery of all the Sukkot material.

Hebrew language teachers may want to experiment with some of Robert Slavin's methods. STAD (Student Teams-Achievement Divisions) works well with subjects for which there are well-defined teaching objectives with single right answers. In STAD, students are put into heterogeneous four-member groups. The teacher presents a lesson frontally, then students work within their teams to make sure that everyone has mastered the material. Each student individually takes a quiz in which they may not help each other.

The teacher compares quiz scores to students' past averages. Then he/she awards points based on the degree to which students can meet or exceed their own past performances. Students receive team scores based *on their individual improvement*. Teams which improve receive certificates or rewards.

By basing team success on individual improvement, students are encouraged to help each other prepare for the quizzes. STAD makes it easy for a weaker student to succeed, since she is competing with herself, not her brighter teammates. The downside of STAD are the objections that Alfie Kohn has raised.

Hebrew language teachers might want to experiment with the writing of a group poem.[7] The following exercise uses groups of four students to create a group poem using a procedure developed by Kenneth Koch in *Wishes, Lies and Dreams*. The Procedure:
1. Assign students to groups of four.
2. Assign roles as follows:
   Director: to get materials and keep track of time
   Facilitator: to make sure everyone's ideas are expressed and listened to.
   Recorder: to make a clear, legible copy of the final version of the poem
   Reporter: to read the poem aloud to the class
3. Have the Director distribute 12 index cards (three per team member) and four felt tip pens, one color for each team member.
4. Show an overhead acetate with the following sentence starters for use in creating the group poem. Explain any unfamiliar words.
5. Ask the students to take a piece of scrap paper and fill in the blanks as best they can, making full sentences. Give them five to seven minutes to complete the assignment. (You can use vocabulary words from your reading series.)
6. Ask students to select their two best lines and write them, one per card, on their two index cards.
7. Explain the roles of the director, facilitator, recorder, and reporter.
8. Go over the instructions for the composition of the group poem:
   a. Each person reads her two cards aloud to the group, translating if necessary.
   b. The group gives feedback after each person shares (words they liked, correcting spelling or grammar).
   c. After all have shared, the team must pick at least one card from each person, decide on the order of the lines to create a good

group poem, and finally, determine a one or two word title for the poem.

The group must agree to use at least one card of each person, to modify the lines only with the consent of the author, to agree on the final product, and to sign the poem with their names. This should take about fifteen minutes.

After each of the recorders copies the poem onto newsprint, the poems should be displayed and then read by the reporters. Any member of the group might be called on for explication. Group processing:
1. Ask the students to reflect on the following questions:
   a. How is writing a poem in a group different from writing a poem alone?
   b. How did I feel about my contribution to the group?
   c. How do I feel about my role within the group?
   d. Were everyone's ideas encouraged and listened to?
   e. What could we do better next time?
2. Give the students time to answer these questions in their groups (four to five minutes).

Whatever models you choose to implement, be sure to keep the groups heterogeneous, and change them every four to five weeks. (Students will work with anyone if they know it won't be forever. During the course of the four or five weeks, they may even learn to respect, if not like, "anyone" very much.) Be sure to encourage group autonomy. Make it a rule: no group can call on the teacher until each person in the group has been asked to answer the question or solve the problem. If you find that certain students tend to dominate the groups, give each member of the groups five poker chips. In order to speak, each member has to ante up a chip. When all five are played, the team member forfeits her right to speak. For a group to complete its tasks, each of the members must play its chips. This system curtails the blabbermouths and encourages the *bayashanim* (shy ones).

Don't forget the encouragement of social skills and group processing. You will find two examples of evaluation instruments in Appendix A and B of this chapter. Please Listen to Me (Appendix A) is for students; the Classroom Observation Chart (Appendix B) is for teachers.

CONCLUSION

As a Jewish educator, I am convinced that collaborative learning, or the Kohn/Johnsons school of cooperative learning, has a great deal to offer Jewish schools. Jews live in community. Public prayer is mandated three times daily. A *minyan* (ten people) is required. We pray using collective language. Our Yom Kippur liturgy intones, "*We* have sinned; *we* have transgressed." Our goal is not individual salvation, but the creation of a holy people. Surely the use of individualization and competition is discordant in a Jewish school; the medium is the message — and collaborative learning is a much more appropriate message.

Shapiro and Ravid studied cooperative learning in Jewish schools. Modifying Slavin's Student Team Achievement Divisions (STAD), they assessed the success of the approach in raising student achievement in Hebrew language and Bible. They also noted a change in attitude toward Jewish education on the part of the students, and a change in attitude toward teaching on the part of the teacher.[8]

As important as the Shapiro-Ravid study is in making a case for cooperative learning in the Jewish school, a more important case can be made. As Jewish life becomes increasingly more fragmented, as secularization and modernity erode the foundations of the Jewish home, the Jewish school is increasingly called upon to recreate the Jewish community. Collaborative learning can foster that community.

Collaborative learning reinforces an essential teaching of Rabbinic Judaism, that "All Jews are responsible for one another." That responsibility is what Ronald Tyrrell noted in his research on cooperative learning. He quotes a teacher who says: "My students worked much better together. There seems to be much more acceptance of each other. They are dealing with what differences there are in a more harmonious way. I hear far fewer put-downs and much more encouraging of each other."[9] What this teacher hears is the sounds of a caring community — the essence of Judaism.

As educators, we have to concern ourselves with community as well as content, method as well as message. Elliot Eisner reminds us that school reform begins with the culture of the school. "How we organize the 'envelope' within teaching and how curricular activities occur also matters. That is, how schools are structured, the kind of values that pervade them, the ways in which roles are defined and assessments are made are a part of the living context in which both teachers and students must function."[10]

In a recent ASCD *Update*, Eisner commented on the purpose of schooling. "I don't think that the major aim of school is to help kids do well in school.... *Schools exist for the kind of life that kids are able to lead outside of schools.*"[11] Using Eisner's definition, collaborative education offers the educator an invaluable resource for the teaching of social responsibility. It is equally as invaluable a resource for Jewish schools.

Collaborative or cooperative learning reminds me of the famous *midrash* about the *lulav* and *etrog*. The injunction comes from Leviticus 23:40, "Take ... a cluster of the four species ...." The Rabbis commented on what this phrase meant. The citron, they said, has fragrance and edible fruit. So the Jewish people has members who study and also do good deeds. The palm has an edible fruit and no fragrance. So the Jewish people has in its midst members who study God's word, but do no good deeds. The myrtle has a fragrance, but no edible fruit. So among the Jewish people are those who do good deeds, but do not study. The willow has neither fruit nor fragrance, like those Jews who neither study nor do good deeds. But God says that in order to make it impossible for the Jewish people to be destroyed, each is bound to the other. Each needs the other. (Adapted from *Pesikta Rabbati* 51:2.) This is the message of collaborative education — that it is imperative for us to create communities that value their members for their contributions and their differences, a message which is Jewish to its very core.

Carol K. Ingall, Ed.D. is an educational consultant for numerous Jewish institutions concerned with curriculum and teaching. These include the Melton Research Center, the United Synagogue Department of Education, the Jewish Museum, and the Commission for Initiatives in Jewish Education.

APPENDIX A
Please Listen to Me

1. How well did I listen to others in my group?

1	2	3	4	5	6
I wasn't listening at all		Sometimes I listened to others			I listen very carefully

   I let others know I was listening by . . .

   I could have been a better listener by . . .

2. How well was I listened to by others in my group?

1	2	3	4	5	6
I wasn't listened to at all		Sometimes I was listened to			My ideas were carefully listened to

   Someone made me feel listened to by . . .

   Someone made me feel I wasn't listened to because they . . .

3. Next time I listen to others I will . . .

APPENDIX B
Classroom Observation Chart

NAMES OF STUDENTS IN GROUP: DATE:

MOVE IN ORDERLY FASHION

STAY ON TASK

HANDS TO SELF

STAY WITH GROUP

Group Cooperative Learning Grade:

Grade Justification:

NOTES

1. David W. Johnson, et al, *Circles of Learning: Cooperation in the Classroom* (Arlington, VA: ASCD, 1984), p. 10.
2. Robert E. Slavin, "Cooperative Learning and the Cooperative School," *Educational Leadership*, November 1987, p. 7.
3. Robert E. Slavin, "Ability Grouping and Student Achievement in Elementary Schools: A Best Evidence Synthesis," *Review of Educational Research*, Fall 1987, p. 307.
4. Alfie Kohn, "Group Grade Grubbing versus Cooperative Learning," *Educational Leadership*, February 1991, pp. 83-87.
5. John Myers, "Cooperative or Collaborative Learning? Towards a Constructive Controversy," *Cooperative Learning*, July 1991, p. 19.
6. Thanks to Amy Gerstein for her help in formulating these questions.
7. This exercise is adapted from "Writing a Group Poem: A Cooperative Learning Lesson in Language Arts" in *Cooperative Learning*, Vol. 11, No. 4, July 1991.
8. Sara S. Shapiro, and Ruth Ravid, "Student Team Learning in Jewish Schools," *Jewish Education*, Spring 1989, pp. 12ff.
9. Ronald Tyrrell, "What Teachers Say about Cooperative Learning," *Middle School Journal*, January 1990, p. 17.
10. Elliot W. Eisner, "What Really Counts in Schools," *Educational Leadership*, February 1991, p. 11.
11. Elliot W. Eisner, "What's the Purpose of School?" ASCD *Update*, December 1990, p. 4.

BIBLIOGRAPHY

Cohen, Elizabeth G., and Joan Benton. "Making Groupwork Work," *American Educator*, Fall 1988, pp. 10ff.

Eisner, Elliot W. "What Really Counts in Schools," *Educational Leadership*, February 1991, pp. 10ff.

———. "What's the Purpose of School?" ASCD *Update*, December 1990, p. 4.

Johnson, David W., et al. *Circles of Learning: Cooperation in the Classroom*. Arlington, VA: ASCD, 1984.

Johnson, David W., and Johnson, Roger T. "What Cooperative Learning Has To Offer the Gifted." *Cooperative Learning*, April 1991, pp. 24-27.

Koch, Kenneth. *Wishes, Lies and Dreams*. New York: HarperCollins, 1980.

Kohn, Alfie. "Don't Spoil the Promise of Cooperative Learning: Response to Slavin." *Educational Leadership*, February 1991, pp. 93-4.

———. "Group Grade Grubbing Versus Cooperative Learning." *Educational Leadership*, February 1991, pp. 83-7.

Myers, John. "Cooperative or Collaborative Learning? Towards a Constructive Controversy." *Cooperative Learning*, July 1991, pp. 19-20.

Schaps, Eric, and Daniel Solomon. "Schools and Classrooms as Caring Communities." *Educational Leadership*, November 1990, pp. 38-42.

Shapiro, Sara S., and Ruth Ravid. "Student Team Learning in Jewish Schools." *Jewish Education*, Spring 1989, pp. 12ff.

Slavin, Robert E. "Ability Grouping and Student Achievement in Elementary Schools: A Best-Evidence Synthesis." *Review of Educational Research*, Fall 1987, pp. 293-336.

———. "Cooperative Learning and the Cooperative School." *Educational Leadership*, November 1987, pp. 7-13.

———. "Synthesis of Research on Cooperative Learning." *Educational Leadership*, February 1991, pp. 71-82.

———. "What Cooperative Learning Has To Offer the Gifted." *Cooperative Learning*, April 1991, pp. 22-3.

Tyrrell, Ronald. "What Teachers Say about Cooperative Learning." *Middle School Journal*, January 1990, pp. 16-19.

CHAPTER FIFTEEN

JEWISH CREATIVE THINKING SKILLS

Robin Eisenberg and Zena W. Sulkes

Students in Jewish schools need new models for exciting educational opportunities. Frequently, the basis for such models can be found in secular education. Adapted and redefined, the models can then be used in Jewish classroom environments. This chapter describes the authors' use of the secular literature related to critical thinking as the basis for what will be called "Jewish Creative Thinking Skills."

The goal of helping students become more effective thinkers is fundamental to American schooling and is not really a new idea. As long ago as 1933, John Dewey discussed the training of students to become reflective thinkers as an important educational objective. The current concern among secular educators and the creation of a wide variety of programs for teaching thinking skills is based upon the growing realization that the level of a country's development depends on the level of intellectual development of its people.

Jean Piaget has written: "The principal goal of education is to create men who are capable of doing new things, not simply of repeating what other generations have done — men who are creative, inventive, and discoverers. The second goal of education is to form minds which can be critical, can verify, and not accept everything they are offered."[1]

We need students who are able consistently and effectively to take intelligent and ethical action to accomplish the tasks society legitimately expects of all its members, and to establish and pursue worthwhile goals of their own choosing. How much the more so is this true in a Jewish context.

Intelligent, ethical action is a result of students having gone through a mental process similar to the following:
1. Clarifying what is to be achieved and why; the criteria and standards to be met and why.
2. Obtaining sufficient valid, relevant, and reliable information to assess the current situation and deciding what, if anything, needs to be done.
3. Analyzing alternative courses of action in terms of feasibility and possible short and long term consequences.
4. Choosing the most appropriate, desirable courses of action after considering what is to be achieved and the well-being of those involved.
5. Making and carrying out the commitment to pursue one or more selected courses of action, evaluate the results and the way they were obtained, and accept and deal with the consequences using the same rational, ethical procedures used to decide on the selected course of action.

MODELS OF CRITICAL THINKING

Several models were studied in the preparation of the Jewish Creative Thinking Skills Model. Those which are considered most significant are reviewed here.

Bloom and Guilford

Bloom and Guilford, in their work of over 25 years ago, were early precursors of the current movement. Each of the lists on the following page contains a variety of thinking skills and behaviors students are to learn. These are the dimensions of the thinking skills sequence.

BLOOM'S TAXONOMY	GUILFORD'S STRUCTURE OF THE INTELLECT
Knowledge	Units
Comprehension	Classes
Application	Relations
Analysis	Systems
Synthesis	Transformations

Cognitive Research Trust Program

The CoRT (Cognitive Research Trust) program, developed by Edward de Bono, is designed for four levels of achievement in the acquisition of thinking skills:

Level One – A general awareness of thinking as a skill. A willingness to "Think" about something. A willingness to explore around a subject. A willingness to listen to others.

Level Two – A more structured approach to thinking, including balance, looking at the consequences of an action or choice, and searching for alternatives.

Level Three – The organization of thinking as a series of steps. A sense of purpose in thinking.

Level Four – Observation and comment on the thinker's own thinking. Designing of thinking tasks and strategies, followed by the carrying out of these tasks.

Analytic and Critical Thinking Program

The Analytic and Critical Thinking Program put out by Midwest Publications offers a sequential plan for instruction in analysis and critical thinking skills. These skills are organized into four basic types — similarity and difference, sequence, classification, and analogy.

Basics

BASICS is a program of thinking strategies selected and organized to advance student achievement in each of the five major types of learning objectives of any curriculum — facts, concepts, principles, attitudes, and skills.

Perkins Model

D.N. Perkins presents still another model for creative thinking. He lists six general principles of creative thinking:[2]
1. Creative thinking involves aesthetic as much as practical standards.
2. Creative thinking depends on attention to purpose as much as to results.
3. Creative thinking depends on mobility more than fluency.
4. Creative thinking depends on working at the edge more than at the center of one's competence.
5. Creative thinking depends as much on being objective as on being subjective.
6. Creative thinking depends on intrinsic, more than extrinsic, motivation.

The more the above six principles guide one's thinking, the more creative this thinking will be. This model is certainly an appropriate way of thinking about the nature of the Jewish mind needed to assure Jewish continuity into the twenty-first century.

Beyer Model

Barry Beyer (1988) developed a scope and sequence for thinking skills instruction. It presents thinking and operations in three levels of complexity, and the model described in this chapter is based upon a similar plan of levels of complexity. Beyer's levels are:

Level One – Thinking strategies that involve problem solving decision making, and conceptualization.

Level Two – Thinking strategies that involve both analysis and evaluation.

Level Three – Information processing skills as the most basic thinking operations.

Summary of Models

A review of the models briefly described above reveals that all are based to some extent on the earlier classic models by Bloom and Guilford. While the CoRT and BASICS models are specifically aimed at achievement, the Midwest Publications program organizes skills into basic types, and the Perkins model is based on six principles that guide one's thinking. Beyer, one of the main proponents of critical thinking, developed a model that presents thinking and operations in three levels of complexity.

THE JEWISH CRITICAL THINKING SKILLS MODEL

The Jewish Critical Thinking Skills model is, like Beyer's, based on levels of complexity. The authors of this chapter suggest that the thinking skills and strategies selected for instruction need to be arranged by grade level and subject area. These skills begin in kindergarten with information processing skills. Problem solving strategies and techniques start in third grade. Critical thinking operations can also begin in third grade. Analysis, synthesis, and evaluation can begin in fifth grade. Decision making strategies are appropriate to begin in the middle school, but this process should be expanded during the high school years. Like Beyer, we have concluded that for classroom instruction in thinking to be productive, scope and sequence guides need to be devised and effective programs should contain sample lesson plans and detailed descriptions of the skills.

A RATIONALE FOR USING JEWISH CREATIVE THINKING SKILLS

Eisenberg and Sulkes utilized components of many of the above models in the creation of a model for teaching Jewish Creative Thinking Skills. Their model incorporates the following educational objectives:

Level I – The student will broaden his/her perceptions and build awareness that Jewish creative thinking can enhance and help develop skills useful for the Jewish and secular world.

The student will also be able to utilize a model that demonstrates the following processing skills using appropriate Jewish content areas: compare, contrast, classify, sequence, and observe.

Level II – Students will be able to identify situations which confront them as Jews and utilize Jewish sources from the past and present to understand these situations. These will then be applied to their own life situations.

Level III – The student will be able to utilize a model that integrates the Jewish and secular world and, using appropriate areas of Jewish content, develop the following information processing skills using appropriate areas of Jewish content: analysis, synthesis, and evaluation.

Level IV – The student will consolidate all previously learned techniques and make decisions and plan a course of action in keeping with Jewish teachings and tradition. This course of action will include the following skills: define goal, identify options, analyze options, rank options, evaluate top options, and choose the best option.

These objectives are planned to be an overlay onto existing curriculum plans and can be meaningfully incorporated into both day school and supplemental school time frames. The program may also serve as the basis for enrichment programming for more able students or as independent units of study. The program ideally should be introduced at the primary grade level and is developmental through high school and adult levels.

Developing Jewish Creative Thinking Skills within our students and in our school programs can be useful in addressing the question "what is missing in our current system?" It provides an answer to our need to challenge our students. It provides for the need to combine the efforts of the home and school. It provides a unique way of looking at traditional Jewish content areas. In addition, it is a model that is applicable to a wide variety of settings and existing curricula.

Why Teach Creative Thinking Skills?

On the following page is a diagram (figure 1) that supports the theory that the family is the setting for human development, while the Jewish school is the setting for cultural transmission. The center section represents those shared values between home and school. The left circle represents nurturing, home, shelter, love, and sense of family belongingness.

The right circle represents cultural transmissions, such as the values of God, Torah, Israel, Identity, Prayer, and how to have Jewish celebrations. It is the area of shared values that is at the core of Jewish education. These include: Jewish self-concept, identity, ethics, holidays, celebrations, life cycle, history, and acts of prayer.

As previously stated, a country's development depends on the level of intellectual development of its people. Likewise, the future of the Jewish people depends on the religious intellectual development of its people.

SKILLS FOR EACH GRADE LEVEL

The chart on page 140 (figure 2) describes the Jewish Creative Thinking Skills at each of the four levels and their grade appropriate content areas.

> **J.C.T.S. IS BASED ON VARIOUS SECULAR MODELS.**

Venn Diagram:
- Left circle: Jewish Family as a setting for development
- Overlap: Shared Values for Jewish Education
- Right circle: Jewish School as setting for cultural transmission

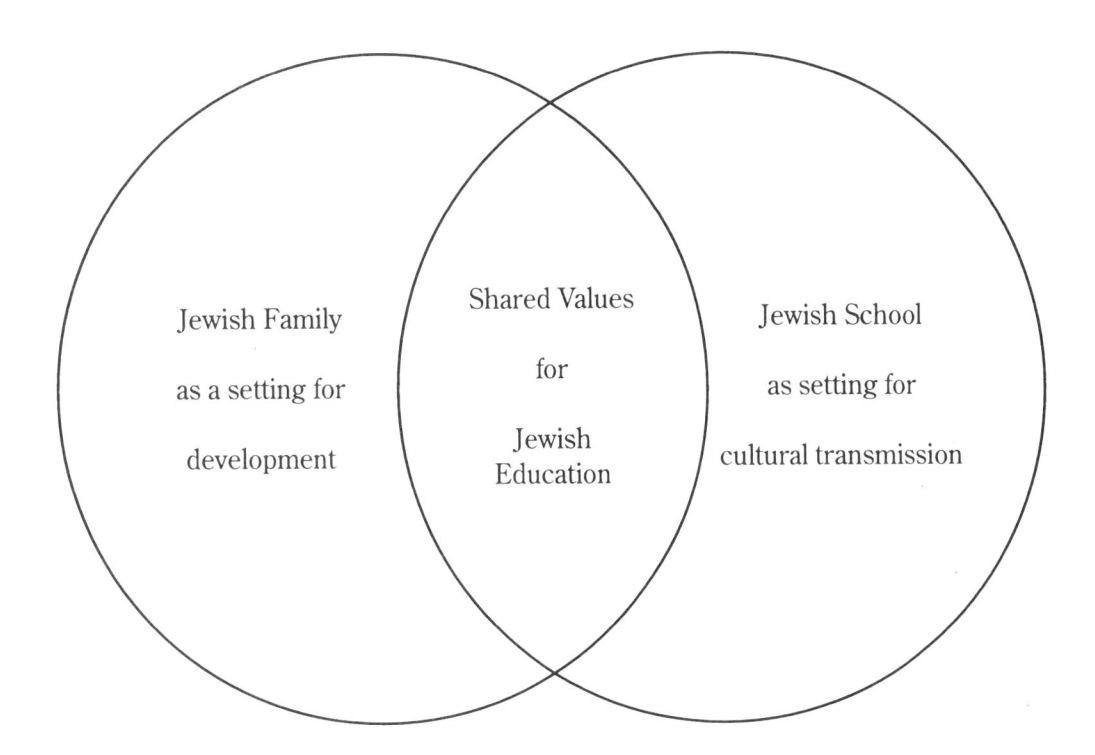

Figure 1

HOW TO ADAPT THE METHODOLOGY
A Variety of Methods

In designing a creative thinking skills program, Jewish educators must consider a number of factors: the characteristics of the learner, the classroom environment, the teacher as facilitator, and the integration of this program into the school curriculum. Considering these variables, the authors suggest a number of modalities for integrating a creative thinking skills program.

1. Use specially created thinking skill sheets to supplement classroom materials. Create sheets using the techniques outlined earlier (compare/contrast, observe, decision making, etc.). These sheets can be either required classroom work or optional. For example, a sheet comparing the jobs of Rabbi, Cantor, and Educator can supplement a unit on the synagogue.

2. Use specially created sheets for enrichment for special needs students. For gifted students, these sheets can provide a more challenging approach to learning. For students with learning disabilities, these materials can provide an alternative to traditional methods. A sheet involving observation skills such as listing the characteristics of a *Havdalah* candle can help a visual learner.

3. Use specially created sheets to "fill time." Also, use them as transition between subjects or as introductory or culmination to lessons. In these cases, sheets relate to subject matter but also stand on their own. The class has been studying *mitzvot*. A sheet can serve as a transition to the study of prayer.

4. Add creative thinking skills as an overlay to a unit or units. Use the model presented earlier in the article to pinpoint specific skills and subject matter which are appropriate for your age group. For example, as an overlay to a unit on Israel for Grade 3, you would use the skills in Levels I and II. In creating your lessons, you would have activities which include classify (on a chart, list products that Israel exports — farming, manufacturing, etc.) and sequence (give students a description of the stages a new immigrant must go through to become a citizen. Have students place them in the the correct order.)

5. Use creative thinking skills as a unit. For example, create a unit for middle school on making decisions Jewishly. This unit would use the decision making process to help students understand the steps needed to make decisions, as well as how Jewish tradition can provide them important information

EISENBERG/SULKES MODEL FOR JEWISH CREATIVE THINKING SKILLS
Grade Levels (Each box contains the appropriate content areas)

Level	Jewish Creative Thinking Skills	Primary (grades K–2)	Intermediate (grades 3–5)	Middle School (grades 6–8)	High School (grades 9–12)
I	Broaden perceptions and build awareness of the usefulness of JCTS in life utilizing processing skills of: compare, contrast, classify, sequence, and osbservation in Jewish contexts.	Holidays/Shabbat; Synagogue/Symbols; Jewish self-concept; Tzedekah; Prayer; Torah; Hebrew; Ethics.	Israel, K'lal Yisrael, History.	Comparative Judaism	Comparative Religion
II	Observe and identify problems and strategies for solving these problems utilizing Jewish values and sources.	not applicable	all content areas above	all content areas above	all content areas above
III	Integrate Jewish and secular life by using information processing skills which include analysis, synthesis, and evaluation.	not applicable	not applicable	all content areas above	all content areas above
IV	Utilize JCTS to make decisions and plan courses of action.	not applicable	not applicable	not applicable	all content areas above

Figure 2

and insight. For example, use Torah portion *Vayishlach* (Genesis 32:4). Why did it become important for Jacob to make peace with Esau? How did he do it? Ask a series of decision making questions: What were Jacob's motives? How did he strategize for success? What was his plan? Does it fit the model for decision making? How can it be applied to the lives of middle school students who are frequently making and abandoning friends or turning away from them?

In an article entitled "Infusing Thinking through Connections" in *Educational Leadership*,[3] Mirman and Tishman give three examples of how to integrate decision making skills. First, the authors speak of making connections to help students understand strategies in terms of subject matter. Secondly, the teachers can find many ways to integrate strategies into the curriculum. Thirdly, the students can transfer creative thinking skills to daily life as well as subject matter.

In the case of the supplementary Religious School, this addresses one of our most basic objectives — making the connection between our classroom and our students' life experience. The use of Jewish creative thinking strategies can bridge this gap.

TEACHER TRAINING FOR JEWISH CREATIVE THINKING SKILLS

It is essential that JCTS model be studied by school staffs. Teacher training in understanding its philosophy and applicability is essential. Once again, secular models are instructive and can be used in Jewish school settings. Most authors and developers of major cognitive curriculum projects agree that direct instruction in thinking skills is imperative. Costa (1985) has argued for the presentation of a staff development matrix for

thinking skills which divide the process into three parts:
1. Teaching for thinking: creating school and classroom conditions conducive to full cognitive development.
2. Teaching of thinking: instructing students in the skills and strategies directly or implementing one or more programs.
3. Teaching about thinking: helping students become aware of their own and others' cognitive processes and their use in real-life situations.

The authors strongly recommend the training of teachers prior to beginning a model for JCTS, and there are five basic understandings that help teachers learn the art of planning appropriate JCTS lessons. These are:
1. Clarifying the Global Concept – What does it mean to think creatively? How can we describe the Jewish Creative Thinker? What skills does he or she possess?
2. Understanding Component Teaching Strategies that Parallel the Values, Processes, and Skills of Jewish Creative Thinking – What are the values that creative thinking presupposes? What are the skills of Jewish Creative Thinking?
3. Seeing a Variety of Ways in which the Various Component Strategies Can Be Used in Classroom Settings – What do creative thinkers do? Why? What do they avoid doing? Why? When can each level of creative thought be fostered? What questions or activities foster it?
4. Getting Experience in Lesson Plan Critique – What are the strengths and weaknesses of this lesson? What Jewish Creative Thinking principles, concepts, or strategies apply to it? What important ideas underlie this lesson? Are they adequately emphasized and explained?
5. Getting Experience in Lesson Plan Remodeling – How can I take full advantage of the strengths of this lesson? How can this material best be used to foster critical insights? Which activities should I drop, use, alter, or expand upon? What should I add to it? How can I best promote genuine and deep understanding of this material?

In order to adapt this methodology to your own school setting, one might view this model as Four (levels of JCTS objectives) by Four (developmental levels) with thirteen areas of content. The four levels of JCTS are designed to be developmental in nature beginning with kindergarten and continuing through high school and adult study levels. They are:
1. Broadening perceptions and building awareness of the usefulness of JCTS in life utilizing processing skills of: compare, contrast, classify, sequence, and observe using Jewish content areas.
2. Observing and identifying problems and strategies for solving them utilizing Jewish values and sources.
3. Integrating Jewish and secular life by using information processing skills which include analysis, synthesis, and evaluation.
4. Utilizing JCTS to make decisions and plan courses of action. These skills include defining goals, identifying options, analyzing options, ranking options, evaluating top options, and choosing the best option.

SAMPLE LESSONS DEMONSTRATE THE MODEL.

We view the above in conjunction with the four developmental levels:
1. Primary Level – this is recommended for grades Kindergarten, Grades 1 and 2.
2. Intermediate Level – this is recommended for Grades 3, 4, and 5.
3. Middle School Level – this is recommended for Grades 6, 7, and 8.
4. High School Level – this is recommended for Grades 9 through 12 and for adult study.

While one can view these areas of skill and developmental levels in relation to many content areas, the authors recommend especially the following categories: Holidays and Shabbat, Synagogue and Symbols, Jewish Self-concept, *Tzedekah*, Prayer, Torah, Hebrew, Ethics, Israel, *K'lal Yisrael*, History, Comparative Judaism, and Comparative Religion.

CURRICULUM PIECES

The following sample lessons will help the reader see JCTS applied in a variety of ways for different developmental levels.

For Primary Level: Sequencing
Purpose

The student will be able to sequence the events and times in a Rabbi's day.

Procedure
1. On chart paper, list several times before school starts in the morning to the starting time of school.
2. Have students list all the things they did before walking into the classroom. (i.e., wake up, shower, breakfast, carpool, etc).
3. Try to list things by approximate time for students to learn the concept of sequencing.
4. Have students complete the worksheet below individually. Check answers as a group and discuss.

Additional Activities
1. A synagogue is more than a building. It is a congregation — a group of people. Have someone come to class and share the "sequence" of your congregation — the story of the history of its existence.
2. Look at a series of synagogue bulletins. Arrange events listed in sequence. Will the list always be the same? Why or why not?

SAMPLE WORKSHEET
Sequencing

The Rabbi is especially busy on Friday evening. Below, write the time that you think each activity might take place. Use these times to write in the blanks: 4:00 p.m. 5:00 p.m. 6:00 p.m. 7:00 p.m. 8:00 p.m. 9:30 p.m.

MEETING _____

GO HOME _____

ONEG SHABBAT _____

COME TO SYNAGOGUE _____

SHABBAT DINNER _____

CONDUCT SERVICE _____

For Primary Level: Comparing
Purpose
The student will compare the words of prayers and circle those in each line which mean the same.

Procedure
1. Bring a number of different children's prayer services to class. Let the students compare these and make a list of the similarities.
2. Do the worksheet together as a class. Talk about each word and then have the students circle the words that have the same meaning.

Additional Activities
1. Teach the class the Shabbat candle lighting and Chanukah candle lighting blessings. Compare the words. List those words that the same in both prayers.
2. List all the times we pray. What makes these times the same?
3. Create a set of prayer vocabulary cards using the words in the worksheet. Write each of the words which mean the same on the opposite sides.

SAMPLE WORKSHEET
Comparing

Circle the two words in each line which mean the same:

BARUCH	PRAISE	BREAD
MELECH	KING	CANDLE
ADONAI	SHALOM	PEACE
ADONAI ECHAD	TODAY	ONE GOD

For Intermediate Level: Classifying
Purpose
The student will classify names from the Torah by placing them in a listing according to the book of Torah in which their name first appears.

Procedure
1. Have students create a list of names of personalities from the Torah with whom they are familiar. Place the list on the chalkboard.
2. Utilizing the worksheet below, have the students compare their list with the list at the top of the worksheet.
3. Give each student or pair of students a Tanach.
4. Encourage students to work either independently or in dyads to place the name of the personality in the correct column.
5. Check the worksheets together and discuss. Why do some books of Torah have more personalities mentioned in them than others? (For example, Leviticus contains laws and injunctions, etc.)

Additional Activities
1. If the students had names on their own list not included in the worksheet, place these in the appropriate column.
2. Have the students brainstorm other ways in which these personalities might have been characterized (i.e., roles — mother, father, son; successful and not successful, etc.).

SAMPLE WORKSHEET
Classifying

Here is a list of personalities from the Torah whom you may recognize: Miriam, Sarah, Isaac, Aaron, Moses, Reuben, Gad, Joshua, Levi, Eleazar, Abraham, Korah, Dathan, Abiram, Ithamar, Rachel, Leah. Place each in the correct book of the Torah below.

GENESIS   EXODUS   LEVITICUS

NUMBERS   DEUTERONOMY

For Middle School Level: Evaluating
Purpose
The students will evaluate statements about each of the four major branches of Judaism.

Procedure
1. Have students make a list of comparisons between the views of the four major branches of Judaism concerning Torah. What are the similarities and differences?
2. Have the students complete the chart [figure 3 below] and discuss its implications.
3. Invite a guest speaker to class to discuss interpretations of Torah.
4. Look at other similarities and differences among the branches of Judaism. Evaluate the different interpretations.

SAMPLE WORKSHEET
Evaluating

Each of the following sentences states something that is not always true. Read the sentences. Then, using resource material, fill in the chart below with the statements that are true for each movement.
1. The laws of Torah have the same origin according to the four major branches of Judaism.
2. Everything in the Torah is of equal importance according to the four major branches of Judaism.
3. All four branches of Judaism teach that the laws of Torah should be adjusted to modern life.

For High School Level: Decision Making
Purpose
To enable students to apply an outline of decision making skills to a Judaic source.

Procedure
1. This lesson begins with a walk through the steps of decision making presented below. Involve students in giving personal examples of each step from their daily lives.
2. Present the worksheet. Have students work independently and discuss their answers and the process they used to reach their conclusions.
3. Present an example from *Vayera* (Genesis 28:16). Do you think Abraham used decision making steps in deciding whether to bargain with God over the lives of the people of Sodom and Gomorrah? Explain your answer. What do we learn from this? In times of high emotion, how can we react rationally?

Additional Activities
1. Find another biblical example of when decision making skills might have been applied (i.e., the binding of Isaac, Noah and the ark,

	Reform	Conservative	Orthodox	Reconstructionist
Origin				
Importance				
Modern view				

Figure 3

etc.). Would the results have been the same had decision making been applied?
2. Find a modern example of a situation in the current news that might be resolved appropriately through the use of the correct process.
3. Discuss how students can apply Jewish decision making to the ethical and moral issues they may face in their lives. You might ask: If you know a friend is taking harmful drugs and his/her parents are unaware of this, should you tell the parents? How do people make a decision concerning donating or receiving human organs?

SAMPLE WORKSHEET: Decision Making

To decide means to make a choice between two or more alternatives. When you are in a situation that calls for a decision, the use of decision making skills will help you choose the best alternative.

You may not realize it, but you make many decisions every day. These decisions are usually easy to make. However, there will be times when you need to make a more difficult decision. At times like this, use the six simple steps of Jewish Creative Thinking Skills to help you make a good decision:
1. State the question.
2. List your goals.
3. List your alternatives.
4. Gather some information.
5. Consider and compare your alternatives.
6. Make your decision.

Follow-up

You can learn from the decision you made by taking the time to determine whether or not your decision was a good one. Ask yourself these questions:
1. Were the results what I expected?
2. What went right?
3. What went wrong?
4. Did I gather enough information?
5. What would I do differently?

SAMPLE WORKSHEET
Using Judaic Sources in Decision Making

Once again in the Torah, we see examples of achievement-oriented stories. One of our *midrashic* tales tells of a Rabbi who in the last days of his life called his students together for his farewell speech. He told them that when he began his Rabbinic career many years earlier, he set as his goal the improvement of the world. Soon he realized that this was a little too ambitious and, as time passed, he limited his goal first to the improvement of his country, then his local community, then his congregation, then his family.

Now, near death, he told his students, "If I could live my life again, I would change the process. I would begin with myself. Once I achieved a degree of personal success, I could help my family and then, increase the goal of service to humanmankind."

Decision Making Questions
1. What does this story say to you about establishing your own goals?
2. Use the decision making steps above and outline the process the Rabbi might have followed in deciding on his goals.

CONCLUSION

The teaching of Jewish Creative Thinking Skills can help to prepare our students for the realities of being Jewish in a Christian society in the twenty-first century. In 1898, Mark Twain wrote an essay printed in Harper's Magazine. In it he commented on the "marvelous fight" of the Jews throughout the ages. He noted the many splendid civilizations which are no more (Egyptian, Babylonia, Persian, Greek, Roman). He concludes by saying, "The Jew saw them all, beat them all, and is now what he always was, exhibiting no decadence, no infirmities of age, no weakening of his parts, no slowing of his energies, no dulling of his alert and aggressive mind."

If today's young Jews are to live up to Twain's assessment, and if we are to assure Jewish continuity, we must train our Jewish students in Jewish Creative Thinking Skills.

Robin Eisenberg is the Director of Education at Temple Beth El in Boca Raton, Florida. She is a Past President of the National Association of Temple Educators, and has contributed material to *Learning Together: A Source Book on Jewish Family Education* (A.R.E.) and *Compass Magazine* (UAHC).

Zena W. Sulkes, Ph.D. serves as Director of Education of Congregation Rodeph Shalom in Philadelphia. She is a Past President of the National Association of Temple Educators, a member-at-large of the CAJE Board, serves on the Editorial Borads of Agenda: Jewish Education, Shofar, and Compass, and is the author of Mitzvah Copy Pak™ and Proud and Jewish (A.R.E.)

NOTES

1. Arthur Costa, *Developing Minds: A Resource Book for Teaching Thinking.* (Alexandria, VA: ASCD, 1989), p. 7.
2 Ibid., Chapter 11.
3. Jill Mirman and Shari Tishman, "Infusing Thinking Through Connections" (*Educational Leadership*, April, 1988).

BIBLIOGRAPHY

Arredondo, Daisy E., and James H. Block. "Recognizing the Connections Between Thinking Skills and Mastery Learning," *Educational Leadership* 47(5), February 1990.

Christie, Janice. *Classroom Activities in Thinking Skills.* Philadelphia: RBS Publications, 1990.

Costa, Arthur. *Developing Minds: A Resource Book for Teaching Thinking.* Alexandria, VA: ASCD, 1985.

Costa, Arthur, and Lawrence Lowery. *Techniques for Teaching Thinking.* Pacific Grove, CA.: Midwest Publications, 1988.

Dacey, John S. *Fundamentals of Creative Thinking.* New York, Lexington Books, 1989.

de Bono, Edward. *CoRT Thinking.* Tarrytown, NY: Pergamon Press, 1987.

Educational Leadership 45(7), April 1988.

Feuerman, Chaim. *Teaching Skillful Thinking.* Brooklyn: Torah Umesorah, 1990.

Forte, Imogene. *Decisions! Decisions! Thinking and Problem-Solving Activities for Primary Grades.* Nashville, TN: Incentive Publications, 1991.

Hawley, Susan H., and Robert C. Hawley. *A Teacher's Handbook of Practical Strategies for Teaching Thinking in the Classroom.* Amherst, MA: Education Research Associates, 1987.

Lipman, Matthew. "Thinking Skills In Religious Education." *Pedagogic Reporter*, Vol. 35, No. 2, March 1984.

Marzano, Robert J., et al. *Dimensions of Thinking: A Framework for Curriculum and Instruction.* Alexandria, VA: ASCD, 1988.

Mirman, Jill, and Shari Tishman. "Infusing Thinking Through Connections." *Educational Leadership*, April 1988.

Norris, Stephen, and Robert Ennis. *Evaluating Critical Thinking.* Pacific Grove, CA: Midwest Publications, 1988.

Paul, Richard. "Socratic Questioning." In *Critical Thinking: What Every Person Needs to Survive in a Rapidly Changing World.* Rohnert Park, CA: Sonoma State University, 1990.

Perkins, D.N. "What Creating Thinking Is." In *Developing Minds: A Resource Book for Teaching Thinking.* Alexandria, VA: ASCD, 1989.

Presseisen, Barbara. *Thinking Skills throughout the Curriculum: A Conceptual Design.* Bloomington, IN: Pi Lambda Theta, Inc., n.d.

Raths, Louis, et al. *Teaching for Thinking: Theory, Strategies and Activities for the Classroom.* 2d ed. New York: Teachers College Press, Columbia University, 1986.

Resnick, Lauren, and Leopold Klopfer, eds. *Toward the Thinking Curriculum: Current Cognitive Research.* Alexandria, VA: ASCD, 1989.

Saphier, Jon; Tom Bigda-Peyton; and Geoff Pierson. *How To Make Decisions That Stay Made.* Alexandria, VA: ASCD, 1989.

Standish, Bob. *I Believe in Unicorns.* Hamilton, IL: Good Apple, Inc. 1979.

Swartz, Robert, and David Perkins. *Teaching Thinking: Issues and Approaches.* Pacific Grove, CA: Midwest Publications, 1988.

CHAPTER SIXTEEN

CLASSROOM LEARNING CENTERS

Audrey Friedman Marcus and Deborah Levy

There are many reasons why classroom learning centers provide an ideal and appropriate method of teaching and learning in a Religious School setting. Here are a few:

1. Learning centers can inspire children to be creative. They offer many opportunities for creative expression.
2. Teaching with learning centers demonstrates awareness that children learn in different ways — some through hearing, others through seeing, still others by doing.
3. Learning centers help children to learn how to make intelligent choices for themselves.
4. Learning centers give children some responsibility for their own learning.
5. Learning centers offer an excellent method for reinforcing learning.
6. Learning centers give students experience working in small groups.
7. Learning centers foster the development of a sense of community in the class.
8. Learning centers enable students to share their work with others and give them a sense of pride in accomplishment.
9. Learning centers combat boredom by offering a variety of learning experiences.
10. Learning centers allow the teacher to act as facilitator instead of being authoritative.
11. Learning centers offer different visual, auditory, and manipulative modalities for learning.

Children learn best by direct involvement, by experiencing. Educators concur that utilization of sensory modalities such as touching, feeling, and manipulating enables students to internalize the concepts being taught and engenders positive attitudes toward school.

WHEN TO USE LEARNING CENTERS

Learning centers may be used in a variety of ways. Some teachers feel comfortable in a totally open setting, using learning centers during all class hours, allowing students to enter the room and settle down at whichever center they choose. In this kind of structure, children are generally permitted to change centers whenever they wish. When using this open system, it is wise to set up some kind of a contract system with students. This assures that there is a plan for learning and also a follow-up to ascertain if students complete the agreed upon work.

A second way to structure learning centers is to make some assignments of centers, still giving the students a degree of choice. Teachers may wish to prescribe particular centers for certain students based on areas in which the students need improvement. Another way of accomplishing this is to use the "Tic-Tac-Toe" form, figure 1 on the next page.[1] Students can do any three activities that make Tic-Tac-Toe, but they must do at least one task with a bold outline. These heavily outlined squares represent cognitive input. The other squares include tasks which are activity-oriented and represent reinforcement and creativity. All nine centers do not have to be set up on the same day; they can be available on one, two, or three different days.

Some teachers do not feel they have the time or the resources to set up centers every week, or they may feel that students tire of centers if they are overused. These teachers prefer to use centers now and then, once a month perhaps, or at the conclusion of a particular unit. Children look forward to "Center Day," often urging teachers to create centers more often. Some schools have instituted "Theme Sundays" or *Shabbatonim* during which centers or stations

PUZZLE CENTER DO SOME PASSOVER PUZZLES	READING CENTER SELECT ONE OR MORE BOOKS ON PASSOVER AND READ THEM.	DISCUSSION JOIN YOUR TEACHER FOR AN INQUIRY LESSON ON PASSOVER
PUPPET CENTER MAKE UP A PUPPET SHOW ABOUT PASSOVER	WORKSHEETS DO THE WORKSHEETS ON PASSOVER FROM *THE JEWISH HOLIDAY COPY PAK 4-6*	FILM CENTER ARRANGE THE PASSOVER SLIDES AND MAKE A SCRIPT FOR A SLIDE/TAPE SHOW
VIDEO WATCH THE VIDEO ON PASSOVER	COOKING CENTER MAKE PASSOVER MATZAH	GAME CENTER PLAY *THE SEDER GAME* THEN MAKE UP YOUR OWN PASSOVER GAME

Figure 1

are employed for all younger students based on a particular theme, such as a holiday or concept.

There are still other ways to structure the use of centers. Centers can be made available when the class first arrives as a way of involving students immediately and of settling them down to work. Centers can be set up permanently in the classroom to be used by youngsters who finish their work quickly. Centers can also provide a reward for good work or good behavior and as an outlet for those diligent students who would rather be involved in an activity than take a break. Centers offer an excellent way to group Hebrew learners.

Another way to structure centers is to schedule a Center Time that lasts anywhere from 45 minutes to one and a half hours. This should follow an opening Class Meeting. Each session can then conclude with a Sharing/Evaluation Period. These three periods are described in greater detail below.

Class Meeting

During the Class Meeting, the teacher meets with the entire group, setting the stage for the activities of the day, discussing the concepts to be learned. The teacher may read a story or play, teach a song, show a video, or play a game. Previous learnings are reviewed and reinforced, and plans are made for activities and celebrations that involve the whole group. It is during this period that the centers for the day are described and explained to the children.

Activity Period

During the Activity Period (which follows the Class Meeting), children work in learning centers. In the centers they complete individual and small group projects. For the most part, children can be allowed a choice of which centers to attend, but some centers should be assigned in order to assure mastery of particular skills and acquisition of specific knowledge. During a two hour session, each child will be able to participate in one to three or four centers offered. (If time allows, popular centers may be repeated in subsequent weeks to give other children a chance to experience them.)

Sharing/Evaluation Period

The third time block of the day is the Sharing/Evaluation Period, which may be called Sharing Time by the children. At this time, students come together again as a total group to share and evaluate the activities and learnings of the day. Students can make "I Learned Statements" or write notes to their parents telling what they accomplished. They may show off to classmates the work which they completed in the centers. It is important to hold a Sharing/Evaluation Period consistently. The knowledge that they will be sharing their work with their peers encourages the children to become more conscientious during the Activity Period. The Sharing/Evaluation Period provides an excellent indication of what students have achieved and learned during the day's lesson. It is also an opportunity for the teacher to look ahead to the next session and develop enthusiasm for the new activities which are planned. The teacher may pass out materials to be sent home and shared with other family members. This Period is also an ideal time to introduce the concept of prayer. Each Sharing/Evaluation Period can conclude with a prayer by the teacher or one of the children.

THE LEARNING ENVIRONMENT

The learning environment is created by the teacher. It can consist of desks or tables in uniform rows and offer little in the way of displays, excitement and challenge, or color. Or, it can reflect a vital and alive scene, an environment which cries out for discovery and participation. It is a good idea to sketch the room and try various arrangements. It may take a while to make it comfortable and well organized for both teacher and students. (For some suggestions on arranging your room, see Chapter 2, "Designs for Jewish Learning Spaces.")

> LEARNING CENTERS DON'T REQUIRE MUCH ROOM.

When beginning to use centers, start slowly, introducing just one or two centers and adding one each week. Have all supporting materials such as worksheets, books, tapes, records, and supplies readily available. Explain the concept of learning centers carefully to the class and be sure they understand how to use them. Role play with the children one particular center and its procedures. Have them act out taking care of the center, cleaning it up, sharing with others, what to do with completed work, etc.

It is not necessary to have a very large classroom or big area for each center. A center can be a table, an inviting place on the floor marked off with an area rug, several desks pushed together, a space in the hall or out of doors, or simply a shelf with a tape recorder and a pad of paper. Sheets of plywood can be hinged with strong tape. A large piece of chipboard standing between two desks creates two center spaces or individual work areas. Corrugated cardboard taped to desks also makes a useful, private study area. Cable spools can easily be turned into tables by sanding and painting. Tri-wall can be used to make displays, tables, bookcases, and storage shelves, as can bricks, boards, or crates.

A Listening Tent, or Listening Center, can be made easily by draping a sheet over a table and placing a tape recorder inside. Students love to crawl in and listen to tapes of songs or prerecorded tapes made by the teacher related to the subject matter. (See below under "Listening/Viewing Center" for more ideas.) Student-made tapes may also be used. Large refrigerator boxes make ideal individual study carrels. These can also be put to use as storage, dividers, display space, thinking centers, and puppet theaters.

To divide the areas from each other — and this is optional — use screens, boxes, area rugs, drapes, egg cartons taped together, or other imaginative creations of teacher and/or students. Try brainstorming to solve this one! It is essential, in any case, to allow space around each work area for moving about. Corners or the floor may be used for Class Meetings, planning, games, reading period, discussions, workshops, the Sharing/Evaluation Period, etc.

Keep your centers neat, attractive, and inviting. Place a title on them so that students understand immediately what each center is all about. Pictures may be used for non-readers. Label the shelves or tabletop spaces where supplies such as crayons, scissors, paper, and glue belong so that students get in the habit of returning all supplies to the proper place. Again, pictures may be used if necessary. Supplies may be kept in one central location for all the centers or may be provided at the particular center where they are needed. Inexpensive shoe bags, divided liquor cartons, tuck top boxes in various sizes, plastic milk cartons cut down and washed, and Pringle potato chip cans provide good ways to store materials. Paper, plastic, or cloth sacks can be tacked to bulletin boards and used to store lightweight supplies and games.

You will want to provide complete instructions for each center activity so that children will be able to work on their own. These may be given orally or recorded on tape for students to play in the center. Or, instructions can be displayed at the center in a variety of attractive ways. Use simple drawings for non-readers (e.g., an ear meaning listen, an eye for look, lips signifying to tell, a pencil indicating to write, and so on).

Games, activities, and worksheets should be self-directing and self-checking whenever possible. This enables children to receive immediate feedback. Furthermore, this eliminates the need for children to ask the teacher whether each completed activity is correct. Some ways to make materials self-checking follow.

Electric Response Board

Figure 2 is a drawing of an electric response board. For easy directions for making this device, consult *The Lively Jewish Classroom: Games and Activities for Learning* by Kopin. (This book contains directions for making over 50 other manipulative games.)

Figure 2

Basic Manual Quiz Board

The basic manual quiz board (figure 3 below) is a non-electric version of the electric response board above. Write questions, words, or pictures one under the other on the left side of a piece of paper or cardboard. Write answers in a different order down the other side. Place a nail or brad next to each question and response or match. Students connect the correct answers to the questions with wool or rubber bands.

To check answers, students place a plastic transparency over the sheet or board. Holes punched in the transparency match the nails or brads and the proper connections are marked by the teacher with a felt pen or china marker.

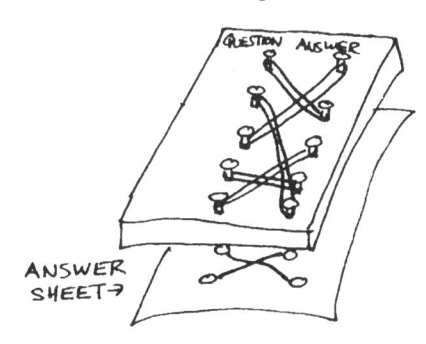

Figure 3

Answer Key

For an answer key (figure 4), write the answers on the back of the game, board, or worksheet. Or, you can write the answers on a separate sheet or card and keep it in an easily accessible file. Students obtain the answer key when they need to check the accuracy of their work. For true-false and multiple choice questions, mark out letters and numbers on the answer key with a china marker. With a damp sponge, students erase the spot they believe corresponds to the correct answer. The right letter or number is revealed, and students know immediately whether or not they answered correctly.

Figure 4

Matching Cards

To make matching cards (figure 5), write a question and answer on a card, one on the left and one on the right. Cut each card apart with a different pattern of zigzag cuts. Only the right answer matches each question.

Figure 5

Series Match

A series match (figure 6) is the same as a matching card above, except that several answers are on each piece of the puzzle.

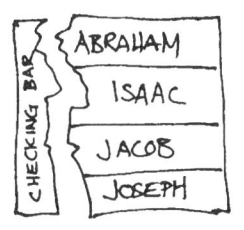

Figure 6

Clothes Pin Wheel

For a clothes pin wheel (figure 7), draw questions or pictures on a round piece of cardboard. Write the corresponding responses on clothespins. Students clip the pins on the cardboard wheel to make a correct match. Using crayon or adhesive dots, color code the clothespins on the reverse side of the wheel to the correct answers.

CHAPTER SIXTEEN 149

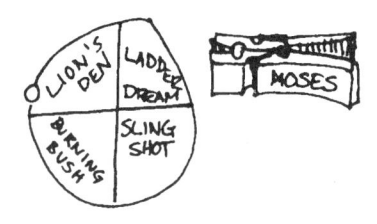

Figure 7

Lift the Flap

When you use the lift the flap technique (figure 8), place the correct answers under a flap of cardboard. Students bend the flap to see if they are right.

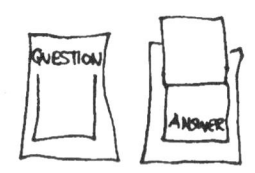

Figure 8

Key Sort

When making a key sort (figure 9), punch a whole under or next to each possible answer. Students place a pencil or golf tee into the hole under the answer they believe is correct. The correct hole is circled or marked on the back.

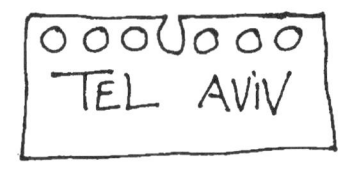

Figure 9

Cellophane Covered Quiz Card

For the cellophane covered quiz card (see figure 10), write questions are written on white 3" x 5" cards in black ink. Write the answers upside down using a yellow felt pen. Each question card is inserted into a small "case" made out of red cellophane or a red transparency. When the card is in the case, only the question will show. A students responds to the question, then slips the card out of the case to see if his/her answer is right.

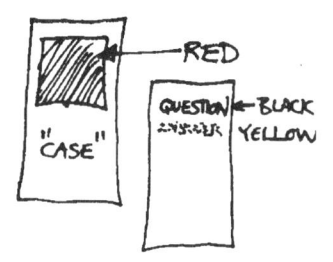

Figure 10

Spin the Wheel

Another way to self-check is by spinning the wheel (see figure 11). Write matching questions and answers in the same position on opposite sides of a round piece of cardboard. Then place the wheel into a manila folder. Fasten these together by inserting a brad through both sides of the folder and the wheel. A slit in one side of the folder reveals the question. A slit in the same position on the other side of the folder reveals the correct answer.

If desired, you can use two wheels and two slits on the same side of a piece of cardboard or a manila folder. Matching questions or pictures can be on the same color background of each of the wheels, thus enabling students to tell if their answers are right.

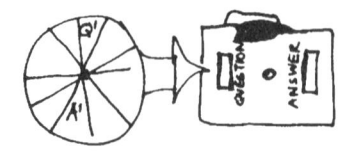

Figure 11

DISPLAYING AND STORING STUDENT WORK

Attractive bulletin boards, a place to display the children's work, and decorated walls near the centers all help to enrich the classroom environment. Student work may be shown off by being tacked on a tower of boxes, on fabric hung between dowels, on a folding screen, or on a large refrigerator box, pinned to a clothesline, or fastened to a large bulletin board. Another way to display student work is by using fishnet. Items can be attached by paper clips opened up into an "S" shape.

Students will need a place to keep their completed work. One easy way to make excellent "cubbies" is to glue Baskin-Robbins ice cream containers on their sides in pyramid shapes (see figure 12). Coffee cans and cereal boxes will also work. Another suggestion is to use tuck top mailers for each child. Still other ways are to use plastic dishpans, orange crates, or divided liquor cartons. Children may keep their stories tacked to a coat hanger with clothespins.

Figure 12

Figure 13

ASSIGNING STUDENTS TO CENTERS

There are many methods of assigning children to centers. Students may be assigned in rotating groups. They may be placed according to diagnosed need. A contract may be developed in which children state their choices, learning methods and the time needed for completion of their work. Or, children may, themselves, make the choice of which centers to work in all or part of the time.

In any event, it is essential to know what the students do each session. You can use a sign-up sheet at each center or place one on the bulletin board or blackboard. Another method is to draw a diagram of the room showing each center and mount it on the bulletin board or on a piece of cork. Children may place a flag with their name on it into the area where they wish to work. A pegboard or board with hooks for namecards or a standard desk chart or library pockets and 3" x 5" cards numbered by centers will also work. Each section of an egg carton can be marked for one center. Youngsters write their names on small scraps of colored paper and place their scrap in the section denoting the center they choose. Another way is for students to make an entry in a "journal" which may be kept in an individual folder. A final suggestion is to draw a caterpillar for each child, adding a ring for each center or task completed as in figure 13.

To regulate the number of youngsters who can be in each center at a time, issue only a certain number of tickets for each center, or have students wear badges which are found in each center. Students can replace badges on hooks when their work is completed. A less complicated method is simply to state that the number of available places at each center are indicated by the number of chairs available there.

RECORD KEEPING

Anecdotal records on each child's progress and participation will be of vital help when going over contracts, when writing evaluations for parents, or when reporting to parents in a conference. It is helpful to keep a 3" x 5" card for each student close at hand (try your pocket). Comments such as, "This is the first day Rebecca read a book about Shabbat, January 29, 1994" are appropriate and helpful. Cards may be kept in a file or placed in each child's individual folder at the end of each session. (For details on Portfolios as a way of keeping track of students' work, see Chapter 40, "Student Assessment: A Rewarding Experience.") Individual conferences with children are also excellent for determining progress and assessing mastery of objectives.

TEACHER'S ROLE

The role of the teacher in a learning center situation is quite different from the role of the teacher in a traditional setting. When learning centers are used, the task of the teacher is threefold: to teach the total class, to teach small groups, and to work with the individual child. Teachers can benefit from the ability to observe and move around the room, helping those students who don't understand directions or who need extra help, praise, or encouragement. It is the teacher who challenges youngsters to attempt more difficult projects, asks stimulating questions, and offers validation.

KINDS OF LEARNING CENTERS

Through the use of multiple modalities, centers reinforce the experiences, concepts, and skills presented at the start of each session. Thus, the purposes of centers are enrichment of specific concepts, development of skills, and/or exploration and discovery. Every center should provide learning alternatives geared to different ability levels, achievement expectations, and interests. This is particularly necessary for multi-age groups. There are primarily two different types of learning centers — Content Centers and Process Centers. Content Centers deal with a specific subject area (e.g., Israel, Heroes and Heroines, Tu B'Shevat, Current Events) or are organized around concepts or themes (e.g., freedom, leadership, *Sh'lom Bayit*). Content Centers can also be organized around a question (e.g., What happened at the Sea of Reeds? Which Jewish heroes/heroines belong in a Jewish Hall of Fame? How is Jewish family life today like or unlike Jewish family life in the Middle Ages?). As in all centers, a variety of learning alternatives and media are offered to enable students to meet the objectives of the particular center.

USE CONTENT CENTERS AND PROCESS CENTERS IN YOUR CLASSROOM.

Content Centers

The following is a list of suggested learning alternatives and resources for a Current Events Center, which is a Content Center. (For other ideas on teaching current events, see Chapter 39, "Teaching Jewish Current Events.")

CURRENT EVENTS CENTER[2]

Suggested Learning Alternatives

1. Examine pictures of newsworthy people who are important in politics, sports, show business, and other areas of endeavor (e.g., the President of Israel, the U.S. Secretary of State, world leaders, athletes, movie stars, etc.). Find these photos in Jewish and secular magazines, and newspapers.
2. Using the pictures, sort them into categories such as sports, politics, military, entertainment.
3. Make up at least one riddle about a person in the news. Put the riddle in the classroom riddle book or on the bulletin board.
4. Look at examples of caricatures and begin your own collection. Start a scrapbook of your classmates' best liked caricatures. Be sure to label each one.
5. Draw a caricature of a person in the news who is important to the Jews. Put the drawing in the caricature pocket in the Classroom Newspaper Learning Center.
6. Listen to the news on TV or radio for one week. Make a list of the major topics discussed each day which are important to Jews. (These need not all be about the Middle East. Such items as helping others, world hunger, poverty, welfare, etc., should also be of interest.)
7. Begin a collection of cartoons about events in the news.
8. Draw cartoons about current events.
9. Begin a scrapbook of news important to you. Include magazine or newspaper clippings or news stories of daily events.
10. Follow the election pools and graph support for the U.S. President/Canadian Prime Minister and other candidates among the general population, among Jews, and among other ethnic and religious groups. Write a news story about which candidate has the greatest Jewish support and why.
11. Examine a newspaper and list all the major sections, such as sports, comics, entertainment, and business. Make a chart or matching game showing each section. Do the Jewish newspapers have these same sections? If so, why? If not, why not?
12. Examine the collection of newspaper clippings and sort these into categories.
13. Interview the editor of the local Jewish newspaper or any other Jewish journalist.
14. Write a letter to the editor, a want ad, a weather report, a sports or news story related to an issue of Jewish importance.
15. Begin a weekly newspaper for the class. Include all the important parts of a paper. Distribute this to parents and other classes.
16. Choose one current event of Jewish interest and collect information about it from as many sources as possible.
17. Plan a radio or TV news broadcast to present to the class on items of Jewish interest. Help plan a daily or weekly news show for the class or the school.
18. Have a panel discussion in front of the class with students taking on the roles of important

anchorpeople, discussing the events and interpreting their significance.

For such a Current Events Center, you will need the following resources and equipment:
1. An attractive sign for the center
2. Many different kinds of newspapers — your local daily newspaper, *The New York Times*, *Wall Street Journal*, *Jewish Week*, *Jerusalem Post*, your local Jewish newspaper, etc.
3. Many different magazines of Jewish interest, such as *Moment*, *Tikkun*, *Lilith*, *Commentary*, *Jewish Current Events*.
4. Radio
5. Video camera
6. Television and VCR
7. Radio and TV schedules
8. Graphs and charts
9. Photographs of people in the news
10. Scrapbooks
11. Newsprint and other supplies for making a newspaper
12. Paper, pencils, typewriters
13. Tape recorder

Process Centers

Process Centers, instead of being geared to subject area and themes, are organized around specific activities, such as listening, discovering, reading, writing, and so on. A brief overview of the kinds of activities that might take place in various Process Centers follows.

Art Center

At this center the children can depict religious ideas and experiences using a variety of media. The emphasis is always on creativity, and children should be encouraged to use and widen their imaginations.

Authors Center

Numerous story starters, writing patterns, blank books, and other similar techniques help children to produce creative writing on Jewish subjects. Children can write or dictate stories, poems, essays, prayers, books, etc. They can work in teams — one child acting as writer, another as illustrator, and a third as editor. They can copy writing done by the teacher or aide. Books written by the children can be bound and typed in duplicate, one for each child to take home and one for the center (and later the school library). Students may also record their books for the Listening/Viewing Center where other children may listen to them.

Since authorship is an important concept in a learning center program, each child should be encouraged to write at least one or two brief compositions. These will give concrete evidence of the content that the child has internalized. Children will also gain confidence in their skills of communication through writing books. They will see themselves as creators of ideas. They will receive practice in basic language skills such as writing, sequencing ideas, using new words, and making clear sentences. In addition, the Authors Center will help children relate to authors or printed books and stories, thus fostering the enjoyment of reading and contributing to the appreciation of books now and as they grow up. (For further ideas on this subject, see Chapter 28, "Creative Writing.")

Cooking Center

In this center children can make traditional holiday, Shabbat, and other Jewish delicacies, as well as Israeli dishes. The final products may be shared during the Sharing/Evaluation Period or at class celebrations.

Dance Center

Children can learn simple Israeli dancing and simple dance movements. (For suggestions on the latter, see Chapter 30, "Creative Movement Activities.")

Discovery Center

This center reinforces use of the sensory-motor modality. Here the children explore, manipulate, and observe new phenomena. Holiday and Shabbat symbols can be placed here with short explanations written about them. A "Feel Box" with Jewish symbols inside may be used. Children reach through a sock, attempting to identify each symbol.

Drama Center

Children have the opportunity to role play, pantomime, improvise, put on skits, and dress up at the Drama Center. (For ideas on this subject, see Chapter 24, "Drama in the Classroom," and Chapter 25, "Theater as an Educational Tool.")

Filmmaking Center

Children make their own slides and filmstrips without a camera. Original sound tracks may be made with a cassette tape recorder.

Flannelboard Center

Children manipulate figures and symbols related to the holidays and symbols being studied, creating stories and explanations about them.

Game Center

Children do worksheets, mazes, and other games which reinforce learning. The games should never be "busy work" or games for the sake of games. Each should help the children to internalize the particular concepts being taught. (For game ideas, see Chapter 17, "Using Games in the Classroom.")

Listening/Viewing Center

Following are some ideas for using a Listening Center.
1. Children can listen to songs, holiday and Shabbat tapes, a story taped by the teacher or classmates.
2. Condense stories from texts, such as *Sidrah Stories: A Torah Companion* by Rosman (UAHC Press).
3. Tape a section of the text, and make a question sheet or a task sheet for students to fill out following their listening.
4. Record a blessing, song you are teaching, a fact to learn.
5. Have students listen to music — Hebrew songs, liturgical music, folksongs, Yiddish songs, modern songs with Jewish implications.
6. One or more students can interview the Rabbi, Director of Education, Synagogue President, Synagogue Board Member, Federation President. Others can then listen to the interview in small groups.
7. Children may listen to taped explanations of symbols made by the teacher.
8. Use a tape recorder for audio-tutorial learning — student listens to a question, then stops the tape, write down the answer.
9. Place on tape information which you have asked the children to research. Some will prefer to listen to the tape rather than read: some poor readers learn better this way.
10. Put the answers to a quiz on tape and have children check their work when finished (could also be a puzzle or such).
11. Language instruction: Use for drill, pronunciation, vocabulary building, practice reading (playing back will give students a real idea of how they sound). Students can record and then let others listen and critique their reading or conversation.
12. Record plays, skits, discussions, and role plays and keep them for future classes as a resource.

Children should be taught to use the equipment in a Listening Center by themselves. A piece of green tape on "go" or "on" and a red piece on "stop" or "off" will help.

Music Center

Original age appropriate songs or existing songs from tapes and CD's can be keyed to each lesson. Each easy-to-sing song should teach some of the important concepts related to the subject matter. Children can also learn traditional *zemirot*, holiday songs, and melodies for *brachot* at this center. (For more music ideas, see Chapter 29, "Music and Jewish Education.")

Nature Center

Here the students can be given an opportunity to study the world of nature, to plant trees or seeds, to take care of their plants or animals, and to learn about ecology and seasonal changes.

Prayer Center

At this center children learn the prayers and blessings said daily, at holiday time, or on Shabbat, plus those blessings associated with particular symbols.

Puppet Center

Children can make puppets or use already made puppets to dramatize stories related to the lessons. Types of puppets can include stick puppets, sock puppets, finger puppets, paper bag puppets, etc. (For ideas on puppet making, see Chapter 26, "Teaching with Puppets.")

Reading Center

Here the children read recreational books, books of information, and books authored by members of the class. They build vocabulary, learn to enjoy reading in a leisurely environment, and do activities which reinforce the concepts being studied. In addition, magazines and newspapers such as *Shofar, Hadassah, Olomeinu,* etc. should be available in this center.

Some suggestions for other centers are: Construction Center, Rhythm Center, Sand Center, Stamps and Coins Center, Let's Find Out Center, Puzzle Center, Picture Center, and Discussion Center.

ONGOING ACTIVITIES

A suggestion for a self-directing and self-correcting activity that will make a real hit with young children is a mock computer in the classroom. Children and teachers make up computer cards with questions and answers on the content of the week. One child enters the computer (a large box) to receive the question card from another child outside the box. The child inside then gives the child outside the proper answer card. A matching number should appear on both the question and answer card.

Another suggestion to enrich your program is to have frequent "Ask the Rabbi" sessions. These can be held in the Rabbi's study or in the classroom. A unique variation is to have a big box in the classroom called "Questions for the Rabbi." Each child is given a chance to address a question about Judaism to the Rabbi and place it in the box. A typed letter addressed to them should be found the following session in answer to their questions.

Use the children's Hebrew names and simple Hebrew words and phrases as frequently as possible — *Ken, Lo, Ayn Li*, etc. Write the Hebrew date on the board each session.

CENTERS FOR OLDER STUDENTS

While centers are most frequently used when teaching elementary school youngsters, students in middle school and junior high also respond well to the use of learning centers. For occasional use, and if prepared in a challenging way and on a more intellectual level, centers can provide a welcome change for this age group.

One creative junior high school teacher successfully adapts mini-courses such as those published by A.R.E. Publishing, Inc. to a learning center setting.

A model lesson plan which provides Task Cards for junior high students can be found in Chapter 18, "Values Clarification." The four activity centers on pages 156 and 157 were designed for an eighth grade classes after several weeks of a mini-course on the Holocaust.

USEFUL HARDWARE

Ideally, classrooms set up for learning centers should have their own cassette tape recorder(s), CD player(s), overhead projector and screen, computer(s), TV and VCR, slide projector, and small filmstrip viewer(s). While this may not be feasible in every school, at the very least the classroom should have easy access to these materials when they are needed.

A camcorder is an excellent teaching tool for students intermediate and older. A Kodak Ektagraphic Visualmaker (a 35 mm. camera on a stand for taking slides from books and maps and charts) also adds a great deal to the media-making potential of the class. Many central agencies have such equipment. Hopefully, your school can afford a few throw-away cameras, now available at a very reasonable cost.

DESIGNING A LEARNING CENTER

Here is a simple seven step method for designing a learning center.

1. Decide on the target age group and whether your center will be a Content Center or a Process Center.
2. Pick a topic — a holiday or a period of Jewish history or other content area, theme, or question.
3. Write an objective or two for your center. Write it in behavioral terms (see Chapter 19, "Planning Lively Lessons"). In other words tell what you want the students to be able to do after they have spent time in the center (to explain, identify, tell, list, compare, draw, etc.).
4. Determine what kinds of activities and learning experiences will enable students to reach the objectives. Include activities at various levels of difficulty and be sure there is diversity in your center.
5. Write down all the supporting materials you will need for your center — books, audiovisual materials, worksheets, etc.
6. Write the instructions for your center. Make them concise and simple and age appropriate.
7. Decide what method of evaluation you will use to determine whether the objectives

Name _____

READING CENTER

Directions: Pick a book or pamphlet that interests you and read as much as you can of it for at least 40 minutes. Then spend 15 minutes answering the questions on this sheet.

1. Which book or pamphlet did you choose? Why did you pick it?
2. Did you think it was well written? Explain.
3. Would you like to finish it? Why or why not?
4. Tell about what you read as if you were talking to a friend and sharing an interesting book.
5. If your reading was a story, with which character in the story did you most closely identify? Why? Write a description of that person.
6. If your reading was a history of the Holocaust, or a pamphlet, list some of the important facts you learned about the Holocaust. Do you think the Holocaust could occur today? Why or why not?
7. Close your eyes and imagine something that involves you happening to one of the characters. Just let your imagination wander and let the event finish before opening your eyes. Tell about what happened. If you read a history, imagine that you were part of an actual event that took place and then describe it.
8. Write any other thoughts and feelings that you have about the reading you did today or about the previous class discussions and activities on the Holocaust.
9. On the back of this sheet, either draw an illustration for the book you read or write a poem, story, or essay about the Holocaust using as the basis something you learned about in your reading today.

Materials Needed:
A variety of history books, pamphlets, and novels about the Holocaust.

Name _____

ART CENTER
Tissue Paper Art

Directions: Cut or tear colored tissue paper. Place it as you wish, making a picture or design on the chip board related to the Holocaust. Then cover with the glue. (Or, put the glue down first, whichever you prefer.)
  When you are finished, please complete the questions and projects on this sheet. Your project should demonstrate your feelings about the Holocaust or reflect some facts which you have learned about it.

1. Is your project abstract or representational? (Abstract is not a pictorial representation. It is not specific, but formless. Representational art is realistic, portraying something as it is.)
2. Describe how you happened to choose this method, how you picked the colors you used, what the colors themselves symbolized, what it felt like to make this picture.
3. How would you explain your picture to a small child?
4. From where do you think the ability to create comes? Explain why you think so.
5. How is it possible that children in such places as Terezin and other concentration camps still drew pictures and wrote poetry?
6. Which is easier for you, expressing yourself in art or in words? Why?
7. Please use the back of this sheet and write a poem, a story, or essay about the Holocaust, using some of the ideas suggested to you by the classroom discussions and activities. In some way, use the image of your picture in the poem or story.

Materials Needed:
Art tissue paper in various colors, chip board, white glue, scissors.

Name _____

VIEWING CENTER

Directions: Watch the video *Act of Faith*. Then, with a partner, answer the following questions:

1. Had you heard about the Danish rescue of the Jews before or was this the first time you learned about it?
2. If you knew about it, how did you first hear about it?
3. If you didn't know about it, why do you think no one ever told you or taught you about it?
4. Why do you think the Danes were the only ones to rescue their entire Jewish population?
5. Why do you think the Church in Denmark spoke out against the Nazis, whereas this did not happen in other countries?
6. If you went to Denmark, how would you want to express your thanks to the people there for what they did during World War II?

By yourself, on another sheet of paper, write a letter to the Danish people expressing how you feel about what they did.

Materials Needed:
Video: *Act of Faith* (Anti-defamation League, 28 min.)

Name _____

LISTENING CENTER

Directions: Listen to the tape, which consists of a panel discussion among several survivors of the Holocaust. When it is finished, answer the questions on this sheet.

1. Which of the stories that you heard interested you most? Why?
2. Some people lost their faith during the Holocaust. Others seemed to gain faith when they had none before. Which do you think is the most logical? How do you think you would have reacted? Why?
3. Do you think it was worth six million lives in order that the Jews have a homeland in Israel or is the price too great, as one of the panelists on the tape asserts? Explain your answer.
4. Do you think God had anything to do with the Holocaust? Explain.
5. Why do you think survivors such as these are willing to talk about their experiences?
6. Do you think we are overly preoccupied with the Holocaust, that we should just forget about it because such a thing will never happen again?
7. On the back of this sheet, write a poem, story, or essay from the point of view of a survivor.

Materials Needed:
A tape recording of a previous program of survivors before group of Junior High students.

have been met. (Some suggestions: model building, dramatizations, creative writing, taped reports, art projects, tests.)

PARENTAL INVOLVEMENT

To succeed with learning centers, parental involvement is essential. The concepts and rituals discussed and experienced in school need follow-up and reinforcement at home. Since this is a direct experience approach to learning which stresses a "hands-on" approach, the children will frequently bring their work home and tell parents about their classroom experiences. For this reason, it is highly advisable to call a meeting of parents to explain the program. An excellent idea would be to have a "mini-class" during which the parent group experiences a Class Meeting, Activity Period, and Sharing/Evaluation Period. In any case, a letter from the teacher(s) should go out to the parents outlining the objectives of the program and the concepts which underlie it, and explaining the materials you will send home and describing the home reinforcement you hope for.

If you can deal comfortably with it, Parent Visitation Days and Open Houses should be scheduled on a regular basis. Parents can look at examples of children's work, see their journals, experience a learning center, helping their children complete a project or activity. Parental volunteers make excellent classroom aides. They can be typists in the Authors Center, monitors in the Listening/Viewing Center, assistants in the Art Center, etc. The children will be very proud to have their parents as part of the program. Parents can also work on special programs and projects such as a Shabbat dinner or classroom *Seder*. They can also be encouraged to donate their "scrounge" for art projects, book covers, and classroom decorations. (For more ways to involve parents in your classroom activities, see Chapter 3, "Parent Involvement.")

AIDES AND TEACHING ASSISTANTS

There is no doubt that extra help will be needed if you are planning to introduce learning centers into your class. High school aides can provide youngsters with good role models of varying ages, and are generally very willing and enthusiastic volunteers. Some suggestions for the use of aides are included here. You and your aide will undoubtedly think of additional ideas.

Aides can:
1. supervise centers.
2. make games and center materials.
3. design and create new centers.
4. play games with students.
5. work with individual students who need extra help or encouragement or attention.
6. take dictation from younger children as a way of writing stories and poems.
7. help bind books.
8. read to students individually or in small groups.
9. keep centers and supply shelves neat and well stocked.
10. help buy and bring supplies.
11. help you plan.
12. explain the use of hardware such as projectors, tape recorders, and CD players to children. Even first graders can use these alone once they understand how.
13. help with evaluation, add their comments to records, report specific difficulties children are having to the teacher, and attend open houses and parent conferences.

(For more creative ways of using teenage aides, see Chapter 32, "Working with Teen Aides.")

CONCLUSION

Certainly learning centers require more work of the teacher than traditional teaching. When using centers, teachers need to plan a choice of many activities each session. They need to be prepared to carry many items back and forth from home and store to synagogue. If your class shares a room with another group, centers have to be dismantled after each session and recreated each week. (One suggestion is to use separate large grocery bags for each center. A stick-on label on the outside of the bag can list all the items needed for that center. Each item may be checked off as it is put into the bag prior to the session.)

Despite the amount of work involved in planning and executing centers, teaching and learning in this kind of environment will add an exciting dimension to your classroom. Learning centers will be well received by your students if you are enthusiastic about them. In such a personalized program, your students will enjoy Jewish learning experiences. Jewish celebrations, symbols, and history will come alive. The youngsters will soon know, even at their young age, why they come to Religious School — to be a part of something very important. They will find their interests enriched and expanded, their intellectual and emotional growth nourished, and their knowledge of Judaism widened in a vibrant and meaningful way.

Audrey Friedman Marcus received her M.A. in Jewish Education from Hebrew Union College-Jewish Institute of Religion. She is Executive Vice President of A.R.E. Publishing, Inc., and the author and editor of teacher manuals, mini-courses, children's books, and articles.

Dr. Deborah Levy served as a Consultant for HEW in Reading and Learning Disabilities for *Encyclopedia Brittanica*'s reading project. Previously Vice Principal of Hillel Community Day School in North Miami Beach, she maintains a private practice as an Educational Diagnostician and Remediator.

NOTES

1. Adapted from a suggestion found in *Teaching Teachers To Teach* by Donald L. Griggs (Livermore: Griggs Educational Service, 1974).
2. Adapted from *One at a Time All at Once: The Creative Teacher's Guide to Individualized Instruction without Anarchy* by J.E. Blackburn and W. Conrad Powell, (p. 68). Copyright © 1976 by Goodyear Publishing Co. Reprinted by permission. (Now published by Scott Foresman & Co.)

BIBLIOGRAPHY

Blackburn, Jack E., and W. Conrad Powell. *One at a Time All at Once: The Creative Teacher's Guide to Individualized Instruction without Anarchy*. Glenview, IL: Scott Foresman & Co., 1976.

Carroll, Jeri. *Learning Centers for Little Kids*. Carthage, IL: Good Apple, 1983.

Classroom Ideas and Activities for Teaching Jewish History. Baltimore: Board of Jewish Education, n.d.

Dunn, Rita S., and Kenneth Kenneth. "Footloose and Free To Learn." *Principal*, January 1991, pp. 34-7

Espinosa, Leonard J., and John E. Morlan. *Preparation of Inexpensive Teaching Materials*. 3d ed. Carthage, IL: Fearon Teaching Aids, 1988.

Griggs, Patricia. *Creative Activities in Church Education*. Nashville, TN: Abingdon, 1982.

Grundleger, Barbara. *Hands On! Teacher-made Games for Jewish Early Childhood Settings*. Denver: A.R.E. Publishing, Inc., 1991.

Holman, Marilyn. *Using Our Senses: Hands-on Activities for the Jewish Classroom*. Denver: A.R.E. Publishing, Inc., 1984.

Kaplan, Sandra, et. al. *Change for Children: Ideas and Activities for Individualizing Learning*. 2d ed. Glenview, IL: Scott Foresman, 1980.

Kopin, Rita. *The Lively Jewish Classroom: Games and Activities for Learning*. Denver: A.R.E. Publishing, Inc., 1980.

Kramer, Shana. *Making Classroom Materials*. Brooklyn: Torah Umesorah, 1989.

Lee, Rachel Gillespie. *Learning Centers for Christian Education*. Valley Forge, PA: Judson Press, 1982.

Marx, Pamela. *Classroom Museums: Touchable Tables for Kids*. Glenview, IL: Goodyear Books, 1992.

Moreland, John, et. al. *Classroom Learning centers*. Carthage, IL: Fearon Teaching Aids, 1973.

Moskowitz, Nachama S. *Games, Games and More Games for the Jewish Classroom*. New York: UAHC Press, 1993.

Pearson, Craig. *Make Your Own Game Workshop*. Carthage, IL: Fearon Teaching Aids, 1982.

Poppe, Carol, and Nancy Van Matre. *Language Arts Learning Centers for the Primary Grades*. Englewood Cliffs, NJ: Prentice-Hall, 1991.

Rappaport, Virginia, and Mary N.S.W. Parker, eds. *Learning Centers: Children on Their Own*. Wheaton, MD: Association for Childhood Education International, n.d.

Simons, Robin. *Recyclopedia*. Boston, MA: Houghton-Mifflin, 1976.

Wierzba, Ellen. "Compass Idea Book." *Compass* 16(2), Winter-Spring, 1984. (A pullout section between pages 16-18).

TEACHING METHODS AND STRATEGIES

CHAPTER SEVENTEEN

USING GAMES IN THE CLASSROOM

Joel Lurie Grishaver

In ancient times, man captured knowledge by playing out magic rituals, telling myths, and by competing in games. In contemporary life, man like his ancestors, will continue to need the playing out of cultural meaning. For man is destined to play with the ideas and the skills of civilization before he can inherit them. As long as civilization incorporates playfulness within its culture, its supporting knowledge and practices will continue to develop. (Mary Reilly)[1]

Sitting in most of our homes is a closet shelf which is stacked full of experiences. Going into it, we can remove a box and find ourselves quickly immersed in becoming an Atlantic City real estate tycoon. Or we can busy ourselves with finding out if Colonel Mustard did it with the lead pipe in the library. Our kitchen and card tables have served as the battle grounds for countless military expeditions, and our living room and bedroom floors provided the foundation for countless quests for fame, money, and happiness. We all share memories of removing cards and game boards from a box and conjuring up an experience for ourselves and a few friends. This is part of both our formative moments and our recreational repertoire.

Board games and card games are part of the American experience. All of us have played *Monopoly, Careers, Candyland, Clue, Scrabble, Old Maid, Master Mind* and a host of other games. Games are a normative social experience. We have filled family evenings and rainy afternoons with them. They have provided common experiences and the means through which we have made friends and extended relationships. They have provided countless learning experiences. Through them we have mastered colors and numbers, we have learned about mortgages and deeds, evolved a sense of logic and entered into a number of worlds and cultures. Games have expanded our imaginations by letting us play and experience roles and situations which our own "real" lives could never provide.

I.

Over the past dozen years, secular educators have begun to understand the value of games as learning experiences. While "hang-man" and the "spelling bee" have been a part of most teacher's bag of tricks since the horn-book days, cards, dice, and game boards have today found their ways into most classrooms. Jewish educators, too, have begun the process of adapting learning games to their own instructional situations. While games offer many advantages in most educational settings, they have many specific advantages which suggest their use by Jewish teachers.

1. Games are fun. Games are highly motivating and provide a relatively painless way of learning facts and drilling skills. Jewish teachers need all the "fun" tools they can amass, especially when these can help them deal successfully with content.
2. Games are social experiences. For many Jewish teachers there is a growing awareness that our classrooms need to engender a sense of community within them. Games provide an educational strategy which allows for the evolution of relationships while dealing with content.
3. Games allow for individualization. Games enable students to master material and demonstrate proficiency at their own level and pace. Games allow teachers to work with many levels within the class through the use of a single tool.
4. Games create realities. As Jewish teachers, we are often called upon to describe

moments or settings which have no concrete reality for our students. The world of the Rabbis, King David's court, and the shtetl are foreign to most of our learners. They aren't part of our cities, our movies, or even, for the most part, our fantasies. Games can build a gestalt, a simulation of these worlds, which can make it possible for our students to experience these situations and settings.

II.

Games are effective teaching and training devices . . . because they are highly motivating and because they communicate very efficiently the concepts and the facts of the subject. They create dramatic representations of serious intellectual and social problems. In games, man can once again play the exciting and dynamic roles he always enjoyed before society became so compartmentalized. (Clark Abt)[2]

Games are educational tools. Teachers can choose to use a blackboard, projector, textbook or handout. They can also choose to use a game. Games can be used in many ways. They can fit the styles of many teachers and classrooms and are appropriate during various stages of the learning process. Let's take a look at some of the ways a game can be utilized.

Let's start at the beginning. Four people are sitting around a board game on a living room floor. The game is about modern Israel, and as they play, the four participants are both "receiving and feeding back" information about modern Israel. The players are being given information about Israel from the game board and from the cards they are receiving as a result of landing on the various squares along the game-trail. As they land on other squares, the players are asked to answer questions or, in other ways, give back information about Israel.

The game is a method of learning. It could come at the beginning of a learning experience. The players could know nothing about Israel and could nonetheless play successfully, because the game is a closed system and in the long run, it provides all the information needed for players to make it to the finish. (Players learn in order to win.) The game could be used in the midst of a learning process. Here, the participants have been exposed to some of the information, but not all of it. Playing the game reinforces some material and introduces other material. Additionally, play provides a framework in which the learner can understand the interaction of many of the individual pieces of information he or she has been given. The game could also come at the end of an instructional process, serving as a final review, culmination, or even examination of the course of study.

But this game is being played in a living room. Let us move it into several classrooms. In the first classroom, the teacher has six copies of the game. They are passed out to groups of 4-6 students. Each group finds its own corner and spends an hour or so playing. At the end of the hour, the teacher gathers the class together and leads a discussion on what has been learned through playing the game.

In a second classroom, the game is found in a learning center. A group of 4 students comes to the center and reads the instructions for the game. They sit down and play, and afterwards complete a worksheet to which the instructions at the center direct them. They pass in the worksheet and check the game off as their choice of task at the Israel Center.

In a third classroom, four students have finished reading Chapter 13 of their Israel textbook and have answered all the questions at the end of the chapter. Now that they have finished their regular work, the teacher sends them to the back of the room and suggests that they play this Israel game.

Let's look at a second game. Imagine any television game show in which providing information is the key to winning. Imagine it as a small group game, played by 2 or 3 students at the back of the room. Imagine it as a learning kit which one student plays against the instructional materials, or against an audio cassette. Imagine it as an all class experience, with teams playing before a studio audience. Imagine it as an all school competition, with a huge assembly and real prizes.[3] Any of these variations can work well.

Let's look at a third model. This time let us start with a classic camp program — The Bible Hunt. Each team is given a Bible and a clue. The clue is from Deuteronomy 27:2 ("You shall set up great stones") and the whole team goes run-

GAMES ARE EDUCATIONAL TOOLS WHICH CAN BE USED IN MANY WAYS.

CHAPTER SEVENTEEN **161**

ning to a new stone wall to find a second clue. Imagine reducing the game to fit in a classroom. (If you don't like the whole team running around, have them appoint one runner.) Then imagine reducing it to a game board, perhaps about the state of Israel, and have a player (or a team of players) throw the dice in order to move from place to place. (If you don't recognize it, this is the game *Clue*.) Then imagine it as a one-student learning kit, with the student trying to beat the clock.

Next, think of giving your students the responsibility of inventing their own games on a subject. You can give them all kinds of restrictions and requirements and they will probably do a better job than we can. Learning games are flexible instructional tools which can be adapted to many settings and many teaching/learning tasks.

III.

Games are a form of poetry. Like poetry they offer the artist's view of the world interpreted through his/her own feelings and experiences. Like poetry, games must have a regular internal structure. There are several different forms this internal structure can take, just as there are several forms of meter and rhyme a poet can choose . . . a game is a cultural reservoir; it continually captures more and more life as it is played. (Bob Parnes)[4]

Today, there are national chains of supermarket sized toy stores. When you walk into them, the first aisle — one whole long wall — is almost always filled with the boxed games. There are literally thousands of games — games adapted from every major movie and television show, games reflecting every dominant cultural issue, and games utilizing every conceivable historical motif. Yet, the more you walk along past this seemingly endless assortment of games, the more you realize that there are really only four or five games which begin to reappear in endless variation, such as cards, *Candyland*, *Monopoly*, *Chess*, and *Pick-up Sticks*.

All card games are concerned with relationships. Whenever we play with cards, we are always matching, comparing, sorting, and ordering. Any time we are playing with a deck of cards, we are always concerned with the relationships between the elements in the card deck.

Let's look at three card games: *Old Maid, Go Fish,* and *Gin*. Each of these three games is concerned with building packs. In *Old Maid,* players draw cards from each other, forming packs of four which are removed from their hand until one player is stuck with the "old maid" – the one card which can't be matched. *Go Fish* is in essence the same card game. Players are concerned with seeing who can amass the greatest number of packs of four. The difference between *Old Maid* and *Go Fish* is actually the difference between just perceiving relationships (*Old Maid*) and projecting them. (In *Go Fish* you must ask for the cards you are missing.) In both *Old Maid* and *Go Fish* every card has only one relationship – it can be part of only one pack.

Gin is also a pack making game, but the relationships are more diverse. Packs can be formed out of the number of a card (all the three's), the numeric sequence (three, four, five . . .) and the suit (hearts). Thus a card can be part of a large number of packs, and the number of relationships which can be perceived or created is far greater.

Now let's turn these three card games into Jewish educational tools. Let's start with games of the *Old Maid* type. The essence of *Old Maid* is forming packs of four, matching things that go together. We could use this model to match Hebrew words built from the same root, famous Jews with the same roles — Prophets, Kings, Judges, Rabbis, types of *traif* food, symbols which go with each Jewish holiday, etc. Let's build a game out of the last suggestion. We are going to take four Jewish symbols for each holiday: For Chanukah we'll use a *chanukiah*, a *dreidle*, a *latke,* and a Maccabee; for Pesach we'll use a *Seder* plate, *matzah*, *charoset*, and *maror*. We will also add the Thanksgiving turkey as the odd card or "old maid."

In designing the game, we now have to make a choice. We can write the name of the holiday on each card (in addition to a picture and the name of the object) and this will tell the player to which pack/holiday the card belongs. Or we can leave the name off, thus forcing the player to define the relationship between objects.

To switch our holiday card deck to a *Go Fish* game, we need to do just two simple things. First, we must remove the Thanksgiving turkey/old maid from the deck, and secondly we must change the rules. This time players must ask for the cards that they need. In a regular *Go Fish* game, players would ask: "Do you have any threes?" In a straight adaption, our students would ask "Got any Chanukah cards?" If we want to make it more complex, we could establish a rule that players must ask for the specific object they want (e.g., "Do you have a menorah?" or "Do you have any *Shelach Manot?*"

Many card games have "wild cards," cards which can be grouped with all packs, or cards which can be grouped with many of the packs. We could easily add wild cards to this deck. A *Kiddush* cup, a set of candlesticks, a *kipah*, etc. which are each part of many of these holidays.

Designing a *Gin*-type game is more complex. Here are two examples. First, a Hebrew-root game. We choose 13 common 3 letter roots. We then conjugate these 13 roots in each of the four present tense forms of *binyan Kal* or *Piel*. For all practical purposes we have a regular 52 card deck in which packs can be made by grouping either common roots or common constructions.

Let us design a second *Gin*-type game. This one will be a deck of Jewish heroes and heroines. The deck will be designed in clusters of four-town patriarchs: Abraham, Isaac, Jacob, and Joseph; four desert personalities: Moses, Aaron, Miriam and Joshua; four Judges; Kings; Prophets; Rabbis; Medieval Commentators; etc. Packs can be made in two ways. Either they can be the clusters of four or they can be chronological sequences which utilize no more than one card from each cluster of four.

Let us look for a moment at some other educational uses of cards. When I cram for an exam, I use flash cards. I make them up by the thousands. By the time I am finished, all the information needed to pass the exam is clustered in hundreds of 3" x 5" cards. I run through them, I stack them in piles. I sort them in groups. I line them up in all kinds of orders and try out all kinds of relationships between them. I practice writing essays by grouping the facts and ideas I will use. I try solving problems by sorting out all the theorems and postulates I will use. I use and reuse the information until I feel that I (1) know the individual elements and (2) can collectively utilize the bulk of material. My own study process has led me to discover two kinds of drill decks: sequence decks and structure decks.

A sequence deck is a deck you put in order. We Jewish educators have to teach many different sequences: services, the *Seder*, holidays, history, etc. A sequence deck gives the learner the elements of a series and asks the learner to supply the order. Rather than working on paper, it lets him/her manipulate and reshuffle.

Sequence decks can also be used in a values clarification kind of process by asking the learner to sort the elements from the "best to the worst" or the "most important to the least important," etc.

Structure decks work in much the same way. I have been utilizing a deck of about 120 famous Jewish personalities which was originally conceived as a sequencing deck. People were asked to put these personalities into a chronological sequence. Over the years lots of other categories have evolved:

    jobs/roles
    doves vs. hawks
    people who lived in periods which were
        good/bad for the Jews
    people who thought Torah was most
        important (or God, or Israel)
        modern/ancient Jews
    people who should be seated together at an
        Israel Bond dinner
    liberals/conservatives
    opposites
    etc.

Each of these structurings of the content gives us a greater insight into the trends, movements, and ongoing concerns of the Jewish experience. The same kind of structure deck can be established for almost any arena of Jewish learning.

Figure 1 on the following page represents the basic gameboard for a board game. It has a start, a finish, and a number of "spaces" in between. This is a *Candyland* Board, a *Parcheesi* board, the *Game of Life*, *Chutes and Ladders*, *Go to the Head of the Class*, and thousands of other board game boards. The object of any of these games is to be the first player to move along the trail or track of the board and reach the finish. While all these games are based on the same format, they differ in the ways the trails are filled in, the "bolt ons" which have been added to the trail, and the rules for movement along the trail.

A trail consists of a progression of spaces between start and finish. These spaces can be

START							FINISH

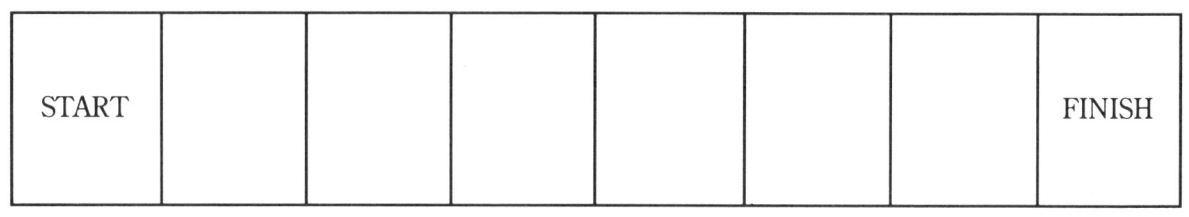

Figure 1

filled in with many different kinds of directions, information, motifs, or tasks. When you land on a space, it can affect your movement — lose 2 turns, advance 3 spaces, etc. When you land on a space, information can be added into the game through the instructions written on the space or through the cards you are told to pick up.

> Your *shtetl* has just had a pogrom. A pogrom is an anti-Semitic riot . . . LOSE 2 TURNS . . .

> It is Shabbat. REST for one turn — no work is permitted on the Sabbath . . .

> *MAZAL TOV!* You have a brand new baby boy. In 8 days he will be circumcised at a Brit Milah. MOVE AHEAD 8 spaces.

When you land on the space, the information and art work can add to the game motif. If your game is designed to represent a community or a period or if it is trying to tell a story, the individual spaces form the elements of these descriptions.

Let's look at some basic Jewish educational formats for "trail games."

The PROGRESSION: A trail provides a logical progression. There are many progressions and sequences in Judaism which we need to teach: the Bible, the prayerbook, the Jewish year, history, etc. It is possible to create a game board which describes the progression and then adds in questions which demand mastery of the progression. This format both provides the content and drills it simultaneously.

THE QUIZ GAME: Here the trail serves as a (1) random question generator, and (2) a score pad. The essence of quiz games is the correct answering of questions. The more questions you answer correctly, the farther along the board you move. This is the *Go to the Head of the Class* format, which is also utilized in the commercial Jewish game *Aliyah*.

THE VALUES GAME: This format uses the metaphor of a board game to create a group process. In these games, most of the spaces require a player to perform a task. These tasks include: value whips, completing sentences, responding to problem situations, participating in role plays, and other group tasks. This basic format can be seen in *The Jewish Values Game*.

The basic difference between *Candyland* and *Monopoly* is what it means to win. In *Candyland* (and all of the above games), you win by being the first one to finish. In *Monopoly, Careers,* and many other board games, you win by being the player who has collected the most money, points, cards, etc. This kind of game tends to be a simulation. Simulation means that the process of playing in some way attempts to simulate a real life experience. For example, in *Monopoly*, the kinds of decisions you must make help you to understand the decisions made by actual real estate tycoons. *Going Up: The Israel Game* and *Expulsion* are both *Monopoly* type games.

A second kind of simulation is called a role playing simulation. Here you not only play at being in a certain situation, but you take on a role and a persona within that situation. Many role playing simulations deal with conventions, meetings, and trials in order to give many players specific roles. *Gestapo: A Learning Experience about the Holocaust* is a commercially available Jewish simulation published by A.R.E.

As we have already seen, board games can be far more complex than card games. Designing a board game means playing with the board, the moving process, the collectible-expandables, and rules. We have already seen that the board can take on a great number of meanings and forms. In addition to those "educational" formats already mentioned, a game board can branch (giving options of trails to follow), it can recycle (you go round and round it), it can have short cuts ("chutes" and "ladders").

In most games, players move with what is called a "randomizer." In plain English this usually means dice or spinners. It can however mean question cards (where you move a specified number of spaces if you answer the question correctly) or other modes. Someone once invented a Purim game in which the players draw lots and I have designed a Chanukah game which utilizes a *dreidle.*

If we go back to *Monopoly,* it is easy to understand what we mean by collectible-expendables. In *Monopoly* we use deeds, money, houses, hotels, chance cards, and community chest cards. These are collected, transformed, and expended in the course of play. Board games can utilize all kinds of ways of feeding in and taking out information, materials, and experiences from the game trail.

When we looked at card games, we said that the essential difference between *Old Maid* and *Go Fish* was the rules. Subtle changes in rules have an ability to affect the playability of a game in a major way. One quick example. Most of our game play has been conditioned by a rule which began in an Indian chase game we know as *Parcheese.* The rule is usually known as "the bump." The rule states that when you land on the same square as another player, you get to send him/her back. In *Alpaim*, the rule has been transformed. It reads, "It is so rare that two Jews have a chance to get together that each of you should be rewarded with another turn."

Chess is the war game par excellence. It is one of thousands which are on the market. War gaming has become almost a cult and games exist for every past and potential battle. Games exist on Iron Age chariot wars in Canaan, on the Sinai campaign, on Golan's tank battles. If such are of interest to you, there is bound to be at least one hobby show in your town which carries the games, magazines, and paraphernalia for war gaming. (If your kids are talking about D. & D. (*Dungeons and Dragons*), it is a fantasy/war game which is a spinoff of the above plus Tolkein).

As you wander along the gaming wall of the toy store/supermarket, you will also notice that about one third of the total games on sale involve not markers, dice, or cards, but physical dexterity. There are endless adaptions of *Pick-up Sticks* and *Tiddlywinks*, etc. Any adaptions you want to make for Jewish education will certainly be original.

IV.

A game is an activity between two or more independent decision makers seeking to achieve their objectives in some limiting context. A more conventional definition would say, a game is a contest with rules played among adversaries trying to win objectives... in some games, players cooperate to achieve a common goal against an obstructing force or natural situation, which is itself not really a player, because it does not have objectives. (Mary Reilly)[5]

Almost every Jewish teacher has confiscated at least one computer game. Today, many of our students regularly play games against computers and television sets and other machines. *Solitaire* is now no longer a lone, single person game. In educational terms, we talk of one person games or tasks as "manipulatives." These learning opportunities are playful, yet they have a predefined goal. The challenge comes from achievement, and completion rather than competition and winning.

Manipulatives offer a large number of educational usages, and there are an infinite number of manipulative formats. In Section III, we discussed flash cards and other kinds of card decks. All of these are manipulatives. However, Montessori, the open classroom, and the use of learning centers have demonstrated a new kind of manipulative — the self-checking manipulative. Self-checking manipulatives are physical study aides which allow students to move things around to get the right answers. Then, after the student has decided upon the right answer, the device informs him/her if the decision was correct. The classic example is the light board. The student touches one wire to a question and a second wire to an answer and the bulb lights up if the match is correct. All kinds of slots, folds, and zig-zag cuts can be used in designing self-checking materials. (See Chapter 16, "Classroom Learning Centers" for examples of ten different ways to make a game or activity self-checking.)

V.

I have found that de-emphasizing the winning and losing aspects of games by creating new games or by changing old games, or by looking at games as interesting models to study, helps students to respond with curiosity rather than competitiveness. They begin to comment on well played games, analyze mistakes, look upon losing as a natural thing to happen in learning something new, They change things around just to see what will happen and don't look upon rules as holy and unalterable. In other words they play and don't merely compete ... It is possible for two people to respect each other's skill, to test themselves and then finish with the game and not consider the outcome a judgment on the moral or intellectual capacities of the winner and loser. (Herbert Kohl)[6]

In this section we will take a look at game design as both an art and a technology.

When I walk through a toy store and am flooded by a million different impulses, I am thinking how this game could be transformed into this topic, how *Chutes and Ladders* could become kosher and *traif*, and so on. It is not so much an analytical insight as it is a moment of awareness. The best way to create games is to know them, to be playing them and looking at them, to be flooding yourself with formats and rule options and all kinds of possibilities. As you do so, you will begin to see how games are transformed and how they reproduce. When you understand that *Parcheesi, Sorry, Chutes and Ladders,* and the *Game of Life* are essentially the same game, it will be much easier to design games.

As a technologist, the process of game design which I use is more systematic:

1. I define the task: At the end of playing this newly designed game _____ number of times, my students who are in grade _____ and who already know _____ about this subject, will be able to demonstrate that they have learned about _____ by _____.

    The final blank space is the key. It must be a behavior I can observe. It could be by "answering 8 out of 10 questions on a quiz," or "listing 32 items on a sheet of paper," or "by drawing a picture, writing a poem, or making a film which shows ... " The key to designing a game is knowing what I expect my learner to be able to do once he/she has played the game.

2. I make a list of the content. I write down all the facts and information – all the issues or concerns – I want the game to cover.

3. I turn my brain loose. The trick is to match the expectations for the game with a game format which will allow the learner to practice the expected outcome of the learning. If I want my students to be able to answer questions, the game should have them answer questions. If I expect them to solve problems, the game should enable them to solve problems, etc.

4. Once I have found a model format for my game, I begin with paper and pencil. No game is ever made in one draft. I begin sketching. I make models of the board, lists of cards. I try to plan everything. I have a basic blueprint of my game long before I ever try to make it.

5. Next it is time for arts and crafts. We use scissors, glue, markers, self-adhesive labels (these are much faster and prettier than drawing in countless game squares), photocopy machines (for making multiple copies), and an almost endless variety of arts and crafts (scrounge) and recycle material. In the Bibliography you'll find several books which deal with the arts and crafts aspects of game making. In the end you'll (a) evolve your own method, and (b) learn to laminate (cover) your games with clear Contact paper so that they have a chance for survival.

6. Then I test-play the game. My classroom is never the first audience. Games almost always have bugs, traps, or flaws. They need new, rules or have other problems which at first make them functionally unplayable.

7. Back to the drawing board. I revise and rework the game, eliminating all the problems I have found.

8. Into the classroom. While using the game I evaluate (a) any other flaws in the game's design, and (b) how well the game is teaching what it is supposed to teach.

9. Having looked at the game in my classroom, I return to step 7. Most games are never finished; they are usually stuck somewhere in the process of revision.

10. I share my games with other teachers, put them in teacher centers, and show them at faculty meetings. In the same way, I hope other teachers will share their creations with me.

Using both of these methods, and with constant improvisation, most of my games ultimately manage to design themselves (given a lot of help from my students and from the countless friends I ask to play them with me)!

VI.

Play is competitive
Play is relaxing
Play is often rhythmic
Play is spontaneous
Play is ritualistic
Play has humor
Play is make-believe
(Filis Frederick)[7]

AN EPILOGUE

There are many good reasons for using games in the classroom. The large amount of academic research on gaming seems to say that games can teach just as effectively as any other instructional medium, except that they tend to be more fun. There is, however, a deeper reason for my personal commitment to the Jewish use of educational games.

When I was 17, I went to Israel for a year. The first six months of that year were spent studying in Jerusalem. I can remember sitting in my room and struggling to translate some text which had to do with Chanukah while some kids outside were playing Maccabees and Greeks. I remember being very jealous. Later that year I visited a friend who was a Rabbi in Ramat Gan. While spending Shabbat at his home, I noticed his five-year-old son playing Rabbi with a toy *tallit* and a toy Ark which my friend and his wife had made. Again I experienced a pang. My own childhood was filled with Jewish experiences and real Jewish moments — a *sukkah*, Friday night dinners, countless Jewish books and stories. It was a good Jewish upbringing, a committed, involved, and active Jewish upbringing. But, since that year, I've always regretted that I never had an opportunity to also come to my Jewishness via play. The children you teach have that possibility. It is my hope that, with the help of this chapter on games, you will provide it for them.

Joel Lurie Grishaver is the Creative Director of Torah Aura Productions and the author of a myriad of materials for Jewish schools, including *The Life Cycle Workbook* and *Tzedakah, Gemilut Chasadim and Ahavah* (A.R.E.) He also teaches Bible and Rabbinics at the Los Angeles Hebrew High School.

NOTES

1. Mary Reilly, *Play As Exploratory Learning* (Beverly Hills: Sage Publications, 1974), p. 114.
2. Clark C. Abt, *Serious Games* (New York: The Viking Press, 1970), p. 13.
3. Ingeborg Prause Huber, "Games and Other Classroom Activities which Motivate the Foreign Language Student" (M.A. paper, California State University Northridge, 1975).
4. Filis Frederick, *Design And Sell Toys, Games and Crafts* (Radnor, Chilton Book Co.), p. 8.
5. Reilly, op. cit., p. 36.
6. Herbert Kohl, *Math, Writing and Games in the Open Classroom* (New York: New York Review of Books, 1974), p. 218.
7. Frederick, op. cit., p. 1.

BIBLIOGRAPHY

Books

Abt, Clark C. *Serious Games*. New York: Viking Press, 1970.

Blackburn, Jack E., and W. Conrad Powell. *One at a Time All at Once: The Creative Teacher's Guide to Individualized Instruction without Anarchy*. Glenview, IL: Scott Foresman and Co., 1976

Gamemaker Kit. West Palm Beach, FL: The Learning Plant.

Goldberg, Sally. *Growing with Games: Making Your Own Educational Games*. Ann Arbor, MI: University of Michigan Press, 1985.

Idea Book. New York: UAHC, 1990.

Isaacs, Ron. *The Jewish Family Game Book for the Sabbath and Festivals*. Hoboken, NJ: Ktav Publishing House, 1989.

Kaye, Marvin. *The Story of Monopoly, Silly Putty, Bingo, Twister, Frisbee, Scrabble, et cetera*. New York: Stein and Day, 1977.

Kopin, Rita. *The Lively Jewish Classroom: Games and Activities for Learning*. Denver: A.R.E. Publishing, Inc., 1980.

Pearson, Craig. *Make Your Own Games Workshop*. Belmont, CA: Pitman Learning, 1982.

Simons, Robin. *Recyclopedia*. Boston, MA: Houghton-Mifflin, 1976.

Distributors of Ready-made Games

A.R.E. Publishing, Inc., 3945 South Oneida, Denver, CO 80237

Czigler Publishing Co., 331 Beardsley Rd., Dayton, OH 45426

The Learning Plant, P.O. Box 17233, West Palm Beach, FL 33416

Torah Aura Productions, 4423 Fruitland Ave., Los Angeles, CA 90058

Game Supplies

The Learning Plant, P.O. Box 17233, West Palm Beach, FL 33416

Chips:
Crisloid, Inc., Eddy and Porter Sts., Providence, RI 02902

Spinners:
American Teaching Aids, P.O. Box 1406, Covina, CA 91722

TEACHING METHODS AND STRATEGIES

CHAPTER EIGHTEEN

VALUES CLARIFICATION

Audrey Friedman Marcus

The term "values clarification" has a definite 1970s ring to it. In recent years, values clarification has fallen out of favor in secular schools. Those on the far right have attacked it as the personification of secular humanism and situation ethics. Calling it an invasion of privacy, these critics have also asserted that the use of values clarification in the classroom usurps the parental perogative to teach values. In the wake of such criticism, many teachers have become wary of employing this methodology in the classroom, and many of the classic reference works on the topic are no longer in print. Why, then, you may wonder, is a chapter on values clarification included in this book?

Simply put, although they may not call it values clarification, many teachers in both secular schools and Religious Schools still use this technique to enrich their classrooms! The author of this chapter is still called upon to train teachers in the methodology. Thus, values clarification still has a place in the arsenal of teaching tools. When used in moderation, values clarification can add spice and excitement to a class and can foster independent, in-depth thinking on issues of import to the Jewish people.) For related topics, see Chapter 14, "Cooperative or Collaborative Learning," and Chapter 15, "Jewish Creative Thinking Skills.")

Here is our first example of a values clarification strategy:

Pretend you are going on a trip to another land far away. You will never return to the land of your birth. You will have to go on a long journey over an ocean. You can take only one suitcase, and you need to be able to carry it by yourself. If this were actually happening to you, what would you put in the suitcase?

Think about it for a minute. Jot down on a piece of paper the first few things that enter your mind.

Now analyze your list. Did you remember to bring a toothbrush? Is there anything on your list that would help you to celebrate Shabbat? What about a diploma or certificate to show your professional training? And pictures of old friends and family? What can you learn about yourself from your list? Are you practical, sentimental, intellectual?

Can we really imagine this happening to ourselves? Yet, countless times in Jewish history, Jews have faced this identical problem. We have truly been a people "on the move" — we moved with Abraham, were led out by Moses, were carried away by Babylon, expelled by the Christians in Spain, had to flee Eastern Europe, were deported by Hitler. For all of these historical events, the so called "Suitcase Strategy" outlined above can help us get in touch both with having to leave our roots behind and with knowing what's important to us. Comparing our responses with those of our parents and grandparents and with historical realities has the makings of an exciting lesson plan. The Suitcase Strategy is just one example of a technique called values clarification.

WHAT IS VALUES CLARIFICATION?

Values clarification is a series of classroom strategies which give students an opportunity to state where they stand on issues which have relevance in their lives or to make evaluative statements about the issues. These strategies enable students to make choices in non-threatening situations, to try on for size various viewpoints and see how they fit, to compare their ideas with their peers.

The theoretical underpinnings of the technique lie in John Dewey's theory of valuation and its interpretation by Louis E. Raths. The book *Values and Teaching* by Raths, Harmin, and Simon is the seminal text on the matter and represents must reading.

These writers assert that in today's pluralistic society, young people receive many conflicting value messages. Where there was once consistency between family, school, and religious institutions, there is now a confusing array of alternatives. Students are confronted with many inconsistent models and with a society that is becoming increasingly complex. They are exposed to a variety of media stimuli and live in a frighteningly mobile environment.

Values clarification strategies provide students with a process for arriving at values. The strategies teach them the skills they need for sorting out values and applying them in their own lives. Youngsters need to examine issues critically and develop a method for arriving at their own outlooks. And we need to help them to do this.

Values clarification theorists have outlined seven criteria which a belief or opinion must meet in order to be considered a value. If a belief or opinion falls short of all seven of the following criteria, then it is a value indicator (e.g., an attitude, belief, worry, activity, interest, feeling, goal, or aspiration) and not a value.

I. PRIZING, AFFIRMING
   1. Cherishing and being happy with the value
   2. Publicly affirming the value
II. CHOOSING
   3. Something you chose freely
   4. Something you chose from among alternatives
   5. Something where you weighed the consequences thoughtfully
III. ACTING
   6. Taking action on your choices
   7. Taking action repeatedly and consistently, with a pattern

A further aspect of the theory which underlies values clarification relates to what has been called Four Level Teaching. We can teach in the area of academic inquiry (facts and concepts) and on the level of personal values inquiry (experiences and values).

The facts level represents the teaching and learning of specific information — facts, details, occurrences, events, and actualities. The basic rudiments of learning a skill are also included here. In other words, this fact-centered area has to do with content. It is obviously vital for students to learn facts. Yet, if they learn only facts and do not know how to use them to build concepts, then a vital part of the educational process is missed.

The concepts level relates to the processes of the subject matter. We teach on this level when we are concerned with making the facts meaningful to our students. We link the facts together and establish relationships between them; we explore the principles behind them and draw generalizations from them. At this level, which is relationship-centered, the more complicated processes of a skill are learned and practiced.

The concepts which students learn, while vital, must not be studied in a vacuum, however. They must be related to the personal experience of students if they are to be internalized. Thus teaching must take place at still another level — the experience level. It is here that students are given the opportunity to relate the facts and concepts to their own lives and personal experiences.

Finally, there is the values level. On this fourth level of teaching, students are directly involved in examining their own values, determining how they will use the knowledge they have gained. Many "you" questions enable them to confront the issues suggested by the content and relate them to their own values and actions. The key question on the values level is: What does this have to do with me? Students explore the connection between subject matter and their own feelings, opinions, and behaviors. Figure 1 below depicts the four levels of teaching.[1]

```
            YOU
           /\
          /VALUES\
         /────────\
        / EXPERIENCES \
       /──────────────\
      /   CONCEPTS      \
     /──────────────────\
    /      FACTS          \
   /──────────────────────\
```

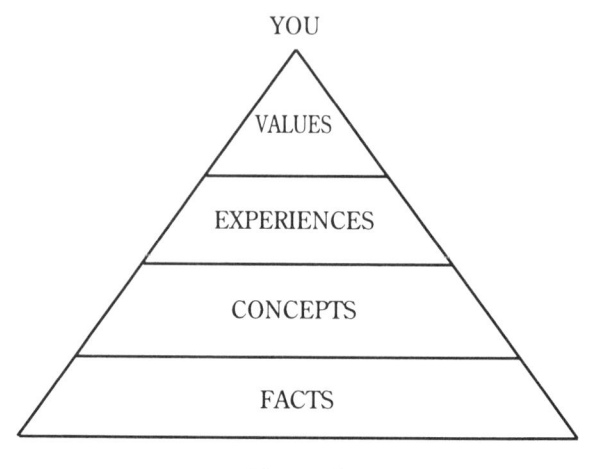

Figure 1

VALUES – enables the student to take a stand or make some evaluative statement on the value issue

EXPERIENCES – relating the facts and concepts to the personal experience of the student

CONCEPTS – the generalizations and principles behind the facts

FACTS – the details of the story or subject matter (content, names, dates, places, events)

Many teachers succeed, of course, teaching only at the fact level. Others teach primarily from the standpoint of concepts. (Many of the current secular social studies programs are concept oriented.) Still other teachers prefer to deal first with all subject matter in terms of personal values inquiry. Much is to be gained by varying the mix and by teaching at each of the levels.

One can work systematically up through the levels, starting with the facts. For example, students might study survival in the shtetl, researching the resources people needed in order to survive — in other words, the facts. Then the question could be posed: What does it take for us to survive? The two life-styles could be compared and then the facts could be highlighted once again.

Or, one can begin immediately with inquiry at the values level. This generally creates a high level of interest and involvement on the part of the students. From here students can be led into the facts as the values issues are resolved. For instance, when studying capital punishment, students could place themselves on a continuum, indicating their views on the subject. Then they might investigate the current status of the death penalty as a method of punishment in various countries, how it was viewed historically, the Jewish view, etc. Then discussion could return to the values issues and to the students' feelings.

It is helpful to practice isolating facts, concepts, experiences, and values so that you can be aware of the level on which you are teaching. Figure 2 (on the following two pages) contains examples of questions that might be asked on each of the four levels on the subject of Passover and the Exodus. The list is not meant to be comprehensive; it is rather a model which demonstrates the application of Four Level Teaching to subject matter. After reading the chart, try making your own list of questions on each of the four levels for the subject matter you are presently teaching. Many teachers have found this to be a very valuable way of planning lessons. You will quickly see that the hard part will be not what to teach about your subject, but how to organize the vast amount of the available material.

VALUES CLARIFICATION IN THE RELIGIOUS SCHOOL

First of all, values clarification is a way of involving the whole student, not just his or her mind, but feelings and emotions as well. It is hardly possible for learning and retention to take place in an atmosphere that is wholly intellectual or cognitive. And this is especially true when the learning is about Judaism, or any religious structure, which involves affect.

Secondly, a major goal for Jewish education is that our students will choose to identify in some way as Jews when they are old enough to make the choice to do so. I believe it is up to us to prepare them for their choice of whether to live as active, committed Jews. Obviously, they cannot be forced to do this. There is no way of "instilling" Jewish values in young people by injection. Nor can we succeed by indoctrination or moralizing. Students can be helped to make choices through values clarification as well as by enabling them to participate in decisions related to seating, homework, discipline, aspects of the curriculum, methods of learning, and even the procedure for asking for bathroom permission! This practice in "choosing" will assist them to make better and better choices. They will come to understand and analyze the options which they face before making decisions. And, after all, the big questions in our lives must ultimately be answered for ourselves.

This is not to say that our schools must become "valueless," thereby dodging our responsibility to promulgate specifically *Jewish values*. It is certainly true that our concerns are very different from secular schools. We have an agenda — a life system — which we want to translate to our youngsters. I believe it is incumbent upon us to point out Jewish values in every area and at every step along the way. Further-

VALUES CLARIFICATION INVOLVES FEELINGS AND EMOTIONS, AS WELL AS MIND.

ACADEMIC INQUIRY	
FACTS	CONCEPTS
Why did the Hebrews go to Egypt 3500 years ago? Can you relate the story of Joseph and his brothers? Why did Joseph's brothers dislike him so? Why did the treatment of the Hebrews in Egypt change? What event caused Moses to flee to Midian? What did Moses do in Midian? What incident occurred which called Moses to return and help his people? What are the 10 plagues? Which plague finally caused Pharaoh to relent? What was the miracle which enabled the Hebrews to escape? What happened to the Egyptians as they pursued? How did the Hebrews celebrate their liberation? What holiday commemorates this event?	What kind of person was Joseph? Was the treatment of Joseph by his brothers justified? Describe the differences between being oppressed and being free. Compare Pharaoh to Hitler, Haman, and Antiochus. How are they the same? How different? What would happen if everyone avoided responsibility? Is this easier? Was the murder of the slave justified? Is murder ever justified? What does the writer of the biblical account believe about God speaking to human beings? Is the method of resistance in the story logical under the circumstances? Compare the miracle at the Sea of Reeds to other biblical miracles. Which is the greatest? Can you list other times in Jewish history when Jews were pursued? What happened at those times? Find any expressions of mercy and compassion to one's enemies in the story or in the *midrash*.

Figure 2

more, I believe we must inform students of how we ourselves feel about all issues (not right away in a discussion and not dogmatically, or they will not feel free to offer differing views). In a classroom which is based on trust and mutual understanding and respect, a free exchange of ideas and viewpoints will be natural and beneficial to everyone. In this kind of environment, I feel confident that our students will choose many Jewish responses to the challenges and problems and issues which life offers.

But isn't it risky, you may ask? Of course it is! Can you think of any method which is guaranteed? And would you be willing to trade the freedom of your life-style and your own ability to make value choices for some other society, one in which you were locked into one prescribed set of choices and behaviors?

There are other facets to values clarification. This method also provides a very useful and exciting tool for enlivening classroom teaching. It allows for maximum student participation, while still providing the very important option for any class member to "pass," not to respond or participate in a particular exercise if it seems too threatening or if one simply has nothing to contribute.

The teacher who is tuned in to values clarification will be much more the facilitator than the one always in command. And students in this environment will really come to know their teachers as human beings. Finally, it gives to our classrooms the kind of flow discussed in Chapter 19, "Plannning Lively Lessons," between various sized groups — individuals at work, pairs (dyads), groups of four to six, and whole groups. Children can move around, communicate with many classmates during each session, and have an opportunity to build a real community based on openness and trust and understanding.

A panacea? I don't think so. Values clarification is not the only answer. But as one tool, it can help us reach our youngsters and help them grow. With many such tools at our disposal, we can deal with any situation which arises and turn it into a productive learning experience for our children and ourselves.

While I believe values clarification offers us a chance to enrich our teaching, I would like to offer some cautions. First of all, go slowly. Help your students understand the purpose of what you are doing. Don't go into class and introduce six or seven strategies. Under any circumstances, this would be too many for one class session. Try one or two at a time, always making sure that the strategies relate to the subject matter. I have seen teachers take the book of strategies into

PERSONAL VALUES INQUIRY	
EXPERIENCE	VALUES
Have you ever seen injustice done to another individual? What did you do?	Do you think slavery can ever be a good experience?
Have you ever worked hard at something you didn't like doing? How did you react?	If you were going on a trip, what would you take? Who would you kiss good-bye?
Have you ever felt like a slave — at home? at school? anywhere else? What was the feeling like? What did you do about it?	List the things that would have to be taken away from you to make you want to leave your country.
Were there leaders in the past you admire? In the present? What are some of their special qualities?	If you lived at the time of the Exodus, would you have stayed or left? Would you have supported Moses or rebelled with Korah?
Do you know anyone who is the kind of favored child or spoiled brat that Joseph was? Are you one? Were you one?	List 20 things you love to do. Which could you continue doing if you were a slave? Which would you miss most?
How is your relationship with your siblings the same as that of Joseph and his brothers? How is it different?	List five qualities of a leader.
	List five qualities of leadership that you possess.
Do you accept responsibility or avoid it?	List five qualities of a leader you don't possess.
Have you ever heard God speak to you? If so, what did God say? Did you listen?	List five qualities of a leader you will work to develop.
Did a miracle ever occur in your lifetime? Do you believe miracles happen?	In your opinion, who is the modern Moses? Could you be one? Will you be one?
Do you ever feel pursued because you are Jewish? Oppressed? Disliked? What do you do when this happens?	Write a poem about a personal victory over your "enemies." (Sports event, a fight, a moral victory, getting rid of a bad trait)
Were you ever singled out and chosen for a special responsibility over others? Were you glad? sad? scared?	How can families avoid the sibling rivalry that occurred in Joseph's family? Write a contract for yourself. Send an "I Urge Telegram" to someone in your family.
Have you ever participated in civil disobedience? Would you? For what reason?	What responsibilities are ahead for you? To which do you look forward? Which are disagreeable?
Have you ever rebelled at parental authority? school authority? synagogue authority? Were you proud of your actions? Would you do it again?	What miracle would you make happen first if you had the power?
	How is this theory of values clarification applicable in the Religious School setting?

Figure 2, cont.

class and begin to bombard students with one strategy after another, totally unrelated to curricular concerns. Students became angry and confused and frustrated, and, from my standpoint, such a session is a waste of time. Values clarification is not a subject; it is a technique, a tool, and must be thoughtfully integrated with your curriculum.

Another caution relates to follow-up. Again, don't use these strategies willy-nilly, completing a Continuum or a Rank Order (see list of strategies in this chapter) and going on immediately to something else. These exercises need to be probed and discussed. Students need to be "debriefed," to have an opportunity to share their thoughts and feelings. They will often get the courage to share their views when they find that others feel similarly. Likewise, I have seen students become proud to be the only one in the class who felt a certain way, once they have learned that it is okay to hold unique and differing views. In regard to this, the students' feelings of okayness about their views will depend in large part on you. Be warmly accepting and non-judgmental and allow all shades of opinion to be expressed. This does not mean you must permit students to be irresponsible or silly, or that you should hesitate to express your own views, and the Jewish view, on a particular issue. Just don't propound your view as the only correct one, and wait to express it until your students have shared their own thoughts and ideas.

Finally, if you don't feel comfortable teaching with values clarification, then don't use it! There are dozens of other effective methods of teaching. Many of them you already know. Many of them are found in this book. If you are not at ease, your students will sense it. Very likely what you attempt will not be successful. But if you believe in the process and have a rough time at first, don't give up. Get your students on your side and just keep plugging.

SOME VALUES CLARIFICATION STRATEGIES

On the next few pages you will find described a number of values clarification strategies.[2] In many cases examples are included to show how the strategy can be related to Jewish concerns. In the Appendix, you will find several lesson plans which demonstrate how values clarification strategies can be integrated into what Merrill Harmin calls "zippy lessons." Included are three different types of lessons for three separate subjects and three varying age levels. These models are not necessarily meant to be used as is in your class. They are included to help you as you begin to design your own lessons using values clarification. This chapter is only a start toward understanding and being able to use values clarification. I hope you will read some of the books listed in the Bibliography at the end of this chapter. Further, I hope you will practice some of the strategies in an in-service session with other staff members. There is no substitute for experiencing the strategies firsthand.

Values Voting: Teacher reads questions beginning: How many of you . . . ? Students respond with a show of hands for the affirmative, waving of hands if very positive, thumbs down for the negative, thumbs vehemently down several times if very negative. Those who want to pass fold their arms. No discussion until the whole list is finished. At the end, the teacher can ask: Which would you most like to talk about? Students can talk about it then with a neighbor, in dyads, trios, "6-packs," or in class. Or, save the discussion until after subject matter is completed for the day, or as a break, etc.

How many of you . . .

    Did something Jewish this week?
        Thought about being Jewish this week?
    Feel that religion is an important part of your life?
    Plan to observe Shabbat in some way when you have your own home?
    Think life should be preserved as long as possible even with extreme means? (such as respirators)
    Think being born is the most important event in life? Circumcision? Bar or Bat Mitzvah? Confirmation? Wedding? Death?
    Feel as if you stood at Sinai with Moses?
    Would rather be Jewish than anything?
    Did something for another human being this week?

Nametags: Each students writes his/her name (big) with felt marker on 5" x 8" white cards. In each corner of the card, they are asked to write something. Examples: Favorite Jewish food, single earliest experience in your life that provided a new flavor in your Jewish experience, two Jewish values important to you (may have to define values), your favorite Jewish holiday, two things that bug you, the person living today whom you regard as the most ideal Jew, a Rank Order (see below), two to three people who have influenced your life, five to six words that describe you ending in "ing" or "able," the date on which you first learned to ride a bicycle, when you first knew that you were Jewish, five days in a row when you were deliciously happy, five words that express who you are and what you like to do, three words that describe you as a Jew, etc.

Milling: Students move around the room silently (the silence is very important), reading the nametags, and looking only at the faces and the nametags of other students. Milling can be used for responses at any time, not just for nametags. Students can also be allowed to tell something to everyone they meet (an answer to a problem posed or one response to a question posed by the teacher — vary it as you wish).

Sharing Trios: Students get in groups of three, preferably with two others whom they don't know very well. They are asked to discuss one of the items on the nametag (you may specify one if you wish) or another question, such as a big decision they have made lately, the one single most fun day of the summer, how it feels to be back in Religious School (are you that daring?), etc.

Focus Rules: Explain Focus Rules — this will help them learn to listen to each other. Each person gets to speak for three minutes while others listen. (Someone in each trio should be timekeeper.) Others should give *attention*, eye contact, asking only those questions which do not shift the focus away from speaker (That same thing happened to me), *acceptance* — they should be warmly accepting, show interest by facial expression and body posture, *draw out speaker* — try really to understand him or her, *no fogging questions* (Don't you think that . . . or Wouldn't it be better if ...), *no judgments* (That's a lousy idea), *no put downs, discounts, or vulture statements*.

At the end, you can go around and have each one say to the other: "I liked it when you . . . ," or "I found you likeable when you said . . . ," or "I appreciated it when you said . . . "

Or, the group can feed back to each other on whether they felt really listened to and accepted and appreciated, etc. Or, discuss which was easier, listening or being listened to, and which they preferred, and why.

This exercise enables students to learn to listen attentively, and to respect the views of others. Using it early in the year can help you to establish a warm and respectful classroom atmosphere. What is more, using Focus Rules give some children their only opportunity to get the undivided attention of others. Experiencing this even for a few minutes can help a person really feel good and worthwhile. Many conversations based on unfinished business generated in Sharing Trios can continue outside of class.

Rank Order: The teacher gives the class three or four choices in answer to a question and they rank these according to their own values. Then discuss in small groups or with the whole class.

>If your city were corrupt, what would you do?
> Move away
> Try to change it
> Make the best of it for yourself
>
>What qualities do you look for in a leader?
> Kindness
> Intelligence
> Effectiveness as a disciplinarian
>
>What is the most effective way of combatting injustice?
> Protesting at a rally
> Writing letters to the government
> Raising money
>
>To which would you rather give *tzedakah*?
> Israel
> Meals for the elderly poor
> Red Cross

Variations: Submit some Rank Orders to a panel of three for response. Then ask if anyone not on the panel would like to respond. Form groups of those with like answers to discuss their views. Or, form groups of three, each of whom chose a different response. Have sharing trios using Focus Rules.

One Minute Biography: Form dyads or trios or quartets. Each person in the group has one minute to give his/her life history. Suggest they hit the high points. Then structure some questions for discussion in the groups or as a class: Did you really learn much about the other person? Was everyone really honest? How many of you told about real feelings as opposed to just names, places, and dates? What does it take to get to know someone really? What do we need to do as a class to foster a friendly and accepting atmosphere, etc.?

Values Continuum: Teacher draws a long line on the board indicating two poles of opinion such as Observant and Non-observant. (These can be given intriguing names, such as Observant Ollie and Non-Observant Ned.) Students mark on the line where they fit on the continuum (either with X or their initials and are asked: Why did you put yourselves in that spot?) They then explain their views.

Variations: Teacher can also put masking tape on the floor or have an imaginary line on the floor and ask students to stand on it. The places can be marked on the floor. After a discussion of an issue or the completion of a unit, you can ask them to take their places again and see if there are any changes. Discuss the changes.

>If you lived in Moses' time, would you have been supportive of Moses or would you have been in the camp of Korah?

Moses   Korah

Synagogue affiliation is essential for Jewish survival.

Strongly agree   Strongly disagree

Where would you put yourself on the line if you were called upon to fight for freedom of worship in the time of Judah Maccabbee?

Couldn't-Care-Less-Clara   Dedicated Dan

Ask the same question for a Syrian Jew living at this time in Syria and for yourself, here and now in North America.

Brainstorming: Students call out ideas in response to a given question. The question could be: What do you hope our class will be like this year? or What can we do to establish an atmosphere of learning and fun in our class? or What are some things you want to learn about Jews in the Middle Ages? etc. The rules are that there must be no evaluation of ideas as they are called out. Wild ideas and quantity are encouraged and someone writes down all the ideas. Students may "hitchhike" on the ideas of others by adding to them or enlarging on them. Sorting the ideas out and choosing those which are feasible can be helpful in structuring the curriculum, finding out where the kids are, getting a discussion started, planning learning centers, etc.

Forced Choice: Teacher asks either-or question such as: With which holiday do you identify more, Pesach or Chanukah? Words can be posted on two sides of the room and students go to their choice. They can discuss in the groups at each sign, or find a partner and discuss it. This works well with four signs, one in each corner.

    Which of these best explains what happened at the Sea of Reeds?
        God actually did part it
        The whole story is a legend, it never happened
        Wind and tide conditions caused the sea to part
        Some combination of the other answers

Which Jewish symbol would you most like to be?
    Shabbat candles
    Kiddush cup
    Challah
    Spice box

If someone gave you $5000, would you rather
    Take a trip to Israel
    Donate the money to charity
    Put the money in the bank for the future
    Buy CD's, video games, and tapes

I Wonder: Have students share the things about Judaism or the particular class curriculum or unit you are beginning that they wonder about. Those who wish call out, "I wonder if" or "I wonder whether" or "I wonder about" or "I wonder when," etc. This strategy can also be open-ended and interesting closure for a unit to let unfinished questions hang in the air.

Buttons: Have every student make a button (like a political button) that has a slogan or sentence on it about being Jewish. Show the buttons around and have students explain them. Then ask them to wear them for one whole day, and report back to the class next time on their experiences. Ask questions like: Were there any reactions to your button? Describe them. Was there anyone who ignored your button? How did it affect you? How did you feel wearing your button? Do you believe your button had any influence on people? etc. A good idea would be to have the blank buttons made up in advance or have the kids make them in class out of cardboard rounds, safety pins, and masking tape. Later on, buttons can be made to show student interest in causes such as Syrian Jewry, Israel, human rights, etc. Similar questions can be asked.

Sentence Completion: Teacher gives a list of unfinished sentences. A photocopied sheet is helpful. Students complete the sentences individually, and then discuss in groups. Or they can be answered aloud by whoever wants to do so, or in order around the room (the latter is called a "Whip").

    A time when I feel most Jewish is _____

The person who has taught me what it really is to be Jewish is _____

When I say (or hear) the Four Questions at the *Seder*, my heart _____

Twenty Things I Love To Do: Students are asked to write down 20 things they love to do (reduce the number to 10 for younger children). Then have them code their responses in various ways: Put an X next to all those things you did in the last week, a dollar sign next to those which cost money, a P next to those your parents also love to do, an R next to those of which your Rabbi would approve, a J next to those which express your Jewishness in any way, and so on. Try to get students to discuss and appreciate some of the meanings in this exercise — e.g., why are there not more Jewish things on the list? Why have you not done anything you like doing in the last week? Why do your parents love (or not love) to do the same things you do? What can you do to change the things you have found out that you don't like?

Magen David (Coat of Arms): Have each student draw a *Magen David* (or a Coat of Arms) or teacher reproduces an outline of a *Magen David* for each of them. Ask each student to write something in each point of the star (questions similar to those used in the Nametags exercise above are good). Then discuss in groups or as a whole.

Value Lists: Students make a list of items they value, prize, or cherish. This may be done in class or completed as a homework assignment. Jewish examples of lists: List Jewish values that are important to you, list the Jewish symbols that have special meaning to you, list Jewish events in your life that were significant, list Jewish people you admire, and so on. Lists can be coordinated with subject matter (e.g., list things about Judaism that a Marrano in Spain or a Jewish prisoner in a concentraton camp might cherish, etc.). Help students get started by suggesting a few things that would appear on your list or by writing your list on the board as they are working on theirs. If desired, students can read items on their lists and share something that they learned about themselves.

Variations: Students can keep a running list of Jewish things they do over a period of days or weeks, of *mitzvot* they perform, of actions of which they are proud, etc.

Creating the World: Ask students to close their eyes. Say: Think about what it would be like to be the creator of the world. What kind of a world would you create? Would it be warlike or peaceful? Heavily populated or sparsely settled? Would there be animals, trees, oceans? Would there be different races and religions? Would there be evil in your world? Small groups then decide what they wish to include in their newly created world. Be sure that everyone's ideas are included. Each group can then present its world to the total group. Similarities and differences between the various worlds can be discussed. Themes can be written on the subject. Other follow-ups might include listing the five to ten things they like most about their new world. Next to each item students can list ways of making the existing world more like the world they "created." Action projects can be initiated by groups of class members. This strategy is excellent for use at High Holy Day time or when discussing messianism and *tikun olam*.

> **ALWAYS RELATE THE STRATEGY TO JEWISH CONCERNS.**

Variations: Create a new Religious School, a new synagogue, a new religion, a new Jewish community, a new prayer book.

Paper Memorials: Form groups of five to seven. Each student submits individually arrived at ideas for someone or something (Jewish) he or she wishes to honor. Each group decides on one of the suggestions by consensus. Groups are given a time limit during which they must plan and build a memorial structure out of newspaper and masking tape. When the memorials are completed, they can be named and a dedication statement written and attached to them. Discuss the experience both in the small groups and with the whole class. Students can determine which values their memorials represent, how the values and memories chosen differ, how decisions were made, and what they would change if they were to repeat the exercise.

Values Auction: Each group of six students must bid on (Jewish) values as they attempt to transmit the most important ones to a civilization beginning on a new planet. Only 14 values can be passed on and no two civilizations may have the same values. Each group receives 1,000 points to use to purchase values on the list of 14 which are sold at auction to the highest bidder. Each group buys as many values as possible until their points are used up. The teacher acts as auctioneer, selling each value until all are sold. Afterward, discuss whether agreed upon goals were reached, the values each group purchased, how students decided what to bid on and the nature of a civilization that operated with the values they bought.

Values Dilemmas: Small or large groups of students are given case studies and asked to decide how they would resolve the problems posed in each. This can be done individually as a writing project and then shared in small groups. Or, endings can be role played instead. Choose situations that relate to your subject matter and that reflect Jewish dilemmas and values. Students can also write their own dilemmas.

Collages: Have each student make a collage that reflects his/her Jewish self. Or have groups of students work together to make a collage about Judaism, Jewish values such as peace or *K'lal Yisrael*, family, community, or synagogue. Pictures, words from ads, yarn, and scraps can be used. Collages may be flat or made out of a box or a cylinder such as a Baskin-Robbins ice cream container. Students can present and describe their collages. Hopefully, the teacher will also make a collage and share it with the group.

My Favorite Person in History: Tell your students: You are climbing up a hill to watch the sun set. As you near the top you sense that something important is about to occur. Then all at once you see your favorite person in (Jewish) history coming down the hill toward you. Students can respond individually to such questions as: Why do you think the person was on the top of the hill? What would you say to the person? For what would you thank the person? If you met your best friend on the path, how would you introduce your favorite person in history to the friend? How would you say goodbye to your historical character? How would you describe your favorite person to your friends and family? How would you tell people what happened on the hill?

Journals: Students can keep ongoing diaries of personal (Jewish) experiences that occur at home and in class. They can make and decorate their journals. Usually the teacher reads the journals periodically and comments in writing before returning them to the students. (Be sure to be non-judgmental and ask lots of clarifying questions, e.g., were you proud of how you responded? Was there some other alternative you might have chosen? How will you act the next time this happens? And, of course, give your students as much validation as possible.) If desired, students can share their journal entries with classmates.

Heroes and Heroines: Tell students that they have the ability to talk to any five Jewish persons they want to, alive or dead. Ask which five persons they would talk to? Why? Variations are to say they have only 15 minutes and can ask only three questions of each person. Have them write down three questions for each person. Share these. Another variation: What three things would you tell them during the 15 minutes? Or tell each person what you appreciate about them, or why you are angry with them.

Magic Box: Teacher describes a magic box that is special. It can be very large or very small and can contain anything they want to put in it. Ask students a question such as: If you could put one thing in the magic box which would help us have a good class this year, what would you put? or Imagine there is something in the magic box which will make this the best class you ever had. What is it? If you could find one thing in the magic box to hasten the peace process, what would it be?

Proud Line: Students are asked to state what they are most proud of about Judaism or about their Jewishness or about their synagogue.

Teacher can ask why they think Judah Maccabee was proud (or King David or Abraham). Were their reasons the same or different from ours? Teacher whips around class and students respond. Often Proud Lines make excellent murals or tape recordings or readings for worship services, assemblies, and programs.

I Urge Telegram: On a 4" x 6" card, or a telegram blank, students write a telegram to a real or imagined person beginning with the words, "I urge you to . . ." The telegrams should be 15 words or less and students should sign their names. These can be read, discussed, or posted in the classroom, or actually sent. Another variation is to send a telegram which begins, "I urge me to . . ." (This is particularly good on Yom Kippur!)

> Send an I Urge Telegram to Pharaoh.
> (Would he listen?)
> Send an I Urge Telegram to God.
> (How is it like or unlike a prayer?)
> Send an I Urge Telegram to _____.
> (Mail it!)

Alternatives Search: Students are presented with a problem (how to help new youngsters in the class, how to celebrate Chanukah more meaningfully, what to do with the *tzedakah* money, how to reach out to old people in the community). They brainstorm individually as many alternatives as they can in three to five minutes. Then, in teams of three or four, they are to develop a list of alternative solutions by combining their individual lists and adding any solutions generated in the group. When all the alternatives are exhausted (ten minutes or so), each group chooses the three alternatives they like best and rank orders them. They may then report the results to the class as a whole and discuss them.

Public Interview: A volunteer is interviewed on his or her beliefs, feelings, and actions. The volunteer sits at the teacher's desk or in a chair in front and the teacher joins the rest of the class. Teacher (and/or other students) may ask any question about the life or values of the volunteer. If he or she answers, it must be an honest answer, but he or she may pass any question.

The interview is over when the student says, "Thank you for the interview."

Variations:
Interview Whip – the teacher "whips" around the classroom, in order or at random, asking interview questions of each student. The same question, or a different question can be asked.

Interview Chain: Teacher asks one student a question. He/she answers and then asks another student a question. (Remember, students may always pass. Even after a pass, they should be allowed to ask a question.)

Group Interview: Students form groups of five to ten. One member volunteers to be interviewed by the others and calls on them to ask questions. The volunteer may ask the reason for asking a question if he or she wishes.

Jewish Characters: Have the class interview a famous Jewish person who can be researched either by the teacher or a student. Or, interview the Rabbi, Cantor, Sisterhood President, Men's Club President, Youth Group President, Golden Age Club President, etc.

Variation: Ask only questions related to the volunteer's Judaism. Answer correctly or incorrectly and have the class vote on whether the answer was true or not. Students answer as their parents or grandparents or as themselves when they are older.

I Learned Statements: Good way to end a discussion or unit or introductory exercise . . . Go around the room and each person says: I learned that I . . . , I relearned that I . . . , I discovered or realized that I . . . , I am surprised that I . . . , or I am pleased that I . . . (Students pick whichever fits for them.)

CONCLUSION

You are now armed with dozens of strategies to have at the ready as you teach. Whether or not you call it values clarification, using these strategies will enrich and enliven your classroom, provide variety in your teaching methods, and give students an opportunity to involve themselves intensely in the values which have held our people together.

Audrey Friedman Marcus received her Masters Degree in Jewish Education from the Rhea Hirsch School of Education of Hebrew Union College-Jewish Institute of Religion in Los Angeles. She studied values clarification under the tutelage of its creators, Sidney Simon and Howard Kirschenbaum. She is the co-founder of A.R.E. Publishing, Inc. and the author of many children's books, mini-courses, and articles on Jewish education.

APPENDIX
Three Sample Lessons

LESSON PLAN #1

HOLIDAYS - PASSOVER
2 hours
Grades 4-6

INSTRUCTIONAL OBJECTIVES:

Students will be able to:
- tell in their own words or write the story of the Exodus.
- compare the Exodus of Soviet Jews to the Exodus from Egypt.
- describe what things are important to them that they would want to take with them if they were forced to move.

KEY CONCEPTS:

It is difficult to leave the place of your birth.
Once we were slaves in the land of Egypt.
Jews are still striving for freedom in some places in the world.

ACTIVITIES:

1. Pretend you are going on a trip to another land far away. You are not going to return to the land of your birth. You will have to go on a long trip over an ocean. You can take only one suitcase, and you need to be able to carry it yourself. What would you put in the suitcase? Individuals make lists. Put on butcher paper. Post around the room, and take a walk around reading each other's lists.
2. Discuss the experience in #1. Discuss what it must be like to have to do this. Who has had to leave home? Tell about it.
3. Read the story of the Exodus in the Bible or show a video.
4. Compare the kind of leaving in the story to that in the exercise. Compare it with Jews who are oppressed today.
5. Learning Centers (choose one of the following):
   a. Make your own filmstrip or slide/tape show on Exodus either from Egypt or Russia.
   b. Write a contemporary freedom Haggadah and illustrate it.
   c. Read Moses' Song in Exodus 15. Make up a song that might be sung by a newcomer from Yugoslavia after reaching Israel.

RESOURCES: Paper, pencils, butcher paper, Bibles, video on Exodus, filmmaking kit, projectors, extra bulbs, sample Haggadot, construction paper, drawing paper, crayons, paints, felt-tipped pens.

Note varied activities: Listening, using imagination, discussing, comparing, making filmstrips, writing, drawing.

Note varying sizes of groups: one, whole class, small groups in learning centers.

LESSON PLAN #2

BIBLE, JEWISH ETHICS, HEROES AND HEROINES
One hour plus party
Grades 1-6

INSTRUCTIONAL OBJECTIVES:

Students will be able to:
- tell in their own words the story of Abraham and the three strangers.
- share some facts and feelings from their own life experience as a host/hostess or guest.
- demonstrate the act of hospitality through acting hospitably toward others.

KEY CONCEPT:

Abraham's hospitality is worth emulating.

ACTIVITIES:

1. Students listen to taped story of Abraham and the three strangers.
2. Discuss. Understand what the text says and what it means.
3. Values clarification exercise: Who comes to your house?

    Draw a line down the middle of the page. On one side of the line list names or initials of all the people who have come to your house recently for a meal or to play. On the other side list all the people who invited you for a meal or to play at their house.

    Code the papers: Put an R if the person was a relative, F if a friend.
    Write a one-word description of each person on your list
    P if the person usually brings a present.
    Star those you think are really happy to see you
    Underline those you are really happy to see
    S or D to show if their religion is the same or different from yours
    SR or DR for same race or different race

4. Talk about learnings from this exercise. Ask: What do you want to change, if anything, about this aspect of your life? Is it more fun to be a host/hostess or a guest? Why? What makes a good host/hostess? How can we be good guests? (small groups of four to six)
5. I Learned Statements about hospitality.
6. Plan a party for another class, or a shut-in, a hospital ward, a Headstart group.

RESOURCES: Cassette with story of Abraham and the three strangers, Listening Post, paper, pencils, party materials, and refreshments, permission slips if necessary.

Note varied activities: Listening, writing, discussing, evaluating, coding, involvement in active class experience.

Note varying sizes of groups: one, whole class, 4-6.

LESSON PLAN #3

JEWISH ETHICS, BIBLE
2 two hour sessions
Junior High School

INSTRUCTIONAL OBJECTIVES:

Students will be able to:
   experience and describe how it feels to be a stranger.
   explain the Jewish attitude toward the stranger.
   list ways they can reach out to strangers.

KEY CONCEPTS:

   It is difficult to be a stranger.
   Jews reach out to strangers because of our own experience.

ACTIVITIES:

1. Sentence completions:
   A stranger is_____.
   When I enter a room full of strangers I feel _____.
   Last time I was a stranger I _____.
   When I meet a new person_____.
   Moving to a new city or a new school is _____.
   I handle loneliness by _____.

2. Find a partner and discuss your sentence completions.

3. Exercise: Form tight circles of five or six. One person outside the circle tries to break in. Those in the circle try to keep the outsider out.

4. Discussion (total group)
   What did it feel like to be on the outside?
   What did it feel like to be keeping the one person out?
   What did it feel like to get inside if you did?
   In what ways are these feelings like real life situations? unlike real life situations?

5. Choose a Task Card and complete the activities on it.

6. Share your work and findings with the whole group.

RESOURCES: Bibles, paper, pencils, information on hunger projects, Commentaries, encyclopedia.

Note varied activities: Sentence completions, discussion, physical exercise, research, writing, Task Cards.

Note varying sizes of groups: Individual work, dyads, groups of five or six, whole class.

LESSON PLAN #3: TASK CARD I

When you reap the harvest of your land, you shall not wholly reap all the way to the edges of your field, or gather the gleanings of your harvest. You shall not pick your vineyard bare, or gather the fallen fruit of your vineyard; you shall leave them for the poor and the stranger." (Leviticus 19: 9, 10)

Do the following:

1. Read a commentary on or explanation of this passage in Rashi, Hertz, Silverman, Birnbaum, or other book on the resource table. Be sure you understand it.

2. Think of a different interpretation and write your own brief summary.

Choose one of the following activities:

1. Draw a square, rectangle, or circle representing your "field" or possessions. Designate the sections (money, clothes, intellect, etc.). Mark off the corners of your field which you could give as gleanings to the poor. Write a story about what might happen if you really did this.

2. Study what modern Jews are doing about the world hunger crisis. (Research Mazon and/or other Jewish and interdenominational efforts to alleviate world hunger.) Write a letter to your classmates or to the synagogue bulletin suggesting things your class or congregation might do about this problem as a group and as individuals (e.g., give *tzedakah* to a group helping hungry people, have a meatless meal once a week, etc.).

3. According to tradition, *peah* (the part of the crop required to be left for the poor) was a minimum of one sixtieth of the harvest. Write an essay on this subject, taking into consideration the following: What might this mean in modern terms? Does it mean that a person earning $60,000 should give $1,000 to the poor? Would this be a good means of determining Federation donations? Is one sixtieth a fair amount now and was it a fair amount in biblical days? How do you think this figure was arrived at?

4. Discuss how service to others has been a strong value in your life.

LESSON PLAN #3: TASK CARD II

"You shall not wrong a stranger or oppress him, for you were strangers in the land of Egypt." (Exodus 22:20)

Do the following:

1. Read a commentary on or explanation of this passage in Rashi, Hertz, Silverman, Birnbaum, or other book on the resource table. Be sure you understand it.

2. Think of a different interpretation and write your own brief commentary.

Choose one of the following activities:

1. Make a list of plans that could be undertaken to welcome strangers into your school or your synagogue. Create a book of guidelines for students your age with a section on "Being a Stranger" and one on "Welcoming the Stranger."

2. During many historical periods, Jews were strangers or were treated as strangers. Do research on one of these periods and report to the class. How were Jews treated? What reasons were there for the treatment? How did Jews respond? What can we learn from these experiences?

3. Place yourself on the following lines where you belong:
   Are you more a stranger or at home in the following places:

	Stranger	At home
School		
Home		
Synagogue		
Parties with your peers		
Homes of your parents' friends		

   What patterns emerge from your placements? What can you learn from these patterns? Do any of your positions have anything to do with being Jewish? Do you want to be in a different place on any of the lines? If so, where do you want to be? If not, why not? Write up your answers in any form you wish.

LESSON PLAN #3: TASK CARD III

"There shall be one law for the citizen and for the stranger who dwells among you." (Exodus 12: 49)

Do the following:

1. Read a commentary on or explanation of this passage in Rashi, Hertz, Silverman, Birnbaum, or other book on the resource table. Be sure you understand it.

2. Think of a different interpretation and write your own brief commentary.

Choose one of the following activities:

1. Find out when there was not one law for the citizens and the strangers (e.g., when Jews were slaves in Egypt, minorities in Moslem countries in the eighth to fifteenth centuries, in Russia under the Czars, in the U.S. in 1654). Look up the facts on two of these or other periods. Compare the situation then in that country with the situation now. Write up your findings in an essay or on a display chart.

2. Look up the Bill of Rights (or your country's equivalent) and see if there is any difference between the native born and the stranger. Find out how these laws compare to those in other countries. Write up your findings for the class.

3. In biblical times, there were two categories of strangers, the circumcised and the uncircumcised. Strangers who were circumcised (and thus considered themselves part of the community) were welcomed and considered to be part of it. The uncircumcised strangers were not. The stranger who should be welcomed was the convert. Do you think this was right (in biblical times)? Why or why not? Is it right now? Why or why not? How does this square with the injunction "Justice, justice shall you pursue"? (Deuteronomy 16: 20)

4. Interview your Rabbi, your teacher, and one of your parents. Read them the quotation at the beginning of this Task Card and ask for their reactions and interpretations. You may tape your interviews. Relate the most interesting statements and reactions to the class.

NOTES

1. Adapted from the 1966 edition of *Values and Teaching* by Louis E. Raths, Merrill Harmin, and Sidney B. Simon (Columbus: Charles E. Merrill, 1966), reissued in Sunderland, Massachusetts by Values Press, 1991, and *Personalizing Education: Values Clarification and Beyond* by Leland W. Howe and Mary Martha Howe (New York: Hart, 1975).

2. Most of these strategies are based on those found in *Values Clarification: A Handbook of Practical Strategies for Teachers and Students* by Sidney B. Simon, Leland W. Howe, and Howard Kirschenbaum (Sunderland, MA: Values Press, 1991).

BIBLIOGRAPHY

Books and Articles

Ballard, Jim. *Circlebook*. Manchester, NH: Irvington Publishers, 1981.

Brooks, B. David. "The School's Role in Weaving Values Back." *Education Digest* 58:67-71, April 1993.

Casteel, J. Doyle. *Learning To Think and Choose*. Glenview, IL: Scott Foresman, 1978.

Dapice, A.N. "Teaching and Learning Values." *Horizons*, Spring, 1990, pp. 168-71.

Harmin, Merrill. *Got To Be Me!* Allentown, TX: Tabor Publishing Co., 1989.

Hawley, Robert C. *Value Exploration Through Role Playing*. Arlington, VA: Educational Research Service, 1974.

Hawley, Robert C., and Isabel Hawley. *Developing Human Potential*, vols. 1 and 2. Amherst, MA: Education Research Associates, 1975, 1977.

Larson, Roland S., and Doris E. Larson. *Values and Faith: Value-Clarifying Exercises for Family and Church-Group*. San Francisco: Harper, 1984.

McFadden, Johnnie, and Joseph C. Rotter. *Values Orientation in School*. Saratoga, CA: R & E Publishers, n.d.

Raths, Louis B.; Merrill Harmin; and Sidney B. Simon. *Values and Teaching: Working with Values in the Classroom*. Sunderland, MA: Values Press, 1991.

Raymond, Susan Gold, et al. *The Jewish Handbook for Group Discussion*. Columbia, MD: National Institute for Relationship Training, 1988.

Schrader, D.E., and J. Millman. "Three Perspectives on Teaching Moral Values." *College Teaching*, Winter, 1991.

Simon, Sidney B. *Meeting Yourself Halfway: 31 Values Clarification Strategies for Daily Living*. Sunderland, MA: Values Press, 1991.

Simon, Sidney B.; Leland W. Howe; and Howard Kirschenbaum. *Values Clarification: A Handbook of Practical Strategies*. Sunderland, MA: Values Press, 1991.

Teaching Values and Ethics. Arlington, VA: American Association of School Administrators, 1992.

Townsend, Katharine. "Not Just Read and Write But Right and Wrong." *Washington Monthly* 21: 30-34, January 1990.

Jewish

Elkins, Dov Peretz.* *Clarifying Jewish Values: 25 Values Activities for Jewish Groups*. Beachwood, OH: Growth Associates, 1977.

———. *Experiential Programs for Jewish Groups Volume 1*. Beachwood, OH: Growth Associates, 1979.

———. *Jewish Consciousness Raising*. Beachwood, OH: Growth Associates, 1977.

———. *The Ideal Jew: A Values Clarification Program*. Beachwood, OH: Growth Associates, n.d. (Leader's Guide and 15 participants' forms)

———. *Why Did Susan Cohen Desert Judaism?* Beachwood, OH: Growth Associates, n.d. (A Values Clarification Program on Intermarriage, Assimilation, Jewish Community Priorities; Leader's Guide and 15 participants' forms)

Israel, Richard J. *Jewish Identity Games: A How-To-Do-It Book*. Los Angeles: Torah Aura Productions, 1993.

Reisman, Bernard. *The Jewish Experiential Book: The Quest for Jewish Identity*. Hoboken, NJ: Ktav Publishing House, 1979.

*Educational materials by Dov Peretz Elkins may be ordered from Growth Associates, 25180 Shaker Blvd., Beachwood, OH 44122.

CREATING AND USING MATERIALS

CHAPTER NINETEEN

PLANNING LIVELY LESSONS

Audrey Friedman Marcus

Each of us knows creative and charismatic teachers who can walk into the class and mesmerize the students for an entire session. These individuals can lecture for the whole hour, use no creative techniques, and still manage to excite the group and impart learning. Teachers of this type exist, but they are very rare. Planning and carrying out exciting and educationally sound lessons is a complex endeavor and a great art. This chapter provides an overview of the components of good lesson plans and some tips to help you plan.

While lesson planning is anathema to many teachers, it is essential to good teaching. What is more, once a person sees how helpful and enriching planning can be, writing lesson plans can be rewarding and even fun. Here are some reasons why lesson plans are necessary:

1. Advance planning can help teachers to make the most out of every lesson.
2. Planning allows time to think deeply about the lesson, to add to it, enrich it, find resources for it, and bounce it off others.
3. The Director of Education or Supervisor to whom lesson plans are submitted can look them over in advance and respond to them in a meaningful way, adding helpful comments and suggestions for enrichment and resources.
4. Planning in advance gives the teacher options from which to choose, depending on the dynamics of the session.
5. Making good lesson plans prevents running out of things to do.
6. Careful planning prevents long delays between activities.
7. Discipline problems which occur because lack of planning can often be avoided. (See Chapter 4, "Classroom Management," for a further discussion of the relationship between discipline and a well organized classroom.)
8. Lesson plans are an invaluable help to a substitute.
9. Lesson plans are essential for next year's teacher. Who knows — that could be you!!

I have heard teachers claim that their best lessons were spontaneous. Certainly we have all had spontaneous successes. In my view, we can continue to do so when using lesson plans. For lesson plans are not meant to imprison us, preventing us from exploring exciting discussions which are not specifically planned. They are rather meant to be a guide, a structure which prevents us from going completely astray, neglecting the assigned subjects and not making the most of the time at our disposal. As one educator puts it, "Good planning is the springboard — not the straight jacket — to creative teaching."[1]

Lessons, like plays and movies and speeches and sermons, need order and flow. They can peak too soon and go flat at the end. They can leave the group, when the bell rings, in the midst of a heated argument or up to the elbows in finger paint. Or they can end before they are supposed to, causing the teacher to cast around hurriedly for time fillers. Lesson planning can avoid these crises.

Lesson plans are not idle exercises invented out of the cruelty of administrators or teachers of education courses. Rather they are like making a shopping list. They help us to remember the items we need and prevent us (for the most part) from impulse buying. A lesson plan helps us to cover the territory we want to cover, or must cover, and to avoid straying into areas which are irrelevant, which belong in some other teacher's curriculum, or which are more appropriately taught in secular school.

THE COMPONENTS OF A LESSON PLAN

Although the lesson plan forms may vary and the terms used may differ, there is usually a space for four main components: key concepts (or main ideas), objectives, learning experiences, and resources. Some forms also provide room to describe the opening and closing activities and to list some questions to ask the students. (See figure 1 for an example of a lesson plan form that includes all of these headings.) Each of the four main components is discussed in detail below.

Key Concepts

Key concepts are the ideas, concerns, or skills which we want to teach our students. They represent the content or subject matter that you will teach. Frequently, these are outlined for you in the curriculum of your school. Sometimes, however, these outlines are very general, and it is necessary to zero in yourself on the concepts you will be teaching.

When isolating key concepts for a lesson plan, it is vital to consider the level of students' intellectual ability. The noted educator Jerome Bruner has said that "any subject can be taught effectively in some intellectually honest form to any child at any statge in development."[2] He goes on to emphasize, however, that the subject matter must be structured so that it is presented in terms of the child's way of viewing things.

For example, a teacher once complained to me of the difficulty in conveying to a prekindergarten child the concept of prayer. I suggested asking such questions as: When your Mom or Dad does something extra special for you, what do you do? When you want them to do something extra special for you, what do you do? When you want them to do something for you sometime in the future, what do you say or do? These questions are asked at the level of the child, yet in the answers to them lies a comparison with the three kinds of prayers — thanks, petition, and praise.

For helpful information on the developmental level of children, see Chapter 6, "About Child Development.")

The content of lesson should be organized around one or two key concepts. If too many concepts are presented at a time, it doesn't allow students sufficient time for synthesis, reflection, and creative expression. Also, it will be very difficult for the teacher to reinforce so many concepts at once.

Concepts are often difficult to teach and to master. This is especially true of concepts such as justice and mercy and the many other abstract qualities of behavior which are so central to Judaism. We need to invest these concepts with meaning for the learner. The best way to do this is by helping the student to experience the concepts in many different contexts and through a variety of activities in which they can become actively involved.

DON'T PRESENT TOO MANY CONCEPTS AT ONE TIME.

Objectives

Objectives are the next component of a good lesson plan. Without well thought out objectives, lessons often appear to be aimless. Learning experiences are not always related, and there is no sound basis for a choice of methods and materials. This can lead to frustration on the part of students and teachers. What is worse, any evaluation of learning becomes difficult, if not impossible.

Students who know what they are supposed to learn can work toward specific objectives, assessing themselves on the way. One of the biggest problems in Religious School is that many youngsters have no idea why they are there and what they are supposed to learn. This situation can be alleviated if teachers will write objectives and share them with their students.

The kind of objectives which we will describe here are called behavioral objectives (or sometimes performance objectives). These are brief, clear statements that describe what kind of performance the student is expected to demonstrate when the lesson is over.

Behavioral objectives are different from goals. Goals are usually created by the Board of Trustees, the Religious School Committee, or the Director of Education. They are more general, often reflecting the philosophical basis of the curriculum. Behavioral objectives, on the other hand, are very specific and reflect the performance of students which evidences that they have mastered the subject matter. These objectives are small steps toward the larger goal.

Following is a brief overview of how to write good behavioral objectives. For those who wish to go into this subject in more depth, several excellent references are cited in the Bibliography.

WEEKLY LESSON PLAN

Teacher _____

Grade _____   Date of Session _____

KEY CONCEPTS [Ideas, concerns, skills you will teach students.]

OBJECTIVES [Statements in behavioral terms — what the students will be able to do after the session.]

LEARNING EXPERIENCES

    Set Induction [The opening activity that will focus students' attention on the lesson, stimulate their interest, and create an organizing framework for the information to follow.]

    Middle Learning Experiences [A list of projects, games, drama activities, songs, field trips, guest speakers, values clarification strategies, lecture, discussion questions, etc., that make up the body of the lesson.]

    Evaluation/Closure [The culminating activity that pulls together the learning, relates it to the objective, and tells you what students learned.]

RESOURCES [Page numbers in textbook or workbook, worksheets, songs, art supplies, pictures or photographs, videos, teacher references, etc.]

Figure 1

As stated earlier, a good behavioral objective specifies the kind of behavior that a student must demonstrate in order to have achieved the objective. It is too vague to say that the objective is "to instill in the students an appreciation of the symbols of Shabbat." Such vague statements need to be transformed into good objectives by using different verbs and by becoming much more specific about the expectations.

Good objectives are written in terms of the student. They state what the student will be able to do at the end of the lesson. And, finally, they are measurable. It is impossible for us to evaluate in a vacuum whether a student appreciates the symbols of the Shabbat. We can, however, measure understanding through his/her identification with and explanation of the symbols.

If desired, the teacher may also impose conditions on the learner which measure the degree of mastery he/she should achieve. These conditions might specify resources or time limits When conditions are imposed, such statements as these are added to the objective: "Given a list of Jewish holidays," "Within thirty minutes," "Without the aid of the text or other books." Teachers may also wish to specify how accurate students must be in order to demonstrate mastery of the objective. For instance, students might be required to answer correctly 75% of the questions, or list correctly eight out of ten possibilities.

Here are some examples of good instructional objectives:

The student will describe to younger children his/her views on the beauty of our tradition.

The student will write the words to the blessings over the wine, candles, and bread.

The student will identify the symbols of the Shabbat and write a brief paragraph on their meaning.

The student will construct a chart which shows the significance of the Torah to the Jewish people.

The student will write a story about the Chanukah celebration as he or she experienced it at home or in class.

The student will explain his or her view of God in poetry, song, or essay.

The student will outline the reasons for giving *tzedakah*.

The student will list reasons for having or not having faith in the goodness of people.

The following list of words reflects specific performance and will help you to write your own instructional objectives in more concrete terms.

List	Diagram
Define	Illustrate
Describe	Create
Identify	Organize
Defend	Relate
Distinguish	Write
Explain	Tell
Give examples	Compare
Summarize	Contrast
Demonstrate	justify
Solve	Interpret
Differentiate	

Many contemporary curriculum materials contain objectives that are expressed in behavioral terms. These objectives are sometimes divided into cognitive objectives and affective objectives. Writing affective objectives is more difficult, but with practice, you can become adept at doing so. In a Religious School setting especially, affective objectives are enormously important.

Learning Experiences

Once the key concepts are outlined and the objectives determined, it is time to design activities which will communicate the concepts and meet the objectives.

In an afternoon or evening program, the students are often tired, restless, and hungry after a long day at school. Many also complain that they are bored in Religious School. A special effort is required to involve and motivate these students. One good way to do so is to employing a variety of learning experiences. Such stimulus variation also helps to prevent discipline problems. Some ways to provide variety in your lessons follow.

Lecture infrequently and keep your lectures short. (A good rule of thumb for the length of a lecture is age plus grade. Thus, if your students are eight years old in the third grade, lecture for only 10-11 minutes at the most. If students are 13-year-old eighth graders, you should be able to talk for about 21 minutes without losing your audience.) Always make an outline for your lecture. (For other suggestions on lecturing, see Chapter 13, "Listening Skills, Lecture, and Discussion.")

Students need to be actively engaged in many different activities, to be doing things, not always to be listening to the teacher. Every learning experience ought to provide an opportunity for each student to become involved, not just those who are outgoing and aggressive or talented.

The existence of different learning styles is another reason for varying the learning experiences. Some children do best when they hear about something, others are visual learners and do best when they see something written down. Still others need combinations of these or other kinds of active involvement. Therefore, don't always read or always discuss. Use reading and analyzing, doing research, observing, writing, experimenting, constructing, tabulating, painting, role playing, dramatization, and as many other processes as possible.

Learning experiences should also be varied in terms of individual, small, and whole group participation. This kind of interaction can cause a whole new atmosphere to pervade a class. For example, students might write solutions at their seats to a problem posed in a case study provided by the teacher. Then small groups of four could meet to share their responses and reach consensus on the best solution. Each "quartet" then shares their ideas with the class as a whole. With this process, every student has moved three times, has had a chance to respond individually, has matched his or her ideas with others, and has had experience problem solving alone and in a group. As reporters, some have had to speak before the entire group. Others have had to learn to be listeners. No one has judged the answers right or wrong, but a free spirit of inquiry has characterized the process. Both cooperative learning and values clarification, among other methods, provide the means for this kind of interaction. (See Chapter 14, "Cooperative or Collaborative Learning" and Chapter 18, "Values Clarification.")

How you physically organize your lessons is also of great importance.[3] Most teachers plan a series of sessions, each with a different focus, always involving the whole class in the same process. A diagram of this type of plan is:

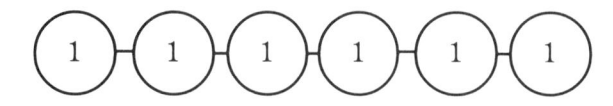

Figure 2

Another way to organize the unit is to start off by introducing all the material. Students are then organized into smaller groups to focus on one area for several weeks. Then they put it all together for a last session summary or review. This model of organizing a unit might be diagrammed as follows:

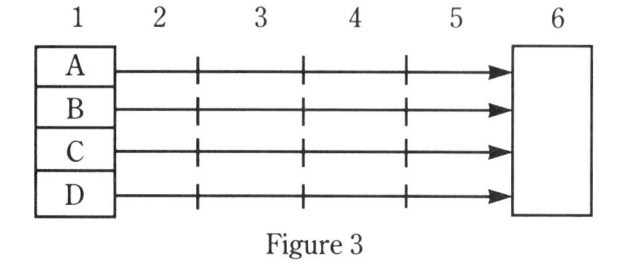

Figure 3

A third way to plan is to introduce a lot of material in the first session, encouraging the students to raise questions, make suggestions, and help decide where to go and what to do in the succeeding sessions. This may be diagrammed as:

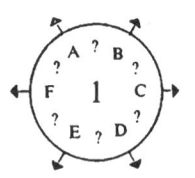

Figure 4

Most teachers find themselves organizing only one way most of the time. It helps to increase the interest of both students and teachers if other models are occasionally used.

Introductory Learning Experience

The introductory activity of any lesson is critical. You want the students to feel a need for the knowledge, to be interested in it, to be prepared for it, to connect it with their own experience. In the past, all of these together were referred to as the motivation. Today, they are more commonly called the "set induction." The set induction develops a mind-set for the material and creates an organizing framework for the ideas, principles, or information which is to follow. It extends the understanding and application of abstract ideas through the use of an example or analogy.

A set induction can be a gripping story, a simulation, a riddle, a hypothetical situation ("Suppose . . . "), a challenging question, a trigger film or segment of a video, or a values clarification exercise. If you are comfortable doing so, you can dash into your classroom shouting something like, "I will not bow down except to God!" Then you can point to a student and say, "Who do I sound like?" Additional ideas for set inductions are limited only by your imagination. Try different ways to set the stage for learning. Consult education books and magazines, your curriculum, and brainstorm with your colleagues.

Middle Learning Experiences

When planning learning experiences, strike a balance between warm-up questions, in-depth discussion, small group activities, and projects. Include affective exercises, as well as cognitive information. Attempt to develop the thinking skills of your students, as well as their creative potential. Include field trips and community activities, simulated experiences, demonstrations, arts and crafts projects. Invite interesting individuals to speak to the class. If using a textbook, stay away from always having a student read a paragraph, then discussing it as a class. (Consult Chapter 21, "Creative Use of Textbooks" for other ways of using a textbook effectively.)

Don't let discussions wander off — keep them tight. Time is too precious to stray off the subject. Yet, you don't want to shut off discussion in areas of deep interest and concern to students. In this, as in all lesson design, it is necessary to strike a balance.

To have a good discussion, you will need to ask good questions. Be sure to ask questions at the various levels of Bloom's taxonomy, e.g., compare, describe, summarize, agree or disagree, make applications, analyze, evaluate, synthesize. (For more on the art of questioning, see Chapter 13, "Listening Skills, Lecture, and Discussion.")

There are hundreds of possible learning experiences you can use in your classroom. For ideas, consult the Appendix where you will find a comprehensive listing categorized into general ideas, games and simulations, audiovisual, arts and crafts, music and dance, dramatics, and creative writing.

Closing Learning Experience

At the end of each session, it is critical to summarize and to anticipate in an enthusiastic way the next get-together of the class. It is essential to end with an activity that ties together and organizes the various aspects of a lesson. One way to accomplish this is to summarize the lesson for the students. Or, closure might take the form of a friendship circle, song, presentation, game, writing a list of key words, a quick quiz, applying the learning, sharing, or "I Learned Statements." A good closure activity will enable you to evaluate your lesson more effectively because you will know what students have learned.[4]

Don't forget to take a moment at the end of your lesson and wish your students a good week, or tie your good wishes into the lesson in some way.

Resources

Resources are the last component of your lesson. These are the textbooks and other materials that you will use in the process of teaching and learning — everything from a text to a tape recorder, an old magazine to a video.

Videos are, of course, very popular with students of all ages. Sources for videos include the Religious School, the central agency, video stores, the public library, and university media centers, as well as commercial distributors of Jewish films. (A list of the latter is included in the section "Resources for Jewish Educators" at the conclusion of this volume.) One other source of films is your public school system. Generally, only teachers in the system are allowed to use the films, but if there is someone on your staff who teaches in a system school, it is possible that arrangements can be made. Many secular films on such subjects as ethics, ecology, behavior, and religion, can be adapted for the Religious School classroom.

Be familiar with the resources available in your community, e.g., places for field trips, Jewish and non-Jewish museums, libraries, video collections, individuals who can donate art supplies, special exhibits, and events. Don't overlook the teacher shelf in your Religious School, the resource center at your central agency, the local newspaper, the local Jewish newspaper, other synagogues, other Jewish organizations, Scripture gardens, and teacher supply catalogs.

Some Final Steps

In the final version of your lesson plan, include the sequence of main teaching points, steps in instructional method, key features of student participation. Estimate the amount of time each activity will take. Write your plan in such a way that you can refer to it easily during the lesson.

When you have completed your lesson plan, look back over it and evaluate it.[5] Show your plan to a colleague and get some feedback before introducing it into your class. Rework it if necessary. Be sure that you don't have too many key concepts, and that the ones you do have are age appropriate and interrelated. Check also to see if your main ideas and objectives are directly connected. Do all of your activities help to fulfill your objectives? Have you planned a

> STRIVE FOR VARIETY WHEN PLANNING LEARNING EXPERIENCES.

variety of learning experiences which will stimulate maximum student interest and involvement? Be certain that your resources also reflect diversity, and that you were realistic about the time needed to teach the lesson.

Especially in Religious School where absenteeism is often high, it is important for each lesson to stand on its own. Students should be able to complete what they are doing and leave with some significant Jewish learning each time they come. Young children enjoy taking home an itemized list of what they did and learned during each session.

In advance of teaching a lesson, arrange for any audiovisual equipment, videos, etc. that you will need for your lesson. Make arrangements with the guest speaker. Be sure the speaker and his/her subject will be interesting to students. Orient the speaker in writing as to the age level of the students, the purpose of the lesson, how long to speak, whether or not to be prepared to field questions, and what sort of questions to expect. Ask him/her to bring a brief bio, and to notify you by a certain date if any special equipment is needed. It is a good idea to help students to prepare a list of questions for the speaker. Remind students to treat the speaker respectfully and always send a thank-you note. Contact field trip sites and arrange for drivers. Make provisions for enrichment for students who have become particularly interested in the topic. Decide on a method of assessment (see Chapter 40, "Student Assessment: A Rewarding Experience" for ideas).

Before teaching your lesson, gather your resources and materials. Prepare any handouts you will need. Reconfirm videos, guest speakers, and field trips.

On the day of the lesson, make your room ready (e.g., straighten it, fix the seating arrangement, put the materials where they are readily accessible, test the audiovisual equipment to be sure it is in good working order, etc.).

Evaluate each lesson after it is over. Determine what was or wasn't effective, what to add or delete. Think of ideas for substitute activities. Assess whether your time frames were accurate. Make notes on your lesson plan for the next time you teach it.

CONCLUSION

Studies show that teachers who plan are more successful in the classroom. Using the tools for planning that have been outlined in this chapter, you will quickly join the ranks of those successful teachers.

Audrey Friedman Marcus is the Executive Vice President of A.R.E. Publishing, Inc. She has been the Curriculum Coordinator at Temple Sinai in Denver. A frequent lecturer on lesson plans and curriculum development, she is a five-time winner of a curriculum award from the National Association of Temple Educators.

APPENDIX
Ideas for Learning Experiences

General Ideas

Organize a mock trial
Conduct a survey
Hold a discussion
Collect/analyze information
Start interest groups/*chugim*
Engage in a celebration
Plan/have a party
Organize learning centers
Promote independent study
Hold a debate
Invite a guest speaker
Go on a field trip
Organize a panel of experts
Have a panel of student experts (a panel of 3; the one who misses is replaced by the one who asked question)
Hold a town meeting
Give a lecture
Present case studies
Teach a lesson to a younger grade
Participate in a group dynamics exercise
Do breakout groups
Drill
Study Jewish sources
Study statements/quotations by famous Jews
Conduct an experiment
Hold a retreat
Read a make-believe letter
Have an all-elective session
Make a web (flow chart)
Engage in values clarification exercises
Do sentence completions
Have a shul-ins
Plan a *Shabbaton*
Engage in small group work
Make an exhibit
Identify sites on a map
Make a map
Trace immigration routes
Create a chart
Make a time line
Cook/bake Jewish food (familiar and from other lands and times)
Hold a bake sale
Taste Jewish food
Make Jewish paper dolls
Plan a personal Jewish library
Plan/share a Shabbat/holiday meal
Involve parents as helpers
Invite students to your home
Have a subject area fair
Hold a bazaar
Have a carnival (Purim or otherwise)
Do an inquiry project
Each student signs a contract
Brainstorm

Solve a problem
Class members respond simultaneously to questions (by raising hands or using other hand signals)
Engage in peer coupling/*Chevrutah*
Collect coins
Collect stamps
Create a Jewish museum
Visit another synagogue
Visit a Jewish library
Analyze a library collection
Check out library books
Prepare a book list for research topics
Do a research project
Make a report
Use a workbook
Complete worksheets
Do a written assignment
Tell a continuous story
Make a time capsule
Engage in a social action project (local, world, national)
Hold a Maccabiah (Sports Day)
Make up a quiz
Take a quiz
Complete a feedback sheet
Make up questions for answers provided
Hold a values auction
Create a history corner
Roll out the Torah
Start an Adopt-a-Grandparent program
Record oral histories
Create a synagogue archive
Hold a demonstration
Attend a rally
Organize a Walk-a-thon
Participate in a Walk-a-thon
Hold an art fair
Attend a cultural event
Discuss in a fish bowl (with a circle of observers)
Take a blind walk
Collect *tzedakah*
Disburse *tzedakah* collection
Do a class *tzedakah* project
Hold a *tzedakah* fair
Teacher plays devil's advocate
Visit community institutions
Volunteer in a community institution
Design a behavior code
Rotate teachers
Team teach
Set goals
Provide an idea box
Create a message center
Conduct an interview
Make a list of questions for an interview
Complete activity/task cards

CHAPTER NINETEEN **195**

Students evaluate themselves
Start an internship program
Take a test
Student gives a lecture
Form a student speakers bureau (speak on Judaism to community groups)
Create a Jewish Hall of Fame
Hold a panel discussion of books
Read from a textbook
Study current events
Make a prayer book
Hold a worship service using *Siddur*
Hold a creative service
Practice meditation
Plant a biblical garden
Have an Israeli nightclub
Salt a dig
Make wine
Put wishes on a paper Sabbath tree
Look up definitions in dictionary
Hold a mock convention
Hold a mock session of Congress
Hold a mock biennial convention of national movements (lay/Rabbinic)
Match story card and script
Sequence pages of story
Work with a magnetic fill-in board
Give a travelogue
Play with a Feelie Box
Make/use kinesthetic letters (sandpaper, corrugated cardboard, yarn)
Read aloud
Participate in a mini-course
Do a non-verbal exercise
Take a pre-test/post-test
Participate in an interfaith activity
Plan a trip
Start a scout troop or "tribe"
Play house, celebrate Shabbat and holidays
Set a holiday table
Do a Jewish show and tell
Create a ritual
Appoint "Reporter of the Day" to summarize class happenings
Start a club
Read Anglo-Jewish papers/magazines
Clip/discuss articles on Jewish issues from secular newspapers
Discuss/perform *mitzvot*
Have a Havdalah service
Look at/discuss pictures, photographs, posters
Plant trees
Design a group motto
Design a group cheer
Design a group T-shirt

Create a logo for the group
Write a song
Visit a Jewish cemetery
Do tombstone rubbings
Compare calendars made in class to published calendars
Design postcards (holiday themes, Israel, etc.)
Design/make holiday cards
Collect food for needy
Tour the synagogue
Lead synagogue tours for visitors
Make vocabulary lists
Adopt and befriend new Americans
Take a nature walk
Go on a hike
Form a learning task force
Create study teams
Use group analysis (small groups solve same problem)
Use a circle of knowledge (students respond to questions in rotation)
Involve students in team learning (small groups teach each other the facts and answer questions on them)
Form listening teams (students listen for particular aspects of a lecture)
Hold a model *Seder*
Make a cause button
Create a family tree
Kids tutor other kids
Hold student-parent panels/discussions
Assign homework
Write Jewish organizations for information/brochures
Students plan a lesson
Students teach a lesson
Students lead discussion
Create a new Jewish society (on the moon/in the 23rd century, etc.)
Attend a life cycle ceremony
Create a new life cycle
Participate in a ceremony for a new life cycle
Determine a class definition (of a concept/symbol/holiday)
Grow seedlings
Plant trees (in Israel/at the synagogue/in the community)
Visit a farm before Sukkot
Solve ethical dilemmas
Have a contest
Memorize (books of the Bible/twelve tribes, etc.)
Compare and contrast (observances in different countries/of different denominations, etc.)
Personalize inanimate ritual objects
Take a guided zoo tour
Adopt a cow on a *kibbutz*
Hold a *kibbutz* town meeting
Engage in Synectics

Games and Simulations

Play a holiday game (manufactured game/*dreidle*, etc.)
Play a guessing game
Play a board game
Students make up own game
Invent a follow the dots

Students fill in missing words
Create and do a rebus
Match columns
Play *Tic-tac-toe*
Play *Probe*

Play Hebrew *Spill & Spell*
Play Hebrew *Scrabble*
Play *20 Questions*
Organize a quiz show (*College Bowl/Jeopardy/Hollywood Squares*, etc.)
Play a game from Israel
Play a game from the shtetl
Play *Shimon Omer*
Make/complete maze
Make/complete a jigsaw puzzle
Design/complete a crossword puzzle
Do a word search
Play *Hangman*
Play *Baseball*
Play *Football*
Play *Concentration*
Play *To Tell the Truth*
Play *What's My Line?*

Play *Dominoes*
Have a treasure hunt
Go on a scavenger hunt
Use flash cards
Have a bee (spelling, etc.)
Hold relay races
Play *Bingo*
Play *Streets and Alleys*
Complete a puzzle map
Play *Go Fish*
Play *Rumor*
Play *Lotto*
Decode messages
Participate in simulations
Unscramble words
Play *Charades*
Play *Who Am I?*
Play *1-2-3 Look and See*

Audiovisual

Show a video
Show part of a film as a trigger
Show slides
Show a filmstrip
See a film in a theater
Attend a play
Take pictures with slide film/print film
Make a slide show
Produce a film
Make a scratch film
Make slides by contact lifting
Make a commercials
Create/use transparencies for an overhead projector
Use an opaque projector
Take Polaroid pictures
Make a photo album
Create a photo essay
Make a "filmstrip" out of overhead transparencies
Revitalize an old filmstrip
Bleach out an old filmstrip and use over

Make pictures using photo sensitive paper in sunlight
Play tapes of famous speeches
Tape record interviews
Make photograms
Create a spot announcement for public service TV/radio
Design a bulletin board
Use a flannel board
Use a flip chart
Make a continuous action "TV" show (roll paper story through a box)
Correspond with pen pal by tape
Show a Viewmaster Bible story
Use a Show 'n Tell machine
Make a photo profile of a famous person
Create a photo exhibit
Make a video
Tape record language practice
Tape record plays/songs/stories
Paste snapshots of children's heads on pictures of adult Jews doing Jewish things

Arts and Crafts

Draw with paint/charcoal/pastels
Make a poster/travel poster
Create a class mural
Write graffiti
Make stickers
Make a woodcut
Draw a cartoon
Draw a comic strip
Make a silkscreen
Draw caricatures
Make a diorama
Construct a model
Create greeting cards
Create postcards
Design stationery with a Jewish theme
Make holiday decorations
Create ritual objects

Design/make costumes
Make a mobile
Create stained glass
Design a book cover/jacket
Create a book mark
Make scenery for a play
Create a jacket for a book
Bind stories into a book
Make a collage
Make a scrapbook
Make a photo album
Make a montage
Do soap carvings
Do potato carvings
Make a flag
Record album covers for Jewish records
Finger paint/foot paint (with finger paint/pudding)

Learn calligraphy
Do seed paintings and boxes
Have an art exhibit
Illustrate stories
Use clay/play dough/sawdust clay/Plaster of Paris
Create using Papier mâché
Use cereal boxes/plastic bottles (to make *tzedakah* boxes, etc.)
Embroider
Create a bulletin board
Make a sculpture (out of metal/wire/toothpicks, etc.)
Make a scroll
Illuminate a psalm/poem
Use a sand table
Make a sand painting
Create a mosaic (out of ceramic/paper, etc.)
Make prints (sponge/linoleum/potato/styrofoam, etc.)
Make Bible toys
Create a banner
Make a flag
Design a Jewish calendar
Make a relief map
Make a model
Make a gift
Make a gift certificate
Design a Jewish quilt
Make a floral decoration for the Shabbat/holiday table
Design/bind a book
Create a booth for a carnival/fair
Do decoupage
Create tissue paper art
Do bottle crafts
Use pipe cleaners
Make a crayon resist
Create a wall hanging
Make junk art

Do stitchery
Create a batik
Tie dye
Weave
Create a string picture
Do nail art
Construct using spools
Make ceramic objects
Make a puppet
Make a puppet stage
Make a chart
Make a map
Design sets for plays
Make a scrapbook
Make a photo album
Make something Jewish to wear
Design a *mizrach*
Learn to do paper cut
Make a plaque
Design a placemat
Make a bookmark
Design wrapping paper/gift tags
Construct a terrarium
Make a mask
Make "Honorary Teacher Certificates" for guest speakers
Design Israeli stamps
Use rice for a project
Make candles (for Shabbat/Havdalah)
Originate musical instruments
Make drawings from slides
Make a card flipping machine
Devise an illustrated Jewish dictionary
Make games/toys
Do a scratchboard drawing

Music and Dance

Listen to music (rock/folk/contemporary/liturgical, etc.)
Listen to/sing Hebrew songs (modern/Israeli, etc.)
Listen to/sing Yiddish and Ladino songs
Compose music
Write new words to a song
Write a parody
Have a song contest
Act out a song
Sing in a choir

Put on a musical/cantata
Do a choral reading
Make a tape
Participate in movement activities
Do Israeli dancing
Vote on favorite Jewish music
Create rhythm instruments
Start a rhythm band
Participate in Jewish karioke

Dramatics

Read a play
Produce a play
Attend a play
Create a radio play/soap opera
Devise a TV show
Tell a story
Role play a story
Create puns
Make up jokes
Reverse roles
Mime/pantomime

Make a puppet (hand puppet/stick puppet/egg carton puppet/sock puppet/mouth puppet, etc.)
Make a marionette
Play "human scenery"
Role play
Carry on conversations between historical/imaginary characters
Act out new endings to a play/story
Reverse heroes and villains
Make miniature stage sets
Put on a skit
Do paper bag dramatics

Listen to/perform dramatic readings
Act out story in new style
Have "historical personalities" visit
Simulate a historical event (life cycle ceremony/board and committee meetings, etc.)
Use a flannel board
Perform a monologue
Play *Charades*

Do a recitation
Make a shadowgraph
Dress up as a famous Jewish person
Do improvisations
Become a symbol
Participate in a guided fantasy
Have a talent show

Creative Writing

Write a report
Write an essay
Organize an essay contest
Write a story
Write a continuous story
Write a class book/story
Put stories together in a book
Create a poem (haiku/cinquain/diamante/acrostic/limerick, etc.)
Finish an unfinished story
Complete unfinished sentences
Complete story starters
Reverse sequence in a story
Rewrite the ending of a story
Start a class or school newspaper/magazine
Write an article for the synagogue bulletin
Write a monologue
Write/send letters (to government officials/pen pals/authors/historical characters/editors/national organizations, etc.)
Write an autobiography
Compose a biography of a famous Jewish person
Do a book report
Write a review of a movie/play/TV show
Compile a Jewish dictionary
Write commentaries
Create *midrashim*
Write *Responsa*
Write a prayer
Write a creative service
Compile handbooks (for new synagogue members/newcomers to the community/new parents/ prospective brides and grooms/B'nai Mitzvah and parents, etc.
Write a first person account of a historical event
Compose character sketches
Write words to a song
Write story as a phone conversation

Write a phone conversation as a poem
Write a phone conversation as the lyrics of a song
Write a story to move someone to action
Tell a tall tale
Complete reaction sheets
Make a book for younger children
Write first person account of an historical event
Write an advertisement
Create advertising slogans
Write a diary/journal (personal/imaginary)
Write a letter to "Dear Abby"
Respond to a letter to "Dear Abby"
Compose an epitaph for a famous Jewish person/for yourself
Write an obituary for a famous Jewish person/for yourself
Write a telegram
Compose a resolution for a Jewish organization
Write a story as an inanimate object (the burning bush/Moses' rod, etc.)
Rewrite a Bible account in dialogue
Create the before/after of biblical stories
Rewrite a Bible story as a newspaper account
Write a modern day story/play of Bible characters (like *Sedra Scenes*)
Create comics
Compare stories/books/TV shows/newspaper accounts
Write a play/skit
Write a script for a student-made slide show/filmstrip
Rewrite the sound track for a film or filmstrip
Write and illustrate a *Siddur*
Write a travel lecture on Israel
Create a travel pamphlet on Israel/other places of Jewish interest
Make up headlines for historical events
Write an ethical will
Write a ceremony for a new life cycle
Write to a Jewish pen pal

NOTES

1. Derwin J. Jeffries, *Lesson Planning and Lesson Teaching* (Sun City, AZ: Home and School Press, 1966), p. 247.
2. Jerome S. Bruner, *The Process of Education* (New York: Vintage, 1963), p. 33.
3. The suggestions on ways to organize lesson are adapted from *The Planning Game* by Donald L. Griggs (Livermore: Griggs Educational Service, 1971). Used with permission.
4. Adapted from an article by Mimi Cohen in the Spring 1990 issue of *The Melton Journal* and reprinted in *V'Shinantam: UAHC Southwest Teacher News*, a publication of the UAHC Southwest Council, Dallas, Texas, August-September 1990.
5. The ways to organize lessons are adapted from *The Planning Game* by Donald L. Griggs (Livermore: Griggs Educational Service, 1971). Used with permission.

BIBLIOGRAPHY

Books

Borick, Gary D. *Effective Teaching Methods*. New York: Merrill, 1992.

Bloom, Benjamin S., ed. *Taxonomy of Educational Objectives: The Classification of Educational Goals. Handbook I: The Cognitive Domain*. White Plains, NY: Longman Publishing Group, 1984.

Bruner, Jerome. *Towards a Theory of Instruction*. Cambridge, MA: Harvard University Press, 1966.

Cooper, James M., et al. *Classroom Teaching Skills; A Handbook*. 4th ed. Lexington, MA: D.C. Heath and Co., 1990.

Dillon, J. T. *The Practice of Questioning*. New York: Routledge, 1990.

Gagne, Robert M., et al. *Principles of Instructional Design*. Fort Worth, TX: Harcourt Brace College Publishers, 1992.

Griggs, Donald L. *Teaching Teachers To Teach*. Nashville, TN: Abingdon Press, 1983.

Gronlund, Norman E. *Stating Objectives for Classroom Instruction*. London: The Macmillan Group, 1985.

Harmin, Merrill. *Inspiring Active Learning: A Handbook for Teachers*. Alexandria, VA: ASCD, 1994.

Henak, Richard M. *Lesson Planning for Meaningful Variety in Teaching*. 2d ed. Washington, DC: National Education Association, 1984.

Jeffries, Derwin J. *Lesson Planning and Lesson Teaching*. Sun City, AZ: Home and School Press, 1966.

John, Peter. *Lesson Planning for Substitute Teachers*. New York: Cassell Publishing, 1993.

Joseph, Samuel. *How To Be a Jewish Teacher: An Invitation To Make a Difference*. Los Angeles: Torah Aura Productions, 1987.

Joyce, Bruce, and Marsha Weil. *Models of Teaching*. 4th ed. Needham Heights, MA: Allyn and Bacon, 1992.

Krathwohl, David; Bloom, Benjamin S.; Masia, Bertram B. *Taxonomy of Educational Objectives: The Classification of Educational Goals. Handbook II: The Affective Domain*. White Plains, NY: Longman Publishing Group, 1984.

Lyons, Paul. *Thirty-five Lesson Formats: A Sourcebook of Instructional Alternatives*. Englewood Cliffs, NJ: Prentice-Hall, 1992.

Mager, Robert F. *Preparing Instructional Objectives*. 2d rev. ed. Belmont, CA: Lake Publishing Co., 1984.

Neibert, Aimee. *Instant Lessons for Substitute Teachers*. West Orange, NJ: Behrman House, n.d.

Sanders, Norris M. *Classroom Questions: What Kinds?* New York: Harper & Row, 1966.

Video

"Teaching Skills for the Jewish Classroom: The Art and Science of Questioning." 52 min. Los Angeles: Rhea Hirsch School of Hebrew Union College-Jewish Institute of Religion, n.d.

CREATING AND USING MATERIALS

CHAPTER TWENTY

EVALUATING AND CHOOSING LEARNING MATERIALS

Ronald Wolfson

On any given day in a Jewish educator's office, dozens of pieces of mail come across the desk, among them, catalogs, brochures, and circulars announcing the latest textbook or video or computer program which, according to its publisher, is guaranteed to revolutionize Jewish teaching forever.

In the 1960s and 1970s, Jewish educators bemoaned the fact that there was precious little to choose from in the way of classroom instructional materials on Jewish subjects. There were the two major private publishers of Jewish textbooks, three ideological commissions on Jewish education, and assorted large and small Jewish organizations which put out materials for "Jewish education" in its broadest sense.

Today, there are dozens upon dozens of publishers of Jewish educational materials, ranging from large, well-established houses to small "kitchen table" operations with something unique to offer. This tremendous growth in sources of instructional materials is in evidence at national teacher and educator conventions, in Jewish bookstores, and in the large number of publicity circulars which are mailed to Jewish schools and teachers. Never in the history of Jewish education has there been such a wealth of instructional material for teaching the subject matter of Jewish schools.

Moreover, the variety and breadth of these new materials are quite impressive. The traditional text books are perhaps still the bedrock of published curriculum offerings. Yet, more innovative forms of instructional materials, including many "teacher-made" materials are available through the emerging network of Jewish teacher centers and libraries. In a word, the Jewish educator of today has a new flexibility to be eclectic in the choice of instructional materials to bring to students.

However, with this new flexibility comes a new challenge — how to evaluate and select the best materials. How are Jewish teachers, principals and school board members to sift through the brochures and catalogs? How are they to make comparisons between various materials designed to reach the same objectives? How are they to judge the quality and effectiveness of expensive media programs? In other words, how do those responsible for selecting instructional materials become enlightened consumers of these products? There are three steps to making informed choices about which materials to use in a classroom or school: (1) identifying and locating what currently exists in any specific area of curriculum — what's available and how do I get it; (2) once located, evaluating the material against some objective criteria — does the material meet our standards; (3) after evaluating what's available, comparing competing materials and reaching a decision regarding which material to use — what shall we buy.

STEP 1: IDENTIFYING AND LOCATING LEARNING MATERIALS

The most obvious source for identifying and locating what materials exist is the publishers themselves. Most companies mail brochures and catalogs on a regular basis to lists of Jewish schools provided by mailing houses or national agencies. If you or your school are missing catalogs, it is a good idea to prepare a short letter asking to be put on the mailing list of publishers from which you want to hear. The most current source of publishers active in the development of Jewish materials appears in "Resources for Jewish Educators" at the back of this book.

In addition to the Jewish publishers of curriculum material, there are many learning materials that may be appropriate for your school or classroom available from publishers and distributors of general educational materials. For example, Weston Woods[1] distributes a series of videos that includes the Isaac Bashevis Singer story "Why Noah Chose the Dove." A national distributor of Social Studies materials, Social Studies School Service,[2] offers a catalogue of materials dealing with religious and values education which includes many items of possible use in Jewish schools, yet produced by secular education companies. A local teacher center, library, or university instructional materials center will usually have catalogs from these publishers.

Other resources for identifying learning materials are magazines, newsletters, and professional journals published by educational organizations. Sometimes publishers will advertise in these journals. Some journals carry columns highlighting new products, for example, *Jewish Education News*[3] publishes critical reviews of materials. *Compass*, published by the UAHC also reviews materials,[4] as does *The Melton Journal*,[5] which is published by The Melton Research Center of The Jewish Theological Seminary of America.

Beyond catalogs, actual collections and displays of materials are certainly an important way to locate materials of possible interest. The first collection to consider is your own school office or library. You may be surprised at what you discover. Next, look at collections of fellow teachers; many colleagues will gladly share resources. The third place to look is other schools and libraries in the area, especially those with teacher resource centers. And don't forget the obvious — a local Bureau of Jewish Education. (If there is no such resource in your immediate locale, it may be well worth the investment in time and expense to fly to a major city so as to sift through the wealth of materials available at a well stocked BJE.) In larger Jewish communities, Jewish teacher training institutions, universities, and independent teacher centers often have extensive collections of published and unpublished learning materials. In some communities, Jewish bookstores carry publishers' materials.

One of the major attractions of the annual CAJE conference is the exhibit of instructional materials offered by publishers. Not only are the materials available for inspection by Jewish teachers and educators, but often a representative of the publisher or even the author of a particular item will be there to discuss materials of interest. Moreover, it is sometimes possible to arrange for a publisher's representative to visit your community to explain the company's products or to conduct a workshop on how to use certain materials. Of course, remember that publishers are trying to sell a product; although most want to be honest about their materials, their claims do reflect a biased opinion.

STEP 2: A GUIDE FOR EVALUATING AND CHOOSING LEARNING MATERIALS

Once the search for materials has been completed, the next task is to subject the products to close scrutiny, preferably by using a set of objective criteria for evaluation.

Using established criteria for evaluating learning materials ensures that the evaluator approaches the task with some guidance and that the results of the evaluation are based on a comprehensive examination of the product. It is so easy simply to "eyeball" material and make quick judgments about its worth. And yet, time and again, in workshops on evaluating materials, participants have changed their opinions after examining materials using the criteria.

The following Guide for Evaluating Instructional Programs and Materials has emerged over years of doing courses and workshops with teachers and educators interested in refining their evaluation skills. It is presented here in outline form, with explanatory comments as necessary. Following the outline, some suggestions for use are offered.

(Note: For a simple form to use when evaluating audiovisual materials, see Appendix. For sources for reviews of videos of Jewish interest, see the Bibliography.)

GUIDE FOR EVALUATING INSTRUCTIONAL PROGRAMS AND MATERIALS

Name_____
Date_____

1.0 Description
    1.1 Title
    1.2 Author(s)
    1.3 Author's qualifications
    Does the publisher detail the background and experience of the author? How much confidence do you have in the author's abilities?
    1.4 Publisher
    What do you know about the publisher? Have you used other products from them?
    1.5 Copyright Date
    How recent is the material? Beware of Social Studies texts with outdated information or pictures — particularly material on Israel.
    1.6 Cost
    Usually cost is available only in publicity brochures or catalogs.
    1.7 Components
    What's in the package?
    1.8 Type of material
    Is it a text, teacher's guide, film, map, transparency, computer program, game, videotape, cassette tape, etc.?
    1.9 Technical characteristics
    Number of pages/size/speed/length/color/sound

2.0 Appropriateness
    2.1 Is the target population specified?
    Does the producer tell you for which learners this material is intended?
        2.1.1 Age
        2.1.2 Grade level
        2.1.3 Special characteristics of learners
        Do the learners need to be bilingual? Is it intended for students with special needs?
    2.2 Is the product appropriate regarding:
        2.2.1 Grade Level
        In your best judgment, will this product be usable in the grade level indicated by the producer? If not, what grade level do you suggest?
        2.2.2 Language
        Will the vocabulary and terminology used in the product be understandable to learners in the grade level indicated? Look at both English and Hebrew words. Are transliterations used? Are the instructions clear to students?
        2.2.3 Is it free from bias, sexist language, and prejudiced attitudes or concepts? Look carefully at materials from the various ideological movements. Can a liberal Religious School use materials published by traditional groups or vice versa?

3.0 Objectives
    3.1 Are the objectives clearly and specifically stated?
    What is the product intended to do? Are there behavioral objectives? Attitudinal objectives? Affective objectives? Social objectives?

- 3.2 Is the value of the objectives substantiated?

    Does the publisher/author state why students should learn this material? Of what value will it be to them?

- 3.3 What outcomes are anticipated by the author if the program is used?

    How much will be learned? What does the author state will happen after students finish the material?

- 3.4 Are there implicit objectives which may lead to unintended outcomes?

    Beware of hidden curricula! Is there anything in the presentation of material which might result in outcomes *not* anticipated?

4.0 Learning Activities

- 4.1 What are the learning activities?
    - 4.1.1 Types of activity

        Projects, lectures, listening/viewing media, discussions, etc.?
    - 4.1.2 Content areas

        What content is presented? What is included? What is left out?
- 4.2 Are the learning activities directly related to the objectives?
    - 4.2.1 Are the learning activities presented sequentially so as to develop student behavior, skills, attitudes?
- 4.3 Will the material and activities be of interest to students?

    Is there sufficient motivation to activate student involvement with the material? Will the material be meaningful to the students?

- 4.4 Does the product communicate information which is accurate?
- 4.5 Are a variety of alternative learning experiences or activities suggested?
- 4.6 Can the product be used in a variety of curricular contexts? Where in the school curriculum can the product be used?

5.0 Utilization

- 5.1 Is there a teacher guide? Does it:
    - 5.1.1 Specify the role(s) of the teacher?

        Is the teacher a lecturer, discussion leader, facilitator, etc.?
    - 5.1.2 Describe special skills necessary for the teacher and provide instruction in those skills? If the teacher is to lead a discussion, does the guide offer tips for leading discussions?
    - 5.1.3 Describe special equipment conditions or materials that are necessary. Do you need a special film projector, craft supplies, etc.?
    - 5.1.4 Is there a bibliography?
- 5.2 Is the material durable and reusable?

    Will the product stand up to the wear and tear of classroom use? Are any components of the product consumable, necessitating replacement?

- 5.3 Does the price reflect the full cost of the program?

    Do you need to buy or rent special equipment to use the product?

6.0 Technical quality

Rate on a four point scale: **Excellent** **Good** **Fair** **Poor**

6.1 Photography
6.2 Graphics
6.3 Color
6.4 Sound
6.5 Music
6.6 Narration
6.7 Script
6.8 Sequence/layout
6.9 Type size

7.0 Evaluation

7.1 Was the program evaluated before publication?

It is rare for publishers to document any field-testing of materials before publication. Nevertheless, write and ask.

7.1.1 If yes, in what different situations, and what kinds of evaluations were done?

If the field-testing was done at camp, why do you think it will work in school? Was it tested in "average" classrooms with "average" teachers?

7.2 Has the material ever been revised?

7.3 Can the effectiveness of the program be evaluated by means provided in the material?

Are student tests provided? Other forms of evaluation?

8.0 Personal Preference

8.1 Does the overall plan, appearance, and content of the product elicit in the educator feelings of

8.1.1 Worth

Is it worthwhile?

8.1.2 Trust

Do I trust it to do what it says it will do?

8.1.3 Reliability

Will it continue to deliver what it promises for a long time (particularly when considering adopting texts or investing in media)?

8.1.4 Potential for approval/disapproval by others

Will the product be controversial if used?

8.1.5 Does the material fit your philosophy of Jewish education?

9.0 General Summary Comments

10.0 Would you purchase it? Would you use it? Not use it?

STEP 3: DECISION MAKING AMONG ALTERNATIVES

There is a variety of approaches to making decisions about curriculum in Jewish schools. In some schools, an education committee decides on the curriculum to be used; in others, this decision is left totally to the professional educator. There are even schools in which teachers are encouraged to decide what materials to use.

In any case, the criteria suggested above should help whoever is charged with the task of evaluating learning materials for use in the school. This Guide is intended as a point of reference and should be adapted to each user's needs and situation. For some, the Guide is very thorough; for others, the Guide may demand more time than is available. The shorter Quick Checklist which follows is offered as an alternative for those unable to study a piece of material in depth.

A QUICK CHECKLIST

1. Is the product appropriate for the grade level specified?
2. Are the objectives clearly and specifically stated?
3. Are the learning activities directly related to the objectives?
4. Will the material and activities be of interest to students?
5. Are a variety of alternate learning experiences or activities suggested?
6. Is there a teacher guide which provides teacher instruction?
7. Is the material durable and reusable?
8. Is the technical quality satisfactory?
9. Was the program evaluated before publication?
10. Can the effectiveness of the product be evaluated by means provided in the material?
    I would purchase it ☐
    Use it ☐
    Not use it ☐

The most comprehensive approach to evaluating and selecting learning materials might take the following form. Appoint a few members of the education committee to take on the responsibility of evaluating material before purchase. Include on this committee the Director of Education and teacher representatives. Acquire copies of the material to be evaluated or, in the case of media, arrange a preview showing to the committee. For each product under consideration, ask each committee member to fill in the "Guide for Evaluating and Choosing Learning Materials." If many products are being considered for one slot in the curriculum, assign one product to each committee member, asking each individual to prepare a summary report to the entire group. When all evaluations have been completed, share the results with the group and come to a consensus on which products should be purchased.

A note of caution: The evaluation of learning materials through the use of criteria is an important step, but even the most thorough examination of materials from an armchair will not substitute for tryout and evaluation in the field. It is entirely possible to rate a particular product high in quality, content, and appropriateness, purchase it and introduce it into the classroom, only to find that it doesn't work. There is no substitute for experience. That is why reports of field-testing are so important. If the publisher cannot furnish evaluations of the material, ask for the names and addresses of other schools or teachers who have purchased and used the material. Contact them directly and ask them about their experience with the product. Beware! Just as asking someone else how they liked a movie carries the risk that your tastes may be different, so, asking colleagues their opinion about materials is also somewhat risky. Yet, the more information you can gather about the product, the better the chances of making the right choice.

One further idea. Some instructional products, especially media, can be previewed before purchase. Or, if the publisher does not offer preview privileges, you might be able to borrow or rent the material from a library, learning center, or neighboring school.

Jewish educators today are indeed fortunate to have an ever increasing variety of learning materials from which to choose for their instructional purposes. Evaluating these learning materials requires an investment of time and energy. Yet, to invest this effort enables the educator to be a skilled and informed consumer and user of educational products. Our field demands no less.

(The author is indebted to dozens of teachers, students, and colleagues who have used and commented on this Guide. A special thanks is due M. Frances Klein, a pioneer in this area of research in public education, whose work has been basic to my own.)

Ron Wolfson is the Director of the Shirley and Arthur Whizin Institute for Jewish Family Life and Vice President of the University of Judaism. He is the author of *The Art of Jewish Living* series published by the Federation of Jewish Men's Clubs and the University of Judaism.

APPENDIX
Audiovisual Evaluation Form

Please indicate your assessment of the materials previewed:

1. Age Level .... primary   intermediate   high school/adult

2. Facts and ideas presented .... accurate   inaccurate

3. Interest: Does the film hold the interest of the age-group for which it is intended? .. always   sometimes   never

4. Narration: Is the tone of voice boring or interesting? .... interesting   acceptable   boring

5. South quality: Clear or muddy; accents hard to understand? .... excellent   medium   poor

6. Background music .... appropriate   inappropriate

7. Overall impression of the film .... excellent   average   poor

8. Would you use this film in your classroom? .... yes   no

9. Would you use this film for entertainment at home? .... yes   no

(Adapted from a form designed by Toby Rossner)

NOTES

1. Weston Woods, Weston, CT 06883.
2. Social Studies School Service, 10,000 Culver Boulevard, Culver City, CA 90232.
3. *Jewish Education News*, CAJE, 261 W. 35th St., Floor 12A, New York, NY 10001.
4. *Compass*, 838 Fifth Avenue, New York, NY 10021.
5. *The Melton Journal*, The Melton Research Center, The Jewish Theological Seminary of North America, 3080 Broadway, New York, NY 10027.

BIBLIOGRAPHY

Association of Jewish Libraries Newsletter. Published by the Association of Jewish Libraries, c/o National Foundation for Jewish Culture, 330 Seventh Avenue, 21st Floor, New York, NY 10001.

Banks, Cheryl. *The Reviews of the Top 100 Videos*. Available from the author, North Suburban Synagogue Beth El, 1175 Sheridan Rd., Highland Park, IL 60035

Broadus, Robert N. *Selecting Materials for Libraries*. 2d ed. New York: H.W. Wilson Co., 1981.

Cabeceiras, James. *The Multimedia Library: Materials Selection and Use*. 3d ed. New York: Academic Press, 1991.

Curriculum Materials Center. *Collection Development Policy*. 2d ed. Chicago: American Library Association, 1993.

Donavin, Denise P. *American Library Association Best of the Best for Children: Software - Books - Magazines - Videos*. New York: Random House, 1992.

Helmer, Dona J. ed. *Selecting Materials for School Media Centers*. Chicago: American Library Association, 1993.

Developing Multi-Media Libraries. New York: R.R. Bowker, 1970.

Hoffman, Preston, and Carol H. Osteye. *Audio Book Breakthrough: Selection and Use in the Public Libraries and Education*. Westport, CT: Greenwood Publishing Group, Inc., 1993.

"Media and the Jewish Community." *Jewish Education News* (CAJE). Special Focus Issue, Spring 1990.

1994 Annotated Bibliography of Videos. Melton Centre for Jewish Education in the Diaspora, Mount Scopus, Hebrew University, Jerusalem, Israel. (Annotations of videos of Jewish interest from around the world)

CREATING AND USING MATERIALS

CHAPTER TWENTY-ONE

CREATIVE USE OF TEXTBOOKS

Stan J. Beiner

It is the first meeting between the Director of Education and the teacher before the start of the school year. The two educators will discuss philosophy, discipline, policies, and complimentary high holiday seats. After the nitty gritty is out of the way, the topic turns to curriculum. The Director of Education explains the subjects to be taught. If he/she holds a masters in anything, some goals and behavioral objectives might be thrown in for good measure. And then comes the inevitable question on the teacher's mind... *NEVER MIND THE OTHER STUFF ... WHAT BOOKS WILL WE BE USING?*

That question is probably the second most predictable inquiry a teacher will make before school begins (the first one being, "When is winter break?"). Ouch! Reliance upon textbooks to teach classes is like an addiction. When we think about it, we know there is something inherently wrong with the dependency, but it's easier just to deny there is a problem. It is, however, the rare textbook that can be so stimulating that it alone can guarantee a successful outcome for the class. The successful teacher has to be creative in the use of books and move away from the notion of a text-based curriculum.

Azriel Eisenberg, author of *Teaching Jewish History* wrote, "You are not teaching a text but teaching... with the aid of a text." That subtle semantic tongue twister strikes at the heart of the matter. The reality is that as a teacher sits down to prepare lessons, he/she is almost always looking at a textbook. The question is whether the class will be organized by what is in the book or whether the book is to be used as a helpful guide. Here are some steps to assist teachers in creating the best set of circumstances in which to use textbooks.

STEP ONE: KNOW WHAT YOU WANT TO ACCOMPLISH

Without getting too involved with the details of goal setting, which is a chapter unto itself, the teacher and Director of Education must first clarify what the goals are for the subject. What is it that the students should accomplish? What information is important to retain? What ethical or moral lessons are to be drawn out? What materials will be available to teach the course?

STEP TWO: ANALYZE THE TEXTBOOK

The text being used should be one that best complements that which the teacher is trying to get across. (Refer back to Step One above.) Keep these points in mind when reviewing a book and deciding whether to use it. The following are questions to consider when analyzing a textbook:

1. Is the book age appropriate in terms of ideas and reading levels?
2. Is it well organized?
3. How is it organized? Is it theme, concept, idea, or biography based?
4. How easy is the book to look at? Does it have attractive and relevant illustrations? Are the pages cluttered with too much information and detail? If the book is confusing for the teacher to read, imagine how the kids will react!
5. Does it come with a good workbook containing challenging exercises? While this is not critical, workbooks can sometimes be wonderful supplements. When a teacher has limited time and resources, why reinvent the kugel?
6. Does it have a teacher's guide? This, too, can be a terrific tool. A good guide will have suggestions, sample lessons, and approaches for transmitting the material to the students.

7. Does the text reflect the philosophy of the school? Books reflect the opinions and ideas of the authors. It is very difficult to be objective.
8. Does the textbook support the school's ideology?
9. Is the information accurate?
If the text does not complement the goals and objectives of the subject to be taught, it is better to discover this before school begins. The teacher and Director of Education would then need to look at alternative books or strategies for teaching the material. Sometimes, the best solution is using several textbooks to cover the topic, focusing in on the strengths that each book has.

(For more suggestions on analyzing materials, see Chapter 20, "Evaluating and Choosing Learning Materials.")

STEP THREE: PREPARATION FOR USING A TEXTBOOK

Congratulations, you have reached Step Three. You are ready to grapple with the challenge of placing a text in front of students who are daring you to teach them something; you are prepared to bring a lesson to life. If you wanted an easy job, you should have become a doctor.

When a teacher feels that the use of the textbook will further a point, careful planning is needed to be as effective as possible. Some suggested guidelines include:
1. Read the passages before presenting them. Textbooks are not a quick fix for those times when you have not had a chance to prepare a full lesson. If a text is used inappropriately, it can turn kids off to the challenges and pleasures that reading can bring.
2. Decide upon the key concepts and points that should be highlighted in the lesson and choose which passages are to be used to do so.
3. Select key words with which students should be familiar, and be sure of their correct pronunciation. Anticipating difficulties with certain words can sometimes prevent a lesson from being lost to students hungering for a belly laugh at anyone else's expense. Without proper warning, "*yarmulke*" can sound like an eskimo delicacy and "*Keren Ami*" becomes a very lucky girl in Israel to whom everyone gives their money.
4. Research other media to complement the text. Videos, filmstrips, magazine articles, games, worksheets, etc.

STEP FOUR: DECIDE UPON A STRATEGY FOR USING THE TEXTBOOK
Reading Aloud

Yes, sometimes it is okay to read from a book. If you feel that a particular passage is appropriate to be read aloud, keep in mind the reading levels in the class so that no one is embarrassed or the point is not lost in the presentation. When a teacher reads aloud from the book, students get a hidden message that this is particularly important. Keep passages to several paragraphs. It should be the rare exception that an entire page would be read to make a point. Examples might be:
1. I am going to read the biblical passage regarding the first day of creation. These sentences contain the explanation of why Jews count their days from evening to evening. See if you can figure it out as I read.
2. I am going to assign everyone a poem from *I Never Saw Another Butterfly*. Read your poem silently and think about what it means. Then each of us will recite the poem out loud and present your individual interpretation.
3. On the board is the phrase "Not by might, not by power, but by My spirit alone." I want you to think about what spiritual resistance means as we open our text, *My People: History of the Jews*, to page 184. We are going to read about two individuals who lived during the Holocaust — Rabbi Leo Baeck and Anne Frank. As we read, concentrate on how their lives epitomize the phrase on the board.

Directed Projects

Many teachers find that students are best motivated to use a text when they are being directed toward a specific goal. Examples might be:
1. Read Chapter 11, "Demanding a Home," in *A Young Person's History of Israel*, and list all the reasons why the British were obstacles to the creation of a Jewish state.
2. Read Chapter 3 on the Jews in the Middle Ages in Rossel's *Journey through Jewish History*. Then create a picture of what life might have been like for a ten-year-old girl, a Rabbi, a merchant.

3. Review the chapters we have covered and create a test that would be fair for the class to take.

Group Work

In directed projects such as these, consider having some work done in groups. Students often enjoy a team approach. Also, it is not always necessary to have everyone doing the same assignment. Groups or individuals can be given a task that is then reported upon to the entire class. A lot can be learned by having groups or pairs work together to outline and decide what the important terms, ideas, and messages are in a chapter. Examples follow:

1. Today we are working in pairs. Each pair will be assigned a reading about a different *mitzvah* hero in *Munbaz II and Other Mitzvah Heroes* by Siegel. Once you have done your reading, create a television interview with that hero/heroine to present to the class.
2. I would like each group to read Chapter 7 in *The Holocaust* by Stadtler and to prepare questions for our upcoming test. I will use one question from each group for the actual quiz.

Other Resources

Another useful strategy when students are doing their own research is having other textbooks available that can fill in gaps or add a different perspective. Following is an example of this strategy:

1. We will be using *Heroes of American Jewish History* to create our reports on famous American Jews. There will be several other resource texts in the classroom for you to look at. Books you may want to use include *The Importance of One* and *Journey through Jewish History*.

Learning Centers

Texts can also be used in learning centers. Chapters can be assigned that are then followed up by worksheets or tasks. Some examples include:

1. After reading chapter two on Sukkot, create a "kit" for building a *sukkah*. What items will be included in the kit? What can be used for the walls and for the roof? What name will you give to the product?
2. Read the chapter on "Conquering Canaan" in *Pathways Through Jewish History*. Using the map worksheet, fill in the names of the tribes and where they were located. Answer these two questions: Why is Dan located in the north and in the south? Why is Manasseh on both sides of the Jordan?

Texts should be seen as a resource for providing information; they are not the authoritative voice on the subject. Part of the challenge is getting students to read the text with the minimum amount of whining and moaning. The greater task is that of determining how to develop the information contained on the textbook pages into an incredible, life changing lesson.

STEP FIVE: FILL IN THE GAPS

All Jewish textbooks are by nature flawed by the fact that people wrote them. Their biases and attitudes have determined what will be included and excluded. The teacher has an obligation to fill in notable omissions. For instance, women disappear from history after Queen Esther (with very few exceptions). Sephardim are virtually non-existent once they are expelled from Spain, making only a brief appearance in Safed before reemerging as part of the ingathering of exiles to modern Israel. Sephardic holiday customs are not mentioned in most texts unless they appear in highlighted boxes. It is the educator's obligation to make Jewish study inclusionary. For example:

1. In two of the most widely used Jewish history textbooks, Jews in Arab lands, Asia, and Africa are not mentioned from the period of the dispersion following the Inquisition until Israel's ingathering of exiles. Since the focus is on Europe and America, the hidden message is that the history of any other Jews is of little consequence. The teacher can rectify this by:
   a. Showing videos that deal with the history of some of the Arab and Ethiopian communities.
   b. Creating lessons based on information from *Encyclopaedia Judaica* and *My Jewish World* about these countries. There are other Jewish history books that cover these areas as well.
   c. Refer to *Our Story: The Jews of Sepharad: A Resource Guide* by Hessel (CAJE, 261

> **MANY TEXTS EXCLUDE WOMEN AND SEPHARDIM.**

West 35th St., Floor 12A, New York, NY 10001). This guide has an outstanding collection of suggested books, videos, and magazine articles to use.

STEP SIX: EXAMINE AT LEAST TEN WAYS TO TEXTUAL PARADISE — SUPPLEMENTING TEXT.

How does a teacher bring the textbook to life? What is out there in the vast oceans of Jewish educational resources that can complement the written word?

Maps

Maps can greatly enhance a lesson because they provide the class with a concrete look at what is being read. Questions such as why Israel was conquered so often or why the Israelites had to fight so many nations before entering the land can be answered when students analyze maps of those periods.

Maps are generally located in libraries and resource centers. See the Bibliography for several resources of note.

Games

Games such as *Charades*, *Twenty Questions*, *Jeopardy*, and *Hangman* can be easily built into textbook lessons. Looking through texts, students can find names of people and places that can be transformed into games. Some useful resources on games may be found in the Bibliography.

Videos

Videos can bring units of study to life. It is not necessary to use an entire movie. Often a short clip will suffice to reinforce learning. Two examples follow:
1. After students have studied wedding rituals, showing the scene from *Fiddler on the Roof* during which Motel and Tzeitel are married.
2. After teaching the historical background on the resistance at Masada, bring that unit to life by presenting the scene from "Masada" in which the suicide pact is made.

Many selections are available at your local video store, as well as in Jewish libraries and resource centers. Other sources are listed in the Bibliography.

Drama

Students can create skits based on personalities or events that they read about in their books. There are many published plays on holidays, Bible, history, and life cycle that can be used to reenforce the text. Some books of plays are listed in the Bibliography.

Pictures

People learn in different ways. Visual presentations are sometimes the most direct route through the complex synapses of a teenager's brain. Posters, slides, and even coffee table picture books can be used to illustrate places, people, or objects.

Song and Dance

The arts can also breathe life into the textbook. For example, "The Partisan's Song" illustrates the passion and power of the Jewish resistance during the Holocaust. There are many songs that describe the *Halutz* period in Palestine. Wedding dances can add to the fun of studying the life cycle. These materials can be found in Jewish teacher resource centers, Jewish libraries, or in the personal collections of songleaders, Cantors, and Rabbis.

Magazines and Newspapers

As teachers, we want our students to find what is being studied to be relevant in their lives. Magazines and newspapers can be used to emphasize concepts. As an illustration, when studying about Israel as an ingathering place for exiles, articles that deal with oppressed Jewry being brought to Israel makes the concept more concrete. Magazines that might be of particular value are listed in the Bibliography for this chapter. A complete list of Jewish periodicals relevant to Jewish education may be found in the "Resources for Jewish Educators" section at the end of the book.

For further resources in this area, see Chapter 39, "Teaching Jewish Current Events."

Speakers

It is one thing to read about history or culture; it is another to hear from people who have been participants. It is very effective to have someone from the Jewish mortuary speak to a class about his/her job after a unit on death and dying. Once students have a good background on the Holocaust, survivors and second generation children can bring this overwhelming subject down to the personal level.

Filmstrips and Slide Shows

Yes, they still exist. In this age of media hype, dust is collecting on some invaluable resources. Though they lack the entertainment appeal of video, filmstrips and slide shows are excellent vehicles to further illustrate a chapter or passage.

The Students Themselves

In *Pirke Avot*, we read that teachers can and will learn from their students. At any age, they are invaluable resources. Questions should be designed to bring out their thoughts and ideas. They bring a wealth of information and of different perspectives to the classroom.

You, the Teacher

In the end, it comes down to the teacher. Your selection of texts, strategies for using them, and choice of supplemental aids all contribute to the quality of the classroom experience. The textbook is your guide for helping organize goals and objectives and is an invaluable source of information. The textbook should never dictate the direction in which you go.

A new teacher is more likely to be dependent at first upon a textbook, because it takes familiarity with a course before beginning to experiment. There is nothing wrong with this. Over time, the book will become a skeleton of what the course is all about, while supplemental sources and programs will become the muscle.

Stan J. Beiner is the Director of Colorado's Central Agency for Jewish Education. He has a BA Ed in Elementary Education, a Masters in Teaching, and a Masters in Jewish Education. He is the author of *Sedra Scenes*, *Bible Scenes*, and *Class Acts*.

BIBLIOGRAPHY

Using Textbooks Creatively
Eisenberg, Azriel, and Abraham Segal. *Teaching Jewish History*. New York: Jewish Education Committee Press, 1954.

United Synagogue Commission on Jewish Education. *A Curriculum for the Afternoon School*. New York: United Synagogue, 1978.

Zusman, Evelyn. *History Is Fun*. New York: Jewish Education Committee Press, 1967.

Maps
Atlas of the Bible Lands. Maplewood, NJ: Hammond, Inc., 1959.

Gilbert, Martin. *Jewish History Atlas*. New York: Macmillan Publishing, 1976.

———. *Jerusalem History Atlas*. New York: Macmillan Publishing, 1977.

———. *Overheads and Transparencies- Vol. 1: Holocaust, Vol.2:*

Europe and America. Milwaukee: B. Arbit Books, 1976. (Out of print; check teacher resource centers.)

Games
Grishaver, Joel Lurie. *Bible Places Ditto Pak*. Denver: A.R.E. Publishing, Inc., 1983.

Grishaver, Joel. "Games and Jewish Learning." (See Chapter 19 in this book.)

Kopin, Rita. *The Lively Jewish Classroom: Games and Activities for Learning*. Denver: A.R.E. Publishing, Inc., 1980.

Moskowitz, Nachama Skolnik. *Games, Games, and More Games for the Jewish Classroom*. New York: UAHC Press, 1994.

The Learning Plant has a number of games for purchase (P.O. Box 17233, West Palm Beach, FL 33416).

Plays
Beiner, Stan. *Bible Scenes: Joshua to Solomon;* A.R.E. Publishing, Inc., 1988.

———. *Class Acts: Plays and Skits for Jewish Settings*. Denver: A.R.E. Publishing, Inc., 1992.

———. *Sedra Scenes*. Denver: A.R.E. Publishing, Inc., 1982.

Gabriel, Michelle. *Jewish Plays for Jewish Days: Brief Holiday Plays*. Denver: A.R.E. Publishing, 1978.

A good source of plays on a variety of topics is the Bureau of Jewish Education in Cincinnati (1580 Summit Rd., Cincinnati, OH 45237).

Magazines and Newspapers
Jewish Current Events, 9279-C Lake Murray Dr., San Diego, CA 92119

Keeping Posted, UAHC, 838 Fifth Ave, New York, NY 10021 (no longer being published; some back issues available)

Shofar Magazine, 43 Northcote Dr., Melville, NY 11747

Videos
Alden Films, Box 449, Clarksburg, NJ 08510

Board of Jewish Education of Greater New York, 426 West 58th St., New York, NY 10019

Critic's Choice, P.O. Box 809, Itasco, IL 60143

Ergo Media, P.O. Box 2037, Teaneck, NJ 07666

HEBREW

CHAPTER TWENTY-TWO

ISSUES IN HEBREW READING INSTRUCTION

Dina Maiben

Any successful program of instruction must necessarily negotiate between the complexities of the subject matter and the special characteristics of the learner. This negotiation is done in part by the teaching method and instructional materials. To a far greater extent, however, the task of mediation falls on the shoulders of the teacher. Because circumstances vary from place to place and change from time to time, no curriculum can be designed to anticipate every unique issue that may arise. The teacher who fully understands both the intricacies of the subject and the nature of the students in a given class is far better prepared to stand at the side of a learner who is struggling to master the material.

The most important subject matter considerations for all reading instruction center on the linguistic qualities of the language being taught and the idiosyncracies of its script. These considerations go far beyond the specific skills focus of most reading programs, for although a number of visual, auditory, and phonological skills are involved in reading, different languages and scripts require the reader to apply these skills in vastly different ways. Hebrew reading instruction should be based on a thorough analysis of these features, employing those structures and sequences that have been shown to minimize potential learning difficulties, and promoting those reading strategies that best enable the beginning reader to apply the basic skills to the unique demands of a Hebrew text.

In the Diaspora, Hebrew reading instruction is complicated by three other factors. These are the extent to which decoding is part of an overall program of Hebrew language instruction, the needs and norms of the school and its community, and a few Hebrew phonemes that can be problematic for native English speakers. The second, broad category encompasses a number of concerns, such as the qualities of the teaching staff, how the teachers reflect the community in which they teach, and the community's standard pronunciation of a few Hebrew phonemes, which may or may not conform to the teachers' pronunciation or that promoted by a given reading program.

On the other side of the equation, developing readers present a number of additional variables. These include age, previous experience with the subject matter, general knowledge, and a wide range of affective considerations, such as interest, motivation, and their tolerance for frustration. The nature of the students' families and the communities in which they live can also effect their ultimate success in learning to read Hebrew. Such factors as the amount of support that students receive for their studies at home, the ability of parents to provide assistance as well as support, and the degree to which Hebrew is valued by the community and its leaders are all very powerful influences that must be addressed.

Because success in Hebrew reading instruction depends on the ways that the teacher and program materials can negotiate between all of these complex variables, a better understanding of each should enable teachers to plan more effectively, diagnose learning problems more accurately, and remediate them more efficiently. It is with these pragmatic goals in mind that this chapter will explore each major issue, examine a wide range of approaches to teaching Hebrew reading and will present a framework for developing new solutions to instructional problems. Fortunately, there is a vast body of research related to general reading instruction and to teaching Hebrew reading in particular, and it is highly valuable to review classroom practices in its light.

This research, however, is not without problems of its own. First of all, reading is a highly complex process. Its complexity has led to a great deal of disagreement among researchers about the best approaches to its instruction, and there are no signs that this controversy will be resolved any time soon. Because secular education has a dual impact on Jewish education, both in the ways that it prepares students for the work they do in Jewish classrooms and in its influence on the development of the methods and materials that are used in Jewish educational settings, it is within the context of this debate that the issues surrounding Hebrew reading instruction must be viewed.

READING INVOLVES FOUR BASIC MENTAL PROCESSES.

An equally significant difficulty with the research lies in the fact that the bulk of it has been conducted with students who are learning to read their native languages. It is difficult to draw any conclusions about the kind of Hebrew decoding taught in most Diaspora schools based on investigations of methods that are designed to teach students to read a language that they already know. For this reason, the suggestions presented here should not be viewed as ultimate answers, but should serve as a stimulus for new thinking about the extraordinary challenges of teaching Hebrew reading.

Before exploring the more technical aspects of Hebrew reading instruction, it is essential to understand the overall process of reading, and the role that each skill plays at every stage.

READING AS A MAGIC LOOM

Mature readers are characterized by the seemingly effortless way that they translate printed symbols into meaningful sounds and words. Because this process has become so automatic, they often fail to appreciate the highly complex nature of reading, and the manner in which many diverse skills are intricately interwoven. Nevertheless, beginning readers frequently have a great deal of difficulty with one or more of these basic skills, and the reading teacher must be prepared to provide assistance at any stage it is needed.

According to Gray (1960), reading involves four basic mental processes — sensation, perception, comprehension, and reaction. The relative importance of any type of skill depends to a great extent on which mental process is in play.

Sensation

Visual skills dominate the first process, which is known as sensation. When a person reads, the eyes move in a series of quick, sideways motions known as saccadic movements. These alternate with short pauses known as fixations. Occasionally, the eyes will skip backwards and fixate briefly before progressing forward along the line of print. This is called regression. It is only during fixations that the reader can actually see the print.

When the eyes fixate on the text, they focus on a set of markings against a contrasting background. Light reflects the patterns of light and dark onto the retina, producing chemical changes. The chemical changes within the retina set off a series of electrochemical impulses through the fibers of the optic nerves, which carry the visual images to the brain. In order for this process to be at all efficient, the eyes must be able to make fine movements in the proper direction, and then focus completely to allow the retina to form a clear image. Adequate lighting, large enough print, and ample space between words and lines of print enable the reader to form more complete visual images.

Perception

Although a number of factors, including the directional flow of the text, can lead to sensory inefficiency, many more problems can arise during the second stage, involving the process of *perception*. The patterns of impulses through the optic nerves transmit the visual information to the brain where it is compared to memory traces of similar patterns. These memory traces are composed of the previous experiences that the reader has had with a particular set of visual images, and generally include auditory, phonological, and linguistic associations, as well as the visual components. Perception requires the meaningful interpretation of what is seen. To accomplish this, the reader must make a number of sensory and cognitive cross-references, combining visual and auditory discrimination skills, visual and auditory memory, and general verbal processing. Because there are so many different skills involved at this stage, there are many points at which processing problems can arise.

Some students have difficulty attending to the distinctive features of individual letter shapes, concentrating only on the overall form of a letter or word. Such students may encode the information improperly, or may have trouble retrieving it. Other students may have similar encoding or retrieval problems because they have difficulty distinguishing between similar sounds, and still others can have trouble with holding a number of images in their memory long enough to make the necessary cross-references. Similarly, some students have trouble with cross-modal processing. While they master all of the basic skills, they struggle with putting them together in combinations. Perhaps the largest set of problems arise not out of specific perceptual deficiencies, but from more general difficulties with visual-verbal integration. For these students, the visual images make little sense because they fail to associate the set of markings with a meaningful word.

It is possible to counteract some of these perceptual problems by providing students with as wide a range of experiences as possible, leading to a great diversity of associations encoded into the memory traces. Multisensory, linguistic, and cognitive experiences all help to reinforce the visual patterns, and increase the likelihood that the reader will perceive the word correctly. In addition, using combinations of sensory and cognitive channels may make the memory traces easier to access.

Comprehension

Closely related to perception is the process of *comprehension*. Reading consists of a series of perceptions firing rapidly, but perceiving a word becomes reading it only when the word is fully understood. Reading is intimately bound up with language, and the process of comprehension draws most heavily on the reader's language skills. At its most basic level, comprehension means understanding the word that is perceived. The visual image of the printed word is compared to memory traces of the reader's previous experiences and is cross-referenced to the language concept that it represents, producing a mental image. It is at this moment that perception becomes comprehension. However, full reading comprehension means that the individual words form a sequence of ideas that the reader can reconstruct. It requires a working knowledge of grammar, syntax, and semantics for the reader to extract meaning from a series of perceptions.

Reaction

The fourth process involved in reading is *reaction*. Here, the type of skills involved depends most on whether the reader is engaged in oral or silent reading, as oral reading requires the phonological production of each word. This approach is slow and deliberate, allowing the reader to process each word fully in order to articulate it properly. By contrast, silent reading is quite rapid. Its pace simply does not allow the reader to process fully every visual image or pronounce each individual word. Still, even experienced readers tend to move their lips when they read silently, with the throat and larnyx making slight movements as well. This is known as subvocal reading, and it is frequently accompanied by an imaginary hearing of the word in the mind's ear. Most people continue to read subvocally all of their lives, and experience other kinds of physical, emotional, and intellectual reactions to what they read.

As Gray's model clearly shows, reading is not a simple act. It combines four mental processes that fire in split-second sequences, and weaves strands of diverse skills into patterns as intricate as a Persian carpet. Gray based this model on his own previous cross-national comparison of reading (Gray, 1956), in which he concluded that reading is essentially the same in every language and script. Nevertheless, even he noted that certain strategies are used distinctively by readers of different languages.

For example, Gray reported that readers of both Hebrew and Arabic employ longer fixations and make more frequent regressions than readers of English. Both of these tendencies can be ascribed to the nature of the writing systems of the two Semitic languages, which lack the visual redundancies of English script. Hebrew decoding appears to require a more fully processed visual image than English, and this necessitates longer fixations and more frequent regressions.

Subsequent cross-national investigations of reading (Downing, 1973; Kavanaugh and Venezky, 1981) have given further support to the notion that both the linguistic and orthographic features of a language can greatly influence the way that beginning readers encode and retrieve its printed words. Hebrew reading teachers must not rely on the strategies that their students have already acquired for decoding English, and must be aware of the unique qualities of the Hebrew language and its system of writing in order to provide their students with those strategies that are most appropriate for Hebrew reading.

IDIOSYNCRACIES OF THE HEBREW SCRIPT AND LANGUAGE

Five general aspects of a writing system can influence the way that mature readers process its written symbols, and should be taken into consideration when teaching beginners. These are the type of script, the directionality it employs, the number of different symbols that the learner must master, the regularity of the sound-symbol correspondences, and the overall visual qualities of the script.

Type of Script

First, alphabetic writing, in which each symbol or combination of symbols represents a sound, differs from both logographic and syllabic systems, where individual symbols represent words or syllables respectively. For example, dyslexia is extremely rare in Japan, where both a syllabic and logographic system are used, and in Taiwan, where the script is wholly logographic (Tzeng and Hung, 1981). It is possible that both logographs and syllables map more directly onto speech than does an alphabetic system from which the reader must be able to abstract the orthographic regularities of the written word in order to master its sound-symbol correspondence rules.

The absence of vowel letters in Hebrew has sparked some debate about whether it originally constituted a syllabic or an alphabetic system. Gelb (1963) claimed that West Semitic writing, including Old Hebrew, was syllabic in nature, and that the transition to an alphabetic orthography began with the development of the *scriptio plene* system, which employed weak consonants like א, ו, and י to stand for vowels. He held that the first completely alphabetic script was Greek, because it consistently used the letters of the old *plene* system to represent vowels. Other scholars disagree, noting that Modern Hebrew is adequately served by consonant representations alone because the vowels play only a minor, inflectionary role.

While Gelb's views have become fairly popular, they suffer from one serious flaw, namely that 22 symbols is not adequate to form a syllabic orthography, especially when the language has between four and eight distinctive vowels. A full syllabary for Hebrew would require at least four markers for each consonant to represent its combination with each vowel. Rather, it seems obvious that Semitic languages did not need to mark the vowels, because Semitic roots are characterized by their consonant schemes, and the vowels simply differentiate grammatical forms. A reader with a command of the language could easily deduce the appropriate vowels from context alone, just as fluent speakers of Modern Hebrew can today.

Although Hebrew script must be considered alphabetic, especially in light of the vowel signs that have been used to vocalize the text for more than a thousand years, the debate over its organic nature does suggest that some non-alphabetic reading strategies might prove beneficial for beginning readers. In the traditional approach to decoding, the reader must abstract single sounds from their printed representations, then recombine them to form syllables and whole words. This approach is analytical, and it requires a degree of linguistic awareness that many students lack. By contrast, the approach to decoding in a syllabic system is synthetic in nature. Students are taught the signs for complete syllables, and then learn to combine these to form whole words.

In the synthetic approach to Hebrew decoding, students are taught to focus on individual syllables, drilling them as units, rather than learning to break them down into their smallest grapheme-phoneme correspondences. Because Hebrew syllables are highly regular, this strategy is particularly attractive. However, such an approach to English decoding has also been suggested by a number of linguists, despite the fact that English syllables are often irregular, on the grounds that consonant sounds are so thoroughly embedded into syllables that attempts to produce them in isolation can lead to such gross distortions that words become unrecognizable (Fries, 1963; Reed, 1965; Liberman, *et al*, 1981).

During the first stage of instruction, students are introduced to the letter and vowel symbols, and master the sound-symbol relationships. Next, they are given lists of consonant-vowel and consonant-vowel-consonant syllables in which one tiny element changes in each example. Research conducted in Israel suggests that these drills should focus on single vowels, with the consonants changing in each example (Feitelson, 1981). The teacher reads a few items to model the process of blending the sounds together. Students then drill the lists, and formulate a set of general rules about the pronunciation of each type of syllable. By combining deductive analysis with synthetic drill, students should become more aware of both the ways that consonants and vowels are blended together to form the natural sounds of speech, and the manner in which the orthography expresses these relationships. This heightened awareness should help to reduce the amount of overly mechanical reading that is so often a by-product of the traditional phonics method. Feitelson (1967) reports that such a scheme for Hebrew decoding was developed in Israel. After only twelve weeks of instruction, the students were able to move directly to an unabridged version of the Bible.

Directionality

Directionality is the second script feature that can have an effect on the way that beginning readers learn. Some languages, such as Chinese, are written from top-to-bottom. Those that use Latin script, including English, French, and German, are written from left-to-right. Hebrew, while written from right-to-left, actually requires a more sophisticated pattern of eye movements than English. In written English, the letters are all printed on a single line, allowing the reader to move his or her eyes in a straight, linear progression from left-to-right. Conversely, Hebrew has meaningful elements that are printed above and below the line of consonants, including most of the vowels and one diacritical mark. A Hebrew reader must not only scan from right-to-left, but in an up-and-down manner as well.

To assist beginning readers with Hebrew's unique directional progression, the teacher can provide a number of tracing activities at the end of the reading readiness program or at the beginning of the decoding program. In these activities, students are given sheets of single syllables and gradually more complex words.

Using a colored marker, the students are asked to trace the progression from consonants to vowels in each example. The teacher should model this procedure, instructing the students to begin on the far right and progress from right-to-left, and top-to-bottom. While the students are working, the teacher should circulate through the room, observing each student, providing feedback or assistance, and keeping a look out for those who attempt to use a left-to-right progression. Once students have mastered the basic concept, the teacher can suggest that they use their index fingers to trace the syllabic configurations of words that they read aloud, eventually weaning them of this technique as their eye movements become more natural and automatic.

Number of Symbols

The third feature that varies in different writing systems is the number of different symbols that the reader must master in order to read. In this area, alphabetic scripts have a marked advantage over both logographic and syllabic systems, as alphabets always contain a significantly smaller number of symbols. It takes the average learner many years to memorize the thousands of individual logographs found in Chinese writing, while mastering the 26 letters of the English alphabet can be accomplished in a matter of hours.

Hebrew has 22 basic consonants, five of which have final forms, nine vowel signs, and a handful of diphthong clusters that represent additional phonemes. Between four and seven consonants are altered by diacritical marks, depending on the pronunciation used by a given community. The phonetic values assigned to certain vowels also vary from place to place, influencing the total number of diphthongs that mark unique pronunciations. Because the variation in this area depends more on the nature of the community than on any inherent qualities of the script itself, it will be discussed further in the section on community needs and norms, below.

Regularity of the Sound-Symbol Correspondences

When comparing logographic, syllabic, and alphabetic systems, the total number of individual symbols that the learner must memorize can be a significant factor in learning to read. When examining an alphabetic script, however, the far more pertinent question is how effectively those symbols map onto the sounds of the spoken language. As mentioned above, both logographic and syllabic systems appear to map more directly onto speech than alphabetic systems. For this reason, logographs and syllables demand far less linguistic awareness on the part of the reader than alphabetic writing (Liberman, *et al.*, 1981).

In the same way, different alphabetic systems make different demands of the reader. Some written languages, such as Finnish, are almost wholly phonetic. Their shallow orthographies comprise nearly perfect one-to-one correspondences between graphemes and the phonemes that they represent. Deep orthographies, like English, require the reader to possess a far greater degree of linguistic awareness, as the grapheme-phoneme correspondences are highly inconsistent. Learning to decode in an inconsistent system can be a very frustrating task, as the novice reader must acquire a seemingly infinite amount of information. While the differences between deep and shallow orthographies are mainly quantitative, they can be qualitative as well. In consistent systems, the knowledge that the reader must acquire is often far less complex than that required for reading in an inconsistent system. Logic dictates that these quantitative and qualitative differences should make a consistent system much easier for the beginning reader.

> ONE THIRD OF ALL ELEMENTARY SCHOOL STUDENTS HAVE DIFFICULTY LEARNING TO READ.

Comparative studies of reading in different countries (Downing, 1973; Kavanaugh and Venezky, 1981) support this notion, documenting a lower incidence of reading disabilities in countries where the system of writing is consistent. For example, Kyöstiö (1981) reports that only 15% of the second grade pupils in Finland suffer from any reading disabilities, and only one university in that country has a department devoted to training special education teachers. The picture of literacy in America is quite different, with reports of increasing reading failures, and estimates that one third of all elementary school students in the United States have difficulty learning to read (Lefevre, 1964).

Hebrew employs a fairly shallow orthography, although not as shallow as Finnish. In written Hebrew, almost every grapheme represents a single phoneme, and most phonemes can be represented by only one grapheme. However, there are a number of exceptions. Lenchner and Dori (1983b) divide these exceptions into four classifications. The first of these contains sets of different letter symbols that mark the same sound. Included in this category are those letters that have regular and final forms, (מ/ם, נ/ן, צ/ץ, etc.), and a variety of unrelated letters that may originally have stood for different sounds, but whose pronunciations have converged over the course of time (ט/ת, ס/ש, כ/ק, ח/כ, ב/ו, and א/ע/[ה]).

In the same way, there are four sets of different vowel signs that receive very similar pronunciations (אִי/אֶ/אֱ, אוֹ/אָ/אֳ, אֻ/אִי, אוּ/אֻ, אֲ/אַ/אָ). Some of these sets contain vowel signs that are visually similar, such as *patach* and *chataf-patach*, and those that bear no visual resemblance to each other, such as *shuruk* and *kubutz*.

The third category of potentially confusing symbols contains those letters that can represent more than one sound. This classification has a number of sub-categories. First, there are the בגד״כפת letters, six letters that originally took different pronunciations depending on their placement within a syllable. Only Yemenite pronunciation retains all six dual forms. Ashkenazic pronunciation retains four dual forms (ב, כ, פ, and ת), while the Sephardic pronunciation has retained only three duals that are differentiated by a *dagesh* (ב, כ, and פ). More confusing are the letters ה, ו, and י. At times, these letters represent the consonant sounds [h], [v] and [y], respectively. At other times, they occur as markers for elongated vowels (e.g., *kamatz*, *chirik* and *cholam*). Finally, the ש can represent [š] or [s], depending on the placement of the dot above it.

The fourth classification is related to the third. It consists of individual vowels that can take distinctly different pronunciations. In Sephardic Hebrew, the *kamatz gadol* represents the phoneme [a], and is virtually identical to the *patach*. However, the visually identical *kamatz katan* represents the phoneme [o], quite similar to the *cholam*. Similarly, the *sheva* can either represent a very short vowel, or the lack of a vowel, depending on where it falls within a syllable. Finally, a *patach* followed by a non-voweled י most often represents the phoneme [ay], like the sound of the English word "eye."

Research conducted in Israel has examined the various ways of arranging the instructional sequences that involve confusing symbols in an effort to determine which approach will enable students to master these items most efficiently. Three specific patterns were examined, concurrent introduction, sequential introduction with confusing items presented one right after the other, and sequential introduction with confusing items separated by strings of neutral symbols.

Classrooms experimentation revealed that concurrent introduction is the most effective strategy for teaching sets of different symbols that represent an identical sound. Both types of sequential introduction resulted in many students learning one symbol while consistently forgetting the other. Conversely, when dealing with symbols that are visually similar or that represent similar sounds, the strategy of separating them with strings of neutral items proved most effective (Feitelson, 1981).

Overall Visual Qualities of the Script

The fifth, and clearly most complicated factor that can influence the process of learning to read, is the overall visual quality of the writing system being studied. In discussing this factor it is necessary to examine three general areas — word shapes, letter resemblance, and the presence of unchanging word forms — as well as any special problems that arise specifically from Hebrew script.

Some instructional methods stress the importance of using ascenders and descenders to assist in word recognition. These are letters that extend above or below the line of print, such as t, h, k, g, p and q. Because these letters often occur at predictable points or in regular combinations within English words, they may assist the reader by providing a shortcut to processing a complete visual image. This technique is especially useful for recognizing whole words rather than phonetic decoding. Words that do not contain ascenders or descenders are considered to lack distinctive features, and are often avoided in the early stages of instruction.

Some scripts, however, have very few ascending and descending letters. Hebrew, for instance, has only one ascender, ל, and only one descender that occurs in every position within a word, ק. The other four descenders are all final letter forms. As a result, Hebrew words lack distinctive shape, and vary mostly in terms of length. Even this distinction is tenuous, as Hebrew's heavy reliance on its root letter system for word-building produces a majority of words that are between three and six letters long. Because most Hebrew words lack distinctive features, it seems clear that the most beneficial approach will emphasize phonetic decoding and single letters, rather than word shape.

Another important aspect of any script's visual quality is how closely individual symbols resemble one another. This is related to the question of how much effort the learner will need to make in order to tell them apart. English, for example, has a few pairs of visually similar letters, most notably b/d and p/q. Hebrew, on the other hand, is filled with sets of printed symbols that are visually similar, although it has none of the mirror-type letters in the English example. Visually similar Hebrew symbols fall into three categories, those that are identical except for one small element, those that are virtually identical when rotated, and those that share only an overall shape.

The first category is by far the largest, and the one most prone to cause problems for the beginning reader: ב/כ/פ, ג/נ, ד/ר, ה/ח/ת, ו/ז, ו/ר, י/ו/ז, ך/ן, ך/ף, ם/ס, ן/ץ. In addition to these visually similar letters, there are also a few pairs of vowels in this category: ָ/ֳ, ֵ/ֱ, and ו/ֹו. As mentioned above, the research strongly suggests that these visually similar items should be introduced sequentially, with strings of neutral symbols separating them. Immediately after introduction, students should drill the sound-symbol relationship, as this is the most important aspect. However, because Hebrew contains so many sets of letters that are identical except for one minute difference, it is essential to train students to concentrate fully on each visual image right from the beginning. This can be accomplished in a number of ways, such as coloring letter forms, creating letters from clay or play dough, and handling three-dimensional letter manipulatives. Feitelson (1968) notes that writing is a valuable reinforcement for reading, and students should be asked to practice writing each new item as it is introduced.

The second category consists of letters that

are similar when rotated, such as ה/כ or פ/ט. Although this is a much smaller category, and one less prone to cause problems for most readers, confusion here can indicate a serious perceptual problem in the area of directionality. Because a multi-sensory approach has been shown to be beneficial for learning disabled students, a learner who exhibits the tendency to confuse symbols in this category should be given activities that employ auditory, tactile, and kinesthetic modalities with visual processing. These include tracing letters in sand, touching wood, plastic, rubber or foam letter manipulatives, and using the body to create letter shapes (Lenchner and Dori, 1983a; 1983b). This list is not exhaustive, and teachers should use their imaginations to find new ways of involving the senses in the learning process. For example, the students can cut letter shapes out of sugar cookie dough, bake the cookies, and eat them as a reward for mastering the grapheme-phoneme corresponces. (This activity also reinforces the traditional Jewish belief that learning is sweet.)

The third category is the most frustrating for many teachers, who are often surprised by students who confuse letters that are clearly quite distinctive. The letters in this category do not share a majority of common features like those in the two previous categories. Rather, they resemble each other in their overall shape or orientation. The most common of these pairs are מ/ט and צ/ע. Students who confuse these pairs are not fully processing each visual image, but are attempting to use minimal visual cues to identify the letter. This strategy is quite similar to that of using overall word shapes mentioned above, and it is inadequate for the task of Hebrew decoding. The remedy for this problem is to remind students that they have to look closely at every letter in Hebrew, and provide practice using any of the acitivities described in this section.

At times, all of the techniques mentioned here will prove insufficient. When this happens, the teacher will have to resort to direct comparisons between confusing items, asking students to examine each and list the ways that they are different. Such a discussion should focus only on the differences, as it is the similarities between the symbols that is leading to the confusion. However, this approach should be used as a last resort, and only after the students have had a great deal of exposure to each of the items that are causing confusion. Using this technique as an introduction may actually increase the likelihood of confusion. Such discussion should be followed by drill work, allowing the students to apply what they have learned, and might also be followed with an activity that allows students to develop mnemonic devices to assist their memory.

The third general aspect of a writing system's visual quality is the availability of unchanging word forms. English is filled with words whose shapes remain constant, and has even more that change in highly predictable ways based on their grammatical function. Because English relies so heavily on word order to convey grammatical role, the reader is able to predict which form a word is likely to take with relative ease. This is one of the key redundancies in English orthography that can assist the reader in processing large amounts of linguistic information without the need for a fully processed visual image.

Unlike Enlgish, Hebrew is an inflected language. Different words are derived from common root clusters, and this process accounts for the greatest amount of Hebrew vocabulary. As a result of creating words in this manner, slight alternations in the vowels, and the addition of affixes can produce dozens of different words, while the most salient part of the visual image, the root consonants, remains the same. The difference is both quantatative and qualitative. Not only can individual Hebrew roots produce many forms, including several words of the same grammatical type, but the visual cues that enable the reader to distinguish between them are often quite subtle. As a result, students who do not focus on the entire visual image may confuse words that are derived from the same root, especially if one form is particularly familiar.

For example, it is not uncommon for novice readers to substitute the word "בָּרוּךְ" for any word derived from the root "ב.ר.ך.", and are even more prone to do so if the word occurs at the beginning of a sentence or if it contains an affix that is visually similar to the letter ו, (e.g. בְּרִיךְ). A student who makes substitution errors of this kind may be trying to process whole Hebrew words at a glance, rather than carefully attending to each visual cue, and should be reminded to look closely at each part of the word before attempting to read it.

In addition to the five general categories of script features that can cause difficulties for the reader, any system of writing can require specific processing strategies, and can be afflicted with a number of problems that are uniquely its own. For example, Hebrew not only requires the reader to fully process every visual image, but appears to demand complete grapheme-to-phoneme translations as well. In other words, Hebrew readers do not identify words by their visual features alone, but recode the graphemic patterns into a phonemic code, then access words according to their phonemic properties. Navon and Shimron (1981) asked adult native Hebrew speakers to identify words by their letters only. They found that naming was equally fast for unvocalized words, those that were correctly vocalized and those that contained incorrect vowels that preserved the phonemic value of the word. However, word identification was significantly slower when words were incorrectly vocalized and the vowel signs did not preserve the sound of the word. A follow-up study (Shimron and Navon, 1982) compared the use of grapheme-to-phoneme translations in children and adults, and found that neither group was able to resist such translations while both groups benefitted from the redundant phonemic information provided by the vowels. The only significant difference between the two groups was that the children were more sensitive to minor alterations in the graphemes even when the phonemic value of the word was preserved, suggesting that the adult readers were able to disregard the vowels to some extent when they were asked to do so.

Because phonemic accessing plays such a crucial role in Hebrew word identification, even for mature readers, the proper phonemic encoding of graphemes should be stressed from the earliest stages of instruction. Further research has explored three questions related to this issue, and has suggested a number of approaches and activities to assist beginning readers with mastering the sound-symbol relationships.

First, the evidence from research in a number of different writing systems suggests that in early decoding experiences the amount of information presented in each lesson should be as small as possible so that the learner is able to focus completely on the task. Initial exposures to the letter and vowel symbols should restrict the total number of items as much as possible. For example, Downing (1973) suggests that concurrent introduction of both upper and lower case English letters can create unnecessary confusion for the learner. For this reason, Hebrew consonants that can take two or more forms and vowel diphthongs should not be introduced concurrently. Rather, the learner should be allowed to master the basic form first, and any secondary form at a later point. In addition to limiting the total number of items presented during the initial exposure, the research suggests that the amount of information about each item should be strictly limited. Because the sound-symbol relationship is of primary importance, all other information, including the names of the letters, should be excluded from the introduction on the grounds that too much information that does not relate directly to the grapheme-phoneme relationship can interfere with the student's mastery of that association (Feitelson, 1965; 1976).

Closely related to the issues of initial exposure is the question of how early decoding sequences should be structured. Here, a balance must be struck between limiting the number of items so that the task is not overwhelming, and providing enough to make the material meaningful. In most of the Hebrew reading programs that have been developed in Israel, the initial decoding sequences are structured to produce meaningful words with an absolute minimum number of letters. Subsequent letter and vowel symbols are introduced gradually in sequences that are designed to produce a maximum number of new word combinations (Feitelson, 1976). In this way, students gain the maximum benefit from their efforts.

Finally, one of the greatest difficulties in teaching the sound-symbol relationships of consonants is that they are much harder to produce in isolation than are the vowels. A number of different strategies have been tried over the years to assist students in learning to associate consonant symbols with their phonemes. Feitelson (1976) traces the development of these strategies, noting that in the earliest one each consonant was introduced in association with a concrete and easily illustrated word that began with it. While the use of key words to illustrate consonants is still the most commonly used approach today, and one that has the added advantage of introducing students to Hebrew vocabulary, it has one distinct disadvantage. The association of a letter with a word that it begins requires the learner to subsequently perform great feats of abstraction in order to apply the letter's sound to other words because the initial association, the key word, is so strong. Although this can be true in any situation, it is most likely to cause problems when the letter occurs in the middle or at the end of a new word.

The second approach introduced each consonant in combination with a vowel. While this plan was more effective than introducing consonant sounds in isolation, and worked quite well during the first stage of instruction when only one vowel was required, the same difficulties with abstraction arose as the students progressed to the more advanced stages where they had to cope with additional vowels.

Because a strong association between each letter and its exact sound value is necessary for success in learning to decode, a third strategy was developed. In this approach, each consonant sound was first introduced through a story in which the sound played an important part and was repeated several times. After the story, the students were shown a letter poster that was illustrated with a picture that reminded students of the story and the sound it contained. Beneath the picture was the letter that represented the key sound. These posters were then displayed in the classroom so that students could refer to them as necessary. Additional reinforcement was sometimes given in the form of songs that reminded the students of the key sound as well as certain elements of the original story. This method proved most effective for students who had certain learning disabilities as well as those who were culturally disadvantaged.

A SET OF SPECIFIC SEQUENCES AVOIDS CONFUSION.

Finally, a system of writing may be afflicted with a number of unique problems. In Hebrew, for instance, the vowels are much smaller than the consonants, and are generally tucked away below or above the line of print. Not surprisingly, vowels have been implicated as a primary contributor to reading failures in Israel. For example, Feitelson (1981) reports that vowel errors were more common than any other single type, accounting for 38% of all errors, in a reading aloud task given to Israeli children at the end of first grade. She goes on to add that the strategy which proved most effective for reducing these errors lay in structuring the learning activities around single vowels, rather than consonants. This approach required students to drill each vowel in combination with every consonant, ([ba], [ga], [da], etc.), instead of following the far more prevalent practice of drilling an individual consonant with every vowel, ([ba], [bɛ], [bo], and so on).

Clearly, a complex relationship exists between learning to read and the idiosyncracies of a language and its script. Since this relationship produces serious consequences for the classroom, Israeli researchers have compared the efficacy of various instructional patterns for dealing with a number of Hebrew script and language features that have been linked to reading failure. A series of systematic classroom experiments revealed a set of specific instructional sequences and approaches that reduce the likelihood of confusion and enable most learners to master the necessary decoding skills more efficiently. Because these factors are directly related to Hebrew orthography, the strategies found most effective in Israel should be equally effective for teaching Hebrew decoding in the Diaspora.

Since every published program represents a compromise between a variety of concerns, great care must be given to the selection of the school's Hebrew decoding program, and a thorough analysis should be made of both its instructional sequences and of the reading strategies that it promotes. In the first case, visually similar symbols (e.g., ד/ר or ָ/ֹ), and those that represent similar but not identical sounds (e.g., ס/צ or ס/שׁ), should be introduced sequentially with strings of neutral symbols separating each confusing pair. By contrast, different symbols that represent the same sound (e.g., ב/ו or ָ/ַ) can be introduced concurrently. Attention should also be paid to the pattern of reading drills, as the focus should be on drilling each vowel with every consonant. In terms of reading strategies, the program should train the reader to focus on every tiny detail of the text right from the beginning and should incorporate multisensory activities, especially those that train students in auditory processing as well as visual skills.

ADDITIONAL SUBJECT MATTER CONSIDERATIONS

While methods that conform to the nature of the Hebrew language and its unique script should form the basis of the decoding program, instructional decisions in the Diaspora must also be informed by three other subject matter considerations. These are the extent to which basic decoding is part of an overall program of Hebrew language instruction, a set of variables related to the needs and norms of the individual community, and a set of Hebrew phonemes that can be problematic for native English speakers.

The first of these issues is by far the most complex, as it has been at the center of a tremendous controversy in Jewish education for more than a decade. There are a number of compelling philosophical reasons to make the teaching of Hebrew language a top priority in every school, such as the link that it forges between Israel and the Diaspora, the fact that language is inherently more interesting than the rote drilling of meaningless syllables, and the feeling on the part of many teachers that it is fundamentally wrong to teach students how to "read" without teaching them what they are reading. These views have been countered with pleas for pragmatism. A not insignificant number of Jewish educators emphasize mechanical reading to the exclusion of language instruction on the grounds that second language acquisition is a lengthy process and it simply cannot be accomplished in the limited amount of class time available in most supplementary Jewish schools.

Philosophical considerations aside, the evidence does not suggest that repetitious drill is necessarily the best way to gain the ability to decode, nor that language acquisition detracts from the students' mastery of decoding skills. In fact, the research lends emphatic support to the notion that a knowledge of the language can greatly enhance the learner's ability to recognize and decode printed words. First, in their recommendations for planning instruction, Lenchner and Dori (1983b) stress the importance of teaching as much spoken Hebrew as possible because oral language provides students who are weak in visual processing with a mechanism for bringing their stronger auditory skills to the task of decoding. An increased involvement of the auditory memory is especially beneficial for students who have difficulty perceiving part-whole relationships. The inability to perceive how the parts of a word relate to the whole word is often cited as a defining feature of learning disabilities, and it can lead students to add, omit, or alter the parts of a word.

On a second level, it appears that the process of comprehension plays a pivotal role in basic decoding by providing the reader with a means of verifying what he or she perceives by cross-checking it with a known lexical entity. It must be remembered that reading is essentially a linguistic activity. It makes unequal demands on the verbal and visual systems, relying far more on the verbal. This has been confirmed by a number of investigations into the kinds of errors that plague beginning readers. A survey of this error analysis (Liberman, et al., 1981) found a remarkable consistency in the patterns of errors commonly made by beginning readers. Not only were these patterns uniform across all studies, but they simply cannot be explained as the result of specific deficits in visual processing.

For example, specific symbols were not constantly confused by individual readers, as one would expect if reading problems were caused by perceptual difficulties. Rather, there were clear differences between the errors that involved consonants and those that involved vowels. Vowel errors accounted for the greatest percentage of errors overall, but could not be linked to any specific location within the word. Conversely, errors made on consonants were often related to the letter's location, with consonants in the final position misread roughly twice as often as those in the initial position. This consistent pattern suggests that the problems of beginning readers are primarily cognitive and linguistic.

In an effort to determine the extent to which reading problems have a linguistic source, a series of experiments was conducted by Frank Vellutino and his colleagues. The subjects were a group of students age 7 to 12 years who had been identified as normal and poor readers of English, and who had no previous experience with learning Hebrew as a language. They were matched by age and grade level to a group of normal English readers who were also learning to read, speak, and write the Hebrew language. Both groups were presented with clusters of three, four, and five Hebrew letters that they were allowed to view for three, four, and five seconds respectively. Immediately after viewing each cluster, the subjects were asked to reproduce its letters in their correct order.

While the performance on letter reproduction was comparable for all groups when the clusters were three letters in length, striking differences were found between all of the groups when the task involved longer clusters. Surprisingly, there were no significant differences between poor and normal readers who did not know Hebrew, and neither of those groups performed as well as the subjects who were learning Hebrew as a language. Additionally, the style of Hebrew block print used in these experiments involved two letters that closely resembled Latin letters in their correct orientation and three that could reasonably be perceived as distorted versions of Latin letters. One particularly impressive finding was that the normal readers who were unfamiliar with Hebrew actually made more orientation mistakes in producing these letters than did the poor readers, while those who were studying Hebrew made far fewer orientation errors in general, and on these items in particular. Finally, both groups who were not learning Hebrew as a language were observed to scan the letter clusters from left-to-right. This was confirmed by the fact that they were prone to omit letters in the far right position, while errors of omission made by those who were studying Hebrew language tended to involve letters in the left terminal position of the words (Vellutino, *et al.*, 1973; 1975).

Although these experiments examined only two aspects of perceptual processing, visual discrimination and visual memory, the results suggest that reading problems are not the result of organic deficiencies in visual memory or perception, but stem from more basic malfunctions in visual-verbal learning. These findings further affirm the notion that a knowledge of the language can play a powerful role in the processing of visual information. For this reason, the Hebrew decoding program should incorporate as much instruction in meaningful Hebrew language as possible. One vehicle for increasing this language instruction is incorporating songs that teach Hebrew vocabulary and simple sentence forms.

Another set of subject matter variables that can influence Hebrew decoding instruction in the Diaspora is related to the specific needs and norms of the individual school and its community. Included in this broad category are such concerns as the qualities of the teaching staff, the extent to which the school's teachers reflect the community in which they work, and the community's accepted pronunciation of a few Hebrew phonemes. Because these factors vary so much from place to place, they will be discussed here in only their broadest outlines.

The teachers who make up any Hebrew faculty are likely to vary greatly in terms of knowledge, experience, and beliefs about the way that Hebrew decoding should be taught. Such diversity can be a very positive force, as teachers can share with and learn from each other. New teachers can benefit considerably from those who have been in the classroom for many years, and experienced teachers can gain equally from the enthusiasm and fresh insights of those who are new to the field. In most successful schools there is an atmosphere of camaraderie that allows teachers to share their frustrations, problems, and successes with each other, and enables them to create solutions to instructional problems in a cooperative manner. This attitude of *esprit de corps* is something that must come from the teachers themselves. The administration can encourage it and nurture it, but cannot mandate it. All that it takes is for one teacher to begin a discussion about one issue or another with his or her colleagues.

It is true that one's fellow teachers can be a very valuable resource for solving specific instructional problems. However, there simply is no replacement for increasing one's own knowledge about the subject matter. This is especially true of teaching Hebrew, which by its very nature is a complex and technical subject. Further, certain programs require specific approaches to instruction or make other demands of the teacher, and often assume that the teacher's background will provide the necessary conceptual framework for understanding the underlying justifications that support a given approach. Fortunately, some programs provide detailed teacher's guides that incorporate a good deal of background information, and one even provides a state-of-the-art teacher training video that shows a master teacher demonstrating actual lessons from the program.

These resource materials provide a starting point for teachers to increase their knowledge of the subject, but they represent the first step only. Improving one's command of the subject is an on-going process, and one that requires more than any teaching guide can provide. In this instance, the Director of Education and the Rabbi can be excellent resources as they can suggest books and articles related to the subject, or direct the teacher to new work being done in the field.

Additionally, many colleges and universities offer courses in Hebrew language as well as second language and reading instruction. These courses may be open to teachers who wish to audit them as well as to those who want to take them for college credit. There is also a wide range of summer workshops and conferences designed for Jewish educators, and many of these include course offerings related to teaching Hebrew. Of note is the annual CAJE Conference held each year in August. Thousands of Jewish educators from all over the world gather together for four days to learn from some of the leading thinkers in the field. Congregations will often provide stipends to assist teachers in their efforts at continuing education, realizing that a small investment in the present can pay big dividends in the future education of their children.

The second and third issues that grow out of community needs and norms are closely related. Teachers who are not members of the community in which they teach may need to make a variety of adjustments in their instructional approach. The clearest example of this involves teachers whose personal affiliation is with a movement other than that of the school. These teachers will likely have to teach versions of certain prayers that are quite different from the versions with which they are most familiar. There are a number of other, more subtle differences between schools that may require further adjustments. This is especially true in the area of performance standards and of pronunciation, for while diversity can be a great strength where knowledge and experience are concerned, it can be quite problematic in these other areas as the overall success of the school's Hebrew program is dependent to a great extent on uniform standards and implementation.

Setting and maintaining standards of excellence in Hebrew reading is as difficult as it is necessary. It goes to the heart of many philosophical conflicts over the nature of Jewish education. Some teachers are resistant to tough grading policies in Hebrew school because they believe that Jewish education should differ significantly from secular education, that it is wrong to fail students where their religion and culture are concerned, or that receiving a poor grade can be detrimental to a child's self-esteem. On the other hand, parents and administrators alike need to know how well a student is actually doing in Hebrew long before it can become an issue at Bar or Bat Mitzvah time.

Consider the following situation. A student who has received good grades in Hebrew begins classes with the Bar or Bat Mitzvah instructor. After the first or second meeting, the teacher calls the parents and informs them that the student will need a great deal of extra tutorial help as he or she simply cannot read Hebrew. The parents will likely become infuriated because they were led to believe that their child was doing fine, and may even feel that they have been swindled out of the tuition that they have paid to educate their child. Such discrepancies between grades and actual performance are not uncommon in Hebrew schools, and they can call the entire process of Jewish education into question. Nothing contributes more to the negative impression that Jewish education is of little or no value than situations like the one described above. Despite all of the philosophical objections and the pragmatic difficulties inherent in the task, there is a clear need for setting and maintaining uniform standards within the school.

SETTING AND MAINTAINING STANDARDS OF EXCELLENCE IN HEBREW READING IS VITAL.

One excellent approach to this task lies in building a consensus between the faculty and administration of the school. Before the beginning of a school year, the Director of Education should gather the Hebrew faculty together for a frank and honest discussion of the issue. This meeting should include everyone who is involved in Hebrew education at every level, from the reading readiness teacher to those who prepare students for Bar and Bat Mitzvah. As the leaders of the school and the community, the Rabbi, Cantor, and school committee chairperson should also be invited to attend this meeting. Their presence will lend credence to the importance of the issues and support for the decisions made. Further, each of them will bring a unique perspective to the problem, providing valuable insights that might otherwise be missed.

As a group, those present should come to some sort of an agreement about what will be required of students at every grade level, how their performance will be tested and evaluated, what sort of remedial help will be offered to struggling students and what mechanism will be used to refer students for this additional assistance. Although subsequent adjustments and refinements will be needed as time goes on, this kind of meeting is an excellent beginning, and the impetus for it can come just as easily from the teaching staff as from the administration.

Closely related to the issue of uniform standards is the question of how evenly a Hebrew reading program can be implemented. Uniform implementation requires not only a set of specific standards, but an increased knowledge of the issues involved in Hebrew decoding and the instructional approaches that best suit each aspect of the subject, as well as a greater awareness of the pronunciation standards of the community. This last issue bears some careful consideration.

Within the Diaspora, there is a great deal of variation in the way that Hebrew is pronounced. Aside from the major differences between the Ashkenazic and Sephardic Hebrew dialects, there are subtle differences in the pronunciations of three separate vowels that can be found in different synagogues that employ Sephardic Hebrew. These vowels are the *Sheva Na* that occurs in the interior of a word, the *Kamatz Katan*, and the *Tzeyrey Chaser*. In addition, there are two Hebrew phonemes that pose particular difficulties for many native English speakers. The first of these, the [ḥ] of ח and כ, is wholly absent from English. The other problematic phoneme is the [ž] of the letter ז. Although this phoneme is present in English, it can never occur in the initial position of an English word.

The *Sheva* (א) can be a very confusing symbol for students of Hebrew reading, as this single symbol serves two very different purposes in Hebrew orthography. At times, the *Sheva* represents a very short vowel. This is always true when it accompanies the initial consonant in a word. At other times, however, the *Sheva* is used to close a consonant-vowel-consonant syllable in which case it indicates the absence of a vowel. Some communities opt to simplify the confusion that this mark can create by viewing virtually every *Sheva* that occurs within a word as if it were a *Sheva Nach*. Thus, in some communities the word הַמְבֹרָךְ is pronounced [ham-vo-rah], and in others it is pronounced [ha-me-vo-raḥ].

Similarly, there are two forms of the vowel *Kamatz* (א). The more common by far is the *Kamatz Gadol*, which represents the phoneme [a], and is pronounced exactly like the *Patach*. The *Kamatz Katan* represents the phoneme [o], and is quite similar in pronunciation to the *Cholam*. Some communities retain both pronunciations of the *Kamatz*, while others simplify decoding by pronouncing every *Kamatz Katan* except the one in the word כָּל as an [a]. Thus, in some communities the word חָכְמָה is pronounced [ḥah-mah], while it is pronounced [ḥoh-mah] in others.

In contrast to both the *Sheva Na* and the *Kamatz Katan*, the two pronunciations of the *Tzeyrey Chaser* did not grow out of an effort to simplify the difficulties caused by using a single symbol to represent two sounds. Rather, the differences grew out of the normal process of linguistic change that affects all languages. Thus, some communities have retained the original long pronunciation [e] for both *Tzeyrey Maley* and *Tzeyrey Chaser* (א and אִ, respectively) while others have adopted the common Israeli pronunciation of [ɛ] for *Tzeyrey Chaser*, making it identical to that of *Segol* (א), and have preserved the long pronunciation in the *Tzeyrey Maley* only.

All of these different pronunciations can be found in various communities throughout North America, and it is beyond the scope of this article to enter into a discussion about which pronunciation is the best or most authentic. For the limited purposes of classroom instruction, it is best to view all of these alternatives as differences in dialect. However, the teacher must be aware of which specific pronunciation is assigned to each of these vowels within the community in which they teach. This is crucial if any school is to approach a uniform implementation of its Hebrew program. If different teachers assign different phonemic values to a single symbol, the students are likely going to become very confused as they progress from year to year. A uniform, accepted pronunciation that is used by every teacher in every grade will greatly reduce the likelihood of confusion. For practical purposes, the pronunciation of the Rabbi and Cantor should set the standard promoted in every classroom.

Finally, there are two phonemes that consistently present problems for native English speakers. The first is the [ḥ] of the letters ח and כ. This phoneme can present problems for the beginning reader because there is no equivalent sound in the English language. As a result, students often attempt to substitute the closest approximate sound that is found in English, producing [h] or [k], and at times alternating the two depending on the phoneme's placement within the word. The other phoneme that can trouble beginning Hebrew readers is the [ž] represented by the letter צ. Although this phoneme is found in English, it never occurs in the initial position of a word, but only in the terminal position of a word (e.g., "hats"). When the צ occurs in the initial, or even an early, position within a word, native English speaking students tend to substitute either [s] or [z], again the closest equivalents found in English.

There is some debate about the cause of this problem. Some researchers (Baratz, 1970; Labov and Cohen, 1973) contend that difficulties of this nature are the result of problems in auditory perception and discrimination. Others, most notably Bryen (1976), insist that this is simply a problem of production, and not one of processing. Experience suggests that it is sometimes a simple matter of production, and that it can be the result of more serious auditory processing problems at other times.

As a first step toward eradicating this problem, it is essential that any time the student hears a teacher pronounce a word that contains one or more of these problem phonemes, that the word receive its full, proper pronunciation. Thus, חַלָּה should never be called "*Hallah*," and צְדָקָה should never be referred to as "*Sedakah*." This should be stressed to teachers at all levels, especially to those who teach the youngest children in the school, as younger children can be particularly adept at mimicking the teacher's pronunciation of the language.

When a student makes one of these common confusions during oral reading, the teacher should provide immediate feed-back, and ask the student to reread the word. If the problem persists, it will be necessary to test the student to determine whether the problem is one of auditory discrimination or simply of production. In one simple test of auditory discrimination, the teacher reads pairs of words to the students. Some of these pairs should be identical, and others should be identical except for the target phoneme (e.g., bass/bass, hits/hiss, less/lets, bass/bats, bets/bess, etc). The teacher should ask the student to indicate which pairs are identical and which are different. A student who can complete this task accurately does not have a problem with auditory discrimination, but may not understand how to produce the correct phoneme. In this case, the teacher should simply describe how the phoneme is made, modeling it in an exaggerated manner, and ask the student to repeat the process. If necessary, the teacher can allow the student to feel his or her throat as the sound is produced.

Remediating problems in auditory discrimination is more difficult. However, several different activities can be used to assist students in developing this skill. First, activities similar to those used to test auditory discrimination can also be used to raise students' awareness of the differences between sounds. The teacher can read pairs of words and ask the student to identify which are the same and which are different, or can use rhyming and non-rhyming words in this task. As a general rule, students are first exposed to similar phonemes that occur in the initial position of a word, and once they can distinguish between them they are presented with words that contain similar phonemes in the final position. As students master each of these types, they can be asked to generate examples of their own, an activity that requires considerable mastery of auditory discrimination. The teacher can ask, "What word begins with the same sound as *Chesed*?" or "What word rhymes with *gets*?" Once students can identify the phonemes in both positions, the teacher can test them again in a more complicated manner by mixing pairs of words that place the target phonemes in different positions.

Hebrew reading instruction in the Diaspora

is a highly complex process, as the teacher must not only contend with the unique problems inherent in Hebrew orthography, but must be prepared to adjust to many additional variables that arise out of teaching students to read a language that they do not speak. In selecting a Hebrew decoding program, the strengths and weaknesses of the teaching staff must be addressed, the norms of the community and its standards of pronunciation must be considered, and ways of incorporating language instruction must be found. Such a sophisticated approach is truly difficult and time-consuming, but the results it can produce are definitely worthwhile, as it can increase the quality of Hebrew reading overall and decrease the number of students who fail.

INDIVIDUAL LEARNER VARIABLES

In addition to the differences that individual learner's may have in the specific visual and auditory skills discussed above, the students in any given classroom may present a wide range of general differences. These fall into roughly four categories: age, previous experience with the subject, general knowledge, and several affective factors such as interest, motivation, and the individual student's tolerance for frustration. Because there can be considerable variation within each of these broad categories, a complete discussion of each is well beyond the scope of this article. However, the teacher must be aware of these issues and the role that they can play in the learning process in order to plan instruction that will best meet the needs of each student.

Of all the variables, age is the simplest, as most supplementary Hebrew schools begin decoding instruction in either third or fourth grade, with either an optional or mandatory year of reading readiness instruction during the year prior to decoding. As a result, most Hebrew decoding programs are designed for use by children age eight to nine years. These programs generally take the cognitive and emotional needs of children at this developmental stage into account, thus solving in advance what would otherwise be the single-greatest instructional difficulty. However, within any grade, there is still going to be a great deal of variation in age, cognitive development, and maturity, and the teacher may need to develop several different ways of explaining the material in order to accommodate these differences.

Where Hebrew is concerned, the previous experience of the students in any class is often far more varied than their ages. Because many schools require students to be enrolled by the year that decoding instruction begins (with the reading readiness year optional), some students may enter the decoding program with no prior exposure to Hebrew while others will have completed one or more years of exposure to Hebrew in one form or another. These discrepancies may be more pronounced at the beginning of the year, or they may have a long-lasting influence. In either case, the decoding teacher must be aware of the approach used to reading readiness and plan his or her presentations of the material to extend what some students have already learned while introducing other students to it for the first time.

One further consideration in this area is also related to incorporating language instruction into the program. When children learn to read their native language, they begin to decode words that they already know. This makes reading a self-reinforcing activity. One easy way of integrating spoken Hebrew into the program lies in teaching the words that students will encounter in the decoding program in advance of the lesson in which they are introduced. This will enable students to bring their linguistic skills directly to the task of decoding. Alternately, the teacher can allow students to practice reading a set of Hebrew-English cognates, words that are identical or highly similar in both languages because they share a common origin. The use of such words for decoding practice allows even those who have no formal background in Hebrew language to apply their linguistic skills immediately.

The student's general knowledge is closely related to his or her previous experience with the subject matter, and can have an equally strong effect on his or her ability to master Hebrew decoding. It is important to remember that beginning Hebrew readers are not beginning readers. They will enter the Hebrew decoding program with three or more years of experience in reading English. In all other subject areas within a Jewish school, such previous experience is not only an advantage, it is a prerequisite for success. Because so few hours are built into the supplementary school program, teachers must necessarily rely on the students' secular education to provide them with the necessary analytical, expressive, and cognitive skills that they will apply to Judaic subjects. Where Hebrew reading instruction is concerned, however, the students' previous experience with English reading can be a double-edged sword.

As detailed at great length above, Hebrew orthography is particularly well suited to approaches that emphasize letter-sound mapping skills, such as phonics. English, by contrast, is so irregular that phonics instruction can be cumbersome and quite time-consuming. As a result, phonics instruction has often been deemphasized in favor of two meaning-emphasis approaches to English reading instruction. The older of these is known as the "whole word method." Early proponents of this method noted that fluent readers do not sound-out each and every word, but tend to process whole words in a single glance. The whole word method is geared to teach students to rapidly process entire words right from the beginning, and its strategies are designed to conform to the nature of English orthography, with its redundancies, and the presence of many ascending and descending letters that lend great distinctiveness to key English words. Such rapid word analysis also requires readers to rely more on their knowledge of syntax and semantics, replacing the slower perceptual cross-referencing mechanisms with an increased use of the more rapid linguistic processing skills. In the whole word method, the mental process of perception is diminished, and comprehension plays a far more significant role. Such an approach is clearly ill-suited for Hebrew reading in general, and for its instruction in the Diaspora in particular.

"Whole language," the newest trend in reading instruction, is not so much a method as it is a philosophical approach to the subject. Where the whole word method stresses the importance of recognizing individual words automatically, whole language places its emphasis on learning to recognize the meanings of printed words as they operate within larger sentence and story structures. Word attack and word recognition skills may be incorporated into the whole language classroom, but they grow organically out of the needs of individual learners, and are never the main focus of the program. Rather, teachers concentrate on motivating the students to become literate by demonstrating the uses of literacy for genuine communicative purposes. Teachers read a great deal to their students, and expose them to a variety of other enriching language experiences. In this approach, the processes of comprehension and reaction receive the greatest attention. While elements of this approach, especially its inclusion of enriching language experiences and motivating activities, may hold a tremendous appeal for Hebrew reading teachers, the whole language approach *per se* is as unsuitable for Hebrew decoding instruction as the whole word method.

It is important for Hebrew teachers to have at least a rudimentary understanding of these reading approaches, not because either of them is suitable for use in the Hebrew program, but because their students will most likely have learned to read English through one of them. Despite the public pleas to go "back-to-basics," heard so often a decade ago, and the recent research that calls both the theoretical foundation and the entire process of whole language into serious question (Byrne and Fielding-Barnsley, 1991; Foorman, *et al.*, 1991; Nicholson, 1991; Vellutino, 1991), whole language and whole word approaches continue to form the basis for much of the English reading instruction that takes place in North America. Because the way that students learn any given skill can predispose them to make certain assumptions and hold specific expectations about that skill, Hebrew reading students may attempt to apply the strategies they have mastered for English reading to the task of Hebrew decoding, regardless of how ineffective the strategies might be. Hebrew reading teachers must be aware of this tendency in order to combat it.

> **MOTIVATION CAN BE THE SINGLE MOST IMPORTANT FACTOR.**

Three affective variations within individual learners must also be considered. The first two of these, interest and motivation, are closely related. Students generally do well in subjects that interest them because they are inherently more motivated to do the necessary work. This single factor can make up for a great many deficits in other areas, especially those in the areas of general knowledge and previous experience. Within any single class, there will likely be some students who are interested in language generally, and Hebrew in particular, but others who are not. Fortunately, people's interests are quite permeable and open to change with time and experience. People can become increasingly interested in a subject as they learn more about it.

One educational factor that has been cited as an agent for increasing the learner's interest in a subject is a high level of teacher enthusiasm. In classrooms where teachers model enthusiasm for learning in general, and especially for their subjects, the students are more likely to develop enthusiasm of their own, to pay greater attention to the material and ultimately attain higher levels of achievement (Rosenshine, 1970; Rosenshine and Furst, 1973). Teachers can model enthusiasm in many ways. They can use voice inflection to convey joy, surprise, excitement, and suspense. They can relate anecdotes about their own experiences with Hebrew, or describe some fascinating facts that they have learned about it. They can use gestures and movement to show that they are alert and vigorous. Some teachers are naturally more dynamic than others, but even shy teachers can find ways to show their enthusiasm for Hebrew.

Of all the individual learner variables that have been studied in relation to second language learning, motivation has been found to be both the most important and the one most open to the influence of the teacher (Savignon, 1976; Gardner, 1980). For example, initial success with language learning has been shown to increase the student's motivation to learn, which in turn leads to greater subsequent success (MacNamara, 1973; Burstall, 1975).

There are two broad classifications of motivation. Intrinsic motivation leads people to engage in activities that are inherently enjoyable, or that fulfill the basic human need of becoming competent and self-determining. Extrinsic motivation involves performing tasks in exchange for receiving an external reward, such as good grades, stickers, or other prizes that are unrelated to the satisfaction that comes from doing something well. Within the classroom, intrinsic motivation rarely exists in its purest form because the demands of the curriculum rarely afford students complete autonomy. However, a related type of motivation that incorporates the positive emphasis on learning for its own sake can be found in classroom settings, and has come to be known as student motivation to learn. Students who are motivated to learn come to value the educational process, and to take pride in their growing knowledge and skill. While they will not find every task to be enjoyable, they will take their work seriously, and try to get as much out of it as they can.

Many Hebrew teachers employ extrinsic rewards to motivate their students to complete certain tasks. However, a vast body of research has demonstrated that when rewards are offered for doing a task that the individual finds interesting, subsequent interest in the activity decreases dramatically. The reason for this may be that offering a reward sends a covert negative message about the nature of the task. As one researcher put it, "To offer a prize for doing a deed is tantamount to declaring that the deed is not worth doing for its own sake" (Neill, 1960). In a landmark study involving 55 Hebrew teachers and more than 500 students, Barbara Rosoff (1990) confirmed that teachers in Jewish classrooms rely heavily on extrinsic motivational strategies, and that teachers who believe that extrinsic rewards are necessary were evaluated less positively by their students. Teachers who had a higher sense of their own efficacy were less likely to use extrinsic motivational strategies, and were evaluated more highly. Those who held a strong belief that their students could learn had students who valued their religious school activities more.

Classroom motivation is complex. Not only must teachers motivate their students to complete specific tasks, but they must often provide them with general motivation for learning the subject as a whole. General motivation can take two different orientations, each of which is related to one of the broad classifications discussed above. The first of these is a performance orientation. General motivation addresses the question of why students need to learn Hebrew. In classrooms that employ a performance orientation, the teacher will stress the necessity of learning Hebrew in order to be able to perform at Bar or Bat Mitzvah. This orientation is parallel to using extrinsic rewards for task motivation.

An achievement orientation closely parallels student motivation to learn. In classrooms that use an achievement orientation, the teacher will address this question by noting that Hebrew is an important aspect of Jewish culture and tradition. It is something that binds all Jews together, and links one generation to another. Knowing Hebrew not only allows one to participate more fully in Jewish life at home and within one's community, but it allows one to participate in services at any synagogue in the world.

Finally, the third affective consideration that must be examined is the individual student's tolerance for frustration. Although most Hebrew students understand that learning often involves some struggle, as they have likely had such an experience in the course of their secular education, there are some students whose coping mechanisms are stronger than others. For students who do not cope well with frustrations it may be necessary to provide more one-on-one attention, to increase the amount of praise that they receive for even the smallest gains in order to bolster their self-confidence, and it may even be necessary to provide tutorial assistance. In addition to these suggestions, research involving culturally disadvantaged children in Israel (Feitelson, 1968) supports using two specific strategies to assist students who have difficulty coping with failure.

First, the program should be structured into a series of small sequential stages. Students are allowed to proceed to a new stage only after they have fully mastered the previous one. Second, the changes from one stage to another should be kept uniform throughout the class, and the rate should be adjusted to the pace of the slowest learners. This approach may slow the progress of the faster pupils, but Feitelson notes that this cost is minimal if a slower pace leads to a real reduction in the number of students who eventually develop serious problems in reading. Such a consideration must clearly be balanced against the amount of instructional time available in Diaspora Hebrew schools.

DEMOGRAPHIC INFLUENCES

Just as variations in the individual can have an impact on classroom instruction, the nature of the students' families and the communities in which they live can present very powerful influences that must be addressed. The two most important considerations related to the students' families are the amount of support that students receive for their studies at home, and the ability of parents to provide instructional assistance. The nature of the synagogue community can also be a considerable factor within the school as a whole, and within the Hebrew program in particular. The degree to which a knowledge of Hebrew is necessary for participation in the life of the synagogue will necessarily determine the kind of support that the community and its leaders will lend to its instruction.

In general, students who receive parental encouragement and support for their studies achieve more than students who do not. This is so because children are very sensitive to their parents' attitudes and actions. Parental approval is one of the strongest motivational forces in any child's life, and children will often go to great lengths to win that approval. At the same time, parents usually want their children to succeed in everything that they undertake, and are particularly anxious to see them excel scholastically. It is a very rare parent indeed who wants to see his or her child fail in English reading, math, or science.

However, where Hebrew school is concerned, there is often a gap between the parents' expectations and the school's. Some parents view Hebrew school as primarily a social or enrichment activity, on a roughly equal footing with little league or dance lessons, rather than as an educational endeavor. As a result, such parents may not place an emphasis on homework completion, regular attendance, or performance evaluations to anywhere near the degree that they do when their child's secular education is involved.

Clearly, this general condition has the greatest consequences for the Hebrew program, as the nature of both Hebrew decoding and second language learning are necessarily complex and unique in the educational life of the child. It is absurd to presume that students can acquire skills without a great deal of practice outside of the few hours that they spend in Hebrew class. In addition, Hebrew specifically suffers from a weakened status in the eyes of even the most supportive parents. Tobin (1992) reports on a number of studies in which parents were asked to rank the importance of a range of curricular elements. Hebrew, while considered important by the majority of those questioned, was consistently ranked as less important than holidays, ritual, ethics, the Holocaust and Israel.

In addressing this issue, the first step lies in educating the parents about the importance of

Hebrew school in the life of their child, and raising their consciousness about the crucial role that they play in their child's Jewish education. It is not enough to communicate the school's policies regarding homework, attendance and other requirements. Rather, these expectations should be presented in terms of how they help to foster the child's Jewish identity and ensure his or her academic success. Parents who understand this relationship are likely to be far more supportive of the school's program than those who perceive Hebrew school requirements as being merely arbitrary.

Specific attention must be paid to the role of Hebrew within the school's program, and its relationship to the development of a positive Jewish identity. In discussing the development of an individual's Jewish identity, Ackerman (1989) notes that values clarification activities alone are not a sufficient basis for the development of either the individual's personal or group identification. Identity is highly malleable. It is subject to change with increased maturity, experience, learning, and growth. The development of an authentic identity requires knowledge and skills in language, history, and literature, and it is on these core content areas that schools must place their greatest emphasis. In a Jewish context, competence in Hebrew is fundamental to most of the skills that are involved in Jewish life. For this reason, Hebrew plays a significant role in many other aspects of the curriculum. Parents may need to be made aware of the crucial part that Hebrew plays in holiday celebrations, ritual observance, and life cycle events, as well as its essential quality of binding all Jews to one another and to Israel.

Closely related to the issue of parental support is the more pragmatic question of whether parents can provide auxiliary instruction for their children. Parents often take an active role in the secular education of their children by assisting them with homework assignments or by providing additional explanations and information. They drill addition facts, multiplication tables, and spelling lists. They listen to their children's reading, and watch them practice their oral presentations. But when it comes to Hebrew homework, many parents feel singularly unprepared to offer any sort of assistance.

Three trends within the North American Jewish community have exacerbated this problem in recent years. They are: the gender gap that has historically led to scant Hebrew education for Jewish women, the rising rates of both divorce and intermarriage, and the shift from the Ashkenazic to the Sephardic pronunciation of Hebrew. Not only can any one of these factors create an obstacle for parents who want to help their children to learn Hebrew, but families may be facing two or more of these issues simultaneously, each one further compounding the problem.

One of the most profound trends in Jewish education over the past few years has been the dramatic increase in equal educational opportunities for girls. In her review of the changing role of women in Jewish education, Monson (1992) cites two sets of past enrollment statistics for American Jewish schools. For example, in the mid-1950s, boys and girls were enrolled in fairly equal numbers in Sunday schools, but boys outnumbered girls by a ratio of two-to-one in day schools and three-to-one in Jewish afternoon supplementary schools. Even as late as 1970, the gender gap had not closed to a very great extent, as girls were as likely to be enrolled in primary education as boys, but by the age of ten, boys were far more likely to attend Jewish schools. Similar studies from the late 1980s and early 1990s reveal that this gender gap has been closed for all intents and purposes, as girls are now as likely to receive a Jewish education as boys (Tobin, 1992). While this trend bodes well for the future, the fact that it is such a recent development suggests that in many families with children currently enrolled in Hebrew school, the mother may not have received any Jewish education beyond the second or third grade, and will likely not have learned to read Hebrew.

Compounding this factor are two other trends within American Jewish families, namely the increasing rate of divorce that reflects a general change in the American nuclear family, and the rising rate of intermarriage. In many communities, single-parent households headed by women have become a very significant segment of the synagogue's membership. In addition to the kinds of financial and emotional stresses that such families may be under, a great many of these mothers did not receive a Hebrew educa-

> **HEBREW IS FUNDAMENTAL TO MOST OF THE SKILLS INVOLVED IN JEWISH LIFE.**

tion themselves, and will not be able to assist their children with Hebrew homework.

At the same time, another important change is taking place within the American Jewish family, and it presents a unique set of challenges for Jewish educators as a whole, and for Hebrew teachers in particular. The 1990 National Jewish Population Survey sent shock waves through the Jewish community, as its reports of a 50% rate of intermarriage and of some 625,000 born Jews who are practicing other religions (Kosmin, 1992) have raised questions about Jewish survival. However, aside from an amorphous feeling that Jewish education ought to somehow become more of a family-oriented enterprise, very little discussion has yet taken place about the implications that the findings of this study have for current Jewish educational practices.

Where Hebrew education is concerned, the growing number of students who have only one Jewish parent presents at least two serious considerations. First, like the situation created by the number of single-parent households, when the parents are an interfaith couple the likelihood that the students will have someone at home who can assist them with their Hebrew studies is greatly reduced. An equally serious concern is that students who have only one Jewish parent are less likely to enter school with the experiential background that forms the basis for Jewish education as a whole, and reading in particular. For example, when one reads the word שַׁבָּת, the visual image of the word is compared to memory traces that contain a record of one's previous experiences with the word, producing a mental image. However, if the reader has never experienced a Shabbat celebration, has never lit candles or had Shabbat dinner at home, this mental image will be deprived of its most important cultural and experiential links. It is difficult to teach Hebrew words with all of their rich associations when the reader's basic mental image is impoverished.

Finally, even if one or both parents received some form of Hebrew education the shift from the Ashkenazic to the Sephardic pronunciation may impede their efforts to help their children with Hebrew. This shift has led to a situation that closely parallels the one that arose in American secular education when the curriculum was changed from "old math" to "new math." Parents were suddenly unable to assist their children with math homework, not because they knew nothing about the subject, but because they did not understand the new approach to it. For many parents, the inability to help their children with work in a familiar subject is far more frustrating than not being able to help them because they do not have a background in it.

In addressing these issues, it is helpful to examine a similar situation that arose in Israel during the 1950s. Feitelson (1973; 1981) details the development of reading instructional techniques that were used in both European Diaspora communities and those that developed in pre-state Israel. It is important to note that the early pioneers rejected the traditional approach to Hebrew reading instruction as part of their overall rejection of Jewish life in Eastern Europe. In its place, they adopted the teaching methods that had been developed by the early educational reformers in America and England for teaching English reading. Despite the fact that these methods were wholly unsuitable for Hebrew reading, there were no widespread reports of reading failure. The mass waves of immigration from Arab lands in the early 1950s brought this happy situation to an abrupt end. Within its first three years of statehood, the population of Israel doubled, and within a short time the majority of school entrants came from Middle Eastern or North African backgrounds, and their families had scant traditions of learning. Suddenly, a reading failure rate of 50% became common. Many schools blamed this rate on the poor conditions in which the immigrant children lived and the lack of motivation on the part of the parents, many of whom were illiterate themselves. However, an independent study implicated the teaching method as a primary cause. Faced with this serious threat to the entire structure of the curriculum, the Ministry of Education set up six teams to explore the situation and develop teaching materials that would rectify it.

These teams based their work on a dual set of considerations, the specifics of the subject matter and the nature of the students for whom the materials were intended. Of greatest significance was the determination that when the children's parents had little or no education themselves, or when the education they had was in a language different from the one used in school, the educational sequences would have to cover all possible contingencies, because the teacher could never rely on the parents to provide auxiliary instruction. In fact, interviews revealed that the old methods had appeared successful only because the students had received a great deal of sophisticated parental assistance (Feitelson, 1981). As a result of these efforts, reading failure in Israel had virtually disappeared by the mid-1960s.

These findings suggest several options for Hebrew teachers who are faced with conditions that negate the possibility of students receiving extra help at home. First, basic decoding instruction can be presented in a framework that reduces or eliminates the need for students to complete assignments outside the classroom. This would require the teacher to slow the pace of instruction considerably, setting it to the pace of the slowest students, and making sure that every student gained a command of each skill before moving on. Such an approach, while probably ideal, may not be possible in schools where instructional time is always at a premium, and teachers struggle to complete each year's curriculum. In this case, several other strategies might prove beneficial.

First, it is possible to create programs that will enable parents to brush up on their Hebrew decoding skills, or to acquire them for the first time. Such programs as day-long Hebrew reading marathons have been used successfully in many communities. They provide an inexpensive introduction to basic Hebrew decoding skills, and can be partially subsidized by the Hebrew school and the synagogue's adult education program. However, such courses provide only a beginning. Like the development of any other skill, fluency in Hebrew reading requires time and a great deal of practice. This is just as true for adults as it is for children.

Some schools attempt to bridge the Jewish educational gender gap in a more direct way by offering programs that lead to adult Bat Mitzvah. Because Hebrew decoding is generally the core of these programs, certain schools offer it directly to the mothers of students who are entering the Hebrew decoding program. Other schools provide similar educational opportunities for parents through a variety of family education models. For example, some schools provide parallel instruction programs for interested parents in key grades. These parents attend classes at the same time as their children, though usually not as often, use the same books, and stay slightly ahead of their children's class. In this way, the parents study exactly the same lessons as their children, but by doing it in advance, they are prepared to provide specific assistance with homework as it is needed. The chief drawback of both of these programs is cost. In order to be attractive to prospective parents, the cost must be absolutely minimal while still covering the teacher's salary and the course materials. Other family education models combine elements of the one-day reading marathon with parallel instructional programs by offering three or four sessions in the school with home study packets. While these reduce the cost of the program, they are clearly not as effective as full reading courses.

Finally, homework packets can be developed that enable parents who do not know how to read Hebrew to work with their children. Items like flashcards that have the Hebrew letter on one side and its equivalent phoneme in English on the other allow parents to drill their children on sound-symbol correspondences without needing to know the letters themselves. Similar flashcards can be developed for drilling syllables and whole words as well as single letter and vowel symbols. As students progress into the prayer curriculum, parents can be provided with transliterations of the passages that their children are studying. In addition, for parents who were trained to read Ashkenazic Hebrew, the school can provide a small packet of information about the differences in Ashkenazic Hebrew and the Sephardic pronunciation taught in the school. By the same token, individualized assignments can be developed for students who are weak in either visual or auditory perception. Although these solutions may not be ideal, they can serve as a first step in assisting parents who care about their children's Jewish education, but who do not possess the skills necessary to help them.

Clearly, programs as ambitious as the ones described above will need the backing of the community to be successful. This is true of any Jewish educational program, but it is especially true of Hebrew instruction, with its unique demands and complexities. Garnering the support of the community and its leadership is not always easy, but it is necessary if the Hebrew program is to receive the financial resources that it requires, and if the school is to be backed in what are sometimes unpopular instructional and administrative decisions. It may be necessary to begin with a program to educate and raise the consciousness of the community's leaders about the important role that Hebrew plays, not only in Bar or Bat Mitzvah preparation, but in the overall development of the child's Jewish identity. It may further require building a coalition in the decision-making process, bringing all of those with a stake in the school's success to a consensus of opinion where Hebrew instruction is concerned.

CONCLUSIONS

Hebrew reading instruction presents a wide range of challenges related both to the subject matter and the needs of the individual learner. In a successful Hebrew reading program, the teacher must be prepared to negotiate between many, often conflicting, considerations. Subject matter considerations, such as the unique qualities of the Hebrew language and its script, the inclusion of language skills, and the norms of the community must be balanced against the learners' previous Hebrew and Judaic experiences, the manner in which they learned English, a variety of affective variables, and the nature of their families and community. The key to the ultimate success in teaching Hebrew reading lies in selecting an instructional program that takes all of the subject matter concerns into account, especially one that presents instructional sequences that have been shown to lead to more effective and efficient learning, and then adapting that program to meet the needs of the learners.

The Israeli experience should serve as both a warning and a model. For when instructional methods are inappropriate for the subject matter, and the parents are unable to provide assistance, failure rates of 50% or more are the result. However, when instructional approaches are developed that take both the specific nature of the subject and the needs of the learner into consideration, the students can and do succeed. Although this approach is quite sophisticated, it is clearly the best way to address all of the issues raised by Hebrew reading instruction.

Dina Maiben is Director of Religious Education at Temple Shaari Emeth of Manalapan, New Jersey. An author, editor, and educational consultant, her work has appeared in *Jewish Education News*, *The Special Educator*, *Shofar*, and *CAJE Bikurim*. She is the author of *Let's Learn Prayer Duplicating Masters* (Ktav Publishing House) and co-author of *Abraham's Great Discovery* and *How Tzipi the Bird Got Her Wings* (NightinGale Resources).

BIBLIOGRAPHY

Ackerman, W.I. "Strangers to the Tradition: Idea and Constraint in American Jewish Education." In *Jewish Education Worldwide: Cross-Cultural Perspectives,* H.S. Himmelfarb, and S. DellaPergola, eds., Lanham, MD: University Press of America, 1989.

Baratz, J.C. "Beginning Readers for Speakers of Divergent Dialects." In *Reading Goals for the Disadvantaged.* J.A. Figurel, ed. Newark, DE: International Reading Association, 1970.

Bryen, D.N. "Speech-Sound Discrimination Ability on Linguistically Unbiased Tests." *Exceptional Children*, 42, 1970.

Burstall, C. "Factors Affecting Foreign-Language Learning: A Consideration of some Relevant Research Findings." *Language, Teaching and Linguistics Abstracts*, 8, 1975.

Byrne, B., and R. Fielding-Barnsley. "Evaluation of a Program to Teach Phonemic Awareness to Young Children." *Journal of Educational Psychology*, vol. 83, no. 4, 1991.

Downing, J. *Comparative Reading.* New York: Macmillan, 1973.

Feitelson, D. "Structuring the Teaching of Reading According to Major Features of the Language and Its Script." *Elementary English*, no. 42, 1965.

———. "The Relationship Between Systems of Writing and the Teaching of Reading." In *Reading Instruction: An International Forum.* M.D. Jenkinson, ed. Newark, DE: International Reading Association, 1967.

———. "Teaching Reading to Culturally Disadvantaged Children." *The Reading Teacher*, vol. 22, no. 1, 1968.

———. "Israel." In *Comparative Reading.* J. Downing, ed. New York: Macmillan, 1973.

———. "Sequence and Structure in a System with Consistent Sound-Symbol Correspondence." In *New Horizons in Reading.* J.E. Merrit, ed. Newark, DE: International Reading Association, 1976.

———. "Relating Instructional Strategies to Language Idiosyncracies in Hebrew." In *Reading, Orthography and Dyslexia.* J.F. Kavanaugh and R.L. Venezky, eds. Baltimore: University Park Press, 1981.

Foorman, B.R.; D.J. Francis; D.M. Novy; and D. Liberman. "How Letter-Sound Instruction Mediates Progress in First-Grade Reading and Spelling." *Journal of Educational Psychology*, vol. 83, no. 4, 1991.

Fries, C.C. *Linguistics and Reading.* New York: Holt, Rinehart and Winston, 1963.

Gardner, R. "On the Validity of Affective Variables in Second Language Acquisition: Conceptual, Contextual and Statistical Considerations." *Language Learning*, no. 30, 1980.

Gelb, I.J. *A Study of Writing.* rev. ed. Chicago: University of Chicago Press, 1963.

Gray, W.S. *The Teaching of Reading and Writing: An International Survey.* Paris: UNESCO, 1956.

———. "The Major Aspects of Reading." In *Sequential Development of Reading Abilities.* H.M. Robinson, ed. Supplementary Educational Monographs, no. 90. Chicago: University of Chicago Press, 1960.

Kavanaugh, J.F., and R.L. Venezky. *Reading, Orthography and Dyslexia.* Baltimore: University Park Press, 1981.

Kosmin, B.A. "The Permeable Boundaries of Being Jewish in America." *Moment*, vol. 17, no. 4, 1992.

Kyöstiö, O.K. "Is Learning To Read Easy in a Language in Which the Grapheme-Phoneme Correspondences are Regular?" In *Reading, Orthography and Dyslexia.* J.F. Kavanaugh and R.L. Venezky, eds. Baltimore: University Park Press, 1981.

Labov, W., and P. Cohen. "Some Suggestions for Teaching Standard English to Speakers of Non-standard and Urban Dialects." In *Language, Society and Education: A Profile of Black English.* J.S. DeStefano, ed. Worthington, OH: Charles E. Jones, 1973.

Lefevre, C.A. *Linguistics and the Teaching of Reading.* New York: McGraw-Hill, 1964.

Lenchner, O., and R. Dori. "Why Jonathan Can't Read: Part I." *Compass*, vol. 6, no. 2, 1983.

———. "Why Jonathan Can't Read: Part II." *Compass*, vol. 6, no. 3, 1983.

Liberman, I.; A.M. Liberman; I. Mattingly; and D. Shankweiler. "Orthography and the Beginning Reader." In *Reading, Orthography and Dyslexia.* J.F. Kavanaugh and R.L. Venezky, eds. Baltimore: University Park Press, 1981.

MacNamara, J. "Nurseries, Streets and Classrooms: Some Comparisons and Deductions." *Modern Language Journal*, 57, 1973.

Monson, R.G. "What We Know About . . . Women and Jewish Education." In *What We Know About Jewish Education: A Handbook of Today's Research for Tomorrow's Jewish Education*, S.L. Kelman, ed. Los Angeles: Torah Aura Productions, 1992.

Navon, D., and J. Shimron. "Does Word Naming Involve Grapheme-to-Phoneme Translation? Evidence from Hebrew." *Journal of Verbal Learning and Verbal Behavior*, 20, 1981.

Neill, A.S. *Summerhill: A Radical Approach to Child Rearing*. New York: Hart Publishing, 1960.

Nicholson, T. "Do Children Read Words Better in Context or in Lists? A Classic Study Revisited." *Journal of Educational Psychology*, vol. 83, no. 4, 1991.

Reed, D.W. "A Theory of Language, Speech, and Writing." *Elementary English*, vol. 42, Dec., 1965.

Rosenshine, B. "Enthusiastic Teaching: A Research Review." *School Review*, 78, 1970.

Rosenshine, B., and N. Furst. "The Use of Direct Observation to Study Teaching." In *Second Handbook of Research on Teaching*. R. Travers, ed. Chicago: Rand McNally, 1973.

Rosoff, B.L. *Student Motivation To Learn in the Conservative Jewish Supplemental School*. Doctoral Dissertation, Rutgers University. New Brunswick, NJ., *Dissertation Abstracts International* 9019758, 1990.

Savignon, S. "On the Other Side of the Desk: A Look at Teacher Attitudes and Motivation in Second Language Learning." *Canadian Modern Language Review*, vol. 76, no. 32, 1976.

Shimron, J., and D. Navon. "The Dependence on Graphemes and Their Translation to Phonemes in Reading: A Developmental Perspective." *Reading Research Quarterly*, vol. 17, no. 2, 1982.

Tobin, G.A. "What We Know About . . . Demography." In *What We Know About Jewish Education: A Handbook of Today's Research for Tomorrow's Jewish Education*. S.L. Kelman, ed. Los Angeles: Torah Aura Productions, 1992.

Tzeng, O., and D. Hung. "Reading in a Nonalphabetic Writing System." In *Reading, Orthography and Dyslexia*. J.F. Kavanaugh and R.L. Venezky, eds. Baltimore: University Park Press, 1981.

Vellutino, F.R. "Introduction to Three Studies on Reading Acquisition: Convergent Findings on Theoretical Foundations of Code-Oriented Versus Whole-Language Approaches to Reading Instruction." *Journal of Educational Psychology*, vol. 83, no. 4, 1991.

Vellutino, F.R.; R.M. Pruzek; J.A. Steger; and U. Meshoulam. "Immediate Visual Recall in Poor and Normal Readers as a Function of Orthographic-Linguistic Familiarity." *Cortex*, 9, 1973.

Vellutino, F.R.; J.A. Steger, M. Kaman, and L. DeSetto. "Visual Form Perception in Deficient and Normal Readers as a Function of Age and Orthographic-Linguistic Familiarity." *Cortex*, 11, 1975.

CHAPTER TWENTY-THREE

GAMES AND OTHER LEARNING ACTIVITIES FOR THE HEBREW CLASS

Hillary Zana

The new school year starts in a week. Your Director of Education has just handed you a copy of the curriculum and your textbook. You know that the time allotted for Hebrew study is limited. Perhaps there isn't time, you think, to include games, songs, dramatic play, art, and other activities into your lesson plans.

These types of activities can be powerful teaching tools, helping to motivate students and to reinforce learning. Whether your curriculum emphasizes oral language, concentrates on phonetic reading of Hebrew (decoding), or stresses reading comprehension, using a variety of activities in your lessons will keep students' attention and allow you to drill new concepts many times without losing their interest. Students learn through different modalities. By using a variety of activities, information can be acquired through all of the senses.

In a traditional Hebrew classroom, a lesson might start with the teacher announcing a new letter of the *Aleph Bet* or a vocabulary word, and then calling on individual students to read. Following the reading, students would be expected to sit quietly and to complete follow-up work independently. Some students will perform adequately with this type of instruction; they enjoy any type of academic pursuit, wish to please the teacher, or find the study of Hebrew to be intrinsically motivating. But, for the majority of our students, this type of teaching is a recipe for disaster. After a long day at public school, the Hebrew School student's attention span is limited. Being required to sit quietly, listen to other children respond, or to concentrate on yet another writing assignment breeds resentment and leads to discipline problems as well.

A more effective type of lesson would encourage student involvement. New material would be presented and drilled in a variety of formats. The class would be one wherein students actively participate in the learning process, rather than silently comply with instructions. The following sample lesson shows how this type of lesson is structured, with suggestions for specific types of activities detailed later in this chapter.

Sample Lesson
Warm up (songs)
Oral language review (game with whole class)
Presentation of new material
    (using pocket chart)
Reinforcement activity (with whole class)
Reinforcement activity (with student pairs)
Textbook reading (whole class)
Learning centers:
    Independent seat work
    Game center
Remediation (with instructional aide)

In this sample lesson, each activity takes from 5 to 10 minutes, with the remaining time spent at the learning centers. Activities are changed frequently so that students stay interested. Students are not expected to sit quietly listening or writing for an entire lesson. Instruction varies and includes frontal teaching, whole class activities, student pair work, group work, and independent work.

This instructional model can, of coursse, be adapted, based on your curriculum and the characteristics of each class. For example, a class with a heavy emphasis on decoding might skip the oral language review, while older students working on reading comprehension would not start their class with a warm-up song. Some classes enjoy working in pairs, while in others personality conflicts make dividing the class into pairs very disruptive. Some students who are accustomed to a more traditional classroom feel that songs and games can't be "real" learning. If your students react this way, introduce the more entertaining activities slowly, and emphasize to them that all the fun and games are for an educational purpose and should be taken seriously.

Another potential problem with using games in the classroom is that of competition. Many students (and teachers) love to compete. Trying to be the winner can be highly motivating. Competition can make your class an exhilarating place to be and can add a special excitement to the most repetitious drill. But, competition can also be debilitating. For every winner there must also be a loser. In games involving academic skill (as opposed to luck) the loser will most often be the less skilled student, exactly the one whom you want to encourage. If the class is divided into teams, the less skilled students may be blamed for causing their team to lose. Instead of motivating, you have caused resentment. In a Jewish classroom, we seek to build a sense of community, based on a foundation of Jewish values such as kindness, cooperation, and concern for the less fortunate. Fierce competition can undermine these lessons.

You can avoid these problems by choosing games in which the entire class competes as one unit, trying to "break" their own record each time. If a game must have teams, switch them around each time you play, so that team loyalty never develops and everyone will be on several winning and losing teams. Don't keep score or announce winners. Choose games where chance determines who wins, and make sure students realize that losing is just a matter of bad luck and no reflection of their abilities.

The activities which are described below have all been used successfully in Hebrew language classrooms. Be sure to use the ones that are best suited to your style of teaching, but don't hesitate to experiment or to try something out of character every once in a while. This collection of ideas is by no means exhaustive. For additional ideas, look in teacher guides and educational magazines from both secular and Jewish education, or ask your colleagues to share some of their ideas with you. Keep a notebook of interesting ideas that you can access when your creative juices run dry.

BASIC MATERIALS

The following materials can be used for a variety of activities or on an ongoing basis throughout the year. Don't feel compelled to prepare each one before the school year begins; you can start slowly, purchase some things ready-made, and (most importantly) save things in an organized fashion for next year.

Hebrew Letter Cards

Materials: Card stock or index cards

Preparation: Write the Hebrew letter on one side of the card and the English sound equivalent on the reverse side. Make one set and photocopy additional sets for each student. You can make eight cards on a sheet of card stock, photocopy the sheet, and then cut out the cards.

Use: Give each student a set of cards, adding new letters to their sets as they are learned. Students can drill each other or use the cards with games. You can send the cards home and ask parents to review the letters with their children. Since the English is on the back, the parents don't need to know Hebrew to do this.

> USE GAMES IN WHICH THE CLASS COMPETES AS A UNIT.

Flash Cards

Materials: Card stock, sentence strips, felt markers

Preparation: You will want to prepare or purchase flash cards of all the new letters or words you are teaching. Make sure the writing is clear and large enough to be seen by children sitting in the back of the classroom. If your students can read Hebrew, you will also want to have sentence strips on hand to write a variety of statements, instructions, and questions.

Picture File

Materials: Magazine pictures, construction paper, scissors, glue, laminating machine or clear Contact paper, file folders

Preparation: Collect magazine pictures of objects or situations found in your curriculum. Include everything from words starting with specific Hebrew letters to vocabulary words to amusing situations that lend themselves to discussion. Mount the pictures on construction paper, laminate or cover them with clear Contact paper, and file them by category in file folders.

Uses: Developing such a file is an ongoing project, but is well worth the effort. You will be able to use the pictures with many activities and with all age groups.

Hebrew Letters

Materials: Felt backed letters, magnetic letters, letter stencils in several sizes, foam rubber letters

Uses: You can use all these types of letters when teaching phonetic reading (decoding). These types of movable letters give you more options than just writing on the chalkboard or using a textbook. You can create and decode a word sound by sound. Then you can rearrange the same letters into new combinations, or change only one letter or vowel. Children will enjoy manipulating the letters to create their own combinations or to "write" words that you dictate. The foam and magnetic letters allow students to feel the shape of each letter, as well as see it. The stencils can be used as is (or traced) for bulletin boards, or they can be traced and given to students for decorating, coloring, cutting, and many other purposes. All of these types of letters will be used in many of the games described later in this chapter.

Displaying Cards

There will be many times in your lessons that you will want to display a number of pictures, flash cards, sentence strips, etc. There are several easy ways of doing this (see below). Choose a system based on your ability to find the right materials, the time you have to create something, and whether or not you will need to be carrying whatever you create from one classroom to another.

1. Fun-Tac: This "sticky stuff" is very convenient. You put a small piece on the back of a card and then stick the card onto the chalkboard. At the end of the lesson, remove the Fun-tac and reuse it the next time. Fun-tac can be purchased at stationery or office supply stores.
2. Magnet Board: Many classrooms have magnetized chalkboards or marker boards. Sometimes school have portable magnetic boards. You can purchase magnetic strips that have a sticker side. Place a strip of this on the back of any object you want to display. The strip will be attached permanently.
3. Felt Board: Any card can be backed with felt and used with a portable felt board.
4. Pocket Chart: A pocket chart is hung in the front of the room. It has slitted pockets so that flash cards can be inserted and displayed. Pocket charts can be ordered from teacher supply catalogs or stores.
5. Paper Clip Board: This homemade option actually works quite well. Take a large and heavy piece of poster board. At even intervals (say every 2") make horizontal cuts about the width of a paper clip. Continue making rows of cuts like this the entire length of your poster board. Each row should be about 6" below the other. Insert large paper clips into each cut. Now you can paper clip any card onto the board. Hang the paper clip board in the front of your room.

Student Dictionaries

You may want to have a way for students to keep track of the vocabulary words or Hebrew letters which they have learned. Individualized dictionaries can help students who have forgotten the new word or letter, and they also provide a sense of organization as students realize that they have a systematic record of the material taught. If you are teaching Hebrew language from one textbook only and that textbook has a good glossary, it is preferable to teach your students how to use it, and not spend class time devising your own system.

There are several ways of creating student dictionaries. You can have all your students use the same system, or (particularly with older students) let them choose a system that works for them.

1. File Card Box: Each student purchases a recipe file. Every time you teach a new word, have students write it on a 3" x 5" index card. Words can be translated into English, defined in Hebrew, or illustrated with a picture. Students file the cards in *Aleph Bet* order.
2. Dictionary Notebook: Each student has a notebook in which they list the new vocabulary. Pages should be labeled in *Aleph Bet* order, one letter to a page.
3. Picture Dictionary: This activity is for students who are just learning to read. Make a Dictionary Notebook as described above. Instead of writing words and defining them, have students draw pictures that begin with the new Hebrew letters. You can also supply students with pictures to cut, color, and paste

into their dictionaries. As your students reading ability advances, they can label the pictures in Hebrew, or write in additional new vocabulary.

Bulletin Boards

Bulletin boards can be used to reinforce new material visually, to display student work, as an activity center themselves, or as a way of presenting a theme or topic of study. There are many commercially produced Hebrew language posters that can be ordered through Jewish catalogs. It is well worth your while to laminate anything you will want to reuse on a bulletin board. Many ideas for creating your own bulletin boards are found in *Original Bulletin Boards on Jewish Themes* by Moskowitz.

SONGS

Songs are a wonderful tool for learning a foreign language. Drill and practice is a necessary part of learning new vocabulary. Songs enable you to repeat the vocabulary many times in an enjoyable format. The use of rhyme, rhythm, and melody in music also aid memory. Often children who are uncomfortable speaking aloud in a foreign language will feel less threatened singing the new words. As a warm-up activity, start your Hebrew sessions by singing one or several songs that you have previously taught.

When you teach Hebrew songs to your students, your enthusiasm is much more important than your musical talents. If you have a cassette tape of the song you are teaching, use a tape recorder to help you with the melodies. If your students can read Hebrew, provide them with copies of the words. Before you teach a new song, introduce most of the unfamiliar vocabulary which you want the students to know. There is no need to teach every word in a song; some words and phrases can be quickly translated while you are singing and not specifically taught. Don't worry about the students understanding each and every word of a song, as long as they understand the important words and basic theme of the song. Use body movement, hand motions, or props to act out what different words mean. You can point to pictures you have displayed to illustrate vocabulary.

There are many cassette tapes of Hebrew songs available. You will find songs of Jewish holidays, liturgical music, Israeli children songs for children, and Zionist songs. A.R.E. Publishing, Inc. offers a full line of cassette tapes in their catalog.

A.R.E. also offers a cassette tape of songs specifically written to teach beginning Hebrew language. The beginning vocabulary found in the songs on the *Z'man LaShir* cassette tape by by Fran Avni is designed to correspond with the Hebrew language curriculum of A.R.E.'s textbooks *Kadimah!* and *Z'man Likro*, but can be a valuable addition to any Hebrew curriculum. A Songbook is also available.

If you need a song to teach specific vocabulary, it is a simple matter to choose a well-known English song and compose your own Hebrew words. Even though you won't be able to use a ready-made tape recording, students will catch on quickly because of the familiar melody.

GAMES

The games described below can be used to reinforce all of the skills involved in language learning: listening, speaking, reading, and writing. Some games are for one of these skills only, others involve several skills or can be adapted so that a different skill is being drilled. For example, some of the reading games can be used to reinforce either phonetic reading (decoding) or reading comprehension. Games can be played with the entire class in a frontal lesson, in small groups, in pairs, or by individual students.

Since a single game can be used to teach several skill areas and with many differently sized groups, the list of games which follows is divided into the type of basic materials required to play the game: Card and Board games, Chalkboard Games, Games with Objects, Games with Displayed Cards, and Action Games.

There is a fairly fuzzy line between a bona fide game and a classroom activity, particularly if the games you play are non-competitive. This shouldn't be a difficulty, unless students complain that a certain activity "isn't a real game." If this becomes a problem, continue with the activity, but stop calling it a game! Be sure to emphasize to your students that the real purpose of all the classroom games and activities is neither winning nor amusement, but to aid them in learning Hebrew.

Card and Board Games

Aleph-Bet in the Basket

Materials: 2 sets of Hebrew letters, 2 baskets or other containers for the letters

Number of Players: 2 or more

Purpose: Letter recognition, vocabulary

Instructions: Players or teams take turns picking one Hebrew letter out of their basket. When a letter is picked, the player must say a Hebrew word that begins with the letter and translate it. If your class has not learned all of the *Aleph Bet*, use only the letters they know. You can keep score if you wish.

Board Game with Answer Cards

Materials: Game board, question and answer cards, markers, spinner or dice (or some other means of determining how far a student will move on a turn). Game boards can be made by either teacher or students, or can be purchased at a teacher supply store.

Number of Players: 2-5; a small group

Purpose: Review any content area or skill

Preparation: If you are creating your own game boards, mark the board with a path of squares along which students will advance their markers. Use Judaica themes in designing your boards — for example, a *Find the Afikoman* game where students move their markers from a starting point through a house until they reach the *Afikoman* at the finish line. Laminate your boards or cover them with clear Contact paper.

Prepare a set of question cards. Write the question or problem on one side and the answer on the other. Students can prepare their own card sets if you check their work for legibility and correctness. Questions and answers can be Hebrew letters and their English sounds, Hebrew letters and words beginning with those letters, Hebrew words or sentences and their English translations, a picture and its Hebrew name, etc.

Instructions: The cards are placed in one pile, question side up. All students write down their answer to the question on the top. The card is then turned over and all students with correct answers can move their markers. There is no bonus for being the first one with the correct answer.

Students can move along the board by spinning a spinner, throwing dice, or advancing by color as in the game *Candyland*. Look at other commercial games to get ideas. The winner is the child whose marker reaches the finish line first.

Memory

Materials: Teacher or student prepared cards

Number of Players: 2 to 3

Purpose: Review any content area

Preparation: Prepare 5 to 13 pairs of cards. Each pair consists of two items which can be matched. For example, a Hebrew letter and its English sound, a picture and its name in Hebrew, or a color and its name in Hebrew. Make sure all of the cards are of the same size and that writing can't be seen through them.

Instructions: Place the cards face down in neat rows. The first player turns over two cards. If the cards match, the player takes both cards and gets another turn. If not, the cards are turned face down again in their same spots and the next player has a turn. The game continues until all the cards have been matched. The winner is the one with the most matches. This game strengthens memory and attention in general, as well as reviewing Hebrew subject matter.

Lotto

Materials: Teacher prepared board and cards

Number of Players: 2-5; a small group

Purpose: Vocabulary or reading review

Preparation: For each student playing you will need to prepare a board divided into 8 spaces and 8 matching cards. Take 2 pieces of unlined 8 1/2" by 11" paper or card stock. Divide each paper into 8 rectangles (4 rows of 2) with a felt marker. Cut one paper into 8 pieces; leave the other piece whole.

On each of the 8 spaces on the whole paper, draw or write an item to be matched; for example, a Hebrew letter or a picture. On each of the 8 cards write the matching answer; for example, the English sound or word in Hebrew. If you want several groups to play at once, photocopy the boards and cards

Instructions: Shuffle all the cards together (each student playing will contribute 8 cards). Place the cards face down in a pile. Students take turns picking cards and placing them on the matching space on their boards. If the student chooses a card that he/she has already matched, that card is returned to the bottom of the pile of cards, and the student does not get to make a match that turn. The winner is the one with the first completely matched board.

Bingo

Materials: *Bingo* boards, markers (dry beans, buttons, colored chips), 16 index cards

Number of Players: 2 or more; can be played with entire class

Purpose: Vocabulary or reading reinforcement

Preparation: Give each student a piece of paper with 16 blank squares (four rows of four). For a game that reviews oral vocabulary, on each of the 16 index cards write a Hebrew vocabulary word. Have students draw a picture of each word on their boards. Each student should draw their pictures in different positions so that each board is different.

Instructions: The teacher or a student picks an index card and reads the item. The students place markers on their boards on the matching picture. The first one with four markers in a row calls out "Bingo!" and is the winner. The winning student can read the index cards for the next round.

If you want students to have more practice reading, have them write the 16 words on their game boards. Then prepare 16 matching picture cards which you will show them. These pictures will need to be larger than index card size, so that everyone can see them.

Two Piece Puzzles

Materials: Index cards

Number of Players: 1 or 2

Purpose: Practice in letter sounds, vocabulary, or reading review.

Preparation: Cut about 10 index cards into two pieces. Make the cut shapes unusual. On each half card write an item that needs to be matched.

Instructions: Students have to find the matching pieces. This activity can be done by individual students in a learning center. Have students prepare their own puzzle card sets, store their completed cards in a labeled Zip-loc baggie, and let other students complete their puzzles. Make sure student work is legible and correct.

Chalkboard Games
Dots

Materials: Chalkboard and chalk

Number of Players: 2 to 3 students or teams

Purpose: To reinforce any skill; especially good for drill work

Preparation: Draw a large grid of dots on the chalkboard, 5 rows of 5 dots each. See illustration below:

• • • • •

• • • • •

• • • • •

• • • • •

• • • • •

Students take turns reading a word, or giving a short answer to a question. When a student answers correctly, he/she draws a line connecting two dots either horizontally or vertically (not on the diagonal). If the line drawn completes a small square, the student writes his/her initials in it. Continue taking turns until all the lines are drawn. The one with the most squares is the winner.

You can also play this game with an overhead projector. Prepare a transparency with the grid drawn in permanent marker. Draw the lines in erasable marker. This way you can reuse the same grid over again.

This is a good game to play when you want to make routine drill and practice more interesting.

Chalkboard Tic-Tac-Toe

Materials: Chalkboard and chalk

Optional Materials: picture, letter, or word cards; Fun-tac

Number of Players: 2 students or teams

Purpose: To reinforce any skill

Preparation: Draw a large tic-tac-toe board on the chalkboard. In each square, write a Hebrew word, Hebrew letter, or a picture to name in Hebrew.

Instructions: In order to place an X or an O in a square, a student must answer the question in that square. Students may be asked to say a

> THESE GAMES CAN REINFORCE ALL SKILLS INVOLVED IN LANGUAGE.

Hebrew word beginning with the letter in a square, read, translate, act out, use a word in a sentence, etc.

Optionally, you can use Fun-tac to stick pictures, letter cards, or word cards onto the board.

Chalkboard Races

Materials: Chalkboard and chalk; letter, word, or picture cards

Number of Players: 2 or more; play with the whole class

Purpose: Letter recognition, reading, translation

Instructions: Call two students who are evenly matched in ability to the chalkboard. Show or ask them both a question at the same time. The students race to be the first to correctly answer the question. Questions can be writing the English sound of a Hebrew letter, translating a Hebrew flash card into English, reading and translating a Hebrew word or sentence, etc. It is best not to have students write Hebrew in this game, as they are racing and their writing will tend to be messy. This game can be very exciting in a competitive version with two teams, but you may prefer just to pick two different students to compete each round, and not keep any kind of score.

Individual Slates

Materials: Individual slates, chalk, and something to erase each slate

Number of Players: 1 or more; can be done with a small group or the entire class

Purpose: Reading or vocabulary reinforcement

Preparation: Each student participating will need a slate and chalk.

Instructions: Ask any question that can be answered by writing or drawing. All the students write their answers on their slates. Then have everyone hold up their slates so you can see their answers. Wipe off the answers and ask another question. There is no advantage to being first. You can also encourage students to look around at others slates and change their answer if they think it is wrong. If you allow this, be sure to repeat the question so the students who are changing answers will make the association between the question and the answer they have "copied."

Ladders and Flags: Ways To Record Achievement

Materials: Chalkboard and chalk; with only one student, paper and pencil is fine

Number of Players: 1 or more; works well with whole class

Purpose: Drill and practice

Preparation and Instructions: Draw a ladder with about ten rungs on the board. Have either individual students or the entire class answer a question. If they answer correctly, draw a figure advancing upward on the ladder. The object is for the figure to reach the top of the ladder.

You may draw many kinds of visual representations of advancing: stairs, bridges, rocks crossing a pond, paths reaching a finish line, etc. This simple technique adds another dimension to routine drill.

If you want to work on student accuracy, make your figure return to the bottom of the ladder or stairs if a wrong answer is given. When using this technique, be careful not to frustrate students overly, or to have less skilled students blamed for making the class start over.

You can also start with an empty chalkboard and draw part of a picture every time a correct answer is given. For example, draw lines to make an Israeli flag. Students will enjoy seeing the picture get more elaborate with every right answer; the longer the drill goes on the better this activity gets!

Games with Objects

The games which follow all use actual physical objects to teach oral vocabulary. It is always best to teach oral vocabulary using objects, rather than translation. Pictures are also preferable to translating, and often more practical than objects (just how would you bring snow or an elephant into class?).

What's in the Bag?

Materials: Large paper bag, 5 to 10 small objects that are vocabulary items for your class

Number of Players: 1 or more; good with entire class

Purpose: Oral language reinforcement

Preparation: Place items in paper bag without letting students see them first. The items should be objects which the students can identify in Hebrew.

Instructions: Choose a student volunteer to come to the front of the room and reach into the bag without looking. Have him/her pick an object in the bag, guess what it is in Hebrew, and then remove the object to see if they were correct.

You can use more Hebrew in this activity if your students are advanced. In this instance, give all the instructions in Hebrew and ask students in Hebrew what they think the item is.

Another variation that uses more Hebrew requires the volunteer student to describe the object being felt, without naming it. Then, the other students in the class must guess what the object is without seeing it first. When someone guesses correctly, the object is removed from the bag and another student gets a turn to choose an object.

What's Missing?

Materials: 5 to 10 objects

Number of Players: 1 or more; good with whole class

Purpose: Oral language reinforcement

Preparation: Set out in plain view of all students five or more objects the names of which they know in Hebrew. You can include a couple of items whose names have just been introduced, as this activity is a good way to drill new vocabulary. If all of your items are new words, students will likely get confused.

Instructions: Show and name all the items on display, having students repeat the words after you in unison. Have everyone close their eyes or put their heads down. Remove one item, tell the students to look up, and ask for a volunteer to say what is missing. Replace the object and play again. If you want, the student who correctly guesses what is missing can be allowed to remove the next object each time.

For more advanced classes, give all your instructions in Hebrew and use more objects. If your students say the game is easy, but their language level isn't high, try moving around the objects while their eyes are closed. For a real test of memory, remove an additional item each round until students must remember all the items at once.

I'm Thinking of . . .

Materials: 5 to 10 objects students, the Hebrew names of which are familiar to students

Number of Players: 1 or more; works well with whole class

Purpose: Oral language reinforcement

Preparation: Set out the objects in plain view of all students.

Instructions: Say in Hebrew, "*Ani choshav/ choshevet al . . .*" (I'm thinking of something . . .). Continue describing the object in Hebrew. Tailor your description based on the students' level of Hebrew. This is a good activity for using adjectives and the colors.

In more advanced classes, students can give the descriptions. In this activity, oral comprehension naturally precedes speaking.

Games with Displayed Cards

The activities described below all use cards posted in front of the class. Cards may be letters, words, sentences, or pictures. For suggestions on how to easily display cards see Displaying Cards, page 242 in this chapter.

Find the Match

Materials: 5 to 15 pairs of cards which can be matched; for example, a Hebrew letter and a picture that begins with that letter, a Hebrew letter and its English sound, a Hebrew sentence and a picture illustrating the sentence.

Number of Players: 1 or more

Purpose: Reading or vocabulary reinforcement

Preparation: Display the pairs of cards so that all students can see them. The cards should be arranged randomly.

Instructions: Call on individual students to come to the board and match two cards. When matching, they should read the card or say the name of the picture. They can actually physically move one card next to the other. As the activity continues, it will become progressively easier, since there will be fewer cards to match. Encourage your weaker students to participate at this point.

In a variation of this activity, the matches do not need to be pairs of cards. For example, you can have several sentences that describe one picture, or several pictures that begin with one Hebrew letter.

Where's the . . . ?

Materials: 5 to 10 picture cards

Number of Players: 1 or more

Purpose: To teach or review oral vocabulary

Preparation: Post the picture cards so all the students can see them

Instructions: This is more of an activity than a game, but is a good way to introduce new vocabulary. After this activity, you can continue using the same picture cards for another of the games described in this chapter.

Identify each picture. Then choose a student to point to all the pictures in turn and have the class repeat the names. A student who is shy or slow can enjoy doing the pointing, as he/she will not need to speak. Next, call on individual students to point to the correct picture after you say the word. Finally, call up pairs of students and have one ask the other in Hebrew to point to a certain picture. In this final activity, only one student in the pair is speaking, so you can choose students of differing ability levels.

What's Missing? (Picture Version)

This game is played just like the version using objects (see description in Games with Objects section on page 247.) Instead of showing objects, you will display picture cards. Play this version of the game when bringing the objects into class is not practical. This game will not work with letter or word cards because you would only be requiring students to remember what was written on a card, not what the word meant or the letter said.

I'm Thinking of . . . (Picture Version)

This version is the game is played just like the version using objects (see the Games with Objects section on page 247 of this chapter). Instead of showing objects, display picture cards.

Action Games

The games described below all include physical activity. At the end of a long day sitting in classrooms, Hebrew School students welcome the opportunity to get out of their seats and move around. With the more active games, make sure you set the ground rules so that decorum and learning are maintained.

Around the World

Materials: Any set of flash cards or pictures.
Number of Players: Group or entire class
Purpose: Reinforcement of reading or vocabulary
Preparation: Seat all the students in a circle facing in. One student is chosen to stand behind a seated student.
Instructions: Show these two students a flash card. These two each try to be the first to read, translate, or name the card. If the standing student is first, he/she continues to move "Around the World," standing behind the next student in the circle.

If the seated student answers first, the two students exchange places. The object of the game is for one student to move completely around the circle. This game requires no special preparation and is a perennial student favorite.

Find Your Family

Materials: Flash cards
Number of Players: Entire class; preferably at least 10 students
Purpose: Reading or vocabulary reinforcement; can also be used for oral conversation with advanced groups
Preparation: You will need one flash card for each student. Cards should be divided into categories, with about 3 to 5 cards in each category. A category could be based on the meanings of the words; for example, colors, animals, foods, clothing, or Jewish objects. Categories could also be words, letters, and pictures that begin with the same Hebrew sound; for example, the Hebrew letter Bet, the English letter B, a picture of a banana, and the Hebrew word Bayit (house).
Instructions: Pass out flash cards at random, one per student. Tell students to walk around the room and find all the students who are in their "family." With younger students, or the first time you play, you may want to announce what the different categories or "families" are. After all the students are in groups, redistribute the cards and have the students form new "families." See how much quicker they can complete the activity each successive round.

With more advanced classes, insist that all conversation be conducted in Hebrew. Teach Hebrew phrases that will be useful, such as, "Do you have a ___ card?" or "What card do you have?"

You can conclude the game by drawing the outline of several large houses on the chalkboard and placing the cards for each "family" in a separate house.

Floor Tic-Tac-Toe

Materials: Masking tape, 10 sheets of construction paper
Number of Players: 2 students or teams
Purpose: Reinforcement of any skill
Preparation: Make a big *Tic-tac-toe* board on the floor of your classroom with masking tape. Each square should be big enough for a student to sit in. With a felt marker, write a big X on 5 of

the pieces of construction paper, and a big O on the other 5 pieces.

Instructions: Play this game with two teams. In order to place an X or O in any square, students must correctly answer a question. Unlike chalkboard *Tic-tac-toe*, you will not be able to place the question cards in each square, because students won't be able to see them clearly. When questions are answered correctly, students get to sit in any square they choose, holding either an X or an O. If your students enjoy playing this game, ask your school custodian to leave the tape on the floor, so you won't have to replace it each time you play.

Floor Board Game

Materials: Masking tape, card stock

Number of Players: 2 students or teams; the entire class must play at once as the game will disrupt anyone working on something else

Purpose: Reinforcement for any skill

Preparation: Tape the pieces of card stock on the floor so that they form a path.

Instructions: Play as in a board game, following the path from start to finish. Choose two students to be human markers, moving along the path whenever a member of their team correctly answers a question. Do not write the questions on the path itself, as you don't want students walking on the writing. When a question has been correctly answered, students can spin dice to determine how many spaces they will move. Choose weaker students to be the dice spinners and "markers," so that they will feel an important part of their teams.

Aleph Bet Race

Materials: 2 sets of *Aleph Bet* letters, including finals and letters without a *dagesh*

Number of Players: 2 teams of at least 3 players each; play with the entire class

Purpose: Spelling

Preparation: Spread each letter set out on a separate table. Letters can be facing in any direction and overlapping. Move away the other tables in the class so that there is a clear area in front of these two tables.

Instructions: Students line up in their two teams, single file, as far back as possible from the tables. Call out a Hebrew word they know. Members from both teams rush to their tables, pick out the correct letters, turn and face the rest of their team, holding the letters so that the word is spelled correctly. Each student should be holding one letter only. The winning team is the one that first spells the word.

Do not pick words that use the same letter more than once. You can choose to give the students more guidelines, such as telling them how many letters are in each word, or suggesting that one team member make sure the word is spelled from right to left when facing their team. Or, you can let them figure out a team strategy by themselves.

After each round, the students who held letters go to the back of their team's line. Return the letters to the table.

Human Letters

Materials: None

Number of Players: 1 or more

Purpose: To learn the shapes of the Hebrew letters

Instructions: Students need to be standing, with room to bend and move. Call out the name of a Hebrew letter. Students form their bodies into the shape of the letter, while saying the letter's sound in unison. (This is obviously easier to do with some letters than others.) For some letters you can have students pick a partner and form the letter together.

As a variation, have all the students seated. Call on a volunteer to stand and form a letter. The rest of the class must guess what the letter is.

Tracing Letters

Materials: None

Number of Players: Any number of pairs

Purpose: To learn the shapes of the letters

Preparation: Students sit with a partner. The partners should be friends, as they will be touching each other's backs.

Instructions: Students take turns tracing Hebrew letters on each others backs and guessing which letter is being traced. When a student guesses correctly, they switch roles with their partner.

Ball Toss

Materials: A soft ball that can be thrown in a classroom; cards with the numerals written on them (i.e., 1, 2, 3, not Hebrew), one for each student; a safety pin for each student

Number of Players: At least 5; play with the entire class

Purpose: To learn the Hebrew numbers in the order of the numbers students are wearing

Preparation: Give each student a number card. Pin the cards on the students so they can be easily seen. Students sit or stand in a circle, in order of their numbers.

Instructions: Give the ball to any student. That student says his number in Hebrew, calls out another Hebrew number, and throws the ball to the student wearing that number. That student repeats her number, calls out a third Hebrew number, and throws the ball to the student wearing that number. Play continues until the ball is dropped, or a player makes a mistake calling out numbers. There are several skills involved here that have little to do with Hebrew skill level, so your less able students may find themselves excelling at this game.

You can play this game competitively, eliminating any student who drops the ball, forgets a number, or throws the ball in the wrong direction. But, if you do, you will gradually have fewer students actively participating. A better variation would be to see how long the entire class can go without making a mistake.

Boom

Materials: None
Number of Players: 3 or more
Purpose: To learn the Hebrew numbers
Instructions: Students are probably familiar with this game in English. Go over the rules and play a sample round in English, so that you are sure everyone understands.

Students sit in a circle. They begin counting in Hebrew, one number each, going around the circle. When the number 7, any multiple of 7, or any number containing 7 (such as 17) is reached, the student whose turn it is says, "Boom!" If anyone forgets to say boom, start over again from 1. Since this is a learning game, help out anyone who forgets how to say a number in Hebrew. But don't warn them when the correct answer is Boom, or you'll spoil the fun.

This game can be played competitively by eliminating students who make mistakes, but then your less able students get less practice and are less actively involved.

> **LANGUAGE IS BEST ACQUIRED IF ORAL LANGUAGE PRECEDES WRITTEN.**

Dramatic Play

The activities which follow all teach or reinforce oral language through a game format. Your curriculum may not leave you much time to work on oral language. But, if you do intend to teach anything beyond phonetic reading (decoding), be aware that language is best acquired if oral language precedes written language.

Teaching oral language through a game has several advantages. Students will tend to concentrate on the game itself, and forget any self-consciousness while speaking in a foreign language. The game provides a rationale for using Hebrew to communicate. Language is used naturally and for a purpose; students are not just reciting unrelated sentences using set vocabulary and grammatical forms.

TPR (Total Physical Response)

Materials: Props for vocabulary words you are teaching; preferably objects, but possible to use pictures

Number of Players: Small group or entire class

Purpose: To learn and reinforce oral language, both listening and speaking.

Preparation: Decide which new vocabulary you want to teach. See how you can combine these new words with previously learned vocabulary and sentence structures. Have the necessary objects or pictures ready. Ideally, each student will have a set of objects to manipulate. You can arrange this by asking students to bring things from home, or by supplying everyone with photocopied pictures.

Instructions: TPR is a very effective system of foreign language acquisition which can be applied to Hebrew. It is beyond the scope of this chapter to discuss the system fully, but additional information can be found in teacher resource centers or libraries.

The teacher begins by describing a situation in Hebrew and modeling it, without translating. For example, the teacher might say, "The hat is under the chair." The first time, the students watch and listen. Then, the teacher repeats the sentence, models it, and students mimic his/her action. The teacher varies the instructions, using both new and review vocabulary in a variety of combinations. As the class becomes familiar with the instructions, the teacher stops modeling. Next smaller groups are asked to respond, and finally individual volunteers. Students are not forced to speak, but will often naturally ask to lead the game themselves and give instructions. They particularly enjoy giving humorous instructions, such as, "The teacher is under the table." You will also notice that they will naturally repeat the instructions to themselves as they are carrying them out.

Keep a list of the vocabulary that you teach with this system, so that you can constantly review it.

Simon Says (Shimon Omer)
Materials: None
Number of Players: Small group or entire class
Purpose: Listening comprehension
Preparation: None
Instructions: This classic children's game is a variation of TPR; students are asked to respond to verbal instructions. Have all the students stand by their chairs. Give oral instructions using Hebrew vocabulary that the students know, such as "Hands on head." You can also introduce new words through the game, making sure not to overwhelm the students with too many new words at once.

Students carry out the instruction only if the teacher first says, "*Shimon Omer*," Hebrew for "Simon Says." In the original version of the game, students are eliminated if they do the wrong action, or if they respond to commands that aren't preceded by "*Shimon Omer*." In a classroom, it is preferable to make note of the mistakes, but let everyone keep on playing. An advanced student can take over the teacher's role.

Charades
Materials: letter, word, or sentence cards
Number of Players: small group or entire class; can be played in teams.
Purpose: Reading comprehension, speaking
Preparation: There are several variations of this game that are good to use with beginning language learners. For each variation you will prepare different types of cards for students to silently act out.
Instructions: In the first version of this game, give each student a list of about 10 sentences that can be acted out. Have an additional list prepared and cut up, with one sentence on each piece of paper. Fold the pieces of paper so they can't be read and have a student volunteer pick a piece and act out the sentence. The other students read their lists and try to guess which sentence was acted out. You can play the same game without lists, which makes it more difficult to guess, but takes away the component of reading comprehension.

Another variation is to play the same game but act out only individual words. You can play this version in teams and have several members of a team act out the same word for the opposing team. This team version doesn't need to be competitive; as soon as one team correctly guesses a word, the other team gets a turn to act.

To add an extra element to the "word" version of charades, make each team unscramble the word they need to act out. Write out the words on cards and cut up the cards into individual letters. Leave any vowels that come under letters attached to the letters. Hand each team all the pieces they need to form a word.

To get everyone involved at the same time, write each word on a different color card, or with a different color marker. Then, give each student one piece of card, have them find the rest of the students with that color card, unscramble the word, and decide how they are going to act it out. In this version, students will need to be moving around the room as they find and meet with their group.

What's on My Back?
Materials: Safety pins, letter cards or word cards
Number of Players 2 or more; good with entire class
Purpose: All skills
Preparation: None
Instructions: Pin a Hebrew letter on the back of a volunteer student, without letting the student see the letter. Have the student turn around and show the rest of the group what the letter is. The other students take turns acting out Hebrew words that begin with that letter, until the volunteer can guess what the letter on his/her back is.

The same game can be played with word cards.

While this game is actually very simple, the twist of having something pinned on their backs makes it popular with students.

Arts and Crafts
Many teachers shy away from arts and crafts activities, either because they are time consuming, or because the teacher feels he/she "Isn't

CHAPTER TWENTY-THREE **251**

artistic." However, these activities are usually favorites with students. Parents are also pleased to see projects come home. They aren't witness to all the wonderful moments of learning that go on in your class, and like to see tangible evidence of their child's progress. The activities described below require no special artistic ability. Many of them can be done in learning centers by students who have completed their assignments. If you find that students are spending too much class time embellishing their art work, put a time limit on the activity and tell those who insist that they "aren't finished," that they can complete the project at home.

Decorated Letters

Materials: Large stencils of the Hebrew letters, construction paper, paint, crayons, or felt markers

Number of Players: Any number

Purpose: Letter recognition

Preparation: Trace the stencil of the Hebrew letter you are teaching onto the construction paper. Make a copy for each student.

Instructions: Have students decorate the letters with paint, crayon, or felt markers. Save the letters so that each student will have a complete set. You can also cut out the letters, laminate them, and tie them together with yarn into a chain that the students can hang up in their rooms at home. Use the decorated letters to review the names and sounds of the Hebrew *Aleph Bet*.

Illustrated Letter Cards

Materials: Medium size stencils of the Hebrew letters, construction paper, felt markers or crayons

Number of Players: Any number

Purpose: Letter recognition, vocabulary review, *Aleph Bet* order

Preparation: Using the stencils, trace a Hebrew letter onto each piece of construction paper.

Instructions: Each time a new letter is learned, assign a student to complete the letter card by drawing a picture of a word beginning with that letter and coloring in the card. Hang the completed cards in your class.

Once you have learned the entire *Aleph Bet*, you can drill the order of the letters using these cards. String a clothesline across the room and hang the cards with clothespins. Remove some of the cards and have students replace them in the correct order.

Complete the Picture

Materials: Photocopied worksheets of partially completed pictures

Number of Players: Any number

Purpose: Oral comprehension of vocabulary

Preparation: Make a list of oral instructions that require students to add something to the partially completed picture. Use familiar vocabulary. Your instructions can be entirely in Hebrew, or use Hebrew and English in the same sentence, for example, "Draw *Aba* next to the *Shulchan*."

Instructions: Give each student a worksheet. Slowly read your list of instructions, pausing to give students time to complete the picture.

Judaica Crafts

Materials: Depends on the project

Number of Players: Any number

Purpose: To relate Hebrew language to Judaica concepts

Preparation: Depends on the project

Instructions: Integrate Hebrew language with your Judaica or holiday curriculum. Create ritual objects that have Hebrew writing on them. For example, *challah* covers with Shabbat written on them, *Kiddush* cups, *Haggadah* covers, *Seder* plates or *dreidles*. Make New Year cards with Hebrew greetings in them.

Pictionary

Materials: Butcher paper, felt markers, tape

Number of Players: Two teams

Purpose: Oral vocabulary reinforcement

Preparation: Prepare a list of Hebrew words or phrases that can easily be illustrated. Tape sheets of butcher paper onto the chalkboard if you don;t have a large pad of butcher paper.

Instructions: The first team chooses a volunteer to come forward and quickly illustrate a Hebrew phrase or word which the teacher shows that student. The team tries to guess the word(s) as quickly as possible. You can time them if you want the game to be competitive. If the student who is drawing feels that he can't illustrate the word, he can choose another teammate to take over for him. Once the picture has been identified, the second team gets a turn, using a fresh sheet of butcher paper.

Overhead Transparency Stories

Materials: Blank overhead transparency sheets, permanent felt markers, nail polish remover, cotton balls

Number of Players: Any number; can be done as an individual activity or in small groups

Purpose: To reinforce all skills

Preparation: Each group or individual will illustrate a Hebrew story, either their own, or a story the class has read. Students should decide on the major scenes in the story and draw complete sketches of those scenes before using the markers. When drawing on the transparencies, erasures should be kept to a minimum. If necessary, the teacher can use nail polish remover applied with a cotton ball to erase the markers.

Students use the pictures to help them retell the story. They can write a script, or practice giving an oral summary.

Instructions: Have a show using the overhead projector to project the transparencies. Each group tells or reads their summary of the story.

Special Activities

The activities described below are a way of integrating Hebrew language learning into special occasions. Use these activities as rewards for good behavior or when your class has completed a unit of study.

Cooking

Materials: Depends on the recipe

Number of Players: Works best with small group, but possible with any number

Purpose: To reinforce any skill

Preparation: Photocopy a Hebrew recipe. With beginning students you will need to translate a recipe from English, so that the language is simple. Choose a recipe that is easy to make, is something your students will enjoy eating, and includes lots of tasks in which everyone can share. Prepare all the ingredients and kitchenware.

Instructions: Teach the new vocabulary. Read the recipe together, making sure everyone understands it. Assign tasks to students, conducting your discussion in Hebrew if possible. When doing the food preparation, describe each step in Hebrew.

Fruit salad is a good choice to make; the vocabulary is useful and making it provides many opportunities for students to cut and mix.

Refreshments

Materials: Food!

Number of Players: Any number

Purpose: Oral language reinforcement

Preparation: Assign students to bring various foods to class. Encourage them to choose at least some healthy foods. Conduct this discussion in Hebrew. This is a good activity to do when teaching about Shabbat or holidays; you can teach students what the traditional foods are.

Instructions: When passing out the food, make students ask for what they want in Hebrew. Teach them how to say "Please" and "Thank you" in Hebrew. Recite the Blessings for each food as well.

Parties

Materials: Food, decorations, music, prepared game or activity, special guests, certificates of achievement

Number of Players: Everyone

Purpose: Any skill; to place value on accomplishments in Jewish learning

Preparation: Complete as many of your party preparations as possible in Hebrew. Include Hebrew writing in your decorations. Have students create Hebrew invitations for your guests. If you want your party to be educational (and something your guests will want to come for) you must prepare a program. Hebrew skits, songs, or the presentation of a special crafts project are good choices. Then lead the students in a game or activity. Certificates of achievement can be presented by the Director of Education. Conclude the party with refreshments.

CONCLUSION

This list would not be complete without a final word of caution and encouragement. Hopefully, the ideas in this chapter will serve as springboards to your own creativity. If an idea doesn't quite work for you, change it. Don't be overwhelmed by the number of ideas listed; pick a few simple activities to get you started and build your repertoire over time. Ultimately, you have to be in the classroom day after day. You know the class best: what the students enjoy and what works. You're the expert.

Hillary Zana received a B.A. and teaching credential from Princeton University in 1976. She teaches Hebrew in Los Angeles to students from ages five to 75, using games and activities with all of them. She was Project Consultant for *Z'man Likro* and *Kadimah!* (A.R.E.), and wrote the teacher guides for both programs. She is also the author of the *Z'man Likro Activity Book*. In her spare time, she is the Librarian and computer coordinator at Emek Hebrew Academy.

BIBLIOGRAPHY

Harris, Frank W. *Great Games To Play with Groups: A Leader's Guide*. Carthage, IL: Fearon Teacher Aids, 1990. (P.O.Box 280, Cartharge, IL 62321)

Isaacs, Ronald H. *The Jewish Instructional Games Book*. Cleveland: Bureau of Jewish Education, 1986.

Kaye, Peggy. *Games for Reading: Playful Ways To Help Your Child Read*. New York: Pantheon Books, 1984.

Kops, Simon, and Carolyn Moore Mooso, eds. *Fast, Clean & Cheap*. Los Angeles: Torah Aura Productions, 1989.

Lee, W. R. *Language Teaching Games and Contests*, 2d ed. London: Oxford University Press, 1979.

Moskowitz, Nachama Skolnik. *Games, Games, and More Games for the Jewish Classroom*. New York: UAHC Press, 1994.

———. *Original Bulletin Boards on Jewish Themes*. Denver: A.R.E. Publishing, Inc., 1986.

Rossel, Seymour. *Managing the Jewish Classroom: How To Transform Yourself into a Master Teacher*. Los Angeles: Torah Aura Productions, 1987.

(For a catalog of Jewish teacher supplies, including Hebrew stencils, stickers, game making supplies, etc., write The Learning Plant, P.O. Box 17233, West Palm Beach, FL 33416.)

THE ARTS

CHAPTER TWENTY-FOUR

DRAMA IN THE CLASSROOM

Joyce Klein

Drama is the expression of emotion. It is imitation. It is rehearsal for living. It has many uses — thematic, emotional, educational. Drama can and should be an integral part of experiential learning. If you "escape from Egypt," your interest in the Bible will increase. If you "live in a shtetl" for 30 minutes, your point of view will be a much more involved one. If you "meet Hannah Senesh," you will remember her poetry, and her story.

There are many kinds of drama — creative dramatics, improvisation, role play, pantomime, and play/performances. All can be used in various ways in the Jewish classroom. In this chapter, each will be described and a number of examples will be included. Each teacher will discover through practice the form or forms that are most comfortable and appropriate.

CREATIVE DRAMATICS

Creative drama is well suited to Bible, history, and folklore. A session should last about 45 minutes, consisting of about 15 minutes of warm-up exercises, 10 minutes of storytelling, 15 minutes of acting, and a 5 minute evaluation.

The warm-up gets the students to relax their bodies and their minds. The best way to do this is to combine something that is fun and imaginative with physical relaxation. For example, have your kids be ice cubes slowly melting, latkes frying (don't forget to flip them over), popcorn popping, etc. Or you could move them through a room full of a changing substance: water, clouds, peanut butter, sand, lumpy oatmeal, etc.

After a relaxing warm-up, move to an imagination warm-up. Sit in a circle with some imaginary "magic stuff" in your hands. Create something (a ball, a telephone, a kitten) and, by your interaction with it, let them guess what it is. Then pass the "stuff" to the next person, and around the circle. Or have each child build a house, and you walk around and try and guess what material they are using. For older students, you might want to play mirrors: pair them off and let them take turns playing "mirror" while you try to guess which is the mirror at any given time. Or have them each imagine a house. They are in it when the lights go out and must look for a candle and matches.

You should then devise a warm-up that is emotionally connected to the story you are going to have them act out. For instance, if your story is about the Lower East Side of New York in the 1920s, where the family works very hard, you might have them each think of a hard job done by one person (cleaning an oven, working at a sewing machine, digging a ditch). Then have them do it, encouraging them to get into it so they really feel as though they've worked. Or if your story is about a group of early *chalutzim* (pioneers in Palestine circa 1900), you could do a warm-up about loneliness or hunger. The important thing is the emotional content of the story.

It is then time to tell the story, Needless to say, the story should be appropriate for the age group. It should not be very long, and it should have a central conflict and solution. Have them all sit down while you tell the story. When you have finished, without discussion (discussion now would be vicarious, so wait), begin to act it out.

The acting: Have your kids pick parts, and then let them act out the story. Encourage them and prompt only when they forget what comes next. With young children (grades 1-3), you might want to take a part in the story, especially the first time you do a creative drama session. You might choose a story with a central character you could play (parent, teacher, etc.), do it once, and then do it again with one of the kids taking your role. This will help them see what to do.

If it is a long story, you may want to act out some parts and tell the rest. In this case, stop after the part you want acted; act it out, and then tell the next part. Or, the story may have some segment that you think is particularly relevant involving one character, in which case you could have the whole class do the part together, with each child being that individual at the same time.

For older students, allow them more initiative. I have used letters from *A Bintel Brief* by Metzger very effectively with junior high students in a creative drama session. I divided the students into groups after I read one of the letters. Some groups acted out scenes of the story, while one group was the editorial board of *The Forward*. They composed an answer to the writer. After the scenes were done and their answer was heard, I read them the actual answer. I have also used the story of Masada with this age group, by telling them the story up to the final scene (walls are burning, Romans are ready to attack at dawn). I then divided my students into families. Each one had a meeting to discuss what to do in the morning. After the various scenes were presented, I told them the actual ending as part of the evaluation.

Following the acting, sit down again for a short evaluation. The things to bring out: emotional impact (how did it feel to work so hard, give that up, make that decision), a short discussion about the elements of the story and how it was to live through it. Encourage students to express how they felt as specific characters, as well as what they observed about the other characters. Although you will want to put the story into historical context, or relate it to previous lessons, keep such remarks to a minimum during the evaluation. The lesson will serve your purposes better if you refer back to it during an upcoming discussion. ("Remember how you felt when you were on strike in the story? Well, that's how they felt.")

IMPROVIZATION

Improvisation, or "improv," is spur-of-the-moment drama. There is no script or story, just an idea, a situation, or a character. Improv is excellent for the teaching of ethics, history, contemporary problems, Jewish identity, etc. It is most appropriate for junior and senior high school students, although it can be used for 5th and 6th graders as well.

In my view, role play is a type of improvisation. A role play session should include the same components as any improvisation session. This will be further discussed later.

Improv should always be preceded by warm-up exercises. In addition to those warm-ups described above, there are two exercises specifically designed to prepare students for improvisation. The first of these is called "Scene on Scene." Two volunteers begin the exercise by picking a situation and beginning to improvise action and dialogue. You go to another student and suggest a role to him or her which requires him or her to interact with one of the volunteers. (You're a cop. Go and give David a ticket. You're the Principal. Michelle gets sent to your office. You are opening your Chanukah presents. Susie is your sister. You open your present from her and you absolutely hate it.) The new student enters the scene and, without any explanation, begins to interact with the volunteer you have indicated. The other volunteer leaves the stage, and the volunteer who has been approached must continue the scene. Wait a couple of minutes, then send a new student into the scene with a new role. There should never be more than two students on stage at once.

A word about a stage: always establish a stage area by indicating a part of the room in which all action takes place. I have seen potentially excellent drama sessions fail because all of the acting took place in the middle of a circle of students. If you set up a stage, it creates the correct atmosphere for both the actors and the audience.

Another improv warm-up is called "Freeze." This one is best when it follows "Scene on Scene" since it requires initiative from the students, and "Scene on Scene" will give them ideas. "Freeze" begins the same way, with two volunteers. However, in this case, members of the audience can decide when they want to enter the scene. When a student sees one of the volunteers (A) in a pose or attitude which suggests a new situation, he or she says "Freeze." The two volunteers must stop action and speech. The new student walks onto the stage, taps the other volunteer (B) on the shoulder. B leaves the stage, and the new student begins to interact with A as if they are in the new scene suggested by A's pose. They continue until another student calls "Freeze."

If your students are shy, or your volunteers do not seem to be taking poses that suggest ideas to the audience, you may call "Freeze" and enter the scene yourself. Your purpose is to create a flamboyant scene which will suggest new ideas to your students. Don't be surprised if your students tap each other out in order to act with you!

Incidentally, when I am working with older students, especially junior high, I always begin improv exercises with the statement that racial, ethnic, or sexual stereotypes will not be tolerated as characters. This prevents unwanted situations from arising. If, despite your warning, someone begins such a scene, simply stop the action and remind students of the rules.

These exercises accomplish two things: they accustom your students to taking on roles, and they loosen inhibitions about acting. (They're also fun!) You are now ready to use improvisation as a teaching tool. Improv can help your students relate easily to a problem or to a historical period.

In its simplest form, thematic improv is much the same as the warm-ups. Tell students they are members of a family on the Lower East Side, workers in a sweatshop, a group walking to Palestine from Russia, a group of slaves in Egypt discussing Moses, and so on. You can write character descriptions on pieces of paper, and have them each pick one, or you can just give them the situation. Remind them of things they have already learned while they are improvising. Afterwards, conduct a short evaluation of how students felt in the situation. For older students, the situation and/or characterization can be more complex, with a problem to solve (e.g., a sweatshop with workers, union agitators, and a foreman; a family in a shtetl deciding whether to leave and if so, where to go). Students will be forced to get into the psychological make-up of the people and their times if they are required to solve a problem from their viewpoint.

ROLE PLAY

Role play is similar to improv, except that there is no time for the actors to prepare. This technique works best with current problems. Simply assign roles, suggest the situation, and have students get up and go with it (Examples: "You're the son, you want to go to a party Friday night. You're his mother, you want him home for Shabbat. Go." "You are twelve years old, and don't want a Bat Mitzvah. You're the Rabbi. Go." "Family just moved to a new neighborhood. You're the kid, trying to talk your parents out of putting a *mezuzah* on the door because you don't want the kids in the neighborhood to know you're Jewish. You two are the parents. Go.") The lack of any preparation time means you are dealing with gut reactions, and the results can be very controversial. An interesting thing to do is to stop in the middle of the scene (by calling "Freeze") and having students switch roles. This forces students to relate to more than one viewpoint and can lead to the exploration of all sides of an issue.

Another improv idea is a soap opera. Divide your class into groups of six or so. Have each participant design a character within a framework you give them (family in Egypt, group starting a *kibbutz*). Then, for ten minutes each week, have the groups become their characters and improvise. This enables your students to assume a role and really explore it, since they do it regularly. Chances are they will pick a role they might wish was theirs, or which represents what they're trying to become. However, because it's "drama," this method provides a nonthreatening way to try out the role.

USE IMPROV TO HELP STUDENTS RELATE TO A PROBLEM OR A HISTORICAL PERIOD.

Soap operas can be as loose or as directed as you and the class desire. It might be easiest to give the group a framework and a direction for the unit (e.g., family in the shtetl trying to decide to go to America or Palestine). This will allow them to anticipate later developments. In addition, there will be continuity from week to week and students will probably relate to the whole unit both as themselves and as the role they have chosen. As the group learns more about the subject, their soap opera will reflect what they have retained, and add richness to the content of the weekly episode.

PANTOMIME

Mime is dramatic expression without words: non-verbal communication. It is good for probing the emotional content of a subject, and also for exploring relationships within the group.

When students express themselves with their bodies, facial expressions, and movements, they must internalize whatever emotion they are portraying in a deeper and more significant way than if they are merely asked to discuss it. For example, if a group of students is asked to portray the Children of Israel at Mt. Sinai when the Torah was being given, these youngsters could gain a much more personal relationship to the fear and awe in the story than if they were just asked about it. The discussion which follows such an exercise will begin on a profound level, and the understanding will be commensurate with the experience. This demonstrates an occasion when pantomime is more effective than any other kind of drama, since the emotions are very strong and are essential to an understanding of the story.

Pantomime should, of course, be preceded by warm-up. Warm-ups should be physical and encourage concentration. "Machines" is a good warm-up exercise. Students are divided into groups and asked to create a machine of which each member of the group is a part. Machines can be real or imaginary. Each group performs for the rest, and the audience tries to guess what machine has been created. (Sound can be a part, as long as words are not used, just nonsense sound like those a machine might make.) Another exercise is a facial expression circle. The teacher walks around in a circle of students, and asks them to look at him or her with specific emotions: fear, hatred, love, jealousy, anger, etc.

You can then suggest simple pantomime exercises to individuals, pairs, or small groups: (1) Get dressed while looking in a mirror — you are a specific age and the group must guess it; (2) See a friend off on a ship; the group must determine how you really feel about the friend; (3) Two people go shopping together; the group must decide what their relationship is; (4) Three people in a waiting room who don't know each other; the group tries to guess each person's first impression of the other two. These exercises with built-in tasks for the audience will give the actors immediate feedback, and encourage attention and concentration from audience members.

Here is an example of the first half of a lesson which made use of the technique of pantomime. The lesson was on the transition of the Jews of Eastern Europe to America in the late 1800s. After a few preliminary warm-ups, I divided the group into threes. I told them that another planet had just been discovered. On this planet, the inhabitants looked very much like human beings and their culture and lifestyle was much like ours. There were two major differences: technology on this planet was more advanced than ours, and the people — their hair, skin, fingernails — were bright green. I asked each group to imagine that Earth is sending a couple of people to live on the Green Planet as ambassadors. Each group was to arrive at the three main problems our ambassadors might face on the Green Planet.

After a few minutes, I asked each group to report on the problems they had discussed. Most came up with fear, ignorance, prejudice, lack of skills to function in a more advanced society, language, etc. I then asked for three volunteers. Two people were asked to portray inhabitants of the Green Planet. The third was an ambassador from Earth. The pantomime was the arrival of the ambassador on the Green Planet. Included in their scene were some of the problems suggested by the groups. This sketch was repeated three or four times with different volunteers. After each scene, we identified and discussed the problems we had seen and how they had been conveyed.

I then talked about the arrival of Jewish immigrants to the U.S. I drew parallels to the scenario we had created. For the immigrants, America was like the Green Planet — the people's dress and looks were different, the technology was more advanced, the lifestyle strange. Some of the problems were the same as well. We looked at some pictures of the period (use a book such as *The Jews in America* edited by Cohen). The rest of the lesson involved letters from *A Bintel Brief*, which I briefly described in the section on Creative Dramatics.

The students were able to relate easily to the discussion of immigration. Their emotions had become involved in the pantomime scenes and they cared about the subject because of their involvement. Of course, it helped that so many of them had grandparents or great-grand-parents who were part of that immigration. We talked about that, too, providing them with another emotional hook to get them personally involved in the subject matter. For that is what drama can do so well — provide the personal connection that makes material meaningful and more easily retained.

PLAY/PERFORMANCES

A play with a script is the most structured type of drama. It involves interpretation of the thoughts of the writer, memorization of lines, and working together with others to produce a meaningful theater experience for performers and audience.

Creating a performance in the usual time frame provided in a once-a-week or after school setting can be very frustrating. If the total amount of time (weekly or otherwise) available, from first rehearsal to production, is less than twenty hours, you will find it very difficult to produce anything larger than a very short script play. If you are working with a group of motivated students, try to create the time needed to put on one substantial production. However, for the more common performance needs (the 5th grade will be doing a "play" for the Purim assembly), here are some alternative suggestions for other kinds of productions.

The "Look-Ma-No-Lines" Production

Pick a wonderful, well-written story (Chelm stories are good), and one or two outgoing students. They are your narrators. Everyone else will be pantomiming the story while your narrators read it. Use all of the theatrical devices you can — make-up, costumes, props, and lights if available. Encourage your students to exaggerate their actions, and your narrators to read with a lot of expression. Three rehearsals are all you will need for a very good production.

Make sure you use all the technical parts of the production for the dress rehearsal so your actors are used to them. If you are performing for a holiday and can't find an appropriate story which is worth doing, any Chelm story can be used. Just start with, "It was the week before Purim (or Chanukah or Pesach)" and end with "So all the people of Chelm went home to prepare for (holiday), and it was the best (holiday) they ever had!" Chelm stories are also good because all you need for costumes are parents' clothes.

The "Why-Work-Harder-Than-You-Have-To" Production

Pick any story you have used in a creative dramatics session. (Or, if you haven't already done one, do a story now.) Thus your students will already know the story and will have "performed" it previously for themselves. They may want to switch parts, but they have no lines to memorize. Add costumes, make-up, props, lights, a little narration if necessary, rehearse it three times, and you're ready to perform it.

The "If-No-One-Can-See-Me-I'm-Not-on-Stage" Production

Borrow, buy, or make puppets and a puppet stage. (Two crates on top of a table with material nailed to the top and hanging down like a curtain will work fine.) Pick a story you have done in class, or even a script. This will require a few more rehearsals — perhaps four or five. Your students will have to practice moving puppets realistically and avoiding stepping on each other, but, again, they don't have to memorize lines. Audiences of every age love puppet shows and they are also good for inhibited students who can "act" without being seen. A nice addition is a microphone, if available. This requires your presence behind the stage, frantically putting the mike in front of the right kid at the right time, but it's worth the effort because everyone can hear!

The "Automatic-Emmy-Cause-Mom's-in-the-Audience" Production

Use any of the above ideas, or something from an improvisation session. Videotape it in sections. Divide the sections using imaginary advertisements, created and acted by the students, which pertain to the subject matter or to the historical period. Everyone will be impressed! By the way, this can be done as a "performance" just for your students in class. Divide the class into groups and have each group produce their own TV show. If desired, they can use their soap opera characters. Film each group individually, then have "Sunday Morning at the Movies," when they see each other's shows for the first time. Be sure to invite parents. They'll love it.

THE TEACHER AS DRAMATIST

A note for the teacher: don't let your students have all the fun. You, as dramatist, can add much to a learning experience. Try coming to class in costume and let your students "meet Isaac" in person. Team up with another teacher and have a well known talk show host/hostess "interview Golda Meir," with your class as the studio audience. Teach a class by candlelight about the Marranos. And please, if you teach preschool or primary grades, "invite a tree in for Tu B'shevat" and sing Happy Birthday to it! A few branches up your sleeves and you, like me, can be "Lena the Greena," introducing twenty four-year-olds to all your relatives in the garden, teaching them an ancient tree song, "*Atzei Zeitim Omdim*" (olive trees are standing), and giving them a relationship to Tu'B'shevat that they will never forget.

Joyce Klein is a playwright, director, and educator. She has had more than 30 plays produced in various countries. Her play *The Island of Shabbat* was commissioned by the American Jewish Joint Distribution Committee, created by Russian *olim* in Israel, and performed in 11 cities in the former Soviet Union, as well as in Tel Aviv and Jerusalem. Joyce is currently the director of the Department of Theatre in Education at the Melitz Centers for Jewish Zionist Education in Jerusalem.

BIBLIOGRAPHY

Drama in General

Albert, Eleanor. *Jewish Story Theatre*. Los Angeles: Torah Aura Productions, 1989.

Allen, John. *Drama in the Schools: Its Theory and Practice*. Portsmouth, NH: Heinemann Educational Books, Ltd., 1981.

Cheyney, Jeanne, and Arnold Cheyney. *Finger Plays for Home and School*. Glenview, IL: Scott Foresman, 1989.

Citron, Samuel J. *Dramatics for Creative Teaching*. New York: United Synagogue of America, 1961.

Coger, Leslie Irene, and Melvin R. White. *Readers Theater Handbook: A Dramatic Approach to Literature*, 3d. ed. Glenview, IL: Scott Foresman, 1982.

Cohen, David, ed. *The Jews in America*. San Francisco: HarperCollins, 1989.

DeMille, Richard. *Put Your Mother on the Ceiling: Children's Imagination Games*. New York: Viking Press, 1976.

Hawley, Robert C. *Value Exploration through Role Playing: Practical Strategies for Use in the Classroom*. Amherst, MA: Education Research Associates, 1974.

Hinson, N.M. "Developing Dramatic Activities." *RE:View*, Winter, 1991, pp. 208-9.

Kohl, Herbert. *Making Theater: Developing Plays with Young People*. New York: Teachers and Writers Collaborative, 1988.

McCaslin, Nellie. *Creative Drama in the Classroom*, 5th ed. White Plains, N.Y.: Longman Publishing Group, 1990.

———. *Creative Drama in the Intermediate Grades*. White Plains, NY: Longman Publishing Group, 1987.

———. *Creative Drama in the Primary Grades*. White Plains, NY: Longman Publishing Group, 1990.

Metzger, Isaac. *A Bintel Brief*. New York: Schocken Books, 1990.

Paley, Vivian Gussin. *The Boy Who Would Be a Helicopter*. Cambridge, MA: Harvard University Press, 1990.

Philbin, M., and J. S. Meyers. "Classroom Drama: Discourse as a Mode of Inquiry in Elementary School Social Studies." *Social Studies*, Sept/Oct 1991, pp. 79-82.

Schwardelson, Susan J. *Kadima Drama Manual*. New York: United Synagogue of America, Dept. of Youth Activities, n.d.

"Stories — Telling, Teaching, Understanding." *Melton Journal*, Winter, 1982.

Plays

Beiner, Stan J. *Class Acts*. Denver: A.R.E. Publishing, Inc., 1992.

———. *Bible Scenes: Joshua to Solomon*. Denver: A.R.E. Publishing, Inc., 1988.

———. *Sedra Scenes: Skits for Every Torah Portion*. Denver: A.R.E. Publishing, Inc., 1982.

Cohen, Edward M., ed. *New Jewish Voices: Plays*. New York: SUNY, 1985.

Gabriel, Michelle. *Jewish Plays for Jewish Days: Brief Holiday Plays for Ages 8-12*. Denver: A.R.E. Publishing, Inc., 1978.

Landis, Joseph C., ed. and trans. *The Great Jewish Plays*. New York: Applause Theater Book Publishers, 1986.

A good source of plays on a variety of topics is the Bureau of Jewish Education in Cincinnati, 1580 Summit Rd., Cincinnati, OH 45237.

THE ARTS

CHAPTER TWENTY-FIVE

THEATER AS AN EDUCATIONAL TOOL

Elaine Rembrandt

Drama is a very popular educational tool and it lends itself well to the religious school. But where do you begin? Where do you look for material? How do you utilize class time? Should you think in terms of a production or just classroom theater games? Where? What? How?

THEATER AS EDUCATION

The first commandment is to remember that we are not just drama teachers. We are religious school teachers utilizing drama as a means of educating. And we are educating two different groups — our students and their audience! Throughout all the rehearsals, I try to help the actors to be aware of the fact that they have the task of educating as well as entertaining their audience. What we do is really educational theater.

There are so many good books and articles available on creative dramatics, role play and classroom theater activities. For this reason I am going to restrict this chapter mainly to preparing for production with middle and upper school students. Theater game activities are fine for the lower elementary school child or as an occasional tool in a content course for the older student. However, these do not motivate the older child in a part-time religious school atmosphere as does a goal oriented class. Theater games are great for teaching and reinforcing the actors' abilities to emote, to ad-lib, to think on their feet. But most students at this grade level want to take part in a play, and anything short of that is disappointing.

There is something marvelous and magical in turning ten to twenty individuals into one cohesive working body — and it can happen every semester! Somehow absenteeism (which diminishes as the pressure of production mounts) and lack of adequate time are surmounted and a play or pageant of worth both for the players and for the audience is performed.

PRODUCTION IN THE PRIMARY GRADES

According to Richard Johnson, author of the book *Producing Plays for Children*, the best authorities in the field of children's theater advise that "children should be over 10 years of age before participating as performers in a theater experience. Until at least that age, they will each gain more by being an audience in the formal theater than a participant in creative dramatics." This statement is true if we are thinking in terms of a full-scale production including all the disciplines of formal theater. But my experience is that many very young primary grade children like to perform, too.

When working with young children, common sense tells us to avoid anything that will require attention span, self-discipline, or knowledge above their ability. Most young children learn visually rather than auditorily. In order for them to react to your direction, they have to be able to "see" what you mean. Explain the ideas and actions of your story in terms of their own experiences. Any formal presentation should be based on a story told and improvised in the classroom, rather than on one that is scripted. Not that dialogue cannot be written down. On the contrary, once dialogue has been decided upon by the players and by you, you should make note of it in order to prompt your young actors at successive rehearsals. And plays should be scripted in very short, easily memorized sentences.

Perhaps you are telling the story of Purim. Ask the children, "Do you think Esther might have been nervous or afraid to go before the king and tell him that she was Jewish? Did you ever break something accidentally and then have to go and tell your mother or father? How did you feel? Were you afraid? Why were you afraid? Show me how you might have looked when you told your parents what you did wrong. Did you smile? Did you laugh? Was your head up or down? Did you fidgit? Why? Show me how you stood. Do you think Esther might have looked the same way? Who wants to show me how Esther might have stood before the king to tell him she was Jewish?" Keep up this kind of banter until you have the makings of a playlet. Then ask for volunteers to take the various parts.

Explain to the participants that they are now going to become actors. An actor is someone who has the talent to become someone else while he or she is on the stage. The difference between "playing" and "being in a play" is that at play, a child is still himself/herself, but when acting in a "play," he/she can become someone else for a while. That's why a person can be a "wicked Haman" in a play even though that person is really very nice in real life. And that is why "old Mordecai" can really be a child of only seven or eight. That is acting.

Now its time to bring your actors up onto the stage area and to paint the scene for them verbally. Tell them where the entrances and exits are and fix the sight lines. When this has been done, you are ready to begin to read the story and let your actors create. You may have to do a small amount of blocking or some line coaching, but chances are that with a minimum of rehearsals, you will be able to present something entertaining and worthwhile for all, especially an audience, of enthusiastic parents. Young children, as well as older ones, delight in make-up and costumes and really "come alive" when these are added. Common sense dictates that the primary grade play should be no more than ten minutes long. Even the plays for the middle school child should be kept to 20 minutes so that what you present has been well rehearsed.

Small children relate well in an atmosphere scaled down to their size. Use the classroom as their stage, rather than a large, foreboding assembly hall. The intimate and familiar atmosphere creates a more secure feeling. It is not necessary to present the play to the entire school. The actors' needs are being met with an audience of their parents and perhaps another class of their peers. As children mature, their ability to cope with a larger arena, to memorize more material and to work in a more formal theater atmosphere will also increase.

CHOOSING THE PLAY

The most important first step is choosing the right vehicle both for the actors and the audience. Many times your content will be limited by the calendar (i.e., a Passover presentation or Israel Independence Day, etc.). The nature of the presentation, however, is totally your responsibility. Don't settle for mediocrity just because you cannot find a quality script. Write your own play if necessary. There are many variations possible on the same theme, yet there is a dearth of good plays, especially for the upper grades. Both children and audience are very sophisticated these days, and the typical "I am a Seder Plate" program will not do past the second grade.

Another problem is caused by the necessity of utilizing an entire class in the production. A play with seven parts, no matter how well written, will not accommodate a class of twenty children. Because of this, I always have to write, rewrite, or revise. Quite often, I am still writing the second act while in rehearsal with the first, just to be able to incorporate enough parts for everyone in the class.

When choosing a play, or a theme for a play, try to focus on an aspect of the topic that is unusual or at least not belabored, so that audience and actors will feel as though they are learning something new. Remember, we are performing educational theater. Such a focus will also keep you, as the director, from becoming bored with the same productions year after year. In fact, try not to repeat any play within a four year period. After that time lapse, few will remember having seen it. It will seem as though it is a fresh piece. Eventually you'll have quite a nice repertoire!

An example of adapting my own old material occurred on one Chanukah when I adapted a previously performed short playlet about the establishment of the first settlements in Israel. The play centered around the miracle of finding water just as all hope was lost. Now you might ask, "What does that have to do with Chanukah?" The introductory scene, which I wrote expressly for our purposes took place on a platform in front of the stage. There a brother and sister are playing *dreidle* as they discuss the game and the concept of miracles in relation to the holiday. Their parent enters, picks up the discussion, and proceeds to recount the story of a modern day miracle. At this point, the curtain opens and the action of the "old" script begins, now edited to include mention that it is Chanukah time. The ending of the play shows both groups, the *chalutzim* and the modern family, lighting their candles simultaneously on two different stage levels and reciting the blessings together. The production turned out to be very poignant and meaningful and something a little different from the usual "miracle of the oil" play.

One year I was searching for a Passover play. In *A Passover Anthology* by Goodman, I found the story of the birds sacrificing themselves as food for the wanderers in the desert during the Exodus. Immediately, visions of fantastic costuming danced in my head! I knew we were slated to present this on the *bimah* during a Friday night service. Because there would be no scenery, the idea of more elaborate costuming appealed to me. I adapted the story into play form and the art director at our synagogue made us two fantastic bird heads. The play at once became very interesting to look at.

BLOCKING

Blocking and pacing are probably the two most important elements a director can contribute to the final performance. Both can make the difference between a boring or an interesting production.

Variety in stage direction is crucial to the total well-being of any play. No matter where your play is being presented — on a stage, on the floor level, on the *bimah* — utilize every entry and every architectural structure in the room! Don't be afraid to let your imagination run wild. In our play, "The Freedom Birds," mentioned above, the birds perched on top of the railings which divide the *bimah* from the congregation, delivering their lines from there. The whole effect, including the marvelous paper sculpted heads, was very eye-catching.

Audiences are always delighted when actors enter through the audience or from unexpected places. Use stairs to the stage level for entrances and exits from the audience. Make sure that you differentiate between outdoor and indoor accesses in the same play so as not to confuse your audience. Use ladders and platforms on the stage or performing area to give dimension and variety, especially in a presentational kind of production. Let your actors sit on the edge of the stage (as long as they can be seen), lean against the proscenium arch, face upstage (as long as as they can be heard), and even use the curtain as a prop! For one production, an edited version of the Broadway musical, "The Me Nobody Knows," heads popped out of the middle opening of the curtain at different heights, as well as along the floor line. This happened in unison at a certain point in the music that opened the play. It was startling, exciting, and very effective.

PACING

There is nothing more deadly than long periods of silence during the dialogue of a play while the actors and the audience wait for someone to make an entrance. A long pause need only be three seconds! Actors must be directed to anticipate their entrances so that they are in place and ready to deliver their lines on cue. Silence, like action, should only be there when it is directed into a play. From the opening curtain to the final moment, there should be a fluidity of movement. This differentiates between the very amateurish production and one which reflects some degree of professionalism. This is true even if the only professional thing about the entire production is you! Of course, you must work with your actors so that they understand that picking up a line cue does not mean rushing the lines. In a well paced show, the cast picks up their line cues. All entrances are made with no interminable waits or without an actor or actress too obviously assuming a blocked position before delivering a line. Now you can work for the more subtle kinds of pacing — the pauses for dramatic effect, or the hurried delivery. These give variety to the delivery of dialogue. They serve to enhance the production and keep it from being monotonous.

> **UTILIZE EVERY ENTRY AND EVERY ASPECT OF THE ROOM.**

THE NO-BUDGET SET AND COSTUMES

Here's where you are asked to be a magician! How do you create imaginative sets and colorful costumes with no money and no technical crew to build anything for you? It's always good to enlist the aid of your art department or a parent or two. Perhaps your needs can serve as a project for another class. Nothing need be elaborate — the use of cartons and fabric can produce amazing things.

For "The Rededication," a Chanukah play designed for production on our stage, we used about twenty-five cardboard boxes of varying sizes. The appeal of this production hinged completely around one special effect. The action of the play begins on the floor level. The action takes place at the end of the Maccabean wars. People are finding their loved ones and neighbors and making their way to Jerusalem to give thanks at the Temple. Their arrival at the Temple is signified by the opening of the curtains, revealing the boxes (painted to look like stones) strewn around the stage. Upstage center is an enormous gold idol and a papier-mâche pig's head is laying on a box. Everyone gasps! It is at this point that the cleansing of the Temple and the rededication begin. With a rented strobe light, and some taped silent movie type music, we choreographed the restoration of the Temple. Each box was put in a prearranged place until two walls were created. At the same time, the idol and pig's head were removed and replaced with a large menorah. At practically no expense we created a very exciting effect. Of course, we are fortunate. We are blessed with a real stage, with a traveling proscenium curtain, and basic stage lighting, including a follow spot. If you are working on platforms or on floor level, you will need to be even more creative, but it is possible. Ask your neighborhood appliance dealer for empty refrigerator boxes. Different scenes can be painted on opposite sides of these and, *presto*, change the scene merely by turning the box around. Go to your friendly grocer, wave your hundred dollar register tape at him/her and ask for a trunk-load of empty cartons.

It's especially wise to create items that can be saved and revised over the years. Trees can indicate any outdoor scene. A window flat can be redressed in different fabrics play after play to become the backdrop of many indoor scenes. Other staples are a throne, a small wooden table (when draped with a white lace cloth and holding centerpiece and candlesticks can be the main fixture of many a Shabbat play), and several low stools.

From time to time, something more specific or elaborate has to be made. Always make sure there is some place to store the item. Make a note of when it was made and where it is being kept so that it can be used again when the play is repeated several years later. We have a magnificent gold cardboard idol about eight feet tall that we have used in a couple of different plays. I'm sure we'll find use for it again in the future. We also have an assortment of trees and rocks (papier-mâché), a window flat, and a large scrim. The latter is a fine piece of material, voile or fine cotton, that is stretched taut over a frame. When lighted from the front it will appear solid, but when lighted from behind, it will cast a shadow. A scrim can be used for special effects. With it I created an effect in the final scene of "The Dybbuk." When the dead bridegroom finally appears to Leah, we projected a larger than life shadow of him upstage on the scrim. This was a much more effective way of creating a feeling of the supernatural than the bridegroom's own image would have been. Of course, effects such as this are only possible if you are fortunate enought to have blackout potential and some kind of proscenium staging ability. You do not necessarily have to have a stage to use this, but your actors have to be able to enter and exit out of view of the audience for the proper effect.

Pulpit presentations performed during a regular worship service are never designed to use anything more than a table and chairs or perhaps a couple of easily moved trees. First of all, the stage cannot be preset, and it is too time-consuming and cumbersome to set anything more elaborate than a few props on the stage. I find it better to rely on colorful costuming for this type of play.

Over the years, we have accumulated a nice assortment of basic robes in many different colors and patterns which fit the bill for most biblical plays. You might enlist the aid of a few parents who are talented with a needle and thread to produce some basic costumes for you. It's a good idea to prowl the fabric shops for remnant pieces which might be just the right size for a child's robe. You might not need it right at that moment. But if the fabric is interesting and the price is right, buy it and hang on to it for just the right occasion. Old pieces of drapery or upholstery material make wonderful throws for the throne of Ahashuerus or Pharaoh. Our

Jewish Community Center has a wonderful theater group and is most generous about loaning costumes. We have borrowed many specialty items, such as frock coats and wide brimmed black hats or knickers and even the wedding dress for *The Dybbuk*. Check out your Sisterhood's rummage sale. Sometimes you will find leftover items that would be perfect for costumes.

MUSIC

I love music! And so does the audience, whether it is live or taped. I have found that music can set a mood when nothing else can, especially if you don't have stage lighting. Some taped music to open the show, or act as background to a reading can do a lot to enhance the production. Be certain that it is just the right sound and length and that it does not distract from the speaker or the action.

A UNIFIED WHOLE

Creating a unified whole is really the essence of a well made play. Everything — the acting, the set, the costumes, lights, sound, should work together (with no facet distracting from any other) to produce the single desired effect. Nothing should be unless it is meant to be!

REHEARSING

I have talked about the various aspects of the play itself. Now I will discuss utilizing class time to rehearse.

I usually use the first session with the group to discuss our goals and objectives, hand out performance dates, and try to discern abilities and talents. It is vital to send home the performance dates as soon as possible. Otherwise you may be surprised a week before the performance when your leading man tells you that he will be out of town with his family on the day the play is to be given. If there are to be additional rehearsals, hand out that schedule, too, as soon as possible. In this way you can be notified of possible conflicts and other activities can be rescheduled if necessary, especially for your dress rehearsal.

You might want to schedule extra rehearsals for the students who attend midweek Hebrew at the synagogue. It is often next to impossible to get your cast together on other weekdays because of music lessons, dancing lessons, and allergy shots. Rehearsals should also be scheduled so that there is a minimum of wasted time for each student. Call performances by scenes or work with individual principal players on a lengthy speech or bit of blocking.

I also schedule weekend afternoon rehearsals, asking the students to bring lunch to Religious School and remain until 2:00 P.M. A tremendous amount is accomplished at these intensive rehearsals.

For junior and senior high students, early evening rehearsals seem to be the best because of involvement in sports or other extracurricular activities after school. For us, it is virtually impossible to prepare for presentation without extra rehearsals. We meet for only one 40-minute period once a week and often this is cut short by assemblies that run overtime, fire drills, or treats sent in to celebrate an upcoming holiday. We won't dwell on other difficulties such as the fact that out of a group of twenty students, few have any natural ability and most cannot be heard beyond the first row. Or that if you're lucky, one or two may have looked over their scripts from one week to the next. Or that only about three quarters of the class is present most weeks and it is a different three quarters each time!

CASTING

Since we see students so infrequently, how do we get to know them well enough to cast intelligently? Even among the most practiced directors, it is quite often a matter of intuition and intelligent guessing.

The first time we meet, I will ask the students to tell a little about themselves when the roll is called. I can usually tell from this who is shy and quiet, who has a mature voice and who still sounds like a child, etc. It gives me an immediate idea of who can play mother or father roles, and who are the ingenue types. If there is time, or perhaps at the second meeting, I will have pages for oral readings. Again, I am looking for volume, for vocal range, for expression, for maturity of interpretation. It is good to remember, though, that a poor reader can sometimes be excellent on stage with memorized lines. So don't rule someone out just because of hesitant reading.

Now is the time to work on improvisations. This technique will indicate who is relaxed in front of an audience and who is imaginative. It will demonstrate students' ability to assume a characterization and to think on their feet. It is at this point that we discuss the play we are going to be doing, even if the actual scripts are not ready. The students have a chance to learn the story line and what characters are involved in the play. They can begin forming ideas of what parts they would like to play. It gives me a chance to discuss the concepts in the play and to discern just how much background the students have about the subject matter.

So, as you can see, we have finished our second class and we have still not looked at the script that we will eventually perform. But now I have a clearer idea of the talent present in the class and who will be able to do which parts. (Sometimes I have been quite surprised in the actual tryouts, however!)

Because of the need to get the students to relax and concentrate, I begin almost every class with about three to five minutes of warm-up exercises, physical as well as vocal. Loosen up with simple jumping jacks, flop over like a rag doll, do arm exercises, bunny hops, and duck walks. It's silly and fun. Then count from one to twenty, beginning with a whisper and gradually increasing in volume until students are shouting. Help them become familiar with the feeling of talking loudly. At random, select someone to count from one to ten angrily, then another to do the same thing happily, then sadly, etc. Try some group tongue twisters. Then try them individually. There are some great ones that are not that well-known. Try saying "three tree twigs" very quickly five times. How about "The sixth sheik's sixth sheep is sick"?

For improving concentration, have someone try threading a needle, missing and missing and finally threading it; lifting a very heavy box; opening a very heavy door; or, trying to stay awake during a dull movie, etc.

When the class meets for the third time, I begin with roll call so I can get to know the students. They answer with a tongue twister. (Some students are still barely audible.) We do our group exercises and I speak to them of the necessity of producing volume when they speak. I don't know how many times I have said, "If you can't be heard, you might as well not get up on the stage." I try to make them aware of speaking from deep down so that they can actually feel their abdominal muscles aid in the expelling of air that passes through the larynx and creates the sound we use as our voice. I compare this to throwing a baseball, explaining that if you just raise your arm and let go, the ball is not going to travel very far, but if you bring your arm back far and then let the ball sail, you're going to get distance. The same is true with volume. The lower down the air is projected, the farther it is going to travel when it is expelled and the greater the vibrations against the vocal chords as it passes through. Have them lift a chair out in front of them and hold it with their arms straight as long as they can. It is their abdominal muscles they are using. Help them to be aware of the feeling. Have them exhale abruptly while loudly saying, "Ho, ho, he, he, hoo, hoo, ha, ha," and to use their hands to force the abdomen to contract each time. A few of the students will master these techniques, but you will still have to remind them about volume.

At this meeting, scripts are handed out. I assign people to read the various parts just to have a read through and to acquaint the students with the script. Then I call for volunteers and reread by scenes so that everyone has a chance to read for the part he or she desires. The tryout readings can be only a half page long so that everyone gets a chance to be heard. This is long enough for the director to get an idea of who is best suited for each role. As you read through the play, talk about the characters, their relationships to each other, and discuss the events that made history. By the end of this class session, everyone will have a pretty good idea of the capabilities and the limitations of the class and who is best suited for each role.

The actual casting of the show is exciting for those given major parts, and sometimes heartbreaking for those who are disappointed. Dealing with these traumatic experiences is also a part of your responsibility as teacher/director. Be aware that students will have reactions that vary from indifference to belligerence. How do you surmount this? Fortunately, everyone will be in the play. A discussion in very professional tones about each actor's contribution to the production helps ease the situation. I emphasize that although some parts are larger than others, all parts are necessary to the show, and that all the actors must be serious in their treatment of the part they are playing. "Think about the part," I tell them. "Who are you? Where have you come from? Why are you entering into the scene? What is your relationship with the other people in your scene? And most important, react to what is going on around you."

The fourth class session really begins the rehearsal period. Ask everyone to come up on the stage. Familiarize them with the stage directions and the terminology that you will be using. Insist that everyone bring a pencil to class to write down the blocking. Use pencil rather than pen so that you can change the blocking if your original idea doesn't work. By writing down the blocking, no one will forget or waste precious time with unnecessary questions.

The blocking and your entire conception of the play should be well thought out in advance of rehearsals. Draw a set diagram so the class can "see" exactly what you visualize. As you begin to block the first scene, have the rest of the class watch how you work and learn what is expected of them. As the rehearsal periods progress and everyone is feeling more comfortable, instruct participants in separate scenes to rehearse by themselves in various corners of the room or out in the hall. Everyone will feel they are doing something worthwhile instead of wasting time. It should be impressed upon students, though, that there will be periods of time when just a few people will have to be rehearsed over and over again to reinforce and perfect the scene and the rest of the class will be asked to sit and learn by watching. This is a great test of self-discipline!

The rest of your class sessions until the play is performed will be used for rehearsals. There will be many weeks when you will wonder if the play will ever take shape and become something worth presenting. But as your extra rehearsals begin, you will see a dramatic change in the seriousness of the actors and in the smoothness of the acting.

It is very important to give a deadline for all lines to be memorized, and it can't be too early. Until the "book" is out of the actor's hand, it is impossible to concentrate on facial expression, reacting, or pacing. It is these ingredients that really make the play.

As soon as lines are learned and hands are free from holding scripts, start bringing in all the hand props that will be needed. It is amazing how the simple act of picking up a prop will "throw" a young actor, and he or she will suddenly go blank. Allow the cast as much time as possible to familiarize themselves with props, set, and lighting. They may have to learn to leave or enter the stage during a blackout.

Some of your actors may have to double for technical people by throwing light switches backstage when they are not on stage. These situations should be well rehearsed so there is no foul-up at the last minute. Curtain pulling, light cues, set changes, and any other technical aspects of the show should all be well rehearsed in advance of your dress rehearsal. The final rehearsal of the play, the dress rehearsal, should be handled as if it were an actual performance. Full costumes, makeup, music, lighting, props, and set should be available and everyone must be present. The actors are asked to be there well in advance of "curtain time" so that you can see if your anticipated simple preparation time before the performance is adequate. Do not stop for line cues or mistakes of any kind.

Sometimes it is wise to use a prompter backstage or in the first row of your audience just to relax your actors, though I prefer that actors know the play well enough to be able to pick up anyone else's forgotten line or miscue — in other words, to cover for another actor. Even fifth and sixth graders can do this if they are rehearsed in this way and they expect to have to do it. You or a student director should be taking copious notes all during this final rehearsal and at the close of the final curtain and after the curtain call is blocked, the actors should be called for "notes."

ALL LINES SHOULD BE MEMORIZED AS SOON AS POSSIBLE.

It is very, very important even with adults, but especially with children, to praise the efforts of the cast, pointing out the fine and wonderful things they are doing before any negative criticism is levied. Assure them that the play is going to be terrific and that they are all wonderful and be specific. "Ronny, you have really developed the character of the old man beautifully. Keep him moving slowly throughout the whole play. Don't forget for one minute who you are supposed to be. Don't start walking like a twelve-year-old." Or, "Amy, do you remember how quiet you were when we first began? You really have improved and can be heard so easily now. I'm really proud of you."

This is it. You've done all that you can do. It's now up to your actors and your crew. It's curtain time! Finally, you have achieved your goal. Your audience has really loved the play. The players are proud of themselves for having done something worthwhile (and they are their own best critics). The Director of Education is happy to have tangible evidence that something very positive has taken place in the Religious School.

(Note: For Bibliography on Drama, see page 260.)

Elaine Rembrandt is a professional actress, writer, producer, and director of Jewish theater, and is currently the Director of the Cultural Arts Department of the Jewish Community Center of Cleveland. She has been touring the country with her one-woman show "Courage and Commitment — A Legacy for Jewish Women." She is the author of *Heroes, Heroines and Holidays: Plays for Jewish Youth* (A.R.E. Publishing, Inc.).

THE ARTS

CHAPTER TWENTY-SIX

TEACHING WITH PUPPETS

Rita Kopin
Illustrations by Judye Kopin-Hendlish

A puppet is an inanimate object which is brought to life by human effort and which can be used to communicate or dramatize an idea to an audience. Puppets come in many sizes and shapes. They can be as small as a finger or larger than a person. They can represent human or animal characters, objects or abstractions. In the Jewish classroom, they can be Purim *shpielers* and Bible heroes/heroines, ceremonial objects, historical personalities, Hebrew letters, Hebrew speaking children and animals, trees, and values. A puppet can be a slow learner trying to learn Hebrew, an interviewer, or a singer of Hebrew songs.

Puppets provide a unique and an innovative means of communication, of creative teaching, and of making learning pleasurable.

I first used a puppet in the classroom during my early years of teaching Religious School. It was during the teaching of a unit on scholars to a third grade class, and I was looking for a novel way to introduce the lesson. Filmstrips, storytelling, inquiry method, or artifacts had been used in previous lessons. Although I had never tried puppetry before and I was dubious about my ability to carry it through, the idea of using them intrigued me. Saturday night before class, I began to make my puppet. I stuffed the top of a brown paper bag with tissues to make a head and tied a string around the puppet's neck, allowing room for my index finger to fit into the head. In the robe portion of the bag, I then cut two slits through which I could insert my thumb and middle finger for the puppet's hands.

Absorbent cotton was used to make hair and a beard, felt odds and ends for features, and burlap scraps for a robe and a hat. Now the puppet was complete. To my delight, the students were pleased with my "Hillel." The paper bag was transformed into a personality. Hillel told about himself and then the students asked him questions. The students were involved, excited, and learning. I knew the lesson was a success when David, a shy boy who rarely spoke up, volunteered to play Hillel, and demonstrated that he understood the concepts and ideas being taught.

This chapter will give the "why," "how," and "what" of using puppets in the classroom. Ideas, methods, and techniques will be shared in the hope that some teachers will be stimulated to try some of the suggestions and will go on to develop their own materials to meet the special needs of their own students.

WHY USE PUPPETS IN THE CLASSROOM?

Puppets are a creative means of communicating and instructing. They encourage imaginative thinking and make learning fun. Puppets are seen on television, in live puppet shows, at zoos, in museums, and secular schools. People of all ages are delighted and intrigued by a puppet coming "alive." Further reasons for using puppets in Religious School are:

1. Puppets evoke student interest and reinforce learning. Students listen to puppets attentively.
2. Puppets help students gain self-confidence. Even a shy child loses inhibitions and assumes the identity of the puppet. This is particularly helpful for students who are reticent about using Hebrew or for immigrant children (e.g., Russian, Iranian) who are shy about speaking English. The puppet's errors are more easily tolerated.
3. Puppet productions foster cooperation among students. They integrate different

skills and learning activities and encourage the expression of otherwise hidden talents. An important sense of community develops in the classroom.
4. Puppets allow for multi-sensory as well as manipulative experiences. They introduce variety in methodology and allow for movement and activity during a sedentary class period.
5. Puppets promote independence and responsibility on the part of students for their learning. Research required to prepare sets, costumes, and script can give students a more thorough understanding of a biblical character, hero/heroine, ceremonial object, historical period, or Jewish holiday.
6. Puppets can teach Jewish values and help develop positive feelings of Jewish identity.

HOW TO USE PUPPETS IN THE CLASSROOM

Puppets may be used in a variety of ways according to the teacher's preference, the needs and age level of the class, and the time which can be devoted to the project. An activity can be structured or unstructured, a teacher strategy, or a student performance. Several effective techniques follow.

The Teacher as a Puppeteer

Here is how it works when the teacher is the puppeteer:
1. The teacher narrates a story and manipulates the puppet. Special puppet voices may or may not be used.
2. The teacher may have a dialogue with a puppet. If the teacher is reticent to use a puppet voice, then the puppet may be depicted as a shy personality who whispers into the teacher's ear. All the communicating is done by the teacher in his/her own voice while the puppet does the acting.
3. The puppet (operated by the teacher) may have a dialogue with the students who ask questions. Interaction is encouraged because the greater the involvement, the more effective the learning.

The Student as a Puppeteer

A student may assume any of the teacher roles described above.

Another approach is to provide a puppet learning center within the classroom. Students may use the available puppets in any way they wish. In a more structured format, the students are given a theme like Shabbat, Abraham, *tzedakah*, etc., and are instructed to create a script and to make an informal presentation for the rest of the class.

When teachers think of puppets in the classroom, they often imagine an elaborate student production with stage, sets, puppet making, script writing, etc., and they dismiss it as too complicated and time-consuming for religious school. The teacher, in preparing a student production, must consider his/her objectives and plan accordingly. When time is very limited, teacher-made or commercially manufactured puppets may be preferred. A teacher or student narrates while the students listen, manipulate the puppets, and/or provide sound effects and background music. This type of performance may fulfill the teacher's objective to reinforce the concepts of a holiday, the contributions of a personality, or the requirements of a *tzedakah* project.

For a group of high school students who are studying a particular period in history or a specific Bible personality, the brainstorming and research required to create appropriate costumes, sets, script, etc., may meet the teaching requirements in a very creative and pleasurable way. The production may also evolve into a meaningful *tzedakah* project when it is presented to a group of senior citizens in a nursing home.

More specific teaching strategies and activities using these different formats will be described and examples given.

WHERE TO GET PUPPETS

Puppets may be purchased from stores or mail order firms featuring commercially manufactured puppets; may be produced by the teacher, a paid aide, or adult volunteers; or may be made by students as part of a project.
1. Commercially manufactured puppets are readily available and some are relatively inexpensive. They should be inspected to make certain that they are well made, easily manipulated, and that the features, especially the eyes, hair, and costume decorations, are not easily damaged or lost.
2. "Teacher-made" puppets can be made by volunteer parents, college students, and senior citizens who are enthusiastic about participating in a creative activity which will benefit the education of children.

3. Loan-a-Puppet program – check to see if your community has such a program. It could be located in your school, library, or teacher center.
4. Many students have their own puppets. Encourage the class to bring in their favorite puppet for a class performance, to dramatize a report or to help introduce a book report.
5. Student-made puppets – Creating puppets gives the student a deeper understanding of the personality, dress, setting of the character being developed. Puppets prepared in class should be attractive, simple to make, inexpensive and made of recycled materials. The kind of puppets students make should, of course, be appropriate for their age and ability.

TYPES OF PUPPETS

There are four basic types of puppets:
1. The hand or fist puppet – controlled by the performer's hand inside the puppet.
2. The rod puppet – controlled by rods and often requiring more than one person to operate.
3. Shadow puppets – flat cutout figures shown as shadows on a screen and illuminated from the rear. Traditionally, these puppets had moving joints which were manipulated by horizontal rods and vertical rods and wires.
4. Marionettes – whole puppets with arms, legs, and head moved by strings from above. These are the most complicated to make and operate and are, therefore, beyond the realm of Religious School.

The hand puppet (figure 1), a simplified one rod or stick puppet (figure 2), simplified shadow puppetry or overhead shadow puppetry are all recommended for the Jewish classroom.

The hand puppet is one of the easiest puppets to make and one of the most effective in the classroom. Any material into which you can insert an index finger can serve as a head, and a square scarf or other fabric with slits through which your thumb and middle finger can fit, is a puppet with varied movement capability. It can walk, bow, wave good-bye, cry, clap hands, etc. Other puppets that are very effective are varieties of the above and include finger puppets (figure 3) made of felt, shaped to fit the finger or made from the finger of an old glove.

Figure 1   Figure 2

Figure 3

A story-glove puppet consists of a glove which has velcro sewn on the finger tips. Small felt puppets are stuck onto the velcro or removed as the story progresses.

A "mouth" puppet is moved with the hand inside the head which opens the mouth. Examples of this are a puppet made of a pot holder (figure 4) or from a sock. The Spong-ee designed by Bruce Chesse and described in his book *Puppets from Polyfoam: Spong-ees* (see Bibliography for source) is recommended as a quick teacher-made mascot for your class (figure 5). The head is made from polyfoam using contact cement or staples. Add a rod to the arm and you have a "hand and rod" puppet.

A simplified version of shadow puppetry utilizes a cardboard box for a stage with a light source in the rear shining on the screen. After removing the cover of the box, a window is cut in the bottom and covered with translucent fabric or paper. It is then set on its side and looks

Figure 4   Figure 5

like a TV. Simple puppets are cut out of poster board and a straw or a dowel attached horizontally. For movable joints, attach the two parts with a paper fastener and add an extra rod.

Shadow puppets may also be provided with light and scenery from an overhead projector.

STUDENT-MADE PUPPETS

Before starting the project, a note should be sent to the parents requesting the donation of items which can be used for making puppets. The list should include felt, fabric, beads, trims, sequins, yarn, scarves, fur scraps, and any other objects which will fulfill the requirements of the activity. Items should be sent to the school in a covered box (a shoe box marked with the student's name or the like). The following list of supplies is provided to assist you in planning to make puppets.

Basic Equipment and Supplies

scissors
stapler
needles & thread
hole punch
paint brushes
white glue
tape
sandpaper
poster board
shirt cardboard
tissue paper
crepe paper
construction paper
elastic bands
pipe cleaner
wire
pencils
markers
crayons
paint
paper fasteners
paper clips
toothpicks
pins
tacks
velcro

For Rod Puppets
dowels
wire hangers
tongue depressors
ice cream stick
paint stirrer
tissue paper roll
bike spoke
umbrella rib
chop stick

For Tiny Puppets
plastic spoons
tongue depressors
clothes pin
glove finger

Bodies/ Heads
paper bags
    stuffed,
    mouth on flap,
    eyes on flap
paper towel rolls
toilet tissue rolls
paper cup
plastic bottle
boxes, e.g., salt,
    egg carton,
    spaghetti box,
    oatmeal box,
    milk carton,
    match box
paper strips
ruler
glove
plastic bottles
wooden spoon
    (figure 6)
broom
fly swatter
spatula

Eyes
sequins
buttons
felt
wiggle eyes
ping-pong balls
pompoms
beads
tacks

For Stick/Shadow Puppets
Characters from:
coloring books
magazines
newspapers
greeting cards

Noses
cork
pompon
carrot

Heads
papier-mâche
balls, e.g., tennis,
    ping-pong,
    rubber,
    styrofoam
sponges
fruits
polyfoam
nylon hose with
    polyester filling
sock
pot holder
mitt
boxes
paper plates
foil plates
envelope
gallon milk jugs
large bleach jug

Figure 6

272   TEACHING WITH PUPPETS

Costume and Trims

felt	bottle caps
fabric	sequins
lace	trims
dollies	ribbon
wallpaper samples	velvet
scarves	fur fabric
foil	feathers
cellophane	beads
tissue	glitter
construction paper	pompoms
costume jewelry	

Hair

yarn	cotton fringe
fur	frayed rope
fake fur	steel wool
absorbent cotton	string
wool fringe	felt

Remember that some of the most creative and exciting looking puppets are made from household discards and junk.

SIMPLE STAGES

Instructional puppets do not require a stage. The teacher's other arm, a box on the teacher's desk, or a lap can provide an adequate setting.

When students perform, a simple stage can be constructed by hanging a sheet across a doorway (figure 7), by turning a table on its side (figure 8), by using a chart holder (figure 9), or a screen.

An appliance carton (figure 10) can be converted into an admirable portable theater. The back and top of the carton are removed and a window cut away in the front section. A curtain may be strung across the top of the stage. One or two "portholes" can be cut in the sides to allow surprise appearances of the puppets. String a curtain across these as well. Place hooks on the inside of the walls to hang puppets.

A large poster board scene may serve as a "stage," e.g., Noah's ark (figure 9). Cut out "portholes" in the ark above deck. Puppets appear through these openings. A map of Israel with openings at key places: Jerusalem, desert, Masada, Dead Sea, etc., can serve as a "stage" as well.

For smaller puppets, a basket (figure 11), party hat (figure 12), or cereal box (figure 13) can all serve as "stages," with a Moses hand puppet, Purim jester stick puppet, or Hebrew speaking finger puppet as the respective performers.

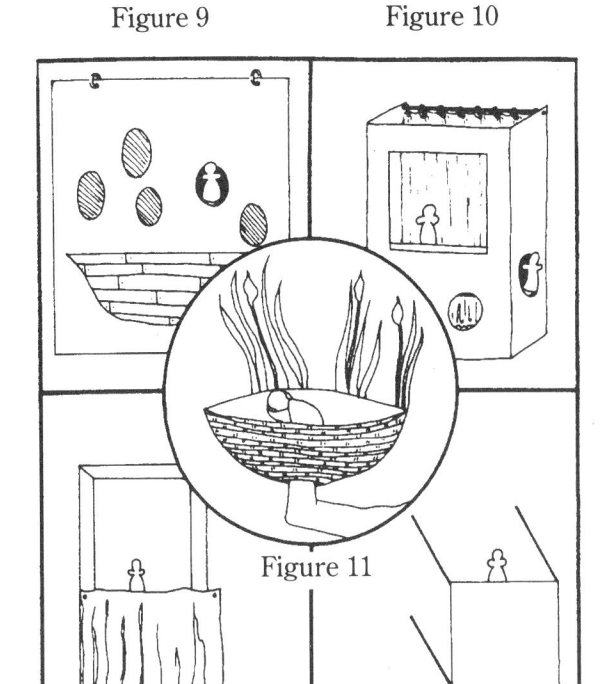

ABOUT MANIPULATION

Manipulation of the puppets brings them to life, creates the mood, and generates interest and excitement for the audience. Even though there is very little time for the students in a Religious School to practice, a little time spent on manipulation will considerably improve the results obtained. Students and/or teachers can practice with a partner and then at home in front of a mirror. This is one homework assignment which students will really enjoy!

The following are a few simple rules which will add elegance to a performance.
1. Puppets should be upright and perpendicular to the stage. They should not appear off balance.
2. Puppets should maintain a constant height. They should not be so low that they seem to be sinking or so high that the puppeteer's arm can be seen.
3. Each puppet should have a distinct personality, its own characteristic movements, tempo, idiosyncracies. The style of movement whether a limp, strut, fast pace, etc., should be consistent throughout the performance.
4. The puppet portrays an impression of life; it is not true to life. Its movements, therefore, should be exaggerated.
5. In general, only the puppet which is speaking should be moving. The others should be stationary. In this manner, attention is focused on the speaking puppet.
6. To enter the stage, the puppet should seem to climb imaginary stairs — otherwise the puppet seems to be popping up out of the floor.
7. Emphasis should be on the action. All parts of the stage should be used. Puppets may also be brought out in front of the stage.
8. Practice moving the puppet.
   a. Use your arm for whole body movements: walk, run, jump, limp, dance.
   b. Use your wrist for trunk or neck movements: nod eyes, turn left and right, sneeze, bow, look for something, pick up an object.
   c. Use your finger for hand movement; wave goodbye, "who me?," play patty cake, cry.

Have students suggest other movements for the class to demonstrate. Practicing these movements can become a game to learn Hebrew verbs. One student picks a card with a printed verb, and with his or her puppet demonstrates the action. The class must guess the movement using the Hebrew word. (See below for more ways to use puppets to teach Hebrew.)

Have the class perform pantomime exercises:
1. Puppet runs, falls, limps off stage.
2. Puppet looks for something, finds it, expresses happiness.
3. One puppet is on stage, a second runs forward, they are happy to see one another, they embrace, and walk off together.

ABOUT VOICE AND SOUND

Hearing as well as seeing the puppet movement is an integral part of the performance. The following suggestions will help enhance delivery.
1. The voice of the puppet should fit its personality and be consistent and distinct.
2. A characteristic sound such as a cough, sneeze, "ahem" (clearing of throat, etc.), before the puppet speaks contributes to giving it a unique identity.
3. With movable mouth puppets, words and lip movements must be synchronized. The lower jaw should be dropped, not the upper jaw lifted, so the eye position does not change.
4. If children are performing behind a stage, be sure they can be heard. Use a microphone, if necessary, or tape record the complete production. For the performance itself, the students should concentrate on listening and manipulating the puppets. The narrator may be up front.
5. Sound effects and recorded or live music enhance the performance and make it more lively and appealing. Encourage students to include these in their presentations. Even preschoolers can create music and sound effects by singing or using rhythm instruments.
6. Practice different voices. Tape record student's voices. Have them listen and try to create greater contrasts. As with manipulation, a little practice and experimentation will go a long way in skills and overall performance.

TEACHING STRATEGIES: WHAT CAN THE PUPPET DO?
Before the Puppet Project

Before beginning a puppet project, especially with high school students, introduced puppetry as an art form. Students should be exposed to *The Art of the Puppet* by Baird, with its beautiful of photographs of puppets through the ages. They should have the opportunity to see museum collections of puppets and to critique puppet shows and report to the class.

Here are some examples of what a puppet can do.

A Puppet Can Teach Hebrew

1. Uri is a Hebrew speaking puppet who speaks no English. Whenever the teacher brings out this child or animal mascot, the students know that only Hebrew is to be spoken.
2. Students welcome play with *mishpachah,* or Hebrew speaking puppets. These can be made of paper plates (figure 14) or can be purchased. They are prepared commercially,[1] and called "a family of puppets."
3. An American puppet family has just made *aliyah* to Israel. They are having a hard time learning Hebrew. The adults are having the most difficulty. The class must help them learn the language.

Figure 14

4. Yossie is having a difficult time learning basic Hebrew even though he is usually very smart. The students help him learn the *Alef Bet*, verbs, etc. He often makes errors. Students have to correct him.
5. The *"Bayt Sichah"* (figure 13, an adapted Conversation House)[2] is made of a cereal box. The house has two open windows. Two finger puppets or tongue depressor puppets manipulated by two students or the teacher and a student have a conversation in Hebrew.
6. Puppets can sing Hebrew songs. Have a puppet teach the class a Hebrew song or have a student manipulate a puppet which leads the class in song. One teacher taught her class a Hebrew song and then asked her students each to bring in a puppet. (Don't be surprised to find that all the children have puppets! If some don't, provide them.) The puppets enthusiastically sang the song while the students sat behind their chairs manipulating the puppets. The class and the audience loved it.

Puppets Can Teach the Alef Bet and Beginning Sounds

Alef Bet stick puppets (figure 15) are made by gluing a tongue depressor to the laminated letter, cut out of bright colored poster board.

1. Children sit in a circle and are each given an *Alef Bet* puppet. As the teacher says the sound of a letter, the student holding that puppet must display it. If the student is right, all the students pass their letter puppets to the right and the teacher continues.
2. The teacher may play the same game using the name of the letter instead of the sound.
3. After students know the letters of the *Alef Bet*, then teacher proceeds by telling a story about *Alef, Bet*, and *Gimel*, etc. Students show their puppet when their letter is mentioned and form words. Some humor can be introduced by having the teacher make an error, by introducing the shy letter *Alef* who keeps dropping out of sight. Don't forget the letter who is always sneezing, the jumpy letter, the slow moving, etc. Students will enjoy listening carefully to the narrator.

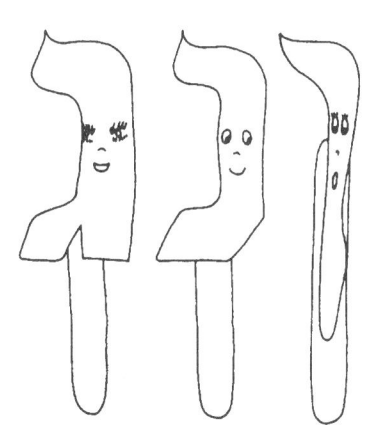

Figure 15

4. Teach the students an *Alef Bet* song. When the student's letter is sung, that puppet must perform a dance or do something in step with the music.
5. Make an *Alef Bet* box by cutting 2" holes on the large side of a box. Write a different letter of the *Alef Bet* over each hole. When a little finger puppet, "Achbari" (a mouse) appears in the hole, the student must say

the letter or sound of the letter. Students may take turns using the mouse puppet (figure 16).
6. Make a *Ken-Lo* box by cutting two 2" round holes in a box. Write "*Ken*" (yes) over one opening and "*Lo*" (no) over the other. The mouse appears at one of the openings to show whether or not a Hebrew phrase or sentence is correct. The box may be used for any subject.

Figure 16

Puppets Can Teach Holidays/Bible/History
1. An animal or person puppet can tell a Bible story or story of a holiday. A puppet (e.g., Noah) can introduce a story which is completed by the teacher.
2. Puppets can enact one event of the story of a holiday, or puppets can show how the holiday is celebrated.
3. The class can interview the dominant figures of a holiday (e.g., Esther and Haman are interviewed by the students who serve as reporters). This technique can be used for teaching students how to ask questions which obtain information rather than yes/no answers.
4. Puppets can be the interviewers while students act as the personalities (e.g., students can be Moses, Miriam, Pharaoh, the princess, etc.).
5. A puppet can be taught about a holiday. An animal puppet knows nothing about Lag B'Omer. Questions are directed by the puppet to the class to find out more about the holiday.
6. Tree puppets can perform for Tu B'Shevat (see sample lesson).

7. Using the *mishpachah* puppets, students role play the customs and ceremonies of a holiday. (One of my classes added a cat and dog puppet to the family.)
8. Each student is assigned to research one ceremonial object: what it is made of, its shape or form, its use, its history. The student then designs and creates a stick puppet representing the object. The setting or stage may be a Jewish home or a synagogue. The dialogue reflects the knowledge gleaned. It may be in verse, set to music, etc. Students are instructed and helped to present their information in an interesting way.
9. "You Are There" format may be used with puppets for Bible, history, or a contemporary hero.
10. Life in the shtetl, on the Lower East Side, on a *kibbutz* can all be portrayed by puppets (see sample lesson).
11. The JTA (Jewish Telegraphic Agency) puppet (any puppet with JTA on its hat) reports current events about Jewish affairs and Israel. Students will enjoy relaying their news while manipulating this special puppet.
12. Puppets can be part of the class *Seder*. At our class *Seder*, I always have a group of 4-5 students tell (in a creative way) the story of Moses. One year, the students prepared the script and used small puppets made of plastic spoons and clothespins. Simple sets were set up on a desk. The students told the story moving the little puppets around to illustrate the different important events in Moses' life.
13. A map of Israel with circles cut out at key cities and other points (e.g., Jerusalem, Tel Aviv, Masada, the Sinai, etc.) is mounted on the outside of the appliance box stage. Have appropriate puppets tell about themselves. A bedouin or a camel in the desert; an Israeli soldier at Masada, etc.
14. Cut out pictures of the builders of Israel. Laminate and make them into stick puppets. Have students develop a script, select music and do a presentation for the class. This is one way of making a report more interesting.
15. Design puppets to accompany cassette taped stories (e.g., Noah, Creation, etc.).

Puppets Can Tell Stories
1. A puppet can tell a story (e.g., have Naftali tell one of the I.B. Singer stories).

2. Have K'Ton Ton, a finger puppet, tell or introduce a story.
3. Encourage students to prepare book reports in a creative way. Suggest that they make a puppet of one of the characters who will introduce the report. This can be a project for Jewish Book Month. Make a display of books and their puppets.

Puppets Can Portray Values

More advanced students can design puppets representing values. These can be clever, abstract creations.

Puppets Can Be Used With Behavior and Discipline

1. A puppet can help with behavior problems of young children. The puppet whispers to the teacher about something that upset him (e.g., two children are fighting on the playground or someone knocked down David's blocks). The teacher asks the class what they think about it. A child puppet is sad because no one will play with him. How can the class help?
2. A puppet can teach about *kashrut*. Miss Piggy can be interviewed on the subject of *kashrut*. Kermit the Frog can also be added, as an ardent proponent of *kashrut*.

Puppets Can Teach about Tzedakah and the Jewish Community

Students can bring puppets to hospitals, nursing homes, apartments for the elderly, etc. A puppet performance can be part of a *tzedakah* project. At the same time, students receive firsthand knowledge of some Jewish situations in the community.

Puppets Can Teach about the Shetetl

This unit is designed as an integrated Social Studies unit for junior and senior high students which requires them to brainstorm, research, and learn the subject content. The wide variety of activities involved allows each individual to participate in those skill areas which are most attractive because of the person's special abilities or interests. This is an opportunity for independent study as well as sharing information in a creative way.

The students have already had a introduction to the shtetl. They have had several reading assignments and have seen a video on the subject. Many of the students have seen the movies *Fiddler on the Roof* and *Hester Street*. This is visually reinforced in the minds of the students by a class bulletin board entitled "The Shtetl: Soul of a People" which has been prepared by the teacher and/or students using pictures by the artist Ezekiel Schloss.

Procedure
1. Brainstorming: The teacher and students prepare a flow chart of all aspects of shtetl life which can be portrayed in a puppet production. The students decide which scenes would most effectively convey an understanding of life in the shtetl.
2. Research: The students divide into small groups to research and design costumes and sets, to find music and literature, to research the history, and to begin planning a script.
3. Creating Materials: The class may regroup if they wish. The script is written, the puppets are made, and sets are prepared. Background music, Yiddish songs, and special sound effects are taped. The students are encouraged to be original and yet accurate.
4. The Puppets: Hand puppets with soft sculpture heads are particularly appropriate. Soft sculpture art is taught in high school and this medium is particularly suitable for showing the lined faces of shtetl inhabitants. Heads made of "instant papier mâché" are also suitable and may be produced to be very expressive.
5. The Performance: While brainstorming, planning the research, and preparing the materials makes this such a meaningful learning experience, it is the performance and sharing of this knowledge with parents and other students which is the highlight. Furthermore, the students can also use the puppet production to fulfill a *tzedakah* project by presenting it to a group of senior citizens in a nursing home or a hospital.

A Tu B'Shevat Puppet Unit

The purpose of this unit is to motivate students to learn about the holiday of Tu B'Shevat and to reinforce the concepts and ideas which have been learned.

Instructional Objectives

The students will be able to:

1. list the other names and meanings for Tu B'Shevat.
2. tell why trees are important, especially in Israel.
3. name and identify some of the trees and fruits of Israel.
4. tell the story of Honi and the tree.
5. recognize biblical quotations relating to trees.
6. sing at least four songs about Tu B'Shevat and Israel.

Pre-lessons

Prior to the puppet lesson, the teacher and students will prepare a bulletin board showing a map of Israel and pictures of trees found in Israel. Appropriate biblical quotations relating to the particular tree will be placed beneath its picture. The students will design a chart listing the reasons that trees are important in Israel. They will find or draw pictures to illustrate their chart. They will read stories and learn songs about trees in Israel.

Procedure: Brainstorming

The class and teacher will list possible puppet skits that they can prepare about Tu B'Shevat. Examples:
1. Importance of trees (in verse if desired)
2. The story of Honi and the tree
3. Customs of planting trees at birth and using branches for *chupah* at wedding
4. Skit which shares Bible quotations with the audience
5. Tu B'Shevat celebration in Israel and North America
6. Puppet show incorporating songs learned
7. Other ideas

Four skits are selected. Two topics may be combined.

Creating Materials

The students divide into four groups, according to the skit they select. They write simple original scripts and prepare puppets.

The Puppets

Trees are made of paper towel rolls covered with construction paper or tissue paper. A wide variety of materials are provided for branches (wires, pipe cleaners, tree branch, etc.) and for foliage (construction paper, tissue paper, styrofoam chips, scrap foam rubber, etc.). Students are encouraged to make trees that look authentic but also to introduce some humor by creating trick effects, e.g., pop-up palm tree (figure 17).

Figure 17

Movable mouths or eyes in the trunks of other trees are produced by inserting a smaller roll into the paper towel roll. An opening is made on the outer roll tube to expose the mouth or eyes drawn on the inner tube. When the tube is moved up, the mouth or eyes close. People puppets would be simple hand puppets.

The Performance

Each group performs for the rest of the class. Another grade and/or parents may also be invited to a Tu B'Shevat puppet show party. Refreshments would be fruit grown in Israel.

A PURIM UNIT FOR PRESCHOOLERS THROUGH GRADE 2

Objectives
1. The children will be able to recognize the characters of the Purim story.
2. They will be able to identify symbols of Purim: *megillah, gragger, hamantashen*.
3. They will be able to follow the story of Purim.

The students have already heard the story of Purim and can identify some of the symbols of Purim.

Procedure

The students sit in a circle. The teacher shows the class each puppet and asks the children to identify each personality. When everyone seems to know the characters, children are selected to be puppeteers. They face the rest of the class to whom *graggers* are distributed. The teacher proceeds to tell the story of Purim. Then the name of a character is mentioned, the child holding the puppet has to manipulate it appropriately. When the name Haman is said, all the children respond with their *graggers* until the teacher indicates stopping by raising a hand.

The puppets are prepared by the teacher, aide, or volunteer. Pictures are cut out of a Purim coloring book, pasted to a poster board, and cut to shape, laminated and glued to a paint stirrer or tongue depressor (figure 2). If time permits, preschoolers can make their own puppets. They should be very simple and made from precut materials prepared in advance. For Bible stories and other holiday stories, team each puppeteer with a child playing a rhythm instrument. Have puppeteers face the musicians. When a character is mentioned, the puppeteer manipulates the puppet and the musician plays the instrument to match the character of the puppet. This activity sharpens listening skills and reinforces the story.

Miscellaneous Activities
1. A puppet can open the class and greet the students by saying, "*Shalom Yeladim*."
2. A puppet can close the class by leading the students in "*Shalom Chaverim*" or another song.
3. A puppet can relay reminders: "Don't forget your notes for the field trip."
4. A puppet can add interest to a record or cassette.

PUPPET RESOURCE CORNER AND LOAN-A-PUPPET PROGRAM

If your community does not have a puppet resource facility, perhaps you would consider starting one. It may be located at your teacher center, in your school library, or in your classroom. The resource corner should be an attractive area which houses and displays puppets, portable stages, patterns, and materials for making puppets, suggestions for puppet plays, and any available scripts. There should be books and displays on how puppets can be used as an educational tool.

The puppets may be teacher-made or well constructed commercial puppets. They can be displayed on a table, puppet rack, hung on a clothesline, or placed in shoe bags or hang-up bags.

The characters represented could be Bible and history personalities, shtetl figures, book characters, animals, people, Hebrew letters, ceremonial objects, etc.

Puppets are catalogued for checkout. Checkout time is for one week.

Teachers should be required to participate in an orientation before being admitted to the Loan-a-Puppet program. Ideally, teachers should also attend a workshop in which they see a demonstration and participate in a hands-on experience showing the correct way of caring for, holding, and manipulating puppets, as well as learn techniques for using puppetry in the classroom.

The workshop should also provide an opportunity for each teacher to create a puppet (mascot or other).

CONCLUSION

Whether you purchase or borrow puppets, make them yourself, or work with students to create them, be sure to look into the possibilities of using puppetry in your classroom. You'll be glad you did!

(The author is indebted to Carol Sterling, author of *Puppetry in the Classroom*, currently out of print, for her help with this chapter.)

Rita Kopin has a Masters Degree in Museum Education. She is Director of the Educational Resources Division of the Board of Jewish Education of Greater Washington and the author of *The Lively Jewish Classroom: Games and Activities for Learning* (A.R.E.).

NOTES

1. Available through Hammett's Educational Supplies, or other supply house.

2. Judy Sims, *Puppets for Dreaming and Scheming – A Puppet Source Book* (Santa Barbara, CA: The Learning Works, 1988).

BIBLIOGRAPHY

Baird, Bill. *The Art of the Puppet.* New York: Plays, Inc., 1966.

Bailey, Vanessa. *Puppets: Games and Projects.* New York: Franklin Watts, 1991.

Buchwald, Claire. *Puppet Book: How To Make and Operate Puppets and Stage a Puppet-Play.* New York: Plays, Inc., 1990.

Chesse, Bruce, and Beverly Armstrong. *Puppets from Polyfoam: Sponge-ees.* Walnut Creek, CA: Early Stages Publications, 1975. (Available from the Puppetry Store, see below for address.)

Cheyney, Jeanne, and Arnold Cheyney. *Finger Plays for Home and School.* Glenview, IL: Scott Foresman, 1989.

Cohen, N. "Ceramic Finger Puppets." *School Arts*, January 1991.

Engler, L., and C. Finjan. *Making Puppets Come Alive.* New York: Taplinger Publishing Co. Inc., 1980.

Ferguson, Helen. *Bring on the Puppets.* New York: Morehouse-Barlow, 1975.

Flower, Cedric, and Alan Forney. *Puppets, Methods and Materials.* Worcester, MA: Davis Publications, 1983.

Forte, Imogene. *The Puppet Factory.* Nashville, TN: Incentive Publishing, 1984.

———. *Puppet-Parade: Easy-To-Make Imaginative Puppets from Readily-Found Materials.* Nashville, TN: Incentive Publishing, 1992.

———. *Puppets.* Nashville, TN: Incentive Publishing, 1985.

Galte, Frieda. *Easy To Make Puppets.* Spokane, WA: Treehouse Productions, 1981.

Holman, Marilyn. "Sense Puppets." In *Using Our Senses: Hands-on Activities for the Jewish Classroom.* Denver: A.R.E. Publishing, Inc., pp. 16-18.

Hunt, Tamara, and Nancy Renfro. *Puppetry and Early Childhood Education,.* Austin, TX: Renfro Studios, 1991.

Larson, J. "Shadow Puppets." *Reading Teacher*, October 1990.

Payton, Jeffrey L. *Puppetools: Introductory Guide.* Richmond, VA: Prescott Durrell & Co., 1986.

Philpott, V., and M.J. McNeil. *Puppets: A Simple Guide To Making and Working Puppets.* Tulsa, OK: EDC, 1977.

Renfro, Nancy. *Puppet Shows Made Easy.* Austin, TX: Renfro Studios, n.d.

Renfro, Nancy, and Beverly Armstrong. *Make Amazing Puppets.* Santa Barbara, CA: The Learning Works, 1979.

Rottman, Fran. *Easy To Make Puppets and How To Use Them: Early Childhood.* Ventura, CA: Kegal, 1978.

Shelton, Catherine. *Puppets, Poems, and Songs.* Carthage, IL: Fearon Teacher Aids, 1993.

Sims, Judy. *Puppets for Dreaming and Scheming.* Santa Barbara, CA: The Learning Works, 1988.

Warshawsky, Gale Solotar. *Creative Puppetry for Jewish Kids.* Denver: A.R.E. Publishing, Inc., 1985.

Video

Beauregard's Bottle Buddies: Plastic Bottle Puppets Made Simple. 30 min. Hands On Productions, P.O. Box 25268, Arlington, VA 22202.

Organizations/Stores

Nancy Renfro Studios, P.O. Box 164226, Austin, TX 78716

Puppeteers of America, 15 Cricklewood Path, Pasadena, CA 91107

Puppetry Store, 1525 24th St. S.E., Auburn, WA 98002

Regional Puppetry Guilds – Write Puppeteers of America for addresses.

(Note: For plays that can be adapted for puppets, see the Bibliography for Chapter 24, "Drama in the Classroom." For stories to adapt, see Chapter 27, "Storytelling: Role and Technique.")

THE ARTS

CHAPTER TWENTY-SEVEN

STORYTELLING: ROLE AND TECHNIQUE

Peninnah Schram

In the beginning there was storytelling. Before there was television, there was storytelling. Before the printing press, there was storytelling. Before there was the written word, there was the oral word. Storytelling has been a form of entertainment and of social and moral instruction since ancient times. In other words, the value of the tale is in the telling and the story has served as the link between the generations. In this age of mass media, when television has taken over as storyteller, live storytelling exists, but in limited ways. Those who share their stories and those who listen continue to experience the power and magic of storytelling. It is my hope that the Jewish teacher will begin/continue to place an even greater emphasis on using stories in and out of the classroom by learning how to tell stories well and by regenerating interest and excitement for this art.

In this chapter, I will discuss the art of storytelling in two ways. First I will briefly explain what storytelling is and note the role and value of storytelling in Jewish life. Secondly, I will explore in more depth various techniques of how to prepare oneself in order to tell stories, how to select stories to tell, how to prepare the telling, and then how to tell a story.

Once upon a time there was the story, and the teller, and the people who listened. These people shared the experience of the teller relating the story. Depending on the place and time, the plot may be invented spontaneously or perhaps shaped on the spot by combining remembered elements (much like a *badchan* — the wedding entertainer of shtetl days). Other times, the story may have been written down and memorized verbatim or read aloud without changing a syllable or accent (as in the Torah readings or reading the *Megillah*). Still other times, the teller remembers or learns the story (oral or written) and recreates the story in his/her own style, adding and deleting and editing according to his/her own interpretation; such is the technique of many storytellers today. Indeed, we are all storytellers.

Since storytelling can be defined in many different ways, depending on the purpose of the storytelling event, it is necessary to adapt a definition which is broad enough in scope to encompass all peoples. I would suggest for consideration the definition proposed by Anne Pellowski in her book *The World of Storytelling*:

> ... the definition of storytelling is the art or craft of narration of stories in verse and/or prose, as performed or led by one person before a live audience; the stories narrated may be spoken, chanted, or sung, with or without musical, pictorial, and/or other accompaniment, and may be learned from oral, printed, or mechanically recorded sources; one of its purposes must be that of entertainment.[1]

The three key elements contained within this definition are the story, the teller, and the listener. Storytelling is defined as an art (which means there is a creative process at work) or a craft (which means there are techniques and skills that can be learned and practiced). The word "live" is important in reference to the audience because interaction between the teller and the listener is necessary. Storytelling is a shared experience. (Storytelling does take place on radio, television, and recordings, but that is storytelling in a different sense.)

As we continue to look at this definition, the words "performed or led by one person" indicate that the storyteller may be either one person or a group led by a main storyteller. When more than one person is telling the story, the experience takes on different dimensions. The definition calls for the narration of stories to be "spoken, chanted, or sung," but it does not specifically indicate "read." The emphasis remains on the oral, however. The final part of the definition, "one of its purposes must be that of entertainment," does not preclude other purposes, such as the instruction of values, tradition, and so on. It is good to keep in mind that entertainment is of prime importance so as to "please" an audience. When instruction is also intended through the use of a story, then that lesson is learned better when it is also pleasing.

For the Jew, storytelling has been a way to transmit Jewish learning, traditions, customs, laws, and values from one generation to the next. As Jews traveled from country to country and settled in many lands, they spoke different languages and adapted different modes of dress. However, they continued to pray in Hebrew and to cling to their main unifying idea of one God. In addition, they studied and shared the stories of the Jewish people which went with them and with the traveling Rabbis, the occasional *Maggid*, *Badchan*, and messengers. The stories created a bond between Jews everywhere.

For generations, storytelling has given the Jewish child an opportunity to experience the Jewish heritage directly through the spoken word. Since there is now a renewed interest in oral tradition and genealogy, storytelling can play an important part in this search for one's past. However, to discover the past is not enough in order to learn about oneself and one's people. The story has to be meaningful so a person can know how to act and live in the present. The story has to serve as a reference point for the future as well — a map for what kind of person to become. In other words, stories are a link to the past and the future.

While this link can be achieved by reading the story silently, it is the spoken word — the voice which carries the meaning in sound that creates the shared experience which is more lasting, more immediate, more imaginative, more exciting. The child does not feel alone. He or she is not the only one who has experienced the feeling of pain, sorrow, rewards, joys, and thoughts found in stories. In addition, there develops a special bond between the storyteller and the listener. Both are drawn into a magical space.

They are taken out of the everyday and then returned with more courage and optimism. Think how much more effective the story of Esther is when it is chanted aloud and shared on Purim. The spoken word is in the Jewish tradition.

Bruno Bettelheim expresses this benefit of the shared story in his book *The Uses of Enchantment*.

> ... Here reading (to oneself) is not the same as being told the story, because while reading alone the child may think that only some stranger — the person who wrote the story or arranged the book — approves of outwitting and cutting down the giant. But when parents tell him the story, a child can be sure that they approve of his retaliating in fantasy for the threat which adult dominance entails.[2]

Who has not had the inner experience of a feeling of anticipation when a story is about to be told ... and of something beautiful happening when a story is being told? A new balance of tension, expectation and relaxation sets in. Audiences suddenly lean forward, open facial expressions replace the more withdrawn occupied looks, and people find a new place for themselves in their seats or on the floor. Pen and notebooks or other objects are put down. Everyone is ready for a journey — an adventure — to add to their imaginative reserves in a more creative way.

For the storyteller, the faces which are so ready to receive, create, in turn, a desire to share the stories. The give and take stirs up an energy which passes between the storyteller and the listeners. The imaginative participation of the audience reflects the highly interactive nature of communication in storytelling. The storyteller searches for the response of the audience which can help shape the telling of the story.

Bettelheim emphasizes that "the telling of a fairy story (add legend/fable/*midrash*) should be an interpersonal event into which adult and child enter as equal partners...."[3] The storyteller shares something of him/herself in the telling, not just the tale itself. The success of the telling depends a great deal on the teller's feelings about the story and the values and images therein. Baker and Greene explain more about this "sharing of selves" which focuses on the special storyteller-audience interaction.[4]

Storytelling flows from a deep desire to share, the desire to be open about something that has touched one deeply. The choice of story and the manner in which it is told reveal one's inner self. Although the storyteller may be recreating a traditional tale, it is his or her experience of life that enters the telling and makes the story ring true.

In this sense, the teacher/storyteller serves as a necessary role model for the teaching of values. A special bond is forged and at this point the story belongs to all the listeners to keep in their memories and to pass on to others who are ready to listen.

Who are the storytellers? All of us are storytellers. All of us have a natural expressiveness. Can we all create the magical time? Yes. Storytelling is an art, a demanding art, which can be learned and must be practiced frequently. One has to keep in mind that just as in playing a musical instrument or painting or acting, there are skills to be learned and mastered. Some have a greater feeling and talent for the art, some need to work harder on the drill work and scales. Nevertheless, one does not have to be an actor in order to become a storyteller (although actors do tell stories).

TECHNIQUE

What does a storyteller need to do? First it is necessary to sharpen communication skills. These tools of the trade are the voice, the body, and the imagination. Along with these, sincerity is a necessity. These are the same tools of the trade for an actor and the tuning of these tools is necessary for both the actor, and the storyteller. But each profession uses them with a different approach and following different conventions. Certainly some of the differences will become clearer after reading this chapter. Keep in mind that storytelling is a process. It is a combination of literature/folklore and the person. Therefore, in order to be an effective storyteller, one has to prepare oneself by training the voice, the body and the imagination.

The Voice

Let us begin with the first component, the voice. The voice is a musical instrument. It has the capability of stirring our imagination, of creating excitement, of putting pictures in our minds, of conveying emotions, and of putting us to sleep. All of this can be done without words, but given the words and the voice together, the possibilities for the storyteller are infinite. Voice training, while desirable, is not essential. However, as teachers, a voice evaluation may be a good idea. Some aspects of your voice to consider are: Are you using your optimum pitch? Is your articulation sharp? Is your voice clear and pleasant to listen to? Do you have regionalisms that cause distractions? Do you use vocal variation? Keep in mind that speaking is a learned activity and that, therefore, poor breathing and speaking habits can be unlearned.

Vocal exercises are beneficial for everyone and good exercises will help you know what your voice can do. The voice is flexible in pitch, volume, and rate. In other words, you can say the same words in a higher or lower pitch range, a louder or softer volume, and a faster or slower rate. These are your choices. No one can tell the same story in the exact same way because we each have a unique voice. Also we each give different interpretations to the story by emphasizing words and phrases of our own choice through the use of the voice.

> **WE ARE ALL STORYTELLERS.**

In order to illustrate emphasis, try saying the following sentence giving a different reading, as suggested in the parentheses, each time.

No you cannot borrow the car tonight,
(but your sister can)
(nor ever again)
(you can have it as a gift)
(but you can borrow my bicycle)
(but you can borrow it tomorrow)

You will discover that the emphasis changes with each reading depending on the meaning of the sentence which in turn depends on what precedes and what follows it.

As an example of pitch range, try saying "Oh," in ways which express the following meanings:

surprise
shock
"I always thought so!"
"I get it!"

Pitch, volume, and rate are interrelated so that they work together to communicate meaning. If you were to say, "The old man spoke softly as he related the incident," in order to capture the meaning and set the scene vocally,

CHAPTER TWENTY-SEVEN   283

you would probably say this sentence slowly. On the word "softly" you might soften the volume, perhaps to a whispery level. Knowing the context of this sentence would, of course, add another dimension to it. On the other hand, the sentence, "The young scoundrel grinned and quickly told his scheme to his friend," would be said at a faster clip. The word "quickly" cannot be said in the same way as the word "slowly." The word "slowly" needs a longer vowel duration time. The different rate has to give us an added level of meaning which we must mentally interpret instantaneously. In listening to a story, the listener has no chance to go back and reread as when one is reading by himself or herself. The story is told and the fully intended meaning must register in the listeners' minds through the hearing of the word and the voice together. The voice has to give us the immediate clues to the meaning. That is why vocal color (variations of pitch/volume/ rate) is so important.

A good book on voice and articulation contains exercises to increase the resonance, the flexibility, and the vocal color, all necessary for more effective storytelling and teaching. (Several are listed in the Bibliography at the end of this chapter.)

It is the voice that is the medium to carry the message. Both voice and message are important in storytelling. A vibrant voice, a voice that helps us to listen and understand, a voice that is pleasant, and a voice that carries the love of the story to the audience — that is the kind of voice we need for telling. Everyone has that kind of voice, or has the potential for that kind of voice. The voice is an essential tool of the storyteller.

The Body

The second component for preparation as a storyteller is the body. As a communicator, the storyteller does not speak with just a voice, but with the face, the eyes, and the body. Communication goes on even when we are not talking. Therefore, we can give nonverbal message cues which are in the story through nonverbal channels utilizing our body and face.

Characterization can be created in this way. For example, if you wished to show a character hesitating before speaking, you could shift your eyes downward while you pause, this indicates a hesitation or reluctance to speak on the part of the character (as opposed to a hesitancy on the part of the storyteller). If you were telling or speaking as a king, your head and shoulders should be upright to indicate pride and authority, and so on. The nonverbal communication can be powerful and yet subtle as a result of an expressive face and body. By suggesting clear nonverbal cues, you can trigger the listeners to see and feel the rest of the scene. An expressive face captures the attention, too. An audience watches the face of the storyteller. A face that is expressing the mood and ideas of the words helps realize and reinforce the meaning of the story.

The single most important difference between acting and storytelling is that a storyteller must establish eye contact with the listeners. What a good feeling it is to know someone is telling you a story! That is the feeling that direct eye contact can help create. And when you tell a story, you can look at the faces of the listeners and respond to their reactions. Sometimes a child will become restless or distracted during the story. At that point, if you touch the arm of the child and direct your eye contact to that child while continuing to tell the story, that can bring that child back to the moment. As a result, there is seldom need to remove the child from the program. Eyes communicate all kinds of emotions, concerns, wonder, thoughts. Eyes create interest and attention and personal interaction.

A storyteller does not move around (at least not to any great extent) and "act out" the story. Gestures, however, can be used which are natural and expressive. On one hand, it is important to remember that making too many gestures or gesturing in a busy fashion creates only distraction. On the other hand, gestures that are too small or that seem hidden are unnecessary and are not noticed. Instead, find gestures and a posture that are comfortable. Practice telling the story without gestures at first and then allow natural spontaneous gestures to come out in later rehearsals. Sometimes, it is more effective to have your hands in your lap or at your side and let only your voice and face tell the story.

There are other times when a gesture can create a vivid picture in the minds of the listeners. An arc formed by the arm and hand as if painting the rainbow across the sky can illustrate a rainbow. Moving the fingers while lowering the hand can indicate snow or rain falling. Gestures such as these do not distract, but rather add to the story. If a gesture you have practiced does not feel natural during the actual telling, then avoid using it. Work for simplicity and sincerity. As I mentioned before, storytelling continues to be a dynamic process rather than a set, staged piece. Work for flexibility and spontaneity within a rehearsed and polished telling.

The size of the audience, the space, and you determine whether you stand, sit on the floor, or use a stool. I prefer to sit on the floor with the audience seated all around me in a semicircle. If the audience is large (more than 50), then I sit on a stool so that everyone can see me and I can see everyone. For audiences of more than 100 people, I might stand on the level floor (if the audience is seated on chairs) or on a low stage, again for the purpose of sight lines. However, on a stage higher than one or two feet, the event becomes more of a performance than a storytelling event. The stage changes the dynamics of the relationship between a storyteller and the listeners. Storytelling is by nature a close personal experience and not a theatrical event. Yet, like an actor playing all the parts, the storyteller must project the mood and characters and plot of the story through the face and body, and of course, the voice. He or she needs to be constantly aware of communicating directly with the people sitting around him/her.

There are many styles of storytelling. No one style is the correct one and no one style is more effective than another because the three elements of storytelling still have to be considered — the teller, the story, and the listener. Included in this consideration must also be the occasion. Let us look at several descriptions of a storyteller in action:

> A serpent is just what Mrs. Torrance is pretending to be, with her shoulders hunched and her eyes leering upward. She lolls her tongue toward the audience, flicks it swiftly from side to side, then hisses. "B'rer Possum," she whispers invitingly . . .[5]

Sabadu was unequalled in the art of storytelling: he was fluent and humorous, while his mimicry of the characters he described kept everybody's interest on the alert. To the Rabbit, of course, he gave a wee voice, to the Elephant he gave a deep bass, to the Buffalo a hollow mooing . . .[6]

She uses gestures sparingly, her face rarely betrays occurrences and emotions involved in the story she is creating, and her approach to her audience seems condescending.[7]

She performs with quiet skill, Hers is instead a calm, assured competence often concealing by its very smoothness the complex strands that combine to create the illusion of a single textured production.[8]

Obviously much affected by his narrative, he uses a great deal of gesticulation, and by the movement of his body, hands, and head, tries to convey hate and anger, fear and humour, like an actor in a play. He raises his voice at certain passages, at other times, it becomes almost a whisper. He speaks fairly fast, but his enunciation is at all times clear.[9]

From these brief and sketchy descriptions of the various styles, diversity is the common denominator — different styles even within one culture. Does one kind of style make a better storyteller? Not at all. Each person has to find one style that is comfortable and good for that person. The story gains life through that style, but in a different way with each telling. Some use a dramatic and exaggerated verbal and body language. Some use a more subtle mixture of verbal and body language. All styles are effective if the storyteller knows which style suits him/her the best. However, keep in mind that there are variations within any particular style. For instance, a storyteller will be more declamatory and dramatic in one story, but quite subdued and calm in the telling of another story. The style must fit the story as well as the storyteller.

Relaxation is the key to attaining the most effective telling. Whether you use a lot of gesture or not, whether you sit on the floor or stand, the body (face, hands, shoulder, feet, etc.) must be relaxed and responsive to how you want to use it in your presentation.

There are many good relaxation exercises. These include stretching, the "Rag Doll" exercise, yoga exercises, dance exercises, any warm-up exercises for dance or sport activities. Here is a simple, yet effective exercise.

Rag Doll Exercise Plus

Standing straight and as relaxed as possible with feet slightly apart, let your body fall from the waist as though you were a rag doll. When you are completely relaxed, your arms are dangling with no energy in them, so that if anyone were to pick them up and drop them, they would fall lifeless. Now, slowly raise your body from the trunk to a standing position. Your head and arms remain limp and without energy. Rise slowly until your head is still resting on your chest and your arms fall into position at your sides.

The head is like a limp ball on a string. The head is now slowly rolled clockwise, touching the right shoulder, around to the left shoulder, until it has completed a circle. Then, yawn slowly and fully. This relaxes the vocal cords completely. Repeat several times. Now say "ah" on a yawn, taking a good breath, maintaining the same feeling as when yawning, the mouth wide open. Repeat several times.

Now take a short breath and release it, take another and release it. Take a big breath and sound a relaxed "ah" yawn sound, but this time slowly closing your mouth until your lips close on an "mmmm" sound. With lots of breath left, let your lips and face vibrate to this "mmmm" sound. Your lips will tingle if you have succeeded in doing this exercise properly.

Imagination

The third aspect of preparing yourself to tell stories is imagination. A storyteller must use the senses and create mental pictures in order to tell the story using vivid verbal and body language. It all starts in the mind. How much more lively the picture is received by the listener when the storyteller "sees" the scene being described, or "smells" the challah baking as he/she tells about it, or "hears" the sound of the closing doors or the horses or whatever is being related, or "feels" the velvet or cactus he/she is mentioning. The senses play a vital part in the telling. The process of imagining helps the storyteller internalize and personalize the story. What begins as an image in the storyteller's head gets translated into words/sounds/movements and subsequently into images in the heads of the listeners. That is the process of sharing stories.

Just as a good actor works on sensory recall exercises, so must a storyteller.

THE SENSES PLAY A VITAL PART IN STORYTELLING.

1. Listen to the sounds and silence around you. Make mental notes of what you hear.
2. Observe everything around you — light changing during the day and at different seasons, people and their reactions, animals and children, plants and the wind, etc.
3. Eat different food (lemon, wine, etc.) and then try to recreate the experience of tasting without the actual food.
4. Smell various objects (flowers, spice box, etc.). Close your eyes and try to recall the smell of that object.
5. Touch various objects (cloth, plants, trees, etc.). Close your eyes and try to sense the feel of that object on your fingertips/hand.

Remember, you will not be acting out in pantomime an entire eating scene. But the way you look and sound and the gestures you make should be different when you tell about a child eating honey as opposed to a lemon, touching a kitten as differentiated from a porcupine. The storyteller needs to have a storehouse of sensory images for ready recall in telling a story. Through imaging the storyteller can find the words that describe the moment more vividly, and together with the storyteller, the audience "sees" and "hears" and "smells" and "feels" and "tastes" the experience.

Don't be discouraged, however, if the recall doesn't begin to work immediately. It could take months and years of concentrated work. What will happen almost immediately is a keener sense of observation and mental activity of a new kind. This imaging takes a great deal of energy, effort, and concentration, but it is tremendously exciting when these sense images appear in your telling.

STORY SELECTION

Now you are ready to choose a story to tell. How does one go about selecting the right story? A consideration of external selection criteria will help narrow the possibilities. The first is the occasion. (Is it a *Yom Tov*? Are you studying a particular person in the Bible or Talmud, etc.?) Secondly, is there a particular value you want to stress in class? The time you have for the story is the third factor to consider. Do you have ten minutes for the story or a half an hour? Some stories require a longer time period and others can be told in a shorter time. Never try to rush through the second half of a story because class ends during the telling. If you cannot continue, then it is better to stop at that point, especially at a high point of the story. The excitement and suspense will build and hold until the next session. Allow for storytelling without rush. Storytelling must be viewed as a special event.

The audience will also determine the kinds of stories you select. This is the fourth factor to consider. Younger children love stories about small things — small animals, young children, etc. Except for certain considerations, a good story is good for all ages. While some stories are too sophisticated for younger children, I maintain that any story for a young person is also a story to be told for adults. A fifth consideration pertains in the event that you find several versions of the same story. Choose the version to which you relate best or combine the elements of each so as to create a new story, your own. This is, after all, the folkloric process.

In looking for stories, the key is to find a story you love and that has meaning for you. Begin thinking of the stories you loved as a child. Try writing down the names of the stories that have remained with you and then try to find a printed version of these. How do these versions (your own and the printed text) compare and differ? What elements stayed with you all these years? You will find out some more about yourself and rediscover and tap the child in yourself. When a story touches you in some way — touches your imagination — then that story can really become "yours."

There are three internal criteria in choosing a good story.
1. A good plot, one that you love and understand — sometimes a fuller understanding comes on a deeper level with each telling. The plot should make you want to ask, "What happens next?"
2. Interesting characters – characters to whom you can relate and who will mean something to the audience, who are not ordinary people.
3. A worthwhile theme (value), e.g., sharing, charity, justice, freedom, hospitality, love for family, Jewish peoplehood, etc.

In choosing stories for telling, keep in mind first of all that we need to give youngsters more imaginative, creative exercises through folklore and fantasy. Albert Einstein stated that the gift of fantasy meant more to him than his talent for absorbing positive knowledge. Therefore, search for stories that contain elements of the unusual rather than those that deal with everyday life.

Encourage kinship with animals in stories such as those found in the Solomon and David legends. The stories, when they contain universal elements and Jewish values, will help a person live the everyday life with more courage and hope. There is a need to carry the audience to different worlds as they let their imaginations soar and delve and explore and probe.

Secondly, find elements in the story that evoke a love of beauty. This can be found in the language and form of the story. On the one hand, there should be humor in some of the stories. Laughter is part of the Jewish heritage. It has strengthened our people and helped us to survive. On the other hand, death and sorrow are also a part of our heritage. Often teachers and parents avoid sad endings or death in stories. By doing so we deprive our children. Death is part of life. It is important to teach about life by telling stories that include death. Seek a balance when choosing stories.

The best aid for story selection is to read many, many stories. Until a background of experience can guide you, use storytelling lists and suggestions from friends. Looking for the right story is often frustrating. If you have a certain holiday or ritual in mind, there may be a limited number of appropriate stories which fit the occasion. For this reason you will need to think in terms of letting your imagination make connections — spin-offs — to that specific theme or holiday on which you are focusing. For example, if you are searching for stories for Shavuot, think in terms of the theme of learning and the Ten Commandments. Not all stories that incorporate one of the commandments may be labeled as such. "The Pocketknife" by Sholom Aleichem is a story that deals inadvertently with the idea of stealing and its result for a young boy who had so wanted to have his own pocketknife. This story fits in with the teaching of the eighth Commandment "You Shall Not Steal." However, I have also told this story during Passover when the theme of freedom is stressed. When the young boy "steals" the pocketknife, he becomes a "slave" to fear and cannot enjoy the long desired knife or tell anyone about it or show it off. There are all kinds of slavery or freedom besides the physical form.

On Sukkot, when we pray for dew and rain, free associate. Rain, dew, flood, rainbow, clouds, desert wind, snow, frost, water wheel, condensation, irrigation farming in the Negev, cacti, storm, a well, the sea, ocean, springs, stream, river, lake, and so on until you come full cycle to Torah, which has been compared to water. Stories of all kinds involving water can be found, such as the Rebekah story, the story of Noah, Elijah stories that deal with asking for water and bread from the widow, Abraham bringing water for washing the feet of the angels, the Job story, the story of King Solomon and the sack of flour, and the story of Rabbi Akiva and the fish. Through the use of a parable, Akiva makes the point that Torah is to the Jew as water is to the fish; in other words, that a Jew cannot live without Torah.

When you use this approach, history becomes more interesting and vital because it is presented in a context, not just as historical facts strung together. The children will remember the stories longer than the facts. By believing in the story, the teacher relates the story so that others can enjoy it, too. It will allow the audience to feel other people's feelings and ideas. The mental pictures of the people in the story and where they lived will remain in the listeners' storehouses of memories.

> **STORIES STRENGTHEN THE MORAL TEACHING OF JUDAISM.**

Through stories, we plant seeds which will grow later on. We will strengthen the moral teaching of Judaism by telling stories because the dramatic appeal to the imagination and the heart is quicker than the moral appeal to the conscience. In the Bible, wisdom is associated with the heart and not with the head or brain. So it is to the heart we must direct the stories. It is in stories that truth and wisdom are to be found.

When you find a good story, a story you want to tell, note it on an index card in a story file. Write down the title of the story, author, where it is found (in an anthology? in which library? etc.), publisher, city, date of publication. Then write a synopsis of the story (outline the sequence of the story). List the characters and place and time period. Also write down any special rhymes, important riddles, or key words which appear. It is amazing how we "lose" stories if we do not keep some sort of written file. The information you record will also help you recall the story after you learn it, but do not retell it for a long while.

PREPARATION

After finding and noting the stories to tell, the key question is: how does one prepare the story for telling? Although there are no set formulas, there are some technical steps to follow. One should keep this in mind: telling includes a rehearsal process. Baker and Greene point out two approaches to learning stories in their book *Storytelling: Art and Technique*.

Storytelling is an individual art. Storytellers develop different methods of learning stories. However, there seem to be two basic approaches: the visual and the auditory. In the visual approach, the storyteller sees the story in a series of pictures, much like the frames of a filmstrip . . .

In the auditory approach, the storyteller is conscious of the sound of words and their arrangement. A break in the rhythm is a warning that the telling is off the track. Those who use this approach often record the story on tape before learning it.[10]

Each person has to find what works best and to trust his or her instincts. However, preparation is essential to the success of storytelling. Storytelling can be tense and demanding. It can take a week and even a month to learn a single story. Patience is definitely an ingredient in the learning process.

What I have listed here are some positive strengths and guidelines to work on in order to develop further the tools of the storyteller and the knowledge of the story.

1. Know about the setting of the story and something about the main characters. Study the ideas in the story and do additional reading if necessary. A good Jewish history book can fill in some of the background. Additionally, the three Teachers' Guides that accompany *Stories from Our Living Past*, *Lessons from Our Living Past*, and *Exploring Our Living Past* (see Bibliography at the end of this chapter) are extremely valuable sources. When you know more than is necessary to be included in the actual telling, then you can present the story more vividly and it will mean more to you as well. More will come through in the telling.
2. Read the story out loud. Read it five times, or even 15 times, out loud. Know it and understand it, but do not memorize it verbatim. Memorization of a story can make it sound mechanical. Memorize instead the sequence of events in the story. With each reading,

focus on different elements in the story, for example, the beginning and ending, the characters, the language, repeated phrases, etc.

3. Outline the story after you have read it several times. The outline can include the beginning-action-climax-resolution-conclusion. In other words, break the plot into units of action. Study the structural elements as well as the words, phrases, sentences. Include repeated phrases, riddles, etc., if there are any.

4. Rehearse out loud, and time your story. After reading it many times, you will commit much of it to memory, but then begin to paraphrase the story in your own words. It will be fresher in the telling when you do this. You may want to edit (shorten or lengthen) a story. However, time your stories in order to have some idea of the time it takes to tell in your version. Telling the story orally to yourself and to friends will help you learn the tale.

    While you may update archaic English, avoid slang, modernisms, or modern euphemisms. "Thou" should become "you"; but "he failed" should not become "he messed it up" or "he blew it." The tone of the story can be abruptly changed and the story turned into a comedy routine. (Bill Cosby's story of Noah is wonderful, but then he has a special talent for this kind of comedy.) Edit but remain faithful to the tone, intent, and the plot of the story. If the storyteller brings to his/her interpretation sensitivity to the time, place, and people in the story, then this creative art will reflect another dimension of beauty and understanding.

5. Rehearse the story mentally, before you go to sleep or while you are on a train or walking in the park. Become saturated with the ideas and characters.

6. Work out natural, spontaneous gestures that add meaning to the story.

7. Concentrate on using eye contact with your listeners. This connotes pleasure and interest in the communication taking place.

8. Work with transitions, pauses, contrasts, silence before you begin and when you end the story (more on this later). The use of pause is extremely important even when telling an exciting, fast paced episode. A pause can be compared to a rest bar in music. There are rest bars even when the tempo is *vivace* or *presto*. The pause in a story heightens the suspense and the tension and helps the listener better interpret the meaning of the sentences.

9. Practice breathing exercises so as to be able to use fluid phrasing and to speak long phrases on one breath. Breaking a phrase in the wrong place can change or interrupt the meaning of a sentence.

10. Use an active voice with variety in pitch, rate, volume, and emphasis. Pace the telling so as to keep the interest and gain momentum as the story progresses.

11. Be sincere.

12. No matter what the age of the audience, do not use a condescending tone. Avoid accentuated vowel elongation, especially with younger children. Exaggeration can be fun, though, depending on the story. However, be careful not to confuse exaggeration of character with elongation of all the words. This tends to sound "babyish."

13. Enjoy the experience of telling stories. Tell the story each time as if it were a first telling. Storyteller Jackie Torrence reveals that she still gets stage fright. Before she goes on, her palms start to sweat, her chin starts shivering. But once on stage, she feels transported. "I can't wait to tell the stories," she says.[11] In order to handle the nerves, work on breathing and physical exercises for relaxation of the vocal cords and the body and the mind.

Many storytelling students ask for suggestions as to how to remember the stories. Certainly attention is immediately lost when a storyteller forgets what happens next in the story. A storyteller must think positively and do his/her homework in order not to forget. Thinking about what you are saying, in other words, telling it actively and not by rote, keeps the concentration focused on the telling and the images and the feedback. If a lapse does occur, improvise, pick up the book, go back a little in the story or learn to "play the pause" so the audience is not aware that you have forgotten.

Each person has to find what works best for himself/herself. Some people learn better by using visual methods and some by using sound methods, as has been already discussed. One idea is to type out the story and learn it that way by seeing it in print and saying it out loud at the same time. The visual and oral reinforce each other. Another method is to associate, or visualize, each part of the story, each transition or beat, with a part of the house or other location (for example, the introduction with the entrance, and so on). Certainly it is necessary to divide the story into parts — the sequence of the story (what happens first, second, etc.) — in order to understand and "see" the development of the story. This will help you pace the story and build to the climax. Another way to learn the story is by seeing the story as a series of pictures, as in a picture book or in the frames of a movie and learning the story incident by incident and picture by picture.

I find that it helps me to commit the story to memory by reading the story aloud several times and then working through it out loud by continuously referring back to the "book." In this way, I hear the sound of the words and the arrangement of the words and sentences and connect the sound to the sense of the words. I also hear the rhythm of the story. Rhythm and sound are important so that the language comes alive. If there is a work or play scene or an activity in the story that requires movement, then the rhythm and sound should coincide to capture this scene. For example, if in the story there is a tailor sitting and sewing, the telling could pick up the rhythm of this work. Sewing by hand would be a different rhythm from sewing by machine. It would also call for a different posture. Go out and observe a tailor with a needle in his hand (or a potter, or children spinning *dreidles*, or a carriage driver). There are Jewish stories that contain all of these activities and more. Remember, the storyteller can never fully become the tailor or driver. There is not the time to do so. Rather the storyteller must only suggest the character and the activity because in the next sentence or so the storyteller may shift to another character or activity or description. The teller is a juggler of many parts and worlds all at the same time. By using the mental pictures of the characters and what they are doing, in addition to the sound of the words describing the scene and the dialogue, you combine the visual and the auditory. One reinforces the other and the story becomes yours for the telling.

TELLING

Let's get to the telling. A story is a journey. On the journey we meet new characters, visit new places, discover new ideas. It is an exciting journey into other worlds and cultures and traditions.

One of the most difficult, but one of the most crucial, moments in telling stories is the beginning. It is important to have a good beginning, a clear transition from the introductory comments to the story itself. Usually I do not tell the title of the story, but it is an option which may help you make the transition. Try it. But do not introduce every story with the title. Vary the openings.

"I want to tell you a story" works very well as a transition into the story. It sets the tone and mood that gets the listeners ready to listen and to go on the journey. The silence/pause before you begin the actual story is also important to help set up the expectation of going on a journey. It is a magical moment and similar to the moment when the conductor lifts his baton in anticipation of the first note of music. Allow for this mood. You will see the audience physically move forward with open faces, all ready to receive the gift of the story. Use this pause by taking a deep, slow breath. Release it slowly to help you get ready for the beginning of the story.

The opening words "Once upon a time," "Once there was . . . ," "Many centuries ago . . .," "A long time ago. . . , " "In a far away country . . . ," are some of the most effective openings because they immediately capture the attention of the listeners. They serve as a bridge to transport the imagination of the audience from the here and now of the telling to that of the story itself. Of course, never start the opening words until you are ready.

Another suggestion as to how to begin a story is to invite the audience to participate. Ask them to help you tell the story by joining in on any sound and motion cues in the story. For example, tell them that when you begin to describe how the wind blew more and more ferociously, they are to begin to make a wind sound which grows ever louder. Or if you tell how the angels yawned, then they might also yawn. Instruct the audience to follow your hands which will signal when the sound is to grow in volume, or when the sound/motion should end. Try out a few sounds and motions before you actually begin the story. The audience will usually be very responsive and will participate well during the telling. Everyone knows how enthusiastically the audience participates in blotting out Haman's name during the

Esther story at Purim. This is an example of controlled participation in the storytelling experience. The listeners become storytellers with you and thereby become even more attentive waiting for their "parts."

Once you begin the story, continue remembering the sequence and building the story as you did in rehearsal. Stay with the moment in the story and do not think ahead to what is coming. Otherwise your mental flow will be interrupted.

During the telling, several other occurrences may distract you. Children may want to interrupt you with questions or comments. A school bell may ring. A fight may break out between children, and on and on. How can you learn to concentrate so that you can continue the story and still handle these distractions? First of all, it takes a great deal of energy to concentrate on telling a story, even without any distractions. But when there are interruptions, it is as though your mind is on a split track. Unless there is imminent danger to a person, or unless it is a fire bell that is ringing, it is the story that is most important, along with its enjoyment for the people listening. The decision of what to do at that moment of distraction is a tenuous, subjective one. Sometimes touching the arm of and for a few moments directing the story to that child who is causing a problem may be enough to get him or her back to the story.

Stopping a moment while the bell rings and then continuing, if you have time, may get you through that disruption. If there is no more time and you will meet that same class in the next day or so, summarize quickly up to where you are ending for the day, and set up a question of suspense or challenge before you stop. Motioning to another teacher to remove a restless child may be the answer to another kind of disruption. All the while, the story and the eye contact with the audience has to continue so that the thread of the story is not lost. Try the best you can to keep the story going, stopping only to say something to a child when it becomes impossible for you to continue. However, if a child asks a question such as "What does that word mean?" it is important to answer. Respond with a synonym, rather than a lengthy explanation. A storyteller needs to anticipate some of these questions by explaining words, names, concepts before the story begins if these are unfamiliar to the group. This should not be confused with explaining the story. Other sincere questions by a child can be often put off until the end of the story. Show the child that you heard the question, giving a quick "under the breath" answer or with a gesture assure the child that you will answer when the story is finished.

When interruptions occur, knowing the sequence of the story well becomes even more advantageous. Ideally, nothing else should exist but the story. Nothing outside of the story should stop the telling, and if it does, then by your concentration and imaging, you can continue the telling without losing the attention and interest of the audience or your train of thought. Admittedly it does take tremendous energy and concentration to do this.

As a storyteller, you are the recreative artist, the interpreter who is between the author and the audience. And more than just an interpreter, you are a composer as well. You are all the characters as well as the narrator. You are a juggler who makes clear who is speaking as well as any change of scene and passage of time. This can be done through pause, change of voice, use of transition phrases (e.g., "Many years have passed . . ."), emphasis, change of physical stance, etc. All of this, of course, must be tried out and polished in rehearsal. (More specific suggestions can be found in the books on storytelling in the Bibliography.)

Now we come to the end of the story. How does one end? With definiteness. End with words and vocal inflections that signal to the listeners that this is the conclusion of the story. The audience has to be ready for the conclusion, so that the story does not finish abruptly and take them by surprise or fade away so the last sentence can hardly be heard. Listen to music and note how compositions come to an end, how the composer and musicians signal to the audience that the ending is approaching. Whether the ending is ". . . and they lived happily ever after," or ". . . and this is how the little bee helped the great King Solomon," it is not only the words themselves, but the voice that plays a big part in bringing the story to an effective end.

A good guideline is generally to avoid ending with the moral of the story or at least not to

DON'T OVEREMPHASIZE THE STORY'S MORAL.

accentuate it in such a way that the story is diminished. The meaning of the story will come through without overemphasizing the moral. If this does not occur on the first hearing, then it surely will after the second telling. Almost every Jewish story has a moral, but do not spell it out so that the audience does no work at all in searching for the meaning. Instead, incorporate the moral into the story. It is so much more effective and lasting when one discovers the moral lesson by oneself.

After the story ends, allow a few moments of silence as private time for the story to settle in the heads of the listeners. Returning from a journey, one needs time to readjust. If the story has been humorous, then laughter may be the right transition. If the story has been serious and poignant, then the audience needs, and even demands, a moment or two of quiet introspection before any other words or sounds crash into their own thoughts. Hopefully their channels of awareness and responses have been expanded by the story. Give them the necessary time for this to happen.

There are many facets of storytelling with which I have not dealt. Some are either not within the scope of this chapter (such as initial and follow-up activities which include arts and crafts, springboard discussion topics, creative dramatics, relating personal experiences, etc.). Other areas were dealt with in brief due to the space limitations. The Bibliography at the end contains several books which deal in greater detail with the techniques of storytelling and creative dramatics.

The teacher becomes a storyteller first of all by telling stories and also by hearing others do so. Listen to records of other storytellers. Go to hear other storytellers whenever you can. Analyze their styles. Experiment to find your own style and the types of stories you love to tell. With further reading and experience and trusting your intuition, you can judge the best time for telling, how to use stories for improvisations, role playing, and so on. Experiment in using the audience to help you tell the story by contributing sound/actions at appropriate times or by stopping at a high point in the story to see how the audience would develop the rest of the story.

Teaching creatively with stories is both imaginative and within the Jewish tradition. Stories enable the teaching and learning processes to become very exciting both for the teacher and the student. Elie Wiesel once said that what is most important in Jewish education is to give the child something beautiful and not boring. What can be more beautiful than to teach our children our Jewish values and culture with a story? So let us continue to tell tales.

Peninnah Schram, storyteller, author, and recording artist, is Associate Professor of Speech and Drama at Stern College of Yeshiva University. Her books include *Jewish Stories One Generation Tells Another* and *Tales of Elijah the Prophet.* She is founding Director of the Jewish Storytelling Center and Network.

NOTES

1. Anne Pellowski, *The World of Storytelling*, p. 15.
2. Bruno Bettelheim, *The Uses of Enchantment*, p. 28.
3. Ibid., p. 152.
4. Augusta Baker and Ellin Greene, *Storytelling: Art and Technique*, (New York: R.R. Bowker Company, 1977), p. 25.
5. Anthony Ramirez, "Meet Jackie Torrence - A Profile" in *The Wall Street Journal*. Excerpt reprinted in *The Yarnspinner*.
6. Pellowski, op. cit., p. 111.
7. Ibid., p. 111.
8. Ibid., p. 113.
9. Ibid., p. 119.
10. Baker and Greene, op. cit., pp. 40-41.
11. Ramirez, op. cit., p. 8.

BIBLIOGRAPHY

Resources for the Storyteller

Barton, Bob. *Stories in the Classroom: Storytelling, Reading Aloud and Roleplaying with Children.* Markham, Ontario: Pembroke Publishers Limited, 1990.

———. *Tell Me Another: Storytelling and Reading Aloud at Home, at School and in the Community.* Markham, Ontario: Pembroke Publishers Limited, 1986.

Bauer, Caroline Feller. *New Handbook for Storytellers.* Chicago: American Library Association, 1993.

Benjamin, Walter, and Hannah Arendt. *Illuminations.* H. Zorn, trans. New York: Harcourt Brace, 1968.

Bettelheim, Bruno. *The Uses of Enchantment: The Meaning and Importance of Fairy Tales.* New York: Vintage, 1989.

Bosma, Bette. *Fairy Tales, Fables, Legends, and Myths: Using Folk Literature in Your Classroom.* New York: Teachers College Press, 1992.

Cooper, Pamela J., and Rives Collins. *Look What Happened to Frog: Storytelling in Education.* Scottsdale, AZ: Gorsuch Scarisbrick, 1992.

Danan, Julie Hilton. *The Jewish Parents' Almanac.* Northvale: Jason Aronson Inc., 1994.

Egan, Kieran. *Teaching as Storytelling: An Alternative Approach To Teaching and Curriculum in the Elementary School.* Chicago: University of Chicago Press, 1989.

Griffin, Barbara Budge. *Storyteller Guidebook Series.* Medford, OR: Self-published. (10 South Keeneway Drive, Medford, OR 97504)
Book One: *Students as Storytellers: The Long and the Short of Learning a Story*, 1989.
Book Two: *Student Storyfest: How To Organize a Storytelling Festival*, 1989.
Book Three: *Storyteller's Journal: A Guidebook for Story Research and Learning*, 1990.

Kinghorn, Harriet R., and Mary Helen Pelton. *Every Child a Storyteller: A Handbook of Ideas.* Englewood, CO: Teachers Idea Press, 1991.

Livo, Norma J., and Sandra A. Rietz. *Storytelling: Folklore Sourcebook.* Englewood, CO: Libraries Unlimited, Inc., 1991.

———. *Storytelling: Process and Practice.* Littleton, CO: Libraries Unlimited, Inc., 1986.

———. *Storytelling Activities.* Littleton, CO: Libraries Unlimited, 1987.

McCaslin, Nellie. *Creative Dramatics in the Classroom.* 5th ed. White Plains, NY: Longman Publishing Group, 1990.

Myerhoff, Barbara. *Number Our Days.* New York: Simon and Schuster, 1980.

Paley, Vivian Gussin. *The Boy Who Would Be a Helicopter: The Uses of Storytelling in the Classroom.* Cambridge, MA: Harvard University Press, 1990.

Pellowski, Anne. *The World of Storytelling: A Practical Guide to the Origins, Development, and Applications of Storytelling.* New York: H.W. Wilson Co., 1990.

Rosen, Betty. *And None of It Was Nonsense: The Power of Storytelling in School.* Portsmouth, NH: Heinemann Educational Books, 1988.

Sawyer, Ruth. *The Way of the Storyteller.* New York: Viking Press, 1965.

Shedlock, Marie. *The Art of the Storyteller.* New York: Dover, 1951.

Spolin, Viola. *Improvisations for the Theatre: A Handbook of Teaching and Directing Techniques.* rev. ed. Evanston, IL: Northwestern University Press, 1983.

Stone, Elizabeth. *Black Sheep and Kissing Cousins: How Our Family Stories Shape Us.* New York: Times Books, 1988.

Zeitlin, Steven J.; Amy J. Kotkin; and Holly Cutting Baker. *A Celebration of American Family Folklore.* New York: Pantheon Books, 1982.

Jewish Story Collections

Adelman, Penina. *The Aleph Beit Bible: For Young Children and Grown-ups.* Los Angeles: Aleph Design Group, 1994.

———. *Miriam's Well: Rituals for Jewish Women Around the Year.* (rev. ed.) Fresh Meadows, NY: Biblio Press, 1990.

Ausubel, Nathan, ed. *A Treasury of Jewish Folklore.* New York: Crown, 1989.

———. *A Treasury of Jewish Humor.* Lanham, MD: M. Evans & Co., 1988.

Bar-Itzhak, Haya, and Aliza Shenhar. *Jewish Moroccan Folk Narratives from Israel.* Detroit: Wayne State University Press, 1993.

Belth, Norton, ed. *The World Over Story Book.* New York: Jewish Education Press, 1970.

Bialik, Hayim Nahman, and Yehoshua Hana Ravnitzky, eds. *The Book of Legends: Sefer Ha-Aggadah.* New York: Schocken Books, 1992.

Bin Gorion, Micha Joseph. *Mimekor Yisrael: Classical Jewish Folktales*. Bloomington, IN: Indiana University Press, 1990.

Brodie, Deborah, ed. *Stories My Grandfather Should Have Told Me*. New York: Bonim Books, 1977.

Brody, Ed, Jay Goldspinner, et al, eds. *Spinning Tales, Weaving Hope: Participation Tales for Peace, Justice and the Environment*. Philadelphia: New Society Publishing, 1992.

Buber, Martin. *Tales of the Hasidim: Early Masters*. New York: Schocken Books, 1987.

———. *Tales of the Hasidim: Later Masters*. New York: Schocken Books, 1987.

Buxbaum, Yitzhak. *Storytelling and Spirituality in Judaism*. Northvale, NJ: Jason Aronson Inc., 1994.

Carlebach, Shlomo, and Susan Yael Mesinai. *Shlomo's Stories: Selected Tales*. Northvale, NJ: Jason Aronson Inc., 1994.

Certner, Simon. *101 Jewish Stories for Schools, Clubs and Camps*. New York: Jewish Education Committee, 1961.

Cone, Molly. *Who Knows Ten*. New York: UAHC Press, 1965.

Eliach, Yaffa. *Hasidic Tales of the Holocaust*. New York: Oxford University Press, 1982.

Epstein, Lawrence. *A Treasury of Jewish Inspirational Stories*. Northvale, NJ: Jason Aronson Inc., 1993.

Frankel, Ellen. *The Classic Tales: 4000 Years of Jewish Lore*. Northvale, NJ: Jason Aronson Inc., 1989.

Gellman, Marc. *Does God Have a Big Toe? Stories About Stories in the Bible*. New York: Harper & Row, 1989.

Geras, Adele. *My Grandmother's Stories: A Collection of Jewish Folktales*. New York: Alfred A. Knopf, 1990.

Ginzberg, Louis. *Legends of the Bible*. Philadelphia: Jewish Publication Society, 1992.

———. *The Legends of the Jews*. (7 vols.) Philadelphia: Jewish Publication Society, 1909-38.

Gold, Sharlya, and Mishael Maswari Caspi. *The Answered Prayer and Other Yemenite Folktales*. Philadelphia: Jewish Publication Society, 1976.

Goldin, Barbara Diamond. *A Child's Book of Midrash: 52 Jewish Stories from the Sages*. Northvale, NJ: Jason Aronson Inc., 1990.

Goodman, Philip. *The Hanukkah Anthology*. Philadelphia: Jewish Publication Society, 1992.

———. *The Passover Anthology*. Philadelphia: Jewish Publication Society, 1993.

———. *The Purim Anthology*. Philadelphia: Jewish Publication Society, 1988.

———. *The Rosh Hashanah Anthology*. Philadelphia: Jewish Publication Society, 1992.

———. *Shavuot Anthology*. Philadelphia: Jewish Publication Society, 1992.

———. *The Sukkot and Simhat Torah Anthology*. Philadelphia: Jewish Publication Society, 1992.

———. *The Yom Kippur Anthology*. Philadelphia: Jewish Publication Society, 1992.

Hautzig, Esther. *The Seven Good Years and Other Stories of I.L. Peretz*. Philadelphia: Jewish Publication Society, 1984.

Howe, Irving, and Eliezer Greenberg, eds. *A Treasury of Yiddish Stories*. (rev. ed.) New York: Viking Press, 1990.

Jaffe, Nina. *The Uninvited Guest and Other Jewish Holiday Tales*. New York: Scholastic, Inc., 1993.

Jaffe, Nina, and Steven Zeitlin. *While Standing on One Foot: Puzzle Stories and Wisdom Tales from the Jewish Tradition*. New York: Henry Holt and Co., 1993.

Katz, Michael Jay. *The Night Tales Trilogy: Night Tales of the Shammas*. Northvale, NJ: Jason Aronson Inc., 1988.

———. *Night Tales Remembered: Fables from the Shammas*. Northvale, NJ: Jason Aronson Inc., 1990.

———. *Night Tales from Long Ago*. Northvale, NJ: Jason Aronson Inc., forthcoming.

Kranzler, Gershon. *The Golden Shoes and Other Stories*. New York: Feldheim, 1982.

Krohn, Paysach J. *Around the Maggid's Table: More Classic Stories and Parables from the Great Teachers of Israel*. Brooklyn, NY: Mesorah, 1989.

———. *The Maggid Speaks: Favorite Stories and Parables of the Maggid of Jerusalem*. Brooklyn, NY: Mesorah, 1987.

Labovitz, Annette. *Secrets of the Past: Bridges to the Future*. Miami: Central Agency for Jewish Education, 1983.

Labovitz, Eugene, and Annette Labovitz. *Time for My Soul: Jewish Stories for the Holy Days*. Northvale, NJ: Jason Aronson Inc., 1987.

———. *A Touch of Heaven: Eternal Stories for Jewish Living*. Northvale, NJ: Jason Aronson Inc., 1990.

Millgram, Abraham E. *An Anthology of Medieval Hebrew Literature.* New York: Abelard-Schuman, 1961.

———. *Sabbath.* Philadelphia: Jewish Publication Society, 1965.

Newman, Louis I. *The Hasidic Anthology.* Northvale, NJ: Jason Aronson Inc., 1988.

Noy, Dov. *Studies in Jewish Folklore.* Hoboken, NJ: Ktav Publishing House, 1981.

Patai, Raphael, ed. *Gates to the Old City.* Ann Arbor, MI: Books on Demand, n.d.

Polsky, Howard, and Yaella Wozner. *Everyday Miracles; The Healing Wisdom of Hasidic Stories.* Northvale, NJ: Jason Aronson Inc., 1987.

Prose, Francine. *Stories from Our Living Past.* West Orange, NJ: Behrman House, 1974.

Rabinowicz, Tzvi. *The Prince Who Turned into a Rooster: One Hundred Tales from Hasidic Tradition.* Northvale, NJ: Jason Aronson Inc., 1994.

Rosman, Steven M. *Sidrah Stories: A Torah Companion.* New York: UAHC Press, 1989.

———. *The Twenty-Two Gates to the Garden.* Northvale, NJ: Jason Aronson Inc., 1994.

Rossel, Seymour. *Lessons from Our Living Past.* West Orange, NJ: Behrman House, 1972.

Rush, Barbara. *A Book of Jewish Women's Tales.* Northvale, NJ: Jason Aronson Inc., 1994.

Rush, Barbara, and Eliezer Marcus. *Seventy and One Tales for the Jewish Year: Folk Tales for the Festivals.* New York: American Zionist Youth Foundation, 1980.

Sadeh, Pinhas. *Jewish Folktales.* Hillel Halkin, trans. New York: Doubleday, 1989.

Sanfield, Steve. *The Feather Merchants and Other Tales of the Fools of Chelm.* New York: Orchard Books, 1991.

Schram, Peninnah. *Elijah the Prophet Study Guide.* (Instant Lesson) Los Angeles: Torah Aura Productions, 1994. (Story and Participatory Activities)

———. *Jewish Stories One Generation Tells Another.* Northvale, NJ: Jason Aronson Inc., 1987.

———. *Tales of Elijah the Prophet.* Northvale, NJ: Jason Aronson Inc., 1991.

Schram, Peninnah, ed. *Chosen Tales; Stories Told by Jewish Storytellers.* Northvale, NJ: Jason Aronson Inc., forthcoming.

Schram, Peninnah, and Steven M. Rosman. *Eight Tales for Eight Nights; Stories for Chanukah.* Northvale, NJ: Jason Aronson Inc., 1990.

Schwartz, Cherie Karo. *My Lucky Dreidel: Hanukkah Stories, Songs, Poems, Crafts, Recipes, and Fun for Kids.* New York: Smithmark Publishers, Inc., 1994.

Schwartz, Howard. *Adam's Soul: The Collected Tales of Howard Schwartz.* Northvale, NJ: Jason Aronson Inc., 1992.

———. *The Captive Soul of the Messiah: New Tales about Reb Nachman.* New York: Schocken Books, 1983.

———. *The Dream Assembly: Tales of Rabbi Zalman Schachter-Shalomi.* Nevada City, CA: Gateways, 1989.

———. *Elijah's Violin & Other Jewish Fairy Tales.* New York: Oxford University Press, 1994.

———. *Gabriel's Palace: Jewish Mystical Tales.* New York: Oxford University Press, 1994.

———. *Imperial Messages: One Hundred Modern Parables.* New York: Overlook Press, 1992.

———. *Lilith's Cave: Jewish Tales of the Supernatural.* New York: Oxford University Press, 1991.

———. *Miriam's Tambourine: Jewish Folktales from Around the World.* New York: Oxford University Press, 1988.

Schwartz, Howard, ed. *Gates to the New City: A Treasury of Modern Jewish Tales.* Northvale, NJ: Jason Aronson Inc., 1991.

Schwartz, Howard, and Barbara Rush. *The Diamond Tree: Jewish Tales from Around the World.* New York: HarperCollins, 1991.

Serwer-Bernstein, Blanche. *In the Tradition of Moses and Mohammed: Jewish and Arab Folktales.* Northvale, NJ: Jason Aronson Inc., 1994.

Sims, Laura, and Ruth Kozodoy. *Exploring Our Living Past Storybooks.* West Orange, NJ: Behrman House, 1979.

Simon, Solomon. *More Wise Men of Helm.* West Orange, NJ: Behrman House, 1965.

———. *The Wise Men of Helm and Their Merry Tales.* West Orange, NJ: Behrman House, 1945.

Singer, Isaac Bashevis. *The Power of Light: Eight Stories for Hanukah.* New York: Farrar, Straus & Giroux, 1967.

———. *Stories for Children.* New York: Farrar, Straus & Giroux, 1984.

———. *When Shlemiel Went to Warsaw.* New York: Farrar, Straus & Giroux, 1968.

———. *Zlateh the Goat.* New York: Harper & Row, 1966.

Sobel, Samuel, ed. *A Treasury of Sea Stories*. New York: Jonathan David, 1965.

Staiman, Mordechai. *Niggun: Stories Behind the Chasidic Songs that Inspire Jews*. Northvale, NJ: Jason Aronson Inc., 1994.

Teller, Hanoch. *Above the Bottom Line*. New York: New York City Publishing Co., 1988.

———. *The Bostoner*. New York: Feldheim, 1989.

———. *Give Peace a Stance: Stories and Advice on Promoting and Maintaining Peace*. New York: New York City Publishing Co., 1992.

———. *"Hey, Taxi!"* New York: New York City Publishing Co., 1990.

———. *A Matter of Principal*. New York: New York City Publishing Co., 1994.

———. *Once Upon a Soul*. New York: New York City Publishing Co., 1994.

———. *Soul Survivors*. New York: New York City Publishing Co., 1985.

———. *"Souled!"* (Books I & II) New York: New York City Publishing Co., 1986.

———. *13 Years*. New York: New York City Publishing Co., 1994.

———. *Welcome to the Real World*. New York: New York City Publishing Co., 1994.

Waskow, Arthur, and Phyllis Berman. *Tales of Tikkun*. Northvale, NJ: Jason Aronson Inc., forthcoming.

Weinreich, Beatrice S. *Yiddish Folktales*. Leonard Wolf, trans. New York: Pantheon, 1988.

Wiesel, Elie. *Sages and Dreamers: Biblical, Talmudic, and Hasidic Portraits and Legends*. New York: Summit Books, 1991.

———. *Somewhere a Master: Further Hasidic Portraits and Legends*. New York: Summit Books, 1984.

———. *Souls on Fire: Portraits and Legends of Hasidic Masters*. New York: Summit Books, 1982.

Collections Which Contain Several Jewish Stories

Best-Loved Stories Told at the National Storytelling Festival. Jonesborough, TN: National Storytelling Press, 1991. (See stories contributed by Doug Lipman, Syd Lieberman, Steve Sanfield, and Peninnah Schram)

Brody, Ed, et al, eds. *Spinning Tales, Weaving Hope: Stories of Peace, Justice & the Environment*. Philadelphia: New Society Publishers, 1992. (See stories contributed by Hanna Bandes, Heather Forest, Marcia Lane, Nancy Schimmel, and Peninnah Schram)

Holt, David, and Bill Mooney. *Ready-To-Tell Tales: Surefire Stories from America's Favorite Storyteller*. Little Rock, AK: August House, 1994. (See stories by Judith Black, Steve Sanfield, and Peninnah Schram)

Lippert, Margaret H., Comp. *Teacher's Read Aloud Anthology*. 9 vols. New York: Macmillan/McGraw-Hill School Publishing Co., 1993. (See stories by Peninnah Schram and Isaac Bashevis Singer)

More Best-Loved Stories Told at the National Storytelling Festival. Jonesborough, TN: National Storytelling Press, 1991. (See stories contributed by Syd Lieberman and Peninnah Schram)

Williams, Michael E., ed. *The Storyteller's Companion to the Bible. Volume Four: Old Testament Women*. Nashville, TN: Abingdon Press, 1993. (See stories contributed by Betty Lehrman)

Williams, Michael E., ed. *The Storyteller's Companion to the Bible. Volume Five: Old Testament Wisdom*. Nashville, TN: Abingdon Press, 1994. (See stories contributed by Peninnah Schram)

Cassettes Containing Jewish Tales

Adelman, Penina. *This Is the Story: Original Songs and Midrashim about Jewish Women*. (Penina Adelman, 243 Upland Rd., Newtonville, MA 02160)

ben Izzy, Joel. *Stories from Far Away* and *The Beggar King and Other Tales from Around the World*. (Joel ben Izzy, 1545 Acton St., Berkeley, CA 94702)

Black, Judith. *Glad To Be Who I Am, Waiting for Elijah, Adult Children of . . . Parents*. (Tidal Wave Productions, 33 Prospect St., Marblehead, MA 01945)

Bresnick-Perry, Roslyn. *Holiday Memories of a Shtetl Childhood, A Real American Girl: Stories of Immigration and Assimilation*. (Roslyn Bresnick-Perry, 401 West End Ave., New York, NY 10024)

Carlebach, Shlomo. *The Best of Shlomo Carlebach*. (5 double audiotapes) (Samuel Intrator, 401 West End Ave., New York, NY 10024)

Danoff, Susan. *Enchantments, The Invisible Way: Stories of Wisdom, Women of Vision*. (Susan Danoff, P.O. Box 7311, Princeton, NJ 08543)

Etshalom, Yitzchak. *Rest Area: Tales of the Road.* (Los Angeles Hebrew High School, 14937 Ventura Blvd. #201, Sherman Oaks, CA 91403)

Fierst, Gerald. *Jewish Tales of Magic and Mysticism, Tikun Olam: Stories To Heal the World.* (Gerald Fierst, 222 Valley Rd., Montclair, NJ 07042)

Forest, Heather. *Tales Around the Hearth, Sing Me a Story, Songspinner: Folktales and Fables Sung and Told.* (Cartoon Opera, P.O. Box 354, Huntington, NY 11743)

Frankel, Ellen. *Classic Tales: Traditional Jewish Stories.* (Ellen Frankel, 6670 Lincoln Dr., Philadelphia, PA 19119)

Golden, Karen. *Tales and Scales: Stories of Jewish Wisdom.* (Golden Button Productions, 6152 W. Olympic Blvd. #9, Los Angeles, CA 90048)

Grayzel, Eva, with Buzzy Walters. *Proud To Be Jewish.* (Eva Grayzel, 4245 Farmersville Ct., Easton, PA 18042-2346)

Harrison, Annette. *Lilith's Cave: Jewish Tales of the Supernatural.* (Annette Harrison, 6370 Pershing Ave., St. Louis, MO 63130)

Ilsen, Eve. *Tales of Mystery and Mussar, Windows to Another World: Chassidic Story and Song.* (Eve Ilsen, 3201 Wellington St., Philadelphia, PA 19149)

Lehrman, Betty. *Watermelon! and Other Stories, Tales for the Telling, Jewish Tales from the Heart.* (Betty Lehrman, 88 Flanagan Dr., Framingham, MA 01701)

Lieberman, Syd. *The Old Man and Other Stories, Joseph the Tailor and Other Jewish Tales, A Winner and Other Stories.* (Syd Lieberman, 2522 Ashland, Evanston, IL 60201)

Lipman, Doug. *The Forgotten Story: Tales of Wise Jewish Men, Folktales of Strong Women, Milk from the Bull's Horn, One Little Candle: Participation Stories & Songs for Hanukkah, Now We Are Free: Passover Participation Stories & Songs.* (Doug Lipman, P.O. Box 441195, West Somerville, MA 02144)

Mara. *Storysong.* (Mara, P.O. Box 20181, San Jose, CA 95160-0181)

Rosman, Steven M. *Sidrah Stories: A Torah Companion. Vol. I: Genesis.* (UAHC Press, 838 Fifth Ave., New York, NY 10021)

Rubinstein, Robert. *The Rooster Who Would Be King & Other Healing Tales, The Day the Rabbi Stopped the Sun and Other Jewish Tales, Tales of Mystery/Tales of Terror.* (Robert Rubinstein, 90 East 49 Ave., Eugene, OR 97405)

Rush, Barbara. *Barbara Rush Tells Stories from the Diamond Tree.* (Barbara Rush, 24 Gaymor Ln., Commack, NY 11725)

Sanfield, Steve. *Could This Be Paradise? Steve Sanfield Live at the Sierra Storytelling Festival.* (Backlog Book Services, Box 694, North San Juan, CA 95960)

Schachter-Shalomi, Zalman. *Le Chayim — To Life, The Seven Beggars: A Tale of Rabbi Nachman of Bratslav.* (ALEPH, 7318 Germantown Ave., Philadelphia, PA 19119-1793)

Schwartz, Cherie Karo. *Worldwide Jewish Stories of Wishes and Wisdom, Miriam's Tambourine: Jewish Folktales from Around the World.* (Cherie Karo Schwartz, 996 S. Florence St., Denver, CO 80231)

Stavish, Corinne. *Women: Willful, Witty, Wise.* (Corinne Stavish, 26150 W. Twelve Mile Rd. #C-54, Southfield, MI 48034)

Stone, Susan. *The Angel's Wings and Other Stories from The Diamond Tree: Jewish Tales from Around the World.* (Susan Stone, 1320 Wesley Ave., Evanston, IL 60201)

Sutton, Joan. *The Jewish Holidays.* (5 audiocassettes) (Joan Sutton, 2349 Funston St., San Francisco, CA 94116)

Teller, Hanoch. *The Sound of Soul I, The Sound of Soul II.* (New York City Publishing Co., 37 West 37 St., New York, NY 19918)

Wolkstein, Diane. *The Story of Joseph.* (Cloudstone, 10 Patchin Pl., New York, NY 10011)

Cassette Anthologies that Feature Jewish Storytellers

Best-Loved Stories Told at the National Storytelling Festival. (2 audiocassettes, recorded live at various festivals, includes stories told by Steve Sanfield and Peninnah Schram) (National Storytelling Association, P.O. Box 309, Jonesborough, TN 37659)

A Storytelling Treasury: Tales Told at the 10th Anniversary - National Storytelling Festival. (5 audiocassettes, includes stories by Judith Black, Heather Forest, Syd Lieberman, Doug Lipman, Steve Sanfield, and Peninnah Schram) (National Storytelling Association, P.O. Box 309, Jonesborough, TN 37659)

Storytelling Organizations

National Storytelling Association (formerly the National Association for the Preservation and Perpetuation of Storytelling), P.O. Box 309,

Jonesborough, TN 37659. Publishes *National Storytelling Magazine*.

The Jewish Storytelling Center, 92nd Street Y Library, 1395 Lexington Ave., New York, NY 10128. Founding Director – Peninnah Schram. Publishes *The Jewish Storytelling Newsletter*.

Jewish Storytelling Coalition of the Boston Area, c/o Bonnie Greenberg, 63 Gould Rd., Newton, MA 02168.

Jewish Storytelling Arts of Toronto, Canada, c/o Leslie Robbins, 96 Chudleigh Ave., Toronto, Ont., Canada M4R 1T3

THE ARTS

CHAPTER TWENTY-EIGHT

CREATIVE WRITING

Audrey Friedman Marcus

Creative writing as a classroom activity provides variety, stimulates involvement, encourages critical thinking, and enables every student to experience success. When we initiate such activities, we help our students develop their ability to express themselves on Jewish subjects and enable them to expand their awareness of and appreciation for Judaism.

Success with creative writing depends on good planning, a good repertoire of projects, and the ability on the part of the teacher to provide acceptance and validation to students for all their efforts. Unify each activity around a holiday or other topic of Jewish interest in your curriculum, and build one writing exercise upon the other. At the next session, review what was learned.

The following section contains a variety of creative writing activities. The list is meant to be suggestive rather than encyclopedic. Once you are up-to-date on some possible projects, you will be able to design other projects of your own. A Bibliography of useful books on the subject concludes the chapter.

STORIES AND BOOKS

Stories can be written on any topic of Jewish interest. They can be written about real people and actual events or about imaginary individuals and happenings. Help your students get started writing stories by providing motivation. For younger children, hold up a photograph or illustration, asking them to write a caption or a story about what they see. Story Starters represent another excellent way to suggest topics and ideas. These can take the form of sentence completions, situations, words and phrases, titles, questions, writing a paragraph from several different points of view, and continuous stories. Some examples in each category follow.

Sentence Completions

Have students complete sentences, such as:
1. When Joseph was sold into slavery by his brothers, he thought . . .
2. If I were a Jewish astronaut, I would . . .
3. The most meaningful Jewish experience I ever had was . . .
4. If Yochanan ben Zakkai hadn't started the academy, I think Judaism would have . . .

Situations

Present unusual and challenging situations and ask students to respond to them in writing.
1. You are someone from outer space. Your spaceship is hovering over someone's Passover *Seder*. You have never seen such a thing before. Write a letter back to your planet and describe what you have seen.
2. Your music teacher forces you to sing Christmas carols. Write an editorial for your school paper explaining why this might not be fair to some students.
3. You are an archaeologist working several hundred years from now. You discover a Jewish home. Write in your journal about the Jewish objects you unearth.
4. Your parents have offered you a trip to Israel for your birthday. If you go, you will miss your sister's wedding. Your schedule does not permit making the trip at any other time. Write a list of the advantages and disadvantages of each choice. If you were "Abby" of "Dear Abby," what would you write to someone in this situation who asked you for advice?

Words and Phrases

Ask students to write a paragraph or two using four phrases that you supply.

1. ships crowded with people hoping
   freedom close at hand
   featherbeds and Shabbat candlesticks
   greenhorn

2. red apple on a stick
   Rabbi going round
   flying flags
   happiness and joy

3. family together
   starry night
   eye appealing fruits
   waving lulav

Titles

Provide titles of essays and ask students to write on the topic. (As a variation of this, give students the last sentence of a paragraph and have them then write the paragraph.)
1. How To Stop Hamans from Arising in the World
2. If I Had Been with Moses at Sinai
3. Honor Your Mother and Your Father
4. The Most Important Jewish Person in My Life
5. I Was a Marrano in Fifteenth Century Spain.

Questions

Ask provocative questions and have students react in writing.
1. What color is Shabbat?
2. If you met Hitler walking down the street, what would you say to him?
3. Is Passover mostly a time of remembering, of celebrating, or of looking ahead?
4. What three things would you suggest to Israel and her neighbors to foster a lasting peace?
5. What is your favorite Jewish holiday?
6. If your *mezuzah* could speak, what would it say?

Be sure to share everyone's writing with the whole class. If your students are shy about this, then don't read the names of the authors. Younger children who do not yet know how to write can dictate their stories to a teacher, an aide, or a parent helper.

Student stories, books, and picture dictionaries can be typed and bound for the class library. Here are the steps necessary for "publishing" a book:

1. The children decide on an idea for a story. They write it individually or as a group.
2. Class members edit and rewrite the book as necessary, checking to be sure it says what the author wanted it to say and that others will understand it. They go over punctuation and spelling and make sure that all sentences are complete.
3. Youngsters plan the book in detail. They decide where pictures are needed, what type of illustrations are suitable, how big the book should be, what goes on each page, and how to bind it.
4. Students write the final copy on the actual pages of the book or dictate it to an adult who will type it or print it legibly. A table of contents, dedication, and copyright should all be included.
5. Students illustrate the book and bind it. For a brief overview of the process of making books, consult *Book Craft* by Pluckrose or other books on the subject in your public library.

Writing from Differing Points of View

Set up situations or topics and have students write three separate paragraphs, each from a different point of view.
1. Describe an act of *tzedakah* from the point of view of the giver, the recipient, and an outside observer.
2. Speak for or against gender equality in prayer language from the point of view of a woman, a man, a Rabbi.
3. Describe Joseph's brothers selling him into slavery as Joseph, as one of his brothers, as the head of the caravan.

Continuous Stories

On three separate pages, have each student start three stories or poems on Jewish topics, one serious, one humorous, one imaginative. (They should write just 20-30 words and put their names at the top of each page.) Put all of these in a box. Each student takes out a page begun by someone else and continues it with another 20-30 words. After five or six students have written on the same page, return the page to the original writer who adds a conclusion. Read the stories.

POETRY

Children are wonderfully free and imaginative. These qualities enable them to write poetry that is both original and creative. To get started, they sometimes need guidelines for the structure of their poem or some help finding a subject. Reading aloud good poetry by ancient and contemporary Jewish poets will inspire them and provide them with models (e.g., biblical poetry, Spanish poets, Yehuda Amichai, Danny Siegel). Establish a mood for poetry writing by playing soft background music. And be sure to remind your group that it is not necessary for all poems to have a set rhyme, meter, or sentence structure. Here are a few different types of poems your students can write.

Class Poems

Poems written as a class or as a two-person collaboration are enjoyable and often are surprisingly lyrical, touching, and descriptive. First outline "rules" for each poem. For example, ask students to put into every line a color, a comparison, a sound, a comic strip character, a foreign language word, a city, or a country. Or suggest they begin each line with the same phrase ("I wish . . . ," or "Sometimes . . . ," or "If I were . . . ,") or that they alternate between two different beginnings for odd and even lines. Each child writes one line according to the rules and turns it in. Then all of the lines are put together and read aloud as a poem.[1]

All of these suggestions are adaptable for Jewish settings and subject matter. Use the phrase "If I were . . . " for poems about symbols or people. Begin odd lines with "Jews used to . . . " and even lines with "But now . . . " Or, suggest that each "I wish . . . " line contains a wish for the Jewish people. Suggest that youngsters include some Hebrew words in their poems.

Cinquain

The cinquain, a form of poetry that originated in France, has five lines:

Line 1 – 1 name word, or noun. This word represents the title of the poem and is usually a person, a place, or a key word in a lesson.

Line 2 – 2 description words, or adjectives. These describe the noun in line 1.

Line 3 – 3 action words, usually verbs or participles (words ending in "ing" or "ed"). These words tell what the noun is, or does or is like.

Line 4 – a 4 word comment, usually a phrase that tells how the writer feels or thinks about the noun.

Line 5 – One word that refers back to the noun in line 1. This may be a synonym.

One example of a cinquain follows:

Akiba,
Determined late-bloomer,
Studying, sharing, suffering,
A model for all,
Hero.

Haiku

A haiku is a non-rhyming poem consisting of three lines. The first line has five syllables, the second has seven syllables, and the last line has five. The form, which originated in Japan, often describes nature or the seasons. Here is an example of a haiku:

Bursting into bloom
The tree outside my window
Welcomes Tu B'shevat.

Diamante[2]

The diamante (pronounced dee-ah-MAHN-tay) is a slightly more complicated type of poem. It is a seven line poem written in the shape of a diamond.

Line 1 – one word subject: noun, opposite of word in last line

Line 2 – two words: adjectives describing the subject in the first line

Line 3 – three words: participles (words ending in "ing" or "ed" about the subject in the first line)

Line 4 – four words: nouns about the subject in the first and last lines

Line 5 – three words: participles about the subject in the last line

Line 6 – two words: adjectives describing the subject in the last line

Line 7 – one word subject: noun, opposite of the work in the first line

Acrostics

Various types of acrostics have been written by Hebrew poets since biblical times. In some, the first letters of the lines spell out the alphabet or variations thereof. Sometimes, they spelled a name of the poet or the name of God. Today we write acrostics for fun, using our own names, a Hebrew word, the name of a holiday or symbol, or a Jewish concept.

To begin an acrostic, write the title or subject vertically from top to bottom. Students start each line with a word that begins with the same letter as the acrostic. This is a good technique for summarizing key concepts or giving students a chance to express their feelings on a particular subject.

Of course, students may also write poems that rhyme and have meter. Older students may enjoy writing more complex forms of poetry, such as sonnets. One form of rhymed poetry which always makes a hit is the ever popular limerick. A limerick has five lines. Lines one, two, and five rhyme and lines three and four (the short lines) also rhyme. The final line often ends with a humorous twist.

Concrete Poems

In a concrete poem, the placement of words on the page is related to the meaning of the poem. For example, a Chanukah poem could be written in the shape of a *chanukiah*, a poem about Jonah might be in the shape of a great fish.

LETTERS AND TELEGRAMS

Letters are another enjoyable form of creative writing and can be related easily to specific content. Students can write letters to government officials, national organizations, famous authors, and editors of Jewish or secular newspapers on issues of concern to Jews. When these letters are mailed, it encourages youngsters to be active and caring members of the Jewish community.

At a more fanciful level, students can pretend to be someone living in a particular historical period writing to relatives elsewhere. For example, a new immigrant in America at the turn of the century writes home to the family in Poland, or a Yeshiva student in Vilna writes to his betrothed in a shtetl a hundred miles away. Students can imagine themselves to be an historical character writing to a contemporary or to another famous person who lived in a different era.

Letters can be written to real pen pals or to imaginary individuals in which students describe their daily lives and Jewish activities. One book suggests, for variety, that some of these letters be written with alphabet noodles glued on paper.[3]

Students can also write "I Urge Telegrams" of fifteen words or less to others, to themselves, or to God.

All of these writing exercises can also be done on a computer if one is available in your class or school.

MISCELLANEOUS IDEAS

The list of creative writing ideas is seemingly endless. Students can interview the Rabbi, the synagogue staff, its members and leaders, as well as interesting people in the community. The interviews, as well as personality profiles of the interviewees, can be written up in detail and bound into a book. Another good project is to involve students in creating helpful manuals for newcomers to the synagogue or the community, for new parents, for prospective brides and grooms, for B'nai Mitzvah and their parents, and for people who have experienced a death in the family.

Class members can initiate a school newspaper with news articles, features, editorials, cartoons, various columns, and advertisements. A good way to begin such a project is to study a variety of secular and Jewish newspapers, analyzing the contents, and deciding what elements are needed in a school paper.

Youngsters can write travel brochures for trips to Israel or to European communities of interest to Jewish travelers. They can design greeting cards for various Jewish holidays or write ads, such as the two which follow, which were written by seventh graders asked to "sell" Shabbat:

> ATTENTION: Atheists and other people bored with their present religion. For Sale: Sabbath, centuries old, yet like new, available in Orthodox, Conservative, Reform, and Reconstructionist versions. For further information, call 613-JEWS.

> Sabbath — free to anyone who wishes to be open with others, or who wants to have time to find himself/herself in relation to God and to the world. Enjoy peace, love, and rest for everyone. The Sabbath wants you!

For a more tactile experience, have students sit in a circle with their eyes closed. Pass a loaf of fresh *challah* around several times. The first time it goes around, ask participants to touch the object, feeling its texture and imagining what it is and what it looks like. The second time, have them smell it. Finally, let them break off pieces and taste it. When the exercise is over, ask students to open their eyes and write about the experience and their feelings.

Many Values Clarification strategies can be followed up with writing projects (see Chapter 18, "Values Clarification," for a list of these exercises). Students can describe their feelings following participation in discussions and role plays. They can analyze in writing their responses to decisions they made during exercises such as Rank Orders.

Older students can keep a journal about their growth as Jews or write anecdotal feedback sheets about Religious School. Stimulating and value laden situations may also be presented for written response.

Many of our youngsters are science fiction fans, but few are aware that there is a considerable body of Jewish science fiction. Introduce the excellent collection, *Wandering Stars: An Anthology of Jewish Fantasy and Science Fiction*, edited by Dann. (While out of print, this book can be found in some secular and Jewish libraries.) Then have students write their own science fiction, adapting stories from the Bible or *midrashim* or making up their own. They can also write about their future lives as adult Jews or about the Jewish community and family issues in the next century.

Don't neglect rewrites of songs, poems, articles, story endings, and the Bible. Try having students rewrite the latter in the first person, or in dialogue, or describe the events just before and just after those that are included in the Torah. Or, rewrite the Bible as newspaper accounts, similar to *Chronicles: News of the Past*, or as a CNN on the spot report. Bible events can also be rewritten in a contemporary manner, such as in the musical *Joseph and the Amazing Technicolor Dreamcoat* and the play *J.B.* by Archibold MacLeish.

Finally, there are many creative writing possibilities using cartoons and comic strips. Students can write and draw original comic strip versions of historical events. Another suggestion is to cut out the words in the balloons, mount the strip on cardboard, and cover it with clear Contact paper. Students then write in their own dialogue with a water soluble felt pen or china marker which can later be erased with a damp sponge.

CONCLUSION

After reading this chapter you have a good beginning repertoire of writing projects. Your colleagues can be a valuable source of other imaginative ideas. Plan carefully (see Chapter 19, "Planning Lively Lessons") and strive for variety, being careful not to overuse creative writing (or any other teaching technique). And most important, be accepting and show enthusiasm for every child's creative efforts. With your help, students can become creative and committed authors.

Audrey Friedman Marcus received her Masters Degree in Jewish Education from the Rhea Hirsch School of Hebrew Union College-Jewish Institute of Religion. She is the co-author of a series of children's books on the Jewish holidays published by UAHC Press, of many materials for teachers and students, and of numerous articles on Jewish education.

NOTES

1. Kenneth Koch, *Wishes, Lies, and Dreams: Teaching Children To Write Poetry* (New York: Random House, Inc., 1980).
2. Arnold B. Cheyney, *The Writing Corner*. (Glenview, IL: Scott Foresman, 1979), p. 97.
3. Gary Grimm and Don Mitchell, *The Good Apple Creative Writing* Book (Carthage, IL: Good Apple, Inc., 1976), p. 30.

BIBLIOGRAPHY

Carlson, Ruth Elizabeth. *Sparkling Words: Two Hundred and Twenty-five Practical and Creative Writing Ideas.* Geneva, IL: Paladin House, 1979.

Cheyney, Arnold B. *The Writing Corner.* Glenview, IL: Scott Foresman, 1979.

Cowie, Helen, ed. *The Development of Children's Imaginative Writing.* New York: St. Martin's Press, 1984.

Dann, Jack, ed. *Wandering Stars.* New York: Harper & Row, 1974, o.p.

Dow, Marilyn S. *Teaching Techniques that Tantalize.* Dubuque, IA: Kendall-Hunt Publishing Co., 1990.

Forte, Imogene. *Composition and Creative Writing for the Middle Grades.* Nashville, TN: Incentive Publications, 1991.

———. *Writing Survival Skills for the Middle Grades.* Nashville, TN: Incentive Publications, 1991.

Grimm, Gary, and Don Mitchell. *The Good Apple Creative Writing Book.* Carthage, IL: Good Apple, Inc., 1976.

Hawley, Robert C. *Writing for the Fun of It: An Experienced-Based Approach to Composition.* Amherst, MA: Education Research Associates, 1974.

Hawley, Robert C., and Sidney B. Simon. *Composition for Personal Growth: A Teacher's Handbook of Meaningful Student Writing Experiences.* Amherst, MA: Education Research Associates, 1983.

Koch, Kenneth. *Rose, Where Did You Get That Red? Teaching Great Poetry to Children.* New York: Random House, Inc., 1990.

Koch, Kenneth, et al. *Wishes, Lies and Dreams: Teaching Children To Write Poetry.* New York: HarperCollins, 1980.

Maid, Amy. *Write, from the Beginning.* New York: Irvington Publishers, 1982.

Milgrom, Jo. *Handmade Midrash: Workshops in Visual Theology.* Philadelphia: Jewish Publication Society, 1992.

Pluckman, Henry. *Book Craft.* New York: Franklin Watts, 1992.

Polette, Nancy. *The Best Ever Writing Models.* O'Fallon, MO: Book Lures, Inc., 1989.

———. *Literature-Based Spelling and Writing Activities for Primary Grades.* O'Fallon, MO: Book Lures, Inc., 1993.

———. *Pick a Pattern.* 4th ed. O'Fallon, MO: Book Lures, Inc., 1992.

THE ARTS

CHAPTER TWENTY-NINE

MUSIC AND JEWISH EDUCATION

Jeffrey Klepper

Music touches and embellishes every facet of Jewish life. It is our spiritual language. It can create memories which have a lasting impact on us and on our students. Music can also be a means of communication — an educational tool.

The purpose of this chapter is to suggest ways of bringing Jewish music into our classrooms and from there into the lives of our students. There is an immediate connection between Jewish music and Jewish life; therefore, a regular program of Jewish music in the school can enrich both a sense of Jewish identity and a sense of community. Through music, we help our students express themselves Jewishly. With songs, we give them the means to celebrate Jewish life and to grow culturally and spiritually as Jews.

Children who come from traditional homes or those who attend Jewish day schools and summer camps understand music as part of the rhythm of Jewish life. But for the vast majority of our students, their entire repertoire of Jewish songs will come from the synagogue via their Cantor or Religious School music teacher.

Should we be trying to give students as much *traditional* Jewish music as we can, the wonderful music *we* learned as children? More and more it seems we can't figure out *whose* tradition to impart, for the Jewish music tradition is not monolithic. In the past, everyone within a specific Jewish community knew and sang the same melodies. This was so because they lived together and shared decades, if not centuries, of experiences together. The influence of the outside world was not as pervasive as it is now.

Today's North American Jewish community is unique, as Jews come from many diverse traditions to form something of a musical *cholent*. In many cities, synagogues across the street from each other might sing their prayers to different melodies. Families gathering together for Pesach *Seder* may find they have few melodies in common. Today each school, each camp, each family has a unique Jewish music tradition, or worse, no Jewish musical tradition at all.

During the past 25 years, a new Jewish repertoire has emerged, as songwriters such as Debbie Friedman, Craig Taubman, and this author search for a musical idiom which will capture the imaginations of Jews, young and old. Embracing familiar musical styles such as folk, rock, and popular music, this trend represents the natural process of evolution in Jewish music which has taken place throughout history in many Jewish communities.

In the distant future, a uniquely North American Jewish music may emerge, perhaps a synthesis of all the styles we hear and sing today. Yet, because modern media, tapes, CDs, and video present us with so many different choices, it is most likely that there will always be diversity. In the meantime, we *should* nurture and pass on to our students those musical traditions which can be meaningful and useful today.

Today, our new generation of students, has been raised on rock and rap videos in a future shock world; they are streetwise and sophisticated. Many have a non-Jewish parent. Some endure the strain of divorce. All are under pressure to excel at studies, sports, and artistic pursuits. Therefore, to reach our students effectively, given the little time we have, the music we teaching in our synagogues and Jewish schools and camps must be either songs for singing or songs for learning.

SONGS FOR SINGING

At happy or sad times, Jews derive great strength from singing together. From earliest times, Jews have chanted the liturgy, because singing a prayer affects us more deeply than simply reading it. Music focuses our attention. It creates a mood, a special atmosphere. The music actually helps us to pray; it adds beauty and a sense of the spiritual to the worship experience for many. But, most important, singing together makes us feel part of the larger community.

Regular services should be an integral part of every Religious School program. The melodies must be age appropriate and participatory. Work closely with your congregation's Cantor or music director to correlate liturgical melodies taught in the Religious School with those used in the repertoire of the adult congregation. Some congregational responses could be simplified for school use if necessary. If the students' repertoire is different, the Religious School melodies should be used in the synagogue for family and children's services. For children, it is very important to lower the keys, if possible, so the singing range lies between the B to B octave.

> SINGING TOGETHER MAKES US FEEL PART OF THE LARGER COMMUNITY.

Over the past generation, new styles of synagogue music have changed the way many congregations worship. Beginning first in camps and youth groups, dozens of new melodies have found their way into the synagogue and Religious School. Most of the new songs are in a rhythmic folk style which appeals equally to children, teens, and adults. Unlike Cantorial or choral compositions, the music can be arranged exactly as you wish — it can be sung a cappella, with guitar, keyboard, or other instruments — keys, harmonies, dynamics, and repeats are determined by you.

SONGS FOR LEARNING

The classroom teacher will find that many of the Jewish songs now available are effective tools in teaching and reinforcing Jewish subject matter including history, values, concepts, and even Hebrew. Since most of the songs are in English, there is little need for translating the lyrics. They are ready to use and enjoy.

The songs usually employ the musical styles which our students now most enjoy — folk, jazz, rhythm & blues, calypso, bluegrass, rock, etc. The music is available on cassette tape or CD's so that students may listen as a class, or individually in learning centers, in a car, or at home. The wide acceptance of this music by educators is evidence of how valuable it is in making Jewish subjects come to life.

BRINGING MUSIC INTO YOUR CLASSROOM: SUGGESTIONS AND STRATEGIES

Finding New Songs

Always be on the lookout for new and interesting songs to enrich your lessons. Ask around to find out what songs are currently popular in the community, and tape record friends who will share their songs with you. Don't be shy! Potential sources of new songs include your Cantor, Rabbi, music professional, youth group and camp song leaders, music teachers from other congregations, songbooks, tapes, and CD's (see list of resources).

Make Lists of Songs

Compile two song lists as follows: List #1 should consist of all the Jewish songs you know. Decide which of these might be appropriate to use in your class, considering the grade and curriculum. Try to stress the songs that will actually be used at services or at home on Shabbat, at camp, youth group, or community gatherings.

List #2 should comprise songs you wish to learn, or songs you have come across which might add meaning to a subject you will be teaching. Share ideas with other teachers in your school. Ask at a teachers meeting, "Does anyone know a good song about . . . ?" To aid you in learning to sing the song, "dub" it onto a cassette and sing along at home or in the car. Practice until you are comfortable with it and can sing or play it without having to look at the music. As you learn these new songs, move them over to List #1.

Language

A well-rounded repertoire includes songs both in Hebrew and English. Each school will have a different ratio of Hebrew to English songs. Let local tradition and the wishes of your Cantor or Director of Education be your guide. Because Jewish tradition places great emphasis on the words of a religious text, make sure the music of a given song is appropriate to the meaning of the words. It is very helpful to know the general meaning of every Hebrew song in your repertoire.

Melody and Rhythm

Assuming the words are appropriate, an interesting melody and a captivating rhythm are the most important qualities of any good song. Even a slow song should move along with a certain spirit. Varying the tempo of a song helps keep it interesting. If a song seems to drag, just pick up the tempo. Generally, upbeat songs are more successful with children than slow ones.

The Correct Key

Your songs must be in a comfortable key for children to sing. Sometimes the best key for our own voices may not be the best for our students. Songbooks usually pitch songs too high, going up to E flat or E above middle C. These should be transposed down. Although higher keys may be used with young choral singers, most children have to strain to sing above B flat or B below middle C. If it feels uncomfortable because the range is too high, kids will often give up and stop singing altogether. When first teaching a song, lower the key, thus eliminating the need to strain. Later, using a slightly higher key for singing brings out more volume and spirit.

Space

The classroom can be a very easy setting in which to teach songs. I like to sit on a low stool or chair with the children on the floor. When a small number of children are in a large room (which is sometimes unavoidable), move everyone into one corner, (facing the wall and not the open room). This enables everyone to hear the reflected sound. In general, group singing sounds best when the room is just large enough to accommodate everyone comfortably. A small group in a large space may inhibit singing, as you will be deprived of the sound bouncing back off the wall. It is this reverberation which makes everything sound so good.

PLANNING AND PACING A SONG SESSION

When planning a music session, the most important thing is to keep it moving along at a brisk pace. It is helpful to begin each session with a song everyone knows and enjoys and then go into the teaching of a newer song. It is also nice to close each session with a favorite song. The remainder of the class should be well paced to include a variety of keys, styles, tempi, and a balance between Hebrew and English songs. It's a good idea always to have some extra songs ready in case the ones you planned don't go as well as you had hoped. Try the following game idea. Play *Name that Tune* to reinforce songs learned; simply play the first few notes of a song and see who can be first to guess what song it is.

Using a Microphone

When teaching songs to a very large group, consider using a microphone. Used correctly, a mic keeps the music teacher's voice from getting hoarse because it eliminates the need to strain. The mic allows Hebrew words to be heard clearly by the students. A mic also permits the music teacher to "orchestrate" the song as the group is singing — you can have one grade sing alone by just asking. It happens without shouting or missing a beat. Leading rounds becomes a simple matter. Another wonderful use of the microphone (learned from Pete Seeger) is to sing a harmony part while the group sings melody. When this works right, it sounds fantastic.

Electronic Keyboards

Music teachers who play piano should seriously consider using an electronic keyboard. These are portable with built-in speakers, and offer numerous sounds and rhythms. Some models allow you to pre-program an entire song and to play it back at the touch of a button. Tempo and even pitch are easily changed. Students love the different sounds.

Playing Tapes in Class

When playing cassette tapes or CD's in class, use a boom-box with stereo speakers if possible. The music will sound better and the students will pay more attention. Also, prepare the students with information about the music they are about to hear. Before playing the recording, ask several questions which require careful listening to the music or words. Have the words printed on the board or on a large poster, or hand out song sheets. Students will listen better if they can see the words.

Synagogue Music Tour

The synagogue music tour is a good activity for younger grades. Visit the Cantor's study and speak with the Cantor about music in your synagogue. Ask the Cantor (or Rabbi) to take you to the choir room, the organ loft, the *bimah* (to see where the Cantor or choir sings). Demonstrate how instruments such as guitar, organ, piano, shofar, etc., add to the services.

Comparing Different Melodies

Jewish musical traditions vary widely around the world. Sing the four versions of "*Mah Tovu*" found in *Shaarei Shirah*. Each was influenced by the culture of a particular time and place: #18 by Louis Lewandowski (nineteenth century Germany), #19, a Chabad melody from Eastern Europe (Chasidic influence), #16, an Israeli folksong (mid-twentieth century), #17 by Jeffrey Klepper (contemporary American influence). Demonstrate how each melody can create a different mood in the service. Can there be more than one *right* melody for a prayer? Absolutely! This exercise can be done with any prayer or song (it works well with "*Hiney Mah Tov*" and "*Adon Olam*").

Musical Memories

Ask older students to interview their (Jewish) grandparents about the Jewish songs they sang as children at home or in the synagogue. These melodies or stories can be taped using a portable recorder, then portions played for the class, along with a brief oral or written report. The interviews should be planned for a time when the family gets together for a Jewish holiday such as Chanukah or Pesach, when memories take us back to childhood. Have the students think about *their* childhood and the role that music has played in helping them to feel Jewish at different times, such as at camp, synagogue, Shabbat, and Pesach *Sedarim* at home. (Remind students to save the tapes — years later, they will be valuable documents of their family's history.)

Top Ten List

At the end of each school year, a week before the last day of classes, the entire Religious School might vote to choose the "Top Ten Jewish Songs of the Year." In years past, I handed out printed ballots. Now I visit each class and request a show of hands in answer to the question, "Which of the following is one of your very favorite songs?" Then I read down a list of 20-30 songs — pre-chosen by me from the past year's repertoire — singing the first line of each song to jog their memory. The teachers help me count hands. Then the votes are tabulated and a song sheet of the "top ten" songs is prepared (the songs are out of order, naturally).

There is always great excitement as we prepare to count down and sing the ten winning songs on the last day of school. It gives the students a real sense of accomplishment to realize how many Jewish songs they know and enjoy. To hear them sing with such spirit and joy is our reward for a long year of good learning. Next fall we will start all over again. Maybe some songs will be forgotten, but the spirit will remain.

CONCLUSION

When we sing, we affirm the values of our heritage. We bring healing to our bodies and souls, we bond together, we become one in spirit. There are no more beautiful sounds than the happy voices of children singing. To hear these sounds is to know that just as the old traditions endure, so will today's creations become the sacred tradition of a new generation.

Jeffrey Klepper has been Cantor of Beth Emet The Free Synagogue in Evanston, Illinois since 1982. He has composed and recorded over 100 original songs, including settings of "*Shalom Rav*," "*Mah Tovu*," and "*Oseh Shalom*," which are regularly sung at synagogue services, camps, and Religious Schools throughout the country. He is also half of Kol B'seder, the popular Jewish folk-rock duo. Kol B'seder has recorded six albums of original music and performs throughout the country.

RESOURCES

Cassette Tapes

Joe Black (*Alef Bet Boogie* and *Everybody's Got a Little Music*)*
Rabbi Joe Black's music is charming and infectious, especially his holiday songs and tunes for morning and evening.

Doug Cotler (*It's So Amazing!* and other titles)*
Doug Cotler wondered what would happen if his students wrote lyrics about being Jewish and the holidays — he wrote the music, sang, and produced the rockin' collection *It's So Amazing!*. (A songbook is available.)

Debbie Friedman (*You Shall Be a Blessing*; *Live at the Del*; *The World of Your Dreams*, and many other recordings)*
Debbie Friedman has penned the Jewish anthems of our age with "L'chi Lach," "T'filat Haderech," "Miriam's Song," and so many other unforgettable songs. (Songbooks are available.)

Jeff Klepper and Susan Nanus (*Especially Jewish Symbols*)*
Popular, upbeat songs about Jewish leaders and symbols of synagogue and home. (Cassette tape and songbook)

Jeff Klepper and Jeff Salkin (*Bible People Songs*)*
Joyful, sing along songs about biblical events and about our ancestors. (Cassette tape and songbook)

Kol B'seder (*Growin'*, *Sparks of Torah*, *Shalom Rav*, *In Every Generation*)*
What does this author do when not being a Cantor? He writes songs and records and performs with Rabbi Dan Freelander as Kol B'seder. *In Every Generation* is the newest release, and *Growin'* vols. I and II will please the whole family when played in the car! (Songbook is also available)

Steve Reuben (*Especially Wonderful Days: Sing Along Jewish Holiday Songs for the Primary Grades*)*
Foot-tapping songs that teach young children about the Jewish holidays. Contains "The Sing Along Song," and 12 others. (Cassette tape and songbook)

Craig Taubman (*Journey*, *Encore*, *Yad B'yad*)*
He knows how to connect young Jews to their heritage with a musical and lyrical message they understand. (Songbooks are available).

Songbooks

Israel in Song**
Great Songs of Israel**
Effie Netzer Songbook**
Songs from Israel are an important part of any Jewish music repertoire. These songbooks contain most of the essential songs through the 1970s.

Manginot (Songbook from UAHC)***
If there is one essential song collection (over 200 songs!) for the Jewish classroom, this is it.

NFTY's 50 (Songbook from UAHC)***
Fifty contemporary songs popular among Jewish youth, many published for the first time and available only in this collection.

Shaarei Shira (Hymnal from UAHC)***
While more of a reference work than a teaching tool, this book contains melodies to most commonly sung prayers in the Shabbat evening and morning services.

Miscellaneous

Tucker, JoAnne. *Creative Movement for a Song: Activities for Young Children*. Denver: A.R.E. Publishing, Inc., 1993.*
Explains 30 simple and advanced movement activities for lively songs by Kol B'seder, Fran Avni, Julie Auerbach, and Steve Reuben. Provides an overview of using movement in the early childhood classroom.

* Available from A.R.E. Publishing, Inc., 3945 South Oneida St., Denver, CO 80237.
** Available from Tara Publications, 29 Derby Ave., Cedarhurst, NY 11516.
*** Available from UAHC Press, 838 Fifth Avenue, New York, NY 10021

THE ARTS

CHAPTER THIRTY

CREATIVE MOVEMENT ACTIVITIES

JoAnne Tucker and Susan Freeman

"That's how Sarah must have felt when God told her she would have a baby at ninety years old!" ... "It's amazing how consoled I felt when I imagined I was a mourner, and you came, and with your whole body and self expressed comfort towards me." These are typical comments heard in classes in which teachers employ the enriching experience of creative movement activities.

Undoubtedly, movement activities offer stimulation, change of pace, and a new avenue of learning, making a unique contribution to the Jewish education curriculum. In this chapter, you will be given an abundance of ready-to-use ideas. In addition, you will be exposed to "tools" and ways of looking at movement which will help you to develop an approach to movement in the classroom that is workable and comfortable, as well as exciting and fun!

Experience has taught us that creative movement activities have the potential to: (a) increase self-awareness and self-knowledge; (b) stimulate creative and imaginative thinking; (c) change the pace/energy in the classroom; (d) provide for cooperative interaction among classmates; (e) help students make a personal connection to what sometimes are remote experiences to them; (f) be accessible at all academic levels from special education to high school/adults; (g) help reinforce the idea that Judaism is *the students' heritage*, and that they can be part of shaping its future.

TWO WAYS TO INCORPORATE CREATIVE MOVEMENT ACTIVITIES

We suggest the following two ways of incorporating creative movement activities into the classroom: (1) Quickies, short five minute activities; and (2) the Developed Movement Session, a four part movement activity lasting 15-45 minutes. Each of these is described in detail below.

Quickies – Short Five Minute Activity

One of the simplest ways to begin is to add movement as a five minute "change of pace" activity to reinforce the regular curriculum. Not only is the energy level changed in the classroom, but this new dimension added to the lesson is shared by the students. This approach is very non-threatening for a novice "movement" leader. We refer to these short movement explorations as "Quickies," and as the chapter continues, we provide you with lots of specific activities that can be used in this way.

Developed Movement Session

A Developed Movement Session can last from 15 to 45 minutes. Such a session usually consists of four parts in the following order:

1. Introduction – the idea and concept are explained. For example, if you are dancing the biblical character of Moses, you might begin with a brief overview of Moses' life.
2. Motivating Movement – needed movement tools are explored so that the participant will have some skills and some practice to use in the later dance improvisation. For example, if you are doing a session on the prophetess Deborah, you might begin by exploring slow controlled arm movements contrasted with bold explosive percussive arm gestures.
3. Movement Improvisation Illustrating the Lesson's Theme – This is the heart of the session. The students experience the lesson's theme by being given specific movement instructions. For example, they are all Moses at the moment he comes down from Mount Sinai and sees the Israelites dancing

around the golden calf. The students are to portray Moses' emotion at this time.
4. Making Connections – relates the theme to the overall curriculum. The teacher leads a discussion with the participants asking relevant questions on how a particular experience relates to their own lives. For example, using the situation of Moses described above, the teacher might ask if there are current examples in our society of a group of people not following a leader's instructions or, taking a different approach, ask if anyone has felt the same emotion that Moses felt at that moment and for what reason.

While most sessions have these four parts in the order given, teachers are encouraged to be flexible and imaginative in how they plan and lead the session. In other words, it's okay to start with movement right away and later introduce the concept, or begin with "Making Connections" by relating to students' personal experiences before doing the actual movement improvisation.

SUGGESTIONS FOR LEADING CREATIVE MOVEMENT SESSIONS

There is a wide range of leadership styles one can use for guiding a group in creative movement. While each leader and situation are unique, we have found that there are some commonly asked questions:

1. *I would love to incorporate creative movement activities in my classroom. To what extent is previous dance experience necessary?*
   While being able to draw on some dance background is very helpful, it certainly is not necessary. If you don't have dance experience, familiarize yourself with various movement "tools" elaborated on in this chapter. In particular, study the response to the next question. Also, spend time becoming comfortable with the movement concepts which introduce each section on ideas for curriculum development — *rhythm, quality/style, space*, and *movement that gathers in and opens out*. (The first section on movement concepts begins after these leadership questions.) Perhaps most important of all, give yourself permission to move and to feel comfortable exploring Jewish ideas through movement. If you are enjoying yourself and having fun with this activity, so will the class.

2. *How should I introduce movement to my students for the very first time? I want to get them excited about the prospect of creative movement activities being a regular part of our classroom experience. What are some easy, safe, and "never fail" ways to get started?*

   BE FLEXIBLE AND IMAGINATIVE IN YOUR PLANNING.

   Here are some suggestions that we find are easy to lead and also quickly get the students involved in moving.

   a. Expanding ritual movement – Sitting in chairs, explore the candle lighting hand movements of circling the flames and covering the eyes. Progress to standing, and explore ritual movement in Jewish worship, such as bending and bowing, lifting (rising onto the ball of the foot) for the *Kedushah* prayer, and ritual movement associated with taking out and putting away the Torah.
   b. Different kinds of walks – Explore walking in a variety of ways based on emotions, intentions, direction and movement quality. Go across the room with a pair (or triplet of students) beginning, and the others lined up in back of them. Have each set begin in an appropriate starting position before moving at all! Another format is to do the various walks in a circle, everyone moving at the same time. A sample walk assignment might be to walk like Jacob and then switch to walking like Esau.
   c. Sculpture – One example is making the shape of a Hebrew letter with your body.
   d. Poses become movement – Strike a pose, another, and another on a particular theme. Continue striking poses until the group is gradually moving from one pose to another without stopping.
   e. Emulating movement – Ask for a volunteer to show a movement phrase. For example, ask to see how Moses might have moved in an angry way when he saw the Israelites dancing around the golden calf. Have the others imitate the movement.
   f. Movement which travels through the body – Ask the class to put a movement idea in just one hand, (i.e., show Moses' anger in only the right hand). Progress

to both hands. Continue by showing Moses' anger in the feet, in the hips . . . in the hands and hips at the same time, the shoulders and feet, and finally in the whole body.

g. Mirroring – Divide the group into pairs. In each pair, there is one leader and one follower. They are facing each other. The leader begins and the follower moves *exactly as the leader does.* Coach the leaders to do slow movements. Reverse roles.

3. *I have a small classroom, and there are no other large rooms in the synagogue building available during my class time. Yet, I want to get the kids moving! Any suggestions?*
Try any of the following:
   a. Have students move in their chairs.
   b. Have students stand in place, and emphasize upper body and torso movement rather than "traveling" movement.
   c. Alternate small groups moving at one time while the others watch.
   d. Move chairs and/or tables to make space.
   e. Go outside and do movement activities.
   f. Give students dance/movement "homework" to try at home or in any space they find comfortable. Later, share experiences (either verbally or physically in class).

4. *Once I get the class up and moving about, how do I keep control over the group?*
It's important to establish guidelines and set clear parameters from the very beginning. Get a "contract" from the group regarding important safety rules such as: no one will hit, or hurt another person; and no one will attempt movement that is unsafe (i.e., jumping off of a shaky table). It is normal for a group to get excited; however, wild or crazy behavior is not appropriate. When someone is acting out of control or disruptive ask the person to stop and watch on the sidelines until he/she is calmed down. Know your class and if doing things in pairs, assign partners so that two disruptive kids aren't working together. If you have a large class, have an assistant with you when leading movement activities. Have an agreed upon signal or word to quiet the group and stop activity. Establish this from the very beginning.

5. *How do I strike the right balance between structure to a movement activity and freedom to improvise?*
Meaningful improvisation grows out of very specific instructions and a structure. Asking a beginning group to improvise without giving them movement tools is not a good idea, and the results are usually poor. Even very advanced dancers want clearly defined parameters for improvisational movement. In the Developed Movement Sessions in this chapter, the motivating movement section provides the tools for the dance improvisation. Providing structure to a movement activity is not the same as stifling creative responses. A judgmental attitude, heavy criticism, or making fun of someone is what hinders freedom to improvise.

6. *At the end of the day, all the students get together for some community activity, such as singing. Can a large group participate in creative movement activity in meaningful ways?*
Yes! Movement is a wonderful activity to help engender a feeling of community because physicalizing an idea together generates enthusiasm for learning. Also, like singing, all ages can participate in meaningful ways. If you have a large group, plan carefully, making sure that the space is large enough so that everyone can participate. Also, plan your instructions so that they will be understandable to children of all ages. Begin simply, with clapping, for example, then expand the movement idea into torso and upper body. Finally, if desired, expand into traveling movement after giving clear instructions about "traffic patterns."

7. *I have some boys in my class who can get wild and are not always open to new experiences. Any ideas on how to reach them using creative movement activities?*
Grabbing their attention with an idea targeted at their interests is essential. Once they become fascinated with an idea, their energy can be channeled into wonderfully creative movement. Relating to the interest of both boys and girls in sports is one way to begin.

For example, start with the verse from Torah about Jacob wrestling with a man (Genesis 32:25). Explore how real wrestling holds can motivate movement by doing them with an imaginary person, or in very slow motion. Develop this activity by relating this wrestling movement to Jacob.

Occasionally, there will be a child, boy or girl, who is simply very reluctant to get involved. Ask the child to play the drum or any other percussive instrument so that while not moving he/she is involved with the class and focused on the activity.

8. *How can I encourage an awkward or self-conscious student to feel comfortable during movement activities?*
Here are some suggestions: Have the student begin with small movements, such as using arms only. Reinforce his/her movements by noting, praising, and repeating a specific move or shape he/she is making. Ask the other students to try the same movement (which sends the message to the student that his/her movement is good enough for everyone to try). Ask the student to make the movement a little bigger and/or to try the same movement using other body parts. Then, ask the student to make the movement as big as possible — covering as much space as he/she can.

Another idea: Have student "shadow" another student's movements. The whole class should be paired into "movers" and "shadows" so that the one student doesn't feel singled out. The shadows can even be encouraged to exaggerate the movers' movements. When it seems the student is more comfortable, have the pairs switch roles. Especially when the student is one of the movers, make sure the movement assignment is simple and straightforward. As confidence builds, movement assignments can become more complicated.

As mentioned in the answer to the previous question, you may want to ask a very reluctant child to play accompaniment for the movement activity as a way of involving him/her.

MOVEMENT CONCEPTS APPLIED TO THE CURRICULUM

When we think in movement concepts, the range of possibilities for insightful curriculum development is limitless. To illustrate our point we will show how to explore *holiday and life cycle events* through *rhythm*; *heroes and heroines* (from the Bible and beyond) through *movement quality/style*; *history, language, and culture* through *spatial elements*; and *mitzvot* through *movement that gathers in and opens out*. For purposes of this chapter, we have applied one movement concept to one area of curriculum. We encourage you to go beyond what we begin with here. Apply rhythm to history, different movement qualities to biblical characters, gathering and opening movement to holidays, and so on. This is only the beginning!

Holidays and Life Cycle Events through Rhythm

"In the beginning was noise, and noise begat rhythm and rhythm begat everything else"[1] Rhythm is a part of each of us and essential for our very existence. The way we breathe, from restful to panting and of course our heartbeat have rhythmic patterns. In this section we look at how rhythm can be an exciting source of inspiration. Motivation for movement may come from the rhythm of our own bodies, the rhythm of music, poetry, a single word, or the rhythm of specific activities. Some characteristics of rhythm are: (a) Rhythm is usually repetitious with an underlying pulse, beat or meter; (b) Rhythm has a tempo (fast or slow) and/or changes of tempo; (c) Rhythm has accents or stresses; and (d) A given note or movement has a specific duration.

Quickies for Life Cycle Events and Holidays through Rhythm

1. Shofar sounds – Put their rhythmic pattern into movement.
2. Preparing for Shabbat – Clap a pattern of six beats with a rest or no clap on seven. Now walk this pattern. Take it into busy movement for 5 beats/or measures, 1 beat of transition, and 1 beat of restful movement.
3. Be *challah* dough – Be kneaded according to rhythm of emotions of a person preparing for Shabbat.

4. Pound nails (imagine it or actually do it) into *sukkah* in rhythm that reflects *z'man simchataynu* (time of our rejoicing). Pound with different body parts. Make a happy rhythm. Also wave the *lulav* in rhythm.
5. Jewish agricultural holidays – Explore the rhythms of planting and harvesting and relate them to the Jewish agricultural holidays.
6. A family is gathered together to celebrate a Bat/Bar Mitzvah. Experiment with the different tempos that each person moves in as they celebrate, e.g., quick darting of a child, slow steady proud walk of a great-grandfather, nervous walk of the Bar or Bat Mitzvah before the ceremony and confident walk afterwards.
7. At the beginning of the wedding service, the bride circles the groom 3 or 7 times. At the end of the ceremony the groom stomps on a glass. Expand the circling and/or stomping into a rhythmic pattern that reveals the different emotions of the moment.
8. Morning prayer. Each morning, as we get up, there is a prayer we recite thanking God for our breath. Pretend you are just waking up and are conscious of your breathing. Let the breathing rhythm take you into some simple stretching movements.

Two Developed Movement Sessions
Preparing for Bat/Bar Mitzvah: A Rhythmic Exploration
Introduction

Today, in most communities, the Bar/Bat Mitzvah ceremony is one that has been prepared for carefully. From first attendance at age five or six in religious school to the intensive few months prior to the ceremony, the participant has encountered a number of different teachers. Each teacher guides in a unique way, and it is possible to look at the learning from a rhythmic point of view. For example, maybe the teacher emphasizes repetition, with the student repeating a phrase over and over. Perhaps the teacher introduces a theme, then allows the student to expand on it in the student's own way. The teacher/student relationship can be explored through movement using rhythm as the jumping off point.

EXPLORE THE TEACHER-STUDENT RELATIONSHIP THROUGH MOVEMENT.

Motivating Movement
1. In a circle, have each person clap his/her name. The group responds by repeating the clapping of the name. After everyone has had a turn clapping, repeat the activity by having each person move his/her whole body to the rhythm of his/her name and with the group repeating the movement.
2. Have the group explore movement that shows "impatience." Particularly coach the group to do quick short rhythmic movement in a hurried manner. Contrast this by exploring "patience" — movement that is slow, with comfortable pauses and a relaxing manner.

Movement Improvisation

Divide into pairs. One person is the teacher and the other is the student. Have the pairs improvise the learning situation with at least three different learning styles in the improvisation. An example of three might be: the pair begins with repetition with the "teacher" doing a movement pattern and the "student" repeating it. Next, they explore question and answer with the "teacher" dancing the rhythm of a short question and the "student" dancing a long detailed rhythmic answer. They end with the "teacher" dancing a hard long question and waiting patiently for the answer, and the "student" taking his/her time to develop a dancing answer. Have the pairs change parts so each person gets to experience being both teacher and student.

Making Connections

Ask students about teachers who have made important contributions to their lives. Ask in what way the teacher made an impact. Encourage students to express their opinions on teaching styles and how they learn most effectively. Discuss that learning different kinds of things may require different styles of teaching. Talk about how the student can impact the teacher's style of teaching.

Beyond the Gragger: A Purim Rendition of Esther
Introduction

It is traditional to read *Megillat Esther* (the Scroll of Esther) on Purim. One of the most memorable and engaging customs of this celebratory ritual is the noise made with a *gragger* when the name of Haman is mentioned. By taking this custom and expanding upon it — introducing more sounds and adding movements — the reading of Esther becomes an even more involving activity.

Motivating Movement
1. Have students go across the floor in pairs or triplets practicing various walks: that of a hero or heroine (confident and steady), a villain (sneaky and irregular), a king (proud and grand), a new queen (tentativeness mixed with growing confidence).
2. Have students stand in a wide circle ready to do any kind of movement in place. Have several instruments ready to use, such as a triangle, a drum, your clapping hands, a keyboard or xylophone, and so on. As the students hear you play different rhythms on different instruments, they should reflect what they hear by responding in movement. Change instruments and rhythms frequently.

Movement Improvisation
With the students, come up with different rhythms on different instruments with associated movement patterns for each of the people in the story of Esther. For example, use the *gragger* for Haman (perhaps, three fast whipping twists followed by two slow plotting twists), triangle for Esther (a light, majestic walk on tiptoes with head looking from side to side), clapping for Mordecai (two low walks forward, a careful jump like a burst of information, two walks backwards). Now read the story of Esther, either from the Bible or an abridged version. When the name of a character is mentioned, play the rhythm of the instrument and do the rhythmic movement associated with the character.

Making Connections
Ask students if they can think of what rhythms and rhythmic movements might be associated with characters significant to other Jewish holidays (for example, Moses at Passover and Shavuot, Judah Maccabee at Chanukah, the Israelites at Sukkot). How might the rhythms change at various times (for example, Moses approaching Pharaoh versus Moses leading the Israelites across the Sea of Reeds to freedom). Ask them what rhythms they associate with their own feelings at different holidays during the year. If there is interest, have students choreograph different rhythmic movements for each holiday, either individually or in groups, based on their own feelings and experiences.

Heroes and Heroines through Movement Quality/Style

When we use the term "quality of movement" we are referring to the essential characteristic of the movement. This is determined by "the amount of effort and the way the energy is released."[2] There are four basic qualities of movement.[3] They are: (1) swinging – movement which goes back and forth or side to side in an even rhythm; (2) percussive – sudden explosive release of energy. When it is quick and short, we may refer to it as staccato; (3) sustained – a steady even release of energy; and (4) collapsing – giving into gravity or falling.

Quickies for Heroes and Heroines through Movement Quality

1. Sarah laughing – Explore staccato/percussive and collapsing movement, illustrating her reaction to the messengers.
2. Contrast how Jacob and Esau might move — Esau, the hunter, with percussive movement and Jacob, who is gentler, with more sustained or swinging movement.
3. Moses and Pharaoh meet. Moses demands, "Let My People Go." Pharaoh refuses. Show the way each character moves in this encounter.
4. Miriam and the women celebrated the new freedom of the children of Israel after the crossing of the sea. Using primarily swinging movement, improvise what their dance of celebration might have been. (Option: Choose a "*Mi Kamochah*" setting to accompany this.)
5. Moses was often upset with the actions of the children of Israel as he guided them through the desert. Sometimes his response was "he fell on his face" (Numbers 16:4). Explore how he might have fallen (collapsing movement).
6. Prophets (Jonah, Jeremiah) waver about their role as prophets — swing back and forth between wanting to follow God's will and wanting to escape.

7. As Hillel, say your own explanations of Judaism while standing on one foot (sustained movement). Students write definitions beforehand without knowing they will read them while standing on one foot. Then read what Hillel said while all stand on one foot.[4]
8. Golda Meir, traveling about, calling out plea to Jews around the world (sustained and percussive movement) to help contribute to efforts to fight to establish State of Israel.

Two Developed Movement Sessions
Deborah: Prophetess and Judge
Introduction

Deborah was a unique woman in the Bible. As prophetess and judge, she achieved greatness based on her own merits. "She used to sit under the palm tree of Deborah . . . and the Israelites would come to her for judgment" (Judges 4:4). In addition, she led the Israelites in war to a victory over enemies led by Sisera, who eventually was killed by a woman named Yael. The following activity will guide students in using various movement qualities in an exploration of who Deborah was.

Motivating Movement
1. Have students practice sustained movements by imagining they are in water. First, have them move their arms as if they are under water. Next, have them walk as if they are walking through water. Finally, have them imagine they are boneless water creatures moving their whole bodies in smooth and sustained movement.
2. Share with students the definition given for percussive movement — sudden explosive release of energy. Have students improvise possibilities for percussive movements. Choose some of the percussive movements created by the students. String several (up to 8 or 10) of the movements together for everyone to learn. Start by doing the same string of movements gently. Repeat several times until the string of percussive movements is as explosive as possible.

Movement Improvisation

Divide group into pairs. Together, each pair represents Deborah. Have each person in the pair decide who will depict one of two prominent aspects of Deborah — as judge or as leader in battle. Have the pairs improvise duets in which Deborah the Judge performs sustained movements under the tree as she listens to people, and Deborah the leader in battle performs percussive movements.

Making Connections

Talk about how Deborah's qualities helped her achieve what she did. How did the two aspects of Deborah's personality explored in the improvisation relate to each other? Are there other qualities about Deborah that were significant? How would one portray other qualities in movement? Name other Jewish heroes and heroines students have studied. Ask them to name two prominent roles or qualities exhibited by the heroes or heroines named. Have the students name two qualities or roles that best describe themselves, and how these qualities or roles relate to each other.

Elijah: A Whirlwind of Surprises
Introduction

Elijah was a prophet in Israel in the ninth century B.C.E.[5] In both the biblical account, and in the number of folktales that have developed about him through the ages, Elijah appears at just the right moment, helps someone in need, and then disappears again. In fact, in his final dramatic exit in the Bible, he ascends to heaven in a whirlwind on a chariot of fire. Elijah is very important to us today as a symbolic figure. We remember him each year at our *Seder* with a cup of wine and by opening the door so that he may enter our homes and hearts — a reminder always to be hospitable and not to judge people by their appearance. A beggar might just be Elijah in disguise.

Motivating Movement
1. Experiment with swinging movement such as: the arms swinging back and forth and side to side, a leg making a swing movement, and step skip with the arms swinging upward on the skip. Add the image of the wind as the group explores swinging movement. Finish with the students creating swinging phrases covering space as if the wind is carrying them.
2. Standing in a circle, begin with one person and pass a blessing around the group using a sustained movement quality. In other

words, the first person blesses the person on his/her right using sustained gestures. That person then dances a blessing to the person next to him/her. Each person should be encouraged to find his/her own way to dance the blessing.
3. Continuing to stand in a circle, have the group imagine that they have just seen someone act in a very stingy way in the center of the circle (no one is actually in the center, the person and act are imaginary). Go around the circle and have one person after another do a strong percussive movement expressing displeasure at the stingy act.

Movement Improvisation

Everyone in the group is to create a solo dance about Elijah. Divide the room in half. Designate one area as "above" (or where Elijah ascended in his fiery chariot) and the other space as our modern world. Ask all participants to begin in the area designated as "above" and to imagine that they are looking down on earth seeing how people act. Perhaps they "bless" or "curse" a person from above, or they make a sudden whirlwind movement over to the area designated as "the modern world" and take on a disguise (beggar, traveler) and interact with an imagined modern person by blessing or cursing the person. When their imaginary interaction is over, they quickly return to the other part of the room. Encourage them to make several journeys back and forth. Using music, particularly clarinet Klezmer music,6 is fun for this improvisation. (This is an advanced improvisation. An alternative simplified improvisation is to divide the group in pairs. One person is Elijah and the other person is someone in need. Elijah sees the person in need from a distance, appears suddenly beside the person, blesses and helps the person, and quickly leaves.)

Making Connections

Discuss the current problem of homelessness. Ask students to share their reactions to seeing people begging for food and money in the street or watching television reports of people who don't have food or a place to live. What can they do to help in their own community? Make a list of ways they can be like Elijah.

History, Language, and Culture through Spatial Elements

Space is the visual dimension or design that is a result of the way the body moves through a certain defined area. Spatial elements include:
1. Amount of space covered. Is the movement mainly in one place or does it cover a lot of ground?
2. Direction – Forward, backward, sideways, diagonal.
3. Level – moving on the ground, close to the ground, standing level, or off the ground.
4. The pattern or design in space we make as we cover space – a circle, straight line, zigzag pattern.
5. The shape which the body makes while moving – symmetrical and asymmetrical, curved or angular.

Quickies for History, Language, and Culture through Spacial Elements
1. Hebrew Letters. Pretend your feet have ink on them, and on the floor in the front of the classroom is a big paper sheet. Make a Hebrew letter with your feet as if creating the first Hebrew letter. Pose the question, "What letter do you think God created first?" Relate to the *midrash* on this issue (*Beresheet Rabbah* 1).
2. Geography of Israel. The space is a map of Israel. Select two different cities or places on the map and move between them in ways that reflect their "personality."
3. Move along footprints illustrating *the wandering of Jews*. Choose a typical path that a person might have followed such as moving first northeast, then south, and finally settling in the east.
4. "Knots."7 In circle grab right hands (not someone next to you); then grab left hands (not the same person grabbed with right hands). "Untie" knot without breaking hands. Everyone needs to duck under and climb over a lot of tangled hands. Relate this to how people spoke all kinds of languages and came from many different cultures during the First and Second Aliyah to Israel. Though there were many "knots" to unwind in order to absorb so many new immigrants, the idea that all Jews are part of one unbroken community remained strong. There are now people from many different cultures living together in Israel.

5. Jew hidden by righteous Gentile during Holocaust. Experience moving in a big space which gets smaller and smaller until it is a space the size of a closet, cave, or attic.
6. Creation. Explore how light enters the universe. Enter space — in a burst (covering much space quickly, as a thin line, as a zigzag bolt, etc.).
7. Assume the shapes of Hebrew letters with your body individually and/or in pairs.
8. Spanish Expulsion of 1492. When the Jews were forced to leave Spain in 1492, they migrated to other lands. We have many examples of love songs from this Diaspora in which the longing for a distant lover is a metaphor for longing for Spain. Dance this longing paying attention to focus and direction.

Two Developed Movement Sessions
Retracing an Immigrant's Journey
Introduction

Jews have been immigrants time after time from the very beginning of Jewish history. After the Fall of the Second Temple, many Jews emigrated to Babylonia. In Medieval times, Jews moved to new places in order to avoid some of the horrors of the Crusades. Jews emigrated to new places during the Spanish Inquisition. During the last century, many Jews emigrated to Israel and the United States during an era of pogroms, and before and after the Holocaust. Most of our more direct Jewish ancestors came to the United States during the last 100 years.

Motivating Movement
1. Have students imagine the whole floor is a giant map of the world. Ask them to think of two places. Tell everyone to go to one of the two locations they have in mind. Then ask them to go to the second location. Have students share where they traveled to and from. Repeat (with the same or two different locations), this time asking students to travel between the two locations in different ways — on a supersonic jet, walking with a baby on their backs, hurriedly, leisurely, and so on.
2. Ask students how they felt when (or to imagine how they would feel if) they moved to a completely new place. Have them come up with at least three different emotions, either individually or as a group. Then, prepare students to travel across the room in pairs or triplets. Ask them to express, as they move, the emotions they came up with, going back and forth between the emotions as they feel is appropriate.

Movement Improvisation

Have the group imagine an immigrant's journey either to Israel or to the U.S. or Canada, for example, how grandparents may have traveled from Russia to the United States around 1910. Begin by making a map of the journey on a large piece of paper. Get as detailed as possible and add descriptive words. Here is one example: Grandfather has to wait here for two years for papers to be processed. Translate into movement in place which alternates between being slow/careful and being nervous to signify this time period. Another example: The journey on the ship across the ocean is crowded, the waters are rough, and sickness is prevalent. Translate into pacing movement which begins strongly and gradually becomes weak. After the journey has been mapped out satisfactorily, have students take the journey as described and translated into movement.

Making Connections

Ask how students felt taking the journey. What do they think would be most difficult and what most exciting about being a new immigrant? Share stories about how their own ancestors came to this country. How would they have dealt with some of the issues their immigrant ancestors would have faced?

Creating Movement to a Holocaust Poem
Introduction

During the Holocaust, children and young adults in the concentration camp of Terezin expressed their feelings in poetry. One of the most stirring poems is called "I Never Saw Another Butterfly."[8] Read the poem to the group.

Motivating Movement
1. Ask students to draw an imaginary circle around themselves no bigger than a foot from their body. They are only allowed to move in this limited space. Ask them to move in the space as if they are frustrated by being in such a small area and want to cover lots of space but are unable to do so. Tell them the space has gotten even small-

er. Ask them to show what happens to their movement as they have less space.
2. Make sure you are in a large open space for this part of the activity. If you have a big group, divide it into several sections. Tell students to imagine the room is a large meadow and they are to run, turn, spin, leap, and jump covering as much space as possible in a free enthusiastic manner.
3. If possible, pass out pictures or see a short video excerpt of butterflies. Ask the students to pretend they are butterflies. Suggest that their arms are butterfly wings. Ask them to make fluttering and gliding movements with their arms. Ask them to be the butterfly resting on a flower and then contrast this with the butterfly freely moving around a meadow.

Movement Improvisation

Everyone pretends to be the young poet who wrote "I Never Saw Another Butterfly." They are to portray the words and emotions. Point out the contrast in the poem: the first part describes the butterfly moving freely, and perhaps the young poet is watching it or trying to catch it. The second part speaks of being "penned up inside this ghetto." Encourage the students to move freely covering a lot of space during the first part, contrasted with limited movement in a small space for the second part.

Making Connections

Talk about the fact that the children in concentration camps were not just "statistics or numbers." Discuss the different kinds of feeling they might have had. Point out that in spite of how horrible their situation was, they were still often able to have optimistic and positive thoughts. Share other examples with them, such as passages from *The Diary of Anne Frank*. Ask how these children's feelings were similar to feelings students in the class might have had.

Mitzvot through Movement that Gathers in and Opens out[9]

By referring to movement as gathering in or opening out we mean movement on the horizontal axis, inward and outward as contrasted with the vertical axis of moving up and down. An inward movement starts with a reach of one of the limbs and pulls into the body, while an outward movement begins close to the body's center and reaches outward.

Quickies for Mitzvot through Movement that Gathers in and Opens out

1. *Tzedakah*. Put on music and ask each person to do movement that represents giving *tzedakah*. Work on very generous movement that opens out.
2. Leaving the Gleanings – *Peah*, *Leket*, and *Shich'chah*. Half the group do opening movement depicting planting and large gathering/harvesting movements. Then, the other half does smaller gathering/harvesting movements.
3. *Bikur Cholim* – Visiting the Sick. There is the saying that visiting the sick removes 1/60th of a person's illness. Create movements that "gather" illness away from a person.
4. Comforting Mourners. One person be a mourner, one be a comforter. The comforter uses opening comforting movement; the mourner draws and gathers the comforting energy into him/herself.
5. Loving the Proselyte – *Ahavat HaGer*. Use welcoming movement going backwards leading a newcomer into a room/part of room.
6. Loving God – *Kiddush HaShem*. Come up with movements of receiving love as expressed in the *Ahavah Rabbah* prayer which tells of God's love for us; and movements of giving love as expressed in the *V'ahavta* prayer which tells us to love God with all our hearts, all our souls, and all our might.
7. Imagine you are a homeless person on the streets in an urban area. Find different ways to ask for help.
8. Imagine you are very discouraged and unhappy. You feel better by doing gathering movements into yourself. These movements represent receiving the gifts/help of others.

Two Developed Sessions
Abraham Welcomes Guests
Introduction

Share the following from Torah about Abraham when God appeared to him by the terebinths of Mamre: "Looking up, he saw three men standing near him. As soon as he saw them, he ran . . . to greet them . . . and said, 'Let a little water be brought; bathe your feet and recline under the tree. And let me fetch a morsel of bread that you may refresh yourselves . . .'" (Genesis 18:2).

Motivating Movement
Practice movement that opens out:
1. Have students imagine that a giant bowl of food is in front of them. They must dip into the bowl and serve children sitting close by. Have them dip and serve using various body parts (elbows, knees, hips, heads . . .).
2. Have students imagine they are part of a Red Cross unit dispatched in a war torn area where there are many starving individuals. They must distribute large quantities of food as quickly as possible to as many people as possible. Have them try to use as much of their bodies as they can. Remind students that they are distributing food to *people*, and that though they must distribute the food quickly, they must try to do so in a dignified manner.

Movement Improvisation
Jewish tradition understands the three "men" who visit Abraham to be angels, some sort of messengers from God. They should be served in the most elevated way. Have students come up with a series of very refined opening out movement phrases. (Remind students of movements they came up with and can refine from the Motivating Movement section.) Coach students to go beyond opening movements which are pantomimed arm gestures, and to come up with opening movement which travels. When students have come up with and precisely learned an eight to ten movement phrase, have them imagine they are Abraham. Have them repeat the phrase several times, preserving the precision and elegance demanded by the nature of the guests (angels!), but speeding them up to reflect Abraham's eagerness to fulfill the *mitzvah* of hospitality, *Hachnasat Orchim*.

DANCE THE EIGHT LEVELS OF CHARITY.

Making Connections
Share reactions to the movement experience. Did being Abraham come naturally to them?

Discuss hospitality, receiving guests — *Hachnasat Orchim*. What experiences have the students had hosting guests and being guests? What makes a guest truly feel welcome? Why is it important to be welcoming?

The Ladder of Charity: A Dance Interpretation
Introduction
Maimonides, perhaps the greatest scholar of all time, lived from 1135 to 1204. Among his outstanding contributions to Jewish thought is the idea that there are levels of *tzedakah*.[10] He identified eight such levels and placed them in an order. Going from the highest to the lowest, they are: (1) to help a person become self-sufficient; (2) when the person giving doesn't know the person receiving, and when the person receiving doesn't know who gave; (3) the giver knows the receiver, but the person receiving doesn't know the giver; (4) the giver doesn't know the receiver, but the person receiving knows the giver; (5) a direct donation to the hand of the needy (given without being asked); (6) a direct donation of sufficient size (given after being asked); (7) a direct donation of small size, given cheerfully (after being asked); and (8) a direct, small donation given grudgingly (after being asked).

Motivating Movement
1. Divide the class into pairs. Ask each pair to create a sculpture in which one person, in need, is receiving something from another person who is willing to give. Have the group share the different poses with each other.
2. Play music that is easy and fun to move to. Ask the students to move from one side of the room to the other in the following way: (1) giving away *as many as possible* imaginary $100 bills, (2) gathering up an endless supply of $100 bills, (3) holding on tightly to their last $100, (4) selectively giving away a last $100, and (5) graciously receiving this last $100. Music is important to add a more imaginative element to this exercise. Any lively instrumental selection from jazz to classical will work for this. Coach the students to be imaginative in their movement adding turns, jumps, and stops to their phrases.

Movement Improvisation

Divide the class into eight groups. Pairs or trios are fine. Assign each group to portray one of the rungs of the ladder. They are to find three poses that illustrate their assignment. After they have their three poses, they are to create transition phrases that link the poses together. Have them practice their three poses with linking transition movement several times until they can confidently perform them. When all the groups have completed the task, have them share with the whole class. If you have a class smaller than sixteen, divide into four groups and give each group two "rungs of the ladder" to illustrate.

Making Connections

Lead a discussion during which the group takes each of the rungs of the ladder and comes up with real life examples that they have seen, participated in or know about.[11]

CONCLUSION

Creative movement activities generate an excitement and freshness to the curriculum. We have provided you with some solid tools with which to work as you begin to incorporate movement into the classroom. You have ways to address the questions you may have as you launch into this exciting teaching technique. You have movement principles which, as you apply them, will enrich participants and challenge them to consider approaching ideas in completely new ways. And, most importantly, you have many examples of activities, both quick and expanded, which are ready for you to use as early as your next class!

If you are new to movement activities, start with one of the Quickies in this chapter that really appealed to you and try it. Before you know it, you will be thinking up lots of movement ideas on your own. Most important, know that while we have provided many suggestions in this chapter, there are no hard and fast rules or magic lesson plans. Each class is different and each leader's background and style are unique.

Keep a pioneering spirit! Your willingness to plunge in and be adventuresome is the first step in getting started. We encourage you to think about the curriculum in ways that lend themselves to movement activities. Focusing on the rhythm of life cycle events and holidays, the spacial dimensions of history, the qualities of our heroes and heroines, and the gathering or giving of *tzedakah* enables us to discover new insights in familiar material. These movement activities can take on a spiritual dimension as you and your students learn more about yourselves, your community, your heritage, and God.

JoAnne Tucker is the artistic director and choreographer of The Avodah Dance Ensemble. She studied dance at The Juilliard School, and has a Ph.D. in creative dramatics and movement from the University of Wisconsin. JoAnne leads workshops on the use of movement in Jewish education and on *midrash*. She is the author of *Creative Movement for a Song* and co-author of *Torah in Motion: Creating Dance Midrash* (A.R.E.)

Susan Freeman was ordained at Hebrew Union College-Jewish Institute of Religion in New York. She serves as Educational Director of Congregation B'nai Israel in Northampton, Massachusetts. She is co-author of *Torah in Motion: Creating Dance Midrash* (A.R.E.), and is a former member of The Avodah Dance Ensemble.

NOTES

1. *Drumming at the Edge of Magic* by Mickey Hart with Jay Stevens, p. 231.
2. *Moving from Within* by Hawkins, p. 61.
3. *Dance: A Creative Art Experience* by H'Doubler, pp. 81-82.
4. A heathen once came before the sage Shammai and said: "I will convert to Judaism if you will teach me all the Torah while standing on one foot. Shammai pushed the man away, telling him he had no time for such foolishness. The man went to see Hillel and repeated his request. Hillel said to him, "What is hateful to you, do not do to your neighbor. That is the whole Torah. The rest is commentary — go and learn it." (*Shabbat* 31a)
5. Suggested reading: *Tales of Elijah the Prophet* by Penninah Schram.
6. Suggested music: Section entitled "*Nigun*" on side 2 of *The Magic of Klezmer* by Giora Feidman, Rom Productions, 101.
7. "Knots" may be found in *New Games*, Andrew Fluegleman, ed. (Tiburon, CA: The Headlands Press, and New York: Doubleday and Company, Ltd., 1976), p. 69. It is adapted here with the addition of Jewish content.
8. This poem can be found in *I Never Saw Another Butterfly*, Hana Volavkova, ed.
9. For ideas on *mitzvot*, see *Teaching Mitzvot* by Barbara Binder Kadden and Bruce Kadden, and *Tzedakah, Gemilut Chasadim and Ahavah: A Manual for World Repair* by Joel Lurie Grishaver and Beth Huppin.
10. See *Tzedakah, Gemilut Chasadim and Ahavah*, p. 17.
11. See *Tzedakah, Gemilut Chasadim and Ahavah* for additional ideas.

BIBLIOGRAPHY

Fluegleman, Andrew, ed. *New Games*. Tiburon, CA: The Headlands Press, and New York: Doubleday and Company, Ltd., 1976.

Grishaver, Joel Lurie, and Huppin, Beth. *Tzedakah, Gemilut Chasadim and Ahavah: A Manual for World Repair*. Denver: A.R.E. Publishing Inc., 1983.

Hart, Mickey, with Jay Stevens. *Drumming at the Edge of Magic*. San Francisco: Harper, 1990.

Hawkins, Alma M. *Moving from Within: A New Method for Making Dance*. Pennington, NJ: a cappella Books, 1991.

H'Doubler, Margaret N. *Dance: A Creative Art Experience*. Madison: University of Wisconsin Press, 1966.

Humphrey, Doris. *The Art of Making Dances*. New York: Random House, 1959.

Kadden, Barbara Binder, and Bruce Kadden. *Teaching Mitzvot: Concepts, Values, and Activities*. Denver: A.R.E. Publishing, Inc., 1988.

Klagsbrun, Francine. *Voices of Wisdom*. New York: Pantheon Books, 1980.

Mettler, Barbara. *Materials of Dance as a Creative Art Activity*. Tucson, AZ: Mettler Studios Inc., 1960. (Available directly from Mettler Studios, 3131 N. Cherry Ave., Tucson, AZ 85719)

———. *Dance as an Element of Life*. Tucson, AZ: Mettler Studios Inc., 1985. (Also available from Mettler Studios)

Milgram, Jo. *Handmade Midrash*. Philadelphia: The Jewish Publication Society, 1992.

Morgenroth, Joyce. *Dance Improvisation*. Pittsburgh: University of Pittsburgh Press, 1987.

Schram, Penninah. *Tales of Elijah the Prophet*. Northvale, NJ: Jason Aronson Inc., 1991.

Tucker, JoAnne. *Creative Movement for a Song: Activities for Young Children*. Denver: A.R.E. Publishing, Inc., 1993.

Tucker, JoAnne, and Susan Freeman. *Torah in Motion: Creating Dance Midrash*. Denver: A.R.E. Publishing, Inc., 1990.

Volavkova, Hana, ed. *I Never Saw Another Butterfly*. New York: Schocken Books, 1979.

SUPPORTS FOR THE TEACHER

CHAPTER THIRTY-ONE

USING THE LIBRARY CREATIVELY AS A DOOR TO THE FUTURE

Barbara Y. Leff

As you teach children about Judaism, do you create lessons for them which peak their curiosity — to the point where they want to find out more for themselves? Do you encourage your students in the lifelong habit of reading Judaica and using a Jewish library as the learning place for being inquisitive about Jews and Judaism? Do *you* use the library — for yourself and as a role model for your students? This chapter represents a challenge to you to encourage students to continue the process which you start — to seek Jewish information so that your students will grow up to become informed Jewish adults.

This chapter will help Jewish teachers understand what to expect from a Jewish library and a librarian. If your library is less than standard and you must "make do," this chapter will also help you . . . to help yourself and your students.

I have made the following observations about students in a supplemental school:

1. Students who read Jewish books are frequently the better students. Students who start to read Jewish books at a young age continue to do so.
2. Students are overwhelmed by a Jewish library until the books become familiar. They need guidance and continuous exposure to find the "right" books — the ones that interest them. Those who make one or more poor choices tend to stay away from Jewish books altogether.
3. Students seek information to satisfy curiosity. When teachers and parents hand down information as "what you need to know" about Jewish holidays and other curricular subjects, the individual and independent challenge to seek for themselves is greatly reduced or eliminated.
4. Students do *not* automatically apply learned research skills to a Jewish library; many need help to translate the process from secular to Judaica. Example: Students easily research Abraham Lincoln, but few realize that the same skills apply to research Golda Meir. They think that a Jewish library is "different."
5. Students cannot learn how to use a Jewish library in a few sessions. Jewish "information literacy" takes years to acquire because the library is a "process" as well as a "place" in a school. When students learn the *process*, are exposed to specialized Judaica resources in all formats, and feel comfortable in the *place*, many return; they purposely select Jewish research topics in high school and college, and they teach their children.

ACCESS TO A LIBRARY COLLECTION

Do you have a library in your school? If yes, explore it — to save you time and effort, to keep you current, to promote creativity, and to serve your students! If no, then ask, even insist, that your school create one. If all teachers want one, a school will most often try to comply. "Increased funding for school resource centers affects teaching and learning in the school."[1]

The quality of the library does not depend on location but rather on content, access, and use. Some combination of the next two paragraphs will effectively give you access to the resources you need, where and when you need them:

One-stop Selection Center

If all library material and equipment resources are in a central location, skip to the next section.

If not, read on. To be able to select the BEST resources for a lesson rather than the most expedient, request that all resources and equipment be gathered in one place instead of your having to run to two or more locations to find things. The school should try to collect in one room all library materials, including the following: books and curricular materials from the Director of Education's office, reference books from the Rabbi's office, audiovisual materials and equipment from closets, and textbooks and other books from various classrooms and homes, as well as a good computer. This will be the start of an excellent, convenient, multi-media resource center library that is accessible to everyone at all times.

> STUDENTS ARE DRAWN TO COMPUTERS LIKE TO MAGIC.

One-stop Selection Catalog

If the gathering of all materials and equipment is not feasible because of space or funding, then request an alternative: a detailed library catalog, following national library standards, in a central location. The catalog should include *all* school and institutional resources and indicate on site and off site locations for each item. This inventory will, in itself, be a useful and often used resource for everyone.

KINDS OF LIBRARY RESOURCES

You should expect a library collection to contain Jewish materials in all the formats currently available. The line between print and non-print materials no longer exists. Non-print illustrations are found in printed books; text is read on a computer screen. I view all library materials as interactive, whether people use their own imagination to interact with the words of the story or manipulate computerized interactive media programs. Library materials also include the extensive information files and indexes which can be created and customized for your school needs; they can be the result of a collaboration between librarian, teachers and school. The variety of exciting and interesting library materials are listed in Appendix C.

COMPUTERS IN LIBRARIES

Supplemental schools in the same institution as Jewish day schools have, or will have, computerized libraries because information technology is standard in private schools. Other supplemental schools are beginning to automate as well.

Students are drawn to computers like to magic. They don't need to wait for teachers and librarians to teach them how to find information via computers. They already know or they will play around with a computer until they figure it out. They are moving ahead on their own because so many have home computers.

As educators, we need to build on this. If we encourage students to interact with computers in our Jewish library, then the Jewish component will become a part of their everyday home life with their families.

As of this writing, we can retrieve and use Jewish information resources via computer software, CD-ROM discs, video (laser) discs, interactive media programs, and networks. We can access off site Jewish databases, and secular databases with Jewish information, and "talk" to Judaica news groups, all via telecommunications software and modems. Classes are part of global communities and students communicate worldwide about Judaism via the Internet, electronic bulletin boards, etc. This *information age* will spawn many, many more means of accessing Jewish electronic resources and networks.[2]

If your library does not yet have computers and you have limited computer knowledge, then you may be overwhelmed by all that is happening. Don't be afraid to try it. Go slowly. Visit a Jewish day school library, a local private or public school library, or a college with an educational resource center; they will give you hands-on experience. You will discover through this visit what is available and how useful it will be for you. Remind yourself that you are a role model for your students; if they are using computers, you need to learn to use them, too.

LIBRARY CATALOG

A library catalog unlocks the door to the location of items both on and off site. If your library catalog is not up-to-date, request that it become so. There are two options for catalogs:
1. Card Catalog. The card catalog has been around for centuries and is familiar to all. Librarians liked them and used them; most students didn't. Most teachers didn't like them either. Card catalogs are time-consuming to create, maintain, and update. Even

with a limited budget, I don't recommend them. They are not efficient, nor are they cost-effective.
2. Online Patron Access Catalog (OPAC). A computer catalog has many more advantages: It is easier to use and provides more successful access and quicker retrieval than a card catalog. Students use libraries more when they are automated. "Students prefer information searches using computer technology to print searches even though they experience difficulty performing this form of information retrieval."[3] Patrons return library items more readily because they know a computer won't forget them. Schools network and share resources via computers. Online catalogs are less time-consuming to create and maintain and very easy to update; they cost the same as card catalogs to set up, but operational costs are less. (Online means you are ON a direct communication LINE to a central data bank; OPAC is the term used worldwide.)

So, if your library has an online catalog, don't be intimated by it! Teachers find these easy to use because they are geared for children. Ask for in-service training so that you can feel comfortable. And do have patience when the computer is "down" (not working) or during the lengthy process when the librarian is converting from a card to a computer format.

LIBRARY STAFF

Do you have a librarian in your school? If yes, then consider yourself fortunate, and enjoy the services a librarian can provide. If no, then again ask, even insist, that your school provide one. Even with limited funds, some money may be forthcoming when teachers collectively request a librarian. "Having a school librarian makes a difference in the amount read."[4]

Convince your Director of Education that a room full of books is overwhelming and static to children and teachers. But, a room full of books *and a librarian*, who knows the contents between the book covers, is inviting and dynamic. The librarian is the human element, organizing and providing access to the materials, and making a *shidduch* between books and readers/users.

The best person to head a Jewish library is a professional librarian with a Jewish Studies background and either (a) a Master's Degree in library and information services and a teaching background, or (b) a library-media certificate (which is granted to teachers with appropriate library training). This prize combination is almost impossible to find; besides, few schools will pay a salary commensurate with such knowledge and skills. Thus, instead, you may meet master-degreed librarians with minimal Judaica and education backgrounds, hard-working para-professionals taking courses, untrained volunteers who love books and learning, etc.

For convenience, the person who is serving in the capacity as a librarian will be referred to as "librarian" in this chapter. But, no matter what a librarian's education or background, don't hesitate to work with them. He or she cares, will work in a professional manner, and will try in every way to find what you want. Get to know this person — his/her background, training, experience, knowledge, areas of expertise, involvement with community. This will help you to know what to expect from him/her.

In most schools, the librarian is on the faculty list, but has a limited role in the school. Help broaden the librarian's scope by suggesting greater use of librarian's considerable talent and knowledge as listed in the Library Services section below.

LIBRARY SERVICES

This section will focus on the many useful services that the librarian can provide for you, the teacher. Feel free to ask what is available. The extent of library services depends upon librarian's knowledge, work load, and hours of assistance from clerks, typists, school secretaries, or volunteers. If your school does not have a librarian, then read the following carefully because you can adapt many of these services to serve yourself. Here are some examples of library
services:
1. Library orientation. Request a library orientation workshop either during faculty orientation or a personal tour. This hands-on instruction in library use will acquaint you with the easiest way to find what you need quickly and efficiently — the library layout and resources, special curricular and enrichment materials, useful reference and elec-

tronic tools. Few people know how to use a library properly. Most teachers do *not* know the depth and breadth of a Jewish library collection. A tour is very satisfying and always sparks wonderful ideas for classroom teaching.

2. Faculty and curriculum consultations. "Students whose library media specialists participate in the instructional process are higher academic achievers."[5] Suggest that librarian be invited to faculty meetings and curriculum planning sessions. As librarian becomes familiar with needs and curricula, he/she will seek new supplemental materials in professional library journals, vendor catalogs, and book stores. Ask librarian to display new items at faculty meetings or in the library. If librarian has a minimal background, all the more reason for that person to be included in your meetings so that he/she can listen and learn.

3. Resource sharing. If your library does not have enough resources, ask librarian to investigate other libraries/resource centers and arrange either inter-library loans or for you to go and borrow what you need. Many libraries already cooperate with other libraries on an informal basis to share resources and save money. Networks and resource sharing will grow as more synagogue and Jewish day school libraries become automated, following national library cataloging standards, known as the MARC record (MAchine Readable Cataloging)

4. Flexible circulation rules. Feel free to request special circulation privileges. Librarian will give you long-term loans on materials not in constant demand, reserves for a specific date and time, and the loan of an uncataloged new item because it is "perfect" for your next lesson.

5. Current awareness services. Ask librarian to keep you informed of new acquisitions — to help you stay current on teaching techniques and topics of interest. For example:
   a. A "What's New in the Library?" list prepared by the library and also posted on the teacher bulletin board and in the library;
   b. Continuing library displays of new books and materials, professional journals, reviews of new materials, and catalogs of publishers, vendors, distributors, booksellers, etc.

6. Selective dissemination of information. Librarian can selectively disseminate information to you about your special interests or needs, e.g., advance preview of new books, new AV materials, reviews, catalogs.

7. Bibliographies and book lists. With adequate advance notice and an online catalog or computer database program, librarian can prepare book lists and bibliographies and update them annually. Also, librarian can contact the Association of Jewish Libraries and Central Cataloging Service for Judaica Libraries for subject bibliographies before spending time preparing one from scratch.

8. Periodical services. Librarian can help you keep current with the following:
   a. Library displays of current subscription periodicals — educational, teachers, students, and general Judaica.
   b. Photocopies of tables of contents of new issues of subscription periodicals — circulated to the Director of Education and also posted on teacher bulletin board and in library.
   c. Circulation to classrooms of multiple copies of student periodicals. (This could be a school budget saver.)

9. Indexing services. See Customized Indexes in Appendix C.

10. Photocopy services/copyright laws. The library and librarian are expected to follow copyright laws — as are you. It is the law and the ethical thing to do, especially in a religious school setting! Do not ask librarian to photocopy books for you or duplicate commercial tapes. [If you were an author, would you want someone freely taking something that you worked so hard to produce?] Ask your librarian for the loan of the current copyright laws so that you will know what is considered "legal."

11. Individualized services. The library responds to the whole child and to the whole teacher; it is not limited to the curriculum. Feel free to ask librarian for books or materials to satisfy your own personal interests, e.g., novels, biographies, archaeology, art, music, cooking, sports. Also, encourage your students to do the same.

12. New library services and a user-friendly library. If you have any requests for library services not listed above or in the Appendix, feel free to suggest them. If librarian has the time and staff, he/she will be pleased to accommodate you. If you have difficulty locating materials within the library, request more directional or instructional signs and manuals. The library must be user-friendly in order to provide good service. Be sure to give continuous feedback on whether library and librarian are serving faculty needs.

13. When library needs help! At times, you may wonder why librarian has to say "no" to you, when the schedule appears "free." Librarians need unscheduled time for administrative work. A "no" does not mean a lack of desire to help you; it means he/she must do behind-the-scenes librarian tasks: scan new books and periodicals, preview new AV and computer-related materials, select and order new library materials, do subject and descriptive cataloging, organize, think, plan, process, confer, help individual patrons, do research, read professional journals, attend meetings and conferences, create catalogs and special indexes, keep current on national library standards, network with other libraries, solve problems, supervise volunteers, etc.

Whenever you can, try to recruit parent volunteers for the library. Their tasks will be to help at the desk and phones, file, clip, glue, cover books, laminate, input data, type, sort, compile, etc. The more help a librarian gets for these clerical tasks, the more professional services you can expect in return. Without this help, librarian must do these tasks alone!

STUDENTS AND A JEWISH LIBRARY

Your students need to know about Jewish libraries because there are so many Jewish library treasures which they can access, learn, and enjoy for a lifetime. But, most students are unable to visit a Jewish school library on their own, unless it is within walking distance or a bus ride from their homes. Therefore, it's up to you, their teacher and mentor, to make the *shidduch* between your students and a Jewish library — *during class time*, starting at a young age, and on a regular basis.

CLASSROOM TIME VS. LIBRARY TIME

Time in a supplemental school is so precious that many teachers ask, "Why should I take classes to the library to help learn a topic that I can teach more quickly in my classroom?" The answer is simple: quicker is good for many things, but it is not best for all things. Find a comfortable balance between classroom teaching and library exploration. The Library Objectives chart (Appendix A) and the Library Lessons section on the next page will give you the clues. In essence, when you use the library for some of your lessons, you will be providing students with valuable tools for continuing to learn about Judaism on their own — when they are ready to do so — in a month, a year, or many years from now. Without this exposure, their knowledge is limited to the time spent in your classroom.

Reading Jewish library books also affects your students' future as Jews. Students who voluntarily take a Jewish library book into their homes show a personal interest in Judaism; they will be better students because they have a positive attitude and will know more. Listening to stories in the library promotes the library and reading. "The class that was read to checked out more books and better books . . . "[6] "Children get much of their reading from libraries."[7] "Access to a school library results in more reading."[8] Even in a technological world where students read from a screen, attitude and familiarity with the subject make a difference.

THE JEWISH LIBRARY CAN BE EXCITING AND CHALLENGING.

CLASS USE OF THE LIBRARY

Classes can find the Jewish library an exciting and challenging experience. Like any good educational experience, advance thought, creativity, planning, and preparation make it happen. If your library is inadequately staffed, please substitute yourself for the role of "librarian" in the rest of this chapter. But first, consider the following.

LIBRARY CURRICULUM — GOALS AND OBJECTIVES

If your school curriculum does not include a library component, here are some guidelines.

Library Goals

The library goals in a Jewish supplemental school are to ensure that students and staff are effective users of the ideas and information concerning the "Jewish world." This is accomplished:
1. by providing intellectual and physical access to library materials of Judaica anywhere in the world.
2. by providing a carefully selected and sytematically organized collection of diverse resources covering the broad range of Judaica, in all formats.
3. by providing user instruction to foster competence and stimulate interest in reading, viewing, and using Jewish information and ideas
4. by working with teachers, specialists, and other educators to design learning strategies to meet the needs of individual students, and to promote in them a commitment to lifelong Judaica learning.
5. by encouraging students to carry on our Jewish traditions of study and learning and to value our Jewish texts and resources.
6. by providing a facility that functions as the information center of the school, and is conducive to study, learning, research, and recreational reading.

Library Objectives

The library objectives are many. The Specific Library Objectives (Appendix A) indicates the major subject and research areas. As you read through these, target what is appropriate for your curriculum and for your grade level.

LIBRARY LESSONS

Library lessons are learning activities conducted in the Jewish library setting based on the combined goals and objectives of both teacher and librarian. The teacher is interested in the student *"learning a specific topic or answer."* Librarian is interested in the student *learning the process and using the resources in order to* "learn a specific topic or answer."

Example: You want students to go to the library and "learn how people lived in biblical times." Librarian wants students to go to the library . . . use the library catalog . . . search under appropriate terms . . . note the best resources . . . locate the right section and shelves . . . read the spine labels . . . find the books . . . and use the table of contents or index to find the pages where they can then "learn how people lived in biblical times." As you can see, library tasks are more extensive, but the end result is that students learn a process that can be applied to *all* subjects. You will benefit as the year progresses, and other teachers will benefit in the future.

Role of Teacher

Librarian conducts the library lesson. The teacher participates by: listening as a model student, clarifying and interpreting, handling discipline, and assisting librarian while students individually search the catalog and select/check out books. (Conversely, if you use library time to do your own work, e.g., to grade papers, do personal research, or select and check out your own books, you are undermining the library program and leaving students without adequate supervision.)

Planning a Library Lesson

You and librarian should meet two to three weeks in advance to plan the lesson. Work with librarian to plan and teach collaboratively and imaginatively. As with any lesson, leave room for adaptability and creativity. The Library Planning Worksheet for Teacher and Librarian (Appendix B) should include: Subject and focus, your teaching objectives, librarian's teaching objectives, your motivational activities before and/or after the library lesson, library approach to be used (research, story, AV, computer, etc.), and logistical problems to be solved. Librarian will then search the resources to be certain that there are enough interesting resources, on the correct reading level, to create an exciting lesson. Librarian designs and outlines the lesson on the Worksheet, lists the materials to be used, and returns a copy of the Worksheet to you a week before the lesson. This will give you enough time to review it and prepare your students for the library visit.

Keys to Successful Library Lessons

The following are keys to successful library lessons:
1. School curriculum. Library lessons should relate directly to the school curriculum. "Meet students on their turf; try to reach

them when they care, and when the information is most relevant."[9] When appropriate, plan related class activities to integrate the library into the school learning experience.
2. Lesson frequency and lengths. Meet with librarian at the beginning of the school year and map out where library lessons fit best. Plan six to eight class library lessons per year. Flexible scheduling ("as needed" basis) will probably best serve your curriculum. Vary lesson lengths according to grade level attention spans: Approximately 20 minutes for Kindergarten to Grade 2; 30 minutes for Grade 3; 35 minutes for Grade 4; 45 minutes for Grades 5 to 7; one hour for Grades 8 and up. For some research, you may want to lengthen the time and schedule lessons on sequential school days or sessions.
3. Choice of topic and logistics. Give librarian a choice of several topics or a theme to explore for a class library lesson. Library lessons require easy access to a topic and adequate resources for the number of students. Not all subjects work well.
   a. Most subjects lend themselves to research, i.e., they are terms itemized in encyclopedias, indexes, or tables of contents. Some topics are difficult to find, e.g., "values" or specific values, because those terms are not usually itemized.
   b. Many resources (generally one per student) are required for a full class research project. Broaden or narrow the subject to allow for this. To illustrate: "Bible" is too broad a research topic (too many books, too large a topic); "Deborah" is too narrow (not enough books or encyclopedias); however, "Women in the Bible" is just right for a library with a good collection.
   c. Logistically, one or more resources per student works well. When copies of resources are limited, consider alternatives: Assign students to work in pairs; divide class in two and repeat the lesson; divide lesson into two parts with each half doing something different, and then switch, or have each doing a related lesson; borrow resources from another library; project the printed page from an opaque projector or make transparencies; use other formats and resources to increase the number of items, etc.
4. Library skills. There is no time to teach general library skills in a supplemental school. The librarian's task is to teach students to apply library skills, learned elsewhere, to a Jewish library setting. To overcome varying student proficiencies, librarian looks at the skills assigned to different grade levels of your city/state recommended library curriculum and plans to incorporate that library skill during the year following the one designated. This extra year allows time for students either to be taught these skills elsewhere or to mature enough to assimilate them quickly. To teach Judaica library skills well and interestingly means to teach them sequentially over several years, with continuous review and reinforcement — following the Library Objectives list (Appendix A). Trying to cram lots of skills into a few sessions each year is an unpleasant library experience and defeats the purpose.
5. Autonomy. Work with librarian to gear your lessons toward students becoming independent users in a Judaica library through repetition of Judaica skills.
6. Library activities. Library activities flow from the subject matter, not from the library skills; library resources are the tools. "The acquisition of library use skills require active participation or hands-on experience."[10] Skills should be taught as part of enjoyable hands-on activities that you and librarian plan, e.g., assign research topics in a dramatic way, create games or puzzles, plan team activities, ask questions in a challenging way, use multi-media resources including computers, insert a "fun" question on student worksheets, read a poem or story to set the scene, let the final report be in an interesting format. The sample library lessons below can help you get started. Also, work with librarian to divert some students to another activity so that all students do not converge on the library catalog at the same time.
7. Research. As you know, students frequently react negatively to research assignments. Don't let this discourage you from assigning them. Research is a very important learning experience; it is the only way that

students will become familiar with the resources and learn how to use them. To start, librarian encourages young children to find information in picture books. As they get older, they find information in words and phrases and they explore tools such as the library catalog and indexes. When approached sequentially and repeatedly, the process helps students to grow intellectually.

This does not diminish the fact that research is complex; it involves communication and information literacy. Most patrons are afraid to ask questions because they do not want to appear ignorant; they frame questions based on what they know, rather than on what they don't know. To isolate the actual question, librarian tactfully conducts a "reference interview," i.e., refines the question, limits its scope, translates it into the library system of coding, scans the collection, and selects what the patron wants — on the reading level, in the amount, and with the specific focus needed. Thereafter, patrons read, evaluate, select, organize, and use the information. Of course, students don't realize all of this. All they think about is that they want what they need quickly and with very little effort. As they gain more experience, however, their confidence does improve and the process becomes easy.

> **USE PRIMARY SOURCE MATERIALS AND CD-ROMS.**

8. Authentic resources. Whenever possible, choose topics that involve research in primary source materials, e.g., diaries, personal narratives, eyewitness accounts, spoken words and images. Many video recordings, video (laser) discs, and CD-ROM formats contain newsreels or footage of actual events.

To instill a reverence for Jewish books, students must touch and explore in order to experience and remember. Some teachers talk about the Bible, but never show one. Rabbis frequently refer to the Talmud, but few children (or adults) have actually seen a Talmud or touched one. Do expose children to the originals.

9. Multi-resources. "Students learn in different ways, therefore, it follows that a variety of media and methods should be employed since no one method is likely to be effective with all."[11] The beauty of the library is that the various kinds of materials and equipment are right there and easy to access. Students enjoy having the choice of media, especially for independent research. For those formats that are sequential and lengthy, assign research to view/listen and specify filmstrip frames, slide numbers, specific transparencies, and approximate tape counter number for audio or videotapes, etc. Compact discs, video (laser) discs and other digital software are easy to access and make excellent resources.

10. Research Variations. In a Jewish research project, students become frustrated if the following are not discussed in advance: (a) transliterations and spelling inconsistencies in the reference tools, e.g., Hanukkah vs. Chanukah; and (b) name variations used during different time periods, e.g., biblical names (Moses — no last name), medieval personalities (Moses ben Maimon — found either under the first name or Maimonides, Moses), modern Israeli names (David Ben-Gurion — found under Ben-Gurion, not Gurion). In the Jewish library field, *Encyclopaedia Judaica* is considered the subject and name authority.

11. Special resources. Ask librarian to introduce a brief "special treat" into the lesson when appropriate, e.g., a pictorial work of great significance, or a quotation — to enrich, intensify, authenticate.

12. Outside class research assignments. Outside reading and research assignments are effective and can go very smoothly, but only if you plan ahead. Here are some suggestions:
    a. If you expect librarian to reserve books on library shelves for an outside class assignment over a 2-3 week period, check with librarian first to see if library has enough resources, enough reserve book shelf space, and enough staff and time to select and pull the books and return them to the shelves. If not, discuss options.
    b. If you expect students to visit any library on their own time (including your own supplemental school library), send a note home at the beginning of the semester alerting parents to plan for such activity,

and then give students enough time to do the assignment. Special library visits take extra planning for parents — to work around car pools, bus schedules, divorced and separated families living in two locations, other schedules, etc. A courtesy letter in advance tends to alleviate the stress.

13. Book talks. Librarians usually plan "book talks" near the end of each library lesson to promote reading. Book talks are brief 30 to 60 second descriptions of story and characters in a book. Some narrative or dialogue may be read from the book to give the flavor. But they never tell the ending — this is a "teaser!"

14. Selection and check-out time. Allow 10 to 20 minutes for students to select and check-out books, which might include searching the library catalog. When faced with rows of books, floor to ceiling, no one can find the "right" book without a starting point and some experience. Once children have read a few enjoyable or interesting books, they build on their successes by looking for others. This exploration and discovery takes time, assistance, and patience. Both you and librarian need to work together to help students walk through this procedure because the search and select process promotes student independence. Your joint teamwork sends a positive message to students, allows the lesson to run smoothly, and enables more to be accomplished in a shorter period of time. (If you are functioning as the sole librarian, then ask someone to assist you during this time — it's a two person job.)

15. Follow-up and Book Activities. The best way for students to understand that classroom and library are integrated is to plan follow-up activities to a library lesson. Discuss with librarian in advance. Another option is to plan activities around books you have borrowed from the library. A good teacher source for this is *Jewish Literature for Children: A Teaching Guide* by Grossman and Engman.

16. Discipline. Classroom discipline problems are usually carried over into the library; you should anticipate this and plan accordingly. On the other hand, some "problem" students, especially bright ones, may "shine" in libraries because they are challenged in a different way.

17. Cancellation of library time. Don't be a "no show" for a library lesson and do not cancel at the last minute. Library lessons take *lots* of planning time besides the lengthy physical labor of pulling books/sorting/replacing them on the shelves. Cancel only when necessary and do give librarian the courtesy of advance notice.

OTHER LIBRARY CONNECTIONS

Besides library lessons, you will also connect with the library during your classroom lessons.

Spontaneous Research

If a spontaneous question arises in class, send students to the library with a *written* question and full details; do not rely upon their memories. (Many a librarian has sent back the right answer to the wrong question.)

Small Group Research

When you plan to send small groups of students into the library for research, give librarian advance notice of the topic so that the best resources may be pulled and reserved for them. If you expect librarian to work with your students, schedule it. If you have to cancel for any reason, do it early.

Pleasure Reading and Book Reports

Promote recreational reading, and assign reading as enjoyable homework or for extra credit. "Library media centers can play a positive role in developing positive self-concepts in children."[12] A library helps children learn about themselves, and their likes and dislikes. When students find Jewish books that are good reading choices, they feel successful.

Set aside five minutes of class time for students to share their reading in small groups. "Young people's reading choices are influenced by their peers."[13]

Encourage students to read Jewish literature, folklore, and fiction for pleasure and learning, Jewish biographies and diaries for inspiration and role models, and non-fiction Jewish books to expand their knowledge of topics discussed in class or to pursue personal interests. Historical fiction is especially good reading because children identify with family characters and events, live vicariously through periods of history, and learn about people, places, and cultures. Ask librarian for help in finding Jewish reading to supplement your curriculum

Assign book reports occasionally, not routinely; otherwise students will begin to resent reading. (Do not assign "100 page books" because they don't exist.) Before assigning reading on a specific subject or genre of literature, check with librarian to be certain that there are enough books on that topic.

Encourage students to report on books in creative ways, for example: (a) book characters telling the story in a graffiti-type poster; (b) student as narrator, and friends reading dialogue, in a dramatic presentation on audiocassette; (c) making a presentation with appropriate musical background or slides of scenes that correspond with the book setting; (d) a computer-generated newsletter incorporating story and character details. Check teacher and librarian materials for other creative book report projects.

Reading Programs

If library sponsors a reading program, support it. If library does not, plan one for your class and ask librarian for assistance. The purpose of this program is to promote reading of Jewish books. The steps are: Create a theme and design the program to include reading parameters, publicity, motivation, and recognition. Plan clever themes, reasonable expectations for number and/or kinds of books or number of pages to read, attractive flyers, reporting forms or a large chart or graph to record student names and progress, and a reward (certificate, appropriate prize). "The Sefer Stars Reading Incentive Program" by Suzan Caplan, Temple Emanu-El, Oak Park, Michigan, is a good example (see *Judaica Librarian*, Association of Jewish Libraries, Spring 1992-Winter 1993, pp. 142-144). For quality children's Jewish books, write to Jewish Book Council and Association of Jewish Libraries; they have lists of recommended and award winning children's books. A list of children's Jewish books published annually is in the *Jewish Book Annual* (New York: Jewish Book Council).

Distance Education

In secular schools, K-12 "distance education" courses are thriving. Teachers and students in different locations are interacting via telecommunications and phone, fax, etc., and libraries are becoming the central conduit for this activity. Students also "attend" special events and field trips electronically. As Judaica courses become available, supplemental schools could benefit greatly from this.

OTHER HELPFUL DO'S AND DON'TS
Scheduling Time To Exchange Books

Do schedule time for students to exchange books on a regular basis, separate from library lessons, especially if you are on a flexible library lesson schedule. Plan 10 to 20 minutes for students to place returned books on the counter and find, select, and check out new books. Be sure to help students with this process.

Don't assume that students, especially younger ones, can return library books on their own. If exchanging books is *not* part of your schedule, then books frequently become overdue, fines are charged, parents become upset, and borrowing library books becomes an undesirable activity.

Reading Aloud

Do read aloud in class as often as you can. Students love to hear teachers read a fiction chapter during each session. "Children read more when they listen to stories, discuss stories."[14] Do read from the book itself rather than from photocopies; students gain a feeling of authenticity from your holding a book while you read. Reading aloud is very important in today's world because children brought up on visual TV sometimes have difficulty imagining pictures in their own minds. Reading aloud promotes inner visual imagery.

Drop-in Library Visits

Don't expect librarian to be available when your class unexpectedly drops in. Librarian serves the entire school needs — individuals, classes, grade levels — and has many deadlines. Be thoughtful and plan in advance.

Non-library Activities

Don't use the library for non-library activities. It is common for teachers to view the library as "supervised space" for students who need to be separated from the class temporarily for whatever reason. Teachers send students to the library expecting them to settle down and be influenced positively by their surroundings. This does not happen! Students carry their anger, resentment, discontent, or uncaring feelings with them, and without warning, librarian has to deal with these emotional young people, often with unfavorable results. This is unfair to students and librarian; and the library's image suffers. Do discuss alternatives with your Director of Education.

Also, don't use library as an unsupervised study hall — even the best of students tends to get bored and create distractions for others. Students will transfer their negative feelings to the library and these feelings are difficult to change.

SAMPLE LIBRARY LESSONS

There are endless possibilities for library lessons. Some of these were created by colleagues, who kindly shared their lessons with me. Once you scan these, in conjunction with the Library Objectives chart (Appendix A), you will have a sense of which of your classroom subjects will make good library lessons. Again, the essence of library lessons deals with the genre of Jewish literature, multi-media resources, research skills, the library process, and promoting reading.

If your school does not have a skilled librarian to teach your class, do not despair. I have purposely included lesson details so that you can work alone, if necessary, and still be successful. The following lessons are designed to be adapted to different grade levels and topics:

Introducing the Library

It is crucial to introduce the Jewish library to children at a young age (pre-K to Grade 1). The lessons should be entirely pleasurable — reading stories or legends, telling flannelgraph stories, talking about facts in picture books — while students sit comfortably in a library setting. Jewish literature is introduced through Jewish authors and illustrators of Jewish picture books. Emphasis is on a warm and intimate experience, on books that are beautiful and enjoyable, and on establishing a close relationship with the librarian as another synagogue person who is a friend. These experiences provide a solid foundation for lifelong positive attitudes toward a Jewish library. This is also the time to establish good library habits, to help youngsters learn how to care for books, locate books on shelves, check out materials, etc. The goal is for children to internalize that the Jewish library is a wonderful place to be!

Introducing a Topic through Jewish Literature

Read appropriate short selections from literature as an introduction to the library lesson topic. Poetry examples: A variety of holiday poems for different reading levels are in the JPS Holiday Anthology series by Philip Goodman, i.e., Rosh Hashanah, Yom Kippur, Sukkot and Simchat Torah, Chanukah, Purim, Passover, and Shavuot, and also *Sabbath: The Day of Delight* by Abraham E. Millgram (Philadelphia: Jewish Publication Society). (Idea from Judith Katz, Religious School Librarian, Stephen S. Wise Temple, Los Angeles)

Variations on a Theme

Some stories inspire authors and illustrators to write and illustrate their own versions and also motivate librarians to help children compare them. A Grade 1 example: Tell the biblical story of Noah. Then, read one or two picture book versions of Noah's ark, and show others. Encourage children to point out similarities and differences.

INTRODUCE THE LIBRARY TO CHILDREN AT A YOUNG AGE.

Jewish Values in Fiction or Folklore

Stories to teach moral and ethical lessons are part of our Jewish heritage. Children enjoy and learn from outstanding Jewish fiction and folklore books. A Grade 2-3 example: The beautifully illustrated award winning children's picture book *Something from Nothing* by Phoebe Gilman (Ontario, Canada: North Winds Press, 1992), teaches creativity and the concept of *Bal Tashchit* ("do not be destructive or wasteful"). This intergenerational folktale shows how Joseph's favorite baby blanket, as it becomes worn, is remade into smaller garments for Joseph, and finally a covered button, by his loving grandfather. Even when the button is lost, what remains is still something — a story! Children also enjoy the wordless sub-story about a mouse family that lives under the floor boards and practices *Bal Tashchit* by using the discarded scraps of Joseph's blanket and the lost button, for their own family and home. Plan follow-up activities and discussion on how students and their families practice *Bal Tashchit*. (Lesson by Toby Rossner, Media Coordinator, Bureau of Jewish Education, 130 Sessions St., Providence, RI 02906. Write for a copy of this and other book activities.)

Setting a Mood Using Library Media

As students enter the library, play a musical recording appropriate to the topic of your library lesson, e.g., Sephardic music for a lesson on Sephardim. Also, use related realia for students to see and touch, e.g., a shofar, a pot from an archaeological dig.

Jewish Versions of Universal Stories

Meet students "where they are" and take them to where you want them to be! Students relate to Jewish versions of familiar folktales, e.g., Little Red Riding Hood, Tom Thumb. Grades 2-4 example: Read one or two authentic Jewish tales from *The Diamond Tree: Jewish Tales from Around the World*, selected and retold by Howard Schwartz and Barbara Rush, illustrated by Uri Shulevitz (New York: Harper-Collins Publishers, 1991).[15] Ask children to name stories they know that are like the ones read. Discuss how all people have folk tales; such tales are a way of passing on family stories and traditions. Talk about Jewish folktales as part of the whole picture of literature. Consider the influence of differing cultures on host communities, and vice versa. Stories enrich and extend their Jewish experience in meaningful and relevant ways so that it fits into their own mainstream American culture. Stories help Jewish children gain a sense of pride and respect for their unique heritage. (Lesson by Helen W. Rogaway, Day School Librarian, Stephen S. Wise Temple, Los Angeles)

Multi-resources and Realia Authenticate a Factual Event

Some annual themes, e.g., holiday stories, tend to become a tale retold instead of reality. By introducing resources and formats that represent facts, the event becomes more authentic for children. For example, after reading or reviewing the Chanukah story to Grades 3-4, light the *chanukiah* and say the blessings together in the library. Then show, read, and/or discuss the following from the Maccabean time period: Some large illustrations showing maps, coins, artifacts, etc.; a volume by or about Josephus, the Jewish historian; brief excerpts from *I and II Maccabees* in the Apocrypha. Conclude by showing students illustrations of *chanukiot* in Jewish ceremonial art books and asking them to count the number of different designs they see.

Teaching Jewish Tradition

The concept of Jewish tradition is easier to teach with these resources:

For Grades 2 through junior high school, Patricia Polacco's true story, *The Keeping Quilt* (New York: Simon & Schuster Books for Young Readers, 1988), will touch everyone who hears it and sees it. This award winning children's picture book describes the making of a quilt by her Russian Jewish immigrant family and how five generations used it, cherished it, and kept it, as the world changed. Wearing a babushka or appropriate hat, start the lesson by showing a quilt (borrow one if necessary). After reading the story, focus discussion on immigration, family traditions passed down through generations, values, and what belongs to a family, how something does not have to be costly to be of value, the quilt as an art form, etc. (Lesson by Helen W. Rogaway, Day School Librarian, Stephen S. Wise Temple, Los Angeles)

For junior and senior high students, the 15-minute *Gefilte Fish*, videotaped by Karen Silverstein (Teaneck, New Jersey: Ergo Media, 1987), is a humorous approach to how three generations of women prepare this Jewish dish. Encourage discussion on other ways that Jewish tradition is passed down from generation to generation.

Library Skills in a Jewish Library

Here is a simple five minute game to introduce students to a variety of Judaica books and help them see the relationship between call numbers and Jewish subjects. Example for Grade 4: Prepare a list of your library's classification scheme divided into its 10 major divisions, with a few key subjects listed under each division. Place on a book truck some interesting books from each division. For example, using *A Classification System for Libraries of Judaica* by David H. Elazar and Daniel J. Elazar (2nd edition,

Jerusalem: The Jerusalem Center for Public Affairs/Center for Jewish Community Studies; Lanham, Md.: University Press of America, 1988), the 600 divisional list might look like this:

600 Jewish Community, Society and the Arts
636 Synagogue
652 Marriage and Family
662 Anti-Semitism
670-682 Art
685-689 Music
690-695 Public Entertainment
696 Sports
699 Cooking

Then, from the book truck, hold up and read off the book titles, one at a time; ask students to refer to the list and tell you the classification number for each book. Segue into the library lesson by saving for last the books from the topic that you are teaching. After the lesson, encourage students to check out the books.

Researching Periods of Time through Printed Visuals

Some Jewish topics are expressed beautifully through different types of pictorial formats, e.g., book illustrations, calendars, pictures, posters, maps, art reproductions, illuminated manuscripts, historical atlases. When students are exposed to these, they begin to view the topic as multi-dimensional and dynamic. Jewish time periods that are rich in pictorial works are: Life in biblical times, Eastern Europe, Lower East Side New York Life, Holocaust, Pre-Israel Palestine, Israel, etc. If resources are limited, divide the class into groups, each researching a different period. Then follow with class discussion comparing the ways of life based on their "picture/caption reading."

Example of biblical environment research: In a library with a strong Biblical history section, an end-of-the-year, Grade 4-5 library lesson on the *Bible* brings the *Torah* to life. Search children and adult books (including reference works, *Haggadot*, art books, etc.) for illustrations and readable captions that show life in Bible times. Prepare at least one question per student, e.g., on shelter, tools, clothes, animals, furniture, transportation, jewelry, medical help, etc., and place these books on a book truck in call number order. Introduce the lesson by showing some large illustrations of life in Bible times. Then give each student a half sheet of paper on which is printed a question and the *location* of the answer (i.e., the book's call number, author, title, and page number). Student locates book on book truck by call number, finds page, records answer, and shares results with the class. Example:

Question: Describe or draw bowls and pots probably used by Abraham and his family.

Answer: See (Ref. 900 Enc) *Encyclopaedia Judaica*, volume 3, pages 307-308, Archaeology — Middle Bronze Age — 2100-1550 B.C.E.

(In my library, one teacher had her class come back several times to allow each student time to research *all* the questions and draw colored pictures of the answers. She gathered all into a handmade book, and sent a photocopy home with each student. Recently, a college student told me that she still had her fourth grade "Biblical Life Book" and she would always keep it!)

Biography Research

Biographical research makes great lessons because students need heroes and role models. Be sure to check ahead to be certain that the library has enough resources on the people you want researched. Here are some ideas:

1. Role play the introduction to Jewish personalities. Wear different hats, bits of clothing, assume various accents, etc., while writing names of people on the board and telling some very brief but fascinating tidbits from their lives. Students choose one to research. Enthusiasm runs high when students are motivated to do research about someone whose life sounds interesting. (Introduction by Stan Beiner, while Hebrew School Teacher at Stephen S. Wise Temple, Los Angeles; currently Director of Central Agency for Jewish Education, Denver)

2. The Hollywood approach — "Celebrities in the News." Prepare an interview sheet to research a Jewish personality: Name of person, date and place of birth, city of residence, marital and family status, occupation, and claim to fame — what events caused them to rise to prominence — and sources for information. Students research a famous person using any source. Students pair up, one posing as the "celebrity" and the other as the news reporter who completes the

interview sheet. Then, they switch roles. Photocopy or draw a picture of the celebrity and attach to the sheet. Post results on bulletin board for all to read and enjoy. (Used by Abigail Yasgur, Day School Librarian, Stephen S. Wise Temple, Los Angeles)

3. "Break the Code" Biographical Research: A simple motivational tool is to write the research subjects' name in a code. Assign research on important Jews worldwide — from ancient to modern, specific subjects such as the Zionists to today's Israeli leaders, people after whom local synagogues are named, etc. Students can search the library catalog, browse the biography book shelves, search the *Index to Jewish Periodicals*, and use biographical dictionaries devoted to a subject, e.g., Talmudic Rabbis, people in the arts (music, film) or general biographical dictionaries, e.g., *Dictionary of Jewish Biography* by Geoffrey Wigoder (New York: Simon & Schuser, 1991); *Who's Who in World Jewry: a Biographical Dictionary of Outstanding Jews*, ed I. J. Carmin Karpman, ed. (Tel Aviv: Olive Books of Israel, latest edition.)

4. Compare and Contrast. Assign or discuss readings that show different perspectives of the same or similar topics; use both fiction and non-fiction. Students can:
   a. describe cultural patterns or similar activities in different countries. Example: Report on how fictional and real families in different countries celebrate Jewish holidays and life cycle events.
   b. view people as multi-dimensional characters through the eyes of others. Example: Select readings about King David — as a leader, a poet, a writer, a musician; as viewed by King Saul (when David was younger and older), by his wives, by his children, by his friends and enemies.
   c. view a topic from a different perspective, using a single pictorial book.
   d. share experiences vicariously through reading. Examples: The Ellis Island experience through immigrant diaries; the series of events found in historical fiction sequel books.
   e. choose your-own-adventure stories (compare student choices and results)
   f. compare lives of people who went to a new country with those who stayed behind; movie version vs. book version of the same story.

(Lesson ideas by Ellen G. Cole, Temple Librarian, Temple Isaiah, Los Angeles)

Creativity and Research

Create imaginary situations to make research fun! For example, ask students to design an advertising campaign for a wealthy philanthropist who wants to promote *kashrut* in the Jewish community. First, while in the classroom, discuss the dietary laws as written in the Bible and Talmud. Then, students go into the library to do research in secondary sources. Using the library catalog, they find whole books and pamphlets about *kashrut* as well as chapters in cookbooks, books on customs, Jewish home, guides to Jewish living, and also encyclopedic entries. Search terms may be *kasher*, kosher, *kashrut*, dietary laws. Working in pairs, students write a radio or TV commercial. They perform their commercials (with props, sound, etc.) before a video camera and an impartial committee, who select the winning commercial. All participants receive an award. (Lesson by Martha Globerman, Librarian, Temple Ramat Zion, Northridge, California)

Publish a Newspaper

Have students browse through the 3-volume set of *Chronicles: News of the Past*, Israel Eldad and Moshe Aumann, eds. (Jerusalem: Reubeni Foundation, 1970), noting the various formats — current and feature articles, maps, illustrations, bulletins, boxed summaries, advertisements, quizzes, letters, etc. Example: For a Maccabees newspaper, students go to the library catalog and research topics, e.g., Maccabees, Chanukah, History, Roman Empire, etc. Students read about the topic and write about it in their format of choice. If doing an advertisement, they must do three interesting ads. Combine the results and publish a newspaper. (Lesson by Susan Dubin, Day School Librarian, Temple Valley Beth Shalom, Encino, California)

Current Jewish News

Help students become more aware of current Jewish news sources. (Few students seek Jewish information in the daily newspaper, or scan the Jewish publications to which their parents subscribe.) Advance lesson preparation: Save those sections of the daily newspaper which include Jewish news (local, national, international); this may take several weeks to collect one per student. Also save copies of your community's Anglo-Jewish newspapers, one per student.

The lesson: Review with students how to scan a newspaper for articles of interest — demonstrate how your eye can quickly scan headlines for either "J" (Jewish, Jews) or "I" (Israel), among other things. First, distribute sections of the daily newspaper, and ask students to scan these and to select an article of Jewish interest. Ask each student briefly to describe the article and to write on the board some key words that characterize it. Next, distribute the Jewish papers, and ask students to choose an article of interest and to make another list of key words on the board. Key words might be: Israel peace talks, Maccabiah games, Jewish homeless, Yiddish play, etc. Compare the two lists and discuss. (Students will discover that articles in the daily paper cover fewer topics and only "popular" topics; articles in Jewish press have much more variety and cover smaller yet important issues, etc.) Thereafter, teacher should assign weekly current event reports or devote a class bulletin board to newspaper clippings.

Jewish Educational Software

Create library lessons around the various topics found on computer software, e.g., Bible, holidays, Jewish calendar.

Jewish Folklore and Legends

To appreciate Jewish folklore and legends, do a comparative study. Have students read several versions of the same story and compare facts and style via class discussion and a chart. Set the stage by comments on how the Rabbis used legends to communicate with the Jewish people. Look for popular folklore that has been published as separate children's books and in collected works, e.g., *A Treasury of Jewish Folklore*, Nathan Ausubel, ed. (New York: Crown, 1948, 1975):

"It could always be worse" (pp. 69-70)
"The wisdom of Chelm" section (pp. 326-342)
"Schlemihls and Schlimazls" section (pp. 343-361)

Varying Viewpoints of a Single Large Topic

This lesson helps students understand the full scope of a large topic and its many parts. Place on a book truck a number of books (at least 1-2 per student) on a major topic. *Without* an introduction, distribute the books and ask students to examine their books and prepare to describe in brief the content to their classmates. As they share their resources, students gradually begin to comprehend the magnitude of this topic because the books speak for themselves. Hold up audiovisual and other media on the subject to intensify the experience even more. Then, ask students to discuss why so many books have been written on this topic, frequently in many different genres of literature. Encourage students to check out the books.

Using the Holocaust as an example for this lesson, check the library catalog and select a wide variety of titles to cover this topic, e.g., pre-Holocaust life in Europe, ghettos, resistance, concentration camps, people in hiding, Righteous Gentiles, Denmark, Nazis, genocide, liberation of camps, war crime trials, resettlement, etc. Select also from among the variety of genres, e.g., diary, personal narrative, atlas, novel, short story, poem, play, chronology, biography, art, comprehensive work, etc.

Check your library catalog for other topics that can use this approach effectively, e.g., United States or Israel — history and immigration.

(Adapted from a Holocaust lesson by Dorothy Steiner, Librarian, Temple Ner Tamid, Downey, California)

Trivia Hunt through Reference Sources

For a pleasurable introduction to a variety of Jewish reference sources, try this. Create trivia questions; use Jewish symbols for graphic designs, e.g., six questions (for six points on a Jewish star); seven questions (for seven candles in a *menorah*); ten questions (for the Ten Commandments). In the top half of the page, list a number of reference book titles, e.g., encyclopedias, dictionaries, almanacs, trivia books, directories, etc., and identify them as A, B, C, etc., as many as possible to handle class logistics. In the bottom half of page, list your trivia questions in "fill in the blank" format, each question followed by the letter A, B, C, etc., corresponding to the reference book in which they will find the answer. Be sure the questions peak student interest, e.g.,

Jewish sports figures (Sandy Koufax, Suzanne Lenglen), Statue of Liberty (Emma Lazarus), Nobel Prize winners (Albert Einstein, Nelly Sachs, Elie Wiesel), secret tunnel in a synagogue, blood libel, Jewish genetic diseases, source of "*Hatikvah*," etc. This could be an individual or team activity, or an optional independent activity as a Jewish Book Month Challenge.

Assignment for the Trivia Hunt: Students use library catalog to find call numbers of reference books and locate books on shelves, find the answers and fill in the blanks, then return books to proper place on shelves before going to next source. At the next class/school assembly, reward students who found all the answers by proudly announcing their names.
(Lesson by Abigail Yasgur, Day School Librarian, Stephen S. Wise Temple, Los Angeles)

Definition of "Jew"

Compare definitions of the word, "Jew," in Judaic and non-Judaic dictionaries. Some appear to indicate that "to jew down" is acceptable.

Biblical Citations

To give students experience in working with the Bible, distribute copies and teach students first how to find citations — chapter and verse. For practice, try familiar citations such as Deuteronomy 6:4 (*Sh'ma*), Exodus 20:2-14 (Ten Commandments), and Exodus 23:14-16 (pilgrimage festivals). Next, distribute copies of the Jewish calendar. Have students look up the Torah portion for the current week and find the citation in the Bible. Show them the *Tikkun* and a miniature or real Torah scroll and discuss similarities and differences between the Bible/Torah, the *Tikkun*, and Torah scroll. Conclude with a discussion on the weekly *parashah*.

Compare Versions of the Bible

As a follow-up lesson to biblical citations above, read introductions and prefaces of a variety of Bibles of the Jewish denominations. Help students note differences in title, version, focus, and bias. Now, add a Christian Bible to the mix. Make sure that students have a clear understanding of the differences between what Jews call *Tanach* and/or the Hebrew Bible and what non-Jews tend to refer to as the Old Testament. Christian editions of the Bible usually contain what they refer to as the New Testament, and the order of the books of the Hebrew Bible is significantly different from that in a *Tanach*. Discuss how this changing of the order accommodates Christian philosophy. (Many students and parents do not know this.)

Bar/Bat Mitzvah — Introduction to Speech Research

Students will appreciate a library lesson on the process for finding their Torah portions, understanding them, and trying to relate to them personally. Assign students the portion of the week (or a *parashah* of your choice). Review with students how to find biblical citations. Next, have students find the *parashah* in a book of the Bible or Torah and read it. Then, show them the resources listed below and explain the assignment, which they will do with a partner. Thereafter, demonstrate with one student how to approach the resources and how to formulate questions partners can ask each other. The goal is to get a better understanding of the *parashah* and find its contemporary and personal relevance. Finally, provide adequate time for partners to use the resources and complete the assignment. After students have explicated the *parashah*, open class discussion so they can share their various interpretations. Resources may include:

A variety of Bibles/Torahs with commentary and/or with the Haftarah, or commentaries alone, e.g., the Hertz *Pentateuch and Haftorahs.*

Chiel, Arthur A. *Guide to Sidrot and Haftarot.* Hoboken, NJ: Ktav Publishing, 1971.

Lipis, Philip L., and Louis Katzoff. *Torah for the Family.* Jerusalem: World Jewish Bible Society, 1977.

Loeb, Sorel Goldberg, and Barbara Binder Kadden. *Teaching Torah: A Treasury of Insights and Activities.* Denver: A.R.E. Publishing, Inc., 1984.

Stern, Shirley. *Exploring the Torah.* Hoboken, New Jersey: Ktav Publishing, 1984.

Specific resources that illuminate a topic — for example, if the *parashah* is about the Tabernacle, use the library catalog to find books on the Tabernacle.

(Lesson by Rita Frischer, Director of Library Services, Sinai Blumenthal Library, Los Angeles)

Biblical Concordance

Students look up an assigned subject, select a citation from the Concordance, and find the passage in the Bible. Also, assign different definitions of the same word, e.g., light. Follow up with class discussion, perhaps tying the various selections to contemporary issues.

Full-Text Sources on Computer

Give students time to explore the resources of Bible, Talmud, Jewish literature, etc., in computer software, CD-ROM, laser (video) disc, other electronic media sources, etc.

Quotation Sources

Quotations and philosophical types of readings are important for students to know about — for speeches, creative readings, and parental blessings dealing with Bar/Bat Mitzvah; audio or video productions; and any occasion where special words and phrases will enhance a presentation. For the lesson, gather quotation sources and philosophical readings on a book truck; include Proverbs from the Bible, *Sayings of the Fathers* (*Pirke Avot*) from the Talmud, compendiums of Jewish thought, poetry, etc., and computer software quotation programs. Discuss the variety of sources. Following are two sample lessons.

1. A simple acrostic assignment to become familiar with several sources: Have students write their first or last name vertically on a sheet of paper. Then ask them to find and copy a quotation or saying that begins with each letter of their name. Upon completion, students select one quotation to share with the class. (I found that students are very selective when linking quotations with their own names.)
2. A more thought provoking assignment: Ask students to select one quotation and write a brief paper about its meaning and applicability to their personal lives.

Global Classroom

Students discuss Jewish issues or share Jewish activities with others globally. Grade 3 and up classes link locally or worldwide via the Internet and other networks, using computers, modems, and telecommunications software

An actual Grade 6 telecommunication example: For a joint 1994 Tu Bishvat celebration, ten schools were linked together. The locations were Boston, Los Angeles, New York, Cleveland, Philadelphia, Jerusalem, and the Negev. Classes selected from a variety of planned activities and their responses were incorporated into local Tu B'Shevat celebrations at the different locations. Some spontaneous activities occurred, too, and these also became part of the records. Then, schools reported electronically about their own celebrations; the shared data gathered over the network was printed into a newsletter and sent to participating schools. Some of the activities for the global classroom project were:

1. Israeli children researched trees native to Israel and selected those trees that had qualities with which students could identify. Then they planted a symbolic forest in Israel.
2. Kids at different sites shared information and customs that they learned about Tu Bishvat at their own schools. This became a resource base showing different perspectives of the holiday.
3. Another class focused on the Torah as the tree of life. Questions answered were: What do trees and the Torah have in common? Why do you think planting a tree in Israel to honor a living person or as a memoral to someone who died is a meaningful act? etc.
4. One class prepared and shared an extensive bibliography on Tu B'Shevat.
5. Another class compared the life of a tree with the life of a person, e.g., how a tree has roots and a person's roots are family, a tree needs nourishment and people also need nourishment, etc.
6. Children at all schools wrote a variety of different kinds of poetry about themes of nature.

This global classroom project inspired classes to initiate their own activities, e.g, some American schools sent an electronic message to Israeli schools with questions about fruits commonly grown in Israel, and compared them with their own local fruits. Also, actual happenings in January 1994 — the unprecedented eastern U. S. cold weather and the Los Angeles earthquake — generated electronic discussions about uprooting experiences of living through a natural disaster and ways to replant.

LINK YOUR CLASSES LOCALLY OR WORLDWIDE VIA INTERNET.

As part of their parent-child Tu B'Shevat *Seder*, the Jerusalem school decided to set up a computer at the *Seder* table and share their experiences electronically with one of the Los Angeles schools. They wrote messages on the screen about the *Seder* progress. The Los Angeles teacher had prepared a few inspirational messages in advance and sent those along while keying in real time responses. Unexpectedly, the Negev school joined in for a three way "conversation" about the beginning regrowth of the desert. The Los Angeles class watched the screen and were very excited to be participating. The Jerusalem school signed off after 20 minutes in order to telecommunicate in Hebrew with other Israeli schools during their Tu B'Shevat celebration.

A future telecommunications project with different schools may be about planning an imaginary trip to Israeli sites for Yom HaAtzma'ut.

(Projects by Judy Eber, Computer Specialist, Abraham Joshua Heschel Day School, Northridge, California)

Jewish Encyclopedias

Students are to do a comparative study among Jewish and general single and multi-volume encyclopedias. Prepare a chart comparing number of volumes, copyright date, place of publication, availability of index, and some sample subjects to research (always include "Israel"). Students will discover that Jewish encyclopedias are better than general encyclopedias for coverage of Jewish topics (especially smaller topics), that most single volume Jewish encyclopedias are better than general encyclopedias for Jewish topics, that the State of Israel can only be found in encyclopedias published after 1948, that coverage of American Jewish topics is generally better in encyclopedias published in the United States, and that they must use the *Index* to the *Encyclopaedia Judaica* to find all topics listed therein (see notes in Appendix A). Assign a follow-up research assignment to reinforce this lesson.

Another lesson is to compare coverage of Jewish topics in printed encyclopedias with those in CD-ROM format.

Responsa Literature

To show relevancy of Bible and Talmud, have students select readings from the Responsa literature and trace the references back to the Bible, Talmud, etc.

Year Books and Directories

Year books and directories contain a wealth of information, frequently overlooked. Let students examine them for content and use. Prepare a word search puzzle on national Jewish organizations and have students find the organization and determine its purpose. Some sources are: *American Jewish Year Book* (New York: American Jewish Committee; Philadelphia: Jewish Publication Society, 1899/1900- .); *World Jewish Directory*, Edmond Y. Lipsitz, ed. (Downsview, Ontario: J.E.S.L. Educational Products, 1991, 2 volumes).

The Haggadah as a Microcosm of Jewish Life

Gather together as many *Haggadot* as possible. Include illustrations and reproductions of *Haggadot* in Jewish art and illuminated manuscript books. Plan a presentation to show why there are thousands of editions of this book, which Jews use only two nights during the entire year. Discuss and show the *Haggadah* as a reflection of: Jewish history, art, prayer, calligraphy, languages, literature, social action, cultures in many lands, concepts of freedom and redemption, stories from the Torah, topics of archaeology, women's liberation, Holocaust, Israel independence, vegetarianism, growth, nature, etc.

History of Jewish Books

Enrich your students experiences by introducing them to the history of Jewish books in print; include reproductions of magnificent manuscripts, *ketuvot*, *Haggadot*, *Siddurim*, and other Hebrew illuminated manuscripts, etc.

Archives and Research

Borrow framed facsimiles of American history documents free from American Jewish Archives (3101 Clifton Avenue, Cincinnati, OH 45220) and have students select one as a basis for research. Display their results in a school exhibit; hang facsimiles on the wall with the student research beside it.

Holidays through Cookbooks

Use cookbooks to revitalize the subject of Jewish holidays to older students. Ask students to read the narratives in Jewish cookbooks. Many are very informative while warmly describing holiday backgrounds and customs. An exceptional example of such a cookbook is *Jewish Cooking in America* by Joan Nathan (New York: Alfred A. Knopf, 1994). Students could make recipes and share the food along with some interesting tidbits about the holiday as a fun class activity.

Student-produced Shows

Assign Jewish subjects for student-produced shows. Students may work in library using whatever production equipment is available, or they could use own offsite equipment. They could present a sound/slide show using illustrations in library books, a photographic essay exhibit, a video production using real people and props, an interactive media presentation using video disc and computer and hypercard stacks, a computer presentation using presentation software, etc.

Pathfinder Culmination Project

The last student library lesson before Confirmation could be to prepare a "pathfinder." Pathfinders are short introductions to topics. They provide patrons with general information on how they can become familiar with a topic. Usually two columns on one page, a pathfinder contains the following parts, listing very abbreviated resource citations:
1. Scope (select a topic, e.g., Israel 1945-1948, Jewish baseball players, Art in the *Haggadah* — 1945 to current, and describe its scope
2. Background (encyclopedias with good background information on the topic)
3. Texts (books or other media that provide good information on the topic)
4. Library call numbers (identify sections of library where the topic is housed)
5. Library subject headings (subject headings in library catalog about the topic)
6. Current materials for an update (subject headings in periodical index; almanacs, yearbooks, etc.)
7. Electronic resources on the topic and the electronic tools to access them
8. Special materials (archives, special collections on the topic, if any)
9. Other resources (people specialists or other libraries, e.g., Holocaust Centers/ Museums)

As you can see, this project pulls together all the library learning through the years. When a student can prepare a good quality pathfinder, then you've reached the goal of helping students become "comfortable" in a Jewish library.

JEWISH BOOK MONTH AND OTHER ACTIVITIES

Jewish Book Month occurs the month before Chanukah, and is the perfect time to focus on reading and other Jewish book activities. This is a joyful international event — and there are hundreds of ways to celebrate Jewish books. Talk with your librarian for ideas; call other Jewish libraries. Write to the Jewish Book Council and the Association of Jewish Libraries for book month programs and materials. Think of it as fun, exciting, interesting and challenging, and your students will respond accordingly!

LIBRARY CONFERENCES AND WORKSHOPS

Be sure to discuss resource problem areas (e.g., current maps of Israel) with librarian; he/she can search for solutions at library conferences and workshops. At library conferences, your librarian meets other librarians and gets new ideas, talks with publishers, and shares school needs, views new sources and resources and ways to use them, updates information technology skills, etc. A librarian in a school setting is an isolated position — there is no one else on-site with the same perspective. If your school's budget supports librarian's professional development, then librarian will be able to attend conferences — for the benefit of all.

SERVICES TO PARENTS

The more Jewish reading, listening, and viewing that children do at home, the better students they are. Join the librarian in promoting library use to parents. When you have the opportunity — during open houses, parent conferences, etc. — encourage family reading, viewing, and read aloud time; recommend your supplemental school library as a good source for materials. If you are involved in planning parent education programs, include a library component to stress the importance of taking books and media home to share. Encourage parents to browse library shelves for Shabbat and Jewish holiday family reading and activities. When a family crisis occurs, recommend the library for support materials. Encourage parents to do parallel reading, i.e., read (on their level) about the subjects their children are studying in your class and share together. When parents establish a habit of borrowing library books for their young children, they frequently become regular library users themselves. When parents read Jewish library books and watch media on Jewish themes, so, too, do their children. You know the value of parent cooperation and participation.

CONCLUSION

Books are friends, and we are the "People of the Book." Remember, the Jewish library will be here long after today's teachers and librarians move on, and it will be there in other communities when your students move on. What greater educational gift can you give your students than the ability to seek and find Jewish reading and information independently, wherever they are, throughout their lives.

Barbara Y. Leff has an M.S. in Library Science from the University of Southern California, and is Library Director at Stephen S. Wise Temple, Los Angeles. She is a past national President of the Association of Jewish Libraries, and is Chairperson of the AJL Library Education Committee. A library consultant, Barbara teaches classes and workshops in Judaica librarianship and microcomputers for libraries.

APPENDIX A
Specific Library Objectives for Jewish Supplemental Schools Library Curriculum

Students will learn to adapt and apply learned library and research skills to a Jewish library setting. They will become familiar with genres of Jewish literature and multi-media Judaic resources and be encouraged to borrow them for home pleasure and information. They will learn the library process via library lessons and independent library activities in the Jewish library.

LIBRARY AND RESEARCH SKILLS AND PROCESSES
Library Rules and Procedures
Students will learn the rules and procedures regarding care of materials, borrowing and returning materials, etc.

Evaluating and Selecting Materials
Students will learn how to evaluate and select Jewish materials for research and pleasure, in all formats, through repeated hands-on library activities.

Kinds of Materials. Students will be able to distinguish between fiction and non-fiction, and will become familiar with the multi-media resources in a Jewish library, including books, periodicals, pamphlets, audiovisual materials, electronic media materials, etc. They will also become familiar with the classical Jewish texts and genres of Jewish literature.

Library Catalog. Students will become proficient in the use of the card and/or computer online catalog in order to find Jewish information and ideas.

Classification Scheme
Students will become familiar with library's classification scheme as a means for finding Judaic material easily and comfortably.

Locating Materials
Students will be able to locate Jewish topics of interest on the library shelves, including the following: Bible stories, Bible (Torah, *Nevi'im, Ketuvim*), biblical aides/commentaries, archaeology, *Halachah*, Jewish thought, folklore and legends, Jewish religious movements, guides to Jewish living, liturgy, Jewish calendar, holidays and life cycle, comparative religion, Hebrew/Yiddish language dictionaries and books, Jewish literature, Jewish communities, marriage and family, Jewish art, music, sports, cookbooks, social conditions and problems, Jewish history worldwide, Holocaust, biography, Zionism, Israel, Middle East, Judaic reference works, etc.

Search Strategy
Students will learn search strategies, including special instructions regarding transliterations and Jewish names, in order to access the library catalog, Jewish dictionaries, encyclopedias, indexes, etc. Where telecommunications is available, they will learn to search the electronic media using electronic tools, and use other methods of finding Jewish information and ideas via emerging information technology tools.

REFERENCE RESOURCES
Almanacs, Yearbooks, and Directories
Students will become familiar with the contents of *American Jewish Year Book, Jewish Book Annual*, and other Jewish year books, almanacs, directories, and trivia books.

Atlases
Students will become familiar with atlases, and especially Jewish historical atlases, e.g., biblical, Holocaust, Israeli, Jewish history, diaspora, which serve as mini-encyclopedias.

Bibliographies
Students will learn how to find bibliography sources in encyclopedias, yearbooks, periodicals, and other databases in order to do further Jewish research.

Biographies
Students will learn to use Jewish biographical works, e.g., *Who's Who in World Jewry, Dictionary of Jewish Biography,* collective and individual biographies.

Chronologies/Time Lines
Students will learn where to find and how to read Jewish history chronologies and time lines.

Dictionaries/Encyclopedias

Students will gain experience in looking up words in Hebrew language dictionaries, English transliterations of Yiddish phrases, and name dictionaries.

Students will become familiar with various children and adult Jewish encyclopedias, dictionaries, compendiums of Jewish knowledge—single and multi-volume, CD-ROM, etc.

Older students will learn to use *Encyclopaedia Judaica* and *EJ Year Book* updates, as well as *EJ Index* (Vol.1) and *EJ Year Book Indexes*. [These Indexes provide access to A-Z Supplemental Entries in the U-Z Vol.16 (pp. 1258-1662), e.g., Hebrew Language, Masorah, Ottoman Empire; and also to other variations, e.g., Isaac Bashevis Singer found under B for Bashevis]

Periodicals and Index

Students will become familiar with adult and children Jewish periodicals—newpapers, magazines, and current sources in the electronic media —and learn to use *Index to Jewish Periodicals*.

Quotations Sources

Students will become competent in using English language quotation books from Jewish, Yiddish, and Hebrew sources, and other quotation-type resources, in all formats.

Vertical Files

Students will learn to use Library's Vertical Files containing pamphlets, clippings, pictures, booklets and other ephemeral materials about Jews and Judaism.

MEDIA AND TELECOMMUNICATIONS

Students will view/hear/use a variety of Jewish audiovisual and computer-related materials, including electronic media, databases, news groups, the Internet, and other networks, etc., for Jewish information.

Students will use telecommunications worldwide and participate in global classroom activities, and use emerging information technology, as it relates to Jews and Judaism.

SPECIALIZED JUDAICA RESOURCES
Jewish Art

Students will be introduced to art in Jewish picture books and to Jewish artists in all media, and the wide range of Jewish art, e.g., ceremonial/synagogue art, Bible art, museum art, illuminated manuscripts, Holocaust art, art in the *Haggadah*, Hebrew calligraphy, photographic essays (e.g., New York's Lower East Side, Eastern Europe, Israel), etc.

Biblical and Talmudic Study

Students of Bar/Bat Mitzvah age and thereafter will become familiar with different versions of the Bible; biblical aides/commentaries on parashah/haftarah; biblical and Talmudic concordances and dictionaries; Talmudic commentaries; Bible and Talmud full text and study aides on CD-ROM and other electronic resources; etc.

Jewish Literature

Students will be introduced to Jewish authors and all genres of Jewish literature, e.g., Bible stories, Biblical and Talmudic legends, Hassidic tales, Jewish folklore and legends, Rabbinic literature, Jewish humor, Holocaust literature, Jewish poetry, Jewish primary sources, Jewish thought, Israeli legends and literature, American and East European literature, anthologies, criticism and analysis, and Jewish fiction (including historical fiction) for all ages, etc.

Jewish Liturgy

Students will become familiar with liturgy of the different Jewish religious movements.

Special Collections

Students will become familiar with special library collections of their school, and their library's customized indexes created for access to Jewish information and ideas, etc.

APPENDIX B
Library Planning Worksheet for Teacher and Librarian

Today's Date _____

LIBRARY SESSION: Date _____ Time _____ Librarian _____

Teacher _____ Class _____ No. of Students _____

GENERAL TOPIC _____

    Specific Focus _____

TEACHER — LEARNING OBJECTIVES _____

MOTIVATIONAL ACTIVITIES: BEFORE Library Session _____

                            AFTER Library Session _____

LIBRARY APPROACH	ADVANCE PREPARATION	HANDOUT
☐ Audiovisual	Teacher _____	
☐ Stories	_____	☐
☐ Research	Librarian _____	
☐ Computer	_____	☐
☐ _____		

POSSIBLE PROBLEMS (Logistics . . . Discipline . . .) _____

                              *

LIBRARIAN — LEARNING OBJECTIVES _____

OUTLINE OF LIBRARY SESSION:	LIBRARY MATERIALS TO BE PRESENTED:
_____	_____
_____	_____
_____	_____
_____	_____
_____	_____

COMMENTS _____

APPENDIX C
Varieties of Library Materials

Library Collection
A library collection should include the traditional print and non-print formats and also current information technology formats. Other very useful library materials are *customized* information files and indexes — the result of collaborative efforts of librarian and teachers in your school. Some wonderful and interesting varieties of library formats, both commercial and "homemade," that you can help promote are as follows:

Material Resources
Traditional library print and non-print materials include books, periodicals, vertical files (i.e., pamphlets, clippings, booklets, pictures, stored vertically in file drawers) — AV materials such as filmstrips, films, posters, flannel graphs, maps, charts, slides, realia, kits, transparencies, art prints and reproductions, videotapes, audio tapes/recordings/compact discs, and games; information technology tools and materials, e.g., computer software, CD-ROM discs, video (laser) discs, interactive media programs, and telecommunications to off site databases, the Internet, electronic bulletin boards, other libraries and networks, etc.

Equipment Resources
Portable equipment to use in classrooms or library are projectors, viewers, recorders, VCR's, and other AV equipment; and information technology equipment, e.g, computers, CD-ROM players, laser disc players, LCD display panel to project computer image to a classroom screen via an overhead projector.

Teacher-made Materials
Encourage your colleagues to share their "homemade" resources. Talented teachers provide creativity and labor for games and study units. The school supplies raw materials and equipment for creating and reinforcing the items so that they are sturdy, and the library acquires the finished product (or a duplicate) and catalogs it as part of the library collection. Materials made from ideas in educational publications and teacher center kits are also ideal for sharing in the library. Also, materials in the Coalition for the Advancement of Jewish Education (CAJE) Curriculum Bank are available via *Bikurim*. Remember to give proper credit to each source and observe copyright laws.

Human Resources Files
Skills and expertise of faculty members, synagogue staff, congregation and community, can be saved on a rolodex or card/computer file as a great help to the school.

Information Files
Other kinds of information, sources or materials available locally, regionally, and/or nationally, organized in a rolodex or card/computer file, can be an asset to the school and community.

Customized Indexes
This is an extraordinary memory tool for teachers and a simple way to expand the library collection without buying more resources. Ask librarian to supervise a "subject analytics" project — analyze a book and save references to unexpected subjects found in parts of the book, e.g., a *mezuzah* story in a book on the Jewish home, a two page color photo of a *sukkah* in a book on Jerusalem. This fun library project allows you and other teachers to share your favorite chapters, paragraphs, illustrations. The easiest way to handle this: teachers read or scan books and make notes, including page numbers, following standard library indexing formats. With the help of typists, librarian prepares a special card or computer indexes referring to the book *and* its interesting parts. Here are some exciting results:

1. *Short Story Index*. Teachers always need stories! Teachers analyze each story in short story collections for content and use; librarian creates a special index for all to share. Examples:
   a. CHANUKAH: Cite five stories associated with Chanukah in Isaac Bashevis Singer's classic, *Zlateh the Goat and Other Stories*, (New York: HarperCollins Children's Books., 1964).
   b. VALUES, TORAH, etc.: Nina Jaffe and Steve Zeitlin tell stories about love, courage, wisdom, Torah, etc., in *While Standing on One Foot: Puzzle Stories and*

346 USING THE LIBRARY CREATIVELY

Wisdom Tales from the Jewish Tradition (New York: Henry Holt & Co., 1993).

2. *Collective Biography Index*: An invaluable source for teacher and class research are brief biographies of important Jewish personalities, especially those about whom whole books have not yet been written. Teachers or volunteers and librarian can jointly produce this biography index. Alternatively, you could have immediate access to all biographees' names if the library has the appropriate software to list them in the note area when a collective biography book is entered into the online catalog.

3. *Illustration Index*: Illustrations, drawings, paintings, charts, maps, etc. make excellent supplemental teaching aids. Create an index by subject, book, and page numbers. One example: would you think to look in an *atlas* for a color chart showing the relationships of Jewish holidays and Shabbat to each other and to the Jewish and secular years? The library catalog entry for this analytic would read:
   a. HOLIDAYS: *A historical Atlas of the Jewish People; From the Time of the Patriarchs to the Present* Eli Barnavi, ed. New York: Alfred A. Knopf, 1992; pages 72-73 (chart) (A similar entry would be made for SHABBAT.)

4. *Excerpts from Books*: Sydney Taylor's popular award winning series has wonderful read-aloud chapters on family holiday celebrations. For example, the first of the series, *All-of-a-Kind Family* (New York: Taylor Productions, 1988 reprint), includes:
   a. SHABBAT: "The Sabbath" — pp. 63-81
   b. PURIM: "Purim Play" — pp. 91-103
   c. SUKKOT: "Succos" — pp. 166-175

5. *Chronologies*: An excellent Holocaust chronology, written in terms that children understand (e.g., no more milk or pets allowed), can be found in Hans Peter Richter's *Friedrich* (New York: Viking/Puffin, 1987), pages 139-149.

6. *Poems:* A thoughtful poem by Constance Gemson explains why "Lot's Wife" looked back in *Four Centuries of Jewish Women's Spirituality, a Sourcebook*, Ellen Umansky and Dianne Ashton, eds. (Boston, Beacon Press, 1992), pages 226-227.

Customized Pictures and Posters

Supplement the library poster/picture files by saving appropriate theme gift wrap and exhibit posters (frequently found in museums) and by clipping photos from pictorial magazines (giving source and date).

Customized Sound and Video Recordings

Record in-house teacher workshops, save with explanatory materials, and circulate to absentee teachers via the library or store in the library collection for new teachers or future in-service sessions. Make similar arrangements, with permission, for teacher conferences, educational workshops, class field trips, and in-house sermons/lectures for use by teachers and teen aides.

Customized Visuals

Select illustrations from books for a lesson and make slides (using a copy stand and camera) for class discussion. Photograph games and teaching aids from other libraries, teacher centers, and the CAJE Curriculum Bank, and donate to your library for a "Teachers' Idea Book." Encourage artistic teachers to donate copies of their original transparencies, story illustrations, or flannel graphs to the library. Again, be sure to give proper credit and follow copyright laws.

Student Projects

Save outstanding student reports to use as teaching aids and for vertical file reference; also laminate their posters, charts, and maps, and store in the poster file for decorating classrooms. Be sure to give credit on each item. Students enjoy reading and seeing other student projects, and learning from them.

Compilation Notebooks and Pamphlet Files

Collect some excellent ephemeral resources, and your librarian (with clerical help) can organize and store them in notebooks or vertical files. (Be aware of copyright laws.) Examples:
1. New Topics, about which there are no books — this is especially appropriate for new, late-breaking stories of interest to the school curriculum.
2. Current Continuing Information, e.g., data about Israel, its leaders' names, the most current map — up-to-the-minute data that is

difficult to find. Faculty can clip from general and Jewish periodicals, indicating source and date on each, and give to library. Besides articles, include political cartoons, illustrations, letters to the editor, etc.

3. Information in Student Periodicals. These articles are brief enough to use for class library research. Ask your school to order two extra copies of student periodicals, e.g., *Shofar* magazine, *Jewish Current Events*, and clip topics of interest for library files.

(You will need two copies so that both sides of the page can be saved.) Back issues of UAHC's *Keeping Posted* — each issue devoted to a single topic — are still available and can be placed in vertical files.

4. Organizations and Charities Research: Create special vertical files using organizational brochures gathered during visits to local Jewish community centers. Use as resources for organization research and *Karen Ami* or other charity research.

NOTES

1. Ken Haycock, *What Works: Research about Teaching and Learning Through the School's Library Resource Center* (Seattle: Rockland Press, 1992), p. 57.
2. *Jewish Computing Catalog: A Guide to Jewish Computing Resources including Software and Telecommunications* (Boulder, CO: Springwells Company, 1991).
3. Haycock, *What Works*, p. 27.
4. Stephen Krashen, *The Power of Reading: Insights from the Research* (Englewood, CO: Libraries Unlimited, Inc., 1993), p. 34.
5. Keith Curry Lance, Lynda Welborn, and Christine Hamilton-Pennell, *The Impact of School Library Media Centers on Academic Achievement* (Castle Rock, CO: Hi Willow Research and Publishing, 1993), p. iv.
6. Krashen, *The Power of Reading*, p. 39.
7. Ibid., p. 37.
8. Ibid., p. 34.
9. Judy Clarence, "LIRT at Midwinter: Managing Library Instruction," A Small Informal Session Which Turned into a Large Informal Session. January 24, 1993, Denver, CO. *Library Instruction Round Table News* of the American Library Association, March 1993, p. 9.
10. Marilyn P. Whitmore, "Aims of User Education in School Libraries: Results of a Nationwide Survey" *Library Instruction Round Table News* of the American Library Association, December 1993, p. 23.
11. Ibid.
12. Lance, *The Impact of School Library Media Centers on Academic Achievement*, p. 7.
13. Krashen, *The Power of Reading*, page 45.
14. Ibid., p. 39.
15. *The Diamond Tree* includes Jewish stories that have variants of universal tales: "The Magic Pitcher" (Little Red Riding Hood); "Katanya" (Tom Thumb/Thumbelina); "The Water Witch" and "The Diamond Tree" (Hansel and Gretel); and "The Bear and the Children" (The Wolf and the Seven Kids).

SELECTED JUDAICA LIBRARY RESOURCES

ASSOCIATION OF JEWISH LIBRARIES
c/o National Foundation for Jewish Culture
330 Seventh Avenue, 21st Floor
New York, NY 10001
  (recommended lists of books, media, and computer-related items; programs; other library info)

CAJE CURRICULUM BANK
JEWISH EDUCATION NEWS
Coalition for the Advancement in Jewish Education
261 West 35th Street, Floor 12A
New York, NY 10001
  (teacher resources, bibliographies)

CENTRAL CATALOGING SERVICE FOR LIBRARIES OF JUDAICA
10400 Wilshire Blvd.
Los Angeles, CA 90024
  (bibliographies, acquisitions, cataloging data)

JEWISH BOOK COUNCIL
15 East 26th Street
New York, NY 10010
  (book lists, Jewish Book Month, *Jewish Book Annual*)

AUDIOVISUAL AND COMPUTER RELATED SOFTWARE RESOURCES
Contact Association of Jewish Libraries for current resources.

For Book Selection

Grossman, Cheryl Silverberg, and Suzy Engman. *Jewish Literature for Children: A Teaching Guide*. Denver: A.R.E. Publishing, Inc., 1985.

Holtz, Barry, ed. *The Schocken Guide to Jewish Books: Where To Start Reading about Jewish History, Literature, Culture, and Religion*. New York: Schocken Books, 1992.

Atlases

(includes historical atlases, which also serve as specialized mini-encyclopedias)

Aharoni, Yohanan, and Avi-Yonah, Michael. *The Macmillan Bible Atlas*. New York: Macmillan, 1993.

Barnavi, Eli, ed. *The Historical Atlas of the Jewish People, from the Time of the Patriarchs to the Present*. New York: Alfred A. Knopf, 1992.

Beinart, Haim. *Atlas of Medieval Jewish History*. New York: Simon and Schuster, 1992.

de Lange, Nicholas. *Atlas of the Jewish World*. New York: Facts on File, 1984.

Friesel, Evyatar. *Atlas of Modern Jewish History*. rev. from the Hebrew ed. New York: Oxford University Press, 1990.

Gilbert, Martin. *Atlas of the Arab-Israeli Conflict*. New York: Oxford University Press, 1993.

Gilbert, Martin, ed. *Illustrated Atlas of Jewish Civilization: 4,000 Years of Jewish History*. New York: Macmillan, 1990.

Encyclopedias for Children

Ben-Asher, Naomi, and Hayim Leaf. *Junior Jewish Encyclopedia*. New York: Shengold Publications. Current edition. (no index)

Chaikin, Miriam. *Menorahs, Mezuzas, and Other Jewish Symbols*. New York: Clarion Books, 1990.

Junior Judaica: Encyclopedia Judaica for Youth. Jerusalem: Keter Publ./Encyclopaedia Judaica. 6 volumes. Index. (out-of print, but available)

Encyclopedias

Birnbaum, Philip. *Encyclopedia of Jewish Concepts*. rev. ed. New York: Hebrew Publishing, 1979.

Abramson, Glena, ed. *The Blackwell Companion to Jewish Culture*. Oxford, England: Blackwell Publishers, 1989.

Alpher, Joseph, ed. *Encyclopedia of Jewish History: Events and Eras of the Jewish People*. New York: Facts on File, 1986.

Bridger, David, and Samuel Wolk. *The New Jewish Encyclopedia*. New York: Behrman House, 1976.

Cahn-Lipman, David E. *The Book of Jewish Knowledge: Basic Facts about Judaism*. Northvale, NJ: Jason Aronson, 1991.

Cohn-Sherbok, Dan. *The Blackwell Dictionary of Judaica*. Oxford, England: Blackwell Publishers, 1992.

Encyclopedia Judaica. Jerusalem: Keter, 1972- . 16 vols. (with yearbook supplements)

Fischel, Jack, and Sanford Pinsker. *Jewish American History and Culture: An Encyclopedia*. New York: Garland Publishing, 1992.

Frankel, Ellen, and Betsy Platkin Teutsch. *The Encyclopedia of Jewish Symbols*. Northvale, NJ: Jason Aronson Inc., 1992.

Jewish Encyclopedia. New York: Funk and Wagnalls, 1901-05. (out of print, but available)

Reich, Bernard. *Historical Dictionary of Israel*. Metuchen, NJ: Scarecrow Press, 1992.

Sirof, Harriet. *Junior Encyclopedia of Israel*. Middle Village, NY: Jonathan David, 1980. (out-of-print, but available)

Telushkin, Joseph. *Jewish Literacy: The Most Important Things To Know About the Jewish Religion, Its People and Its History*. New York: Morrow, 1991.

Wigoder, Geoffrey, ed. *The Encyclopedia of Judaism*. New York: Macmillan, 1989.

Wigoder, Geoffrey, ed. *The New Standard Jewish Encyclopedia*. New York: Facts on File, 1992.

Other Reference Works

Gribetz, Judah. *The Timetables of Jewish History*. New York: Simon and Schuster, 1993

Isaacs, Ronald H. *The Jewish Information Source Book: A Dictionary and Almanac*. Northvale, NJ: Jason Aronson Inc., 1993.

Olitzky, Kerry M., and Ronald H. Isaacs. *A Glossary of Jewish Life*. Northvale, NJ: Jason Aronson Inc., 1992.

Unterman, Alan. *Dictionary of Jewish Lore and Legend*. New York: Thames and Hudson, 1991.

Note: The author is indebted to the following resources for help with this Bibliography:

Charles Cutter and Micha F. Oppenheim. "Recommended Judaica Reference Works, 1991-1992" in *Judaica Librarianship* of Association of Jewish Libraries, Spring 1992-Winter 1993, pp. 111-118.

Rita Frischer and Rachel Glasser. "Selected Cataloging Data" in Central Cataloging Service for Libraries of Judaica. Los Angeles: Sinai Temple Blumenthal Library, January 1992-December 1993.

SUPPORTS FOR THE TEACHER

CHAPTER THIRTY-TWO

WORKING WITH TEEN AIDES
Helene Schlafman

Developing a program for teen aides in the Religious School can be a wonderfully rewarding experience for teachers, parents, young children in the school, for the aides themselves, and for the congregation and community, too.

Through an aide program, Jewish teenagers can play meaningful roles in Jewish education. They are encouraged to share with others what they have learned and to continue to enrich their own Jewish education. Such a program helps the teenager to view Jewish education as an important focus in Jewish life and to appreciate the process of education. It enables the teenager to be a part of the process rather than apart from it. Furthermore, involvement in an aide program reduces significantly the post Bar/Bat Mitzvah/pre-Confirmation drop out rate.

In this chapter, I will outline briefly the training necessary for teenage classroom aides, point out some guidelines for teachers as they work with aides, identify potential problem areas, and list some suggested tasks that teen aides can perform in the classroom and the school. I have also included a Code of Ethics for student aides, as well as a list of suggestions for aides to help them with their classroom responsibilities. A short Bibliography concludes the chapter.

TRAINING

Before entering the classroom as an aide, the teenager requires specialized and extensive training. Such training should be organized by the Director of Education and/or Rabbi and should include an introduction to child development and group dynamics, as well as an overview of educational processes and techniques. This general background must then be related to the Religious School/Hebrew School setting.

The course should provide the participants with actual experience in lesson planning, teaching techniques, discipline, and classroom management. It should also include a review of all the cognitive information which aides need to master in order to be prepared to teach — Hebrew vocabulary, history, prayer, holidays, and other basic components of the school's curriculum.

Upon completion of the training period, the aide is then ready to enter the classroom where the important process of learning to be a teacher begins. From then on, the aide will look to the classroom teacher for support and guidance.

This chapter can serve as your orientation on working with an aide. In addition, it would also be beneficial to get together formally and informally with the other teachers in your school to share suggestions, pool ideas, and consider potential problems that might arise when working with an aide.

HOW CAN AN AIDE HELP YOU?

An aide in your classroom can open endless creative opportunities. First, you will want to examine how an aide can help you.

Before meeting with your aide for the first time, list the ways you think an aide could be utilized in your classroom based on your teaching style. For example, one teacher may use Learning Centers. In that teacher's classroom an aide could be responsible for one particular station. Another teacher might use grouping. In such a setting the aide can work with one of the small groups. Still another teacher might have an individualized program. For him/her, an aide could help supervise and check assignments. For the frontal lecturer, the aide might tutor individual children. So, ask yourself these questions:

1. How can my aide be helpful to me and to my students?
2. How can my aide provide an opportunity to try something different? (Remember that having an aide means there is a lower teacher-student ratio. This gives you the chance to experiment with new methods.)
3. What are some of the difficulties I face in the classroom? How can my aide help in these areas? (Examples: A first grade teacher might need extra hands for art projects, snack time, etc. A fifth grade teacher might have students who work much faster than the average and so become easily bored. An aide could do enrichment projects with these students. An aide can work with someone who might not catch on as quickly as other students. An aide can take over the class while the teacher deals with a problem situation.)

Once you have established some possibilities for the utilization of your aide, it is then time to meet together.

MEETING YOUR AIDE

It is very important for you and your aide to get to know each other before the first day of class. The first meeting is usually awkward. The aide may feel somewhat uncomfortable and insecure. Try to set the aide at ease. You may want to invite the aide to lunch or to your home. You could also meet at school and work together to prepare your classroom.

REMEMBER, YOUR AIDE IS ALSO YOUR STUDENT.

When you first meet your aide, be sure to share backgrounds and experiences. Through this exchange you will both gain insight into working together. Find out about interests, talents, and future plans. You may have an undiscovered song leader. Perhaps your aide is interested in Israel or in archaeology . . . which could lead to an exciting unit.

During this first interview, you will also discover something about your aide's personality. You might decide that this person would work better in small groups or on a one-to-one basis rather than with the group as a whole. This initial meeting is a good time for you to share your needs and goals. Your particular interest may be to provide students with individualized attention, to offer more projects, or strengthen emphasis on reading skills. Discuss how you and your aide might work together to achieve your aims. Listen for new ideas and approaches from your aide. Don't forget, your teenage helper is closer to your students' point of view and he/she may have some interesting ideas or different approaches to offer.

Have copies of your curriculum available. Your aide should have a copy of all textbooks and the complete curriculum outline to study. You might also want to suggest some extra readings. Your aide will probably not have an in-depth background in the subject matter, but should be encouraged to expand existing knowledge. Remember, your aide is also your student.

Be clear about your approaches to classroom management and outline your expectations of both your students and your aide in this important area.

Find out your aide's expectations for the year. How does he/she envision working in the classroom? Is he/she willing to take responsibility for a ten minute segment during each class period? Will he/she be more comfortable working with a small group or on a one-to-one basis? What is your aide's daily school schedule? What kind of time is available to prepare for class?

Before the meeting ends, try to establish a "possible plan" and agree on a procedure. For example, you might suggest that your aide observe the class and work with individual students for the first few sessions and/or be responsible for a closing game based on vocabulary review. Then, plan to meet again soon to explore future possibilities.

THE ONGOING RELATIONSHIP

Working with your aide is an ongoing process. It requires flexibility on both parts because there is no set division of tasks. It is often difficult to find the right expectations for an aide. This naturally differs with each teacher/aide situation. On the one hand, your aide needs to be challenged. There is no satisfaction in being a "flunky," assigned to do only the menial tasks. On the other hand, the aide is not qualified to take over a major portion of the curriculum, to be responsible, for example, for teaching the entire history section.

One teacher may choose to take roll while the aide does a warm-up Hebrew game. Another might have the aide preparing flashcards while she herself introduces a new lesson. Another may split the class in half for Hebrew, the teacher teaching reading, the aide supervising writing. If you work and talk together you will uncover a process that is appropriate for both of you. Don't be afraid to experiment.

TRAINING AND SUPERVISION

It is extremely important to carry on an ongoing training program with your aide. Aides are not professional teachers; they will need help and guidance. You can share important insights with your aide on a daily basis. Explain why you chose to handle a situation in a particular way. For example, say "I chose Johnny to be in charge of our Chanukah mural because I think we should encourage him to take a more responsible role in our class." Or, "Did you notice that I sat with Lori while you were playing the *Around the World* game with the class? Well, she was absent last week and didn't know the new vocabulary, so I took the opportunity to go over the words with her. She might have felt uncomfortable playing the game."

Share problems with your aide so that he/she can be involved in the processes and solutions. "I'm not pleased with our students' behavior in the sanctuary. Let's figure out a plan of action so that we can change this." Or, "Richard seems so withdrawn. How can we encourage him to become more involved?"

Explain fully your approach to discipline. Give specific suggestions for maintaining the desired control. Work on positive reinforcement techniques and preventive discipline. Help your aide to know when and how to step into a situation. (For ideas, see Chapter 4, "Classroom Management.")

Keep your aide up to date on the latest programs and materials and what is happening in the school. You and your aide should attend teacher workshops, seminars, and staff meetings together. Help your aide to be aware of the various policies and procedures of the school as a whole. He/she should know whom to call in the event of absence, what to do in an emergency, etc.

Suggest that your aide read some of the chapters in this book.

Arrange a daily meeting time with your aide, as well as monthly planning sessions. It is very rewarding to watch your aide develop into a capable and responsible young teacher.

In the beginning, your aide will probably function best in a support role. Look to your aide to help with projects, to tutor, read stories, and to work with small groups. As confidence develops, you can encourage a more outgoing role. Your aide can begin with a simple lesson such as teaching a game or a song. When this is successful, he/she can begin to develop short lessons and eventually work on teaching an ongoing unit.

The amount of time needed to become a capable teacher will vary with the individual aide. Some aides will be ready for a frontal teaching experience after the first few days. Others will need to develop confidence and may not be ready for months. Your encouragement and backing will be an important factor in your aide's development.

When your aide is ready for the "big step" be supportive and encourage creativity! Let your aide try out ideas even though they may not be in your style. And help your aide always to feel that what he or she is doing is important.

The lesson plan guide in Appendix A will help your aide to plan a complete lesson. Be sure to review the plan and make suggestions before the actual lesson occurs. Guidance will probably be needed in the setting of goals. (Also see Chapter 19, "Planning Lively Lessons.")

You can help to insure your aide's success during his/her lesson by remaining in the classroom. This usually eliminates discipline problems and enables your aide to complete the lesson plan without extraneous interruptions. After your aide becomes more secure and capable, your presence is no longer absolutely necessary.

Lesson evaluation by the aide is a very important step. Your aid should sit down after the lesson and complete an evaluation form (see Appendix B for a sample form). Meanwhile, you can jot down any comments you might have. Set a time, preferably soon after the lesson, to meet privately with your aide. First, listen to the aide's evaluation of the lesson. The points you were going to make may have already been covered. The aide will gain a great deal from determining areas that need improvement in a self-evaluation process. Your aide will look to you for encouragement. So be positive! Always begin and end your comments with the positive aspects of the lesson. "You really had their attention with your relay game — it's a terrific idea! Next time you might want to divide into more teams so that everyone can have several turns." Ask your aide to make suggestions. "Can you think of a way to clarify your instructions? Some of the children seemed to be confused at first. Once they understood what you wanted, they really enjoyed the game. I was pleased to see that everyone became excited about reviewing the new vocabulary words." Be careful — criticism can be devastating. You and your aide will grow and develop through this evaluation process.

Remember that your aide depends on you for guidance. Your approaches to education, your attitudes and mannerisms will often be emulated. You are an important role model for your aide.

PROBLEM AREAS

Sometimes the teacher and aide are mismatched and personalities clash. Some personalities just do not mesh into a working relationship. If this occurs, I strongly suggest switching aides. It's important for both the teacher and aide to be honest about this so that a change be made. It is sometimes helpful for the teacher to compose a help wanted advertisement and for aides to submit job resumes.

> **BENEFITS OF A TEEN AIDE PROGRAM OUTWEIGH THE PROBLEMS.**

The relationship between the teacher and aide is crucial. The students in the class are quite sensitive to this relationship. Mutual respect and admiration will be felt by your class. Criticism and correction should not occur in front of others. Make suggestions privately and work out solutions together. If you show respect toward your aide and give him/her a feeling of authority, the students will react in the same way toward the aide. And remember, don't take your aide for granted. Always show appreciation for your aide's work.

It is important to be honest with your aide. When you are direct, misunderstandings are minimized. Be assertive. Let your aide know what you expect.

The aide is caught in a dual role as both a student and a teacher. Often this becomes difficult for both aide and teacher. The teacher may sometimes expect too much, or may not expect enough. The aide may find it difficult to relate to a former teacher and to accept the responsibilities that are expected. The teacher may feel that his/her role in the classroom is being usurped. The aide may feel treated "like a child." The aide may try a power trip, using his/her position unfairly in the classroom. The aide may become bogged down with homework and other activities and not attend class on a regular basis.

If situations such as these do occur, the solution can be found through communication. Encourage your aide to be direct with you. Feel free to state your concerns. Seek solutions together.

The benefits of the teen aide program far outweigh the problems that may occur. You will find that the enthusiasm generated from the aides will be felt throughout the entire school. Your programs will be revitalized. Your students will look to the aides as positive role models.

Your own aide will help you to gain greater perspective of the students' viewpoint. Because they are not authority figures, aides are often especially successful at communicating with and encouraging students. They can free you to work in small groups, individualize, and provide enrichment programming. You will help your teen aide to be involved in Jewish education during the high school years, enabling him/her to gain insight into the workings of the synagogue. Aides themselves become better students and feel a loyalty and responsibility to the congregation. They tend to participate in Jewish summer camps and Israel programs. They will often choose to incorporate Jewish themes in their public school term papers and to take advanced courses in Jewish studies.

Teens who have been aides in Religious Schools often become active in Jewish affairs on the college campus and frequently rise to leadership positions. They are better prepared for responsibility than most people of the same age. As college students, they may develop as full teachers in your program or if they attend out of town colleges, they will always be able to find positions in other congregational schools.

The following lists detail some of the tasks that teenage aides can perform in the classroom and in the school. The list is meant to be suggestive; you will surely think of other duties which relate to the needs of your particular classroom and school.

TASKS FOR TEENAGE AIDES
In the Classroom
- Tutoring
- Working with students on individual projects
- Working with small groups
- Staffing Learning Centers
- Acting as a reading partner
- Designing and creating bulletin boards
- Correcting papers
- Supervising work
- Leading games
- Supervising recess
- Telling stories
- Helping with drama
- Developing materials
- Working with gifted students
- Reinforcing Hebrew
- Helping with art projects
- Helping with music
- Leading dance
- Presenting the weekly Torah portion
- Spearheading preventive discipline
- Creating a student poetry book
- Choosing "hero/heroine of the month"
- Organizing treasure hunts
- Creating photo montages

In the School
- Working with the newspaper
- Making Hebrew signs
- Designing and carrying out *tzedakah* projects
- Leading songs
- Leading Junior Choir
- Directing art projects
- Designing and creating displays/bulletin boards
- Conducting a reading clinic
- Helping with school open houses
- Tutoring
- Producing materials
- Creating flash cards
- Creating worksheets
- Designing Games
- Organizing slide presentations
- Showing films and slides
- Making tapes
- Creating posters
- Making signs
- Working in the library
- Introducing new books
- Staffing the bookmobile
- Cataloging
- Doing research
- Helping in the office
- Helping with Hebrew enrichment
- Leading dance
- Leading photography projects
- Running a Hebrew store
- Designing Hebrew sayings of the week
- Leading outdoor games
- Conducting services
- Leading history tours
- Acting out historical events
- Staffing field trips
- Staffing camp weekends/Shabbatonim/family education programs
- Running A/V equipment
- Planning holiday skits
- Designing game shows
- Organizing Israeli stamp club
- Organizing Israeli coin club
- Helping with puppet shows
- Doing magic shows
- Supervising individualized projects
- Helping with all-school projects
- Listening to Bar/Bat Mitzvah chanting/speeches
- Directing small group projects
- Helping with class projects
- Supervising murals
- Preparing resource material
- Leading holiday workshops Programming
- Organizing and staffing Purim Carnival
- Cooking
- Conducting interviews
- Developing educational videos
- Leading school worship services
- Conducting library research projects
- Planning a walk through history
- Programming (immigration, Maccabiah, games shows, family education, etc.)
- Leading *mitzvah* projects
- Organizing chronicles
- Helping with family worship services
- Developing a congregational history

CONCLUSION

Appendix C is a suggested "Code of Ethics" for student aides. Appendix D contains a list of helpful suggestions for aides. You may wish to add some of your own suggestions to this latter list and pass it along to your aide. Your interest and encouragement can help your aide grow as a learner and as a teacher. You, too, will learn and grow in the process, becoming more effective in the classroom and in interpersonal relationships as well.

Helene Schlafman has been the Director of Education at Congregation Beth Israel in San Diego since 1977. She has received curriculum awards for her Madrichim Classes, Camp Programming, and Beth Israel's children's performing troupe, SHOW B.I.S. She lectures throughout the country on Hebrew enrichment, teacher training, teenage programming, and camping education.

APPENDIX A
Student Aide Lesson Plan Outline

NAME: _____

1. **WHEN?** (day and date of lesson)

2. **WHO?** (grade and age of students; name of teacher; type of class)

3. **WHY?** (purpose of lesson: goals to be accomplished)

    A. General Goals

    B. Specific Goals

4. **HOW?** (methods to be used)

5. **WHAT?** (equipment: audiovisual, craft supplies, teaching aids, etc., to be used)

APPENDIX B
Student Aide Evaluation

1. Were your goals accomplished? (Explain)

2. How did you use your methods and equipment?

3. How did the class respond?

4. What, if any, changes did you make on the spot?

5. Would you make any changes in your plan if you were to give this lesson again?

PLEASE WRITE ANY ADDITIONAL COMMENTS ON THE REVERSE SIDE.

APPENDIX C
Student Aide "Code of Ethics"

REMEMBER:
1. Teachers are responsible for everything that takes place in the classroom and they must make all decisions on program and behavior.

2. Classroom work is always kept confidential, except between the teacher and the aide.

3. Problems that may arise in your hours of work should be discussed with your teacher and/or supervisor.

4. Aides are always faithful and prompt. They know that no program works if only half the people show up only half the time. Please be sure to call in advance in case of an absence.

5. Aides know that they are there to help the children.

6. Aides set a good example for the students. Remember, you are a role model!

NEVER:
1. Belittle a child or make comparisons between children.

2. Hit a child under any conditions. Also, "rough housing" can be dangerous.

3. Visit with other aides while on duty.

4. Do children's work, such as drawing pictures for them or telling them answers.

5. Rush children or nag at them.

6. Criticize the teacher to children or to parents. (Instead, tell the teacher your criticism.)

7. Start projects with children that you cannot finish.

APPENDIX D

Suggestions for Student Aides

1. Call the child by name at each opportunity.

2. Listen attentively to the child. Encourage him/her to watch you as you talk. (Working across from each other helps reinforcement of speech better than working side by side.)

3. Start where the child is successful in the subject matter and proceed slowly into new material. Always end the session with a successful experience.

4. Praise the child for even the smallest success.

5. Observe the total child and carefully watch his/her responses as you work.

6. Approach a subject in a very specific way. In planning with the child, have few expectations and express them clearly. Present alternatives instead of "no-no's."

7. Remember that each session is also a language experience with speaking, listening, reading, and writing. As an example, speak in a quiet, controlled voice.

8. Be relaxed and confident — the student will relax with you!

9. Teach appropriate behavior by example. Show by demonstration, such as the quiet way of entering a room, how to behave during services. When you are polite to the child, you are helping the child learn manners.

10. Be prepared — know your material, but . . .

11. Be FLEXIBLE! Don't be afraid to admit your mistakes. No one is perfect or knows everything and students are delighted at such honesty. It gives them a chance to become a teacher to you or an opportunity for the two of you to learn together, both of which are important academically and personally.

12. Be PATIENT! Remember that teachers are human — they will have good days as well as bad and will not be operating at 100% efficiency all the time. No one can.

13. Be ENTHUSIASTIC! It's contagious!

14. BELIEVE IN YOURSELF! We are all more believable when we do!

BIBLIOGRAPHY

Joseph, Sam. *Madrikhim Handbook*. Los Angeles: Torah Aura Productions, 1990.

Perl, Michael. *Teacher Aide Handbook*. Dubuque, IA: Kendall-Hunt, 1993.

Welty, Don A. *Teacher-Aide and the Instructional Team*. New York: McGraw-Hill, 1976.

SUBJECT MATTER

CHAPTER THIRTY-THREE

THE CHALLENGE OF TEACHING ABOUT GOD

Sherry H. Blumberg

The experience of God is the source, the wellspring, from which Judaism as a religion and, later, as a way of life, grew. The individual's relationship to God, and the community's response has nurtured, challenged, and shaped Jewish history; it continues to do so. While actions are considered more important by Jews than belief, it is the belief which enables the actions to have meaning. Our ability to experience a relationship with the sacred and the divine, our partnership with God, have created the context for Jewish values, ethics, symbols, etc.

Each Jew, therefore, is responsible for confronting his or her beliefs and feelings about God. As teachers in Jewish schools, we have the privilege of facilitating this experience for our students, of creating the context for the exploration, and of making available the content. It is also our responsibility to confront our own doubts, questions, feelings, and ideas.

An individual's experience of God will change and grow during his or her lifetime. The experience of God is connected to the "faith development" of the individual. How a person experiences God will help determine how one grows in a religious tradition, and even how one makes sense of the world. Faith development is a process unique to each individual, but there are some elements in common for all people as they develop and grow as human beings. (For more on this subject, see Chapter 8, "Faith Development: A Jewish View.") If we as Jewish educators want to help influence the faith development of our students, then we must help them to experience God in a Jewish context. There are many paths to God, each as different and special as the person who is seeking.

This chapter will present the terminology needed to teach and discuss God, then will outline some overall approaches to teaching God, and finally, will suggest some specific strategies that can be used and adapted in the classroom. These definitions, approaches, and techniques, along with the annotated Bibliography at the conclusion of the chapter, will help teachers facilitate their students' exploration of the subject, as well as their own.

No one method of teaching about God is correct, and there are obviously many more ideas than can be included here. Hopefully, this material will provide a starting point and will serve to encourage teachers to create their own approaches and techniques. It is wise to be aware that every student will respond uniquely to the activities teachers choose, an indication of the richness of this area of our tradition, and of the mystery and wonder of God.

TERMINOLOGY: VOCABULARY AND SYMBOLS

As we begin to approach teaching the ideas and concepts connected with God, or the experience of God, one of the gravest difficulties is the problem of words and language. Words are symbols. We must determine whether the words used in our tradition to speak about God still have the same meaning today or whether we must create a new vocabulary to express our "God-talk" (a term coined by John MacQuarrie in his book of that title). Further, we must understand the statements of faith from other eras in the context of modern secular and technological times — perhaps not in exactly the same way, yet language is the tool we use. Because this is so, here is a list of words that the teacher should be able to define or explain:

Belief Systems
Theism – belief in the existence of God

Atheism – a view which denies the existence of a God
Agnosticism – the view that we cannot know whether or not God exists
Monotheism – a belief that there is one God
Pantheism – God is equated with the forces of nature; God is in everything

Nature of God
Omniscient – all knowing
Omnipresent – all present, everywhere
Omnipotent – all powerful
Transcendent – above and separate from human beings and the earth, a force, a power
Immanent – close and personal, immediate, a God that cares
Creation – the act of bringing the world into existence
Revelation – the act of communication by God to human beings, and the content of the communication
Redemption – a religious concept expressing a striving by human beings for personal improvement. When related to God, synonyms include saving, salvation, etc.
Covenant – in theological terms, a binding agreement between God and human beings.
Holiness, Sacredness – that which is set apart, special, or unique; not common; imbued with religious meaning (Hebrew: *kodesh, kadosh*)

OVERALL APPROACHES TO TEACHING GOD

Often, we convey to students messages about our own values through the importance we attach to a particular area of the curriculum. These messages are reflected in the amount of time spent, the methodology we use, and in the overall approach we take to the subject. We also give our students messages from what we do not include. Therefore, it is essential to consider carefully how, when, and in what way we teach about God in our own classroom and in the school.

In the following section we will consider the impact of each of several possible approaches to teaching about God.

Responding to Questions as They Arise

The subject of God is often left unexplored until a question arises from a student. Then, depending on where the teacher is in the lesson or unit, or where the class is, the question may be answered or may be postponed.

It is best to explore questions about God as they occur. One advantage of doing so is the high level of interest which is already present (i.e., the student is ready to explore this question). A disadvantage of this approach is more subtle: often the students do not know what question to ask. They are afraid to seem ignorant, especially when talking about God.

When using this approach, plan experiences that create questions. Try to integrate ideas about God into the teaching of history, prayer, customs and traditions, and values. Don't be afraid to mention the word God during the course of discussion. When the ideas and experience of God are introduced as an integral part of all Jewish life, students will be encouraged to talk freely on the subject.

> **INTEGRATE IDEAS ABOUT GOD INTO ALL YOUR TEACHING.**

Feelings and Emotions Connected with God

One of the most frequent ways of approaching God is to explore the question of God through the emotions. Emotions such as love, wonder, awe, mystery, security, doubt, and others, provide openings for discussions and experiences connected with God. Jewish literature, especially Psalms and passages from Prophets, can reinforce this type of exploration.

An advantage of this approach is that it is appropriate for many different age groups. Another is that it can instill love of God and demonstrate that feeling and faith are important parts of Jewish life. However, if the teacher is uncomfortable with this, or if the students are too resistant, the students can become silly and the session meaningless. If there is an adequate preparation, both younger and older students can benefit greatly from approaching the subject of God through the emotions.

Historical Approach

For the older students who understand time and conceptual development, a historical approach to the subject of God is appropriate. Source materials can be arranged chronologically. An emphasis on the developing idea of God will encourage students to continue the chain of tradition by adding their own ideas. This approach is primarily cognitive. However, it can be combined with an expression of feelings that will enrich the explorations of the students. It conveys to the students a message that God is present and active in Jewish history whenever we have a relationship with God.

It is not advantageous to use this approach before students are ready to assimilate the attendant complex intellectual ideas and concepts. It is important to focus on questions and concepts that are specifically geared to the age level you teach.

Theological Approach

An exploration of, and confrontation with, the ideas about and experiences of God by theologians is also appropriate for older students. The ideas of different theologians (e.g., Rambam, Buber, Heschel, etc.) are presented to students. This approach reinforces in students the fact that people think deeply about God and then write about their thoughts and experiences. This, too, is a cognitive approach and, in combination with the historical approach, can be very effective.

The centrality of God in Jewish life obliges us to consider carefully how and when we present the subject to our students. Whatever the approach, a decision must be made in advance and only after a great deal of thought and study. Being clear about the overall approach will facilitate the creation of lessons which will accomplish their intended goals and objectives. If a decision is made to integrate the teaching of God into all aspects of the curriculum, students will, in the course of their years in religious school be able to experience each of the approaches outlined above. Thus the context and content for a variety of experiences related to God will be present and students can carry on their search throughout their adult lives. However, even if a choice is made to answer questions about God as they arise, some forethought about the answers and familiarity with sources, concepts, and strategies is necessary.

SOME SPECIFIC STRATEGIES

Below are some examples of strategies for presenting ideas, concepts, and experiences about God. Whenever possible, credit is given to the originator.

Experiences with Props: Sugar in the Water

Using two glasses of water (one plain, and one with some sugar dissolved in the water so that it cannot be seen) have students taste the contents of both glasses. Do they look the same? (Yes.) God is like the sugar in the water. We cannot see God, but God's presence sweetens the world and our lives. Ask students how God sweetens their lives.

Analogies: Rabbi Akiva and the Skeptic

A skeptic asked Rabbi Akiva to prove the existence of God. Akiva answered him by asking, "Who made your suit of clothes?" The skeptic answered, "Why, the tailor, of course." Rabbi Akiva asked him to prove it. The result of the discussion was the realization that no proof was necessary, since the suit obviously could not have made itself. Then Akiva pointed out that the universe could not have created itself anymore than could the suit of clothes.

Have the students find other proofs of God's existence that relate to Rabbi Akiva's explanation (love, a tree growing from a seed, etc.).

Essays on Classroom Doors

Stop in the middle of a high school class to ask students to write a 200 word essay about the door of the classroom. Each essay will be different, yet the door exists. Make the analogy that our views of God are different, yet one God exists. (Rabbi Wolli Kaelter)

Cartoons

Using cartoons can be fun and challenging and can result in stimulating, often illuminating, discussions. Peanuts, Broomhilda, Kelly and Duke, and Feiffer are good sources for cartoons. Students can also create and share their own cartoons to express their ideas about God.

Nature of God

Place six signs around the room, each of which expresses one idea about God:
1. Master of the Universe – God pulls the strings and works miracles.
2. Watchmaker – God put the world together, wound it up, then left it running
3. List Maker – God takes notes on what we do and rewards or punishes us for our acts.
4. Still Small Voice – our conscience, the voice of right and wrong.

5. God is order, gives order – God is nature and scientific rules.
6. Personal God – God is a presence which comforts us and has a personal relationship with us.

Have students choose the idea that best describes their belief about God. In small groups, discuss why they arrived at the choice. Bring the groups together to share. (Shirley Barish)

For a similar exercise, see the beginning of the Leader Guide for the mini-course *God: The Eternal Challenge* by Bissell.

Art Projects

Art projects are among the best strategies for teaching about God. Have students make collages or use clay or other media to express feelings about God which words cannot describe. Concepts that lend themselves particularly to art projects include Oneness, Creation, Revelation, and Holiness. Begin by using shapes and colors in abstract designs. It is also effective to have students draw the ways in which they are partners with God.

1. For older Students: Share the various names of God with the students. Alone or in small groups, pick one of the names and draw it on a small piece of paper. Then take the smaller pieces and create the shape of the number one, or place the names together in a circle. This illustrates that all the names of God are part of "One God."
2. Ask students what color or shape they think of when they hear the word God. Using colored crayons and all kinds of shapes, have them create an abstract expression of their thoughts about God.
3. Using clay, have the younger students pretend that they were present at creation and partners with God as the world was created. In what ways would they have helped God? How does creation continue each day? How can they help God now?
4. Using Maimonides "Thirteen Attributes of God," create collages to represent each of the attributes. This is especially effective with older students who can conceptualize the qualities. Make sure the collages reflect a wide variety of interests.

Music and Poetry

Music and poetry are like two doorways into the beliefs of others about God. Students can begin by reacting to songs, sounds, and words. This is often safer than starting with an exploration of one's own beliefs. (Don't forget that many prayers are also poems.) When using these media, be creative yourself. Use music and poetry as triggers, then add dance, art, discussion, and other activities.

As a follow-up, have the students create their own songs and their own poetry about God. Both older and younger students can achieve beautiful expressions.

Excellent poems for the older students may be found in the section on God in *A Time To Seek* (UAHC Press). Especially appropriate are Jacob Glatstein's poem "Jewish God" and "The Great Sad One" by Robert Mezey. Younger children can find the poetry in *Let's Talk About God* by Dorothy Kripke (Behrman House) to be a stimulus. Also, don't forget to use the Psalms, which through their poetic imagery and their depiction of our relationship with God have provided inspiration to Jews and non-Jews through the centuries.

There are many beautiful songs about God which can be used appropriately as teaching tools. Some examples are: "*Lo Ira,*" "*Eyli, Eyli*" (in both Hebrew and English), "*Eleh Chamda Libi,*" and the album *Sing Unto God* (Debbie Friedman). A teacher of older students may wish to compare Jewish liturgical music with that of other religions, e.g., Gregorian chants or Christmas carols.

Role Play

The enactment of encounters between God and human beings can be an exciting and stimulating strategy. Biblical and *midrashic* stories present a rich source for short plays or role play situations. Updating the incidents to today's world can be especially meaningful. Here is an example of a role play situation:

Enact the argument between Abraham and God about Sodom and Gomorrah. Have students switch roles. Add the private, inner voice of both God and Abraham.

One caution regarding role playing: unless the students are experienced in the technique and unless the stage is carefully set, the group may lack focus and the point of the exercise may be lost. It is also important to ask follow-up questions which will reinforce the goals of the lesson. For example, how did you feel when you played God? Was it difficult to have so much responsibility? How do you think God "feels" when human beings don't follow the laws and commandments?

Fantasy Trips

The use of fantasy can create the mood and the context for an exploration and confrontation with God. Such fantasy trips also help people to learn to pray. Ask students to close their eyes, and then begin to create an experience. It is very important that students learn to accept their fantasies and not to judge responses. Sharing should also be optional. Here is a suggestion for a fantasy:

> Close your eyes and go to one of your favorite spots in the whole world — a beach, the mountains, your room, wherever you are comfortable and safe and loved. Picture the place, smell its odors, listen for its sounds.... Relax there.

USE FANTASY TRIPS TO EXPLORE AND CONFRONT GOD.

You may invite someone to be with you, or you may be alone....

You feel love and feel loved....

You feel healthy and strong....

You feel safe and happy....

Listen quietly to your breathing. Now listen as a voice fills your thoughts: *Sh'ma Yisrael Adonai Eloheynu Adonai Echad*...

You sense the meaning of the Oneness of God... Unique, Alone, Special, God....

You may ask any question of God that you wish....

Perhaps you may be answered, perhaps not. You can say anything you wish to God....

You may ask for something... for yourself, for the world, for friends.... You may be answered yes or no....

Say your favorite prayer. The feelings about God will leave you in peace and happiness.... When you are ready, open your eyes....

Process the experiences of the students.

Journals

Keeping a journal can be a very important way for students to express their thoughts about God, enabling them to keep a record of their growth. The teacher can structure the nature of the entries, or material can be freely generated by students. A combination of these approaches is best.

To help students begin their journals, ask them to complete such sentences as: I believe in God when _____. I doubt God when _____. Have them describe their reactions to poetry or short stories about God or to your lesson. Suggest that students list their doubts, questions, ideas, and feelings.

It is important that each student share his or her journal with you in an ongoing way. Sharing it with others must be up to you and the student. Your written comments and reactions to the journal will foster growth and provoke further thought about the issues raised.

Guest Speakers and Interviews

Interviewing different people with varying views about God can be an exciting and worthwhile undertaking. Invite believers, agnostics, and atheists to speak to older children. Have students prepare questions for the speakers in advance. Have students interview the Rabbi, their parents, the Director of Education, Cantor, etc. Compile the responses and compare the similarities and differences between the views. Find out with whom the students most agree. Which person differed most from the students' beliefs? What did the class learn from the exercise?

Creating Audiovisual Materials

Create a filmstrip, slide show, or video of your favorite stories about God. Show them to younger classes. Pick music and words that express creation, revelation, and redemption and create a sound tape to accompany the presentation. Shirley Barish suggests using books by Molly Cone for this activity. (See the Bibliography at the conclusion of this chapter for titles.)

Discussion

The major consideration when conducting discussions is the establishment of a climate of openness to all ideas, concepts, and materials. If desired, a Jewish context can be set up for the discussion which includes Torah, Covenant, Israel, etc. However, do not exclude from the discussion the struggles of students as they wrestle with the complexities of the God idea. If a student is resistant during discussion, simply help the student to be aware of his or her resistance. It is important for students to feel that their views are not wrong and to know that Jews have been struggling for centuries with the very same ideas.

Use a continuum to initiate a discussion. Have students stand along a line in the classroom at the point that best represents their views between two poles. Some examples:

God will redeem Israel if we deserve it	God will redeem Israel because God is God, and chose us
God will send a personal messiah	If all human beings are considerate, we will achieve a Messianic Era
God created the world as it says in the Bible	Science will reveal how the world was created

Other topics for discussion:
Primary Grades:
I feel close to God when _____.
I pray to God when _____.
I think God should _____.
I thank God for _____.

Intermediate Grades:
Why do bad things happen?
How can I let God work in my life?
Why do people believe different things about God?
Upper Grades:
Which of the two, faith or reason, is more important for Jews when trying to understand God?
Has ritual kept us close to God or separated us from God?

CONCLUSION

To write a brief chapter on strategies for teaching about God may seem presumptuous. People devote their lives to the questions we have dealt with in these few pages. But we must begin somewhere.

While there is no right way to teach about God, we must use every opportunity to encourage our students to reach out for a spiritual dimension in their lives. We hope these ideas will help you begin this vital task. The Bibliography contains an annotated list of books and materials which can reinforce and expand the ideas and suggestions which have been presented.

Sherry H. Blumberg is Assistant Professor for Jewish Education at Hebrew Union College-Jewish Institute of Religion in New York. She is the author of *God: The Eternal Challenge* (A.R.E.) and the Leader's Guide to *Renewing the Covenant* by Eugene Borowitz. Prior to joining the staff of HUC-JIR, she directed Religious Schools in California, taught, and led youth groups and camp programs.

BIBLIOGRAPHY

Elementary Level
Jewish
Cone, Molly. *About God*. The Shema Story Books IV. New York: UAHC, 1973.

This book uses stories to answer fundamental questions about God. These include: What is God? Why can't I see God? Does God know me? The lovely illustrations, the good paper binding, and the large and readable print make the book appealing to children. Values statements are simple and not trite, and the use of Jewish sources from the *Tefilot* make the overall effect honest and exciting. The view that God is personal and caring is put forth without the use of stereotypical answers. Recommended without qualification for primary and even intermediate, children.

———. *Who Knows Ten: Children's Tales of the Ten Commandments*. New York: UAHC Press, 1965. Chapters 1-3.

For an older age group than *About God*, this book uses a similar format — stories to make the point. Unfortunately, the author sidesteps the issue of God, dealing with freedom and responsibility in the first commandment, rather than "I am the Lord, Your God." The book is delightful and the illustrations well done in Uri Shulevitz's inimitable style. It can be used as supplementary material, but not to answer questions about God.

Bogot, Howard I. and Daniel B. Syme. *I Learn About God*. New York: UAHC Press, 1982.

Specially designed for young readers and preschool children, this book demonstrates that the things we do (e.g., helping a friend, seeing a butterfly come out of its cocoon, trying our best) are ways of learning about God. In lovely black and white pencil drawings, the book leads up to reading a Jewish book and saying the *Sh'ma*.

———. *Prayer Is Reaching*. New York: UAHC Press, 1982.

This beautiful book explores prayer as an approach to the experience of God for the younger child. It is a book which can be used to answer such questions as: Why pray? Does God answer our prayers? Or, it can be used as an integrated part of the curriculum to introduce the idea of God. Illustrated in brown and white, the book is a welcome addition to the materials for elementary age students.

Groner, Judyth, and Madeline Wikler. *Thank You, God! A Jewish Child's Book of Prayers*. Rockville, MD: Kar-Ben Copies, Inc., 1993.

Presents common *brachot* in Hebrew, English, and transliteration. Soft, colorful illustrations introduce prayer and set the stage for a child's traditions about God.

General
Ingram, Robert D. *Who Taught Frogs To Hop? A Child's Book About God*. Minneapolis: Augsburg, 1990.

This delightful book for young children and parents chooses some unusual images starting with the question: who made the world round instead of square? The book plays with the imagination and encourages the reader to play. The illustrations contain all kinds of faces, including oriental and people of color. The book attributes many things to God without ever saying the word.
    Jewish teachers need to be aware that the book does use the word "church" in one place. However, this can be adapted, and the theology is consistent with Jewish thought. This is well worth using.

Sasso, Sandy Eisenberg. *God's Paintbrush*. Woodstock, VT: Jewish Lights Publishing, 1992.

In sharing how God may be perceived in our world and in our lives, *God's Paintbrush* is a wonderful book for young children and their families. This colorful book will spark many ongoing discussions about God, since it presents a metaphor and then asks a question directly in the text. The metaphorical content is very personal, and can appear to be personification for the older reader, but the images and questions are very true to the younger child's development. If the book is seen as metaphor, the older reader will gain greatly. In it, God is explored through emotions (anger, laughter), actions (painting the leaves during fall, hiding), and in the connection of God to everyday life. It is very sophisticated and yet also readily accessible.

Wood, Douglas. *Old Turtle*. Duluth, MN: Pfeifer-Hamilton Publishers, 1992.

This is my favorite book about God. Not only is it a very special story, but the illustrations are so beautiful that they will amaze you. The story is a fable about a time when all the beings of the world could speak and understand each other. They had an argument about "what is God?" Old Turtle stops the argument with the statement God is . . . then says that human beings will come to be reminders of all that God is. But when the people come, they forget and begin to hurt and destroy until Old Turtle again says, "Please stop." The people listen, and begin to see God in one another. I recommend this book for all ages, especially teens and adults.

Intermediate
Jewish
Kushner, Lawrence. *The Book of Miracles: A Young Person's Guide to Jewish Spirituality*. New York: UAHC Press, 1987.

A collection of *midrashic*, Talmudic, and biblical stories to lead young readers to basic Jewish experiences.

Pasachoff, Naomi. *Basic Judaism for Young People. Volume Three: God*. West Orange, NJ: Behrman House, 1986.

Introduces fundamental Jewish concepts of history, belief, ritual, *halachah*, and tradition.

Secondary and Adult
Bissell, Sherry; Audrey Friedman Marcus; and Raymond A. Zwerin. *God: The Eternal Challenge*. Denver: A.R.E. Publishing, Inc., 1980. Student Manual and Leader Guide.

An experiential mini-course based on student questions about God. The course, for Grade 7 and up, explores many areas, and the Leader Guide contains exceptionally fine background material and supplementary strategies.

Borowitz, Eugene B. *Liberal Judaism*. New York: UAHC Press, 1984.

An exploration of the varieties of Jewish thought and ritual practice from a liberal Jewish perspective. Included is a section on "The God We Affirm."

Buber, Martin. *I and Thou*. Walter Kaufman, trans. New York: Scribner, 1970.

Buber's difficult, original work probes the possibilities of a direct or immediate relationship with God.

Dorff, Elliot N. *Knowing God: Jewish Journeys to the Unknowable*. Northvale, NJ: Jason Aronson Inc., 1992.

In an attempt to move adults beyond their childhood images of God, the author probes what adults can know about God through human reason, human and Divine words, and human and Divine action.

Gellman, Marc, and Thomas Hartman. *Where Does God Live? Questions and Answers for Parents and Children*. New York: Ballantine Books, 1991.

The idea to do a book based on questions is not new, but to have the book written by a Rabbi and a Monseignor is very unusual. The book speaks a lot of love. It is a warm and usable book that both parents and intermediate readers will enjoy. It uses idioms that the young person will relate to (Elmo the hamster and calling miracles "weird," and most of the talk is straight answers.

Gillman, Neil. *Sacred Fragments: Recovering Theology for the Modern Jew*. Philadelphia: Jewish Publication Society, 1990.

Gillman is a favorite teacher at the Jewish Theological Seminary because of his ability to link theology to the human being. His book accomplishes the same thing as his teaching.

While not a systematic theology, the book addresses questions such as: What is the reason for rituals? How can we define and believe in revelation of Torah? How do we speak about God? In his afterword, Gillman addresses the reader and encourages each to write his/her own theological reflection.

Green, Arthur. *Seek My Face, Speak My Name: A Contemporary Jewish Theology.* Northvale, NJ: Jason Aronson Inc., 1992.

Presentation of basic faith claims of Judaism in spiritual and poetic terms.

Heschel, Abraham J. *God in Search of Man: A Philosophy of Judaism.* Northvale, NJ: Jason Aronson Inc., 1987.

This classic outlines Heschel's philosophy of religion in general and Judaism in particular.

Kerdeman, Deborah, and Lawrence Kushner. *The Invisible Chariot: Introduction to Kabbalah and Jewish Spirituality.* Denver: A.R.E. Publishing, Inc., 1986. Student Workbook and Leader Guide.

A workbook for Grades 9 to adult. Contains the major ideas of Kabbalah, the connection of Jewish mysticism and spirituality to students' daily lives, and extensive opportunities for self-reflection. The Leader Guide features step-by-step instructions, many additional activities, and a Bibliography.

Konowitz, Israel. *The God Idea in Jewish Tradition.* Shmuel Himelstein, trans. Jerusalem: The Jerusalem Publishing House, 1989.

This book presents a very traditional view about God as found in *Aggadah,* Talmud, *Midrash,* and Torah. It is organized into 90 short chapters that are the statements about God as found in the prayer book and Bible, such as "The Lord Robes Himself in Majesty" and "The Lord Will Be King over All the Earth." For anyone wanting a quick reference, and the sources of traditional God concepts, this book is very important.

Kushner, Lawrence. *God Was in this Place & I, i did not know.* Woodstock, VT: Jewish Lights Publishing, 1991.

In a blend of scholarship and imagination, psychology and history, the author gathers an inspiring range of interpretations of Genesis 28:16 by a variety of sages. Through these, we learn what each of these spiritual masters discovered about God's Self and ourselves.

Olitzky, Kerry M.; Steven M. Rosman, and David P. Kasakove. *When Your Child Asks Why: Answers for Tough Questions.* Hoboken, NJ: Ktav Publishing House, 1993.

The authors pose and answer questions relating to God, as well as to Jewish identity, the Torah, deal and evil, relationships with family and friends, and Jewish study and ritual practice.

Salkin, Jeffrey K. *Putting God on the Guest List: How To Reclaim the Spiritual Meaning of Your Child's Bar or Bat Mitzvah.* Jewish Lights Publishing, 1992.

Guide to the spiritual meaning of a Bar or Bat Mitzvah.

Sonsino, Rifat, and Daniel Syme. *Finding God: Ten Jewish Responses.* New York: UAHC Press, 1986.

The authors explain the different ways that Jews have spoken of God throughout history. Views of great Jewish thinkers are presented, including Philo, Maimonides, Spinoza, Buber, Steinberg, Kaplan, and others.

"What Does God Require of Us: A Symposium." *Reform Judaism*, Vol. 22 (1): 9-21, 70-71, Fall 1993.

Articles in this issue describe various approaches to God, and are by such authors as Rabbi Roland Gittelsohn, Rabbi Daniel Syme, Rabbi Bernard Zlotowitz.

Wolpe, David J. *The Healer of Shattered Hearts: A Jewish View of God.* New York: Henry Holt and Co., Inc., 1990.

Through texts and traditions, Wolpe examines the role of God in our daily struggles, fears, needs, and questions.

———. *In Speech and Silence: The Jewish Quest for God.* New York: Henry Holt and Co., Inc., 1993.

Explores how each of us can use the complexity of language and simplicity of silence to communicate and react to God.

———. *Teaching Your Children about God: A Rabbi Speaks to Concerned Parents.* New York: Henry Holt and Co., Inc., 1993.

A fresh view of talking with children about God from the brilliant young author of two other books on the subject.

Audiovisual

Anyone Around My Base Is It. 28 min., color. Jewish Chautauqua Society, 838 Fifth Avenue, New York, NY 10021.

A man who is searching for God tries to tell a boy whose father was killed where God is.

Clay (Origin of Species). 8 min., black and white. Contemporary Films McGraw-Hill, Princeton Rd., Hightstown, NJ 08520.

A visual variation on Darwin using clay animation.

The Creation. 15 min., color. Obtain from central agencies.

The first segment of The New Media Bible, a film version of the entire Hebrew and Christian Bibles.

Crimes and Misdemeanors. 107 min., color. Facets Multimedia, 1517 W. Fullerton Ave., Chicago, IL 60614.

This serious full-length drama asks questions about the nature of good and evil and how each is rewarded or punished. For sophisticated audiences.

I Asked for Wonder. 57 min., color. Jewish Theological Seminary, 3080 Broadway, New York, NY 10027.

Several people who are studying about God talk about dealing with serious illness or pain as they also learn from theologians. Excellent for adults and older teens.

Oh, God and *Oh, God, Book II.* 104/94 min., color. Available at video stores.

The 1977 film (and sequel) stars George Burns as God. In the films, God calls upon John Denver, who plays a supermarket employee, to be a prophet. Theology and philosophy are mixed with humor.

SUBJECT MATTER

CHAPTER THIRTY-FOUR

OF PRAYER AND PROCESS – ONE MODEL FOR TEACHING JEWISH PRAYER

Stuart Kelman and Joel Lurie Grishaver

For many years, each of us independently has been working on ways to teach Jewish prayer. In fact, several years ago, each of us independently began an article which tried to correlate the "content" of the liturgy with the "process" of prayer: the "what" with the "how." At that time, an ongoing discussion between the two of us began. In this chapter, we hope to share some of the results of that dialogue.

FEAR OF PRAYING/FEARS OF TEACHING PRAYER

For some of us, there is something scary about teaching prayer. We tend to fear it more than most other areas in the Jewish curriculum. Some of that fear stems from our own insecurity regarding our "liturgical performance," and much of the fear anticipates our students' probable reaction to having to study prayer . . . boring! Yet, the prayers themselves are probably the most frequently taught piece of Jewish content. For years, they have been the classic battleground and training field for the skill of mechanical Hebrew reading. They were a great source for identifying the roots of Hebrew verbs and they provide an endless supply of Hebrew one-liners for song leaders. We sing prayers. We read prayers. We go through prayers, but we rarely talk about praying. We discuss the tension between *Keva* (the fixed regimen of prayer) and *Kavanah* (prayer with intention), but we don't get involved in what one actually does. We avoid the "how you do it," because we are either unsure ourselves, or we are convinced that it is personal, "Something you can't really talk about."

Our own insecurity with prayer is only part of the problem. There are some other difficulties:

1. Prayers as found in the *Siddur* are Hebrew literature — a genre often foreign to us. Even for those of us fairly familiar with Hebrew, the prayers are a technical literature which conforms to formal and stylistic conventions. The literature is subtle. It is permeated with illusions, allusion, and nuances, many of these drawn from Rabbinic literature (the Talmud and the *Midrash*) — also areas in which we may not feel particularly comfortable. Often, when we read the *Siddur*, we know that the text is doing something, but we aren't sure what.

2. Prayers talk about God. Sometimes, prayers even ask us to talk to God. And God is a problem for many modern individuals. There seems to be a direct connection between "God-concept" and "ability to pray." We and our students feel that we need a cosmic setting — a theological blueprint of what we are "actually doing" when we pray, before we can risk praying. The "try it — you might like it" popular mystical approach to prayer has lost some of its effectiveness in the face of the pragmatic hedonism of today's kids.

3. Prayer has "bad press." Prayers are used in "services." Most of our students have had negative (boring) experiences with services. When our students have had positive worship experiences (usually in summer camps or youth programs), these are attributed to special people, or special places, and not to the process of praying. Meaningful prayer is seen as having nothing to do with real (or even weekly) life.

4. Prayer seems difficult. Most of the student texts are just not adequate. The secondary literature (which seems to be filled with end-

less Hebrew terms in transliteration) can be hard to master, especially without a good basic knowledge. Prayer seems difficult to learn, unless you grew up in a circle of people who actually pray regularly (and who seem to understand what they are saying).

5. Deep down, both teachers and students intuitively know that prayer is a process, not just a content area. At some point, though, we have to get past the structure, history, and order of the prayers and into the process of praying. Because prayer seems to be a dynamic-intra-psychic-communicative-evocative-associative-personal process, we don't know how to teach it.

Ironically, the prayers themselves do teach us how to pray, once we learn how to read them. Reading them successfully has as much to do with an attitudinal awakening as it does with a series of fact and skill learnings. To understand this abstraction, consider the following analogy, a common occurrence in many family rooms throughout the country.

The parent is listening to Gershwin on the FM radio. Enter the child, a typical 12 to 14-year-old. Disliking "classical music," the child puts a favorite disk into the CD player. The parent quickly complains about the "noise." Neither has any insight into the other's music. The child is unable to distinguish between Bach and Gershwin; both are long pieces of orchestral music without any discernible melody. For the parent, the latest teen group plays unintelligible music which the child turns on too loudly. These usually employ distorted guitars and a driving (annoying) electric bass.

In facing the *Siddur*, we are like both parent and child. We lack the combination of technical insight and experiential enrichment to involve ourselves in the art form. We need to learn how to perceive the melody, the themes, and variations, the jargon, the feeling, and even the dance steps. We need to know the contextual setting of prayers, and to add to our own experiences some moments of closeness to prayers and some moments when praying creates a sense of closeness.

In this chaper, we will (1) consider the liturgical material itself and make explicit the process of praying which it suggests, (2) look at one prescriptive model of providing students with both a cognitive background and an experiential resource for internalizing the liturgy, and (3) provide the teacher with realistic tools to comprehend #1 and #2.

TOWARD A WORKABLE MODEL OF JEWISH PRAYER

Most models of praying assume that a true prayer conforms to Newtonian physics, e.g., that "every action has an equal and opposite reaction." A "reaction," though, is not a reasonable expectation. Jewish worship is a mundane, ongoing process. Rather than seeking a single special moment, a "religious experience," a sudden insight into the "other," Jewish prayer attempts to create a regular community process through which the individual can evaluate and plan for new moments. Traditionally, the Jew prays three times a day, and uses the same basic text continually. The Jewish worship experience is rooted in the regular application of an intricate, multi-leveled framework of questions, images, and symbols to each new day of living. Jews pray by gathering in groups and participating in a fixed process. Jewish worship is a structured attempt to evolve a community lifestyle and to evoke self-evaluation. It seeks both a sense of community and the development of the individual. In this way, it evolves — rather than reveals — a sense of "the holy."

The *Siddur* is a text which was designed for constant reuse. The Rabbis who shaped and crafted the *Siddur* didn't know the word "*gestalt*," but they did understand its impact. They didn't see the endless renditions of the liturgical cycle as merely a holding action, a waiting for a time of need or for a moment of breakthrough or insight. Rather, they saw the daily passage through the regimen of prayer much the way a weight-lifter/body builder looks upon his/her endless exercise reps, or the way a jogger justifies the continuous laps, or the way a singer practices *arpeggios*. The effect of any single "training experience" is hard to identify, but the total impact of all "training experiences" is manifest in the present state of the person.

OF PRAYER AND PROCESS — ONE MODEL FOR TEACHING

Philo, an ancient Jewish philosopher living in a Greek sphere of influence in Alexandria, Egypt,

> **THE PRAYERS THEMSELVES TEACH US HOW TO PRAY.**

used this image when he described the Jew as being an "athlete of virtue."[1] While he didn't specifically delineate the role of praying in the "ethical-athlete's" training, he does describe the Jewish life-style as one which is constantly in preparation for doing right (in classical terms: doing *mitzvot*).

Max Kadushin, a twentieth century American Jewish scholar, did draw this connection. In *Worship and Ethics,* he describes the constant ethical underpinning of the liturgy. He sees the regimen of the *Siddur* (as well as *brachot* such as *Birkat HaMazon*) as reinforcing and developing ethical insights and sensitivities.[2] He makes explicit the "training process" which Philo implies. Kadushin's work was the foundation of our own. We started with his insights into the pedagogic nature of the *Siddur* and then began exploring. We thought that if the prayer process was indeed a "learning experience," then perhaps the use of various learning models might help us to understand its nature. Ironically, or perhaps self-evidently, the most fruitful analogy to the process of prayer was a Rabbinic model of Jewish learning.

Paradise and Prayer

The Middle Eastern mind saw paradise as a rich, lush orchard. In many Semitic languages (including Hebrew) the root *PaRDaiS*, which means "orchard," also came to mean paradise. Jewish biblical commentators used the word *PaRDaiS* as the basis of a model of Torah study. They believed that studying the biblical text was in a way like modern archaeology — that to discover truth one must dig through layers. For them, each layer brought one deeper into the text and deeper into oneself. They defined these four layers as (1) *P'shat* – the literal/plain meaning of the text; (2) *Remez* hints or allusions found in the text, especially about political events (in a future spiritual history); (3) *D'rash* – interpretations of the text (related to *Midrash*); and (4) *Sod* – secret or mystical meanings. The nature of these four can best be clarified through an example. First, we take half a biblical verse. This one comes from the story of Jacob's dream about the ladder reaching from earth to heaven. It says: "And behold the angels of God ascending and descending on it" (Genesis 28:12).

P'shat

It is hard to study *P'shat* — the plain meaning in English — because the translation has already told us what the words mean. The Hebrew text is far richer. The word *hiney*, which was translated as "behold," could also have been rendered as "and here," "and there was" or, it may even be skipped. The word *"malachim"* which was rended as "angels" could also have been translated as "messengers."

The text, however, contains a problem. It states that angels were ascending and descending. If we assume that angels begin in heaven and come to earth, the order seems backwards. To solve this problem in the "*P'shat*" of the text, the Rabbis moved through the other levels.

D'rash

D'rash is an explanation which is to be given within the context of other biblical material. Jacob was about to leave the land of Israel. What is happening is a changing of the guard. The Israel angels ascend and the Diaspora angels descend. The moral: life in Israel is different from life elsewhere.

Remez

Remez is a hint of a future spiritual history. Each individual angel went up and then down. Each angel represented the rise and fall of earthly kingdoms, especially Assyria, Babylonia, Rome, and then the Messianic rule of David — which is yet to come. The moral: the future of the world is redemption through Israel.

Sod

Sod represents mystical insight. Like the angels, each of our spiritual ascents also contains descents. As we move up the ladder (toward union with the Deity), we will make progress and slip back, but the overall direction of our growth should be upward.

According to the Rabbis, a person did not have to choose between these explanations of the text. There was truth in each of them singly and in all of them collectively. A text has a *P'shat*, a *D'rash*, a *Remez*, and a *Sod* — a *PaRDaiS*. There is literally a little piece of heaven in every verse. Notice, however, that the learning wasn't necessarily linear. The reader could start anywhere and proceed everywhere. For the fullest understanding, though, all the levels needed to be touched individually and put together collectively.

Of the four layers of interpretation, *Sod* was the most difficult to reach, for *Sod* was found not in the text, but through the text. *Sod* was the personal, private path of association: our version of what the prayers said to us at that moment. Collectively, like the jogger, the weight lifter, the singer, each experience served as preparation for the next.

The text, for the Rabbis, was not merely a listing of ethical precepts, but rather a complex puzzle which forced the reader to guess and compare, to associate and intuit, to ferret out the meaning(s). In making life a conscious, careful search for meaning, the medium mirrored the message. How the text was to be learned was a reflection of what the text had to teach. It is this process of study and learning which we believe defines a model for decoding the liturgy, and which ultimately establishes the vectors for Jewish worship.

TOWARD THE TEACHING OF PRAYING — DECODING AND ENCODING

Facility with the *Siddur* is only one prerequisite for successfully praying. If prayer is both a drawing together of previous Jewish learning and an interweaving of personal metaphors with traditional images, students of prayer must be able to "associate" on two levels: analytical and personal. In an analytical association, connections are made relative to specific contextual connections. In a personal association, an emotional free association is required in order to link images. To reach these two associative processes, we need to add a facility with the prayer book: a general Jewish literacy, a working Judaism concept, and personal experiences which give emotional depth to our knowledge.

P'shat utilizes formal analysis. It concerns itself with the structure of the prayers. We want to know the format of each prayer and the sequence which all prayers follow. We are interested in the words which form the prayers. We are concerned with their meaning and the possible ambiguity in their meaning. The *P'shat* level is the development of basic competency at using the *Siddur*. It is having the student reach the point where he/she can open the book, find the right place, know what's there, feel comfortable with what's there (including knowing the names of most of the parts and pieces), and be able to function as a participant in services (reading, chanting, doing the appropriate movements, etc.).

D'rash applies content analysis. It concerns itself with basic Jewish literacy. We have established that Jewish liturgy is a literature of allusion. *D'rash* provides the students with the background to recognize and appreciate the images which are referenced in the *Siddur*. That means that he/she can read "Who with a word brings on the evening" and recognize it as a reference to the first story of creation; or when reading "God of Abraham, God of Isaac, and God of Jacob," the student knows that the Patriarchs (and the Matriarchs) each had a unique relationship with God. *D'rash* provides the background to appreciate from where the prayers have emerged.

Remez uses conceptual analysis. It involves identifying and correlating the themes in the *Siddur*. We recognized the fact that Rabbinic "spiritual-history" underpins the structure of the liturgy, and that it emerges as we probe the prayers. In order to appreciate this, and formulate their own insights, students have to be able to weave the Jewish knowledge they have amassed into Judaism concepts. We are used to talking about God-concepts, but these form only part of an understanding of being a Jew. To apply Jewish knowledge to real life (which is indeed one of the key functions of prayer), one has to have an understanding of key Jewish concepts. *Remez*, therefore, involves the study of Jewish thought and the evolution of concepts that are at the core of what we call Judaism.

Sod is experiential. It is the process of connecting the conceptual to the actual. In *Remez*, biblical stories and Rabbinic legends have coalesced in-to "creation," "revelation," "redemption," "covenant," "*mitzvah*," etc. The *Sod* level is where we move from the intellectual to the real. Prayer is concerned with human connection to the Divine. Part of the challenge is to demonstrate the experiential reality of the Divine. A quick example: Rabbi Lawrence Kushner reported the following interaction with a group of young students. He asked, "How many of you believe in God?" He was shocked to find that the majority of the class didn't believe in God. He later asked the class, "How many of you have ever felt close to God?" The response was a classroom full of stories. While the concept of God was difficult, the experience of God was real.[3] In a secular society, the role of *Sod* is to conjure the Divine which is present in ordinary life, and to acknowledge its presence. It is the experience of being created, of connecting to revelation, of expecting redemption, etc. *Sod* is both the mystical level and the real connection of the prayer process.

While these four levels provide a background for praying, they don't guarantee that the learner will choose to apply them toward prayer. They are sort of a "praying readiness" process. While nothing will insure the production of students who readily gravitate to services, the combination of these four levels of insight, coupled with regular chances to participate in "good" services and the availability of appropriate adult and peer models, may give someone a chance to become a praying person. While the classroom can prepare a student to worship, the sanctuary is the place where the background and training coalesce into prayer. If you are teaching prayer, you must also provide settings for praying. Reciprocally, services are places to pray, but the needs of the liturgy are complex enough to warrant classroom time.

To better understand this *PaRDaiS* model of praying and prayer instruction, let us examine a single prayer (*Mah Tovu*), reveal the layers of insight, and then move into some instructional designs. *Mah Tovu* is an opening prayer or meditation traditionally said quietly as one enters a sanctuary. This prayer deals with the relationship between an individual and God. It explores the nature of Jewish prayer which takes place in specific locations, at fixed times, and through a proscribed ritual.[4] Let's see how the prayer develops these themes. To begin, let's read the text of the prayer.

מַה־טֹּבוּ אֹהָלֶיךָ, יַעֲקֹב,
מִשְׁכְּנֹתֶיךָ, יִשְׂרָאֵל!
וַאֲנִי, בְּרֹב חַסְדְּךָ אָבֹא בֵיתֶךָ,
אֶשְׁתַּחֲוֶה אֶל־הֵיכַל קָדְשְׁךָ
בְּיִרְאָתֶךָ.
יְיָ, אָהַבְתִּי מְעוֹן בֵּיתֶךָ,
וּמְקוֹם מִשְׁכַּן כְּבוֹדֶךָ.
וַאֲנִי אֶשְׁתַּחֲוֶה וְאֶכְרָעָה,
אֶבְרְכָה לִפְנֵי־יְיָ עֹשִׂי.
וַאֲנִי תְפִלָּתִי לְךָ, יְיָ, עֵת רָצוֹן.
אֱלֹהִים, בְּרָב־חַסְדֶּךָ,
עֲנֵנִי בֶּאֱמֶת יִשְׁעֶךָ.

1. How goodly are your tents, Jacob, your dwelling place (Tabernacle), Israel. (Numbers 24:5)
2. As for *me*, through Your abundant kindness I will enter Your House (Temple). I will incline toward Your Holy Sanctuary (Temple) in awe of You. (Psalms 5:8)
3. Lord, I love the refuge of Your House (Temple) and the place where Your glory dwells (Tabernacle). (Psalms 26:8)
4. *I* will incline, and I will bow, I will kneel before the Lord my Maker. (Psalms 95:6)
5. May *my* prayer to You, Lord, be at a favorable time; God, in the abundance of Your kindness answer me with the truth of Your deliverance. (Psalms 69:14)

The P'shat
1. *Mah Tovu* is made up of five biblical verses. Four of them are taken directly from the Bible, and the fifth is reworked (Psalm 95:6) from first person plural (we) to first person singular (I) so as to fit with the prayer's syntax. Four of the verses are in poetic parallel, a literary device in which both halves of a sentence say the same thing in different words.
2. If we look at the way words are used and reused, we will learn something about the message of this prayer. The following terms are repeated:
   Me-I-My – *Va'ani* – 3 times
   Lord – *Adonai* – 3 times
   Abundant kindness – *B'rov Chasdacha* – 2 times
   I will incline – *Eshtachaveh* – 2 times
   House (Temple) – *Bayt* – 2 times
   Dwelling (Tabernacle) *Mishkan* – 2 times
   This kind of word count can be a key to understanding a Hebrew text. In this case we learn the number of times the word *Va'ani* (Me-I-My) is used, equals the number of times the word *Adonai* (Lord) is used. This

helps to define the prayer, showing us that it deals with *My* relationship to *God*.
3. When we look at the nouns used by this prayer, we discover a second insight. Looking closely, we find a progression of nouns: tents, dwelling place, Your House, and Your Holy Sanctuary. Each of these represents a specific place the Jewish people set aside for communicating with God. They are: The Tent of Meeting, The Tabernacle, and the Temple (twice). The repetition of *Mishkan* (Tabernacle) and *Baytecha* (Your House) in the third line seems to reemphasize this progression.
4. Finally, if we look at the "active" verbs, we discover one more factor:
   (a) I will enter (*Ah'vo*)
   (b) I will incline (*Eshtachaveh*)
   (c) I will incline (*Eshtachaveh*)
   (d) I will bow (*Echra'ah*)
   (e) I will kneel (*Evr'chah*)
   (f) (You) answer (*Ah'naynee*)

   The middle three verbs — incline, bow, kneel — describe three specific physical postures for worship, each a bit harder, lower, and more complex. These three actions are introduced by a verb denoting entry (*Ah'vo*) and a foreshadowing of the first gesture (*Eshtachaveh*). They are followed by the single verb (*Ah'naynee*) which requests Divine rather than human action. All of these actions have been performed by *me*, except for the final request that *God* answer me. Thus the text describes worship as a progression of actions which become harder, deeper, and more complex.
5. By examining segments of the prayer, we have seen that *Mah Tovu* concerns itself with: the relationship between God and an individual, specific places of worship, and the fixed process of worship. If we look at the whole prayer, we will see their interrelationship. Verse #1 is an external description of the place of worship. Verse #2 describes the entry into the place of worship. Verse #3 verbalizes the feelings generated by being in the place of worship. All of these are states of preparation. Verse #4 describes the threefold postures of prayer and culminates with "before the Lord my Maker." This is not a casual or distant description of God, but rather an acknowledgment of the most intimate and essential kind of relationship between God and people. The last verse has a shift in focus from I, the subject, to the impact of my feelings, perceptions, and actions on God. In essence, I am asking God to move from being my Maker — a fact which has been accomplished — to becoming my Redeemer, a truth which yet needs to be revealed.

The D'rash

We have seen that this prayer is drawn from five biblical verses. To further understand their impact, we need to look at their context.

1. Numbers 24:5 – This verse is the culmination of the story of Balaam. It is the focal line in the blessing which he gives to Israel, rather than the curse which he intended. Dr. Reuven Kimmelman points out that this is an example of energy transformation: Balaam sets out to do one thing (curse) and ends up doing something different (blessing).
2. Psalm 5:8 – This Psalm is introduced as a "Psalm of David." It begins with the "prayer relationship," but essentially focuses on God's desire for ethical actions — "For Thou dost bless the righteous" (verse 13).
3. Psalm 26:8 – This also is "of David." It begins "Judge me, O Lord . . . Examine me . . . Test my reins." The middle of this Psalm describes David's strivings for ethical action, and it ends: "Redeem me, and be gracious unto me." This Psalm echoes the concerns of Psalm 5, but adds the themes of judgment and redemption.
4. Psalm 95:6 – This Psalm is not specifically assigned to David. It begins with a general description of "praising the Lord," and then moves into (a) a description of God as creator, and (b) the historical relationship between God and Israel, particularly the conflicts in the wilderness. This is the verse which was changed from plural to singular, and it makes no specific reference to a "place of worship."
5. Psalm 69:14 – This is also a "Psalm of David." It begins: "Save me . . ." and then lists the dangers which David feels surround him, and the remorse he feels for the evil he has done. The middle of the Psalm contains our

> **I AM ASKING GOD TO MOVE FROM BEING MY MAKER TO BECOMING MY REDEEMER.**

verse — "let my prayer . . . answer me with the truth of your deliverance." It is followed with deliver me, answer me, draw my soul near, ransom me, etc. It then moves through repentance to a description of the establishment of God's Kingdom. The Psalm ends: "For God will save Zion and build cities for Judah . . . The seed also of His servants shall inherit it; And they that love His name shall dwell therein."

When *Mah Tovu* was assembled, the Jewish people knew their sources via an oral tradition. Much the same way in which we identify a strand of a popular song and know the whole tune and lyrics, they could be given a single line of a Psalm and know its entirety. Thus, our searching the context of these verses merely reestablishes the initial impact of this composition. While it has a rhetorical meaning (that which we found in the *P'shat*), it also has a contextual meaning. We know that the prayer concerns itself with human relationship to God within the context of worship. To that we have added ethical behavior, Divine judgment, a God of creation and of history, and a God who will redeem via the process of repentance. In addition, we know that much of this prayer represents the personal artistry of King David. The more we know of his life and struggles, the more we can appreciate his statements of need and faith. Finally, we realize that the sources used to assemble this prayer overtly connect David and the "Sanctuary." We are thus drawn toward the story (II Chronicles 22:6-16) in which God refused to allow David to build the Temple because — "You have spilled much blood on the earth before me." David is instructed that Temple building will be the task and honor of his son, whose name will mean peace — Solomon.

The Remez

Our entry into the *Remez* of a text comes via Rabbinic literature. That literature comes in two forms: *halachah* (legal material) and *aggadah* (exegetical and homeletic material). To understand the *Remez* of this prayer, we will need to look at the passage in terms of both of these categories.

1. We know that it is the Jewish custom to recite *Mah Tovu* as one enters a synagogue. The second line of *Mah Tovu* contains ten words and serves a particular function. Jewish superstition prohibits the counting of people by numbers, so counting was accomplished by reciting verses — matching words with objects. The second line of *Mah Tovu* became the formula through which the *minyan* was established. Thus while the prayer contextually connects the individual with God through personal prayer, it functionally connects the individual with the other members of the community.

2. Near the end of this prayer, the pray-er asks: "May *my* prayer to you, Lord, be at a favorable time." The notion of an appropriate time for prayer is an important Jewish concept. Jews have set time periods for worship, and the legal literature is extensively concerned with defining the parameters of favorable, or appropriate time.

3. This concept of acceptable worship time provides another connection. Balaam is the soothsayer who is employed to curse Israel and who finally issues the blessing which forms the first line of the *Mah Tovu*. In Talmud *Berachot* 2b, the Rabbis suggest that even though Balaam was a non-Jew, his invocations could greatly influence God because he knew the proper times to pray.

4. *Mah Tovu* concerns itself with "places of worship." In the *P'shat* we recognized the progression from Tent of Meeting, to Tabernacle, to Temple. The Temple Mount is an important location in Rabbinic "salvation history." In various *midrashim* the Temple Mount is the center of the universe, the foundation stone of creation, the place where Adam was created, the corner of the Garden of Eden, the place where Noah sacrificed after the flood, the location where Abraham bound Isaac, the bottom of the ladder in Jacob's dream, the source of the Ten Commandments (where the stones came from), the place David bought for the Temple (because of the love demonstrated there by two brothers), and the spot from which the Messiah is to begin his campaign.[5]

5. Jewish concept of "holy space" is defined by the introduction God gives Moses at the burning bush: "Take off your shoes, because the ground on which you stand is holy ground" (Exodus 3:5). The legal literature sets down a whole number of conditions regarding the proper treatment of a place of worship (Talmud *Megillah* 29b). As one enters

the sanctuary, the legal obligations of being in Temple come into play (head coverings, saying *Mah Tovu, minyan,* etc.). These activities set the tone and begin a process of association.

The Sod

Mah Tovu is a journey. It is a pilgrimage. That is the motif which has underpinned each of the previous layers. On the *P'shat* level we (1) moved through a series of verbs into a state of worship, and (2) followed a historical progression from the desert Tent of Meeting to our own sanctuary. In *D'rash* we recognized the "Davidic" connection and saw worship expanded to include a number of Jewish themes moving from creation to redemption. Following David's own struggle with faith and ethical living, we are led into the dialogue with the Divine. In *Remez* these connections were made more explicit. From a *halachic* standpoint, a number of required physical tasks bring the intellectual process of the words into the real world — symbolic sanctuaries connect to real synagogues. We touch the *mezuzah* upon leaving the house and quicken our pace as we near the synagogue. In the *aggadah,* the real synagogue is connected to historical events, both actual and yet to be actualized. In all of these there is a movement. The person praying follows the *Mah Tovu's* paths and matches the "guided imagery" with his/her own. Among the issues the individual must consider are:

1. The nature of "sanctuary." What is a holy/special place?
2. What is prayer? I am about to engage in a process which has a long historical tradition. How do I relate to it?
3. *Mah Tovu* is a prayer about relating to God in prayer. What is my sense of that relationship? Most of all, the person praying must define his/her own journey. As he/she enters the sanctuary and recites the words of *Mah Tovu*, the individual struggles with the meaning of entering the synagogue at that given moment of life.

The matrix below summarizes the layers of insight into the *Mah Tovu* prayer which have been revealed by using the *PaRDaiS* model:

PLANNING LESSONS

While all of these biblical-Rabbinic pyrotechnics seem a little scholarly, they do provide us with a number of instructional possibilities. The the matrix (figure 1 below) shows the vast variety of knowledge, conceptualization, and experience a student should have. All of these may not need to be covered by the "prayer" teacher. Some may come from earlier learning, some may come in later schooling, and some may never be formally transmitted. That kind of decision is made by the teacher in concert with the school curriculum. What this concept matrix does show us is that there are a number of good starting places for getting into the *Mah Tovu*.

P'SHAT	D'RASH
1. 5 Biblical verses: Num. 24:5, Ps. 5:8, 26:8, 95:6, and 69:14 2. The progression of nouns: Tent, Tabernacle, house, Temple 3. The progression of verbs: enter, prostrate, bow, kneel, answer 4. Prayer process – from external viewing to anticipating God's answer	1. Numbers 24:5 – Balaam's story 2. Psalm 5:8 – Psalm of David, Ethics 3. Psalm 26:8 – Psalm of David, Judgment and Redemption 4. Psalm 95:6 – God of creation, God of history 5. Psalm 69:14 – Psalm of David, Redemption 6. The David Saga – including the refusal to let him build the Temple.
REMEZ	**SOD**
1. *Ma Tovu* and *minyan* 2. Fixed time for worship 3. History of Temple Mount 4. Regulations of holy space	1. Making a pilgrimage 2. "Sanctuaries" – holy places 3. "Holy times" 4. Relationship with God/Prayer

Figure 1

From *P'shat*, we can begin with the way words are used, and establish (1) my relationship with God, (2) the history of Jewish worship places, (3) the physical component to praying, and (4) the overall movement of the prayer. We can also start with the four basic places for Jewish prayer: The Tent, The Tabernacle, The Temple, and the synagogue and compare the ways of worshiping in each.

From *D'rash* we can study two personalities: Balaam, a professional soothsayer who felt no concern over using his ability to pray successfully and King David, who was hypersensitive to his human weaknesses and used prayer to try to overcome them. From these "contexts," these biblical verses now used as prayers take on added life.

From *Remez* we can draw on the history of the Temple Mount, and see in that one location a connection between the act of prayer and the process of history from creation through revelation to a final redemption. We can also examine the legal literature, finding out how required and prohibited actions shape spaces and times, generating certain kinds of processes within them.

From *Sod*, we can enter into the student's own quest. We can lead the student to define and connect with his/her own sense of pilgrimage, and use it to define sacred space, sacred time, prayer, and the relationship between people and God.

What this means is that a number of possible lessons present themselves to us. From the standpoint of goal statements, the following are objectives that a person teaching the *Mah Tovu* (completely) should want his/her student to accomplish:

1. That the student can identify the basic patterns in the prayer. These include: (a) the overall structure, (b) the progression of nouns and verbs, (c) the number of times certain words are used, and (d) the change of perspective and movement.
2. That the student is familiar with the basic places and ways Jews have worshiped and feels some connection to them.
3. That students know the stories of Balaam and King David, and can see how the verses used in assembling this prayer (and perhaps the large literary sources from which they are drawn) reflect their personal struggle with the meaning of prayer.
4. That the students know some of the events which the *midrash* locates at the Temple Mount, and can explain why the Rabbis want to find that sense of connection between a place and world history.
5. That the students study some of the rules regarding behavior and entry into the synagogue and connect the actions to the text through the meaning/process they embody.
6. That the students explore their own view of holy space and time through a connection to the concept of pilgrimage/quest. (The ongoing popularity of *Dungeons and Dragons*, *The Lord of the Rings*, and the King Arthur legends should make this one easy. Quest is a popular notion among young people.)

From this point on the teacher should have no problem in developing lesson plans. Once an achievable set of goals for the lesson has been isolated, all a teacher needs to do is apply the whole menu of instructional devices and styles. All of the trade secrets, from worksheets to multimedia, from role play to computer programs, can be applied. The hard part is in deciding which things about the prayers (the content) you will select to teach.

Starting with P'shat

In our presentation of the *Mah Tovu*, we demonstrated the sequential approach by which a teacher can, layer by layer, reveal the meanings of this prayer. The following represents other potential instructional sequences.

Starting with D'rash

The students spend several sessions studying the history of King David. They understand the basic struggles David has gone through in his life: his rise to power, the conflicts with Saul, his friendship with Jonathan, his marital problems, the struggles against Achitophel and Absalom, his desire to build a Temple. They know that he has high points and low points in his life: King and fugitive, lover and sinner, poet and participant in numerous power struggles. The students then sit down with (1) an outline of the major events in David's life, and (2) a number of verses from Psalms 69, 26, and 5.

LAYER BY LAYER, THE MEANING OF A PRAYER IS REVEALED.

They are asked to try to determine what personal event David was thinking of when he wrote each verse. Here are several examples:

Thou destroyest them that speak falsehood; the Lord abhorreth the man of blood and deceit.

But as for me, in the abundance of Your loving kindness will I come into Thy house. (Psalm 5:7-8)

Gather not my soul with sinners, nor my life with men of blood. (Psalm 26:9)

I am become a stranger to my brother, and an alien to my mother's children. Thou knowest my reproach, and my shame, and my confusion: My adversaries are all before Thee. (Psalms 69:9, 20)

As the students look at these verses, some may think the "evil person" in the first verse is Saul; others might think that it is Abner. Some may decide that David didn't want to be a sinner after Nathan reproached him for taking Bathsheba; others will think it was when God refused to let him build the Temple. Some might suggest that the third verse referred to the time when David hid from Saul. Others may argue that it was when Absalom drove him out of Jerusalem. The discussion will be intense. But more than deciding that a specific moment was behind each verse, the class (with the teacher's direction) can realize that the poetry which forms these Psalms (and consequently *Mah Tovu*) came from a real person (*davka*, a soldier, warrior, lover, King) and was generated out of real critical moments in his life.

In the next step, the students are asked to describe David's concept of prayer. Slowly a model emerges: (1) prayer can affect God, (2) praying can affect people, (3) *teshuvah* (repentance and real change) is possible, and (4) faith and praying make a difference in a person's life. Then the teacher can ask, "Did David really believe in all this stuff or was he simply a King putting on a good show?" The argument will again be intense, but the class will probably agree that David really did listen to Nathan when confronted, and he really did devote a lot of effort toward establishing a Temple.

In the following session, the class stages a debate between Balaam, who believes that anyone's prayers can work (if they pray at the right time and aren't against God's will), and David, who believes that people really have to be sincere. Finally, the teacher passes out a copy of *Mah Tovu*, and the class does the word counts and form analysis. They recognize the verses as coming from stories and texts they have already studied, and discover that the debate they had on the meaning of prayer is contained in this prayer. When they come to the prayer's text, it is already infused with meaning from their insights into David and Balaam.

Starting with Remez

In this classroom, the teacher has pushed back the desks and taped a 4' x 4' square in the middle of the floor. After the class has entered and commented on the square, the teacher asks them to imagine that this square is a piece of sidewalk. The teacher picks pairs of students, asks them to "meet on this square" and create any scene regardless of content. After the whole class has participated, the teacher begins to "mix and match" scenes, bringing characters and situations from one into another. In the course of fifteen minutes, the improvisations have been woven into a play. The teacher then asks the students to work in small groups and diagram the play. In sharing the diagrams and discussing them, the question is raised: "Is the location of the square important, or is it merely coincidental that all these things happened here?" As they begin to discuss this, the teacher clarifies by asking: "What thing caused all the other things in our story to happen?"

The teacher then shifts the focus, and asks the students to imagine that this square was the most important location in all of Jewish history. The teacher asks every student to pick a partner and act out, in the square, the event which makes the location important. As the students act out the scenes, the teacher lists them on the board. The list will include such items as receiving the Ten Commandments, Adam and Eve, crossing the Red Sea, etc. Looking at the list, the teacher asks which of them happened in the same place. Very few of them seem to have a geographic connection.

The teacher then passes out a page of texts which describes the various activities which took place on the Temple Mount. (If the class is in the right mood, the teacher may have them dramatize each of the events to make sure that all the students know what happened in each.)

Then the teacher asks: "Why did the Rabbis want to have one spot connect so many events?" The class comes up with lots of answers: the ground is holy, they wanted the events to be connected, something else about the place connected the other events. The teacher establishes that all of these are correct, and then introduces the significance of the Temple in Jewish life. Among other things the teacher quotes, "For from Zion shall go forth the Law, and the word of the Lord from Jerusalem." Through a combination of lecture and discussion, the class learns that the Temple was a place which (1) unified the Jewish people, (2) connected the Jew to God, and (3) was the center of the Jew's becoming a "light to the nations." Then the question is asked: "So why connect the Temple to creation, Adam and Eve, Noah, the Messiah, etc.?" With the teacher's help, the class comes to understand the connection the Rabbis want to make between prayer and history. They also understand that the Rabbis believed that history had a direction.

THE RABBIS WANTED TO CONNECT PRAYER WITH HISTORY.

When the teacher distributes the text of *Mah Tovu*, the class is able to find many connections between the events listed in the *midrash* and the things mentioned in the prayer. Once the class understands that this prayer is really the history of a relationship between God and people, and that the Temple is the place where the two regularly meet, someone is able to conclude that these events represent the major moments which shaped the relationship. Some one else might suggest: "It's like going to see grandparents you don't see all the time. On the way there, you remember lots of other visits; that helps you to get ready."

Starting with Sod

In this session, the teacher has asked the students to relax, close their eyes and concentrate:

> Imagine that you can see a very special location. It is a place you have never been, but it is a place which feels wonderful. It is a place which is full of peace and beauty . . . it is a place which is hard to reach. Walk around the place, and get to know it. (The teacher pauses for a minute or so.)
>
> I want you to imagine that a number of things are hidden in this special spot. In this spot there is a secret message written just for you. In this spot there is a mirror which can let you know who you are, and who you can be. In this spot is a crystal ball which can answer many of your questions. In this spot is a clue to your past — something which belonged to your family for generations, but which has been lost for a long time. Hidden in this spot are things which can make you wiser, things which can make you rich, sayings which can make you feel connected, things which can help you to become happy. Look at all the things and find them hidden in this secret spot. (The teacher pauses after each of these sentences, and then waits for a minute after the last sentence before going on.)
>
> This spot is a very special place, but it is hard to get to. There are many struggles and obstacles in getting there. Some people don't even really believe that this place exists. Imagine all the things you would have to do to come to this place, and find the special things which are hidden there.

The teacher has the students look around this special place, hear its sounds one more time (so as never to forget it), and then "wake up back in the classroom." Without letting them talk, the teacher asks the students to write a story about leading an expedition to their special place. After the stories are written, the group begins to share some of their adventures. As they do so, the teacher notes some of the key elements from each story on the blackboard.

Having gone through all of these stories, the teacher then asks the class to compare these stories to other stories they know. The class responds with various fantasy stories and fairy tales. The teacher establishes the idea that most people have dreams of a quest hidden inside of them.

The teacher explains that Jews have long had dreams of a return to the Temple, the place which held those kinds of treasures. The teacher then compares the list of things which could be found in this special place to things Jews expected to find in the Temple. The class then goes back and studies the layers of *P'shat*, *D'rash*, and *Remez* and sees how each is a quest for the treasures which can be found in the Temple.

THE EPILOGUE

Our students are the products of visual rather than verbal imagery. Walt Disney has implanted within most of us the image of a mirror which can reflect back to us our deepest thoughts and aspirations. Via the "Wicked Witch of the West," we understand the workings of a crystal ball which can reveal happenings from other places. Such fantasies have a very powerful reality.

The prayer book is indeed a mirror, a crystal ball — a map. Through it we can see reflections of our own thoughts and aspirations (*Sod*), things happening at other places (our ethical responsibilities), lost civilizations (*D'rash*), and a map which leads us from creation toward redemption (*Remez*).

And what of the teacher? It would seem that to teach a prayer, a teacher must be a biblical scholar, a Talmudic expert, well versed in *midrash,* and able to lead students safely into their own dreams and hopes. Teachers, however, can join the ranks of Merlin, Yoda, and the Rabbis. None of those mentors had all the answers. If they had, there would have been no need for Arthur, Frodo and Bilbo, Luke Skywalker, and us. The teacher of prayers need only share a few secrets with his/her students: (1) that each student is a hero or heroine engaged in a struggle to let good overcome evil, to bring peace, prosperity, completion, and redemption to creation, (2) that the *Siddur* is indeed a magical tool which can open many pathways within and between us, and (3) that there are ways to decode the *Siddur* and find its meanings, both private and communal. From these starting points, teachers and students can start their quest through the *Siddur* and beyond.

Stuart Kelman is Rabbi of Congregation Netivot Shalom in Berkeley, California. He has a Ph.D. from the University of California and an Honorary Doctorate and Rabbinic ordination from Jewish Theological Seminary. Formerly Executive Director of the Agency for Jewish Education in Oakland, California, Dr. Kelman is the editor of What We Know About Jewish Education (Torah Aura Productions).

Joel Lurie Grishaver is the Creative Director of Torah Aura Productions and the author of a myriad of materials for Jewish schools, including The Life Cycle Workbook and Tzedakah, Gemilut Chasadim and Ahavah (A.R.E.) He also teaches Bible and Rabbinics at the Los Angeles Hebrew High School.

APPENDIX A

A Taxonomy of Behavioral Objectives for the Mastery of Jewish Liturgy

P'SHAT – Literal Meaning
Prayer Level:
I. That for each prayer in the service the learner can:
   A. State the name
   B. Describe the structure
   C. State the theme
   D. Translate
      1. From Hebrew to English
      2. From "English" to his/her own language
   E. Read, Sing, *Daven*, etc. (e.g., congregational participation)

Structural Level:
II. That the learner can:
   A. Identify the major sections of a service
   B. State which sections make up each service
   C. State the sequence of prayers in each section

D'RASH – Biblical Interpretation
Prayer Level:
III. That the learner can explain the denotative meanings of the images/metaphors of the prayers:
   A. Find and trace the biblical allusions
   B. Find and trace the historical background

IV. That the learner can accept the Prayer-Theme as a Jewish category of significance:
   A. That the learner can organize and correlate material to the theme
   B. That the learner can correlate personal experiences to the theme

Structural Level:
V. That the learner can describe the structure of the service and:
   A. Trace the interaction of imagery between prayers
   B. Describe the "flow" of the structure of the service
      1. as a progression of images
      2. as a progression of themes

REMEZ – Clues/Salvation History
Prayer Level:
VI. That the learner can explain the connotative meanings of the images/metaphors or the prayers:
   A. Find and trace the *midrashic* allusions
   B. Synthesize the *midrashic* allusions with the Prayer-Theme.

Structural Level:
VII. That the learner can describe the structure of the service
   A. Trace the interaction of *midrashic* imagery between prayers
   B. Describe the "flow" of the structure of the service
      1. as a progression of *midrashic* images
      2. as a progression of *midrashic* themes

SOD – Secret/Internal/Meanings
VIII. That the learner can integrate learned material with personal experience
    A. That the learner can integrate his/her own symbol system into his/her perceptions of the liturgy and its structure.
    B. That the learner can integrate the structure and symbol system of the service into his/her own life and perception of reality.

IX. That the learner can use the liturgy as a tool to shape, direct, and evaluate his/her own actions, feelings, beliefs, and lifestyle.

APPENDIX B
Content Analysis of Basic Prayers

THE PRAYERS	P'SHAT	D'RASH	REMEZ	SOD
Birchot HaShachar These are a string of "one-line" *brachot* which were originally designed to be said individually as one woke up each morning. They later became part of the introductory ritual in the synagogue.	The following are the sequence of blessings and issues: (all present tense excepting #1):	These Biblical verses are in some cases clear sources for the blessings, and in others merely image-linked	This sequence of blessings is described in the Talmud (*Brachot* 60b). Each blessing is connected to an action.	This series of blessings correlates the process of physically waking up to a spiritual awakening.
	1. rooster (or heart) power to distinguish	Job 38:36	hearing rooster crow	
	2. not a heathen	Deuteronomy 10:19	(not in Talmud)	
	3. not a slave (or made me Israel)	Leviticus 25:55	(not in Talmud)	
	4. not a woman (or made me according to will)		(not in Talmud)	continued...
	5. sight to blind	Psalm 146:9 / Lev. 19:14 Genesis 3:5	opening eyes	continued...
	6. free prisoners	Psalm 146:7	stretches and sits up	
	7. clothe naked	Genesis 3:21	dressing	
	8. raises the bowed	Psalm 145:14 / 146:8	getting out of bed	
	9. spreads earth on the waters	Psalm 136:6	feet on ground	
	10. directs people's steps	Psalm 37:31	first steps	
	11. all my needs		tying shoes	
	12. girds Israel with strength	Jeremiah 13 Psalm 65:7 / Job. 38:3	tying belt	
	13. crown Israel with glory	*Pirke Avot* 2:1/4:1 Psalm 103:4 / Is. 49:3	covers head	
	14. strength to weary	Isaiah 40:28-31	(not in Talmud)	
	15. removes sleep from my eyes		washes face	

THE PRAYERS	P'SHAT	D'RASH	REMEZ	SOD
Pesukay d'Zimrah Verses of Song:	Compare the present order of these to the Talmudic formula.		Most of these can be sorted into Creation, Revelation (Ethics), and Redemption.	
	This is a string of biblical verses — essentially songs of praise — which are woven into an introduction to the morning service. It has an opening blessing (*Baruch She'amar*), and a closing blessing (*Yishtabach*). We will focus on 4 of the 15 prayers.			
1. *Baruch She'amar* This is the introductory *brachah*. it begins the first third of these "hymns."	This is a string of God names preceeded by "*Baruch*," introducing a long blessing. 1. The One who spoke and the world was 2. Who does creation. 3. Who says and does. 4. Who decrees and fulfills. 5. Who has mercy on the earth. 6. Who grants fair reward . . . 7. Who grants fair reward . . . 8. Who lives forever. 9. Who redeems . . . . 10. Whose name is blessed.	These diverse God names are drawn from diverse (and non-specific) biblical verses. The Bible expands on the idea of God's names: Exodus 3:1-5 (Burning Bush) Exodus 6:2-4 (History of God's names)	David creates Psalms: At midnight the strings of his harp, which were made of the gut of the ram sacrificed instead of Isaac, began to vibrate in the wind. David would awaken, study Torah and write the Psalms. (Ginzberg, 545) "Why does Israel pray in this world without being heard? Because it doesn't know the Holy name of God." (*Midrash Psalms* 91)	Personal associations: 1. Attributes of God 2. Role of names 3. Identity Continued . . . .
2. David's song – (I Chronicles 16:8ff) 3. *Rommemu* – collection of verses from Psalms 4. Psalm 100	The second half of this prayer is the long blessing. It contains two words: *Hillul* and *Shevach*, both of which are related to "praising."	Many biblical verses in Psalms. It may be good to foreshadow the *Hallel* Psalms.	Montefiore: pp. 10-12 also, index note - 822 Notice structure – 1-6 Creation 3-8 Revelation 7-10 Redemption Rabbinic literature is full of images of the angels being involved in praising God . . . . See Montefiore – p. 642	Associations with: 1. Praising 2. Learning from giving praise.

THE PRAYERS	P'SHAT	D'RASH	REMEZ	SOD
5. *Ashray* – Psalm 145 The Psalm most frequently used in the liturgy. 6. Psalm 146 7. Psalm 147 8. Psalm 148 9. Psalm 149	*Ashray* is made up of Psalm 145, with 2 verses (Psalm 84:5, 144:15) added at the beginning, and 1 verse (Psalm 115:8) added at the end. The Psalm is an acrostic — the sequence of verses are alphabetical (with the letter *Nun* missing). They are in poetic parallel. All the Psalms in this series begin and end with *Halleluyah* (except *Ashray*) which only ends with it.	The structure of the prayer invites these questions: 1. Why the two introductory verses? 2. Why is the *nun* missing? 3. Why is the verse added at the end? Part of the answer is to link *Halleluyah*. Also, notice the use of *Bless* – beginning, middle, and end of piece. And, the word *all* – 10 times.	Importance of the Alphabet: Ginzberg – pp. 2-3 Ben Shahn – *Alphabet of Creation* Kushner – *Book of Letters* *Ashray* in Talmud – *Ber.* 4b. *Midrash* – *Nun* is missing because it stands for *naphelah* – fallen (cf. Amos 5:2), but it is lifted up in the *Samach* verse.	Progressions, orders, and sequences in our lives. Poetic parallel in our lives – two things which mean the same thing which happen differently. Exceptions from our orders. Lifting up the fallen – (*Tzedakah*, etc.) the needs and effects.
10. *Halleluyah* – Psalm 150 This is the last Psalm; it is also the last in this series of 6 Psalms. 11. *Baruch HaShem* verses from: Psalms 89:53, 135:21 and 72:18-9 12. I Chron. 29:1 - 3 13. Nehemiah 9:6 - 11 14. Exodus 14:50 - 15:18	This Psalm is built around the word *Hallelu* – praise. It appears 13 times. It appears 15 times when the last line is repeated (as is the custom). The repetition is attributed to it being the last verse of a biblical book.	This Psalm is present without modification. It is worth noting its role as the culmination of the Book of Psalms. Look at how it echoes the previous 5 Psalms. The context of the Psalm is the Levitical rite in the Temple.	The number 13 is equated with the 13 articles of faith – by Maimonides. The *Zohar* identifies it with 13 attributes of God. Investigation of the Temple ritual.	Use of music in praise – celebration. Non-verbal (instrumental praise). Relating to *all* life praising. Personal articles of faith and attributes.
15. *Yishtabach*	This is the closing blessing in *P'sukay d'Zimrah*. It is a short blessing. It contains a list of 15 verbs reflecting praise.	The Bible describes the Temple as having 15 steps. The Levites worked their way up the steps, singing one Psalm at each step.	The number 15 is associated with God, because (*Yud* – *Hey*) the core of Divine name (The Lord) adds up to 15. The *midrash* describes God's throne as having 15 steps – Ginzberg, pp. 556-8 (Under parallel of Solomon's throne)	Create your own list of 15 steps of ascent

THE PRAYERS	P'SHAT	D'RASH	REMEZ	SOD
Barchu The call to worship – *Brachah* which introduces the *Shema* and its blessings.	Consists of two lines: A command to bless in the plural, followed by an individual statement of blessing.	Compare to Psalm 149:18 the next to last Psalm in *Pesukay d'Zimrah*.	Montefiore: On "*Minyan*" – 97, 107, 348 On "Blessing" – 375-8	Individual/Community

CHAPTER THIRTY-FOUR

NOTES

1. Hans Lewy, Alexander Altman, and Isaak Heinemann, *Three Jewish Philosophers* (Cleveland: World Publishing Co., 1960).
2. Max Kadushin, *Worship and Ethics* (Chicago: Northwestern University Press, 1964).
3. Lawrence Kushner, "Holier Worlds Than This," *Keeping Posted*. Volume 25, No. 3. (New York: UAHC, 1979).
4. We are grateful to Dr. Reuven Kimmelman of Brandeis University for his illuminating insights into the understanding of this prayer.
5. Zev Vilnay, *Legends of Jerusalem* (Philadelphia: Jewish Publication Society, 1973).

BIBLIOGRAPHY

Books on Prayer/Teacher Guides

Arzt, Max. *Justice and Mercy*. New York: Hartmore House, n.d.

Bernstein, Ellen, and Dan Fink. *Let the Earth Touch You Teacher's Guide*. Wyncote, PA: Shomrei Adamah, 1992.

Bialik, Hayim Nahman, and Yehoshua Hana Ravnitzky, eds. *The Book of Legends: Sefer Ha-Aggadah*. New York: Schocken Books, 1992.

Braude, William G., trans. *Midrash on Psalms*. 2 vols. New Haven: Yale University Press, 1959.

Buxbaum, Yitzhak. *Jewish Spiritual Practices*. Northvale, NJ: Jason Aronson Inc., 1990.

Cohen, Jeffrey M. *Serve the Lord with All Your Heart: A Comprehensive Guide to Jewish Prayer*. Northvale, NJ: Jason Aronson Inc., 1993.

Davis, Avroham. *The Metsudah Siddur*. New York: Metsudah Publications, 1981.

Donin, Hayim Halevy. *To Pray as a Jew*. New York: Basic Books, 1991.

Elbogen, Ismar. *Jewish Liturgy: A Comprehensive History*. Philadelphia: The Jewish Publication Society of America and The Jewish Theological Seminary of America, 1993.

Feuer, Avrohom Chaim. *Shemoneh Esrei: The Amidah/The Eighteen Blessings*. Brooklyn: Mesorah Publications, Ltd., 1990.

Ginzberg, Louis. *Legends of the Bible*. Philadelphia: Jewish Publication Society, 1992.

Greenberg, Sidney, ed. *A Treasury of Thoughts on Jewish Prayer*. Northvale, NJ: Jason Aronson Inc., 1989.

Grishaver, Joel Lurie. *And You Shall Be a Blessing: An Unfolding of the Six Words that Begin Every Brakhah*. Northvale, NJ: Jason Aronson Inc., 1993.

Hammer, Reuven. *Entering Jewish Prayer: A Guide to Personal Devotion and the Worship Service*. New York: Schocken Books, 1994.

Heinemann, Joseph, with Jakob J. Petuchowski. *Literature of the Synagogue*. West Orange, NJ: Behrman House, 1975.

Jacobson, B. S. *The Weekday Siddur: An Exposition and Analysis of its Structure, Contents, Language and Ideas*. Tel Aviv: Sinai Publishing, 1978.

Hertz, Joseph. *The Authorised Daily Prayer Book*. New York: Bloch, 1955.

Hoffman, Lawrence A. *The Art of Public Prayer: Not for Clergy Only*. Washington, D.C.: The Pastoral Press, 1988.

———. *Beyond the Text: A Holistic Approach to Liturgy*. Bloomington: Indiana University Press, 1987.

Kadden, Bruce, and Barbara Binder Kadden. *Teaching Tefilah: Insights and Activities on Prayer*. Denver: A.R.E. Publishing, Inc., 1994.

Klein, Isaac. *A Guide to Jewish Religious Practice*. New York: Jewish Theological Seminary, 1979.

Kirtzner, Yitzchok, and Lisa Aiken. *Art of Jewish Prayer*. Northvale, NJ: Jason Aronson Inc., 1991.

Kushner, Lawrence. *The Book of Letters: A Mystical Hebrew Alphabet*. 2d rev. ed. Woodstock, VT: Jewish Lights Publishing, 1990.

———. *The Book of Words: Talking Spritual Life, Living Spiritual Talk*. Woodstock, VT: Jewish Lights Publishing, 1993.

———. *Honey from the Rock: An Easy Introduction to Jewish Mysticism*. 2d rev. ed. Woodstock, VT: Jewish Lights Publishing, 1990.

Midrash Rabbah. 5 vols. London: Soncino Press, 1959.

Moskowitz, Nachama Skolnik. *A Teacher's Guide to A Bridge to Prayer: The Jewish Worship*

Workbook Volumes One-Two. New York: UAHC Press, 1989.

Munk, Elie. *The World of Prayer.* 2 vols. New York: Feldheim, 1961.

Nulman, Macy. *The Encyclopedia of Jewish Prayer: Ashkenazic and Sephardic Rites.* Northvale, NJ: Jason Aronson Inc., 1993.

Or Chadash: (A New Light): New Paths for Shabbat Morning. Philadelphia: ALEPH: Alliance for Jewish Renewal, 1989.

Siegel, Seymour, and David Bamberger. *Teaching Guide for When a Jew Prays.* West Orange, NJ: Behrman House, 1973.

(Note: Check the Artscroll Series for books on prayer and the *Siddur.*)

Classroom Texts

Berman, Melanie. *Building Jewish Life: Prayers and Blessings.* Los Angeles: Torah Aura Productions, 1991.

Brown, Steven M. *Higher and Higher: Making Jewish Prayer Part of Us.* New York: United Synagogue of Conservative Judaism, 1980.

Fields, Harvey J. *Bechol Levavcha: With All Your Heart.* New York: UAHC Press, 1976.

Grishaver, Joel Lurie. *Basic Berachot.* Los Angeles: Torah Aura Productions, 1988.

———. *Building Jewish Life: The Siddur Commentary.* Los Angeles: Torah Aura Productions, 1992.

———. *19 Out of 18: The All New Shema Is for Real Curriculum.* Los Angeles: Torah Aura Productions, 1991.

———. *Shema and Company.* rev. ed. Los Angeles: Torah Aura Productions, 1991.

———. *Shema Is for Real: A Book on Prayers & Other Tangents.* Los Angeles: Torah Aura Productions, 1993.

Karp, Laura. *Student's Encounter Book for When a Jew Prays.* West Orange, NJ: Behrman House Inc., 1975.

Moskowitz, Nachama Skolnik. *A Bridge to Prayer: The Jewish Worship Workbook Volume One: God, Prayer, and the Shema.* New York: UAHC Press, 1988.

———. *A Bridge to Prayer: The Jewish Worship Workbook Volume Two: The Amidah, Torah Service, and Concluding Prayers.* New York: UAHC Press, 1989.

Rossel, Seymour. *When a Jew Prays.* West Orange, NJ: Behrman House, 1973.

SUBJECT MATTER

CHAPTER THIRTY-FIVE

BEYOND BIBLE TALES: TOWARD TEACHING TEXT

Joel Lurie Grishaver

The central goal of every Bible teacher is to reveal to his/her students that the Holy Scriptures are haunted — that indeed something is lurking behind the words, phrases, and metaphors. Every time we open the text, we try to encounter the force which inhabits each ancient phrase. It does not matter whether we are seeking God's true voice, the ghosts of Rabbinic sages past, the secret identities of the "real" authors, or simply the echoes of ancient footsteps. What is important is that we encounter the text itself, that we allow it to conjure from our past, from ourselves, from its past and from its own reality, a dynamic relationship. What we are seeking is a text with which, and over which, we can talk.

To search for the text's inner voice, we need to know how to probe the text, how to listen for its response. In doing so, it is necessary to go past the story to the way the story is told. The depth of the biblical material lies not in the intricacies of plot, but in the complex workings of the words themselves.

The Bible is well suited for this probing. In fact, it demands it of us. Regardless of our vision of the text, be it divine or exquisitely human, we can see that its style is unlike any other great literature. For it is like a marvelous haunted mansion, carefully crafted. It is filled with individual works of art, which are both more beautiful and more puzzling because of their age. It is alive with echoes and glimmering light sources, and its construction is riddled with secret connections and hidden passageways.

In the course of this chapter, we will first examine five patterns which enable us to engage the text in dialogue. (While there are at least five other such patterns,[1] we cannot cover them all here because of space constraints.) Following the analysis of the five patterns, we will discuss the steps necessary in the preparation of good lessons on the Bible.

The kind of biblical investigation we are suggesting is not limited to the adult or to the sophisticated learner. All who like to engage in dialogue and all who are fascinated by mystery can be involved. Students of all ages will be intrigued when exposed to these patterns and become aware of their significance. So let us take candle in hand and begin our investigation of some haunted passages.

PATTERN ONE: REPETITION

We open the Bible and start reading. One of our first impressions is that the text frequently repeats itself. We see the same pattern over and over: God tells someone to do something, and then (more or less repeating the same phrases), the narrator tells us that the deed has been done. Or, a character is told to tell someone something, and then (more or less repeating the same phrases), the character delivers the message. Additionally, we find incidents when the narrator describes a character's actions, and then (more or less repeating the same phrases), that same character or another character describes the action. Such is the biblical style, but there is more to it. The narrative portion of the text is basically made up of narration and dialogue. The two are very carefully structured; it is the variation, not the repetition, which is significant. The repetitions focus our attention and build our expectations. But the subtle variation in the pattern holds the author's hidden message.

Let us look at some examples. The first consists of two passages about Abram and his family

> **FIVE PATTERNS ENABLE US TO ENGAGE THE TEXT.**

as they leave certain places. One passage describes leaving Haran and going to the land of Canaan; the other describes leaving Egypt and returning to the land of Canaan.

> And Abram took
> Sarai his wife,
> and Lot his brother's son
> and all their substance...
> (Genesis 12:5)
> And Abram went out of Egypt
> He, and his wife
> and all that he had,
> And Lot with him...
> (Genesis 13:1)

What seems to be the change in Lot's status? (Clue: Lot's position in the description is not the only thing. Look also at what the syntax suggests about collective ownership of property.)

Genesis 13:1 immediately precedes the fight between the shepherds of Lot and Abram which results in their split. What might the narrator be trying to tell us about that incident? What lesson or message can be drawn from this insight?

A second example from the book of Numbers describes Moses turning the leadership of the people over to Joshua... and the Lord answered Moses, "Single out Joshua, son of Nun, an inspired man, and lay your hand upon him. Have him stand before Eleazar the priest and before the whole community, and commission him in their sight. Invest him with some of your authority..." (Numbers 27:18-20)

Moses did as the Lord commanded him. He took Joshua and had him stand before Eleazar the priest and before the whole community. He laid his hands upon him and commissioned him, as the Lord had spoken through Moses. (Numbers 27:22-23)

Some questions to ponder: Moses follows God's instructions, but there is one major shift in sequence as the instructions are carried out. The order which Moses uses to carry out the instructions is the logical sequence. Why might God have inverted the order when instructions were given to Moses? (Clue: What insight into Moses' character might God have acted upon?) What lesson can be drawn from this inversion of the repetition? Explain why Moses decided to add a hand to his installation process. This explanation can be used as the basis of a moral lesson.

Rashi poses this solution to the case of the extra hand (after all, we are exploring a haunted house):

And he laid his hands generously; meaning in much greater measure than he had been commanded — he did it with both hands to make him as a vessel which is full to the brim and overflowing, and so he filled him with a generous helping of wisdom.

Rashi, in his own way (as all of us do) distorts the text slightly for his own purpose. Consider this: In the text, what does God tell Moses to use as he invests Joshua? What does Rashi suggest that Moses used? Is there a correlation? Are the two identical? Should they be identical? Can another lesson be drawn, this time from Rashi's comment?

In each of the above examples, we have found that behind the apparent repetition and use of formula in the text, a message is conveyed through that which is not repeated (more or less using the same phrases) and through that which is altered. This kind of analysis is a form of literary criticism, which is technically known as form criticism. It is used by literary scholars, as well as by the commentators Umberto Cassuto (1883-1951) and Benno Jacob (1862-1955). It is also standard procedure for the *Midrash* and for Rashi. In spite of its "scholarly" roots, any of us can participate in this process.

Classroom Applications

Here are a few possibilities for adapting the pattern of repetition to classroom lessons. You can generalize these suggestions to other passages.

1. Using an inquiry format, have your students find the clues in the text by a) providing them with the portions of the text laid out in such a way that they can easily see the variations, b) having them color code their texts with circles and arrows and other markings, or c) having them read the two versions out loud. As we have done here, emphasize both the finding of the clue and the creation of lessons to be learned.
2. Adapt the childhood exercise, "What is wrong with this picture?" Create (or have students create) pictures which go with each version of the story. Then have the students match phrase and illustration.
3. A standard vaudeville sketch format occurs when the protagonist repeats the dialogue directed by the narrator:

Narrator: And then God said: "Let there be light."
God: Let there be light.
Narrator: And there was light.

Write skits which exploit this device to reflect the changes in the text.

4. The first text dealt with the relationship between Abram (and Sarai) and Lot. Our reading of the text suggested that relations had begun to break down before the shepherds fought. Have your students act out or creatively write the scene inside Abram's tent when he and Sarai talk about Lot, and the scene inside Lot's house as he discusses Abram. Use these scenes to evaluate the solution to the conflict arrived at by Abram and Lot.

5. In the text on the installation of Joshua by Moses, we found a significant issue revolved around the laying on of hands. After studying this passage, have the students invent a ceremony during which they grant gifts to each other through the laying on of hands.

6. In Rashi's solution to the text, we saw that there is a question of the relationship between knowledge and authority. Have your students play *Blackjack* (or any other game). Have them adjust the rules so that the dealer (or the leader) has varying amounts of knowledge and authority. Discuss what happens to the game if the dealer gets to see everyone's cards before he or she plays, or what happens to the game if the dealer can decide for each player how many cards they may (or must) take. Then discuss the question in the passage.

PATTERN TWO: TWICE TOLD TALES

Most events in the Bible are told at least twice. Deuteronomy retells many of the accounts in Exodus, Leviticus, and Numbers. Chronicles I and II retell a great deal of history, especially what has already been reported in the books of Samuel and Kings. The Prophets and the Psalms echo many of the accounts in the Torah and especially the portions of Genesis which precede Abram. Often, the second version of a story imparts new information.

Consider, for example, the fourth commandment as it appears in the two versions of the Ten Commandments.

1. Remember the Sabbath day and keep it holy. Six days shall you labor and do all your work, but the seventh day is a Sabbath of the Lord your God: you shall not do any work — you, your son or your daughter, your male or female slave, or your cattle, or the stranger who is within your settlements. For in six days the Lord made heaven and earth and sea, and all that is in them, and He rested on the seventh day; therefore the Lord blessed the Sabbath day and hallowed it. (Exodus 20:8-11)

2. Observe the Sabbath day and keep it holy, as the Lord your God has commanded you. Six days you shall labor and do all your work, but the seventh day is a Sabbath of the Lord your God: you shall not do any work — you, your son or your daughter, your male or female slave, your ox or your ass, or any of your cattle, or the stranger in your settlements, so that your male and female slave may rest as you do. Remember that you were a slave in the land of Egypt and the Lord your God freed you from there with a mighty hand and an outstretched arm; therefore the Lord your God has commanded you to observe the Sabbath day. (Deuteronomy 5:12-15)

Determine which portions of the text are the same in both versions. Which are parallel (more or less the same words in the same place)? The central difference between the two versions of this commandment is in the reasons given for celebrating the Sabbath. The starting words for each of the two commandments (the active verbs) are different. The closing formulas are also different. In Exodus, God is the subject and the Sabbath is the direct object. In Deuteronomy, God is the subject and "You" is the direct object. All of the Exodus version of this commandment is contained in the Deuteronomic version. However, the commandment as found in Deuteronomy has two major additions as can be seen in the following lists:

Exodus	Deuteronomy
Remember	Observe
Creation	Exodus (freedom from slavery) command
Bless	
Extra material on commandments	Extra material on slaves resting

How are the elements of each list consistent? Do the two versions of this commandment contradict each other? Do they complement each other? If so, in what way? What lesson can be drawn from the fact that the two versions outline different reasons for celebrating Shabbat?

The first verse of "*Lecha Dodi*," the song with which we welcome the Shabbat, begins: "'Observe' and 'Remember' were said together in one breath . . . " Is the "lesson" of "*Lecha Dodi*" similar to the one drawn above?

Now we look at a second example, the two versions of the story about sending spies into the land of Israel (Numbers 13:1-3, 27-32 and Deuteronomy 1:22-28). Unlike other repetition patterns, these two stories confront us with significant contradictions rather than literary variations. In Numbers, (1) the Lord instructs Moses to send spies, (2) the spies are princes of the tribes, (3) the land is "flowing in milk and honey," (4) Moses is credited with bringing the people there, and (5) the spies spread an evil report "that the land consumes its inhabitants."

In the book of Deuteronomy, (1) the people ask to send spies, (the spies are simply "twelve men," (3) the land is "good," (4) God gave it, (5) the inhabitants are "greater and taller than we," and (6) God brought us there because He "hated us." Now we have to resolve these differences. Here are some "popular solutions." Consider the evidence for each.

1. The "documentary hypothesis" suggests that the Bible was assembled by collecting various documents/texts which had been written by different groups, under different influences, in different time periods. What evidence is there that these two editions might indeed be two different accounts (from different sources) of the same event?
2. Several commentators say that there is no real contradiction between the two accounts. Like two news reporters, the writers are simply choosing to focus on different details. Can you explain how both versions could be "factual?"
3. A commentator named David Hoffman suggests that the two accounts had different intents. The account in Numbers was created to preserve an historical reality, while the edition of the story found in Deuteronomy was structured to teach a "moral truth." What is the evidence for this point of view?
4. The Ramban (Nachmanides) suggested that the two versions of the story were designed to fit the needs of two audiences. The first was written about (and for) the generation which left Egypt and the second was written for the generation which was about to enter the land of Israel. Is there evidence to support this point of view?
5. Why do you think the Bible includes two separate accounts of this incident? What are we supposed to learn from the two accounts? Do you accept one of the above explanations or a combination of them? Do you have a different point of view? Many portions of the biblical text appear in more than one location. The Bible seems to preserve multiple testimonies about specific occurrences and legal concepts. Sometimes these experiences are nearly identical; at other times they seem significantly different. In either case, we are drawn into the material. We find ourselves looking for the "true" version and, like good detectives, we begin to sort out the various testimonies and piece together our version of the truth. Frequently we discover that it is not the facts of the event that have changed, but the nature of the conversation. Different people tell (and retell) stories differently, and different audiences call for different ways of telling. In confronting conflicting accounts, we must realize that the resolution may never be clear. Often the presence of two (or more) voices expands rather than confuses our image of the text; at other times the ambiguity enhances our involvement in the material. It is as if the Bible is asking us, "Nu, so what do you think?"

Other examples of the pattern of twice told tales may be found in the accounts of the story of Saul's death in I Samuel 31 and I Chronicles 10. Look also at Psalm 105 and find the three stories retold there.

Classroom Applications

Let's explore a few possible lesson formats for this pattern. Some of these will deal with the nature of confronting two sources; the remainder will draw on the insights gained from the passages.
1. As with the repetition pattern, use written or oral inquiry techniques to find clues in the text.

2. A particular professor was famous for staging a "murder" in his class once a semester. At some point, when everyone least expected it, an assistant would burst through the door, shoot the professor, and disappear. The class would then be asked to write an account of the incident. Reports varied as to the size, height, age, race, and dress of the "murderer." Adapt this (in a less violent format) to your classroom. Use the various reports to talk about the nature of human testimony.
3. Do the same kind of thing with a past event. Analyze a significant event which took place last year or a while ago and compare the results of "historical memory."
4. Bring in two articles about the same news events or two reviews of the same film from sources such as *Time* and *Newsweek*. Use the two accounts to try to reconstruct the "true" event.
5. Do guided imagery with your class. Have students close their eyes and imagine an event you describe. Then have everyone write down a description or draw a picture of their experience. Compare the diverse impressions of a single experience.
6. Have someone tell a story to a group of adults and then to the first grade class. (Videotape this if desired.) Compare the versions of the stories told. Decide if this situation is analogous to the two accounts of the same story found in the texts you have studied.
7. Compare the other differences in the two versions of the Ten Commandments. Also, look at the structure of the Ten Commandments. For background and activities, see *Bible People Book Two* by Grishaver.
8. That there are two versions of a commandment about Shabbat could serve as the basis for explaining why Shabbat is celebrated with *pairs* of candles; two *challot*; angels who, in the *midrash*, escort people home. Explore the pairs theme. A good reference is *The Sabbath* by Abraham Joshua Heschel (New York: Harper and Row, 1952).
9. Imagine what Shabbat would be like in the Garden of Eden and what it was like for the slaves in Egypt. Simulate these experiences with your class, then reread the two sets of commandments.
10. Organize a debate on which version of the incident of the spies is most true (or create a *60 Minutes* type report on the topic).
11. Two versions of the story of the spies represent an interesting literary format: we are presented with "mixed reports" of the land, from "mixed reports" of spies. Have students respond to the reports from the point of view of Joshua, of one of the spies, of Moses, of an ordinary Israelite, of Moses 30 years later, of an ordinary Israelite 30 years later, of one of the spy's children or grandchildren, of Joshua's mother, of a history teacher 75 years later, etc.

PATTERN THREE: CONVENTIONS[2]

Certain kinds of events seem to characterize the lives of many biblical characters. Biblical women, for instance, have a difficult time getting pregnant. What is more, it sometimes seems that no self-respecting biblical hero is ever born of a mother who got pregnant on the first try. Aliases (and other name changes) run in biblical families. Many good biblical marriages (and many poor ones) began at a well. And, in almost every generation, the "wrong" child — the one who is qualified by skill but not by order of birth — takes over the leadership of the Jewish family/people.

The idea of standard events (or technically, "type-scenes") is familiar to us. In movies and television shows we are used to certain basic "conventions." Lightning storms at night (especially around castles and abandoned houses) and full moons (accompanied by ominous string music) are certain clues to what will transpire. It is universally accepted that the first place every western hero goes when he gets to town is through the swinging doors into the saloon. We all know that his entry into the saloon will reveal both the degree and style of his machismo.

Whenever we watch a western movie, we have a number of expectations. We expect to meet many of the following types: a good sheriff trying to tame a bad town; a good sheriff fighting bad guys with the people of the town; a bad sheriff and gang controlling a town; the lovable prostitute; a retired gunman who will not pick up a gun, but who somehow does, just in time to resolve the storyl an ex-bad guy, gone straight, who is discovered and soon thereafter dies fighting for right (usually in his son's arms) having finally paid his debt to society; the kid who wants to be a gun fighter; lots of cowardly town folk who make their living by walking back and forth across Main Street in period clothing; etc. In poor westerns, these stock incidents become cliche's. In a good western, such conventions are used to establish and define the hero. Similar conventions exist in biblical literature. How the characters behave within the type-scenes, and how they live up to or confound our expectations reveals their unique, dynamic personalitites.

Two characters who provide good examples of conventions and expectations are Samson and Isaac. Both are strange biblical heroes. Samson is strange because he does little that is heroic and less which conforms to normative Jewish values. Isaac, "the silent one," according to the Rabbis, is a quiet presence who intensely occupies, but doesn't fill, his portions of the text.

As we compare some key events in the lives of Samson and Isaac, be aware of how the tension between our expectations and what actually happens shapes our insight into the characters' humanity.

1. The Mother's Inability To Get Pregnant

Our Expectation – The mother will be unable to get pregnant. She will appeal to God, and because of her merit or piety, God will "open her womb."

Samson – Samson's mother can't get pregnant. She is not named, but identified only as Manoah's wife. There is no statement of merit, and no demonstration of any positive qualities.

Isaac – In Isaac's case, neither Abram or Sarai ask God for the pregnancy. Abram appears to merit the pregnancy, and not Sarai. (See Genesis 12:7, 15:1-7, 16:1-4, 17:1-7, 18:9-15.)

2. Annunciation and Naming

Our Expectation – Either God, an angel, or an agent will inform the mother of her "open womb" and project the nature of the child. The child is given a name either when notice is given or at birth. The name reflects the condition of birth and usually projects part of his character.

Samson – An angel appears twice, because Manoah doubts the credibility of his wife's report and wants to be told "how to act with the child that is born." The angel predicts that the child "shall be the first to deliver Israel from the Philistines." Something else is also foreshadowed in this portion (which is another example of pattern one, repetition). When the angel first speaks to the wife, she is given the following three warnings: (1) let no wine touch his lips; (2) let him not eat anything unclean; and (3) let no razor touch his head, because he is to be a Nazirite. When she tells the instructions to Manoah and when the angel/man restates them, wine and unclean food are repeated, but the razor is forgotten.

Isaac – Abram, and not Sarai, is informed of Isaac's impending birth. Yet, it is Sarai's reaction to the news which determines his name. (See Genesis 17: 21, 18:9-15 and 21: 1-7.)

3. Sibling Rivalry

Our Expectation – The younger brother will struggle with the older brother, and eventually take over the key role. The older brother is usually the outdoor type, and the younger more "homespun."

Samson – No example

Isaac – It is mother Sarai who does Isaac's fighting. (See Genesis 21:9-14.)

4. Leaving/Fleeing from Home

Our Expectation – At some point in our hero's development he will leave home (usually because he needs to flee), and will develop his own lifestyle. The break with the family usually reflects the development of the character's own identity.

Samson – Samson is described leaving home (for no particular purpose) and then returning to his parents once he has seen a woman he wishes to marry.

Isaac – Isaac remains at home upon the decision of his father. His wife is brought to him. (See Genesis 24: 1-9.)

5. Initiatory Trial

Our Expectation – Our hero, having left home, encounters a challenge which forces him to demonstrate his strength, courage, faith, and abilities.

Samson – Samson wrestles the lion and proves his strength for the first time. When it states "the spirit of the Lord gripped him, and he tore (the lion) assunder with his bare hands," the text informs us that Samson lost control. Rather than applying the minimal force necessary, he uses all his strength. The same will be true at his death. The text tell us, "Those who were slain by him in his death outnumbered those who had been slain by him when he lived." When he returns to the "scene of the crime" a year later, the lion's bones become a source of honey. Thus some good does come from his violence.

Isaac – Isaac left home for his trial when he went to Mt. Moriah with his father. But Abraham is really the star of Isaac's trial. (See Genesis 22.)

6. The Betrothal at the Well

Our Expectation – Our hero should go to a town well. There he should meet the girl of his future dreams. The two of them interact. He may do something for her. She will draw water for him. Then, straight from the well, they go to her tent to meet the family and arrangements are made.

Samson – Samson's betrothal scene is aborted; the anticipated marriage is never consummated. He sees the girl (presumably at the well) and then, instead of interacting with her, he goes home and has his parents work out the details.

Isaac – Isaac's marriage is arranged by Abraham's servant Eliezer. He meets Rebekah at the well and then interacts with her family. (See Genesis 24.)

7. Dying Testament

Our Expectation – Unlike western heroes, biblical heroes die in bed surrounded by their families. They usually know they are about to die and gather the family for a "closing benediction."

Samson – Samson doesn't have a family. He dies alone, asking God for the strength to take revenge. His closing remark is, "Let me die with the Philistines." This is a reversal of the set formula in which the hero usually asks to be buried with the family.

Isaac – Isaac's final benedictions do not go as he wishes them to. Indeed, he has no control over the situation; his wife sets the stage for the blessing. His actual death is reported in a matter-of-fact manner. Esau and Jacob bury him.

We began this comparison with the notion that Samson was less than the ideal biblical hero. Our study has revealed that he consistently fails to fulfill the expected conventions. His annunciation scene foreshadows his fall, his initiatory trial demonstrates the out of control violence which will determine his death, and the aborted betrothal scene defines his alienation both from his people and from most human contact. Samson is the Jewish leader who is born to "deliver Israel from the Philistines," and who dies "among the Philistines." For the biblical narrator, Samson is a tragic hero who does kill Philistines, but who dwells in the same gulf of human relations which existed between his unnamed mother and his doubting father. He has to die in order to reach peace with his people.[3]

Isaac, on the other hand, was a quiet figure. If we look at the type-scenes which come into play here, we begin to understand why. Others dominate each of Isaac's key moments. His parents are the central focus of the annunciation. His father dominates the story both when Isaac leaves home and when he goes through his initiatory trial. His betrothal is arranged by his father's servant. And his testament is in the hands of his wife and youngest son. This leaves us with an impression of Isaac as a weak individual who has no control over his own life.

Classroom Applications

The analysis of type-scenes and conventions provides us with many possible lessons. Here are a few suggestions:

1. Each of the type-scenes is like a key life cycle moment. We can bridge from the moments to teaching about birth, courtship, marriage, death. and other similar events in the lives of the biblical characters and of our students.
2. We can look at characters via the type-scene. In doing so, we can go beyond comparing Isaac (Eliezer), Samson, and Moses at the well. What, we might ask, would John Wayne, Humphrey Bogart, and Mork from Ork do there? Write or act out type-scenes in which non-biblical characters experience biblical conventions. These would be appropriate to videotape.
3. Imagine biblical characters experiencing American conventions, e.g., Moses walks into the saloon, etc.
4. Write biblical conventions for characters in the Bible who don't experience them, e.g., Abram and Sarai at the well, etc.

5. Create dioramas (shoe box scenes) of various character's type-scenes. Stack them to form a 3-D chart of these characteristics.
6. Use the insights gained into the biblical characters you study to project other incidents: Abraham fighting with Isaac, Samson talking to his brothers, etc.

PATTERN FOUR: LEADING WORDS

Read the following text:
When your brother sinks down beside you and his hand falters beside you
>hold him fast
>sojourner and settler
>let him live
>beside you

You may not take from him interest or multiplication
>Stand in fear before your God
>your brother shall live beside you

Do not give him your money on interest for multiplication do not give your food
>I am your God
>who brought you out of the land of Egypt to give you the land of Canaan
>to be God to you

When your brother sinks down beside you and sells himself to you
>you shall not make him serve the service of a serf
>As hired-hand
>as settler
>shall he be beside you
>Until the year of Recall he is to serve beside you
>then he is to go out from beside him
>he and his children beside you
>and return to his clan to the land plot of his fathers
>he shall return
>For they are my servants
>whom I brought out of the land of Egypt
>they shall not be sold in servant-selling
>>Leviticus 25:35-42
>>(Translated by Everett Fox in *Response*. Winter 1971-1972. Reprinted with permission)

Think about these questions: What two laws does this passage teach? What theological rationale is given for both commandments? What is the lesson of this passage? Note how often the phrase "beside you" appears. Noticing this phrase can affect our understanding of the passage or our view of the text's lesson.

Let's look at a second text:
His word was to Yona son of Amittai, saying: Arise,
>go to Nineveh, the great city,
>and call out concerning it
>that their evil-doing has come up before my face.

Yona rose
>to flee to Tarshish, away from His face.

He went down to Yafo, found a ship traveling to Tarshish, gave (them) the fare,
>and went down aboard it, to travel to Tarshish, away from His face.

But He hurled a great wind upon the sea,
>so that the ship was on the brink of breaking up.

The sailors were afraid, they cried out, each man to his god,
>and hurled the implements which were in the ship into the sea, to be lightened from them.

Now Yona had gone down into the hindmost deck, had lay down and had gone to sleep.

The captain approached him and said to him: How can you sleep!
Arise, call upon your god!
>>Jonah 1: 1-6
>>(Translated by Everett Fox
>>*Response*, Summer 1974
>>Used with permission)

Does the text tell us anything about what Jonah is thinking or feeling? Note each usage of the verbs "to arise" and "to go down." The use of these leading words can give us clues to Jonah's psychology. This example and the previous one have provided us with some understanding of the ways the biblical text uses words.

The *Leitwort* (leading word) is a pattern in biblical style, defined first by Martin Buber. Biblical texts resemble poetry in many ways, especially in their conscious use of words. This amounts to serious punning. In the biblical text, puns form a subliminal guide, an internal commentary on the text.

Classroom Applications

While the pattern of leading words is hard to generalize (and very difficult to recognize in the usual English translations), your students can feel the presence of the leading words and then recognize their role. They do so by working with a passage, understanding what it says and how it feels, then finding out the significance of repeating phrases. Here are a few ways that this pattern can be used with your students:

1. To convey the idea of word obsession, designate a word for the day. Give out a piece of candy, a point, or some other reward for each time the word is used in class. Encourage puns, variations, and other word plays.
2. Do as Groucho Marx did and hang up a magic bird (duck) with a secret word. Give out play money every time the magic word is said. (Use a cigar and a grease pencil moustache if you have the gumption.)
3. Upward and downward movement is central in the Jonah story. Create a comic book or a calligraphic version of the text which reflects these movements.
4. Give your students a story to tell or write and a leading word to utilize.
5. Compare one of Everett Fox's translations with either one of the Jewish Publication Society translations (see Bibliography). See which words emerge.

PATTERN FIVE: MOTIVATION

The pattern of motivation is similar to what happens in detective movies. A crime, or other action, has occurred and our job is to figure out why. We know who did it (usually), we know exactly what was done. The problem is, we almost never know the motivation. This pattern is a direct outgrowth of the biblical style. As we have noted previously, the biblical text is essentially made up of two components — dialogue and narration. The dialogue is usually minimal; it captures the essence of the story. That which is said out loud is usually the character's central action or concern. The narration is used to establish and define the action, usually describing it while providing few other details. Whatever explanation of motive that is given is usually spoken "in the heart." Let's look at an example:

Now Aaron's sons, Nadab and Abihu, each took his fire pan, put fire in it, and laid incense on it; and they offered a strange fire before the Lord, which He had not requested of them. And a fire came forth from the Lord and consumed them; thus they died before the Lord.

Then Moses said to Aaron, "This is what the Lord meant when He said: Through those near to Me I show Myself holy, and assert My authority before all the people." And Aaron was silent.

(Leviticus 10:1-3)

Notice that most of the passage is narration. We have only one line of dialogue, spoken by Moses to Aaron. The narrator gives us no clues as to the motivation of Nadab, Abihu, or Moses, or the reason for Aaron's silence. We are given a behavioral description of the incident; yet we have no insight into the emotions and feelings — the motivation.

First let us establish the facts:

1. Nadab and Abihu offered "strange fire" that was not requested before God. We don't know if the fire is strange because of its timing or because of the kind of fire used.
2. The fire which killed the two men "came forth from the Lord." Notice that we are not told that God "sent forth" the fire. We don't know if their deaths were caused by the conditions of the fire or by God's reaction to the fire.
3. We do know that Moses goes and talks to Aaron. We know that he quotes God. We do not know if God directed Moses to instruct Aaron, or whether this piece of "instruction" is Moses' reaction.
4. We do know what Moses says to Aaron. We do not know if he intended it to mean
   a. I'm sorry — we all know how hard it is to be a public servant, or
   b. they got what they deserved: if you misuse power, you pay the price, or
   c. both responses. The narrator gives no description of Moses' tone of delivery.
5. We know that Aaron's response to Moses is silence; we have no insight into why. It could be shock, grief, anger, or even agreement. Given all the above questions, it is time to play detective. Using the Bible, decide which of the following is the true story of this death/homicide:
   a. GOD did it. Nadab and Abihu violated the sanctity of the Tabernacle and so God punished them.

b. AARON did it. Nadab and Abihu tried to take over his job. They were doing too much exploring of the role, so he rigged the fire pans.

c. MOSES did it. There was an ongoing tension between Moses and Aaron which goes back to the golden calf. Moses was worried that the priests are getting too powerful, so he arranged the accident as a warning.

d. THE FIRE WAS AN ACCIDENT.

In his solution to this mystery, detective Rashi found a suspicious verse, Leviticus 10:8-9: "And the Lord spoke to Aaron, saying: 'Drink no wine or other intoxicant, you or your sons with you, when you enter the Tent of Meeting, that you may not die.'" Based on that verse, this is Rashi's report:

Rabbi Ishmael said: They died because they entered the Sanctuary intoxicated by wine. You may know that this is so, because after their death he admonished those who survived that they should not enter the Sanctuary when intoxicated...

Let's look at a second case, this one from Numbers 20. This is the story of why Moses was not permitted to enter the Promised Land. Most people think this occurred "because he hit the rock," but that's wrong. Previously (Exodus 17:5), God had ordered Moses to hit a rock. Others say that it was "because he didn't talk to the rock" — but that's wrong. Moses stood before the rock and said: "Shall we get water for you out of this rock?" While he didn't talk exclusively to the rock, he did talk about the rock in the rock's presence.

Now let's take a closer look. (Remember, the clues are usually in the dialogue.) From the dialogue we learn that Moses was really "not publicly affirming God's sanctity." Our next question must be: what action(s) or lack of action did not, in God's view, affirm His sanctity?

Here are several possibilities (suggested by the classical commentators):

1. Getting angry at the people and not responding to them even to reprimand them (with respect). Think about what he says to them. (Rambam)

2. Letting the people think that Moses and Aaron, and not God, were bringing them the water. (He says: "Shall we bring you forth water?") (Rambam)

3. Missing an opportunity to teach the people. It was not geting angry, hitting the rock, or saying "we," but rather not using this opportunity to show the people that God would take care of them. This situation wasn't like the first time, when the people were coming straight from being slaves in Egypt. This was the new generation who were about to enter the land. (Ibn Ezra)

Classroom Applications

The pattern of motivation is clearly the most fun, and the most accessible of the five we have looked at. It is easy and challenging to play detective and the text provides us with both an abundance of mysteries and a plethora of clues.

Here are a few exciting classroom activities:

1. Use the same kind of inquiry approach described above in the presentation of this pattern.

2. Have your class script and present the Nadab and Abihu story as an episode of "Quincy" or any other detective series. Present it live, as a radio play on tape, or videotape it.

3. Develop a new set of cards and play *Clue* with biblical problems.

4. Have a panel discussion between various commentators on a biblical issue.

5. Create (in any number of media) Moses and Aaron questioning God on what they really did wrong.

So far, in this chapter, we have considered ways to approach the text through repetition, twice told tales, conventions, leading words, and motivation. For each pattern, a number of classroom applications has been included. The remainder of the chapter will be devoted to an examination of how to prepare for teaching the Bible. This next section will include Terminal Objectives for Pre-Academic Bible Study, Preparing the Text: The First Reading, Preparing the Text: Reference Work, Organizing Research into a Lesson, and Choosing Activities: Assembling the Lesson.

ANALYSIS OF TEXT SHOULD BE THE MAJOR THRUST.

TERMINAL OBJECTIVES FOR PRE-ACADEMIC BIBLE STUDY

In my view, the center of our efforts in Bible study, even with the youngest students, should be analysis of the text. A complete program of Bible study should also include basic knowledge of the document, as well as ways to help students personally to integrate and to actualize the biblical texts. Most contemporary Bible teaching in non-Hebrew settings has focused on the latter, while ignoring the real inquiry into the text. We generally read (or tell) a Bible story and then establish relevant analogies.

Virtually every Bible lesson (and learning experience) should contain all three of these elements: content, process, and the learner. This means that every lesson should somehow touch and interact directly with the text (even if with only one phrase-clause) and should provide the student with a personal opportunity to "manipulate" the text. This model of Bible study is a lifelong process, requiring the commitment and participation of every teacher of Bible in order to provide continuity. We must guard against presenting our students with material that is far too difficult for them; yet it is equally important to avoid an excessively juvenile approach to the text. We must convey to our students that the text represents more than Jewish bedtime stories or cute tales with ethical morals attached. And we must not teach information or conceptions that need to be unlearned at a later date.

In the Introduction to the workbook *Bible People Book One* by this author, I stated:

The Bible is a big, long, thick book. It is a book that many people talk about and study. The Bible is a book which tells lots of stories about lots of people. It tells the story of sisters who really loved each other. And it tells the story of kids who lie to their parents. Stories of parents who favored one child, while older brothers picked on younger brothers. Stories of people who do good things. And stories of the same people doing not such good things. There are stories of people's dreams. And there are stories of people falling in love.

The Bible is full of stories about people. People who cry. People who laugh. People who worry. People who enjoy life. All the experiences and feelings we have, people in the Bible had, too. As we read about their adventures and understand their feelings, we also begin to understand some of the things we feel.

This model of the Bible is appropriate to second or third graders. It is conceptually and experientially within their capacities, while consistent with a far more sophisticated view of the text. It opens doors; it doesn't close them. While that workbook doesn't introduce parataxis, it implies from the start that Bible study is dialogue and that we enter the text to learn with it, not just from it. It states that this kind of study is both communal and reflexive. Second graders will not be able to understand intellectually or to verbalize this adult model of text study. But they can work within this framework and come to value it. As in many forms of learning, the patterns we develop early in life ultimately influence our adult view.

With all of this in mind, then, let us look at one statement of terminal objectives for essential background in the Bible for Jewish students.

Divisions of the Bible
1. The learner can list the three sections of the Bible (Torah, Prophets, and Writings) and can identify with an 80% accuracy in which section a given book is contained.
2. The learner can locate any quotation within the text, given its book, chapter, and verse.
3. Given the names of the books of the Bible, the learner can give a one sentence description of their content.

Familiarization with Biblical Texts
1. The learner has read the narrative material in Genesis, Exodus, Numbers, and Deuteronomy, as well as most of the early prophets, the five *Megillot*, plus Jonah.
2. The learner has read a selection of legal material from the Torah and a basic selection of prophetic documents.
3. The learner has had some exposure to material from Psalms and Proverbs.

Specific Knowledge of Biblical Detail
1. The learner can identify, order, and define the relationship between all major characters in the Torah.
2. The learner can classify characters from the Prophets as either Kings, Prophets, Priests, or Judges with 80% accuracy. (He or she will also be able to sequence key Judges and major figures from the books of Samuel.)

3. The learner can identify 80% of key quotations from biblical stories.
4. The learner can locate on the map: (a) the basic geographic features of *Eretz Yisrael*; (b) the major locations indicated in Genesis, Joshua, Samuel, and Kings; (c) locations of at least five tribal areas (including Judah, Ephraim, and Manasseh); and (d) the borders of David's kingdom and of Judah and Israel.

Text Skills
1. The learner can identify theme and variation from predefined repetition patterns, including multiple repetitions of stories or laws.
2. The learner can identify (a) examples of the expectations of basic type-scenes and (b) appearances of these in the lives of biblical characters.
3. The learner has struggled to define the motivation of key biblical characters in key incidents.
4. The learner can trace some "word-echoes" (themes) through the biblical text.
5. The learner can define *P'shat* and *Drash* and, with 60% accuracy, distinguish between examples of both.

Language Skills
1. The learner can give examples of the problems of studying the biblical text in translation.
2. The learner can give examples of idioms which reflect the Hebrew mind.
3. The learner can describe, identify, and analyze some basic Hebrew literary patterns: poetic parallel, parataxis, and verb chains.
4. The learner can describe personal associations with some key verses or images from the text.

Use of Rabbinic Sources
1. The learner can explain the concept of *Midrash*, including (a) the historical context, (b) an explanation of its assumptions, (c) an identification of its textual problems, and (d) a description of its style relative to the biblical text.
2. Given ten *midrashim*, the learner can, for at least eight of them, successfully identify (a) the textual issues, (b) the solution posed in the *midrash*, and (c) the message of the text.

3. The learner can identify Rashi, the Ramban, the Rambam, Nehama Leibowitz, Cassuto, and several other biblical commentators by name and persona.
4. The learner has participated in comparing conflicting interpretations of a text.

Personal Views of the Text
1. The learner has a history of evolving his/her own interpretations of the text.
2. The learner has a history of correlating the metaphoric material of the text to his/her own experience.
3. The learner has evolved his/her own sense of the importance of Bible study.

PREPARING THE TEXT: THE FIRST READING

The first step for any Bible teacher is to do a first reading of the intended text. The purpose of a first reading is not to decide what to teach or to find deep scholarly insights into the passage. A first reading is a scouting mission. It is a formal introduction or a renewed acquaintance with the text. We are just looking over the terrain, learning the topography, familiarizing ourselves with the characters, the setting, and the words.

Begin by listening to the text. (Everett Fox, a contemporary Bible scholar, suggests that you read it out loud.) What is the first thing it says to you? Is there a special tone? Is there an overt message? Is there an interesting ambiguity?

Next, consider what you already know about this text. Are there some key insights that you already possess? What are your past associations with the text? (Remember your interests, but don't be afraid to discover something new.) Does the text have external connections which are important (e.g., is it the theme of the congregation's stained glass window, or part of the Friday evening service, etc.)?

Then analyze what bothers you about the text, what calls out to you, "Explain me." Does the text contain echoes of other things you want to identify? Is there anything you want to know more about?

Up to now, you have not yet begun to make decisions regarding the lesson you will teach. Now it is time to come up with answers to the following questions:

CHAPTER THIRTY-FIVE

1. What is the text I will be teaching? Which verses will I include? If I am going to be telling a story, or reading a story version of the text, how much of it will I use?
2. What textual issue(s) will serve as the focus of the lesson? If I am working from a text, what will students look for in it? If I am telling the story, what portion of the actual text will I bring to the students?
3. What information do the students need to know in order to handle this text, e.g., previous incidents, social phenomena, vocabulary, or geography?
4. What skills will the students need to handle this text, e.g., how to compare two stories, find extra language, imagine how someone would feel, etc.
5. What information (facts) should the students retain? Is there a line or two (perhaps a passage) which they should know, or almost know, by heart?
6. What will the students "own" from this passage? What will they find interesting in it? What will they believe is important about it?
7. What does my class need right now? What kind of learning experiences are appropriate — more group work, fewer worksheets, a chance to role play, etc.?
8. How can this story relate to past learning and to things students will study next year? If I show them X, will they be able to relate it to Y?
9. What do I want to teach? What is important in the text for me?

PREPARING THE TEXT: REFERENCE WORK

A good working library for serious Bible teachers consists of about 30-35 volumes. These provide the basis for preparing almost any lesson. Ideally these books belong to the teacher. However, a synagogue or community library can be used instead.

To prepare a text, start with a notebook and a photocopy. (The later enables you to mark up the text.) Then complete the following steps:

FOLLOW THESE FOUR STEPS WHEN PREPARING A TEXT FOR STUDY.

Step One

Examine three translations of the text: the 1917 and 1962 Jewish Publication Society translations and a translation by a modern scholar such as Everett Fox (*Response*, Winter 1971-2 and Summer 1974). Compare the translations, noting instances in which the translators differ significantly. Locate idioms which capture something important about the biblical mind. Identify patterns in the language which come through in only one or two of the translations. For questions about the meaning of a word or phrase, consult *Notes on the New Translation of the Torah*, edited by Orlinsky.

You might also look up the verse in the *Anchor Bible*, a non-sectarian, scholarly translation. This work is still in process and volumes do not yet exist for every book in the Bible. The *Anchor Bible* includes an introduction, an original translation, and two sets of notes. The first set discusses the text as a whole, defining patterns and focusing on the possible sources which underlie it. The other set consists of line by line notes in the text itself.

You might also wish to look up some geographical locations in a biblical atlas. One excellent atlas is *The Macmillan Bible Atlas* by Aharoni and Avi-Yonah. One further tool is a concordance, a book which lists all the words in the Bible and every instance that each appears. There are many different ones available; the best is in Hebrew. Use the concordance to locate other places in which the words from your passage appear.

Step Two

Look at what the traditional commentators have to say about the passage. Start with books by Nehama Leibowitz, an Israeli Bible scholar who has authored five excellent books on the Torah: *Studies in Bereshit (Genesis)*, *Studies in Shemot (Exodus)*, etc. Leibowitz presents three to eight sermons/studies on individual issues for each Torah portion. She focuses on one problem in each, defining why the issue is an issue, then quoting a number of commentators and Rabbinic sources.

Next, turn to Louis Ginzberg. Ginzberg was an American scholar who collected *midrashim*. His collection is published in two editions: *Legends of the Bible* and *Legends of the Jews*. *Legends of the Jews* is a six volume work which collects virtually every *midrash*, rewritten in a non-textual format. It consists of four volumes of *midrashim* and two scholarly volumes filled with notes and indexes. These include a list of every biblical verse in the work. Verses can be found in the discussion of your portion, as well as in *midrashim* from other texts. *Legends of the Bible* is a one volume condensation of the larger work without the scholarly materials. Another excellent source for *midrashim* is *The Midrash Rabbah*, translated by Freedman and Simon.

Pentateuch with Targum Onkelos, Haphtaroth and Rashi's Commentary, translated into English and annotated by Rosenbaum and Silbermann is another good source. Here you can check out which problems in the text Rashi addresses and the connections he makes.

Finally, you might take a quick look at the three volumes of *The Rabbis' Bible* by Simon, et al, to see which *midrashim* it includes. There are many other collections of *midrashim* and commentaries, but by now you will undoubtedly have found something worth teaching. Out of all this you may have come up with any or all of the following:

1. Some interesting problems, echoes, or issues in the text.
2. Some interesting images from the *midrash*.
3. Some good *midrashim* you can use in class.

For each *midrash* you consider, make sure that you know the textual question from which the *midrash* stems, the resolution of that issue, and the moral or lesson the *midrash* is teaching.

Step Three

If you don't feel that you have enough to go on, you may turn to what might be called "idea books." These are books about the Bible and provide ideas for teaching. They will also expand your facility with the text. Here are some suggestions of useful books of this type.

The Art of Biblical Narrative by Alter applies literary tools to the Bible. It has chapters on conventions, repetition, leading words, motifs, and other stylistic elements. It contains many examples from texts you regularly teach.

A Commentary on the Book of Exodus and *A Commentary on Genesis: From Adam to Noah and from Noah to Abraham* by Cassuto are difficult, but helpful. While methodical and scholarly, these books are written in readable English with little jargon. Cassuto does an insightful, close reading of the text and is the outstanding revealer of patterns, echoes, structures, and connections within the text.

Text and Texture: Close Readings of Selected Biblical Texts by Fishbane represents another language centered look at the text, a place to find echoes, patterns, and parallels.

The Torah: A Modern Commentary by Plaut is an interesting collection of all kinds of insights into the text.

Step Four

Look now at your collection of teaching materials. Go through *The Rabbis' Bible* again, along with its Teacher Guide and Resource Book. Look at your collection of materials published by A.R.E. Publishing, Inc.: *Bible People Book One, Bible People Book Two,* and *Bible People Book Three* and their accompanying Leader Guides, all by Grishaver; *Bible People Songs* by Klepper; *Sedra Scenes: Skits for Every Torah Portion* and *Bible Scenes: Joshua to Solomon* by Beiner; and *Teaching Torah* by Loeb and Kadden. See the Bibliography at the conclusion of this chapter for a list of books on the Bible for teachers and students, atlases, enrichment materials, tapes, and music books. You might also go to your synagogue library to consult a reference book or encyclopedia and to check out some historical background, especially if you are teaching the Prophets.

ORGANIZING RESEARCH INTO A LESSON

It is likely that you now feel comfortable with the story and have made some basic decisions about what you will teach. You know the text you will teach, how much of it you will use, the textual issue(s) on which you will focus. You have done your research and have the resources to deal with unanticipated questions which might arise. You are now ready to organize your lesson.

At this time you will want to choose one of the patterns to apply to the text, using the examples provided in the early part of this chapter or others you know. Isolate a question or theme for the class to discuss and explore based on what they discover in the text. Carefully formulate how you will encourage each student to manipulate the text and come to "own" it. Sometimes this manipulation will mean that students identify their own solutions to issues in the text. Sometimes it will mean that they evolve their own solutions to issues in the text. And other times it will mean that you foster the creative expression by students to material in the text. The chart (figure 1 below) represents some possible formats for designing Bible Lessons:

The above formats are not the only ones possible, but they are the ones which work most often. It is often effective to include three activities in the course of every session. However, if the material lends itself, you can introduce the three over two, three, or more periods or weeks.

The central issues when organizing a Bible lesson are the nature of the text to be studied its specific difficulties, loadings, and context. If the text needs clarification before your students can approach it, or if it needs extension before its "lesson" can be made clear, then the placement of the text in your sequence of instruction is especially critical. If there are issues to which students need to be sensitized, address yourself first to this. If there is a complex skill needed (one that can't be picked up as it is applied), take time to introduce it and drill it. Once the text has been introduced and probed, don't stop there. You want your students to learn by experience that a biblical text always leads us somewhere — to a reflection of human nature, an insight into ethical relations, or a further understanding of Jewish tradition. Rather than conclude with the text, end by helping students find a way to make the text their own, through individual interpretation and expression.

	Beginning	**Middle**	**End**
I	Study the Text.	Isolate and discuss central issue.	Encourage students to expand their understanding of the material through interpretation/ expression.
II	Define the central issue.	Find that issue expressed in the text.	Encourage students to interpret/express the material.
III	Have the students isolate a problem or theme from their own experience.	Have the class generalize about the theme/ issue based on their collective experience.	Find and explore the same issue in the text.
IV	Same as first step in III	Find the issue in the text.	Clarify and discuss the issue.
V	Introduce and train students in a skill for text study.	Apply the skill to the text.	Draw out the moral found in the issue.
VI	Introduce a text.	Apply a pattern of text study to the passage (e.g., leading word, repetition).	Analyze and discuss what emerges.
VII	Introduce a text.	Use a pattern of text study to identify an issue.	Generalize the skill, practice its application.

Figure 1

CHOOSING ACTIVITIES: ASSEMBLING THE LESSON

With your basic lesson format decided upon, you now begin to select the activities you will use. Some teachers find it helpful to keep a file of 3" x 5" cards, each of which contains an idea for a lesson. These can be collected from a variety of sources — from books, other teachers, your students, workbooks, things you have picked up at conferences and idea exchanges, and from workshops and lectures you attend. Ideas can also be borrowed from other disciplines, and even from other religions. (Many good ideas for teaching Bible can be drawn from such Christian resources as *Twenty New Ways of Teaching the Bible* by Griggs and *How To Teach Bible Stories for Grades 4-12* by Keithahn and Dunshee, both published by Abingdon.)

To spark your own creativity, here are a few activities from my own card file.

LEARNING THE DIVISIONS OF THE BIBLE

Introductory Activities

1. Give a basic lecture on the divisions of the Bible.
2. Make cards with the names of the books of the Bible on them. Have students sort them into the categories of Torah, Prophets, and Writings.
3. See who can locate various books in the Bible first.
4. Let students design their own memory devices. Use these to learn the order of the books.
5. Design a racetrack board game which reflects the order and sequence of the books of the Bible. Design questions which ask where the various books may be found. Students can look at the board to answer.
6. Design a worksheet or chart which students fill in.
7. Have treasure hunt games (finding items inside the text).
8. Give coded messages using the abbreviations for the Bible books.

Application (students demonstrate understanding and competency)

1. Everytime you mention a book in the Bible, have students review where in the Bible it is located.
2. Have students use the correct form for biblical citations at all times.

Individual Expression

1. Have students design charts, posters, games, cards, drills, quiz shows, displays such as a museum of the Bible with each book on exhibit.
2. Have students develop games and coded messages.
3. Have students teach those in a younger grade how to find passages in the Bible.

FAMILIARIZATION WITH BIBLICAL TEXTS

Introductory Activities

1. Identify characters as they are introduced.
2. Have students keep lists, charts, cards, etc., of the characters.
3. Post a visual record in the room, e.g., charts, posters, timelines, etc.
4. Give examinations on the material; have a "College Bowl" type quiz.

Application

1. As characters are introduced, or reintroduced, have students establish their position and relationship.
2. Have students categorize characters by role, personality, or position.

Individual Expression

1. Have students design creative review formats — games, posters, etc.
2. Develop quiz formats.
3. Act out (in any medium) various personalities and their relationships.

TEXT SKILLS

Introductory Activities

1. Lecture/introduce the concept.
2. Develop a visual format to enhance the insights. Use (a) capital letters or underlines to enhance perception (split the text into parallel columns) (b) have students color code the two parts of a document, (c) use circles and arrows.
3. Use two or more photographs/pictures and compare them for differences, similar to "What is wrong in this picture?"
4. Use an outside example to introduce the concept, then have students apply it to the text.

Application

1. Use visual displays to study the text, e.g., posters, charts, timelines, etc.
2. Have two students alternate reading. One reads the first version, the second reads the repetition. Identify and analyze the differences.
3. Once a pattern is clearly understood, have students find examples of the pattern on their own.

Individual Expression

1. Draw "lessons" or conclusions from the repetitions and changes in the text.
2. Compare and evaluate traditional insights.
3. Express the themes and variations creatively through art, music, drama, film, etc.
4. Devise extension activities based on the moral of the story, such as a role play, creative writing exercise, etc.
5. When there are conflicting details in repeated stories, have students see if they can (a) identify ways of deciding which version is right or (b) figure out how both could be correct.

CONCLUSION

In-depth Bible teaching doesn't depend on teachers with years of academic training. Any teacher who is open to growth and willing to invest time can master the skills for exploring texts and transmitting them to his/her students. The developmental process outlined in the second part of this chapter represents a very stuctured series of steps which, when followed, will produce the kind of dynamics outlined in the first section. Feel free to adapt these steps into your own workable form. Using the tools we have suggested for engaging students in textual study will enrich their lives and yours, as well as enhance the interaction that takes place in your classroom.

Joel Lurie Grishaver is the Creative Director of Torah Aura Productions and the author of a myriad of materials for Jewish schools, including *The Life Cycle Workbook* and *Tzedakah, Gemilut Chasadim and Ahavah* (A.R.E.) He also teaches Bible and Rabbinics at the Los Angeles Hebrew High School.

NOTES

1. The patterns not dealt with in this chapter are Metaphor, Translation, Word Echoes, Surplus Language, and *P'shat* and *Drash*.
2. Both the insights and many of the metaphors for this section were inspired by *The Art of Biblical Narrative* by Robert Alter (New York: Basic Books, 1981).
3. For this understanding of Samson, I am indebted to Rabbi Yossi Gordon.

BIBLIOGRAPHY

Aharoni, Yohanan, and Michael Avi-Yonah. *The Macmillan Bible Atlas*. 3d. rev. ed. New York: The Macmillan Company, 1977.

Alter, Robert. *The Art of Biblical Narrative*. New York: Basic Books, 1981.

Beiner, Stan J. *Bible Scenes: Joshua to Solomon*. Denver: A.R.E. Publishing, Inc., 1988.

———. *Sedra Scenes: Skits for Every Torah Portion*. Denver: A.R.E. Publishing, Inc., 1982.

Cassuto, Umberto. *A Commentary on the Book of Exodus*. 3d. ed. Jerusalem: The Magnes Press, The Hebrew University, 1967.

———. *A Commentary on Genesis: From Adam to Noah and from Noah to Abraham*. Jerusalem: The Magnes Press, The Hebrew University, 1961.

Coleman, Lucien E. *How To Teach the Bible*. Nashville, TN: Broadman Press, 1980.

Eisenberg, Azriel. *The Book of Books: The Story of the Bible Text*. New York: Bloch Publishing Co., 1976.

Fox, Everett. *Genesis and Exodus: A New English Rendition with Commentary and Notes*. New York: Schocken Books, 1991.

Freedman, H, and Maurice Simon, trans. *Midrash Rabbah*. London: The Soncino Press, 1977.

Furnish, Dorothy J. *Experiencing the Bible with Children*. Nashville, TN: Abingdon Press, 1990.

Ginzberg, Louis. *Legends of the Bible*. Philadelphia: Jewish Publication Society, 1992.

———. *Legends of the Jews*. Philadelphia: Jewish Publication Society, 1956.

Griggs, Patricia. *Opening the Bible with Children: Beginning Bible Skills,*. Nashville, TN: Abingdon Press, 1986.

Grishaver, Joel Lurie. *Bible People Book One (Genesis)*. Denver: A.R.E. Publishing, Inc., 1980.

———. *Bible People Book Two (Exodus to Deuteronomy)*. Denver: A.R.E. Publishing, Inc., 1981.

———. *Bible People Book Three (Prophets and Writings)*. Denver: A.R.E. Publishing, Inc., 1982.

Heschel, Abraham Joshua. *The Sabbath*. New York: Harper & Row, 1952.

Kugel, James L. *In Potiphar's House; The Interpretive Life of Biblical Texts*. San Francisco: HarperCollins, 1990.

Leibowitz, Nehama. *Studies in Bereshit (Genesis)*. Jerusalem: World Zionist Organization, Department of Torah Education and Culture, Jerusalem, 1980.

———. *Studies in Shemot (Exodus)*. Jerusalem: World Zionist Organization, Department of Torah Education and Culture, Jerusalem, 1980.

Loeb, Sorel Goldberg, and Barbara Binder Kadden. *Teaching Torah: A Treasury of Insights and Activities*. Denver: A.R.E. Publishing, Inc., 1984.

Orlinsky, Harry M., ed. *Notes on the New Translation of the Torah*. Philadelphia: Jewish Publication Society, 1969.

Plaut, W. Gunter. *The Torah: A Modern Commentary*. New York: Union of American Hebrew Congregations, 1981.

Sarna, Nahum. *Exploring Exodus: The Heritage of Biblical Israel*. New York: Schocken Books, 1986.

———. *The JPS Torah Commentary: Exodus*. Philadelphia: Jewish Publication Society, 1991.

———. *The JPS Torah Commentary: Genesis*. Philadelphia: Jewish Publication Society, 1989.

———. *Understanding Genesis: The Heritage of Biblical Israel*. New York: Schocken Books, 1970.

Silbermann, A.M., and M. Rosenbaum, trans. *Pentateuch with Rashi*. 5 vols. Spring Valley, NY: Feldheim, 1973.

Simon, Solomon, and David Morrison Bial. *The Rabbis' Bible. Volume I: Torah*. West Orange, NJ: Behrman House, 1966.

Simon, Solomon, and Abraham Rothenberg. *The Rabbis' Bible. Volume II: Early Prophets*. West Orange, NJ: Behrman House, 1970.

———. *The Rabbis' Bible. Volume III: The Later Prophets*. West Orange, NJ: Behrman House, 1974.

Audiocassettes

Klepper, Jeff, and Jeff Salkin. *Bible People Songs*. Denver: A.R.E. Publishing, Inc. (Cassette Tape and Songbook)

Sounds of Freedom: Exodus in Song. Denver: A.R.E. Publishing, Inc. (Cassette Tape)

Sounds of Creation: Genesis in Song. Denver: A.R.E. Publishing, Inc. (Cassette Tape)

Sounds of Creation and Freedom Songbook. Denver: A.R.E. Publishing, Inc.

SUBJECT MATTER

CHAPTER THIRTY-SIX

EXPANDING THE JEWISH SOCIAL STUDIES

Fradle Freidenreich

For the past several decades, we have been told that participation in public life is essential to the growth and health of any system of community. In order to ensure the continuity and creative future of society, we must educate each successive generation to identify, understand, and work effectively to maintain the values of the community, as well as to solve the many problems that inevitably face a diversified, complex, and interdependent world. Effective Social Studies programs are supposed to do just that: educate future citizens for their roles in society.

The above paragraph could easily have been the keynote charge to a conference of public school educators on "Social Studies Teaching." General education has acclaimed the role of Social Studies to be the linking of knowledge and skills with an understanding of and commitment to democratic principles and their applications in a balanced education.[1]

How is it that something so essential in general education finds so little practical application, or even philosophical acceptance, in Jewish schools? Certainly, limitations of time (even in Jewish day schools with their over-programmed double formula) and the priorities of Hebrew language, prayer skills, holiday observances, and biblical sources are limiting factors. However, we have yet to see students emerge from Jewish schools that do not offer an enriched Social Studies program with a strong sense of Jewish self, a knowledge of the Jewish community past and present, and a willingness and commitment to participate in the continuity of Jewish communal life.[2]

Precisely because our supplementary Jewish schools do not provide a reflection of the community in which the American Jewish child lives, an additional burden is placed upon teachers and curriculum — to train students to understand the nature of Jewish Social Studies and their own roles as future citizens. And this must be done in a relative vacuum, for rarely does the home, and even more rarely does the street environment, reflect and/or reinforce the teachings of the Jewish school. That education which cognitively prepares youngsters to take their effective roles as contributing future members of the Jewish community, emerges from a carefully planned series of courses and activities in the Jewish Social Studies. These must be presented spirally and sequentially over the span of years during which the child attends a Jewish school. Concurrently, these courses and activities must be integrated into the overall curriculum. In this fashion we teach, and more important than that, the student learns, the meaning of Jewish values, our cultural heritage, our history, and the relevancy and application of each to other subject areas being offered. Fine examples of such materials are to be found, among others, in many of the publications of The Melton Research Center.[3]

Studies of Jewish elementary supplementary schools have shown that there has been little change in the curriculum over the past several decades with respect to Social Studies (or any of its subsumed subject areas).[4] It is still in the lowest place on the curricular ladder, both in time allotted and importance in the overall Jewish education picture. Understanding why this presents a serious challenge to our future Jewish citizens is one function of this chapter. Explaining how to integrate Jewish Social Studies in our schools is another. I will be addressing these issues to the Jewish supplementary elementary school primarily. However, much of the orientation and philosophy embodied herein can readily be adapted to both day school and high school situations. In addition, the suggestions are trans-ideational, allowing for application to various denominational as well as communal and independent schools.

As part of a general introduction to this chapter, it would seem in place to define the terms Social Studies, Jewish Social Studies, and Integration.

Social Studies deal with the following areas of knowledge:

History and culture of individual nations

Geography – political, physical, economic, and cultural

Social Institutions – the society, the community, the group and the individual

Economics – theories, processes, and systems

Relationships – interpersonal and intergroup (touching on anthropology, sociology, psychology, and archaeology) between and among institutions, nations, races, and cultures, past and present

The Social Studies teach concepts, generalizations, and skills (both thinking and participation). Social Studies programs are supposed to combine the acquisition of knowledge and skills with an understanding of their application to life through personal participation representing an ideal standard — optimally, the will to take part fully in public affairs.

Jewish Social Studies "personalizes" the above definition within the context of Jewish life. To that end, we refer to Jewish history, a study of Jewish communities of the past and present, and the problems of Jewish civics. The latter necessarily calls into play the issue of Jewish values vis-a-vis Jewish survival. In order to teach these two areas, we must deal thoroughly with customs, ceremonies, and calendar. If general education relies on the basic three R's, then Jewish Social Studies certainly relies on these basic three C's. Of the seven basic disciplines which come under the rubric of Social Studies, history is generally considered the most basic. Oftentimes, it is equated or substituted for the broader umbrella term of Social Studies.

Integration, in the interdisciplinary sense, involves the synthesis of subject areas, affording students opportunities to see interweaving and overlapping relationships. The integrative approach provides a facility for transfer, through the placing of interpretations, attitudes, and meanings into previously unrelated contexts. This offers a natural continuity of associative learning.

For the purpose of this chapter, integration refers to inter and intraschool functions. Within the Jewish school, the curriculum is viewed as interdisciplinary, e.g., helping students understand the relationship of *Siddur* to *Chumash*, of *Chumash* to history, of history to the development of culture, etc., and of all these to each other. Between the supplementary Jewish school and its general studies counterpart (public or private), there is great need to help the student integrate bodies of knowledge as well as discrete subjects, i.e., world history and Jewish history should be seen in parallel. In this way students can begin to recognize appropriate chronological facts and understand the relationships of historical implications from various sources.

Some years ago, there was a symposium devoted to "The Place of Social Studies in the Jewish School."[5] In it, seven renowned Jewish educators addressed problems of time, integration, methods and materials, and Jewish citizenship in relation to teaching Jewish Social Studies. They discussed the goals of Jewish Social Studies and how best to achieve these in light of the problems listed above. All participants agreed that developing a sense of identity and the willingness to act responsibly within the Jewish community and its unique life-style were basic to the definition of Jewish Social Studies.

THE PROBLEM

Statements of broad societal and personal goals in terms of expected student behaviors were in the forefront of the massive revisions of Social Studies curricula which have been ongoing for the past several decades. There is consequently a new view about the content to be taught. "A major emphasis has been placed on identifying basic concepts, principles, and methods of investigation in history and the social sciences, and then using those elements as a basis around which to organize the curricu-

> THE SOCIAL STUDIES TEACH CONCEPTS, GENERALIZATIONS, AND SKILLS.

lum. Student learning is also being reconsidered. Emphasis is shifting from learning as acquisition to learning as utilization; from learning as a process of absorption of givens (from textbooks and teacher) to learning as a process of discovering important relationships and principles inductively; to learning as a way of inquiring and thinking according to the procedures of the social sciences."[6]

Thus, we understand that teaching Social Studies involves consideration of specific subject areas, their interrelationships with other subject areas of the curriculum, their implications for living within our world, and the transferability of the learned material and skills employed to other subjects and life situations.

Such a charge is an awesome responsibility for any full-time school and teacher; how much more so for the very part-time teacher in a supplementary Jewish school. Here, motivation, activities, and methods and materials must all withstand the rigors of such tests as time constraints, competition from sports, TV, creative arts lessons, and extra-curricular activities. In addition, there is a lack of acceptance of the Jewish school as an important given in the child's educational world, and perhaps most detrimental of all, there is no compulsion of consequence from anyone regarding attendance, passing grades, getting into college, earning a living, etc. In this most difficult of situations, we must not only teach skills, but forge links of identity with peoplehood and community as well.

One study by the Jewish Education Service of North America (JESNA) confirmed statements by Yehudah Shabatay that in schools where "Jewish civics are taught, its boundaries are set around the synagogue and the home, with relatively meager efforts made to branch out into the larger American Jewish community and to include the study of other Jewish communities as well. The instruction of history, which occupies almost the totality of the 'Jewish People' course, is definitely past-oriented and it generally concentrates on factual information, more than the understanding of trends and ideas. Virtually no attempt is made to place Judaism into a larger context, i.e., the American, or Western culture, or even to correlate the curriculum of the Jewish supplementary school with parallel materials taught in its secular counterpart. These realities contradict the announced lofty ideals of the Jewish school . . . guiding students toward 'maturity as religious integrated personalities rooted in their faith, preparing them for 'significant roles in the developing Jewish community.'"[7]

This is the problem facing the Jewish Social Studies teacher. What a challenge!

WITHIN THE JEWISH SCHOOL

A working model for all types of supplementary Jewish schools for developing a Social Studies program must be broad in scope. This allows for involving the entire spectrum of defined subject areas which address a Jew's relationship to his or her physical and social environment. Such components would include:

1. Forces in Jewish History - Major personalities, events, movements, and their philosophies, periods of history, and institutions which have shaped our past. Examples of each of these areas of history might be:

Major Personalities	**Groups or Individuals**
The Minor Prophets	Amos
Great Names in Rabbinic Literature	Rambam
Builders of the State of Israel	Theodor Herzl
Resistance Fighters	Mordecai Anilewicz
American Jewish Leaders	Stephen S. Wise

Major Events
Destruction of the Second Temple
Expulsion from Spain
The Kishinev Pogrom
The Dreyfus Case
The Warsaw Ghetto Uprising

Major Movements
Messianism
Hasidism
Haskalah
Political Zionism
Reconstructionism

Periods of History
The Babylonian Exile
The Golden Age of Spain
The Shtetl
Pre-Holocaust Europe

The Modern Diaspora
Institutions
The Sanhedrin
The Kehillah
The Bund
Central Agencies for Jewish Education
The World Zionist Organization

Issues Affecting Jews
Anti-Semitism
Assimilation
Cults
Ecology
Identity
Intermarriage

These topic examples should be structured in units which can be taught as self-contained entities or related to any or all of the other components which follow.

2. Customs, Ceremonies, and Calendar – Those rituals, traditions, and cultural heritage legacies which punctuate our Jewish lives and lend purpose to our Jewish identification.
3. Current Events and Jewish Civics – Those happenings in the world around us which impinge on our present and future lives as Jews. The study of our own Jewish community — local, regional, and national, and those other contemporary Jewish communities existing around the world: the people, institutions, and culture which shape their communal being.
4. The Creative Arts – Jewish literature, music, and art are forces which have contributed to our heritage and culture and which bind us as a people throughout time.

These four major components can be taught, as they usually are, as discrete subject areas of the Social Studies. However, teaching them in an integrated fashion, diminishes the usual bifurcation existing between subjects in the curriculum and builds conceptual bridges and associations. In such a manner, for example, students can understand the place of Jewish history in relation to world history. Of even greater importance, they can identify the meaning of leadership (or slavery, or developing nationhood) whenever, and in whatever context, it applies.

Shabatay summarizes the organization of recent Social Studies curricula into three categories of objectives: (1) knowledge (students need to understand), (2) attitudes (students need to become), and (3) skills (students need to learn how).[8]

Supplementary Jewish schools must, of necessity, deal with all three objectives concurrently. It is expedient to forego the teaching of some Social Studies skills (map, discussion, fact organization, data gathering, etc.), hoping that the public and private schools will assume those time consuming tasks for us. On the other hand, oftentimes Social Studies skills have not yet been introduced to elementary grade students, and our teachers may find it necessary to teach those skills as part of the development of a particular unit. Because of this, it is very important to become familiar with the many skills involved in learning (and teaching) Social Studies subjects, regardless of the particular unit. A partial list is offered here as an outline for understanding the overall Social Studies skills framework:

Thinking Skills
gathering data
decision making
comparing
classifying
questioning
reasoning
drawing conclusions

Participating Skills
observing
working in groups — organizing, planning, decision making, consensus reaching, taking action
compromising, bargaining, persuading
evaluating, etc.

Transmitting knowledge, albeit challenging our creativity in methods and materials, is the stuff of which teachers' jobs are made. Having selected a subject, the quest for texts, print, and non-print materials, and the best methodologies is pursued. There is generally a direct relationship between the amount of effort and care invested into planning and teaching lessons and the amount of knowledge passed on. Some good references on the subjects of both methods and materials as they pertain to the teaching of Jewish Social Studies may be found in the Bibliography. Be sure also to read the pertinent chapters in this volume.

Of the three categories of Social Studies objectives which are mentioned by Shabatay, the most difficult to teach is attitudes. This, translated loosely for the Jewish school, is values teaching. A word or two is in order about this often misunderstood area.

For many years, it was assumed (and perhaps by some still today) that attendance at a Jewish school assures the learning of values, as if... by osmosis. The questions can rightfully be put: Don't all Jewish texts and subjects automatically teach Jewish values? Why should we teach values as a subject when they are inherent parts of all of Jewish education?

Would that the answers were as direct and simplistic as the questions. Unfortunately, the problems of living in a series of heterogenous societies strongly affect the young American Jewish child who is subject to the values and lifestyles of each. Often, they are in conflict. More often, although he/she is a nominal member of more than one community, the child relies primarily on one — the local neighborhood and its larger American societal counterpart — for setting standards in regards to beauty, health, morality, education, business and professional ethics, family life, manners, dress, attitudes towards others, etc. The values which Jews have incorporated and developed for centuries, often embodied in concepts of *Menschlichkeit* and *Yiddishkeit*, are not only unpracticed by our American students, but more alarmingly, are unknown to them as being Jewish in origin.

JUDAISM'S VIEWS ARE CONSISTENT WITH CURRENT PROGRESSIVE THINKING.

Our teens are often shocked to learn that Judaism has long had points of view (consistent with current "progressive" thinking) about ecology, the aged, and other such pertinent contemporary causes. It is this shock which a carefully thought out Social Studies program can lessen. Since the Social Studies aim to educate students about people's relationship to their physical and social environment, values teaching becomes a primary concern. Teaching about values is, as with all good teaching, merely the first step toward providing specific knowledge. The more crucial educational measure of success is how well the student integrates that knowledge in his or her own personal life and, when put to the test of life experiences, how that student reacts. It is rather appalling to note the attitude and behavior of students to each other, to their teachers and parents, and toward property that is not theirs. Being able to answer questions correctly on an exam is obviously no test of acting on an issue. The Jewish Social Studies curriculum must therefore make provisions for the kinds of learning experiences which will teach, explore, clarify, and lend personal meaning to Jewish values.

INTEGRATING THE JEWISH SOCIAL STUDIES

The most basic subject areas taught in the Jewish supplementary school are listed in the left-hand column of the chart (figure 1 on the following page). In the right-hand column are the twenty-nine examples of Social Studies units previously offered.

If each item on the right is used as a possible theme, it is not too difficult to find relationships, interpretations, and direct examples from each area listed on the left. Brainstorming this exercise with faculty or a small group of peers will yield very rich results. Any of the examples from the column on the right could be developed by applying some or all of the items from the column on the left into a full curriculum which for the appropriate age group that could last a month, a semester, or a year.

Once attuned to the possibilities and great rewards of such an integrative process, it is difficult not to teach seeking interdisciplinary connections. Otherwise the student is not able to synthesize the various bits of knowledge presented. When one goes further, and takes the initiative of relating the material presented to the learning taking place in the counterpart school, the effect is even more stunning and leaves the greatest and most lasting impression.

As simple examples of the above, witness the surprise of students when they learn for the first time that: Jews lived and were part of the French Revolution ("Oh, that can't be, that happened in France not Canaan or Palestine!"); the shared characteristics of leaders such as Moses, Abraham Lincoln, Mahatma Gandhi, Franklin D. Roosevelt, and others transcend the very different periods in which they lived and affected each other ("Aw, gee, Moses was from the Bible, millions of years ago — that's ancient stuff."), and other such seemingly unrelated issues.

History	The Minor Prophets – Amos
Hebrew language	Rabbinic Literature – Rambam
Holidays	State of Israel – Theodor Herzl
The Jewish Calendar	Resistance Fighters – Mordecai Anilewicz
Prayer and Synagogue Skills	American Jewish Leaders – Stephen S. Wise
Current Events	Destruction of the Second Temple
Bible	Expulsion from Spain
Law	The Kishinev Pogrom
Ritual and Ceremony	The Warsaw Ghetto Uprising
Israel	Messianism
Ethics	Hasidism
Creative Arts:	Haskalah
Music	Political Zionism
Drama	Reconstructionism
Art	The Babylonian Exile
Dance	The Golden Age of Spain
Literature	The Shtetl
American Jewish Community	Pre-Holocaust Europe
Jews around the World	The Modern Diaspora
Holocaust	The Sanhedrin
	The Kehillah
	The Bund
	Central Agencies for Jewish Education
	The World Zionist Organization
	Anti-Semitism
	Assimilation
	Cults
	Ecology
	Identity

Figure 1

Developing the ability to see a problem, or fact, or concept out of its specific context is a particular Social Studies skill which we as Jewish educators must address in presenting the subjects we teach.

ACTIVITIES AND PROJECTS: THE UNIT APPROACH

A unit approach calls for developmental activities, either in groups or with one individual, which are directed toward helping students find answers to questions and problems that have meaning for them. The following considerations are therefore recommended before developing Social Studies units:

1. What relevance does or could the material and content offered in the class have to the present-day life and experience of the children involved?
2. What are the feelings and personal reactions of the children about and to the content of the materials?
3. In dealing with procedures in teaching for affective learning, much thought must also still be given to the cognitive skills.
   a. Process skills are clearly important for the learner, but they are a means to an outcome.
   b. Basic learning skills are taught in order to employ content vehicles. The process skills are "learning to learn" skills.
   c. The third set of skills are "self and other awareness skills" which address themselves to affective learning.
   d. Social Studies units and, indeed, the curriculum should therefore reflect: attitudes toward self-acceptance and personal identification; a concern for continuity of

the Jewish people and Judaism; knowledge and understanding, skills and attitudes which can be behaviorally translated during childhood, adolescence, and adult life.

Once the unit has been introduced, students should be directed to: recognize and identify general problem areas from which specific problems will evolve; work through a process of teacher-pupil planning by discussion and use of resource materials presented; conference with others (both other students and teachers) to test the validity of the solutions, methods, and materials; and employ any number of the following techniques, depending on the subject, nature of the process (large or small group or individual), time, materials, and resources available. (Many of these suggestions need teacher initiation and/or preparation.)

- using classroom libraries and school library and/or resource center
- using a multi-text approach (taking parallel material from a variety of texts on the same subject)
- creating student-made movies, filmstrips, slides, radio broadcasts, newspapers, dramatic presentations, and music and/or art renditions appropriate to the topic
- writing quizzes
- developing polls and questionnaires
- compiling oral histories, time lines, pictoral displays, scrapbooks, and exhibits
- listing comparisons and differences
- assembling explanatory material for maps and charts
- taking a "show on the road" — presentations of whatever form to other classes and schools
- forming a guest lecture bureau made up of students, parents, and other community members who are prepared to make presentations on specific topics with or without audio-visuals
- developing focal activities such as festivals, fairs, assembly presentations, etc.
- preparing a box of realia
- debates
- forming learning centers within the classroom devoted to particular themes with displays, materials, activities, publications, crafts, resources, etc. (see Chapter 16, "Classroom Learning Centers" for details on centers).
- games and simulations
- audiovisuals
- creating "permanent" presentations — a library of homemade booklets, reports, multimedia presentations, charts, etc., to be used for other classes in the future
- stamps and coins
- role plays and sociodramas
- personality "autobiographies"
- field trips
- using the current press — secular newspapers and magazines as well as publications in English on Jewish topics (see Chapter 39, "Teaching Jewish Current Events" for ideas on how to do this).

In order to implement these units and activities most effectively, there should be:
1. ongoing in-service work and teacher sharing of ideas, materials, and critique
2. communication with parents about the work being conducted with parental feedback
3. class meetings with full student participation
4. continual and careful evaluation including record keeping and student-teacher conferences to assess levels, interest, and achievement (see Chapter 40, "Student Assessment: A Rewarding Experience" for suggestions on how to evaluate students).

Teaching Social Studies strategies which specifically address the Social Studies skills areas must include activities for the thinking processes, student research, informational skills, geography skills, and time and chronology skills. As previously indicated, these cannot fall readily within the strictures of the supplementary Jewish school, and so they are not explored in this chapter.

Teaching strategies for conceptual and informational learning are, however, the focus of this chapter. Consequently, the foregoing suggestions for teaching/learning strategies utilize activities directed toward dealing with concepts and related factual material.

Since concepts are intellectual abstractions and the creative efforts of human beings, they are subject to changes, modifications, revisions, and to new combinations which reflect our growing knowledge.

Concepts exist on various levels of complexity; therefore, it is very important to create teaching units that are age level and intellectually appropriate.

Strategies which will help students to make decisions about personal and social problems will provide the greatest long lasting effect, since that is one of the basic goals of Social Studies education. Social inquiry (utilizing facts, concepts, generalizations, and theories) based on questioning strategies will offer a practical vehicle for classroom use.[9]

Strategies for teaching Social Studies concepts and facts can be clustered:
1. Experimental (participatory)
2. Demonstrational (outcome is known in advance)
3. Organizational (group and coordinated individual activities)
4. Reinforcing (providing additional examples)
5. Provoking (stimulating thought processes through exchange of ideas)
6. Speculative (inspiring imaginative and creative responses to problems and material)

Strategies, other than those directed at specific skills, should build in social process, human relations, historical culture, cultures other than our own, and current events.

One example of such an interdisciplinary Social Studies unit would be a study of the Jewish community of _____. (Select a country reasonably unfamiliar to the students.) In teaching this unit, one might approach it vertically (throughout history, or a period of time in history) and so touch upon chronology, particularly in relation to the rest of the world, and the majority culture of that country. Customs and ceremonies would certainly be a part of the unit. How are they similar to, or different from, our own? What literature and what other creative arts has this community contributed? A study of their synagogue and prayer life will certainly allow for new learning and/or reinforcement of that already taught. How is the Jewish life cycle celebrated there? How do we react to customs that, although authentically Jewish are different from our own? What is happening today in that country? How does that affect the Jews living there today? the Jewish future? Is there a relationship between that community and our own? If so, what is it? If not, why not? Can we do anything about it? Should we? How?

In presenting this example, particular effort was made to suggest questions and statements which stimulate thinking, invite discussion of Jewish values, teach information, recreate history, and allow for personal decision making.

The importance of selecting appropriate questions and materials cannot be overemphasized. Texts or teacher lectures which present facts and information, only begin (and sometimes end) the educational process. Steps must be taken to prepare teachers who, and materials that will, seek to address themselves to the stated goals.

In an article on "Teaching Teachers To Teach Jewish History,"[10] Karbal and Lewis trace the methods used in a course which dealt with the philosophy of Jewish history, the preparation of specific units of instruction for use in the classroom, and the opportunity for utilization of the material in the educational laboratory of the classroom. The lecture sessions provided the historical and philosophical overview to Jewish history and the various approaches to teaching it. These included:

TEXTS AND LECTURES ARE ONLY THE BEGINNING.

I. Secular Approaches to History and Jewish History
   A. Greek and Roman historians
   B. Church Fathers
   C. Humanist Renaissance historians
   D. Economic and political historians of the nineteenth and twentieth centuries
   E. The Oriental view of history
II. Jewish Approaches to History and Jewish History
   A. Biblical views
   B. Talmudic views
   C. Medieval Jewish historians
   D. Haskalah views
   E. N. Krochmal and Luzzatto
   F. Heschel, [Yavetz], Kook
III. Problems in Presenting History in the Classroom
   A. Undeveloped sense of historicity
   B. Students who do not think historically think hysterically
   C. Need to unify diverse "facts" of history in some holistic way
IV. Suggestions for Teaching History
   A. Need to view both world and Jewish history as two sides of the same coin
   B. Need to find meaning in Jewish history
   C. Need to emphasize specific survival traits.

The planning steps needed in creating educational materials for a unit of instruction were presented during the lab sessions of the course. These sessions were directed towards team development of materials, for the sharing, exchange, and enrichment of professional efforts. The results of such a process generally redound most beneficially to the students.

In his article "Trends in the Teaching of Social Studies,"[11] Lewittes outlines these trends as follows:
- History has been replaced by Social Studies.
- Scope and sequence must be clearly defined.
- The multimedia approach has replaced the single textbook.
- Inquiry and critical thinking rather than memorization are emphasized
- Instruction is sometimes organized around small groups and individual research
- Role playing and dramatization are frequently used in the teaching of Social Studies.
- Social Studies teaching aims to develop a variety of skills.
- An interdisciplinary approach has enriched the Social Studies.
- The development of values and the understanding of basic concepts are important objectives.
- Evaluation helps us to determine whether we have achieved our objectives.
- The trends provide much food for thought and represent a fine summary of the suggestions made thus far in this chapter.

THE CONCEPTUAL APPROACH
Developing the Conceptual Approach

In developing the materials for Social Studies, the curriculum should be based on a conceptual approach. Such an approach:
1. uses the generalizations accepted by specialists of the various Social Studies disciplines. These generalizations are called concepts and variants.
2. organizes these generalizations into a manageable, teachable whole, with a sequence of development of the concept, e.g., a holiday, Israel, the synagogue, the life cycle, etc., through the grade levels.
3. encourages within pupils:
   a. an ability to see beyond the facts so that they can recognize the patterns of human behavior and know the relationship of these patterns in time and place.
   b. an ability to think so that they can approach the study of human behavior analytically rather than descriptively.
   c. an ability to act so that they can assimilate the unending mass of specific data with which they are, and will continue to be, faced.

Understanding the Conceptual Approach

In order to implement this conceptual approach, the teacher should understand:
1. The meaning of the selected concepts and their variants in terms of their validity on an intellectual level and their significance for Jewish living.
2. The relationship of subject matter to the teaching of the concepts and their variants. Generalizations cannot be taught in a vacuum. Examples must be given in order to illustrate their meaning to the student personally (What does giving *tzedakah* mean to me?) as well as their humanistic universality (What happens in the Jewish community when no one cares about other people and institutions?).
3. The importance of using skills in context. The skills to be emphasized are those inherent in the individual social science disciplines. Techniques for gathering, organizing, evaluating, and presenting data should be identified and used in context. Above all, pupils should be encouraged to use the skill of critical thinking which is the skill of drawing warranted conclusions from reflective thought supported by valid evidence. (The teaching of skills will be left to the domain of the public school.)
4. The inductive method. This method is particularly applicable to the conceptual approach.

Planning for the Conceptual Approach
1. The teacher should first review the concepts and variants he/she wishes to implement for a given topic or area of study. These generalizations become the teaching objectives of the unit and individual lessons. Carefully selected sources will give the proper support to the objectives of the unit and lessons being designed.
2. Once the selection of material has been made, the teacher should then carefully and creatively design different learning experiences geared to having the pupils discover the truths they contain. These experiences do not have to be revolutionary

in format. Paragraph and essay writing, debating, committee reports, discussions, role playing, flannel board stories, etc., are very suitable experiences.
3. In concluding lessons, carefully formulated questions have to be designed to lead the pupils to arrive at generalizations which they can support, given the knowledge acquired earlier.

Teaching the Conceptual Approach
1. A carefully planned unit or lesson can be easily managed as long as the teacher does not lose track of the concepts, variants, and the learning objectives.
2. Whenever appropriate, during the initial presentation of material, as well as during the concluding questions, be on the alert to ask the type of concluding questions that will enable the pupil to see "beyond the trees."
3. Teachers must also use ingenuity to build upon pupil answers by formulating additional questions of a generalizing nature.
4. The key to success of the conceptual approach, once the unit or lesson has been carefully planned, is asking the proper questions at the proper time.

Resources

The school library, classroom libraries, texts, homemade materials, and audiovisuals must respond to the needs of the subjects and students. The sharing of teacher-prepared material should have a high priority.

As an example, let us explore the concept of Family, a unit of study in the elementary grades, so important to Jewish life (see the chart in figure 2 on pages 420-423). The family, like more complex social units (a culture, or community, regardless of time period), should be viewed with the many components which maintain and substantiate its existence in mind. By charting these components, we can provide focal points for the variants of the concept according to the various Social Studies disciplines.

For each concept or variant above, stories from Yiddish and Hebrew literature could be used to motivate, and/or to describe and give information, and/or enrich, and/or review and reinforce. Other creative arts could similarly be called into play. Verbal expressions in Yiddish and Hebrew that reflect Jewish values and lifestyle can then be introduced.[12] References to appropriate biblical passages and examples from Rabbinic literature will complete the integrated curricular circle.

Following is a list of additional strategies particularly appropriate for enrichment in teaching Jewish Social Studies.
- Mystery map missions – charting Jewish communities
- Yellow pages survey and Anglo-Jewish press – to determine what agencies and services are available to the Jewish community
- What's to see of Jewish interest in our community? – an annotated listing
- Tracking words – inquiring about different Jewish cultures by analyzing language
- Who remembers when? – researching the community's development through oral history projects
- Examining the Jewish community services – a local monopoly board
- Jewish career awareness
- Dateline and byline – writing about important issues and times in the life of the Jews
- Time lines that talk — expanding time lines vertically by adding stories and art work to the various segments
- Can you locate? – places of interest in Jewish history and geography indicated with some particular designation on maps or globes
- Studying statistics – population, demography, etc.
- Fashions of the period – a research project into a particular period of time
- Music of the period
- Art of the period
- Literature of the period
- In the good old days – dramatic history with costumes and personal characterizations
- The story stamps tell.
- Building a future society – simulation of an ideal community developing a Constitution, flag, anthem, government, institutions, etc.
- I'm applying for – job descriptions for various Jewish communal responsibilities and qualifications of persons "applying"
- Current Events Reaction Sheets.
- Let's Look at our Prejudices and Biases.
- Working with primary source materials. (For excellent ways to do this, see Chapter 37, "M'korot: Teaching Jewish History with Primary Sources.")

COMPONENTS OF A FAMILY (OR COMMUNITY)

1. Size and Composition
2. Shelter
3. Relationships Among:
   Family, Relatives, Neighbors
4. Health and Safety
5. Dress
6. Work
7. Values and Goals
8. Education
9. Transportation
10. Communication
11. Food
12. Social Life: Culture and Recreation

Social Studies Discipline	Concept	Variant
History	I. Change in Jewish life is a part of history	1. Family life sometimes differs among various communities around the world. 2. Families of today are different from families of earlier times: e.g., biblical, Middle Ages, shtetl, the *kibbutz,* etc. There must be flexibility to survive.
	II. Jewish experience is continuous and interrelated since we are products of our past and influenced by it.	1. Families celebrate holidays to commemorate their Jewish historical heritage. 2. Family customs and traditions are products of the past. They are transmitted from parents to children.
	III. History is a record of events and problems which people have met with varying degrees of success. The Jewish response has frequently resulted in change and adaptability. Over the long period of our existence, this flexibility has proved successful to our continuation as a people.	1. Being a member of a group requires many adjustments. Change may help some and hurt others. 2. Family roles vary from family to family, in time, place, and community.
	IV. Acts and events have consequences which vary greatly in different cultures. A knowledge and understanding of our Jewish past in meeting the challenges of our present day Jewish community.	1. What people say and do affects others (responsibility, cooperation, concern for others). 2. Families are affected by what is done and said in the communities and nations in which they live. 3. Individuals and families learn lessons from the past.

Figure 2

	V. People tend to judge or interpret the evidence of the past in light of their own times. So too, the historical record is influenced by the times and culture of the historian.	1. Evidence of the past and ways in which it differs from the present can be found in our homes and all around us. 2. Many parts of the Bible have important parallels in writings of and about other ancient peoples of the Near East.
Anthropology and Sociology	I. Human beings are more alike than different. They have physical characteristics, and basic needs, and wants that are similar.	1. People in the same family usually have some similar characteristics. 2. A family of families — e.g., the Jews, also has similarities.
	II. Human beings live in groups. Jews live in groups.	1. The family is the basic social unit in most societies. 2. The family is the basic social unit in most Jewish societies.
	III. People living in groups develop a unique culture.	1. Jews living in the same area usually have similar cultural traits: Language, customs, values, life-styles. 2. Families may interpret these cultural traits in particular ways.
	IV. Jews are in part a product of their culture. In the diaspora, it is a dual heritage.	1. Cultural traits and skills are learned. 2. Jews accommodate to pluralism in particular ways.
	V. Every group tends to develop formal and informal "controls" to lend stability and provide order among its members.	1. Family members have responsibilities to each other. 2. Families have responsibilities to other members of the community.
	VI. Culture change is continuous but takes place at varying rates.	1. People learn new things as they grow older. 2. Changes in the community are a result of this knowledge.
Political Science	I. Every society creates laws commensurate with its customs and values.	1. Families have rules in their homes. 2. Schools have regulations. 3. Communities and neighborhoods have laws for health and safety.

Figure 2, cont.

	II. Governments and voluntary groupings are established to achieve order, actualize power, and implement regulations.	1. Rules have reasons. If change is needed, certain processes have to take place for orderly transitions. 2. Jewish communities in various periods of time and in various places have achieved government by a variety of means, e.g., Kehillah, *Bet Din,* Sanhedrin, etc.
	III. Decision making is a fundamental activity of government and the governed.	1. Families arrive at decisions in various ways. 2. Jews working together are usually more effective when the rights and feelings of others are considered, and where their differences are respected.
	IV. The definition of citizenship varies in different cultures. In the Jewish community, ideally it involves active participation.	1. Members of a family can agree upon rules that will be beneficial to all. 2. Jews who are active within their Jewish community make decisions of responsibility.
	V. All levels of government are interrelated. At the world level, all nations are interdependent. *"Kol Yisrael Arayvin Zeh Ba-zeh."*	1. Some authority is divided between family and the outside world. 2. The rules and welfare of the family and its community are mutually dependent.
Geography	I. Each place on earth (area or specific location) is related to all other areas in terms of size, direction, distance, and time.	(The variants for the two concepts listed fall more into the area of skills teaching, and are therefore not expanded upon here.)
	II. A region is a mental concept useful in organizing knowledge about the earth and its people. It is an area which in one or more ways has relatively homogeneous characteristics such as physical features, cultural features, occupations, or political affiliations, and is in one or more of these respects different from surrounding areas.	Specific examples of variants for teaching geography concepts for the Jewish supplementary school would be: biblical Canaan and its surrounding neighbors, shtetl, Jews in Arab Lands, modern Israel, etc.

Figure 2, cont.

Economics	I. The economic problem is the scarcity of resources relative to human desires. People have exhibited unusual ingenuity in increasing output. Yet, desires continuously outrun the available goods and services. This is because at any moment of time, resources — human beings (land and machines) — are limited, whereas, human desires are limitless.	1. Individuals and families want more than they can have. They are constantly faced with choice. All members of a family are consumers; a limited number are producers of goods and services. 2. Jewish communities have had to exist within the oftentimes restrictive environments of the host countries in which they live.
	II. Basic economic problems have often been answered by many forces and factors that have helped shape the culture of a given society. Among these are its geography, its ethics, its cultural social structure, its political history, the state of its industrial arts and the level of its technical skills.	1. A budget is a form of organization for the efficient use of family income. 2. Jewish communal funding must be appropriated to many needy causes.

Figure 2, cont.

- Classroom learning centers appropriate for Jewish Social Studies in a supplementary school (see Chapter 16, "Classroom Learning Centers" for more details on this topic).

Some suggestions for learning centers are: Your Local Jewish Community, Israel, Let's "Dig" the Bible, When in Rome, It's Not Greek to Me, Holocaust History, Around the Globe, Anti-Semitism, The Written Word, The Jewish Calendar, The Jewish Life Cycle, The Enlightenment, Zionism, Hasidism, The Golden Age, The Talmud, Commentaries, Once Upon a . . . , Heroes/ Heroines of Yesterday, Heroes/Heroines of Today, Immigration to America, Calligraphy Can Show.

The following steps represent the procedure for organizing learning centers:
1. Determine curricular areas.
2. Only set up as many "corners" as:
   a. you can handle at once.
   b. you have time and material for.
   c. you can make attractive and relevant.
3. In each corner:
   a. Prepare ample activities for a number of children to work with simultaneously.
   b. Make certain reference materials are easy to work with and can be identified.
   c. Provide for a variety of materials to meet individual differences in style, rate, and interest in subject matter.
   d. Write instructions for activities in behavioral objectives in language the children can easily understand and relate to make certain there are evaluation and record keeping systems present.
4. Organize the room so that:
   a. there is enough space to allow the students to work comfortably.
   b. the teacher (and paraprofessionals) can be in a position to get to groups and individuals as they work.
   c. several floor plans are possible and flexibility is present.
   d. equipment serves your needs.
5. You will need:
   chairs
   tables
   bookcases or shelves
   bulletin boards
   file cabinets or boxes
   tape recorders
   slide and/or filmstrip projectors
   VCR/television set
   some crafts equipment

some rug remnants
a supplies closet
some storage space for each "corner"
6. Teacher (and aides) are consultants or facilitators or enablers. They direct and help students who work individually or in small groups.
7. Goals include:
   a. high standards of work and accomplishment.
   b. student involvement in the learning process.
   c. identifying contemporary issues affecting the American Jewish child.
   d. indicating to the children that these issues are human concerns and social problems dealing with attitudes, values, identity, continuity.
   e. Social Studies are various disciplines that can be dealt with interdisciplinarily.
   f. Social Studies involve the learning and use of skills.
   Methods include:
   a. research, guided inquiry, problem solving, and creative efforts on the part of students.
   b. use of small group, large group, and individual activities.
   c. stimulating, multi-sensory environments.
   d. careful instructions and group discussion for all activities.
   e. detailed, ongoing evaluation.
8. How to begin:
   a. Try out several physical floor plans.
   b. Set up the room carefully and attractively.
   c. Acquaint your pupils and parents with the program, the physical arrangements, and the record keeping system.
   d. Explain goals and standards.
   e. Describe behavior, guidance, and evaluation.
   f. Discuss care and operation of equipment and cleanup procedures.
   g. Make cards or instruction sheets for each center including:
      - What we want you to learn
      - Instructions for activities
      - Activities
      - Time limitations
      - Assessment procedures
9. Supplies and materials for centers: maps, globes, charts, tapes, texts, magazines, newspapers, games, writing materials, junk box, file box, reference books, boxes, time lines, pictures, media equipment, subject realia and artifacts, filmstrips, transparencies, videos, crafts supplies.

MATERIALS

There is no dearth of good materials for the teacher willing to read, evaluate, and modify to suit his/her own needs. A Bibliography of recommended readings in the field appears at the end of this chapter. In addition, many units and lessons designed by teachers are available through the CAJE Curriculum Bank, 15600 Mulholland Dr., Los Angeles, CA 90077.

Many references have been made in this chapter (as in many other books and articles for the Jewish teacher) on the necessity and advisability of creating homemade materials to augment texts and published works. The references in the Bibliography offer help in this direction, as do the Bibliographies for other chapters in this volume.

CONCLUSION

Under the rubric of Jewish Social Studies are the history, culture, lifestyle, and ethics of our people. Excitement and personal gratification await the ready teacher and inquisitive student when they explore our past and relate it to the present, study others of our people and understand their relationships to us, and think through the application of our religious and cultural heritage to our daily lives. Let us hope that this stimulus of expanded and enriched Social Studies teaching will augur well for our continuity, as individuals, as families, and as a people.

Fradle Freidenreich is the former Director of the Department of Pedagogic Services, Jewish Education Service of North America. She now lives in Israel.

NOTES

1. "Essentials of Education Statement," Washington, DC: The National Council for the Social Studies, 1980.
2. The one exception to this is the network of Yeshiva school systems which the Ultra-Orthodox provide in which there exists a total support system outside of the school. In these instances, school is merely an extension of home and community, and as such, reflects the community's value system, past and present, in a functioning format.
3. Melton Research Center, The Jewish Theological Seminary of America, 3080 Broadway, New York, NY 10027.
4. George Pollak, "Inventory of Curricular Subjects in Supplementary Jewish Schools." *Research and Information Bulletin* #51, New York: JESNA, 1981.
5. *The Pedagogic Reporter* XXIX (2): 2-9, 1978.
6. Hilda Taba, et al, *A Teacher's Handbook to Elementary Social Studies.* (Reading, MA: Addison-Wesley, 1971), p. 1.
7. Yehudah Shabatay, "The Teaching of Jewish Social Studies in the Weekday Afternoon Religious School," unpublished paper, 1975.
8. Ibid.
9. James A. Banks has excellent suggestions in *Teaching Strategies for the Social Studies: Inquiry Valuing and Decision Making* (White Plains, NY: Longman Publishing Group, 1990).
10. *The Pedagogic Reporter*, op. cit., pp. 19-21.
11. *The Pedagogic Reporter*, op. cit., pp. 9-13.
12. A good reference is *Your Jewish Lexicon* by Edith Samuels (New York: UAHC Press, 1982).

NOTES

Akker, J. Van Den, and W. Kuiper. "Implementation of a Social Studies Curriculum." *Journal of Curriculum Supervision* 8:293-305, Summer 1993.

Association of Teachers of Social Studies in the City of New York. *A Handbook for the Teaching of Social Studies*. Needham Heights, MA: Allyn and Bacon, Inc., 1984.

Baloche, Lynda. "Breaking Down the Walls: Integrating Creative Questioning and Cooperative Learning into the Social Studies." *The Social Studies,* January-February 1994, pp. 25-30.

Banks, James A. *Teaching Strategies for the Social Studies: Inquiry Valuing and Decision Making*. 4th ed. New York: Longman Publishing Group, 1990.

Bragaw, Donald H., and H. Michael Hartoonian. "Social Studies: The Study of People in Society." *Content of the Curriculum*. Alexandria, VA: ASCD, 1988.

Brown, Chris, et al. *Social Education: Principles and Practices*. Bristol, PA: Taylor and Francis, 1986.

Bruner, Jerome. *The Process of Education*. New York: Vintage Books, 1963.

Coleman, Robert E. "On Becoming a Social Studies Teacher." *The Social Studies* 85:5-6, January/February 1994.

Davis, James E., et al. *Planning a Social Studies Program: Activities Guidelines and Resources*. 3d ed. Boulder, CO: Social Science Education Consortium, Inc., 1991.

Edeger, M. "A Grade 6 Project in the Social Studies: The Wall of Old Jerusalem." *Canadian Social Studies* 27: 156-6, Summer 1993.

Focus: A Handbook of Classroom Ideas To Motivate the Teacher of Intermediate Social Studies. New York: Educational Services Press, 1977.

Freeland, Kent. *Managing the Social Studies Curriculum*. Lancaster, PA: Technomic Publishing Co., 1990.

Jewish Education 60, 1993. (Includes many articles that relate to teaching Social Studies)

Jewish Education News. Special Focus: Transposing History Scholarship, Winter 1990.

Jewish Educators Assembly. *New Insights into Curriculum Development Volume VII*. New York: United Synagogue of Conservative Judaism, n.d.

Kenworthy, Leonard S. *Social Studies for the 80's*. New York: Macmillan, 1981.

Kochar, S.K. *The Teaching of Social Studies*. New York: Sterling Publishing Co., Inc., 1983.

Livingston, Samuel A., and Clarice S. Stall. *Simulation Games: An Introduction for the Social Studies Teacher*. New York: Free Press, 1973.

O'Conner, John E. *Teaching History with Film and Television*. Houston, TX: American History Association, 1987.

Parker, Walter C. *Renewing the Social Studies Curriculum*. Alexandria, VA: ASCD, 1991.

The Pedagogic Reporter XXIX (2), 1978.

Reichert, Richard. *Simulation Games for Religious Education*. Raleigh, NC: St. Mary's College, 1975.

Stafford, Jan. "How To Teach about Religions in Elementary Social Studies Classrooms." *The Social Studies* 84:245-8, November/Dcember 1993.

Stahl, Robert J., and Ronald S. Van Sickle, eds. *Cooperative Learning in the Social Studies Classroom: An Invitation to Social Study*. Washington, DC: National Council for the Social Studies, 1992.

Wilson, Gerald L., et al, eds. *Teaching Social Studies: Handbook of Trends, Issues and Implications for the Future*. Westport, CT: Greenwood Publishing Group, Inc., 1993.

Woolever, Roberta, and Kathryn P. Scott. *Active Learning in Social Studies: Promoting Cognitive and Social Growth*. New York: HarperCollins College, 1988.

SUBJECT MATTER

CHAPTER THIRTY-SEVEN

M'KOROT: TEACHING JEWISH HISTORY WITH PRIMARY SOURCES

Seymour Epstein

If Jewish history and social studies are to be taught in our schools, we must clarify our objectives, deliberate, and decide on some strategies, and re-train ourselves accordingly. The use of the pronoun "we" in this context is careful and caring verbage. Given the broadest definition of curriculum design that is popular these days, all that goes into teaching and learning Jewish social studies cannot be determined by one single member of the following cast: publisher, text author, principal, teacher, student, or subject matter. The teaching/learning model described in this chapter is designed to bring all of the above factors together in a dynamic instructional instrument that enhances any study of history. In its most imaginative and comprehensive application, *M'korot* could be used as the sole method in a history unit. In any history and social studies class, this model is an effective complementary tool; not merely as a change of pace, but as a new dimension added to the scope of the learner.

The single best criticism of most history lessons now taught in Jewish schools is that they differ little from lessons in Bible, *Mishnah*, or *Siddur*. A model unique to the study of Jewish history must be created (or at least, adapted from the general field) to fit the needs of the Jewish Studies curriculum. With the introduction of this model, the teacher who has mastered it need no longer rely solely on the secondary texts now available from either Israeli or American publishers.

Why do we wish to downplay the use of secondary texts? Are some of them not acceptable if used properly by a knowledgeable teacher? The best of them are plot narratives that give us a decent account of historical events — people, places, dates, etc. They tell us little about the art of historical discovery, the variety of lessons learned from history, the different approaches to the study of any one period or the implications of history and its study for our own time.

The worst of the history texts are used as readers to be recited in class, sometimes by the teacher, at other times by some unfortunate student. If the text is in English, the student hopes that he won't mispronounce "Diaspora." If in Hebrew, the class can become a grammar lesson at the drop of a *hitpael*. There exist elementary Day School classes in which the teacher actually initiates unison reading of a Hebrew history text. In case any bright pupil creates a distinction in his own mind between the study of history, the preceding half hour of prayer, and the hour of Bible yet to come, such foolish notions are dispelled by the common model used for all three.

This model is called *M'korot,* which means primary sources or original documents. It was designed for secondary students, but can be used effectively with younger and older children as well. It makes serious demands of the students and requires even greater commitment from the teacher. The rewards are simple, yet significant. This technique leads one to think like and act as a mini-historian. It may even inspire one to become a full-fledged Jewish historian.

Before we start with grandiose promises, the teacher must make some decisions about his/her own commitment (time, finances, headspace) to the teaching of Jewish social studies. Whether you teach three quarters of an hour Sunday morning or fifteen periods in a day school, you are representing the discipline of Jewish history. This requires seriousness. Your needs may differ because of varying backgrounds, but here are some sine qua non:

1. A few university level courses with a Jewish historian or (for those remote from the center of Jewish learning) exposure to some of the best secondary sources available today.
2. A decent library or access to one — it should include most of the primary source collections listed in the Bibliography.
3. Preparation time — a large chunk of July or August is recommended.
4. Hebrew fluency or a commitment to study the language. This is actually not critical, but is highly recommended.

Now, let's discuss our objectives. When I teach history I wish to achieve the following goals:

1. The transmission of some historical data, i.e., time lines, names, places, events, etc. (What?)
2. An appreciation of historiography, i.e., how an historian does his/her work. (How?)
3. A careful deliberation on consequences of certain events, people, times, etc., and an even more careful projection to contemporary parallels. (Why?)
4. An exposure to the joy of learning (through hard work) that could lead to the love of the study of history. (Oy!)

As an aside, I hope that my first goal satisfied the "back-to-basics" crowd, but I wish to state clearly that the other three goals do not occupy a lesser place in my categories. These are four basic objectives that must color and flavor every deliberate act of teaching on my part.

During the 1960s, a serious re-evaluation of the teaching of social studies took place in North America. Of the hundreds of volumes and articles that were produced then, I especially recommend for reading in this area of curriculum development one text that provides a general survey of the social studies reform movement and a sufficient number of practical guidelines for our purposes. That book is *Teaching the New Social Studies in Secondary Schools* by Fenton.

M'korot is a model that deals with but one aspect of the "New History" of the 1960s. Fenton's book deals with many other aspects of the reform. I will refer only to those passages which are directly relevant to the dynamics of *M'korot*. Teachers interested in the general field of social studies reform might read the entire Fenton volume and also look at the relevant sections of *Models of Teaching* by Joyce and Weil.

Let us begin as Fenton would. Take the history text that you are presently using and reread a chapter that you have not yet taught this year. Now ask yourself the following questions:

1. Why should this chapter be taught? If it is taught, should the emphasis be on factual knowledge, basic concepts, critical thinking, values, or some other objective?
2. If this chapter is to be taught, what methods of teaching are available? How are the ones we use selected?
3. What content emphases (in this chapter) are most important to teach? How should a teacher select content emphases?

The ultimate question will always be: How does this chapter fit into my set of objectives as outlined above? With the average history text (even the newer ones that include some primary material), you will have difficulties in going beyond the "what" objective. Even that material is not always communicated best by a single reading of a text. How many times have you read an article or a chapter of simple material that you could not recall a week later? But, think again of the most complex material you have read that you will never forget, and contemplate what makes the difference.

In an attempt to build a theoretical basis for his inductive approach to teaching history, Fenton makes good use of two notions basic to the 1960's reforms: structure and discovery. One cannot proceed further without referring to Jerome Bruner, the theoretical father of that curriculum reform. Two of his works, *The Process of Education* and *On Knowing* are quoted at length in Fenton's volume, and my selections on the notion of structure and the act of discovery are from that source.

Bruner asserts that the structure of a discipline should shape the classroom study in that area. This will mean that, for instance, in the teaching of Talmud, one would of course be interested merely in the transmission of certain pieces of information obtained through Talmudic discussion, as well as in the final reading of the law. But one should be especially interested in the very structure of Talmudic reasoning and in the approach that the *Mishnah* and *Gemara* take to life problems. Let's hear it firsthand from Bruner's, *The Process of Education*:

"The first object of any act of learning, over and beyond the pleasure it may give, is that it should serve us in the future. Learning should not only take us somewhere; it should allow us later to go further more easily. There are two ways in which learning serves the future. One is through its specific applicability to tasks that are highly similar to those we originally learned to perform. Psychologists refer to this phenomenon as specific transfer of training; perhaps it should be called the extension of habits or association. Its utility appears to be limited in the main to what we usually speak of as skills. Having learned how to hammer nails, we are better able later to learn how to hammer tacks or chip wood. Learning in school undoubtedly creates skills of a kind that transfer to activities encountered later, either in school or after. A second way in which earlier learning renders later performance more efficient is through what is conveniently called non-specific transfer or, more accurately, the transfer of principles and attitudes. In essence, it consists of learning initially not a skill but a general idea, which can then be used as a basis for recognizing subsequent problems as special cases of the idea originally mastered. This type of transfer is at the heart of the educational process — the continual broadening and deepening of knowledge in terms of basic and general ideas."[1]

Bruner goes on to claim that "the continuity of learning that is produced by the second type of transfer, transfer of principles, is dependent upon the mastery of the structure of the subject matter." "The more fundamental or basic is the idea he has learned, almost by definition, the greater will be its breadth of applicability to new problems." Bruner illustrates his hypothesis with reference to a classroom experience in one of the "softer" sciences: A sixth-grade class, having been through a conventional unit of the social and economic geography of the Southeastern states, was introduced to the North Central region by being asked to locate the major cities of the area on a map containing physical features and natural resources, but no place names. The resulting class discussion very rapidly produced a variety of plausible theories concerning the requirements of a city — a water transportation theory that placed Chicago at the junction of the three lakes, a mineral resources theory that placed it near the Mesabi range, a food supply theory that put a great city on the rich soil of Iowa, and so on.

In case you're getting impatient with theory at this juncture, let me point out that all of this is directly applicable to our problems of how to teach Jewish history. Bruner's emphasis on the critical importance of teaching the structure of a discipline should caution us against teaching time lines, names, and places without giving equal and simultaneous attention to historiography, so that students can learn, appreciate, and internalize the process of historical study for future transfer to similar problems. For example, if you teach the Spanish period properly, some of the skills that have been learned can be applied to the study of the *shtetl*, or political Zionism, or the Hasmonean period. I'll let Jerome Bruner have the last word on structure.

". . . the curriculum of a subject should be determined by the most fundamental understanding that can be achieved of the underlying principles that give structure to that subject. Teaching specific topics or skills without making clear their context in the broader fundamental structure of a field of knowledge is uneconomical in several deep senses. In the first place, such teaching makes it exceedingly difficult for the student to generalize from what he has learned to what he will encounter later. In the second place, learning that has fallen short of a group of general principles has little reward in terms of intellectual excitement. The best way to create interest in a subject is to render it worth knowing, which means to make the knowledge gained usable in one's thinking beyond the situation in which the learning has occurred. Third, knowledge one has acquired without sufficient structure to tie it together is knowledge that is likely to be forgotten. An unconnected set of facts has a pitiably short half-life in memory. Organizing facts in terms of principles and ideas from which they may be inferred is the only known way to reducing the quick rate of loss of human memory."

Having given us some clear direction in the realm of what to teach, Bruner also has some notions on how to teach. His work on the act of

> **LEARNING THE PROCESS OF HISTORICAL STUDY IS MORE IMPORTANT THAN LEARNING DATES AND EVENTS.**

discovery is prefaced in *On Knowing* by a reference to Maimonides' *Moreh N'vuchim* (*Guide for the Perplexed*). The Rambam decides that of the four forms of perfection, the acquisition of worldly goods, physical fitness, moral behavior, and possession of the highest intellectual faculties, the last is the highest form. Bruner quotes Maimonides: "Examine the first three kinds of perfection; you will find that if you possess them, they are not your property, but the property of others. . . . But the last kind of perfection is exclusively yours; no one else owns any part of it." Bruner uses this quote as a proof text for the further projection that "if man's intellectual excellence is the most his own among his perfections, it is also the case that the most personal of all that he knows is that which he has discovered for himself."[2]

After stating a caveat that discovery is not a chance encounter with knowledge ("Discovery, like surprise, favors the well prepared mind"), Bruner goes on to describe two teaching styles, one of which is more encouraging of discovery. He distinguishes between the expository mode and the hypothetical mode. I recommend reading David Ausubel,[3] Paulo Freire,[4] or Eugene Borowitz[5] on this second mode of teaching. These three scholars plus Bruner have written convincingly of the great benefits of a teaching style which involves students in an ongoing active deliberation with the subject matter rather than a passive receptive role.

Bruner lists four major benefits that accrue from learning by discovery. He claims an increase in intellectual potency; a shift from external motivating factors (grades, outside approval, etc.) to internal, self-confident drives; a learning of the heuristics of discovery (i.e. the dynamics of how a variety of factors lead one to an act of discovery); and an improvement in memory conservation. This convincing argument for discovery as the most effective learning process coupled with Bruner's notion of structure should prepare us for the introduction of primary source material into our Jewish history classes. *M'korot* exposes our students to the research of historians and gives them a chance to participate actively in similar work.

DYNAMICS OF THE MODEL

There are five steps to this teaching model. Before describing and illustrating them, I remind the reader that a number of books listed in the Bibliography at the end of this chapter can reinforce and further elucidate. Also, there are now many collections of Jewish source material in addition to the standard sources — Bible, Talmud, recordings, photographs, and newspapers. Any source that is authentic to its own period is acceptable. Some sources are more reliable than others, but that's one of the problems that lies ahead of us. Now, to begin.

1. The first step involves describing the period under study in terms of dates and places. This can be accomplished by the students with the help of an encyclopedia or a text, but is probably best introduced by the teacher in a directed class where he/she can eliminate all interpretation and transfer only the events and the locations. It is best to prepare a source sheet with the following information on it kept by each student.

B'nai Talmidim Hebrew School
Date:
TOPIC: Mandate for Palestine
PERIOD: April 25, 1920 — May 14, 1948
PLACES: Palestine, Great Britain
PARALLEL EVENTS IN WORLD HISTORY:
   League of Nations, WW II
PERSONALITIES: Weizmann, Ben Gurion, Samuel, Plumer, etc.
REFERENCES: *Encyclopaedia Judaica*, Vol. II, pp. 861-863. Secondary Text, pp. 00-000.

Not much more than this is necessary. The general rule for this first step is that too much will squelch while too little will self correct. A fresh method (not to be used more than once a year) might be a phenomenological approach to the sources. This can be used once students are somewhat adept at working with primary material. Here the teacher starts a new unit by bringing in several documents without an introduction. The students work on them as a puzzle, looking for clues to identify the period, the place, and the principal personalities. While missing details can be filled in via secondary texts, nothing can replace the joy of learning and discovery in such an exercise.

2. The second step is to help students to be aware of the distinction between primary and secondary sources. Use illustrations from material that is familiar to the students. For

example, compare the first prophets (Joshua, Judges, Samuel I and II, Kings I and II) with Bright's *A History of Israel* or compare Dawidowicz's book *A Holocaust Reader* with her *The War Against the Jews 1933-1945*.

A structural technique must be developed for dealing with primary sources. Please remember what Professor Bruner said about discovery favoring the well prepared mind. Edwin Fenton has three chapters (9, 10, and 16) in his book that will help you and your students to deal with primary sources. I will summarize the methodology here, but you would be wise to study the Fenton material carefully.

In a series of six readings Fenton deals with the following concerns: "How the historian classifies information," "How the historian proves a hypothesis," "How the historian decides what is fact," "How the historian asks questions," "How the historian deals with mind set," and "What is history?"

How the Historian Classifies Information

You can teach this best by giving your students a list of eighteen words and asking them to arrange them in groups of things that seem, for some reason, to belong to each other. Tell them to make many different classifications. Fenton uses fish, animals, and birds. You can use *mitzvah* objects, names of Jewish books, and places in Israel. It doesn't matter. Remember that classification can be based on anything from *gematria* to psychological associations. Prepare some classification that the students might never have considered. If, for example, the list is of geographic areas in Israel (seas, cities, rivers, hills, etc.), your classification should be according to the number of letters in the name or according to first letters.

Here are some sample questions for the discussion after the work is done: What do all of your categories have in common? These are my categories. What do my categories have in common? How are they different from yours? What does "frame of reference" have to do with history? Where does one get his/her "frame of reference"? Do historians have a "frame of reference"?

How the Historian Proves a Hypothesis

Fenton makes some specific suggestions for teaching this lesson. Historians never collect data helter-skelter. If they did, they would take notes about everything they read. Historians do not operate in this fashion. They select the data they want to record in notes and then select again from the notes those pieces of evidence (facts) that will be used to prove the point. Every step in the process of writing a book or an article involves selection.

How do historians start to select? They usually start with a question: What caused World War I? Why did the United States become more democratic in the 1830s? What was the most important contribution of the Romans to the western heritage? Then they begin to do research, reading and collecting notes about their topic. Before long, a hypothesis emerges as a tentative answer to the question. As more data is gathered, the hypothesis is revised . . . or abandoned if there is enough evidence against it. In this case, the historian will be forced to develop another hypothesis to guide the ongoing research. Eventually, one hypothesis will emerge that seemingly matches the facts of the case. It is then time to write about these conclusions.

This procedure sounds far more simple than it really is. Where does one get the idea for a hypothesis in the first place? How does one decide when a hypothesis has been proved? How should one arrange supporting evidence so that readers will agree with the thesis?

Once you and your students have "mastered" this lesson you can apply these procedures to every original document that you use in class.[6]

How the Historian Decides What Is Fact

Fenton uses two accounts of the Hungarian revolution (one from *Time* and the other from Radio Moscow) to illustrate this problem. For our purposes, I would refer you to a classic problem in Jewish historiography — the Marranos. Space does not permit reprinting three essays here, but I suggest that you read the following: "The Utilization of Non-Jewish Sources for the Reconstruction of Jewish History" by Ellis Rivkin (*Jewish Quarterly Review* XLVII, 1957-1958), pp. 183-203; review article on "The Marranos of Spain" by Gerson D. Cohen (*Jewish Social Studies* XXIX, no. 3; July 1967); and "The Marranos of Spain: From the Late XIVth to the Early XVIth Century According to Contemporary Hebrew Sources" by B. Netanyahu (New

York: American Academy for Jewish Research, 1966), pp. 1-4.

The problem simply put is: "How Jewish were the Marranos?" If we believe the inquisitorial records, we will hold the traditional view that the conversos were at one with the Jewish people. If we read some of the North African responsa literature we could come to believe the opposite. A careful reading of the three essays will give you some insights into how historians decide what is fact.

How the Historian Asks Questions

To help us formulate good questions that could lead to a hypothesis, Fenton shows us an essay by Carl G. Gustavson on "The Cause of the Reformation." The penultimate paragraphs will give us the beginnings of a list.

The foregoing outline, which by no means exhausts the possibilities of causation in the Reformation, does provide a check list of factors likely to be important in such a phenomenon. When a student is faced with a problem of this nature, a few general questions are of great assistance in analyzing the situation. When these are "tried on for size," some will immediately suggest causes, while others may have little relevance. The following nine should prove helpful: (1) What was the immediate cause for the event? (2) Had there been a background of agitation for the principles victorious during this episode? (3) Were personalities involved on either side whose strengths or weaknesses may have helped to determine the outcome of the struggle? (4) Were any new and potent ideas stimulating the loyalty of a considerable number of people? (5) How did the economic groups line up on the issue? (6) Were religious forces active? (7) Did any new technological developments influence the situation? (8) Can the events be partially explained by weakened or strengthened institutions? (9) Was the physical environment itself a factor in the situation? . . . A systematic analysis of a problem of causation with the aid of these questions will ensure that all the major historical factors have been taken into consideration . . . .[7]

If you now see that these same questions and others like them (and some that no one has thought of yet) can be equally applied to the Hasmonean uprising or the Hasidic movement, you are well on your way to becoming a teacher of *M'korot*.

How the Historian Deals with Mind Set

In order to illustrate the importance of mind set in the perception and analysis of facts (i.e., that no historical research is completely objective), Fenton makes use of an excerpt from *Les Miracles de Saint Benoit*.[8] I Might also suggest a reading of *Shivhei Ha-Besht* or the translation by Dan Ben-Amos and Jerome R. Mintz, *In Praise of the Baal Shem Tov*.[9] Golem literature will serve a similar function. Rational and intelligent adults wrote material from a universe of discourse quite different from ours. To appreciate that kind of documentation historically, one must be able to deal with the difference in mind set.

What Is History?

By now your own notions of what historical study is should have been somewhat altered. I hope that you have come to see the importance of exposure to the process of historiography alongside the ongoing transfer of historical data. The basic objective of this section is to teach the process that will be applied to all original documents. Given your economics of time and curriculum, you may be forced to shorten this step. Do so, but be careful to leave your students with some organizing technique for the analysis of the sources.

You might warn the class of the limitations of this type of scholarship. While it is true that the students are being trained to be mini-historians, they must be made aware of the fact that they lack basic tools, (e.g., ancient languages, experience, a broad base of historical knowledge, sufficient source material to be comprehensive, etc.). These restrictions will, in part, explain some of the inevitable discrepancies between their work and that of the historians.

This entire step is only necessary once. A class that has had this introduction need only be reminded by means of review.

3. The third step of this model has to do with the distribution and classification of the primary sources. Distribute them with as little or as much introduction as necessary. You may decide to have the entire class examine one document (as a class or in groups), or different sources can be distributed to separate groups. This determination depends on class size, the work habits of the students, and the length and quality of the primary sources.

Another possibility is the source box. These boxes are available in a commercially produced form, or they can be developed by the teacher. They consist of a collection of sources on one period. Any particular box could include documents, tapes, photographs, newspaper articles, period novels, artifacts, etc. Teachers should be encouraged to create a box of such sources for each period they teach.

The sources are distributed and the students classify them and their data, ask questions, decide what is fact, and begin work on a tentative hypothesis.

4. During step four, students carefully evaluate the documents. The class must prepare a list of general notions, hypotheses and proven facts derived from the source material. These interpretive notes must then be matched to the dates and places posited at the outset. If there are any conflicts they should either be clarified immediately (if possible, in a secondary source), or noted as unsolved problems.

Please note that any evaluative instrument used (papers, tests, or examinations) in such a setting should reflect the special nature of the work done in class. For example, a test could include a new source previously not seen by the students or an essay assignment could involve the analysis of an original document in the light of work done in class. You might try a debate between two groups that used contradictory sources.

5. Step five takes place at the end of a unit. Make reference to a secondary source and check the interpretation of the period reached by the class with that reached by an historian. If the class is using a history text book, use that as your secondary reference. An excellent volume to use as a check on both your work and your history text book is *A History of the Jewish People*, edited by Ben-Sasson.

CONCLUSION

When learning can involve students in a process as intriguing as a mystery, as absorbing as a puzzle, and as fascinating as a trip to the past, then the study of Jewish history becomes not just a mastery of names and places, but an uncovering of the what, how, and why of a period of time. To search for answers is to make history interesting; to find reasonable answers is to make it important enough to want to continue the search. The use of *M'korot* is but one technique for the study of history — and yet, it is one that can evoke fascinating results.

Seymour Epstein received his Ed.D. from the University of Toronto. He serves as the Committee Director for Morocco of the Joint Distribution Committee.

NOTES

1. Quotations from Bruner on structure are from Jerome S. Bruner, *The Process of Education* (Cambridge, MA: Harvard University Press, 1960), pp. 17-32, 38-40, 46-48, 50-60, 66-68, 71-73, and 80, with omissions. Reprinted with permission.

2. Quotations from Bruner on discovery are from Jerome S. Bruner, *On Knowing* (Cambridge, MA: The Belknap Press of Harvard University Press, 1963), pp. 81-96, with omissions. Reprinted with permission.

3. David P. Ausubel, "Reception Versus Discovery Learning in Classroom Instruction," *Educational Theory* 11:21-24, January 1961.

4. Paulo Freire, *Pedagogy of the Oppressed* (New York: Herder and Herder, 1972).

5. Eugene B. Borowitz, "Tzimtzum: A Mystic Model for Contemporary Leadership," *Religious Education* LXIX (6):687-700, November-December 1974.

6. From Edwin Fenton, *Teaching the New Social Studies in Secondary Schools: An Inductive Approach*, Copyright © 1966 by Holt, Rinehart and Winston, Inc. Reprinted by permission of Holt, Rinehart and Winston.

7. Ibid., p. 153.

8. Ibid., p. 169.

9. Dan Ben-Amos and Jerome R. Mintz, eds. *In Praise of the Baal Shem Tov* [*Shivhei Ha-Besht*]. (Bloomington, IN: University Press, 1970).

BIBLIOGRAPHY

Ackerman, Walter, ed. *Out of Our People's Past: Sources of the Study of Jewish History*. New York: United Synagogue Commission on Jewish Education, 1977.

Adler, Elkan Nathan, ed. *Jewish Travellers in the Middle Ages*. New York: Dover Publishers, Inc., 1987.

Baron, Salo W. *The Contemporary Relevance of History: A Study in Approaches and Methods*. New York: Columbia University Press, 1986.

Baron, Salo W., and Joseph L. Blau, eds. *Judaism: Postbiblical and Talmudic Period*. New York: Macmillan, 1954.

Ben-Sasson, Haim H., ed. *A History of the Jewish People*. Cambridge, MA: Harvard University Press, 1976.

Bright, John. *A History of Israel*. 3d. ed. Louisville, KY: Westminster/John Knox, 1981.

Bruner, Jerome. *On Knowing: Essays for the Left Hand*. exp. ed. Cambridge, MA: Belknap Press of Harvard University Press, 1979.

———. *The Process of Education*. Cambridge, MA: Harvard University Press, 1960.

Chazan, Robert, and Marc Lee Raphael, eds. *Modern Jewish History: A Source Book*. New York: Schocken Books, 1974.

Dawidowicz, Lucy S., ed. *The Golden Tradition: Jewish Life and Thought in Eastern Europe*. Northvale, NJ: Jason Aronson, 1989.

———. *A Holocaust Reader*. New York: Behrman House, 1976.

———. *The War Against the Jews 1933-1945*. New York: Bantam Books, 1986.

Ehrmann, Eliezer L., ed. *Readings in Modern Jewish History from the American Revolution to the Present*. Hoboken, NJ: Ktav Publishing House, Inc., 1977.

Fenton, Edwin. *Teaching the New Social Studies in Elementary Schools*. New York: Holt, Rinehart and Winston, Inc., 1966, o.p.

Gersh, Harry. *Kabbalah*. West Orange, NJ: Behrman House, 1987.

———. *Midrash: The Oral Law*. West Orange, NJ: Behrman House, 1985.

———. *Talmud: Law and Commentary*. West Orange, NJ: Behrman House, 1986.

Glatzer, Nahum N., ed. *The Judaic Tradition*. Northvale, NJ: Jason Aronson, 1987.

Hertzberg, Arthur, ed. *The Zionist Idea: A Historical Analysis and Reader*. New York: Greenwood Press, 1969.

Holtz, Barry, ed. *Back to the Sources: Reading the Classic Jewish Texts*. New York: Simon and Schuster, 1986.

———. *Finding Our Way: Jewish Texts and the Lives We Lead Today*. New York: Panthon Books, 1993.

Joyce, Bruce R., and Marsha Weil. *Models of Teaching*. 4th ed.. Needham Heights, MA: Allyn and Bacon, 1992.

Katz, Betsy. "Creating Community as Text Study." *Jewish Education News* 14(3):40-41, Summer 1993.

Kobler, Franz, ed. *Letters of Jews through the Ages. Volume One: From Biblical Times to the Renaissance*. Rockaway Beach, NY: Hebrew Publishing Co., 1978.

———. *Letters of Jews Through the Ages. Volume Two: From the Renaissance to Emancipation*. Rockaway Beach, NY: Hebrew Publishing Co, 1978.

Marcus, Jacob R., ed. *The American Jewish Woman: A Documentary History*. Hoboken, NJ: Ktav Publishing House, Inc., 1981.

———. *The Jew in the Medieval World: A Source Book 315-1791*. New York: Greenwood Press, 1975.

———. *This I Believe: Documents of American Jewish Life*. Northvale, NJ: Jason Aronson Inc., 1990.

Penslar, Derek Jonathan. *Anti-Semitism: The Jewish Response*. West Orange, NJ: Behrman House, 1989.

Roskies, Diane K., and David G. Roskies. *The Shtetl Book*. rev. ed. New York: Ktav Publishing House, n.d.

Sarna, Nahum. *Exploring Exodus: The Heritage of Biblical Israel*. New York: Schocken Books, 1986.

———. *Understanding Genesis:* The Heritage of Biblical Israel. New York: Schocken Books, 1970.

Schwartz, Barry. *Jewish Theology: A Comparative Study*. West Orange, NJ: Behrman House, 1991.

Stillman, Norman A. *The Jews of Arab Lands: A History and Source Book*. Philadelphia, PA: Jewish Publication Society, 1979.

———. *The Jews of Arab Lands in Modern Times*. Philadelphia: Jewish Publication Society, 1991.

Sugarman, Morris J. *Ethical Literature.* West Orange, NJ: Behrman House, 1988.

Talmage, Frank Ephraim, ed. *Disputation and Dialogue: Readings in the Jewish-Christian Encounter.* New York: Ktav Publishing House, Inc., and The Anti-Defamation League, 1975.

"Using Primary Sources in the Classroom." *Tov L'Horot: Newsletter of United Synagogue Dept. of Education,* Winter 1993.

SUBJECT MATTER

CHAPTER THIRTY-EIGHT

TEACHING ABOUT DEATH AND DYING

Audrey Friedman Marcus

"The world is a beautiful place to be born into," says the poet Lawrence Ferlinghetti, "but then right in the middle of it comes the smiling mortician."[1] Despite the inescapable nature of death to which the poet refers, and the necessity of facing it, we find death hard to discuss and even more difficult to teach. In this chapter, we will (1) analyze the need for death education; learn how to prepare to teach death; (2) discuss what, when, and how to teach it; and (3) conclude with a list of appropriate resources.

THE NEED FOR DEATH EDUCATION

In the past, death education took place in a natural way. People died most frequently at home, surrounded by family and friends. Death was a familiar experience to both young and old alike — infants and mothers died in childbirth, children died of childhood diseases, and animals died on the farm. Today, death is shunted away into hospitals, old age facilities, and nursing homes. Few of us ever see a dead person. This has made the whole subject of death mysterious and scary.

Also, in the nineteenth century, corpses were taken care of by family and the community. This was always the case for Jews. Today few cultures continue this practice and, despite its revival among some Jewish groups, most of us are far removed from contact with death.

Still another factor which points up the need for death education is the fact that death is so depersonalized in our society. It has become little more than a meaningless actuarial statistic. In wartime, we use the word "waste" instead of kill. Sophisticated weapons are an everyday fact of our lives. Video games are not fun unless there is someone or something to "take out." On our television screens actors die and "reappear" next week in another show. Usually it is only the "bad guy" or the enemy who dies. And they copy their television role models and play "Bang you're dead."

Writers on the subject of attitudes toward death point out that grief and mourning are deritualized today, or short circuited. We admired and praised individuals who, like Jackie Kennedy, kept a stiff upper lip and didn't show their real feelings at a time of tragedy. Similarly, some Jews observe only a short period of *shiva*, or none at all, forgoing the opportunity this ritual provides to work through grief and to mourn properly.

Somehow we think of death as an accident or illness which we can avoid, rather than as a natural event. We refer to it euphemistically as "passed away," "gone," "departed this life." We say "I lost my . . . ," "he or she entered eternal rest," or "went to sleep." We substitute interred for buried, memorial park for graveyard, coach for hearse, and remains for corpse. The effects of death are disguised by embalming. Loved ones are placed in a "slumber room." Some funeral parlors even use light blue hearses instead of black. The emphasis we place on youth further contributes to the denial of death.

What is most damaging, however, is our avoidance with children of the subject of death. Not only are young people growing up without experiencing death directly, they are also denied a forum for their questions and their anxieties.

For all these reasons, then, it is apparent that death education is necessary and that our Religious Schools must deal with the subject. We must introduce it throughout our curriculum, helping students to view death as a natural occurrence, and providing them and their parents with the attitudes and skills needed to cope with death as a reality. Children need to learn that good guys also die. Doing so will help them grow up into fully developed human beings. It has been heartening to watch death education come to the fore in the last several decades. We must continue this encouraging trend.

It is possible that one of the reasons that we avoid discussing and teaching death is because most of us haven't yet worked it out for ourselves. Perhaps, too, we don't know the techniques and tools to use. In the remainder of this chapter, we will discuss the goals for death education and how to prepare ourselves to teach about death. This will be followed by some how-to's.

STUDENTS MUST SEE DEATH AS A NATURAL OCCURRENCE.

GOALS FOR TEACHING DEATH

The following represent some overall goals for death education. They grow out of the specific needs mentioned above.

1. To help children face the death of a loved one by presenting the subject early.
2. To make death less fearful and living more enjoyable.
3. To help develop a realistic and accepting attitude toward death.
4. To explain the Jewish rituals surrounding death, burial, and mourning, the rationale and wisdom inherent in these observances.
5. To establish a feeling of trust so children will open up and ask questions.
6. To help children develop mentally healthy ways of coping with separation experiences.
7. To help children to reach out to peers who experience death and grief.

PREPARING TO TEACH ABOUT DEATH

Before dealing with the subject of death in the classroom, we must be comfortable ourselves with the topic. Any anxiety we feel will be conveyed to the youngsters we teach. It is essential to deal matter-of-factly with the students, answering their questions, relieving their fears, and acknowledging difficult areas. It might be helpful to talk over your own feelings with a relative, friend, Rabbi, or colleague before beginning to teach about death.

The first step, when getting ready to teach death, is to read the literature on death and death education and to keep current with it. It is also helpful to attend classes and workshops when they are offered in the congregation or community, at a junior college, a hospital or medical school. Next, it is important to familiarize yourself with Jewish teachings and customs. Besides the *Encyclopaedia Judaica*, two excellent sources are: *The Jewish Way in Death and Mourning* by Lamm and *Jewish Reflections on Death* by Reimer. You will also want to read and analyze the available teaching units for Jewish schools and to preview videos on the subject. The complete citations for the resources above, as well as many others, and a listing of some of the videos on the subject may be found in the Bibliography at the conclusion of this chapter.

Before beginning a unit on death, it is a wise idea to inform parents of your intentions. This may be done by letter, but is best accomplished at a meeting. Make the arrangements for such a get-together in cooperation with your Director of Education and Rabbi, both of whom should be present. Approach the contact with parents in a positive way, assuming that they will be supportive. For the most part, they will be. Describe the course material and give parents a chance to ask questions and to calm their own anxieties. Suggest ways that they can reinforce the learning at home. Give them a few well chosen references and some excerpts from books by Rabbi Earl A. Grollman. Stress the importance of keeping the subject open and of answering their childrens' questions truthfully. A course on death can be a significant aid in opening communication between parent and child and in encouraging a frank discussion of death. Parents need to understand their role as a positive force in helping their children adjust to the realities of life.

Later on, if possible, schedule at least one class for parents alone and also include them in a session with their children.

Rabbi Gerald M. Kane[2] has found that some parents are resistant to having their children learn about death in Religious School. To counter this view, he suggests holding a regularly scheduled (annual or biennial) parent workshop, to be held while school is in session. The library, he believes, is a good setting for such a gathering. The workshop can be conducted by the librarian. A Rabbi or a Jewish helping professional could be on hand to help parents feel comfortable with the topic. Kane believes that by announcing such a workshop as an ongoing activity and by holding it in a non-threatening place, we are able to take the stigma off the subject. This arrangement sends a clear message that, like sex education, this topic is an appropriate one for parents and children to discuss.

Be aware of, and sensitive to, any problems among class members such as a recent death in a family. In these cases, talk to a parent or relative to see how you can most help the child. Assess how to include the child in the discussions without causing discomfort. The best way to handle such a situation is in conference with the student. Ask if he or she wants to talk about it. Convey a message of care and help the child to face the irreversibility of death and to deal with the guilt or anger that often surrounds the death of a loved one. However, don't probe or insist on responses or participation from any member of the class. Let each child determine his/her level of involvement.

With all students, it may be necessary to create distance between them and the subject and to avoid personalizing the content, as we do in other courses. Be calm yourself and monitor the anxiety level of the group by asking students what is going on for them.[3]

Try to establish a climate of sensitivity to the feelings of others and an atmosphere of trust before you begin teaching about death. Help students learn to listen to each other and to avoid putting each other down (see Chapter 13, "Listening Skills, Lecture, and Discussion.") You will find the effort worthwhile to establish a sense of community in the classroom, helping students to be more caring toward their classmates and more understanding of each other's views. (For a series of exercises to accomplish this, see Chapter 1, "Creating Community in the Classroom.") Finally, be accepting and non-judgmental yourself regarding the questions students ask and the opinions they express. It is only by responding in this manner that the necessary climate of openness and trust can be built. Don't hesitate to give your own ideas, but be sure students know that these are your views and that other opinions can also be valid.

OUTLINING THE COURSE

Once you have made up your mind on what you will include in your course and have done your research, decide on the time frame for the course and list age appropriate sub-topics. Let students help you do this by submitting their questions anonymously. Their participation can aid you significantly in formulating the course. Identify resources for the classroom, including books, audiovisual materials, guest speakers (a Rabbi, Minister, psychologist, social worker, funeral director, etc.) and potential field trip sites (cemetery, funeral home, Holocaust memorial, etc.). Then determine your objectives.

The following objectives are reprinted with permission from the Leader Guide for the mini-course *Death, Burial & Mourning in the Jewish Tradition* (A.R.E. Publishing, Inc.)

Cognitive Objectives:

Students will be able to:
1. describe and explain the Jewish customs relating to death, burial, and mourning.
2. compare Jewish death, burial, and mourning rituals and traditions with those of several other cultures.
3. differentiate between traditional and liberal Jewish practices in regard to death, burial, and mourning.
4. describe the emotions which accompany bereavement — grief, anger, disbelief, and guilt.
5. summarize the Jewish views of life after death.
6. give examples of the reverence for life that the Jewish tradition espouses.

Affective Objectives:

Students will be able to:
1. relate their anxieties about death.
2. show awareness that death is a natural part of the life cycle.
3. describe their own experiences with death — pets, nature, friends, relatives.
4. present in writing and discussion their own feelings about death and dying.
5. express the humaneness and psychological soundness of the Jewish rituals associated with death burial and mourning.

The book *Death out of the Closet* by Stanford and Perry provides an excellent list of objectives for death education in the areas of attitudes toward death, the personal experience of death (survival, the process of dying, grief), death rites and rituals, social and ethical issues, death and the humanities, immortality and the hereafter, and death and science. Consult this extensive list if you need help preparing your objectives.

Next, write your course outline, decide on the methods of presentation and on appropriate activities and exercises for each sub-topic. Many excellent activities can be found in the next section of this chapter, and in *Death out of the Closet*, in *Thanatopics: Activities and Exercises for Confronting Death* by Knott, and in *The Chain of Life: A Curricular Guide for Teaching about Death, Bereavement and the Jewish Way of Honoring the Dead* by Isaacs, Arlen, and Wagner. *Thanatopics* features introductory exercises, values clarification and affective experiences, exercises that require pencil and paper, and role plays. Each is followed by instructions for debriefing. *The Chain of Life* addresses many questions children have when a loved one dies, as well as customs surrounding death and mourning. These discussions are follwed by activities, but no age level is specified for these.

The introductory activity you choose will set the tone for the course. There are many interesting ways to get into the subject of death. These include asking questions, sharing thoughts and feelings, using a questionnaire, discussing population statistics, reading a quotation or passage from a novel or poem (such as the one quoted at the beginning of this chapter), watching a video, making a collage or lifeline, comparing plant and animal cycles. You might discuss what would happen if no one ever died. Or, from a list of words such as loss, pain, evil, joy, beautiful, gone, unexpected, peace, nothingness, etc., ask which words students associate with death. Compare choices, analyze the percentage of positive and negative words chosen, talk about euphemisms for death, etc.

Now you are ready to choose the other readings and materials you will use and to decide on the videos you will show. Determine which, if any, guest speakers to invite. Decide if you will include one of the field trips you identified earlier.

Do your time budgeting now. Estimate how long each segment of the course will take and adjust your outline to fit your allotted time frame. Allow plenty of time for open discussion — don't over program. Finally, write good discussion questions, plan lectures, and organize student materials. Order videos and invite guest speakers. Give a lot of thought to closure. You will want to end on an upbeat note, affirming life and its joys and the beauty of the Jewish tradition.

Finally, decide on a method of evaluation. Design opportunities for further study and enrichment, either for the class or on an individual basis. You are now ready to teach the course.

In the next section we will discuss in brief the attitudes of children of various ages toward death. Some teaching strategies, a few age appropriate books, and, where applicable, a listing of teaching units will round out the chapter.

THE CHILD FROM 3-6
View of Death

At ages three to six, death is not understood by children as a final separation. They often believe they are responsible when a death occurs. If they are good, they think, death will not occur. Children of this age often mourn without showing it.

Teaching Strategies

1. Care for pets in the classroom. When pets die, reassure children that they are not responsible, that death just happens and that it is part of nature. Tell them we don't know why the animal dies — we can only guess. If they feel guilty about the death, reassure them that they can do better in the future. Don't replace the pet immediately. Offer sympathy and let the children grieve. Let them touch the dead bird or pet if they wish to do so.
2. Bury a dead pet. Make a marker for the grave, sing songs, plant flowers, and encourage the children to talk about their feelings. Help them to do so by making such statements as, "I will miss our gerbil," "He was our friend," "Our gerbil will never come back — he is dead." "What are some good things you remember about our animal?"
3. Point out flowers that are dying. Touch them. Crumble dead leaves. Draw the leaves and flowers.
4. Grow and observe plants.
5. Draw pictures of animals alive and dead.
6. Use a flannelboard to tell stories of an animal's life.
7. Read books about animals that die, such as *The Tenth Good Thing about Barney* by Viorst. (For other age appropriate books, see the Bibliography.)

THE CHILD FROM 7-9
View of Death

Children of this age are aware that death is final for all living things. They associate death with the disintegration of the body, and are curious about what happens to the body. (When they ask, it is all right to say you don't know.) They also tend to personalize death as a ghost, bogeyman, or skeleton. They begin to question the cause of death. Between seven and nine, children think of death as mostly for old people, but they are beginning to understand that it could happen to adults like their parents, and possibly even to children as well.

Teaching Strategies
1. Caring for and observing pets is still one of the best ways to introduce the subject of death. Keep a pet in the classroom. See items #1 and 2 under the teaching strategies for ages 3-6 above for details.
2. Write an epitaph for a pet that died.
3. Discuss and tell stories about the cycles in nature — birth, death, the seasons.
4. Go on nature walks. Take photographs, then make bulletin boards and collages.
5. Do nature experiments — look at plants under a microscope.
6. Talk about the death of a public figure. Discuss the person's life and how he/she affected the children's lives.
7. Talk about grandparents. Invite them to class. Reminisce about those who have died.
8. Do art projects using various media.
9. Sing folk songs, such as "Go Tell Aunt Rhody."
10. Read and report on books about death. (For age appropriate books, see the Bibliography.)

THE CHILD FROM 10-12
View of Death

By the age of ten, children have completed the basic development of their concepts of time, space, quantity, and causality. Most understand death as final and inevitable, but they fantasize an alternative to death, such as an afterlife.

Teaching Strategies
1. Discuss death and decay as part of the natural life cycle. Study what happens to small animals when they die.
2. Do Rank Orders, such as the following: A favorite pet of yours has a very bad (and very painful) disease. Would you let it die naturally, have it put to sleep, or ask to have its body frozen in the hope of some medical breakthrough?
3. Identify with characters in books and stories (see Bibliography for age appropriate titles).
4. Watch *The Day Grandpa Died,* a dated but appropriate film about a boy of this age.
5. Conduct an interview to find out what the Rabbi does when notified of the death of a member of the congregation.
6. Survey parents on such questions as: Should children attend funerals? Should they be allowed to visit cemeteries? Should flowers be permitted at a Jewish funeral? Should *Kaddish* be recited if there has not been a death in the family?
7. Study the Hebrew terms associated with death — e.g., *Aninut, Avelut, Avelim, Alav HaShalom, Alehah HaShalom, Chevrah Kaddisha, Hesped, Kaddish, Keriah, Matzayvah, Seudat Havra-ah, Shiva, Sh'loshim, Vidui, Yahrzeit, Yizkor.*
8. Involve youngsters in role play. Do it in small groups so they will be comfortable.
9. Write stories and poetry about death, then illustrate them.
10. Do research and write a report on death.
11. Write a condolence letter, real or imaginary, to someone who has experienced a death.

> **OLDER CHILDREN LONG TO TALK ABOUT DEATH.**

Teaching Unit
Death, Burial & Mourning in the Jewish Tradition by Audrey Friedman Marcus; Sherry Bissell; and Karen S. Lipschutz.

THE CHILD FROM AGE 13 UP
View of Death

Young people of this age sense the personal meaning of death. This often leads to a fuller appreciation of life. They may have difficulty applying fears about death in a personal way. They long to talk about death, to share feelings and anxieties.

Teaching Strategies

1. Role play in small groups. Some excellent situations are found in *Death out of the Closet*, page 60.
2. Write condolence letters to real or imaginary individuals who have experienced the death of a close family member.
3. Communicate an early childhood experience with death through writing or art.
4. Determine how attitudes have changed over the centuries in regard to death and immortality.
5. Have a dialogue with death.
6. Read Jewish fiction on the subject of death, such as the book of Job, *The Diary of Anne Frank*, books by Elie Wiesel, the novel *Exodus* by Uris, and short stories, such as "Silent Bontche" by I.L. Peretz.
7. Compare the style and content of obituaries. Rewrite them more appropriately. Have each student write his/her own obituary as if he or she were to die suddenly, listing any unique accomplishments that are worthy of being remembered.
8. Have each student write his/her own epitaph, summarizing their life and expressing how they would like to be remembered. This exercise can help students identify what is important to them and can serve as a stimulus for goal setting in their lives. (Students enjoy hearing W.C. Fields' epitaph: "On the whole I'd rather be in Philadelphia.")
9. Study death, burial, and mourning customs in other cultures. View films on the subject, such as *The Parting*.
10. Read poetry about death. (For good examples from secular literature, see *Death out of the Closet*, pages 92-94.) Then have students write their own poems about death, either as a class or individually.
11. Look up secular and Jewish quotations about death. Collect these in a notebook. Then have students write their own pithy statements and add them to the collection.
12. Visit a cemetery. Make tombstone rubbings.
13. Interview clergy from various faiths about death.
14. Have students outline a *Magen David*. In each of the six points, have them make a drawing to represent their response to the following six questions or statements. (This can be a very heavy exercise and should be used only with older high school students and adults and only when you are sure the group can handle it.)
    a. If you were to die right now, what do you think your friends would miss most about you?
    b. Think of something about which you feel strongly, something for which you would be willing to give you life.
    c. What was the closest you ever came to losing your life?
    d. Think of someone who was close to you who died. What do you miss most about that person?
    e. What are you doing to help yourself to live a long, healthy life?
    f. Imagine that you have one year left to live. What would you do in that year? Share students' responses in small groups then ask for volunteers to share with the whole class. Be sure to be supportive of the thoughts and feelings that emerge.
15. Analyze death as it is "described" in classical music. Listen to a Requiem by Mozart or Verdi, "Juliet's Death" from *Romeo and Juliet* by Prokofief, *Kaddish Symphony* by Leonard Bernstein.
16. Ask students to bring in the lyrics from popular songs which talk about death. Discuss and compare the songs.
17. Watch and discuss the trigger film *The Corridor: Death*.
18. Discuss the attitudes toward death found in such movies as *My Life, Brian's Song,* and *West Side Story*. Also, analyze death as shown on TV.
19. Study the funeral business. Interview a mortician, a salesperson, an embalmer. Visit a funeral home. Discuss the revival of the *Chevrah Kaddisha*. Read and discuss *The American Way of Death* by Mitford.
20. Discuss preparing for death — wills, organ banks, life insurance, living wills.
21. Discuss and research related topics, such as the causes of death, suicide, aging, "small deaths" (separations such as divorce, moving, breaking up), euthanasia, the right to life, cryogenics, cremation, autopsies, and the legal issues surrounding death — brain death, Right To Die Laws, living wills, etc.

(For age appropriate books, see the Bibliography.)

Teaching Units
Death, Burial & Mourning in the Jewish Tradition by Audrey Friedman Marcus; Sherry Bissell; and Karen S. Lipschutz.

CONCLUSION

We are models for children in coping with painful experiences. Children can acquire a fear of death by observing the behavior of fearful adults. Thus it is vital that we deal with death realistically and that we answer our students' questions simply and factually, using the correct words. We must avoid comparing death with sleep or referring to a journey. Such comparisons may cause children to be afraid. Nor should we tell children that God wanted the person and that's why he/she died. Such a statement can lead to a resentment of God. In our attitudes — and even in the tone of voice we use — we must be calm, sympathetic, and warm when discussing this sensitive subject.

Shielding children from the realities of death can stand in the way of emotional growth. The efforts we make to help the youngsters we teach understand and accept death as natural, inevitable and irreversible can have an important impact on their healthy adjustment to life.

Audrey Friedman Marcus received her Masters Degree in Jewish Education from the Rhea Hirsch School of Hebrew Union College-Jewish Institute of Religion. She is the co-author of *Death, Burial and Mourning in the Jewish Tradition* (A.R.E. Publishing, Inc.)

NOTES

1. From *A Coney Island of the Mind* by Lawrence Ferlinghetti (N.Y.: New Directions Books), pp. 88 and 89.
2. Gerald M. Kane, "Teaching Children about Death and Dying" *Compass* 15 (3): 16-17, Spring-Summer 1993.
3. Gene Stanford and Deborah Perry, *Death out of the Closet.* (New York: Bantam Books, 1976), pp. 18, 21, 23.

BIBLIOGRAPHY

For Adults

Brener, Anne. *Mourning & Mitzvah: A Guided Journal for Walking the Mourner's Path through Grief to Healing.* Woodstock, VT: Jewish Lights Publishing, 1993.

Grollman, Earl A. *Concerning Death: A Practical Guide.* Boston: Beacon Press, 1974.

———. *Explaining Death to Children.* Boston: Beacon Press, 1989.

Harlow, Jules. *The Bond of Life.* New York: Rabbinical Assembly of America, United Synagogue of Conservative Judaism, 1983.

Isaacs, Ronald H., and Kerry M. Olitzky. *The Jewish Mourners' Handbook.* Hoboken, NJ: Ktav Publishing House, 1991.

Kane, Gerald M. "Teaching Children about Death and Dying." *Compass* 15 (3): 16-17, Spring-Summer 1993.

Kay, Alan A. *The Jewish Book of Comfort for Mourners.* Northvale, NJ: Jason Aronson Inc., 1993.

Knott, J. Eugene, et al. *Thanatopics: Activities and Exercises for Confronting Death.* New York: Free Press, 1989.

Kolatch, Alfred J. *The Jewish Mourners Book of Why.* Middle Village, NY: Jonathan David Co., 1992.

Lamm, Maurice. *The Jewish Way in Death and Mourning.* Middle Village, NY: Jonathan David Co., 1969.

Mitford, Jessica. *The American Way of Death.* New York: Fawcett Book Group, 1987.

Olitzky, Kerry M.; Steven M. Rosman; and David P. Kasakove. *When Your Child Asks Why: Answers for Tough Questions.* Hoboken, NJ: Ktav Publishing House, 1993.

Riemer, Jack. *Jewish Reflections on Death.* New York: Schocken Books, 1974.

Sonsino, Rifat, and Daniel B. Syme. *What Happens after I Die? Jewish Views of Life after Death.* New York: UAHC Press, 1990.

Stanford, Gene, and Deborah Perry. *Death out of the Closet.* New York: Bantam Books, 1976.

Weiss, Abner. *Death and Bereavement: A Halakhic Guide.* Hoboken, NJ: Ktav Publishing House, 1991.

Wolfson, Ron. *A Time To Mourn and a Time To Comfort.* New York: Federation of Jewish Men's Clubs, 1993.

Curricular Guides

Isaacs, Ron; Susan Arlen; and Richard Wagner. *The Chain of Life: A Curricular Guide for Teaching about Death, Bereavement and the Jewish Way of Honoring the Dead.* New York: Coalition for the Advancement of Jewish Education, 1993.

Marcus, Audrey Friedman; Sherry Bissell; and Karen S. Lipschutz. *Death, Burial and Mourning in the Jewish Tradition.* Minicourse and Leader Guide. Denver: A.R.E. Publishing, Inc., 1976.

Books for Ages 3-6

Aliki. *Go Tell Aunt Rhody.* New York: Macmillan Publishing Co., Inc., 1986.

Brown, Margery W. *The Dead Bird.* New York: Dell Publishing Co., 1979.

Carrick, Carol. *The Accident.* New York: Houghton Mifflin, 1981.

Clifford, Ethan. *The Remembering Box.* New York: Houghton Mifflin, 1985.

Lanton, Sandra. *Daddy's Chair.* Rockville, MD: Kar-Ben Copies, Inc., 1991.

Pomerantz, Barbara. *Bubby, Me and Memories.* New York: UAHC Press, 1983.

Simon, Norma. *The Saddest Time.* Niles, IL: Albert Whitman Co., 1986.

Stein, Sara Bonnett. *About Dying: An Open Family Book for Parents and Children Together.* New York: The Danbury Press, 1974.

Viorst, Judith. *The Tenth Good Thing about Barney.* New York: Atheneum Publishers, Inc., 1971.

Wilhelm, Hans. *I'll Always Love You.* New York: Crown, 1989.

Books for Ages 7-9

Brooks, Jerome. *Uncle Mike's Boy.* New York: Harper & Row, 1973.

Brown, Margery W. *The Dead Bird.* New York: Dell Publishing Co., 1979.

Caseley, Judith. *When Grandpa Came To Stay.* New York: Greenwillow Books, 1986.

Corley, Elizabeth Adam. *Tell Me about Death: Tell Me about Funerals.* Santa Clara, CA: Grammatical Sciences, 1973.

Fassler, Joan. *My Grandpa Died Today.* New York: Human Sciences Press, 1983.

Grollman, Earl A. *Talking about Death: A Dialogue Between Parent and Child.* 3d ed. Boston, MA: Beacon Press, 1991.

Krementz, Jill. *How It Feels When a Parent Dies.* New York: Alfred A. Knopf, 1981.

LeShan, Eda. *Learning To Say Good-bye: When a Parent Dies.* New York: Macmillan Child Group, 1976.

Miles, Miska. *Annie and the Old One.* Boston, MA: Little, Brown and, Co., Inc., 1972.

Rosman, Steven M. *Deena and the Damselfly.* New York: UAHC Press, 1992.

Spero, Moshe Halevi. *Zeydeh.* New York: Simcha Publishing Co., 1984.

Techner, David, and Judith Hirt-Manheimer. *A Candle for Grandpa.* New York: UAHC Press, 1993.

Warberg, Sandol. *Growing Time.* New York: Houghton Mifflin, 1975.

White, E.B. *Charlotte's Web.* New York: Harper & Row, 1952.

Books for Ages 10-12

Blue, Rose. *Grandma Didn't Wave Back.* New York: Franklin Watts, 1972.

Blume, Judy. *Tiger Eyes.* Scarsdale, NY: Bradley Press, 1981.

Buck, Pearl. *The Big Wave.* New York: Day, 1984.

Clark, Brian. *Whose Life Is It Anyway?* New York: Avon Books, 1978.

Grollman, Sharon. *Shira: A Legacy of Courage.* New York: Doubleday, 1988.

Kay. Alan. *The Red in My Father's Beard.* Instant Lesson. Los Angeles: Torah Aura Productions, 1992.

———. *Pebbles on a Stone.* Instant Lesson. Los Angeles: Torah Aura Productions, 1993.

LeShan, Eda. *Learning To Say Good-bye: When a Parent Dies.* New York: Macmillan Child Group, 1976.

Mellonie, Bryan, and Robert Ingpen. *Lifetimes.* New York: Bantam Books, 1983.

Rofes, Eric E. *The Kids Book about Death and Dying, by and for Kids.* Boston: Little, Brown & Co., Inc., 1985.

Smith, Doris Buchanon. *A Taste of Blackberries.* New York: Thomas Y. Crowell, 1973.

Books for Ages 13 up

Agee, James. *A Death in the Family.* New York: Avon, 1971.

Beckman, Gunnel. *Admission to the Feast.* New York: Dell, 1973.

Blinn, William. *Brian's Song.* New York: Bantam Books, 1983.

Caine, Lynn. *Widow.* New York: Bantam Books, 1987.

Girion, Barbara. *A Tangle of Roots.* New York: Scribners, 1979.

Graven, Margery. *I Heard the Owl Call My Name.* Garden City, NY: Dell, 1980.

Greenberg, Jan. *A Season in Between.* Boston: Houghton Mifflin, 1977.

Grollman, Earl. *Straight Talk about Death for Teenagers: How To Cope with Losing Someone You Love.* Boston: Beacon Press, 1993.

Gunther, John. *Death Be Not Proud.* New York: Harper and Brothers, 1989.

Ish-Kishor, Sulamith. *Our Eddie.* New York: Alfred A. Knopf, 1992.

Klein, Isaac. *A Time To Be Born, A Time To Die.* New York: Department of Youth Services, United Synagogue of America, 1976.

Spiro, Jack. *A Time To Mourn.* New York: Bloch, 1985.

SUBJECT MATTER

CHAPTER THIRTY-NINE

TEACHING JEWISH CURRENT EVENTS

Linda K. Schaffzin and Stephen Schaffzin

Why teach current events in the Jewish school? After all, the students are probably studying current events in their Social Studies class. Why clutter up an already overcrowded program with yet another subject area? The reasons, we feel, are compelling. The responsible citizen in a participatory democracy such as ours (and Israel's) is one who is aware of issues and events that concern the community. Reading newspapers and magazines is one way to become informed, and the skills necessary to form a "reading the news" habit should be taught early.

There are Jewish values to be imparted through this exercise. In *Pirke Avot,* we are taught, "Do not separate yourself from the community." In a current events sense, this means we should be well informed citizens.

And as Jews we have special concerns: Israel, human rights, energy and conservation, etc. Again, as Jews we feel responsible for one another, and we feel the need to act on behalf of our Jewish community.

Beyond these underlying values are the specific facts, the processes, the history-in-the-making that contribute to our students' Jewish education and their Jewish identification. So how to begin? We would like to suggest two approaches: The Current Events Period and the Integrated Approach.

THE CURRENT EVENTS PERIOD

Most programs set aside a weekly chunk of time for current events. The class reads one or more student publications, or perhaps students are assigned to bring in a clipping and be prepared to discuss it with the class.

There are problems with this method. It is unlikely that everyone in the class will be able to present his/her article and students may start "gambling" on not being called. Often students do little more than read the article to the class. Instead, try these suggestions: For younger children especially, it might be better for you to pick the topic. Pick a newsworthy personality, a place or an issue, such as Mid-East peace talks or church-state issues. Be specific and make sure it is something that appears in the press currently. Ask students to find out all they can, bring in pictures, poll family members about the issue, etc. Use student findings as the basis for an in-depth class discussion the following week.

Another idea: duplicate a political cartoon, map, chart, or other graphic aid. Ask students to read about the issue for a few days. Then discuss. You may find that the simplest information is the most worthy of your class time: the meaning of separation of church and state, the definition of lobby and who has one, the picture of a personality in the news and his/her specific job.

Have students bring in articles and cut off headlines. The class can guess how headlines relate to the articles. Then bring in only headlines. Ask students what they think the article said. Is headline skimming a good way to find out about what is happening?

If you do set aside a specific Current Events Period, you may want to turn to more than your local press and Anglo-Jewish papers (see below for more resources).

THE INTEGRATED CURRENT EVENTS PROGRAM

Another way to deal with current events is the Integrated Current Events Program. This means that instead of isolating current events, they are brought into the teaching of all aspects of your curriculum. For example, current issues and concerns fit in with almost every holiday theme throughout the year:

Rosh HaShanah/Yom Kippur: Use this time to survey events in the year that passed, or judge the world just as we are judged at this time of year.

Chanukah: Deal with the theme of the few against the many (Israel among the Arab nations, status of minority groups, especially Jews, in the U.S. and other countries); or use this time to look at Jews in sports (e.g., Maccabiah from Maccabees as your tie-in).

Tu B'Shevat: This holiday lends itself to the themes of ecology, energy, and conservation in North America, Israel, and the world (also, oil and water policies).

Purim: Examine the status of Jewish communities all over the world.

Pesach: Through the theme of freedom, lead into a unit on Eastern European and Ethiopian Jewry, etc. Examine the relationship between Israel and Egypt today.

Yom HaAtzma'ut: Can be a culmination of a project or concentrated study of Israel in the news.

Yom HaShoah: Study current issues, such as the hunt for war criminals, neo-Nazism, or the activities and views of Holocaust deniers.

Shavuot: Discuss law — civil law vs. religious law in Israel, the rights of Jews according to U.S. or Canadian law. (There are occasional cases of clashes between school systems, companies, or the military and observant Jews. For example, the issue of prayers at public school graduation ceremonies was brought to the Supreme Court by a Rhode Island Jewish family that objected equally to the minister and the Rabbi invited to give an invocation at their daughter's graduation.)

A current events program could also be integrated into the history curriculum. As each event or period is covered, ask students for evidence of current parallels. Or use history to explore an issue in the news. For example, what are the historical events that have led to the formation of the P.L.O. or to the granting of U.S. citizenship to a Swede named Raoul Wallenberg?

Current events might even be taught in Hebrew language class using Hebrew newspapers for children such as *LaMishpaha* (see below for address). Or they could be taught in connection with a Jewish values course. In this instance, an issue such as capital punishment could be examined from the standpoint of its current political relevance, as well as from the Jewish point of view.

RESOURCES

Whether you designate current events time during each session or decide to integrate current events into all areas of your curriculum, you will need resources. The following is a list of some possibilities:

1. Publications written for children: Look for publications geared to students, such as *Shofar* and Noah's Ark. A publication originated by your students may be your best answer. It is accessible, it motivates, and it helps you teach newspaper skills and raise issues.

2. The Anglo-Jewish Press, local editions: Generally speaking, your Anglo-Jewish newspaper can be a good resource if it is used properly. Its greatest value is its news about the local Jewish community. Students should have a sense of that community, its scope, and the services it offers. The columns, editorials, etc., are often syndicated, strongly pro-Israel and pro-Jewish. Your students should understand this. Most Anglo-Jewish papers get their national and world news from the Jewish Telegraphic Agency (see below).

3. National Anglo-Jewish press: There is no national press as such. Most national publications are periodicals, magazines, or newsletters that appear monthly or less frequently. Many are published by organizations and emphasize issue-related feature articles. Often, however, these contain analyses, background features, or articles on personalities that may be of value to you.

4. General press: The students' job will be to use newspaper skills to assimilate content and check out facts in the general press. Students should be taught to read critically. Do not hesitate to have students go to history books to check out facts and figures. Use the letters to the editor column as a reason to check out historical processes and facts. Let students themselves write in to correct faulty statements or counter opposing views.

Many national news magazines and some local newspapers have special student editions, supplements, or teacher guides and aids. Some offer reduced prices if bought in bulk for a class. If the reading level of your students is not up to *U.S. News and World Report,* but you have 10 or 15 teachers in your school, you may want to order in bulk just for the faculty. The addresses of such weeklies may be found at the conclusion of this chapter. Costs and offers change, so be sure to check on current rates.

5. Press releases: Many organizations routinely send out press releases and they are very interesting. The American Jewish Congress, for example, sends out releases about civil suits affecting Jews. The Anti-Defamation League monitors the attitudes and actions of non-Jews toward Jews — e.g., synagogue vandalism and incidents that can be characterized as anti-Semitic. Have each student write to an organization and ask to be put on its mailing list for press releases. Keep a "mail corner" set up in your room. Have school stationery and envelopes, stamps, and pens on hand. Make it as easy as possible for students to write and mail a letter to an organization, Congressperson, embassy, newspaper, etc. A small telephone address book is helpful. Keep updating addresses so there is no delay between student interest and letter writing.

6. Organizational organs: The newspapers, magazines and newsletters that are put out by American Jewish organizations are a good source for news in a given area, e.g., Zionist groups have magazines with fine features on Israel.

7. Jewish Telegraphic Agency (JTA): This syndicate concentrates on national and international Jewish news. A subscription could be purchased for your class or school. It is an excellent way to get all the Jewish news in daily or weekly capsules. While the JTA has a teletype service, their bulletins would be more appropriate for your purposes. There is a daily bulletin, a weekly (which encapsulates the dailies), and a community news reporter which appears weekly, reporting on local and community news, such as awards and appointments. The JTA bulletins are written clearly and are organized well, enabling students to use them easily or enabling you to present the news to the students. If you look at by-lines in your local Jewish paper, you will probably see JTA entries. For addresses see below.

8. Jerusalem Post: This English language weekly is an excellent resource for the Jewish school for current events and for features about life in Israel. We recommend it highly. While it is probably too expensive for each child to subscribe, there should be a few copies for the school, the number depending on the size of the school. A tabloid with news on every aspect of Israeli life (from sports to stock quotations, from editorials to entertainment), most of the news reports will be understandable to your upper elementary and junior high school students. Editorials and analyses are for older readers.

9. The Jerusalem Report: A few years ago, with new ownership, *The Jerusalem Post* took a perceived turn to the political right. New editorial policies and processes led to the disaffection of staff. Many moved to this new left-leaning biweekly magazine. After a rocky start, *The Jerusalem Report* seems to have stabilized; it includes news from Israel on all fronts as well as investigative reporting and features.

THE STUDENT AS JOURNALIST

Youngsters most often understand news best if they are asked to gather and present it themselves. They can see how facts can be fudged or checked out, how imprecise words can be and how powerful the news (and its writers) can seem. The projects need not be enormous. Here are some suggestions:

1. Let each student individually, or with a partner, follow an issue, once a week handing in an update to be included in a class newsletter. Reproduce the newsletter and share it with other classes in the school.

2. Divide the class into groups. Assign each group one period a month to present to the class, grade, or school a news roundup or and in-depth news report (a la "60 Minutes" or "Good Morning America," depending on how sophisticated and critical you feel they can be).

3. Use school-side surveys to stimulate discussion. Choose a "hot" issue and do some background research on it, either as a class or in groups. Devise a survey to see how other people feel about the issue. When the results are in, discuss them. Present the findings to the school.

RESOURCES

4. You can foster an understanding of and relationship to your community through the creation of a community newspaper. Write to local organizations (Synagogues, Jewish Community Centers, etc.), requesting that they notify you of upcoming events that may be of interest to kids (and their parents). Reproduce your newsletter on a monthly basis.
5. Other techniques for involving students in their community or in local, national, and worldwide issues are letter writing (to newspapers, government officials, etc.), debating, interviewing, and inviting informed guests to the classroom.

THE GOALS OF A CURRENT EVENTS PROGRAM

The goals of any current events program are important:
1. The learning of newspaper skills (reading headlines and text critically, deciphering cartoons, maps, charts, etc.)
2. The establishment of the newspaper habit which should lead to:
    a. a feeling of belonging to a community.
    b. a sense of responsibility as a citizen in a participatory democracy.
    c. an understanding of history as it affects current news.

As Jews we have special problems. A few years ago a particularly disturbing letter appeared on the OP-Ed page of *The New York Times*. Its writer, Andrew Fauld, a member of the British Parliament, clearly outlined the position of the United States in relation to the oil producing Arab nations and Israel. He maintained that it was not in the country's best interest to continue its strong support of Israel and that eventually the incumbent president (then Jimmy Carter) would recognize this. He twisted a few "facts" and argued his case well. He advised Carter to forget about Jewish votes and worry about the realities of the world.

Fauld's letter, predictably, met with cries of anti-Semitism from a number of letter writers in the days that followed. Yet, the letter could have been answered unemotionally, factually, and with a strong, rational case for a pro-Israel, U.S. policy. Our goal is to produce students who could argue the issues, who could call on history with understanding, who could assume their role as Jews facing the constantly changing, often bewildering issues of our complicated world.

Linda K. Schaffzin and Stephen Schaffzin have been involved in Jewish children's publications since 1976 when they founded *Levana Monthly*. After six years as co-editors of *World Over Magazine* and three years in Israel while Linda was a Jerusalem Fellow, they are back in Jewish publishing with, among other things, *Footnotes: An Israel Travel Diary* and *Kids' Notes: An Elementary Level Assignment Book for Jewish Day Schools*.

Newspapers and Periodicals for the Jewish School

JEWISH TELEGRAPHIC AGENCY, INC.
330 Seventh Avenue, 11th Floor
New York, NY 10001-5010

THE JERUSALEM POST, INTERNATIONAL EDITION
211 East 43rd Street, Suite 601
New York, NY 10017

THE JERUSALEM REPORT
P.O. Box 580
Mount Morris, IL 61054

LAMISHPAHA ILLUSTRATED HEBREW MONTHLY
47 West 34th Street, Suite 609
New York, NY 10001

NEAR EAST REPORT
440 First Street, NW, Suite 607
Washington, DC 20001

THE NEW YORK TIMES
(800) 631-2500
No school rate. Individual college rate depending upon where the college is located.

NEWSWEEK
(800) 634-6849
Student subscription rate available on orders of 15 or more. That bulk order also entitles the teacher to a multi-media package available in English, English as a second language, or Social Studies format. An order of 15 copies entitles you to teaching aids including maps, quizzes, worksheets, etc.

NOAH'S ARK: A NEWSPAPER FOR JEWISH CHILDREN
8323 Southwest Freeway, Suite 250
Houston, TX 77074

SHOFAR
43 Northcote Dr.
Melville, NY 11747

U.S. NEWS & WORLD REPORT
(800) 523-5948
Student subscription rate available. Each educator receives a personal representative contact to work with on orders, as well as one free educators subscription delivered to home or school. Choice of three free resource materials. Free wall map and almanac. Free weekly teacher's guide.

Organizations for News Releases

THE AMERICAN JEWISH COMMITTEE
165 East 56th Street
New York, NY 10002

THE AMERICAN JEWISH CONGRESS
15 East 84th Street
New York, NY 10028

ANTI-DEFAMATION LEAGUE
823 United Nations Plaza
New York, NY 10019

AMERICAN RED MAGEN DAVID FOR ISRAEL
888 7th Avenue, Suite 403
New York, NY 10016

CONFERENCE OF PRESIDENTS OF MAJOR AMERICAN JEWISH ORGANIZATIONS
110 East 59th Street
New York, NY 10022

CONSULATE GENERAL OF ISRAEL IN NEW YORK
800 Second Avenue
New York, NY 10017

ZIONIST ORGANIZATION OF AMERICA
4 East 34th Street
New York, NY 20016

IN CONCLUSION

CHAPTER FORTY

STUDENT ASSESSMENT: A REWARDING EXPERIENCE

Norman J. Fischer

Strange as it may seem, student assessment, when done properly, can be a rewarding experience for both teacher and student. It can also serve to motivate a student to higher achievement. However, this can only be accomplished if you are willing to treat assessment as a process, an integral part of each lesson, and not as a "necessary evil" for the purpose of grading at the end of a unit.

What follows is an explanation of the assessment process, some of its advantages, and specific assessment techniques. (If you hate theory and are only interested in the "down and dirty," you may skip to the section "Final Step: Choosing the Right Instrument.")

WHY ASSESS STUDENTS?

There are two very good reasons for a teacher to assess students. The first is obvious but sometimes overlooked; the second is important to know.

1. After all is said and done, the primary purpose of assessment is to determine if you have achieved the educational goals of your school. You have been hired to teach the children, and accountability requires evidence that they have learned the material.
2. Research has shown that within a significant number of effective schools, there is a system for frequent monitoring of student progress.

Therefore, if it is your wish to be effective, i.e., that the students learn what your program requires (#2), it is a very good idea to develop a process of assessment (#1).

WHERE DO I BEGIN?

First and foremost, you must be clear as to the difference between formative and summative assessment. Formative assessment is conducted while the class is "in progress" in order to decide how well *you are doing*. Summative assessment is done at the end of a unit or course, in order to grade the students and judge how well *you did*.[1] Most of us concentrate on summative assessment, yet it is the formative "in progress" assessment that is crucial, especially when considered in terms of the theory of Mastery Learning as proposed by Benjamin Bloom.[2]

Bloom states that the difference among students is not so much their *level* of achievement as their *rate* of learning. Using a variety of formative "in progress" assessments to detect flaws early on ensures that a student is brought to mastery *before* proceeding to the next area of study. When time for the summative assessment roles around, it is not the traumatic experience of a student being "drilled and killed," but a rewarding experience for the teacher who sees the fruits of his/her labor and perhaps more importantly, for the student, who realizes that he/she has made significant progress (and actually learned something!).

Step 1: What Do I Need To Know?

Always remember the following: (1) the key to effective assessment is the match between the task and the intended outcome, (2) the criteria of acceptable performance (C.A.P.) is critical, and (3) assessment design is dependent on the assessment purpose.[3]

Simply stated, if you have properly prepared your student objectives, which cover steps 1 and 2, step 3 becomes clear. What does it take to write a performance objective? Nothing more than knowing your ABC's.

A is for AUDIENCE e.g., The students in sixth grade.

B is for BEHAVIOR e.g., The students in sixth grade will explain some differences between Jacob and Esau.

C is for CONDITIONS e.g., After reading the story of the selling of the birthright, the students in sixth grade will explain some differences between Jacob and Esau.

D is for DEGREE e.g., After reading the story of the selling of the birthright, the students in the sixth grade will explain three differences between Jacob and Esau.

That's all there is to it! You've got your outcomes, you know your C.A.P., you're teaching the lesson. You can now use "in progress" assessments and watch your students achieve. (You'll know if your performance objective is well written if you think of yourself as a substitute teacher and ask yourself the question, "Can I teach from this?")

> Remember student assessment is part of the teaching process, *NOT* the end of it.

Next Step: What Do I Need To Answer?

Consider these questions:

1. Do the *tasks match the important outcomes?*
2. Will the tasks be *meaningful and engaging* so students will be motivated to show their capabilities?
3. Do the tasks *require the kinds of knowledge and skills* that are taught in my class?
4. Do the tasks *include a C.A.P.?*
5. Are the tasks *developmentally appropriate?*
6. Have the students had *sufficient opportunity to learn* what is included?
7. How *many similar tasks* must a student perform in order for me to make a decision?
8. Are any of my tasks *measuring two skills at once* (e.g., asking a content question in Hebrew necessitating a student understanding the Hebrew before addressing the question itself)?
9. Are the tasks *feasible* in terms of time, space, etc.?
10. Is the test *Criterion-Referenced or Norm-Referenced?*

    What, you may be wondering, are Criterion-Referenced and Norm-Referenced tests?

Criterion-Referenced tests:
- are Pass/Fail
- are not scaled
- contain basic knowledge everyone must know
- are scored against a standard or criterion (your C.A.P.)
- contain questions or skills students should be able to answer or perform

Non-Referenced tests:
- are graded (A, B, C, etc.)
- may be scaled
- are designed to spread out scores, with not everyone having to know everything
- are scored against the "norm" of the group
- contain questions or skills that approximately one half of the students should be able to answer or perform

The difficulty with Norm-Referenced tests is that they merely rank students, yet those receiving A's may, in reality, not be able to perform well enough in relation to a C.A.P. Conversely, all the students may have met your C.A.P., yet by definition, some receive A's, others C's.[4]

If you expected outcomes are definite achievement criteria (C.A.P.), then you should be using a Criterion-Referenced format.

> A good way to validate your testing, instrument is to ask a colleague: "What do you think this assessment measures?"

When you are able to answer the above questions which related to assessment design, (1) you are an expert judge of your students' progress, (2) you are in a position to help them improve, (3) you have provided a means by which they will feel good about themselves and their accomplishments, and (4) you've covered yourself in terms of parents and other consumers to whom you may be accountable.

What, you ask, does this have to do with student assessment? Simply, frequent student monitoring with valid instruments provides ample and accurate documentation concerning

a student's progress. Documentation is important because:
1. it enables you to detect reoccurring patterns.
2. it provides you with a total picture of a student's overall growth.
3. it gives you recorded results so you don't rely on "memories."[5]

Documentation is also important because: Whatever you say in parent conferences or in other discussions pertaining to a specific student, you are able to support with evidence, facts related to the specifics of your class requirements (see how important C.A.P. is!).

> Frequent monitoring with properly developed assessment instruments:
> 1. enables the school to achieve its educational goals.
> 2. enables students to achieve and feel good about their accomplishments.
> 3. enables you to be an effective teacher (and a confident communicator).

What if I'm dealing with Affective Behaviors? (How can I tell how the student *feels* about . . . ?) The most frustrating aspect of assessing personal or social development is setting your C.A.P. Once you know what to look for, assessment in this area is not difficult at all. Here are four distinct levels of affective behavior. These range from simply responding, to personal choice, to commitment.[6] Use these as points of reference in developing your own criteria.

LEVEL 1 — The student is aware of, or *passively* attends to, certain activities.

LEVEL 2 — The student *complies* with given expectations, *obeying* or participating as expecting.

LEVEL 3 — The student consistently displays *behavior* in situations in which the student is *not forced* to comply or obey, displaying a high degree of certainty and conviction.

LEVEL 4 — The student is *committed* to a set of values, making judgments and determining relationships based on this value system

What about Psychomotor Behavior? (What kind of C.A.P. will apply to a student's physical development?) Here, too, four levels are provided, ranging from mere imitation to complete spontaneity.[7]

LEVEL 1 — The student *imitates* the action demonstrating the capacity to repeat it, yet often lacking coordination or control.

LEVEL 2 — The student performs the action according to *instruction* and *direction*, though additional practice is necessary.

LEVEL 3 — The student performs the action *independent* of a model or a set of directions with few errors in *accuracy, control, and exactness*.

LEVEL 4 — The student demonstrates a high level of proficiency involving *accuracy* and *control plus elements of speed and time*, a *routine* that is *automatic* and *spontaneous*.

Final Step: Choosing the Right Instrument

There are a great many assessment tools from which a teacher may choose. The following are generic techniques which can be adapted to most any teaching format or structure. whether it is a supplementary or a day school. Depending upon your specific situation, one technique may serve you better than another. For this reason, always remember the limitations and needs of the students you are assessing and adapt accordingly. What is important is that you have enough tools at your disposal from which to make the right choice as to which instrument will best meet your criteria.

FORMATIVE (IN-PROGRESS) ASSESSMENTS
Signaled Answers

Pose a question or statement and have every student signal the answer. Examples:

"Look at the first multiple choice question. Decide which answer you would select and when I say 'Show me,' place the number of fingers under your chin."

"Raise your hand each time you hear (or see) an example of _____."

USE THESE EFFECTIVE WAYS TO DO FORMATIVE EVALUATION.

These techniques allow you to get an overall picture of the level of understanding of the entire class *before* moving on to the next topic. Also, it is best to accompany each response with an explanation as to *why* it is correct. This will clarify the response even further as well as help those who were in doubt about the answer.

Choral Responses

Ask the group a question and get a choral response. The strength as well as the correctness of the response can assist a teacher in knowing whether most students know the answer. Choral responses also help a student who does not know the correct answer to now learn it.

Sample Individual Response

Pose a question to the whole class. Based on the stratum of your class, call on specific students. If a bright student is confused, you might infer that most of the students do not understand. If a slower student responds correctly, you may conclude that it is time to move on.

A second way of sampling individual responses is to require students to write a *brief response*. While they are writing, you can circulate to see if the majority have succeeded in learning the material. You can also select responses to present to the class. This will add variety and increase everyone's understanding.[8]

Questioning

Perhaps the most overlooked, yet most effective, means of "in progress" assessment is questioning. Here's how to handle this type of assessment:

1. Distribute questions so that *many* are encouraged to speak.
2. Balance the kinds of questions and do not ask an inference or assessment question until you have "worked up the ladder."
3. Encourage students to give lengthy responses. Ask questions that require such answers.
4. Allow students ample time to think over the question. (*Do not answer your own question.*)
5. Ask clear and coherent questions. (Do not ask multiple questions as one.)
6. Encourage student-to-student interaction.
7. Ask questions that cannot be answered merely with a "yes" or "no."
8. Ask questions *before* calling on a student to respond.
9. Focus on the trigger or action verb used to describe the problem.

In measuring Thinking Skills, in the classroom, the following can be used.[9]

If you want to measure	Use these key words in the exercise
Recall	define, repeat, identify, what, label, when, list, who, name
Analysis	subdivide, categorize, break down, sort, separate
Comparison	compare, differentiate, contrast, distinguish
Influence	deduce, anticipate, predict, what if..., infer, apply, speculate, conclude

If you want to measure	Use these key words in the exercise
Evaluation	evaluate, argue, judge, recommend, appraise, debate, defend, why, critique

Lapboards

Students are given a question, and asked to write down their answers and hold up their boards. You can see at a glance if everyone has mastered the material and can decide where to proceed next.[10]

Note Taking

When note-taking, have students rule their page as in figure 1.

Capture	Key Word
Questions	

Figure 1

1. In the large upper left section, students "Capture" information from the book, lecture, or class discussion.
2. At regular intervals stop the students and ask them to review their notes.
3. Have the students extract the main ideas and write them as single words or simple phrases in the "Key Word" column.
4. Move around the room and check the columns. This will tell you if the main ideas are understood.
5. Have the students examine the "Capture" information and the "Key Words" and figure out what questions are answered. Ask them to write those questions in the lower left section.
6. While students work on formulating their questions, move around the room to monitor and assist.
7. These questions can be used as homework, starting the next class, review, or even as your summative assessment.
8. The small section in the lower right hand corner is for doodling.[11]

Papers

Assign short papers of one to five pages so that you are able to return them promptly with immediate feedback. Your purpose is to tell students what they need to learn; grades merely tell a student if the paper was acceptable.

Observation of Performance

For learning that can be measured only by direct observation of performance, that performance becomes the test to be assessed. The Criteria for Acceptable Performance (C.A.P.) needs to be made explicit so that feedback can be specific.[12]

Learning Centers

In a learning center students can learn something new, practice something already taught, or develop their own creativity. Learning centers contain materials used to organize instruction so that students learn independently with self-direction rather than teacher-direction. A learning center may contain:
   sorting or matching activities
   dials and spinners
   contracts
   games
   puzzles
   writing assignments
   manipulative devices
   assignment pockets
   resource materials
   audio visual equipment
(For more learning centers, see Chapter 16, "Classroom Learning Centers.")

Contracts or Checklists

Using contracts or checklists, students mark off specific learning goals as they are attained. This tends to minimize competitiveness and enables teachers to individualize work assignments and learning goals.

SUMMATIVE (AT THE END) ASSESSMENTS

Student Self-Assessment: Rating Scales

Before teaching a lesson, you pose the question, "How will we know if we have learned . . . ?" and the class decides on the C.A.P. After the lesson, the students vote to determine if they met their C.A.P. They may rate themselves either individually or as a group.

Self-assessment can become an ongoing activity expanding into many learning areas (even parent-teacher conferences). A key element is the trust built up between students and teachers. It is encouraging to students to know that the teacher values their opinions and ideas.[13]

Portfolio Assessment

When students maintain portfolios of their work, they learn to assess their own progress as learners. Many assessment techniques actually prevent students from becoming constructive judges of their own work.

The following process for motivating students to produce high-quality work is recommended. It is based upon the work of William Glasser.

1. *You ask the students to describe the quality of work to be done and the resources needed to do it.* More specifically, students develop a C.A.P. equating to "great," "good," or "fair." (When it is *their* criteria for good work students can no longer "get off the hook" by claiming they did not know what was expected of them.)
2. *You and students provide clear models of the work to be done.* Students should ask themselves, "Am I done? Does my work meet the standards? How can I make my work better?" You can help students improve by referring to the students' own criteria.
3. *You provide the students with the resources necessary to produce high quality work.* These resources include supportive conferences, skill-building activities, leading questions, praise, and time to practice and think. You must suspend judgment during the process and give students the time they need.

Students need to maintain their own portfolios and continually assess their own work as they produce it. This approach requires that they understand *in advance* what good work is, eliminating the need for students to "guess" what you require.[14]

Written Tests

When giving written tests, it is wise to limit the amount of writing permitted. One sentence, one paragraph, or a one page answer requires very clear understanding. This gives you less to correct and leaves no question as to the student's compensation. In addition, it sets a premium on quality rather than quantity. When using short-answer tests, do the following:

1. Develop criteria for and an outline of a good response, based upon the aspects of critical thinking you wish to assess and on the grade level being tested.
2. When grading a student's response, first read the whole short answer without assigning a grade, in order to get an overview or sense of the student's response. Then reread it, applying the criteria you have developed.
3. Do not allow such things as legibility, grammar, or spelling influence your judgment of students' critical thinking; remember what you are testing.
4. If students' responses differ from the ideal response, try to discern why. Do not mark responses merely right or wrong as in multiple-choice tests, and be open to legitimate alternative responses.

CONCLUSION

What you have here is the briefest of introductions to the assessment process and just some of the many techniques which can be used. Experiment. See what works best for you and your students. If you find that your summative assessments are easy to grade because just about all the answers are correct and your students come away saying, "It was long, but I can't believe how much I knew" — you're on the right track.

Norman J. Fischer received his MFA in Drama from the University of Houston, and is completing his Ed.D. at the University of Alabama at Birmingham. He is currently the Principal of the Community Talmud Torah in Denver, Colorado, and Judaic Consultant to the Rocky Mountain Hebrew Academy, a day school for Grades 7-12.

NOTES

1. Leonard H. Clark and Irving S. Starr, *Secondary and Middle School Teaching Methods* (New York: Macmillan Publishing Co., 1986), p. 348.
2. Pamela R. Aschbacher; Joan L. Herman; and Lynn Winters, *A Practical Guide to Alternative Assessment* (Alexandria, VA: ASCD, 1992).
3. Ibid., pp. 109-110.
4. Cindy J. Christopher, *Nuts and Bolts: Survival Guide for Teachers* (Lancaster, PA: Technomic Publishing Co., Inc., 1992), p. 70.
5. Adapted from the work of Benjamin Bloom.
6. Madeline Hunter, *Mastery Teaching*. El Segundo, CA: TIP, 1982), pp. 59-61.
7. Edys Quellmalz, Evelyn Rubel, and Richard J. Stiggins, *Measuring Classroom Skills in the Classroom* (U.S.A.: NEA, 1988), p. 19.
8. Marilyn Finesilver and Delores K. Solovy, "Evaluation Techniques for the Jewish Classroom," *The Pedagogic Reporter*, September 1985, p. 15.
9. Judy Olson, *Learner Responsibility* (Dubuque, IA: Kendall-Hunt Publishing Co., 1990), pp. 58-61.
10. Hunter, op. cit., p. 62.
11. Finesilver, op. cit., pp. 15-16.
12. Scott Willis, "Quality by Design through Portfolios," *ASCD Update*, October 1993.

BIBLIOGRAPHY

Archibald, D.A., and F.M. Newmann. *Beyond Standardized Testing: Assessing Authentic Achievement in the Secondary School.* Reston, VA: National Association of Secondary School Principals, 1988.

Christopher, Cindy J. *Nuts and Bolts: Survival Guide for Teachers.* Lancaster, PA: Technomic Publishing Co., Inc., 1992.

Clark, Leonard H., and Irving S. Starr. *Secondary and Middle School Teaching Methods.* New York: Macmillan Publishing Co., 1986.

Finesilver, Marilyn, and Delores K. Solovy. "Evaluation Techniques for the Jewish Classroom." *The Pedagogic Reporter,* September 1986.

Fredericksen, J.R., and A. Collings. "A Systems Approach to Educational Testing." *Educational Researcher* 18 (9):2-32.

Glazer, Susan Mandel, and Carol Smullen Brown. *Portfolios and Beyond: Collaborative Assessment in Reading and Writing.* Norwood, MA: Christopher-Gordon Publishers, Inc., 1993.

Harrow, Anita J. *A Taxonomy of the Psychomotor Domain: A Guide for Developing Behavior Objectives.* White Plains, NY: Longman Publishing Group, 1972.

Herman, Joan L.; Pamela R. Aschbacher; and Lynn Winters. *A Practical Guide to Alternative Assessment.* Alexandria, VA: ASCD, 1992.

Hershon, Jerome L., ed. *Tools of the Teaching Profession Book 2.* Miami, FL: CAJE, n.d.

Hill, Bonnie Campbell, and Cynthia Ruptic. *Practical Aspects of Authentic Assessment: Putting the Pieces Together.* Norwood, MA: Christopher-Gordon Publishers, Inc., 1994.

Hunter, Madeline. *Mastery Teaching.* El Segundo, CA: TIP, 1982.

Joyce, Bruce, and Marsha Weil. *Models of Teaching.* 4th ed. Needham Heights, MA: Allyn and Bacon, 1992.

Krathwohl, David R. *Taxonomy of Educational Objectives: The Classification of Educational Goals. Handbook 2: Affective Domain.* White Plains, NY: Longman Publishing Group, 1964.

Madaus, George F., and Ann G.A. Tan. "The Growth of Assessment." In *Challenges and Achievements of American Education.* Alexandria, VA: ASCD, 1993, pp. 53-79.

Marzano, Robert J.; Debra Pickering; and Jay McTighe. *Assessing Student Outcomes.* Alexandria, VA: ASCD, 1993.

Olson, Judy. *Learner Responsibility.* Dubuque, IA: Kendall-Hunt Publishing Co., 1990.

Olsen, M.W. "Portfolios: Educational Tools." *Reading Psychology* 12 (1):73-80, January-March, 1991.

Quellmalz, Edys; Evelyn Rubel; and Richard J. Stiggins. *Measuring Classroom Skills in the Classroom.* Washington, DC: NEA, 1988.

Shepard, L. "Why We Need Better Assessments." *Educational Leadership* 46 (7):41-47, 1989.

Stiggins, Richard J. *Student-Centered Classroom Assessment.* New York: Merrill, 1994.

Willis, Scott. "Quality by Design through Portfolios." *ASCD Update,* October 1993.

Worthen, Blaine R., and James R. Sanders. *Educational Evaluation: Alternative Approaches and Practical Guidelines.* White Plains, NY: Longman Publishing Group, 1987.

IN CONCLUSION

RESOURCES FOR JEWISH EDUCATORS

ANTI-DEFAMATION LEAGUE
823 United Nations Plaza, New York, NY 10017

ADL publishes and distributes materials on human relations, anti-Semitism, multi-cultural topics, Holocaust, etc. Same items in their collection contain specific lesson plan ideas.

A.R.E. PUBLISHING, INC.
3945 S. Oneida St., Denver, CO 80237

A source for innovative Jewish educational materials, teacher manuals, Hebrew materials, workbooks, minicourses, Copy Paks™, clip-art, and games, as well as a full line of cassette tapes for use in the classroom.

BEHRMAN HOUSE, INC.
235 Watchung Ave., West Orange, NJ 07052

Publisher of Jewish textbooks ranging from nursery school to college level. Subjects include: Hebrew, Bible, History, Holidays, Jewish Thought, and Ethics.

B'NAI B'RITH BOOKS
1640 Rhode Island Ave. N.W., Washington, DC 20036

Publisher and distributor of transideological books for adult education and independent study.

BOARD OF JEWISH EDUCATION OF GREATER NEW YORK
426 W. 58th St., New York, NY 10019

This BJE offers a wide range of materials for the classroom in both English and Hebrew. Their catalog consists of a series of small brochures organized by holiday or topic.

BUREAU OF JEWISH EDUCATION OF CINCINNATI
1580 Summit Rd., Cincinnati, OH 45237

This Bureau distributes materials that are useful in the Religious School classroom. They also publish an extensive list of play scripts.

BUREAU OF JEWISH EDUCATION OF GREATER BOSTON
333 Nahanton St., Newton, MA 02159

This BJE is known for curriculum materials for all grade levels, with particularly good material at the junior and senior high school levels.

BUREAU OF JEWISH EDUCATION LOS ANGELES
6505 Wilshire Blvd., Los Angeles, CA 90048

BJE of L.A. publishes a variety of educational materials useful in school settings.

BUREAU OF JEWISH EDUCATION OF METROPOLITAN CHICAGO
618 S. Michigan Ave., Chicago, IL 60605

This Bureau is a source for original classroom enrichment guides, including an extensive listing for the early childhood classroom.

BUREAU OF JEWISH EDUCATION TORONTO
4600 Bathurst St., Suite 232, Willowdale, Ontario M2R 3V2, Canada

This Bureau prepares materials that can be used in your classrooms.

CENTRAL AGENCY FOR JEWISH EDUCATION
4200 Biscayne Blvd., Miami, FL 33137

In addition to student-oriented educational material, this agency distributes curriculum guides on a variety of topics. These guides include experiential activities for student participation.

CCAR (CENTRAL CONFERENCE OF AMERICAN RABBIS)
192 Lexington Ave., New York, NY 10016

Publisher of a new family Haggadah, as well as other books of Reform Jewish rituals and liturgy.

C.I.S. PUBLISHERS
200 Park Ave., Lakewood, NJ 08701

Publishers of books for children and adults, in Hebrew and English, within the Orthodox framework.

COALITION FOR THE ADVANCEMENT OF JEWISH EDUCATION
261 W. 35th St., Floor 12A, New York, NY 10001

CAJE, in addition to sponsoring its annual educators conference each summer, publishes a periodical, *Jewish Education News*. Through the publication *Bikurim*, teachers can access materials from the CAJE Curriculum Bank. In addition, CAJE publishes units on specific topics.

CZIGLER PUBLISHING CO.
331 Beardsley Rd., Dayton, OH 45426

The Czigler catalog includes educational materials, posters, puzzles, and games for both English and Hebrew use.

DAVKA CORPORATION
7074 N. Western Ave., Chicago, IL 60645

The world's largest developer of Hebrew/Judaica software for computers used in homes, schools, and institutions.

EKS PUBLISHING
5346 College Ave., Oakland, CA 94618

EKS specializes in materials to aid adults in learning classical Hebrew.

ENJOY-A-BOOK CLUB
555 Chestnut St., Cedearhurst, NY 11516

Forms are distributed for this club through individual schools, enabling parents to purchase books, games, videos, and tapes for the home. The Company also coordinates book fairs.

FEDERATION OF RECONSTRUCTIONIST CONGREGATIONS AND HAVUROT
Church Rd. and Greenwood Ave., Wyncote, PA 19095

The official body of the Reconstructionist Movement, this organization distributes prayer books, including the Siddur *Kol Haneshamah,* as well as other educational materials.

FELDHEIM PUBLISHERS
200 Airport Executive Park, Spring Valley, NY 10977

Provides Orthodox oriented books for personal library and classroom use.

GEFEN PUBLISHING HOUSE
12 New St., Hewlett, NY 11557

The U.S. address for this Israel-based publisher which, in addition to publishing books on or about Israel, is the distributor for other Israeli publishers.

HADASSAH, THE WOMEN'S ZIONIST ORGANIZATION OF AMERICA, INC.
50 W. 58th St., New York, NY 10019

This organization prepares and publishes topical units that can be used for adults and, with some modifications, for Religious Schools. They distribute *Textures* and *Bat Kol* for adult education.

JASON ARONSON INC.
230 Livingston St., Northvale, NJ 07647

This publishing company includes in their collection both new titles of Jewish interest, as well as reprints of classics.

JEWISH BOOK COUNCIL
15 E. 26th St., New York, NY 10010

The national clearing house for Jewish literature, and sponsor of Jewish Book Month. Publishes numerous thematic bibliographies for educators.

THE JEWISH BRAILLE INSTITUTE
OF AMERICA
110 E. 30th St., New York, NY 11016

This agency provides material in large print, talking books, and books in Braille for the visually impaired and for others with learning disabilities. They have a large collection of books available in large print.

JEWISH EDUCATIONAL SERVICE OF NORTH AMERICA (JESNA)
730 Broadway, New York, NY 10003-9540

The planning, coordinating, and service agency for communal Jewish education organizations in the U.S. and Canada. JESNA provides consultations, has a placement service, does research, and publishes several periodicals, including *Agenda, Media Media,* and *Trends.*

JEWISH LIGHTS PUBLISHING
P.O. Box 237, Woodstock, VT 05091

Publishers of the works of Rabbi Lawrence Kushner and other books on sprituality, as well as on Twelve Step Programs and meditations for recovering individuals.

JEWISH NATIONAL FUND OF AMERICA
Department of Education, 114 E. 32nd St., New York, NY 10016

JNF is the fundraising agency for the reclamation and reforestation of the Land of Israel. They publish classroom materials which explain and enhance the importance of protecting the land in Israel, and run annual school-wide tree planting programs.

JEWISH PUBLICATION SOCIETY
1930 Chestnut St., Philadelphia, PA 19103

The oldest publisher of Judaica in the English language. Selections include Bible translations and commentaries, history, literature, philosophy, poetry, and children's books.

JEWISH THEOLOGICAL SEMINARY OF AMERICA
Dept. of Radio & Television, Dept. of Publications
3080 Broadway, New York, NY 10027

Producers of *The Eternal Light* broadcast series, they present materials, both audiovisual and print, for classroom and adult education use. Many of their programs are available on audiotape or video, as well as on film.

JEWISH WOMEN'S RESOURCE CENTER
National Council of Jewish Women, New York Section
9 East 69th St., New York, NY 10021

The JWRC, founded in 1977, enriches women's involvement with Judaism and the Jewish community through its research library, conferences, holiday celebrations, workshops, and publications.

KABBALAH SOFTWARE
8 Price Drive, Dept. CJ, Edison, NJ 08817

Creators and distributors of Judaic oriented software for home, institution, and school use.

KAR-BEN COPIES, INC.
6800 Tildenwood Ln., Rockville, MD 20852

Kar-Ben publishes story and activity books and tape sets for young children. They have board books, family services for various holidays, in addition to a broad collection of illustrated books for elementary age children.

KTAV PUBLISHING HOUSE
900 Jefferson St., Hoboken, NJ 07030

One of the largest and oldest distributors of texts and learning materials for both day and supplementary schools. Their catalog includes basic curriculum information for use of their texts.

LAYELED
2841 West Estes, Chicago, IL 60645

Distributors of innovative early childhood products, including wooden puzzles and manipulatives, audiocassettes of stories, and teacher guides.

THE LEARNING PLANT
P.O. Box 17233, West Palm Beach, FL 33416

Suppliers of game-making materials, books, learning center items, in addition to teacher idea books, audiocassettes, and art for bulletin boards.

MELTON CENTRE FOR JEWISH EDUCATION IN THE DIASPORA
Mount Scopus, Hebrew University, Jerusalem, Israel

This facility is a repository of educational materials from all over the world. They also publish a list of annotated periodicals from many different countries.

MELTON RESEARCH CENTER FOR JEWISH EDUCATION
3080 Broadway, New York, NY 10027

This Center is dedicated to the general improvement of Jewish education through its work with Jewish educators and the development of materials for schools and families. Materials can be used in informal and formal education settings. Also publishes *The Melton Journal*.

MESORAH PUBLICATIONS, LTD.
4401 Second Ave., Brooklyn, NY 11232-9814

Publishers of the Art Scroll series, in addition to other books. Their collection includes storybooks for children, as well as texts for adults. Publications are written according to strict Orthodox adherence to *halachah*.

MILWAUKEE ASSOCIATION FOR JEWISH EDUCATION
6401 N. Santa Monica Blvd., Milwaukee, WI 53217

This central agency publishes curriculum units, in addition to other items for classroom and home use.

MODAN PUBLISHING
P.O. Box 1202, Bellmore, NY 11710

Publishers of the Telem Series for use in day schools.

MUSEUM OF THE MIKVEH
1360 44th St., Brooklyn, NY 11219

Offers publications and videos on the topic of *mikvah*.

RABBI TZVI BLACK PUBLICATIONS
125 Carey St., Lakewood, NJ 08701

Distributes, among other items, "The Time Line Display of Jewish History."

SCHOCKEN BOOKS
201 E. 50th St., New York, NY 10022

Publishers of books on Jewish history, culture, literature, and religion. Schocken has an extensive back list of Jewish titles.

SHENGOLD PUBLISHERS
18 W. 45th St., New York, NY 10036

Publisher of one volume *Jewish Encyclopedia* and other books about Judaism, Zionism, and Israel.

SIMON WIESENTHAL CENTER
9760 W. Pico Blvd., Los Angeles, CA 90035

Committed to preserving the memory of the Six Million, the Center publishes many materials on the Holocaust, provides speakers, and publishes a magazine, *Response*. The museum provides visitors with an educational experience.

TARA PUBLICATIONS
29 Derby Ave., Cedarhurst, NY 11516

A source for Jewish music for all ages in all forms: audiocassettes, videos, CDs, sheet music, songbooks. A broad based and varied selection in English, Yiddish, and Hebrew.

TEKOA SOFTWARE
415 West Maple, Kalamazoo, MI 49001

Exclusive Takoa Jewish educational teaching aids. Programs include Hebrew, Bible, Jewish/Israeli History, Geography, and more.

TORAH ART FACTORY
P.O. Box 2726, Fairlawn, NY 07491

A source for bulletin board materials, posters, and other items to enhance the classroom and as teaching tools.

TORAH AURA PRODUCTIONS
4423 Fruitland Ave., Los Angeles, CA 90058

Publishers of materials for the classroom, including workbooks, texts, instant lessons, and audiovisual materials. Texts for adults on Jewish education and family education are also available.

TORAH UMESORAH – NATIONAL SOCIETY FOR HEBREW DAY SCHOOLS
160 Broadway, New York, NY 10038

In addition to being the organizational headquarters for Orthodox Day Schools across the country, this organization publishes texts and audiovisual materials for classroom use. Many of their materials are useful for adult education. They also publish the children's magazine, *Olomeinu*.

UNION OF AMERICAN HEBREW CONGREGATIONS DEPARTMENT OF EDUCATION/UAHC PRESS
838 Fifth Ave., New York, NY 10021

The organization headquarters of the Reform movement. Its Education Department offers consultations to member congregations and publishes *Compass* magazine. UAHC Press is the publishing arm for the UAHC. They publish and distribute books for classroom and general use for all ages, as well as audiocassettes and videos.

U.S. HOLOCAUST MEMORIAL MUSEUM
2000 L. St. NW, Suite 717, Washington, DC 20036

This outstanding museum opened in 1993, and is an excellent source for materials on the Holocaust in both print and audiovisual formats. Members receive a newsletter about the museum and Holocaust materials.

UNITED SYNAGOGUE OF AMERICA BOOK SERVICE
155 Fifth Ave., New York, NY 10010

The organizational headquarters of the conservative movement. Its Book Service produces and distributes English and Hebrew textbooks, liturgical and educational materials, evaluative and administrative forms for Jewish schools. Publishes curriculum guides for both Solomon Schechter Day Schools, as well as congregational supplementary schools.

WORLD ZIONIST ORGANIZATION – AMERICAN SECTION
110 East 59th St., New York, NY 10022

As part of its mission as the Aliyah Center and the agent of the WZO in Israel that promotes Israel in North America, they publish and distribute books and videos on all aspects of Israeli life. Various departments publish textbooks in English and Hebrew, e.g., The Department of Education and Culture and Herzl Press. WZO provides options for Jewish educators to travel and study in Israel.

PERIODICALS

ADL ON THE FRONTLINE
Anti-Defamation League of B'nai B'rith
823 United Nations Plaza, New York, NY 10017

A monthly that keeps up to date on human relations issues both in the U.S. and abroad.

AGENDA
Jewish Educational Services of North
America, Inc.
730 Broadway, New York, NY 10003

    Articles focus on Jewish education from a communal perspective.

AMERICAN JEWISH ARCHIVES
Hebrew Union College – Jewish Institute
of Religion
3131 Clifton Avenue, Cincinnati, OH 45220

    A journal devoted to the preservation and study of the American Jewish experience.

AMERICAN JEWISH HISTORY
American Jewish Historical Society
2 Thornton Rd., Waltham, MA 02154

    Scholarly articles that encompass the role of Jews in American history.

CCAR JOURNAL: A REFORM JEWISH
QUARTERLY
Central Conference of American Rabbis
192 Lexington Ave., New York, NY 10016

    A forum for ideas and issues on Judaism primarily from a Reform perspective.

CHILDHOOD EDUCATION
Association for Childhood Education
International
11141 Georgia Ave., Suite 200, Wheaton, MD 20902

    Articles address a broad range of topics on the well-being of children from infancy through adolescence. Includes articles on innovative practices in the classroom and significant findings in educational research.

COMPASS
UAHC Department of Religious Education
838 Fifth Ave., New York, NY 10021

    Devoted to Jewish life and learning for both professional and lay readership.

DIMENSIONS
Published by the International Center for
Holocaust Studies, Anti-Defamation League of
B'nai B'rith
823 United Nations Plaza, New York, NY 10017

    A journal of Holocaust studies.

EDUCATIONAL LEADERSHIP
Association for Supervison and Curriculum
Development
1250 N. Pitt St, Alexandria, VA 22314

    Contains articles on such subjects as curriculum, instruction, supervision, and leadership.

ERETZ
Eretz Ha-Tzvi, Inc.
P.O.B. 8074, Syracuse, NY 13217

    A quarterly that shows the beauty of the land of Israel through articles and full-color photographs. Published with the Society for the Protection of Nature in Israel.

HADASSAH MAGAZINE
50 West 58th St., New York, NY 10019

    Published by the Women's Zionist Organization of America. Includes book reviews, articles on Jewish life, various Jewish communities, etc.

IN PRINCIPAL
Board of Jewish Education of Greater New York
426 West 58th St., New York, NY 10019
    A newsletter directed at day school and Yeshiva principals. Content deals primarily with general studies.

INDEX TO JEWISH PERIODICALS
P.O. Box 18570, Cleveland Heights, OH 44118
    An author and subject index to over 70 English language journals of general and scholarly interest to the Jewish community.

INSTRUCTOR MAGAZINE
Harcourt Brace Jovanovich
545 Fifth Ave., New York, NY 10017

    Includes articles on classroom or all-school programs, effective teaching strategies, new ideas and teaching devices, and art projects.

JERUSALEM POST INTERNATIONAL EDITION
P.O. Box 282, Brewster, NY 10509

Printed in English, this weekly includes news and articles from the Israeli daily of the same name.

JEWISH BOOK WORLD
Jewish Book Council
15 E. 26th St., New York, NY 10010

Published three times a year, this publication includes full reviews of important new books and an annotated listing of over 150 new titles of Jewish interest.

JEWISH EDUCATION NEWS
Coalition for the Advancement of Jewish Education (CAJE)
261 W. 35th St., Floor 12A, New York, NY 10001

Each issue of this quarterly includes articles on a different aspect of Jewish education written for teachers and anyone concerned with Jewish education.

JEWISH PARENT CONNECTION
160 Broadway, New York, NY 10038

Published by the National Society for Hebrew Day Schools, the articles center on the home and school.

JOURNAL OF JEWISH COMMUNAL SERVICE
3084 State Highway 27, Kendall Park, NY 08824

While the emphasis here is on education in informal settings, there are always one or two articles of interest to the educator.

JOURNAL OF PSYCHOLOGY AND JUDAISM
Human Relations Press
233 Spring St., New York, NY 10013

A quarterly that provides in-depth articles on the relationships between religion and psychology.

JUDAICA LIBRARIANSHIP
Association of Jewish Libraries
15 E. 26th St., Room 1034, New York, NY 10010

Includes articles on Jewish libraries and literature, as well as book reviews.

KEEPING POSTED/FOCUS ON
UAHC Press
838 Fifth Avenue, New York, NY 10021

Back issues of *Keeping Posted,* a social studies teaching magazine, are still available. Each issue is on a single theme. It is now replaced by *Focus On,* which is distributed quarterly with *Reform Judaism* magazine.

LEARNING MAGAZINE
Springhouse Corp.
1111 Bethlehem Pike, Springhouse, PA 19477

Contains articles by practitioners which present techniques or materials that have been proven effective, as well as articles that analyze and evaluate educational issues.

THE MELTON JOURNAL
The Melton Research Center
The Jewish Theological Seminary of America
3080 Broadway, New York, NY 10027

Published twice a year and distributed free to educators and individuals interested in Jewish education. Each issue focuses on a different issue or theme in Jewish education. Includes articles, book reviews, and brief biographies. Back issues are available for purchase.

MOMENT MAGAZINE
3000 Connecticut Ave. NW, Washington, DC 20008

A bimonthly publication of Jewish culture and opinion of interest to lay people and educators.

NOAH'S ARK
8323 Southwest Freeway, Suite 250, Houston, TX 77074

A publication for elementary school age children. Includes articles, puzzles, games, recipes for home or classroom use.

OPTIONS
Box 311, Wayne, NJ 07474

> A monthly Jewish resources newsletter describing the who, what, and where of Jewish living. Of particular interest to Jewish educators.

OUR WORLD/OLOMEINU
National Hebrew Day Schools
5723 18th Ave., Brooklyn, NY 11204

> A student magazine with stories about personalities, holidays, and Jewish values.

RECONSTRUCTIONIST TODAY
Church Rd. and Greenwood Ave., Wyncote, PA 19095

> Published by the Federation of Reconstructionist Congregations and Havurot, this is the official magazine of the Reconstructionist Movement.

REFORM JUDAISM
838 Fifth Ave., New York, NY 10021-7064

> The official magazine of the Reform movement, with articles on world issues, as well as movement activities and personalities.

RELIGIOUS EDUCATION
409 Prospect St., New Haven, CT 06511

> Published by the Religious Education Association of the United States and Canada, this journal contains articles on religious education of interest to educators of all denominations.

RESPONSE
The Wiesenthal Center
9760 W. Pico Blvd., Los Angeles, CA 90035

> The articles in this magazine focus on the Holocaust and information about the Holocaust Museum it sponsors in Los Angeles.

SH'MA
CLAL
99 Park Ave., New York, NY 10016

> A transideological newsletter which presents differing views on topics of Jewish interest. Also includes book reviews.

SHOFAR
43 Northcote Dr., Melville, NY 11747

> A colorful magazine for middle school students. Each issue is centered on a topic, such as a holiday or event. A teacher/parent guide is included.

STUDIES IN AMERICAN JEWISH LITERATURE
Kent State University Press, Kent, OH 44242

> A scholarly review of literature.

TRADITION
Rabbinical Council of America
275 7th Ave., New York, NY 10001

> The official magazine of this Orthodox Rabbinical association.

ULTIMATE ISSUES
c/o Dennis Prager
6020 Washington Blvd., Culver City, CA 90232

> Articles cover a wide range of topics of interest to the Jewish community. The format encourages the reader to think about these issues in relationship to his/her own perspective of Judaism.

UNITED SYNAGOGUE REVIEW
United Synagogue of Conservative Judaism
Rapaport House, 155 Fifth Ave., New York, NY 10010

> The official magazine of the Conservative Movement.

YOUNG CHILDREN
National Association for the Education of
Young Children
1834 Connecticut Ave., Washington, DC 20009

The practical articles in this publication are geared to teachers and others who work with children up to eight years of age.

YOUR CHILD: FOR PARENTS OF YOUNG CHILDREN
United Synagogue of Conservative Judaism
155 Fifth Ave., New York, NY 10010

A free newsletter which discusses issues of parenting and the transmissions to children of Jewish values, knowledge, and practices.

DISTRIBUTORS OF AUDIOVISUAL MATERIALS

ALDEN FILMS
7820 20th Ave., Brooklyn, NY 11214

ANTI-DEFAMATION LEAGUE
1580 Summit Rd., Cincinnati, OH 45237

ARIELLA FILMS
4219 Vinton Ave., Culver City, CA 90232

BOARD OF JEWISH EDUCATION OF GREATER NEW YORK
426 W. 58th St., New York, NY 10019

BUREAU OF JEWISH EDUCATION LOS ANGELES
6505 Wilshire Blvd., Los Angeles, CA 90048

CARMI HOUSE
Box 4796, North Hollywood, CA 91617

CRITICS CHOICE VIDEO
P.O. Box 749, Itasca, IL 60143

ERGO MEDIA
P.O. Box 2037, Teaneck, NJ 07666

FACETS MULTIMEDIA, INC.
1517 W. Fullerton Ave., Chicago, IL 60614

ICJM (INSTITUTE FOR CREATIVE JEWISH MEDIA)
152 Simsbury Rd., Avon, CT 06001

JEWISH EDUCATIONAL VIDEO
713 Crown St., Brooklyn, NY 11213

NATIONAL CENTER FOR JEWISH FILM
Brandeis University, Iowa Bldg. #120, Waltham, MA 02254

SIMON WIESENTHAL CENTER
9760 W. Pico Blvd., Los Angeles, CA 90035

TORAH AURA PRODUCTIONS
4423 Fruitland Ave., Los Angeles, CA 90058

Beth Sholom Religious School
805 Lyons Blvd.
Fredericksburg, VA 22406